Communications in Computer and Information Science 1563

More information about this series at https://link.springer.com/bookseries/7899

Yuan Tian · Tinghuai Ma ·
Muhammad Khurram Khan · Victor S. Sheng ·
Zhaoqing Pan (Eds.)

Big Data and Security

Third International Conference, ICBDS 2021
Shenzhen, China, November 26–28, 2021
Proceedings

Springer

Editors
Yuan Tian [ID]
Nanjing Institute of Technology
Nanjing, China

Muhammad Khurram Khan [ID]
King Saud University
Riyadh, Saudi Arabia

Zhaoqing Pan [ID]
Tianjin University
Tianjin, China

Tinghuai Ma [ID]
Nanjing University of Information Science
and Technology
Nanjing, China

Victor S. Sheng [ID]
Texas Tech University
Lubbock, TX, USA

ISSN 1865-0929 ISSN 1865-0937 (electronic)
Communications in Computer and Information Science
ISBN 978-981-19-0851-4 ISBN 978-981-19-0852-1 (eBook)
https://doi.org/10.1007/978-981-19-0852-1

This Springer imprint is published by the registered company Springer Nature Singapore Pte Ltd.
The registered company address is: 152 Beach Road, #21-01/04 Gateway East, Singapore 189721, Singapore

Preface

This volume contains the papers from the Third International Conference on Big Data and Security (ICBDS 2021). The event was held at the Shenzhen Institute of Advanced Technology, Chinese Academy of Sciences, and was organized by the Nanjing Institute of Technology, the Shenzhen Institute of Advanced Technology, King Saud University, the Jiangsu Computer Society, and the IEEE Broadcast Technology Society.

The International Conference on Big Data and Security (ICBDS) brings experts and researchers together from all over the world to discuss the current status and potential ways to address security and privacy regarding the use of big data systems. Big data systems are complex and heterogeneous; due to their extraordinary scale and the integration of different technologies, new security and privacy issues are introduced and must be properly addressed. The ongoing digitalization of the business world is putting companies and users at risk of cyber-attacks more than ever before. Big data analysis has the potential to offer protection against these attacks. Participation in conference workshops on specific topics is expected to achieve progress through global networking and the transfer and exchange of ideas.

The papers submitted to ICBDS 2021 came from researchers who work in universities and research institutions, giving us the opportunity to achieve a good level of understanding of the mutual needs, requirements, and technical means available in this field of research. The topics included in the second edition of this event included big data, security in blockchain, IoT security, security in cloud and fog computing, artificial intelligence/machine learning security, cybersecurity, and privacy. We received 221 submissions and accepted 59 papers. All the accepted papers were peer reviewed by three qualified reviewers chosen from our Technical Program Committee (TPC) based on their qualifications and experience.

The proceedings editors wish to thank the dedicated TPC members and all the other reviewers for their efforts and contributions. We also thank Springer for their trust and for publishing the proceedings of ICBDS 2021.

January 2022

Tinghuai Ma
Muhammad Khurram Khan
Victor S. Sheng
Zhaoqing Pan
Yuan Tian

Organization

General Chairs

Ting Huai Ma   Nanjing University of Information Science and
                                Technology, China
Yi Pan   Georgia State University, USA
Muhammad Khurram Khan   King Saud University, Saudi Arabia
Yuan Tian   Nanjing Institute of Technology, China

Technical Program Chairs

Victor S. Sheng   Texas Tech University, USA
Zhaoqing Pan   Tianjin University, China

Technical Program Committee

Abdullah Al-Dhelaan   King Saud University, Saudi Arabia
Adil Mehmood Khan   Innopolis University, Russia
Alia Alabdulkarim   King Saud University, Saudi Arabia
Amiya Kumar Tripathy   Edith Cowan University, Australia
Babar Shah   Zayed University, UAE
Basmah Alotibi   King Saud University, Saudi Arabia
Chunguo Li   Southeast University, China
Chunliang Yang   China Mobile IoT Company Limited, China
Cunjie Cao   Hainan University, China
Davide Taibi   University of Tampere, Finland
Dong-xue Liang   Tsinghua University, China
Elina Annanperä   University of Oulu, Finland
Eui-Nam Huh   Kyung Hee University, South Korea
Farkhund Iqbal   Zayed University, UAE
Ghada Al-Hudhud   King Saud University, Saudi Arabia
Hang Chen   Nanjing Institute of Technology, China
Heba Abdullataif Kurdi   Massachusetts Institute of Technology, USA
Irfan Mohiuddin   King Saud University, Saudi Arabia
Jiagao Wu   Nanjing University of Posts and
                                Telecommunications, China
Jian Zhou   Nanjing University of Posts and
                                Telecommunications, China

Jianguo Sun	Harbin Engineering University, China
Jinghua Ding	Sungkyunkwan University, South Korea
Kashif Saleem	King Saud University, Saudi Arabia
Kejia Chen	Nanjing University of Posts and Telecommunications, China
Lei Cui	Chinese Academy of Sciences, China
Lei Han	Nanjing Institute of Technology, China
Lejun Zhang	Yangzhou University, China
Linfeng Liu	Nanjing University of Posts and Telecommunications, China
Linshan Shen	Harbin Engineering University, China
Manal Hazazi	King Saud University, Saudi Arabia
Manar Hosny	King Saud University, Saudi Arabia
Maram Al-Shablan	King Saud University, Saudi Arabia
Mariya Muneeb	King Saud University, Saudi Arabia
Markus Kelanti	University of Oulu, Finland
Maryam Hajakbari	Islamic Azad University, Iran
Miada Murad	King Saud University, Saudi Arabia
Ming Pang	Harbin Engineering University, China
Ming Su	Beijing University of Posts and Telecommunications, China
Mohammad Rawashdeh	University of Central Missouri, USA
Mohammed Al-Dhelaan	King Saud University, Saudi Arabia
Muhammad Ovais Ahmad	Karlstad University, Sweden
Mznah Al-Rodhaan	King Saud University, Saudi Arabia
Nguyen H. Tran	University of Sydney, Australia
Omar Alfandi	Zayed University, UAE
Päivi Raulamo-Jurvanen	University of Oulu, Finland
Pasi Kuvaja	University of Oulu, Finland
Patrick Hung	University of Ontario Institute of Technology, Canada
Pertti Karhapää	University of Oulu, Finland
Pilar Rodríguez	Technical University of Madrid, Spain
Qiang Ma	King Saud University, Saudi Arabia
Qiao Lin Ye	Nanjing Forestry University, China
Rand J.	Shaqra University, Saudi Arabia
Sarah Alkharji	King Saud University, Saudi Arabia
Shadan Alhamed	King Saud University, Saudi Arabia
Shaoyong Guo	Beijing University of Posts and Telecommunications, China
Shiwen Hu	Accelor Ltd., USA
Soha Zaghloul Mekki	King Saud University, Saudi Arabia

Sungyoung Lee	Kyung Hee University, South Korea
Susheela Dahiya	University of Petroleum and Energy Studies, India
Tang Xin	University of International Relations, China
Teemu Karvonen	University of Oulu, Finland
Tero Päivärinta	University of Oulu, Finland
Thant Zin Oo	Kyung Hee University, South Korea
Tianyang Zhou	State Key Laboratory of Mathematical Engineering and Advanced Computing, China
Valentina Lenarduzzi	University of Tampere, Finland
Wajahat Ali Khan	Kyung Hee University, South Korea
Weipeng Jing	Northeast Forestry University, China
Xiao Xue	Tianjin University, China
Xiaojian Ding	Nanjing University of Finance and Economics, China
Xinjian Zhao	State Grid Nanjing Power Supply Company, China
Xuesong Yin	Nanjing Institute of Technology, China
Yao Zhenjian	Huazhong University of Science and Technology, China
Yonghua Gong	Nanjing University of Posts and Telecommunications, China
Yu Zhang	Harbin Institute of Technology, China
Yuanfeng Jin	Yanbian University, China
Yunyun Wang	Nanjing University of Posts and Telecommunications, China
Zeeshan Pervez	University of the West of Scotland, Scotland
Zhengyu Chen	Jinling Institute of Technology, China
Zhiwei Wang	Hebei Normal University, China
Zilong Jin	Nanjing University of Information Science and Technology, China

Workshop Chairs

Mohammad Mehedi Hassan	King Saud University, Saudi Arabia
Asad Masood Khattak	Zayed University, UAE

Publication Chair

Vidyasagar Potdar	Curtin University, Australia

Organization Chairs

Chenrong Huang   Nanjing Institute of Technology, China
Yanjie Wei   Shenzhen Institute of Advanced Technology,
                               Chinese Academy of Sciences, China
Yong Zhang   Shenzhen Institute of Advanced Technology,
                               Chinese Academy of Sciences, China

Organization Committee

Pilar Rodriguez Gonzalez   University of Oulu, Finland
Jalal Al-Muhtadi   King Saud University, Saudi Arabia
Geng Yang   Nanjing University of Posts and
                               Telecommunications, China
Qiao Lin Ye   Nanjing Forestry University, China
Pertti Karhapää   University of Oulu, Finland
Lei Han   Nanjing Institute of Technology, China
Yong Zhu   Jingling Institute of Technology, China
Päivi Raulamo-Jurvanen   University of Oulu, Finland
Bin Xie   Hebei Normal University, China
Dawei Li   Nanjing Institute of Technology, China
Jing Rong Chen   Nanjing Institute of Technology, China
Thant Zin Oo   Kyung Hee University, South Korea
Alia Alabdulkarim   King Saud University, Saudi Arabia
Rand J.   Shaqra University, Saudi Arabia
Hang Chen   Nanjing Institute of Technology, China
Jiagao Wu   Nanjing University of Posts and
                               Telecommunications, China

Contents

Artificial Intelligence/Machine Learning Security

Cybersecurity and Privacy

Privacy Preserving Facial Image Processing Method Using Variational Autoencoder

Yuying Qiu[1], Zhiyi Niu[1], Qikun Tian[2,3], and Biao Song[1(✉)]

[1] School of Computer Science, Nanjing University of Information Science and Technology (NUIST), Nanjing, China
bsong@nuist.edu.cn
[2] Nanjing Institute of Technology, Nanjing, China
[3] University of Oulu, Oulu, Finland

Abstract. Over the recent years, a massive number of face images are widely used in each field of Internet, which makes the privacy leakage problem due to the abuse of facial images become more serious. The existing simple face de-identification methods like occlusion or blurring seriously damage the useful information and structure of image, which leads to a poor visual effect and is of little significant in practical application. In this work, we propose a novel privacy preserving facial image processing method. The proposed method removes the identity information of face images by four different measures first, and then fuse these de-identified images through a multi-input generative model based on Variational Autoencoder (VAE) to reconstruct the useful information of image. The proposed method aims to generate images that is close to the real face but does not contain the privacy information in the original human face image, which avoids the disclosure of privacy. We demonstrate the information reconstruction capabilities of our method with contrast experiments on the CelebA datasets. Experimental results emphasize the superiority of our method in terms of maintaining useful information and visual effects over traditional face de-identification methods.

Keywords: Face de-identification · Variational autoencoder · Privacy protection · Deep learning

1 Introduction

In recent years, the development of Internet and transmission technology provides a reliable platform for the uploading and storage of images. Online transferring and sharing of personal images have become an integral part of the modern social life. Every day a massive amount of image data gets recorded and shared on public network platforms. This phenomenon has brought hidden danger of image abuse and posed a threat to the security of our private information, which has major repercussions on our daily lives. As a result, the issue of privacy disclosure is now receiving increasing attention.

The authors extend their appreciation to the Jiangsu Province Students' Platform for Innovation and Entrepreneurship Training Program, 202110300083Y

Since face is an important biometric feature that reveals identifiable characteristics of a person in an image, the protection of privacy information in face images plays an important role [1]. Traditional privacy protection methods, such as occlusion and blurring, although can accomplish the work of privacy protection visually, but other important non-biometric features may also get obscured, along with identity. For example, in the context of social media, privacy protection is necessary, but if the facial structure can be preserved at the same time, it will greatly contribute to the overall expression of information. However, the relationship between removing privacy information and keeping the image close to the real face is likely to be non-linear, or even contradictory. This is the dilemma that the current face de-recognition work is facing. Therefore, how to achieve the two goals of protecting privacy and maintaining useful information of image quickly is a problem to be solved.

The work of face image de-identification, on the one hand, requires blurring the identity information in the face image, and on the other hand requires that the de-identified image can preserve useful information and maintain visual effects. Many recent studies have been devoted to finding the optimal balance the two mentioned above. [2] proposed a method of face de-identification which relies on face and key points detection followed by a variational adaptive filtering, finishing the de-identification of faces with expressions preservation in images. [3] designed novel verificatory and regulator modules for the face de-identification problem to ensure generating de-identified image with retained structure similarity. [4] finetunes the encoding part of a standard autoencoder and finish the work of de-identification in the latent space which can maintain the nature and diversity of the original face images, while generating new faces with different person identity labels. There is still room for improvement in the efficiency and applicability of existing technologies. The need for the development of an efficient and adaptable framework to achieve both privacy protection and utility preservation cannot be over-emphasized.

In order to overcome the limitations outlined above, we propose a novel privacy preserving facial image processing method using VAE. The proposed approach exploits a recent generative model Vector Quantized Variational AutoEncoder (VQ-VAE) [5]. This generative model can generate de-identified faces with high visual quality. We select four traditional protection models [6] to process the images respectively and get four groups of pictures that do not contain private information. Then we modified the loss function for the specific service, so that it has the index of service quality evaluation which guide these images to merge. This method makes it possible to retain specific aspects of quality in the original data, which is relay on the service scenario, while removing the privacy information in the image because the input of the model itself does not contain privacy information.

To summarize, the main contributions of this work are:

- We introduce a novel privacy preserving facial image processing method using VAE, which takes full advantage of existing privacy protection technologies and innovatively takes several private images as the input of generator to achieve the aim to remove private information of original images.
- We design a multi-input generation model based on VAE and VQ-VAE. To achieve the purpose of utility reconstruction, the model training guided by the goal of narrowing the distance between the generated image and the real face.

- We demonstrate the feasibility of our framework on an open dataset. Experimental results show that compared with the traditional methods of de-identification, our method has superior stability and efficiency. and achieves a balance between face de-identification and service quality maintenance.

The rest of the paper is structured as follows. In Sect. 2, We review the related work about de-identification. In Sect. 3, We introduce four privacy protection methods and basic principles of VAE. In Sect. 4, we introduce our novel de-identification framework, which combines four protection modes and VAE. In Sect. 5, a quantitative evaluation is provided to test the performance of our proposed framework and the image results are shown to prove its effectiveness. We conclude the paper with some suggestions for future research in Sect. 6.

2 Related Work

Privacy protection in face image data has been extensively researched in recent years. Traditional face de-identification techniques was focused on the application of standard still image processing techniques like image blurring, image pixilation, adding a black (or white) cover in the image region occupied by the face [7], etc. However, these naive methods are inadequate for removing all privacy-sensitive information from face images [7, 8]. [9] used a deep multitask learning network to detect privacy-sensitive information and provide simple protection by blurring, but it also seriously destroys the visual effects.

The k-Same algorithmic family [10–12] provided de-identification methods with the oretical guarantees of anonymization [13]. In these methods, each de-identified image is represented by an average face image of the k closest face images from the set of images. The images generated by these frameworks are always suffered from ghosting artifacts due to the alignment errors when calculate the averaging of multiple faces. As an improvement, the q-far de-identification approach [14], which is based on Active Appearance Model (AAM) [15], incorporates an additional pose estimation step to align the faces, thus successfully eliminate the ghostly appearance on the de-identified face. K-Same-Net [16] combines k-Same algorithm with Generative Neural Networks (GNNs), which conceals the identity of faces while still enables preservation of selected non-identity-related features. [17] proposed k-Same-Select algorithm where k-Same algorithm is used independently to the mutually exclusive subsets partitioned from the input set and the technologies of semi-supervised learning techniques [18] and co-training [19] are used to learn the expression of original images. k-Same-Select is proved to have more potential for utility preservation compared to both k-Same and ad hoc methods on the FERET database [20]. [21] decomposed the face space into subspaces that are respectively sensitive to face identity and face utility, then processed the latter by the k-anonymity de-identification procedure. In this way, the purpose of image utility preservation of can still be achieved while defying face identity recognition. An disadvantage of each of the techniques based on k-Same algorithm is that these are unable to generate unique de-identified results for different face images.

The development of generative adversarial network (GAN) [22] has opened up a new perspective for the research of face de-identity recognition [12, 23–25]. In [26] GAN is used for facial landmark conditioned head inpainting. This maintains the details of the original face to a certain extent, while generating a facial image of high visual quality which is more effective than pure blurring methods on the task of de-identification. Wu et al. [3] proposed the CGAN-based PPGAN to solve the face de-identification problem by inputting a single face image to output a de-identified image which keeps the structural similarity. The de-identified image generated by PPGAN can retain the emotion present in the input face, but its identity obfuscation quality is not appreciably good [1] To optimize the face de-identification, Li et al. [27] provides a solution called SF-GAN, which construct a variety of external mechanisms to balance the influence of multiple factors on the effect of face de-identification. [4] presented multiple methods for face de-identification based on fully connected and fully convolutional autoencoders, by training the encoder to learn to shift the faces towards other faces with desirable attributes and away from samples with conflicting attributes. Chen et al. [28] combined VAE [29] and cGAN [30] and proposed a method for privacy-preserving facial expression recognition based on the Variational Generative Adversarial Network (VGAN), which learn an image representation that is explicitly disentangled from the identity information. This method effectively create an identity-preserving representation of facial images with expression preserving realistic vision.

Differential privacy (DP) technology [31] is also widely used in face privacy protection. [32] proposed a differential privacy noise dynamic allocation algorithm based on the standard deviation circle radius named SDC-DP algorithm, which is effectively reduce the relative errors and improve accuracies. [33] proposed a novel privacy analysis of training neural networks based on f-differential, which suggests improving prediction accuracy without violating the privacy budget by tuning certain parameters of neural networks. [34] proposed a face image publishing SWP (sliding window publication) and sort SWP algorithm, innovatively transforming the problem of image private into that of data stream private protection. Compared with the LAP algorithm, the SWP algorithm and sort SWP algorithm have better display effect. [35] utilized deep neural network techniques to identify the privacy-sensitive information in images, and then use the synthetic content generated by GANs with DP to protect it. In [36], a privacy-preserving adversarial protector network (PPAPNet) was proposed as a advanced mechanism to add noise to the original image. Experiments show that PPAPNet has a good performance in converting a sensitive image into a high-quality and inversion-attacks-immune [37] generated image. [38] directly modified pixel intensity to achieve DP, regardless of the distribution characteristics of face image. It is also proved that the exponential mechanism proposed by us in this context can provide higher visual quality for pixel space obfuscation using Laplace mechanism and has strong universality. In [39], a privacy-preserving semi-generative adversarial network (PPSGAN) is proposed, which use the self-attention mechanism and selectively adds noise to the class-independent features of each image so that the generated image can retain the original label. PPSGAN has better practicability than other traditional methods, including blur, noise, filtering, and GAN generation.

Current works are mainly focuses on maintaining a specific image quality, and the application scene has been determined in the design of the model. Although this can bring good results, it increases the complexity of the model and is strictly limited to the scope of application. To break the limitations of the above mentioned method, in this paper, we adopt the strategy of destroying the information of the image first and then using the VAE to reconstruct the information, which makes the generated image avoid the disclosure of privacy and close to the real face. In this way, we can achieve the purpose of maintaining the utility of the image with high efficiency and wide adaptability.

3 Preliminary

3.1 Methods of Face De-identification

In order to complete the task of privacy information protection, we use four different existing privacy protection methods to de-identify the original image. The first way is blindfold. In this method, the value of the row in the eye region of the image is set to 0, and the rest of the image remains unchanged. We use T_{eyes} to represent a set that contains all the eye coordinates. The function of blindfold is expressed as:

$$x1_{i,j} = \begin{cases} 0 & \text{if } (i,j) \in T_{eyes} \\ x_{i,j} & \text{other} \end{cases} \tag{1}$$

The second way is facial mosaic. It is to add a mosaic to the face area of the image, which construct a color block with a length and width of 8 pixels based on the value of a point in the original image, covering the values of 64 pixels around it. We use T_{face} to represent a set that contains all the eye coordinates and use the function $g(x)$ to represent the average value of the point in the color block where x is located. The function of facial mosaic is as follows:

$$x2_{i,j} = \begin{cases} g(x) & \text{if } (i,j) \in T_{face} \\ x_{i,j} & \text{other} \end{cases} \tag{2}$$

The third way is to add the Laplace noise with the probability density function as shown in Eq. 3, and in our work, we set λ to 1 and μ to 0. The last method is to animate the image. The pre-trained UGATIT network [6] is used to transfer the image style and transform the image into animation style.

$$f(x) = \frac{1}{2\lambda} e^{-\frac{|x-\mu|}{\lambda}} \tag{3}$$

Through the above methods, we construct four sets of images that do not contain privacy. We suffer from the possible loss of quality when using these de-identified images for further services. Consequently, we need to design fusion algorithms for these images to reconstruct useful information in the image and provide better visual effects.

3.2 Basic Principles of VAE

VAE is one of the most popular methods of unsupervised complex probability distribution learning nowadays, and we use it as the basic architecture when designing and generating models. The basic flow of VAE is shown in Fig. 1.

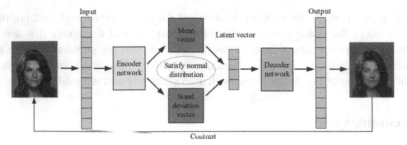

Fig. 1. The basic flow of VAE.

The basic structure of VAE is the same as that of AE, which is divided into two parts: encoder and decoder. Different from the ordinary AE, the encoder no longer generates a low-dimensional vector directly, but generates two vectors, one representing the mean value and the other representing the standard deviation, and then uses these two statistics to synthesize the low-dimensional vector. In this process, we default that the low-dimensional vector obeys the normal distribution, which makes the decoder robust to noise.

The input data is first reduced to a hidden vector through the encoder network, and then the generated data is restored through the decoder network, and then the two data are compared. The parameters of the encoder and decoder in this network are trained by minimizing the difference between them. Finally, a new sample is generated, which is similar to but different from the training set data.

4   Proposed Methodology

4.1   System Model

Face privacy protection considering the quality of service is a complex task. In the pure de-identification process, the potential damage to useful information is not considered, so the image utility tends to decline in this process. In order to address this issue, we propose a novel generative model of image utility maintenance framework based on VAE and several privacy protection methods. We use the mean square error between the original image and the generated image to guide the model to train. The overall structure of de-identification module and utility reconstruction module is shown in the Fig. 2. First, we use four privacy protection modes (blindfold, cartoon, laplace, mosaic) for face images to generate de-identified data sets. Next, we design a new method of image fusion, which is a multi-input image generation model using de-identified data sets as input to generate de-identified face images with guided quality preservation. During the model training process, we calculate whether the result image maintain the useful information in the original image and take this calculation result as part of loss function. Back propagation is performed to continuously update the generated image to achieve the purpose of maintenance the utility of image.

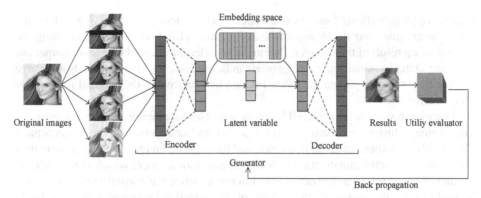

Fig. 2. The structure of de-identification module and utility reconstruction module.

4.2 Architecture and Working

The purpose of our work is to establish a multi-input generation model, using multiple de-identified images to generate a de-identified images with guided quality preservation. Our framework provides an inspiring framework on training self-return neural network to generate realistic and high-definition images samples.

Our framework absorbs the essence of Vector Quantization (VQ) which was first put forward in VQ-VAE, using discrete latent variables as a new way of training. The priority and prior distributions in this model are classified. The index of samples extracted from these distributions are embedded in the table. Then these embeddings serve as input into the decoder network. VQ-VAE defines a latent embedding space e between the input x and the low-dimensional random variables z. The complete parameter set of the model can be divided into three parts: encoder, decoder, and embedding space e.

In order to construct the input parameter x of the model, we stitch the images generated under four kinds of privacy protection modes to keep the image length and width unchanged and increase the number of channels. The encoder products output $z_e(x)$ with the input x. The output $z_e(x)$ does not directly enter the decoder, but finding the nearest embedding in the embedding space e and then using the index of this embedding to represent the latent variable z as shown in Eq. 4. The probability of the posterior classification distribution $q(z|x)$ is defined as follows. This formula means that the index position of the vector closest to $z_e(x)$ is set to 1, and the remaining bits are set to 0.

$$q(z = k|x) = \begin{cases} 1 \text{ for } k = \text{argmin}_j \, ||z_e(x) - e_j||_2, \\ 0 \text{ otherwise} \end{cases} \tag{4}$$

The input of the decoder is the closest embedding vector found in e, as shown in Eq. 5. $z_e(x)$ is mapped to the nearest element in the embedding space through discretization, and then be passed to the decoder.

$$z_q(x) = e_k, \quad \text{where} \quad k = \arg\min_j ||z_e(x) - e_j||_2 \tag{5}$$

In this work, we extracted two-dimensional latent feature space for image data. The model completes the nonlinear process of mapping the latent vector to the embedding vector, copying gradients from decoder input $z_q(x)$ to encoder output $z_e(x)$ at the same time. The gradient push the change of the assignment in Eq. 4 which in turn in affects the discretization result of the encoder. Due to the encoder input and the decoder output use the same D dimensional space, the gradient indicates how the encoder needs to change its output, in order to reduce the reconstruction loss relative to the original image after image fusion.

Equation 6 specifies the overall loss function. The first item is used to optimize the loss of image fusion reconstruction for decoders and encoders, i.e., the Mean Square Error (MSE) between the generated image and the original image. The second item uses the method of vector quantization to learn the embedded space, which is used update the dictionary of vector quantization. The last one is defined as commitment loss, which is used to limit the growth of the volume of the embedded space and can effectively constrain the encoder to prevent its output from deviating from the embedding vector when the encoder parameter update efficiency is too fast. Thus, the total training objective are as follows:

$$L = \log p(x|z_q(x)) + ||sg[z_e(x)] - e||_2^2 + \beta||z_e(x) - sg[e]||_2^2 \qquad (6)$$

where sg is a stop gradient operator which has zero partial derivatives and non-updated operand at forward computation time. The first loss items are optimized by the encoder and the decoder. The second loss term is optimized by embedded space, and the last loss term is optimized by the encoder. Through the above methods, when we train the generation model, we recognize the MSE between the original image and the generated image.

4.3 Method Execution Process

We use the method of first destroying and then restoring utility to maintain utility. The execution flow of our method is shown in Fig. 3.

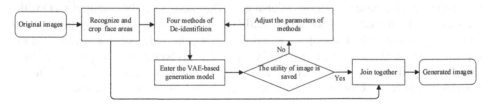

Fig. 3. The execution flow of the privacy preserving method using VAE.

The original image to be processed requires face detection, and the face region is cropped for subsequent processing. Then we use the four privacy protection modes described in Sect. 3.1 to process the face areas. To restore image utility, four de-identified images will enter the generation model based on VAE.

The mean square error between the original image and the generated image evaluates the utility of the generated image, calculates the utility loss, and guide the generation process of the model, finally be accord with privacy removal with utility to generate images at the same time, provide safe application service.

5 Experimentation and Results

5.1 Experimental Setup

We verify our proposed framework model on CelebA dataset [40] which contains 202599 celebrity face-aligned and cropped images. The first 1000 pictures from the original dataset were selected for experiment, and the first 80% of them were selected for training and the remaining 20% for testing.

Our model trained with TensorFlow 1.8 and Keras 2.24 interface on GTX 2070. The results did not vary for values of β in Eq. 6 ranging from 0.1 to 2.0 [20], so we assign β to $= 0.25$ in all our experiments. During the whole system training, we use the ADAM optimizer with a learning rate of 1e-3. The parameters of simulation are shown in Table.1.

Table 1. The parameters of simulation.

Methods	Epochs
Blindfold	\
Mosaic	\
Laplace	\
Cartoon	\
Method based on VAE	from 10 to 40 in steps of 10

5.2 Face Images De-identification

We have made different de-identify processing for the 1000 original face images. According to different methods of face privacy protection, we divide the data into five different data groups: original image, eyes coving image, face-mosaic image, Gaussian noise image and cartoon image. The results of image de-identification are shown in Fig. 4.

Apart from utility preservation, in the problem of face de-identification, we want the generated image to be erased only private information, but its similar performance with the original image can be maintained as much as possible. That is to say, we only delete the data related to the specified privacy but preserve the visual similarity. In order to prove that our proposed model achieves good results in de-identification and utility maintenance, we use MSE to calculate the loss rate of generated images. If the value of MSE is getting smaller and smaller, it shows that the effect of the neural network on image utility service quality maintenance is getting better and better.

Fig. 4. The results of image de-identification.

We measure the average of MSE of all samples in the four protection modes. As shown in Table 2, we can see a clear loss of the useful information, up to 0.0395. Obviously, the utility of these images was affected after being processed in these methods.

Table 2. The utility loss after different privacy protection methods.

Methods	Average utility loss	Standard deviation of utility loss
Blindfold	0.0395	0.01749
Mosaic	0.0024	0.0012
Laplace	0.0046	0.0014
Cartoon	0.0355	0.0220

5.3 Image Utility Maintenance

We take the original image and its four processing images as a set of training data. In each batch of training, we take a set of training data as the input, and finally generate a result graph. For each batch training, we use Eq. 6 as the loss function.

We use the test set to calculate the value of MSE under different training epochs. and finally get the change trend of image utility as shown in Fig. 5.

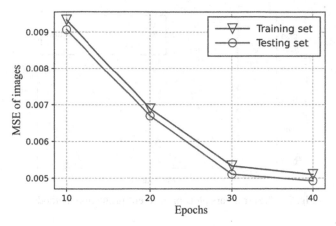

Fig. 5. The changing trend of MSE with model training.

From the above results, when training for 40 rounds, the MSE of both the training set and the testing set is about 0.005 which is less than the methods of blindfold and cartoon.

The resulting images are shown in Fig. 6. Our proposed framework surpasses four traditional methods in visual effects and produces results that are very similar to real faces. This shows that our framework has an obvious effect on maintaining the utility of facial image.

Fig. 6. The result image after utility restoration using a VAE-based generator.

We calculate the MSE of each image in the sample before and after processing, and made error bars and error scatter of four protection methods and our framework, as shown in Fig. 7 and Fig. 8. Combined with visual effects and data, our framework strikes a balance between privacy protection and utility maintenance. Compared with the traditional methods, our framework has stable and superior utility retention ability.

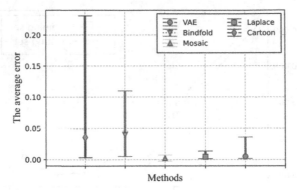

Fig. 7. The error bars plots of different protection methods.

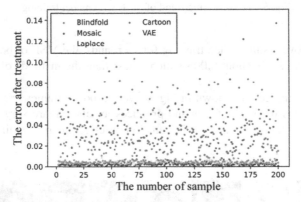

Fig. 8. The error scatter plots of different protection methods.

Figure 9 shows an example process of privacy protection through our method. Compared with the original image, the processed image erases the privacy information of face, which provides a guarantee for the safe use of the image in the application scene. Compared with the traditional method, the image generated by our proposed framework is more similar to the real face than traditional methods, so it has little influence on the expression of image information.

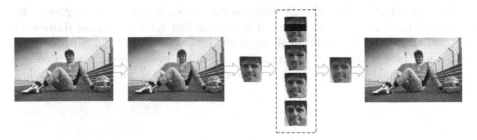

Fig. 9. A case process of private preserving facial image processing method using VAE.

6 Conclusion

In this paper, we have proposed a new face de-identification method using VAE, which integrates multiple existing privacy protection technologies for de-identification. We innovatively use VAE to restore the useful information of face images. In the experiments, we quantitatively demonstrated that our proposed framework has an excellent performance in maintaining the utility of image. We are the first to propose a universal privacy protection framework that combines VAE with multiple privacy protection modes, with flexible adaptability and high efficiency.

In the process of quantitatively calculating the utility retention of the image we only consider the similarity with the real face, that is, the MSE of the image before and after processing without talking about the specific service scenarios. In the future research, it is reasonable to preserve image utility for specific service and adopt more reasonable indicators to measure the degree of privacy protection and utility maintenance. In the future, this method can break through the field of face image and be applied to the privacy information protection in a broader field such as motion, fingerprint and so on.

References

1. Agarwal, A., Chattopadhyay, P., Wang, L.: Privacy preservation through facial de-identification with simultaneous emotion preservation. SIViP **15**(5), 951–958 (2020). https://doi.org/10.1007/s11760-020-01819-9
2. Letournel, G., Bugeau, A., Ta, V.T., Domenger, J.P.: Face de-identification with expressions preservation. In: 2015 IEEE International Conference on Image Processing (ICIP), pp. 4366–4370. IEEE (2015)
3. Wu, Y., Yang, F., Xu, Y., Ling, H.: Privacy-protective-GAN for privacy preserving face de-identification. J. Comput. Sci. Technol. **34**(1), 47–60 (2019)
4. Nousi, P., Papadopoulos, S., Tefas, A., Pitas, I.: Deep autoencoders for attribute preserving face de-identification. Signal Proc. Image Commun. **81**, 115699 (2020)
5. Oord, A.V.D., Vinyals, O., Kavukcuoglu, K.: Neural discrete representation learning. arXiv preprint arXiv:1711.00937 (2017)
6. Kim, J., Kim, M., Kang, H., Lee, K.: U-gat-it: unsupervised generative attentional networks with adaptive layer-instance normalization for image-to-image translation. arXiv preprint arXiv:1907.10830 (2019)
7. Ribaric, S., Ariyaeeinia, A., Pavesic, N.: De-identification for privacy protection in multimedia content: a survey. Signal Proc. Image Commun. **47**, 131–151 (2016)
8. Neustaedter, C., Greenberg, S., Boyle, M.: Blur filtration fails to preserve privacy for home-based video conferencing. ACM Trans. Comput. Human Interact. (TOCHI) **13**(1), 1–36 (2006)
9. Yu, J., Zhang, B., Kuang, Z., Lin, D., Fan, J.: iPrivacy: image privacy protection by identifying sensitive objects via deep multi-task learning. IEEE Trans. Inf. Foren. Secur. **12**(5), 1005–1016 (2016)
10. Gross, R., Airoldi, E., Malin, B., Sweeney, L.: Integrating utility into face de-identification. In: International Workshop on Privacy Enhancing Technologies, pp. 227–242. Springer, Berlin, Heidelberg (2005). https://doi.org/10.1007/11767831_15
11. Gross, R., Sweeney, L., De La Torre, F., Baker, S.: Semi-supervised learning of multi-factor models for face de-identification. In: 2008 IEEE Conference on Computer Vision and Pattern Recognition, pp. 1–8. IEEE (2008)

12. Sun, Z., Meng, L., Ariyaeeinia, A.: Distinguishable de-identified faces. In: 2015 11th IEEE International Conference and Workshops on Automatic Face and Gesture Recognition (FG), Vol. 4, pp. 1–6. IEEE (2015)
13. Newton, E.M., Sweeney, L., Malin, B.: Preserving privacy by de-identifying face images. IEEE Trans. Knowl. Data Eng. **17**(2), 232–243 (2005)
14. Samarzija, B., Ribaric, S.: An approach to the de-identification of faces in different poses. In: 2014 37th International Convention on Information and Communication Technology, Electronics and Microelectronics (MIPRO), pp. 1246–1251. IEEE (2014)
15. Gross, R., Sweeney, L., De la Torre, F., Baker, S.: Model-based face de-identification. In: 2006 Conference on Computer Vision and Pattern Recognition Workshop (CVPRW'06), p. 161. IEEE (2006)
16. Meden, B., Emeršič, Ž, Štruc, V., Peer, P.: k-Same-Net: k-Anonymity with generative deep neural networks for face deidentification. Entropy **20**(1), 60 (2018)
17. Gross, R., Airoldi, E., Malin, B., Sweeney, L.: Integrating utility into face de-identification. In: Danezis, G., Martin, D. (eds.) PET 2005. LNCS, vol. 3856, pp. 227–242. Springer, Heidelberg (2006). https://doi.org/10.1007/11767831_15
18. Seeger, M.: Learning with Labeled and Unlabeled Data (2000)
19. Blum, A., Mitchell, T.: Combining labeled and unlabeled data with co-training. In: Proceedings of the Eleventh Annual Conference on Computational Learning Theory, pp. 92–100 (1998)
20. Phillips, P.J., Wechsler, H., Huang, J., Rauss, P.J.: The FERET database and evaluation procedure for face-recognition algorithms. Image Vis. Comput. **16**(5), 295–306 (1998)
21. Chuanlu, L.I.U., Yicheng, W.A.N.G., Hehua, C.H.I., Shuliang, W.A.N.G.: Utility preserved facial image de-identification using appearance subspace decomposition. Chin. J. Electron. **30**(3), 413–418 (2021)
22. Ian, G., Pouget-Abadie, J., Mirza, M., Xu, B., Warde-Farley, D.: Generative adversarial nets. In: Advances in Neural Information Processing Systems (2014)
23. Cai, Z., Xiong, Z., Xu, H., Wang, P., Li, W., Pan, Y.: Generative adversarial networks: a survey towards private and secure applications. arXiv preprint arXiv:2106.03785 (2021)
24. Han, C., Xue, R.: Differentially private GANs by adding noise to discriminator's loss. Comput. Secur. **107**, 102322 (2021)
25. Hukkelås, H., Mester, R., Lindseth, F.: Deep privacy: a generative adversarial network for face anonymization. In: International Symposium on Visual Computing, pp. 565–578. Springer, Cham (2019)
26. Sun, Q., Ma, L., Oh, S. J., Van Gool, L., Schiele, B., Fritz, M.: Natural and effective obfuscation by head in painting. In: Proceedings of the IEEE Conference on Computer Vision and Pattern Recognition, pp. 5050–5059 (2018)
27. Li, Y., Qianwen, L., Tao, Q., Zhao, X., Yanmei, Y.: SF-GAN: face De-identification method without losing facial attribute information. IEEE Signal Proc. Lett. **28**, 1345–1349 (2021). https://doi.org/10.1109/LSP.2021.3067517
28. Chen, J., Konrad, J., Ishwar, P.: Vgan-based image representation learning for privacy-preserving facial expression recognition. In: Proceedings of the IEEE Conference on Computer Vision and Pattern Recognition Workshops, pp. 1570–1579 (2018)
29. Louizos, C., Swersky, K., Li, Y., Welling, M., Zemel, R.: The variational fair autoencoder. arXiv preprint arXiv:1511.00830 (2015)
30. Mirza, M., Osindero, S.: Conditional generative adversarial nets. arXiv preprint arXiv:1411.1784 (2014)
31. Dwork, C.: Differential privacy. In International Colloquium on Automata, Languages, and Programming, pp. 1–12. Springer, Berlin, Heidelberg (2006). https://doi.org/10.1007/11787006_1

32. Zhou, G., Qin, S., Zhou, H., Cheng, D.: A differential privacy noise dynamic allocation algorithm for big multimedia data. Multimed. Tools Appl. **78**(3), 3747–3765 (2018). https://doi.org/10.1007/s11042-018-5776-0
33. Bu, Z., Dong, J., Long, Q., Su, W.J.: Deep learning with Gaussian differential privacy. Harvard Data Sci. Rev. 2020, **23** (2020)
34. Liu, C., Yang, J., Zhao, W., Zhang, Y., Li, J., Mu, C.: Face image publication based on differential privacy. In: Wireless Communications and Mobile Computing, 2021 (2021)
35. Yu, J., Xue, H., Liu, B., Wang, Y., Zhu, S., Ding, M.: GAN-based differential private image privacy protection framework for the internet of multimedia things. Sensors **21**(1), 58 (2021)
36. Kim, T., Yang, J.: Latent-space-level image anonymization with adversarial protector networks. IEEE Access **7**, 84992–84999 (2019)
37. Fredrikson, M., Jha, S., Ristenpart, T.: Model inversion attacks that exploit confidence information and basic countermeasures. In: Proceedings of the 22nd ACM SIGSAC Conference on Computer and Communications Security, pp. 1322–1333 (2015)
38. Croft, W.L., Sack, J.R., Shi, W.: Obfuscation of images via differential privacy: from facial images to general images. Peer-to-Peer Netw. Appl. **14**(3), 1705–1733 (2021)
39. Kim, T., Yang, J.: Selective feature anonymization for privacy-preserving image data publishing. Electronics **9**(5), 874 (2020)
40. Liu, Z., Luo, P., Wang, X., Tang, X.: Large-Scale Celebfaces Attributes (Celeba) Dataset, vol. 11 (2018). Accessed Aug. 15(2018)

A Survey on Privacy-Preserving Deep Learning with Differential Privacy

Yu Zhang, Ying Cai[✉], Meng Zhang, Xin Li, and Yanfang Fan

Department of Computer Science and Technology,
Beijing Information Science and Technology University, Beijing 100101, China
ycai@bistu.edu.cn

Abstract. Deep learning has been increasingly applied in a wide variety of domains and has achieved remarkable results. Generally, a large amount of data is needed to train a deep learning model. The data might contain sensitive information, leading to the risk of privacy leakage in the process of model training and model application. As a privacy definition with strict mathematical guarantee, differential privacy has gained great attention and has been widely studied in recent years. However, applying differential privacy to deep learning still faces a big challenge to reduce the impact on model accuracy. In this paper, we first analyze the privacy threats that exist in deep learning from the perspective of privacy attacks, including membership inference attacks and reconstruction attacks. We also introduce some basic theories necessary to apply differential privacy to deep learning. Second, to summarize how existing works apply differential privacy to deep learning, we divide perturbations into four categories based on different perturbation stages of deep learning with differential privacy: input perturbation, parameter perturbation, objective function perturbation, and output perturbation. Finally, the challenges and future research directions on deep learning with differential privacy are summarized.

Keywords: Deep learning · Privacy protection · Differential privacy

1 Introduction

With the development of artificial intelligence and the advent of the big data era, it has led to a rapid increase in the amount of data, which has stimulated the research on deep learning. As the frontier field of machine learning research, deep learning has been applied in every aspect it can be used and is gradually expanding its application fields, such as the natural language processing [7,17], LHC physical data analysis [18], biomedical image classification [37], wireless communication [19,22], face recognition [38], and many more.

This work was supported in part by the National Natural Science Foundation of China under Grant 61672106, and in part by the Natural Science Foundation of Beijing, China under Grant L192023 and in part by the project of Scientific research fund of Beijing Information Science and Technology University of under 5029923412.

The main content of deep learning is to study and summarize the laws of the sample data. With its wide application, many sensitive personal data, such as users' physiological characteristics and medical records, are collected by various enterprises and institutions and used for data analysis, which brings greater risks and challenges to personal privacy protection. Therefore, personal privacy protection is also receiving increasing attention and concern. In May 2018, the General Data Protection Regulation [1] became enforceable for all EU countries, and companies are required to obtain users' consent for accessing their personal data. In fact, many scholars have conducted research on privacy protection in this regard. The k-anonymity [41,42] algorithm and its extended model have a deep influence in the field of privacy protection. It lays a foundation for anonymous privacy-preserving algorithms based on grouping of equivalence classes. However, a series of subsequent studies have shown that these models cannot provide sufficient protection for data. For example, in order to resist "Homogeneity" attack, l-diversity [28], t-closeness [27], (α, k)-anonymity [46], M-invariance [47] and other models have been proposed. Many novel attacks such as composition attack [16,45] have challenged grouping-based privacy-preserving algorithms, and these privacy-preserving models are related to the background knowledge possessed by the attacker, and thus always require updated designs to capture novel attacks.

Differential privacy was first proposed as a privacy definition by Dwork [9] in 2006, initially to address the privacy leakage problem of statistical databases. Under the differential privacy definition, an attacker is considered to have maximum background knowledge if he obtains all the data containing within the data except the target data, so the differential privacy model do not need to estimate the amount of knowledge that an attacker can have. The mathematical proof process is rigorous in differential privacy, which, among other things, strictly defines privacy protection and provides how to calculate the loss due to privacy breach. As a result, differential privacy is widely accepted and applied. Several attempts have been made to apply differential privacy to deep learning by combining its rigorous mathematical proofs and flexible composition theorems to protect privacy during training and prediction, and the best protection scheme can be obtained by varying the model parameters to compare different levels of privacy protection. And differential privacy is gradually applied to real-life applications, such as Google's Chrome [13] and Apple's iOS10 [31], which require the extraction of various private data of users who perform machine learning, are necessary to protect users' data and data details regarding privacy. However, there are many privacy attacks in deep learning that want to steal sensitive data and model parameters, and differential privacy interferes with the real data by adding a portion of the noise. Therefore, how to use differential privacy to interfere with the process of deep learning to protect privacy is important, because the availability of data and models must be maintained after noise is added.

The rest of the paper is organized as follows. In Sect. 2, We briefly introduce the basic concepts of deep learning, as well as describe the privacy issues that exist in deep learning. Section 3 introduces some basic theory needed to apply differential privacy to deep learning. Section 4 analyzes the current results on applying differential privacy to deep learning. In Sect. 5, we discuss the challenges and future research directions of differential privacy combined with deep learning. Section 6 provides an overall summary of the entire paper.

2 Privacy Threats in Deep Learning

2.1 Deep Learning

Deep learning has gradually become a key research direction for machine learning because of its advantages such as stronger abstraction ability and higher accuracy rate. Deep learning simulates the human brain by building deep neural networks for analysis, so that the machine can have the ability to learn and analyze like humans. The depth of the model structure is the focus of the study of deep learning compared to the previous shallow learning. The hidden layer usually has 5 layers, 8 layers, or 12 layers. Moreover, it is crucial to perform feature learning in deep learning. The deep learning model transforms the original features into a new feature space by taking the input original features and transforming them through feature transformations between different layers. Thus, it can go to solve some complex problems. Typical deep learning models include convolutional neural network [20,25], deep belief network [21], and stacked auto-encoder network models [8].

Machine Learning as a Service (MLaaS) is a service offered by cloud computing providers such as Google and Amazon. The user simply uploads the data for making predictions to the MLaaS server and obtains the desired results [53]. This service solves the problem of insufficient computing resources for users and the protection of intellectual property rights of service providers' machine learning models. While the MLaaS service is convenient for users, because users need to upload data to the server in plaintext, the uploaded data cannot be encrypted, and the user's data privacy cannot be effectively protected.

2.2 Privacy Attacks

The privacy issues in deep learning are mainly manifested in the following two aspects: First, in the data collection stage, due to the phenomenon of arbitrary collection of personal information without people's permission, illegal processing of data will cause privacy to be compromised directly; Second, In the data analysis stage, there is a phenomenon that the leak-prone information of unknown individuals in the training dataset can be inferred from the interaction with the model. Which will lead to indirect leakage of personal privacy. Privacy attacks in deep learning can be categorized as membership inference attacks and reconstruction attacks depending on the attacker's target.

Membership Inference Attack. An attacker can use a method called inference membership attack to determine whether a sample is in a certain deep learning dataset. That is, to determine whether the sample is a member of the training data. Membership inference attack sometimes causes serious consequences. For example, during the COVID-19 epidemic, there is a medical diagnosis model constructed from the data of many COVID-19 patients. An attacker can determine the likelihood that someone has COVID-19 by inferring which model their medical data belongs to.

The membership inference attack [23] follows a black box configuration. The attacker can use the samples to query the target's model so that predictions can be generated, and thus the model can be built for the attack. To train a model that can perform an attack, the adversary needs to build models that closely resemble the target model. The attacker can then train an attack model that can analyze the accuracy of the data coming from the target model based on the output of a very similar model and the target model. The research of Shokri et al. [40] showed that attacks using inference-related members can infer from which training dataset a certain data originates.

Reconstruction Attack. A reconstruction attack is an attacker's attempt to infer information about a person or a useful model from information already in his possession, corresponding to model inversion attack and model extraction attack, respectively.

The model inversion attack aims to reconstruct individual information. According to experiments already done by Fredrikson[15], model inference attacks against model speculation can infer certain features of the used dataset by using the output of the model after training. Especially in the face recognition, Fredrikson did experiments to verify that attackers can reconstruct the training data from the model [14].

The model extraction attack is aimed at reconstructing the training model. The method of equation solving was mainly used in the early stage, but it is only suitable for simple linear dichotomy models. Tramèr et al. [44] applied this approach to complex models such as nonlinear support vector computers and neural networks, and uses predictive confidence to significantly improve the attack effect.

3 Differential Privacy Protection

3.1 Definition

The prevention of leakage by adding interference noise to the data is the differential privacy technique. It was originally proposed to protect individual information in the database, and it has since been widely accepted and applied. Compared with encryption methods, differential privacy mechanisms are easier to deploy and apply in actual application scenarios.

Definition 1 (ε-differential privacy). A random algorithm $K : D \rightarrow R$ with domain D and range R satisfies ε-differential privacy if for any two adjacent inputs $d, d' \in D$ and for any subset of outputs $S \in R$ it holds that

$$Pr[K(d) \in S] \leq exp(\varepsilon)Pr[K(d') \in S] \tag{1}$$

The parameter ε is the valuation of the loss due to the privacy breach. Normally, the value of the privacy budget is very small, making $\exp(\varepsilon)$ close to 1, that is, for two data sets with only one record difference, the probability of querying them is very close. A smaller valuation of privacy loss indicates higher privacy confidentiality, while a larger valuation of loss due to privacy breach indicates higher data availability. Therefore how to weigh the privacy level and data availability is a very important issue [11].

3.2   Noise Mechanism

Differential privacy is achieved by adding partial scrambling noise to interfere with the data. The size of the noise will affect the security and availability of the data, which is more relevant to the global accessibility of the data [10].

Definition 2 (Global Sensitivity). For a query function $f : D \to R^d$, the global sensitivity is represented by the symbol Δf, Δf is defined as

$$\Delta f = \max_{D_1, D_2} \parallel f(D_1) - f(D_2) \parallel \tag{2}$$

Among them, D_1 and D_2 are any two adjacent data sets. The global sensitivity has nothing to do with the data set, only with the query results.

The perturbation objects of differential privacy can be both data sources and model parameters and output results. That is, participants can add noise to their original data so that the original data never appears in the computation process. Privacy can also be protected by adding noise to the model parameters during the model training process. It is also possible to protect the output results by adding noise before the results are directly output, so as to prevent an attacker from inferring the input data from the computed results.

The implementation mechanisms for adding noise mainly include Laplacian mechanism [26] and Exponential mechanism [30]. The former is often used for functions with numerical output, and the latter is often used for functions with non-numerical output.

Theorem 1. *For a given data set D and function $f : D \to R^d$, if the output result of algorithm K satisfies:*

$$K(D) = f(D) + Lap(\frac{\Delta f}{\varepsilon}) \tag{3}$$

Then the algorithm K satisfies ε-differential privacy.

Theorem 2. *Given an availability function $u : (D, r) \to R$, if the output result of algorithm K satisfies:*

$$K(D, u) = \left\{ r \mid Pr[r \in O] \propto exp(\frac{\varepsilon u(D, r)}{2\Delta u}) \right\} \tag{4}$$

Then the algorithm K satisfies ε-differential privacy.

3.3   Composition Theorems

In some complex problems it is necessary to apply the differential privacy algorithm several times to be able to protect privacy. Therefore, when solving complex problems, it is necessary to consider how the entire privacy budget can be rationally divided to every step of the algorithm. In this way it can ensure that the whole process satisfies the differential privacy for a given total budget. In deep learning, to study how the whole neural network satisfies the differential privacy requires the use of the composition theorem [24].

Theorem 3. *Let K_i each provide ε_i -differential privacy. The sequence of $K_i(X)$ provides ($\sum_i \varepsilon_i$)-differential privacy.*

Where K_i denotes a differential privacy algorithm satisfying ε_i-differential privacy, and $K_i(X)$ denotes all algorithms acting on a data set X. Then the overall composition of all algorithms satisfies ($\sum_i \varepsilon_i$)-differential privacy.

Theorem 4. *Let K_i each provide ε -differential privacy. Let D_i be arbitrary disjoint subsets of the input domain D. The sequence of $K_i(X \cap D_i)$ provides ε-differential privacy.*

Where K_i denotes a differential privacy algorithm satisfying ε-differential privacy, D_i denotes mutually disjoint datasets, and $K_i(X \cap D_i)$ means that the individual differential privacy acts on disjoint data sets. Then the overall composition of these algorithms satisfies ε-differential privacy. Theorem 4 can be generalized to mean that if K_i denotes a differential privacy algorithm satisfying ε_i-differential privacy, then the overall composition of these algorithms satisfies ($\max \varepsilon_i$)-differential privacy [29].

4   Deep Learning Privacy Protection Mechanism Based on Differential Privacy

Applying differential privacy to deep learning allows adding noise to the raw data or intermediate parameters during model training for privacy protection, or adding noise to the output of model parameters to protect the model. There have been many studies combining differential privacy and deep learning. These approaches assume that the training dataset and model parameters are databases and demonstrate that the improved algorithms meet the definition of differential privacy. According to the different perturbation phases, differential privacy for deep learning can be classified into four parts: input perturbation, parameter perturbation, objective function perturbation, and output perturbation. Therefore, we will analyze how differential privacy can be applied to each part according to this classification.

4.1   Input Perturbation

Input perturbation for deep learning can be regarded as preprocessing of the training data set. The original dataset is partially noisy added to generate synthetic data. The synthetic data is released without revealing privacy and can be used for various subsequent applications and analyses. The solution aims to hide or alter sensitive features of the training dataset while keeping the data availability for further analysis of deep learning. Chamikara M et al. [6] proposed a new local differential privacy algorithm called LATENT to train convolutional neural networks (CNN) with high privacy and high accuracy. The algorithm divides the structure of the CNN into three layers, where a randomization layer is introduced to realize that the data is protected before use. Zhang et al. [52] proposed a framework called dp-GAN, which is mainly used for data publishing. Differential privacy protection is introduced in the generative model in this framework instead of publishing the data directly after cleaning. Yang et al. [48] proposed a privacy-preserving framework called dp-WGAN that is mainly used for privacy protection of image data, and differential privacy is used to train generative models with privacy-preserving features. The synthetic data generated by this generative model ensures that it has similar characteristics to the sensitive information to complete further analysis and processing of the data, and also ensures that the sensitive information is not compromised.

4.2   Parameter Perturbation

The earliest way to apply differential privacy to deep learning to solve the privacy leakage problem is to add noise to the gradient of the model. Abadi et al. [2] proposed a new algorithm DP-SGD. The implementation of the algorithm is mainly composed of two components: Sanitizer and Privacy accountant. Sanitizer is mainly used to perform a pre-processing of the gradient. The gradient values are constrained to a range of values by gradient clipping, and then noise satisfying the Gaussian mechanism is added to the gradient before each gradient update. How to calculate privacy loss is an important issue in the combination of differential privacy and deep learning. Privacy accountant is mainly used to track privacy expenditures during model training. Shokri and Shmatikov [39] proposed a deep neural network distributed system that satisfies differential privacy, providing a novel approach for implementing deep learning on mobile devices. Phan et al. [33] proposed a heterogeneous Gaussian mechanism that uses Gaussian noise to interfere with the first hidden layer. And this mechanism adds a new noise scale constraint that relaxes the traditional privacy budget.

Since in neural networks, every input feature has a different influence on the final output result. Phan et al. [36] proposed an adaptive Laplace mechanism (AdLM) to improve the Laplacian mechanism of differential privacy. AdLM applies Layer-wise Relevance Propagation (LRP) to compute the relevance between every input feature of the training data and the model results. Different amounts of noise are added to the input features depending on the magnitude of their impact on the output results. Therefore, the impact on the usability of the model is reduced while ensuring privacy protection.

4.3 Objective Function Perturbation

The deep learning model will output the corresponding output based on the initial value of the input. The loss function is generally used to evaluate the difference between the output result of the model and the true value. The smaller the value of the loss function indicates that the model works better. Zhang J et al. [50] proposed a function mechanism that improves on the Laplace mechanism. This mechanism perturbs the objective function of the deep learning model. Phan et al. [34] improved the traditional deep private autoencoder. The main idea of which is to approximate the polynomial form of the crossentropy error function by using Taylor expansions, and then injecting noise into these polynomials. This scheme applies differential privacy to the objective function itself rather than to the result of the objective function. Phan et al. [35] applies the Chebyshev expansion to deduce the polynomial approximation to the nonlinear objective function used in CDBN, which significantly improves the applicability of differential privacy in deep learning.

4.4 Output Perturbation

Perturbing the output of deep learning can achieve privacy protection by perturbing the model parameters that can be released after training. Yuan D et al. [49] proposes a collaborative deep learning approach for the medical image analysis problem, where hospitals add noise satisfying a Gaussian mechanism to the parameters of a locally trained model when they are uploaded to a parameter server to protect the true parameter values.

We compare differential private methods on deep learning, as shown in Table 1.

5 Future Challenges of Differential Privacy Protection on Deep Learning

With the in-depth research on deep learning, its special structure has brought huge challenges to the privacy of data and network models. Combining differential privacy and deep learning models still faces some challenges. Applying differential privacy to deep learning can prevent the model from revealing some sensitive information, but introducing perturbations can affect the accuracy and usability of the model. In this section, we are going to discuss some challenges of combining differential privacy models with deep learning and possible future research directions.

5.1 Extension of the Definition of Differential Privacy

Differential privacy does not require any assumptions about the attacker's background knowledge, and is defined very rigorously and mathematically proven.

Table 1. Comparison of differential privacy protection methods in deep learning.

Perturbation stage	Perturbation method	Algorithm	Dataset	Related work
Input perturbation	Local differential privacy	LATENT	MNIST/CIFAR-10	[6]
	Generate synthetic data	dp-GAN	MNIST/CelebA/LSUN	[52]
		dp-WGAN	MNIST/CelebA/CIFAR-10	[48]
Parameter perturbation	Gradient parameter perturbation	DP-SGD	MNIST/CIFAR-10	[2]
		DSSGD	MNIST/SVHN	[39]
		Secure-SGD	MNIST/CIFAR-10	[33]
	Input feature perturbation	ADLM	MNIST/CIFAR-10	[36]
Objective function perturbation	Objective function expansion coefficient perturbation	FM	Integrated Public use microdata series	[50]
		dPA	Health social network data	[34]
		pCDBN	YesiWell data/MNIST	[35]
Output perturbation	Output parameter perturbation	Collaborative deep learning with the analysis Gaussian mechanism	Chest X-Ray Images (Pneumonia)	[49]

Therefore, it is often necessary to introduce enough noise to satisfy the requirements of the differential privacy definition, but too much noise may render the data completely meaningless. In response to this problem, some researchers have tried to relax the requirements for differential privacy when applying it, in order to achieve an appropriate reduction in privacy while improving the usability of the results.

As differential privacy is applied in various fields to achieve privacy protection, its definition is constantly being extended to meet practical needs. (ε, δ)-differential privacy is a relaxed definition, introducing a new parameter δ. The possibility of ε-differential privacy being compromised with probability δ is considered compared to the standard definition, thus providing more flexibility in the choice of privacy protection mechanisms. Concentrated Differential Privacy [12] improves the original advanced composition theorem and combines the privacy budget with the advanced composition theorem. Gaussian differential privacy [3] is a privacy representation recently proposed by a research group at the University of Pennsylvania, and the combination with deep learning ensures higher prediction accuracy with the same privacy budget.

We believe that proposing a new privacy definition on the basis of differential privacy is a perfection, and is important for expanding the application field of differential privacy.

5.2 Differential Privacy Combined with Cryptography

The advantage of differential privacy mechanism is that adding random noise will not cause excessive performance cost, while the disadvantage is that the perturbation mechanism will probably make the model accuracy worse and the availability of the output results reduced. Encryption methods [4,5,43,51] can avoid deciphering the content of the data by unauthorized users during the transmission and computation of the data. However, because the intermediate process involves a lot of computation and key transfer, its computation and communication overhead are not optimistic when dealing with complex models. If the strengths and weaknesses of these methods can be used to complement each other, the effectiveness of privacy protection can reach a high level. However, the feasibility of deep learning applications and the effectiveness of algorithms need to be fully considered, which also brings a new challenge for privacy protection in this field. Owusu-Agyemeng et al. [32] proposed an MSDP architecture for privacy protection in deep neural networks that combines secure multi-party compilation and differentiated privacy with better performance of deformation and at a high level of generalization.

6 Conclusion

With the gradual expansion of deep learning application areas, how to protect user privacy has become a pressing issue. There is an urgent need to consider how to guarantee security and avoid various existential dangers in practical applications, especially for some users who often perform irregular operations and are likely to be potential attackers. Currently, to realize the balance between availability and privacy in complex deep learning, relaxed differential privacy definition is often used instead of the traditional strict differential privacy definition, and how to trade-off availability and privacy protection is a very important issue in the future. This paper starts with the privacy issues in the deep learning model. It mainly introduces two privacy attack methods: membership inference attack and reconstruction attack. It explains some basic theories of differential privacy and analyzes some current research results of applying differential privacy to deep learning. We hope this survey could stimulate more research in this field.

References

1. The European General Data Protection Regulation (GDPR). https://gdpr-info. eu/. Accessed 9 July 2021

2. Abadi, M., et al.: Deep learning with differential privacy. In: Proceedings of the 2016 ACM SIGSAC Conference on Computer and Communications Security, pp. 308–318 (2016)
3. Bu, Z., Dong, J., Long, Q., Su, W.J.: Deep learning with gaussian differential privacy. Harvard Data Sci. Rev. **2020**(23) (2020)
4. Cai, Y., Zhang, S., Xia, H., Fan, Y., Zhang, H.: A privacy-preserving scheme for interactive messaging over online social networks. IEEE Internet Things J. **7**, 6817–6827 (2020)
5. Cai, Y., Zhang, H., Fang, Y.: A conditional privacy protection scheme based on ring signcryption for vehicular ad hoc networks. IEEE Internet Things J. **8**, 647–656 (2020)
6. Chamikara, M., Bertok, P., Khalil, I., Liu, D., Camtepe, S.: Local differential privacy for deep learning (2019)
7. Deng, L., Yu, D.: Deep learning: methods and applications. Foundations Trends Sig. Processing **7**(3–4), 197–387 (2014)
8. Du, B., Xiong, W., Wu, J., Zhang, L., Zhang, L., Tao, D.: Stacked convolutional denoising auto-encoders for feature representation. IEEE Trans. Cybern. **47**(4), 1017–1027 (2016)
9. Alvim, M.S., Chatzikokolakis, K., McIver, A., Morgan, C., Palamidessi, C., Smith, G.: Differential privacy. In: The Science of Quantitative Information Flow. ISC, pp. 433–444. Springer, Cham (2020). https://doi.org/10.1007/978-3-319-96131-6_23
10. Dwork, C., Naor, M., Pitassi, T., Rothblum, G.N.: Differential privacy under continual observation. In: Proceedings of the Forty-Second ACM Symposium on Theory of Computing, pp. 715–724 (2010)
11. Dwork, C., Roth, A., et al.: The algorithmic foundations of differential privacy. Found. Trends Theor. Comput. Sci. **9**(3–4), 211–407 (2014)
12. Dwork, C., Rothblum, G.N.: Concentrated differential privacy. arXiv preprint arXiv:1603.01887 (2016)
13. Fanti, G., Pihur, V., Erlingsson, Ú.: Building a RAPPOR with the unknown: privacy-preserving learning of associations and data dictionaries. arXiv preprint arXiv:1503.01214 (2015)
14. Fredrikson, M., Jha, S., Ristenpart, T.: Model inversion attacks that exploit confidence information and basic countermeasures. In: Proceedings of the 22nd ACM SIGSAC Conference on Computer and Communications Security, pp. 1322–1333 (2015)
15. Fredrikson, M., Lantz, E., Jha, S., Lin, S., Page, D., Ristenpart, T.: Privacy in pharmacogenetics: an end-to-end case study of personalized warfarin dosing. In: 23rd USENIX Security Symposium (USENIX Security 14), pp. 17–32 (2014)
16. Ganta, S.R., Kasiviswanathan, S.P., Smith, A.: Composition attacks and auxiliary information in data privacy. In: Proceedings of the 14th ACM SIGKDD International Conference on Knowledge Discovery and Data Mining, pp. 265–273 (2008)
17. Gong, Y., Lu, N., Zhang, J.: Application of deep learning fusion algorithm in natural language processing in emotional semantic analysis. Concurrency Comput. Pract. Experience **31**(10), e4779 (2019)
18. Guest, D., Cranmer, K., Whiteson, D.: Deep learning and its application to LHC physics. Annu. Rev. Nucl. Part. Sci. **68**, 161–181 (2018)
19. Gui, G., Huang, H., Song, Y., Sari, H.: Deep learning for an effective nonorthogonal multiple access scheme. IEEE Trans. Veh. Technol. **67**(9), 8440–8450 (2018)
20. Hao, X., Zhang, G., Ma, S.: Deep learning. Int. J. Semant. Comput. **10**(03), 417–439 (2016)

21. Hinton, G.E.: Deep belief networks. Scholarpedia **4**(5), 5947 (2009)
22. Huang, H., Song, Y., Yang, J., Gui, G., Adachi, F.: Deep-learning-based millimeter-wave massive MIMO for hybrid precoding. IEEE Trans. Veh. Technol. **68**(3), 3027–3032 (2019)
23. Irolla, P., Chtel, G.: Demystifying the membership inference attack. In: 2019 12th CMI Conference on Cybersecurity and Privacy (CMI) (2020)
24. Kairouz, P., Oh, S., Viswanath, P.: The composition theorem for differential privacy. IEEE Trans. Inf. Theor. (2017)
25. Ketkar, N.: Convolutional neural networks. In: Deep Learning with Python, pp. 61–76. Apress, Berkeley, CA (2017). https://doi.org/10.1007/978-1-4842-2766-4_5
26. Koufogiannis, F., Han, S., Pappas, G.J.: Optimality of the Laplace mechanism in differential privacy. arXiv preprint arXiv:1504.00065 (2015)
27. Li, N., Li, T., Venkatasubramanian, S.: t-Closeness: privacy beyond k-anonymity and l-diversity. In: 2007 IEEE 23rd International Conference on Data Engineering, pp. 106–115. IEEE (2007)
28. Machanavajjhala, A., Kifer, D., Gehrke, J., Venkitasubramaniam, M.: L-Diversity: privacy beyond k-anonymity. ACM Trans. Knowl. Discovery Data (TKDD) **1**(1), 3-es (2007)
29. McSherry, F.: Privacy integrated queries. In: Proceedings of the 2009 ACM SIGMOD International Conference on Management of Data (SIGMOD) (2009)
30. McSherry, F., Talwar, K.: Mechanism design via differential privacy. In: 48th Annual IEEE Symposium on Foundations of Computer Science (FOCS 2007), pp. 94–103. IEEE (2007)
31. Novac, O.C., Novac, M., Gordan, C., Berczes, T., Bujdosó, G.: Comparative study of google android, apple iOS and Microsoft windows phone mobile operating systems. In: 2017 14th International Conference on Engineering of Modern Electric Systems (EMES), pp. 154–159. IEEE (2017)
32. Owusu-Agyemeng, K., Qin, Z., Xiong, H., Liu, Y., Zhuang, T., Qin, Z.: MSDP: multi-scheme privacy-preserving deep learning via differential privacy. Pers. Ubiquit. Comput., 1–13 (2021)
33. Phan, N., et al.: Heterogeneous gaussian mechanism: preserving differential privacy in deep learning with provable robustness. arXiv preprint arXiv:1906.01444 (2019)
34. Phan, N., Wang, Y., Wu, X., Dou, D.: Differential privacy preservation for deep auto-encoders: an application of human behavior prediction. In: Thirtieth AAAI Conference on Artificial Intelligence (2016)
35. Phan, N.H., Wu, X., Dou, D.: Preserving differential privacy in convolutional deep belief networks. Mach. Learn., 1681–1704 (2017). https://doi.org/10.1007/s10994-017-5656-2
36. Phan, N., Wu, X., Hu, H., Dou, D.: Adaptive Laplace mechanism: differential privacy preservation in deep learning. In: 2017 IEEE International Conference on Data Mining (ICDM), pp. 385–394. IEEE (2017)
37. Revathi, M., Jeya, I.J.S., Deepa, S.N.: Deep learning-based soft computing model for image classification application. Soft. Comput. **24**(24), 18411–18430 (2020). https://doi.org/10.1007/s00500-020-05048-7
38. Sharma, S., Kumar, V.: Voxel-based 3D face reconstruction and its application to face recognition using sequential deep learning. Multimedia Tools Appl. **79**, 1–28 (2020)
39. Shokri, R., Shmatikov, V.: Privacy-preserving deep learning. In: Proceedings of the 22nd ACM SIGSAC Conference on Computer and Communications Security, pp. 1310–1321 (2015)

40. Shokri, R., Stronati, M., Song, C., Shmatikov, V.: Membership inference attacks against machine learning models. In: 2017 IEEE Symposium on Security and Privacy (SP), pp. 3–18. IEEE (2017)
41. Sweeney, L.: Achieving k-anonymity privacy protection using generalization and suppression. Internat. J. Uncertain. Fuzziness Knowl. Based Syst. **10**(5), 571–588 (2002)
42. Sweeney, L.: k-anonymity: a model for protecting privacy. Internat. J. Uncertain. Fuzziness Knowl. Based Syst. **10**(05), 557–570 (2002)
43. Thambiraja, E., Ramesh, G., Umarani, D.R.: A survey on various most common encryption techniques. Int. J. Adv. Res. Comput. Sci. Software Eng. **2**(7), 307–312 (2012)
44. Tramèr, F., Zhang, F., Juels, A., Reiter, M.K., Ristenpart, T.: Stealing machine learning models via prediction APIs. In: 25th USENIX Security Symposium (USENIX Security 16), pp. 601–618 (2016)
45. Wong, R.C.W., Fu, A.W.C., Wang, K., Yu, P.S., Pei, J.: Can the utility of anonymized data be used for privacy breaches? ACM Trans. Knowl. Discovery Data (TKDD) **5**(3), 1–24 (2011)
46. Wong, R.C.W., Li, J., Fu, A.W.C., Wang, K.: (α, k)-anonymity: an enhanced k-anonymity model for privacy preserving data publishing. In: Proceedings of the 12th ACM SIGKDD International Conference on Knowledge Discovery and Data Mining, pp. 754–759 (2006)
47. Xiao, X., Tao, Y.: M-invariance: towards privacy preserving re-publication of dynamic datasets. In: Proceedings of the 2007 ACM SIGMOD International Conference on Management of Data, pp. 689–700 (2007)
48. Yang, R., Ma, X., Bai, X., Su, X.: Differential privacy images protection based on generative adversarial network. In: 2020 IEEE 19th International Conference on Trust, Security and Privacy in Computing and Communications (TrustCom), pp. 1688–1695. IEEE (2020)
49. Yuan, D., Zhu, X., Wei, M., Ma, J.: Collaborative deep learning for medical image analysis with differential privacy. In: 2019 IEEE Global Communications Conference (GLOBECOM), pp. 1–6. IEEE (2019)
50. Zhang, J., Zhang, Z., Xiao, X., Yang, Y., Winslett, M.: Functional mechanism: regression analysis under differential privacy. arXiv preprint arXiv:1208.0219 (2012)
51. Zhang, S., Cai, Y., Xia, H.: A privacy-preserving interactive messaging scheme based on users credibility over online social networks. In: 2017 IEEE/CIC International Conference on Communications in China (ICCC) (2017)
52. Zhang, X., Ji, S., Wang, T.: Differentially private releasing via deep generative model (technical report). arXiv preprint arXiv:1801.01594 (2018)
53. Zhao, J., Chen, Y., Zhang, W.: Differential privacy preservation in deep learning: challenges, opportunities and solutions. IEEE Access **7**, 48901–48911 (2019)

Research on Security Protection Model of Power Big Data

Lan Zhang[1](✉), Xianjun Wang[1], and Sheng Ye[2]

[1] State Grid Henan Marketing Service Centre, Zhengzhou 456000, China
[2] State Grid Zhejiang Electric Power Company, Ltd., Hangzhou 310000, China

Abstract. As an information carrier, power data contains important parameters of power system operation, and it is also related to the security and stability of power system. In the current big data environment, the study of power system security has important practical value. On account of this, this paper first analyses the data security situation and response of power system, then studies the power data security protection system and power big data security protection strategy from the perspective of big data, and finally gives the power big data information security protection model, architecture and its specific applications.

Keywords: Big data · Security protection model · Power

1 Introduction

At present, the growing demand for energy in all walks of life makes the energy industry face new development opportunities as well as new challenges. As an important part of modern energy system, electric power industry plays an important role in promoting the development of all sectors of society, directly affecting the stability and development of related industries [1]. Power industry has been producing a lot of data in the process of operation, which contains important information and needs further mining and expansion. With the help of big data mining technology, it could effectively explore the value of data, and accelerate the development of power system. As the valuable information carrier, power data contains important parameters of power system operation, and it is also related to the security and stability of power system. In the current big data environment, how to effectively protect the security of the power system has become the focus of industry attention and research.

On the other hand, the application and popularization of computer intelligence technology has laid an effective premise for the intelligent development of power system, especially the application of big data in the field of power system security, which provides effective data support for the rapid development of power industry. In the Internet era, power system big data has been proved to contain important value, which significantly accelerates the development and progress of the whole power industry, and provides effective support for the technology upgrading and industrial structure transformation of the industry. Big data, as shown in Fig. 1, drives the development of power enterprises

© Springer Nature Singapore Pte Ltd. 2022
Y. Tian et al. (Eds.): ICBDS 2021, CCIS 1563, pp. 31–44, 2022.
https://doi.org/10.1007/978-981-19-0852-1_3

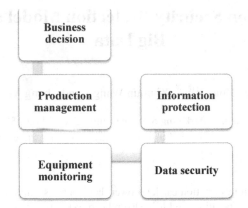

Fig. 1. Applications of big data in power enterprises

in terms of data and science, and has evolved into a key support for the progress of the power industry.

In addition, the contribution of power big data to the power industry is gradually changing from quantitative change to qualitative change, and this transformation is gradually realized in the context of the integration of power big data and information technology. Under the background of the development and transformation of power system networking and informatization, its operation has gradually realized automation and intelligence, and in many links as shown in Fig. 2. The construction of production informatization system has been implemented, a comprehensive information data platform has been established, which connects the power production platform with user end. The data intelligent analysis system of power system can effectively protect the privacy and data security of power users in the distributed and open environment, which brings new challenges to the big data security protection of power system. In the face of information security threats in the networked environment, the power big data architecture and security protection measures need to be further strengthened. Hence, it needs to enhance the data defense level of the power system, changing from passive defense to active defense.

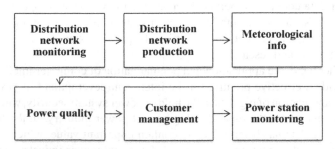

Fig. 2. Elements of integrated information data platform

With the continuous upgrading of big data security protection requirements of power system, higher requirements are put forward for the whole process and life cycle of power system operation. Whether it is from the front-end power grid system planning, power information collection, or the back-end power energy transmission and usage, data protection needs to be further strengthened. Power big data security is mainly in the information security architecture, taking innovative measures to meet the needs of data security protection under the new situation. The in-depth application of intelligent technologies such as IoT, AI and cloud computing in the power system not only significantly accelerates the intelligence progress of the power system, but also makes the data generated in the operation process of the power system more complex. Using big data analysis technology can effectively sort out the rules and values behind these complex data, and find out the shortcomings of data security protection.

In a word, in the big data environment, the data security and privacy protection of power system has become an important premise and guarantee for the stable and healthy development of power system. In view of the realistic threats to the current information security of power system, it is necessary to establish a power big data security protection model to prevent data security risks and effectively protect power information assets.

2 Data Security Requirements in Power System

2.1 Data Security Situation in Power System

In the current digital era, the power system is facing a severe security situation, mainly in that data has become the core production factors and key strategic resources of the power industry. While realizing value creation in the flow of power data, it also faces various risks of leakage, and becomes an important target of network attacks. State Grid intelligent applications provide convenience for users, but its security also needs a long time test, and has an impact on the power system. The industrial control system of electric power industry is a relatively closed system, which is not connected with the Internet, so that as long as a breakthrough is found in the industrial control system, it is possible to go directly to the key parts of the control system, resulting in the leakage and losses of data and information.

In addition, the data security of the power industry not only has an increasingly prominent impact on the security of the whole industry, but also has a more prominent hidden danger of data security due to the large scale and wide coverage of its users. With the construction of power IoT (Internet of Things), the emergence of new business such as power big data and integrated power services, the power business environment is more open and the data sharing is more frequent, which makes the power data security face great challenges. The importance of power system data security makes the relevant countries have introduced important measures to ensure the security of power system, in order to further strengthen the legal process of data security and personal information privacy.

2.2 Challenges Faced by Power Big Data Security Protection

First of all, due to the huge amount of data in the power system, the cost of security management rises, and as an important basic industry, it is easy to become the target of various illegal attacks. Secondly, there are various types of business data in power system, leading to the increased difficulty of security protection due to the different security requirements. In addition, the single data value of power system is relatively low, so that security efficiency for distributed data is reduced, which brings new criteria to security. The data processing speed of power system is fast, which requires high efficiency of security means, bringing huge performance pressure to security. The protection of power big data is usually divided into three levels, namely the trusted layer of data, the security layer of data and the basic layer. Among them, in the data trusted level, it mainly includes transaction security. In the data security level, it mainly includes data access, data storage and data services security. Finally, in the basic level, it mainly includes the node security itself and security between nodes.

Therefore, it is necessary to take the power data security risk management and control as the starting point, actively carry out the exploration and practice of data security, form an integrated data protection framework, and build a data security defense barrier. In this context, the power industry needs to build a data security governance system, data security compliance management and control platform, and establish online dynamic desensitization measures on account of scenarios and user roles. Secondly, it needs to set up the monitoring system of offline distribution process on account of data watermark and the data analysis and testing system on account of virtual database. In addition, data protection on account of database security operation and maintenance should be established, abnormal operation monitoring of industrial control database should be carried out, and real-time alarm should be given, unfamiliar IP address, abnormal connection to database transmitted in the network should be recognized to prevent malicious theft and tampering of power data.

3 Power Big Data Security Protection Model and Technologies

3.1 Power Big Data Security Model

Power Big Data and Security Architecture
The architecture of power big data includes multiple steps such as collection, analysis and utilization, and forms a systematic architecture including data layer, basic platform layer, big data analysis layer, big data application layer and big data service layer. The architecture of power big data implements high-speed data transmission, heterogeneous integration, visualization, data analysis and status analysis. It also implements power data-driven business and big data service mode for internal and external power system. The security of power big data runs through the whole system architecture of power big data. The security system of power big data is jointly established at the levels of authentication, authorization, authority management and data security.

The distributed parallel computing framework of power system big data is shown in Fig. 4. Through this framework, real-time, distributed and high concurrent processing and bearing of power system big data can be implemented [5]. As an inevitable process of power energy technology innovation, power big data involves major changes in the development concept, management system and technical route of the whole power system, and is a leap in the value form of intelligent power system in the era of big data.

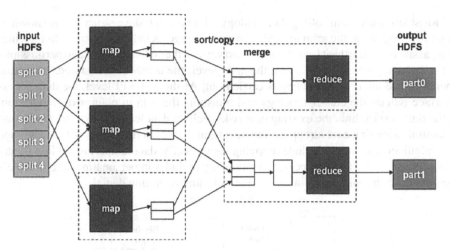

Fig. 3. Distributed parallel computing framework for power system big data

Big data technology can be used to accelerate the pace of intelligent control in the power industry and accelerate the development of smart grid [6]. By arranging sensors for power infrastructure and dynamically monitoring the operation of the facilities, the security risk of power operation can be effectively monitored and predicted. On account of the concept of big data analysis, data mining and visualization technology, the intelligent online monitoring and visualization dispatching management mechanism is constructed by integrating online detection, video monitoring, emergency command, maintenance query and other functions, which can effectively change the power big data security protection means and lower the power big data security risks from the starting stage.

Through the analysis of the historical big data of the power industry, it can effectively predict the behavior of power users to subdivide the user group, so that managers can optimize the power data security architecture and improve its operation mode [7]. Secondly, through the exchange of data with the outside world, the power system mines the hidden relationship between users' power consumption and other factors, so that the power consumption security prediction model is constructed that provides multi-dimensional, intuitive, comprehensive and in-depth prediction data for decision makers at all levels [8]. Power system uses high-performance servers and big data model solutions to support the construction of its security protection model, so as to better carry out power big data security protection decisions.

In addition, through integrating the operation data of production, operation, sales and management of the power industry, the data sharing of the power system is realized, and the resource allocation is optimized by the power big data security drive, the management of power production, operation and maintenance and sales is coordinated, and the safety protection efficiency and resource utilization rate of power data are improved [9]. The integration of data of various departments in the power industry will optimize internal information communication, facilitate the security protection work of power system.

Most storage systems of big data ecology adopt master-slave structure, as shown in Fig. 4. Among them, the primary node contains storage metadata, obtains data information passively by heartbeat from the node, and verifies the coarse-grained and permissions at the operating system level. From the node level, the actual data is stored, the actual operation and the task scheduling is carried out. At the rest API level, the data access interface reflects the cluster topology and transmits the data in plain text. In addition, in the data service link, the existing data risks include data leakage, identity fraud, and communication link eavesdropping and operation denial. In the process of data storage and calculation, it mainly includes copying data directly, data tampering, adding illegal nodes and so on. In the data access link, it mainly includes impersonating other people's identity, eavesdropping on communication links and operation denial.

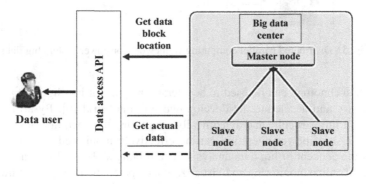

Fig. 4. Master and slave structure of big data system

Through the establishment of a credible, manageable and controllable data lifecycle protection system, the whole process protection of power system business, management, operation and maintenance and the third-party's structured and unstructured data can be realized from the aspects of data generation, data storage, data use and interaction, and data destruction. For power users, CA agent authentication and unified identity authentication system are used to ensure the credibility of users. At the utilization trusted level, the key authentication method is adopted to ensure the utilization trusted. In addition, at the node trustworthiness level, issuing certificates to nodes is adopted to ensure node trustworthiness and prevent malicious users from joining illegal nodes in the cluster to steal data. The trustworthiness architecture is shown in Fig. 5 below.

At the level of access behavior control, the security of big data access is ensured through host hiding. At the level of data usage, users' fine-grained data permissions are set to prevent users from using data beyond their level. In addition, at the level of data encryption, the data is encrypted to ensure the storage security. At the level of storage behavior, the storage security is ensured by authority, encryption, watermark and other measures. At the level of data use, the use security is ensured by watermark, desensitization and so on.

Security Protection Model
Big data security is an important premise to enhance the refinement level of power

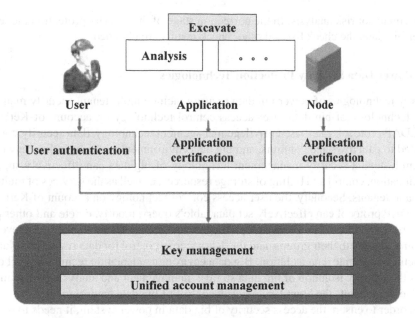

Fig. 5. Trusted architecture of power system security protection

system and the management ability of information security, and it is very important and necessary to build a big data information security system model. The security protection model of power big data should not only meet the needs of resisting the malicious intrusion of external personnel, but also prevent the unauthorized operation of internal personnel [11]. The construction of security protection model of power big data should be initiated from the level of system management and technical management, and the foundation of power big data security should be established in the dimension of system management. In the dimension of technical management, the corresponding authority is established to effectively prevent the occurrence of unauthorized access events. The integration of technology management and system management can effectively prevent most of the data attacks and security threats, and establish a solid shield in the aspects of access control, data encryption and data isolation.

The implementation of security protection model of power big data can be implemented through PDCA cycle. Among them, in the planning stage of power big data security protection model, by building a scientific and reasonable power system big data management framework, the scope of security management is clear, and the overall goal of big data security management system is formulated [12]. Secondly, in the implementation phase of the power big data security model, we fully use access control, data encryption and other big data security technologies to achieve power data protection, and confirm the system standards and data security protection requirements. In addition, in the inspection stage of power big data security protection model, with the help of internal and external review, daily inspection and other routine inspection measures are taken to check the power system big data security management level, aiming at the requirements of risk analysis. In the correction stage of the security protection model of power big data, the check list and other check results are obtained.

3.2 Power Data Security Protection Technologies

The key technologies of power big data security include multi-tenant security management technology of big data, user access control technology on account of Kerberos and LDAP protocol, role-based privilege management technology, data security control oriented to data rows and columns, and big data environment isolation technology [10]. The multi-tenant security management technology of big data can effectively support the allocation, control and billing of storage resources, as well as the services of multiple units and tenants. Secondly, the user access control technology on account of Kerberos and LDAP protocol can effectively set data table's query, modify, delete and other permissions. In addition, the role-based privilege management technology can achieve the mapping of users to their groups, and the data security control for data rows and columns can achieve accurate data isolation. Big data environment isolation technology not only meets the security isolation of big data storage, management and analysis environment, but also implements the boundary security control of big data environment.

In order to ensure the access security of big data in power system, it needs to implement communication encryption, application access management, service access management and data access management [3]. At the level of power big data storage and computing security, it should prevent malicious users from joining illegal nodes in the cluster to steal data. The node trusted architecture to ensure data security is shown in Fig. 3.

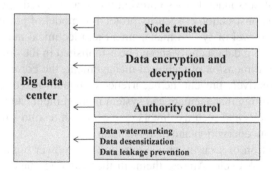

Fig. 6. Node trusted architecture for data security

At the level of unified authorization management, the user's fine-grained data permissions are set to prevent the user from using the data beyond their authorities and other arbitrary access behavior to the data. With the help of unified authorization management, the authorization of data service, collection and queue is carried out, so that permissions of data table, row and column, file reading and writing permissions and queue execution permissions are guaranteed [4]. By means of end-to-end encryption and decryption, sensitive data exists in the form of cipher text in the process of storage and transmission, so as to prevent the data leakage caused by direct copy of files and network eavesdropping. By adding watermark to data, data tampering can be found in time, and the data flow process can be traced. Through replacement, rearrangement, encryption, truncation, mask and date offset rounding, sensitive data exposure can be prevented. In addition, it is deployed at the network export to intelligently analyze and identify the content of the data transmitted through the network, and audit, alarm and block the illegal content according to the policy.

At the level of data analysis and testing protection on account of virtual database, for the risk of power data analysis and testing, virtual database technology is used to provide data use for users through network mapping, so as to avoid direct operation of the original database, and the whole process of monitoring the distribution of data. Through multi-level process approval and flexible permission configuration, the original database cannot be operated directly, and the virtual database can be recycled afterwards. The data analysis architecture on account of virtual database is shown in Fig. 6. Secondly, in the aspect of data protection on account of database security operation and maintenance, for the risk of database security operation and maintenance, we use database security operation and maintenance tools to standardize the approval process of data operation and maintenance, and achieve fine-grained control and audit of database, table and field level, so as to effectively reduce the security risk of database operation and maintenance. Through security research and judgment in advance, multi-level approval, flexible setting of fine granularity of authority, real-time dynamic desensitization of sensitive data and audit of operation and maintenance log (Fig. 7).

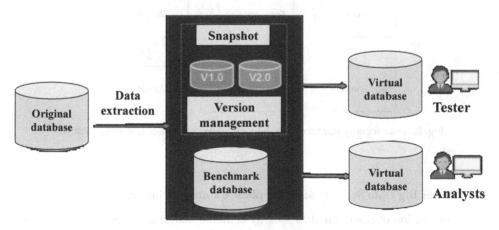

Fig. 7. Data analysis architecture on account of virtual database

4   Power Big Data Security Protection System

4.1   Data Security Management System

First of all, it needs to build a data security governance system covering the whole life cycle security compliance control requirements, security management requirements,

technical research and team building of power data security at the level of key information infrastructure and data security regulations, so as to help the data security protection
capability construction of power industry. Secondly, around all kinds of business scenarios in the power industry, it needs to build a panoramic data security governance system
so as to implement data desensitization, watermark traceability, integrating security technology and equipment to strengthen the risk response ability of all aspects of data. The
data security governance architecture covering the panorama of power system is shown
in Fig. 8.

At the level of building online dynamic desensitization on account of scene and user
role, for the risk of data online real-time access leakage, through the plug-in dynamic
desensitization component of sensitive data, associated with access rights, data sensitivity level, the accurate positioning and flexible online adjustment of differential desensitization strategy under online business access are implemented. At the offline distribution
process control level on account of power data watermark, for the risk of data export, the
data security flow and watermark traceability control tools are developed. On account of
the technology of data watermarking, the whole process control of data and the ability
of responsibility traceability under the condition of data leakage are implemented. The
system architecture of the whole process security control, sensitive data usage authority
management, operation log audit, and the addition of watermark to the outgoing data is
established.

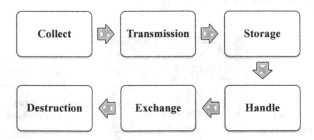

Fig. 8. Data security governance architecture covering power system panorama

4.2 Power Big Data Security and Compliance Control Platform

The construction of power big data security and compliance management and control
platform is on account of the data as the center, facing the needs of the whole process
of data security management, providing integrated solutions, integrating management
requirements and technical measures. At the level of data application, it mainly includes
data analysis personnel, management personnel, approval personnel and operation and
maintenance personnel. At the level of unified data access authority management, with
the help of big data security and compliance platform, through the integration of unified
authority system, the dynamic control of authority and fine-grained control of multi-
dimensional access authority are implemented. With the help of the data authority management system as shown in Fig. 9, the centralized account authority, privileged account
management and real-time control are implemented.

In addition, the power system big data security service capability is built on demand, and the micro service and light deployment architecture are adopted. The data security capability is integrated by standardized interface, and is provided for different business scenarios [2]. It also needs to integrate the advanced and mature data security technologies and concepts of the power industry to create a data security ecology. At the construction level of power data security compliance control platform, through multi business scenarios, the data security compliance control process is flexibly constructed to achieve the collaborative control of different personnel roles. The security capability is called and configured flexibly in the business process, so as to realize the integration of management and technology, online and offline integration. Through static distribution and usage process detection of power data assets, the panoramic view of data security is constructed, and the dynamic of data assets is fully and real-time mastered.

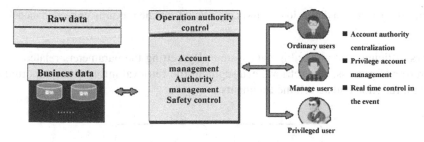

Fig. 9. Power data authority management system

For power data utilization scenarios such as power big data, data sharing and application, it is necessary to further strengthen the research in federal computing, multi-party security computing, multi-source data collaboration, etc., so as to ensure that power big data can be efficiently utilized through encryption exchange mechanism in the case of non-transmission, and meet the requirements of data privacy, security and supervision of power system.

5 Application of Power Big Data Security Protection System

The effective application of power big data security protection system is implemented from several dimensions as shown in Fig. 10, which can effectively resist to security threats and meet the expected power big data security needs. In addition, the power big data information security protection system can be applied to research and development, testing, operation and many other aspects through hierarchical protection, event awareness, early warning scheduling and emergency response, disaster recovery, attack and defense confrontation, so as to effectively deal with the current and future power big data security challenges.

The architecture of power big data information security model is shown in Fig. 11. According to the practical needs of power information data storage and retrieval, the cluster data storage and retrieval algorithm on account of Hadoop and MapReduce can not only significantly enhance the storage efficiency of data, but also ensure the

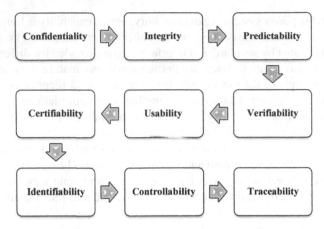

Fig. 10. Utilization dimension of power big data information security protection model

retrieval efficiency of power big data system. By setting the parameters related to the data retrieval process, data retrieval can segment the retrieval information imported by the main function and search the fragments.

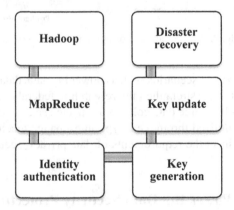

Fig. 11. The architecture of power big data information security model

In view of the typical characteristics of large number of users and strong data sensitivity in power system, it is necessary to develop an effective information security mechanism to ensure the security of power system and power big data [13]. In view of the damage risk of power system data storage equipment, it is necessary to establish an effective disaster recovery system to ensure the safety of data storage. With the help of identity authentication technology, it can effectively prevent illegal users from entering the power system, so as to effectively protect the data security of power users. The process is shown in Fig. 12.

Using key generation and update technology can effectively deal with the risk of private key leakage while preserving historical data. In addition, as an important support and prerequisite to ensure the information security of power information system, the system disaster recovery mechanism can effectively avoid and reduce the adverse impact of big data security events. Generally, the power system disaster recovery mechanism uses local and remote replication to copy the system data to the LAN internal database or remote disaster recovery center for storage and backup.

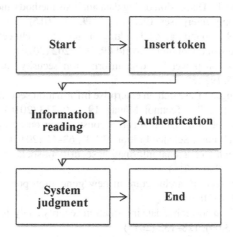

Fig. 12. Identity authentication process

6 Conclusion

In summary, in the face of information security threats in the networked environment, the power big data architecture and security protection measures need to further strengthen the protection, enhance the data defense level, change from passive defense to active defense, and effectively drive the data security of the power system. Through the analysis of the data security situation and challenges of power system, this paper studies the power data security protection system from the perspective of big data. Through the research on the security protection strategy of power big data, the security architecture and key technologies of power big data are analyzed. Through the analysis of power big data information security protection system, the power data storage and processing, power big data security protection and specific application strategies are studied.

Acknowledgement. This paper is supported by the science and technology project of State Grid Corporation of China: "Research and Application of Scenario-Driven Data Dynamic Authorization and Compliance Control Key Technology" (Grand No. 5700-202058481A-0-0-00).

References

1. Cao, B., Fan, Y.: Analysis on personal information security of social networks in the era of big data. Technol. Innov. **11**, 51 (2016)

2. Qiang, C., Li, C., Kai, W.: Utilization of big data concept in power information network management. Power Inf. Commun. Technol. **14**(11), 40–45 (2016)
3. Wei, J.: Discussion on the utilization of big data technology in network security analysis. Network Secu. Technol. Util. **11**, 96–98 (2016)
4. Honghong, J., Tao, Z., Xinjian, Z., et al.: Power information network traffic anomaly detection mechanism on account of big data. Telecom Sci. **03**, 134–140 (2017)
5. Di, L., Jinmin, L., Tao, F.: Discussion on big data analysis methods and ideas for information security of power supply enterprises. Electr. Test. **09**, 73 (2016)
6. Gan, M., Zhaowen, R., Dongqing, Z.: Thinking on security architecture of new generation power information network. Commun. World **09**, 201–202 (2016)
7. Chuan, P.: Discussion on power big data information security analysis technology. Sci. Technol. Shangpin **05**, 198 (2017)
8. Hongmei, S., Ruisheng, J.: Research on enterprise information security management system in the era of big data. Res. Sci. Technol. Manag. **19**, 210–213 (2016)
9. Peng, X.: Perspective of information security construction on account of system view. J. Beijing Union Univ. (Natural Science Edition) **28**(3), 63–65 (2014)
10. Huanpeng, Y.: Research on personal information security of social network in the era of big data. Chem. Manag. **5**, 294 (2016)
11. Hui, Z.: Thinking on security architecture of new generation power information network. Commun. World **9**, 194 (2016)
12. Zhichen, Z.: Research on power big data information security analysis technology. Power Inf. Commun. Technol. **13**(09), 128–132 (2015)
13. Jie, Z.: New challenge of big data to information security. Comput. CD Softw. Util. **13**, 163–164 (2014)

Research on Identification Method of Sensitive Data in Power System

Pengfei Yu[1,2(✉)], Danni Wang[3], and Shijun Zhang[4]

[1] Global Energy Interconnection Research Institute Co., Ltd, Nanjing 210000, China
[2] State Grid Key Laboratory of Information & Network Security, Nanjing 210003, China
[3] State Grid Liaoning Information & Communication Company, Shenyang 110000, China
[4] State Grid Jibei Information & Telecommunication Company, Beijing 100000, China

Abstract. The power system equipment is currently facing more serious risk and threat of data leakage. The online monitoring of power transmission lines, the complexity of power consumption information collection methods and the uncontrollable operating environment make the business data of power system more prone to data leakage. On account of this, this paper firstly analyses the risk of sensitive data in power system, then studies the identification process of sensitive data in power system. The architecture and functional composition of sensitive data identification system for power system are proposed. Finally, the implementation process of sensitive data protection is given.

Keywords: Identification method · Sensitive data · Data security · Power system

1 Introduction

With the iterative progress and maturity of computer technology, it has been widely and deeply studied and popularized in many fields, especially the application of computer technology represented by intelligent sensitive data recognition in power system has greatly accelerated the intelligence and accuracy degree of sensitive data recognition. With the rapid growth of social economy, especially the continuous acceleration of social production, the demand of all walks of life for power system is also constantly strengthening. The power system is not only facing the pressure of security, but also facing the realistic threat of power data information security and protection. In this context, the interaction frequency and interaction needs between power system and multi-source users are constantly deepening, especially the diversification of terminals, which makes the identification and protection of all kinds of sensitive data in power system face greater pressure. How to effectively identify sensitive data in power system has become an important issue to avoid data leakage.

Since the intelligence degree of power system is constantly improving and its functions of data acquisition, processing and storage are growing, it also makes a variety of power system equipment face more serious data leakage risks and threats. The online monitoring of power transmission lines, the complexity of power consumption information collection methods and the uncontrollable operating environment make the business

© Springer Nature Singapore Pte Ltd. 2022
Y. Tian et al. (Eds.): ICBDS 2021, CCIS 1563, pp. 45–57, 2022.
https://doi.org/10.1007/978-981-19-0852-1_4

data of power system more prone to data leakage. With the rapid development of power system integration, the power transmission process in the power grid system integrates various resources and data such as power, data and information, which makes all kinds of sensitive data face the threat and risk of leakage in the transmission process.

In order to better protect the sensitive data in the power system, we need to audit, control and encrypt the sensitive data, so as to better protect the data security. Using computer technology to intelligently identify and automatically protect sensitive data can greatly strengthen the protection methods and efficiency, reducing the dependence on manual identification. We also need to enhance the complexity of sensitive data access control rules, so as to better prevent the leakage of sensitive data. The recognition of sensitive data in power system mainly focuses on several aspects as shown in Fig. 1 below. With the help of intelligent algorithms such as TF-IDF (Term Frequency–Inverse Document Frequency), SVM (Support Vector Machines) and ANN (Artificial Neural Network), the preprocessing of feature selection, the determination of learning threshold and the recognition and verification of sensitive data are implemented.

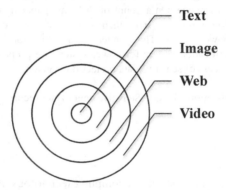

Fig. 1. Identification elements of sensitive data in power system

In addition, sensitive data in power system not only involves a large number of users' privacy information, but also is very important for the stable and safe operation of power system. The leakage of sensitive data in power system will cause serious threats to the core secrets, industry competitiveness and operation security of power system. As the sensitive data of power system covers the whole life cycle process as shown in Fig. 2, various security problems will occur in the process of data flow. It is necessary to strengthen the identification and control of sensitive data. If the identification of sensitive data in the power system still relies on the traditional manual way, it not only has the problem of high missing rate, but also has low efficiency and high labor cost. Therefore, it is urgent and necessary to make full use of modern information and intelligent technology to carry out the identification of sensitive data, so as to achieve efficient identification and processing of sensitive data.

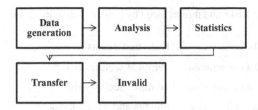

Fig. 2. Life cycle of sensitive data in power system

2 Risk Analysis of Sensitive Data in Power System

2.1 Risks During the Life Cycle of Sensitive Data

Generally, the common architecture of power system is shown in Fig. 3. It can be seen that the life cycle process of sensitive data mainly includes data generation, data processing, data circulation, data utilization and data destruction. The risks and threats faced by the power system at various stages are shown in Table 1. In the aspect of terminal security risks of power system, the causes mainly include the lack of security review for terminal access to the network, illegal data access, system security vulnerabilities, lack of behavior security audit, virus threat and so on. In addition, in the aspect of power system mobile storage media security risk, it mainly includes the spread of virus and malicious code, the lack of effective security authentication.

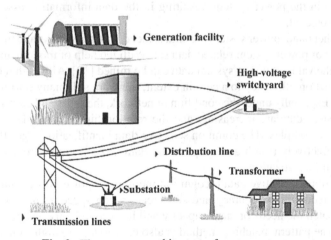

Fig. 3. The common architecture of power system

In the data network transmission stage of power system, the risks it faces mainly include virus attack and hacker attack. At the level of data utilization in power system, the risk causes mainly include authentication defects and abuse of excessive permissions, SQL injection, and buffer overflow attack, denial of service attack, non-encryption of sensitive data, insufficient audit of database and lack of database backup. In the stage of power system data destruction, the main risks are malicious data recovery and malicious data deletion.

Table 1. Risks and threats faced by power system in various stages

Stages	Risks and threats
Data generation	Terminal security risk
Data processing	Terminal security risk
Data circulation	Storage and network risk
Data utilization	Database security risk
Data destruction	Malicious recovery and deletion risk

2.2 Problems of Data Security

With the increasing complexity of power system scale and service objects, its data model is also expanding, which increases the difficulty of data management. In order to better meet the diversified needs of power system end users, it is necessary to continuously iterate the data model of power system to better carry out the adaptive adjustment and optimization. At present, there are some problems such as unreasonable evaluation of system data model, inadequate control mode, leading to the lack of overall consideration of power system data model. Hence, it is difficult to effectively reflect the actual operation situation. In addition, the relevant business departments cannot accurately identify the sensitive data in the power system, resulting in the data information assets cannot be effectively protected.

On the other hand, power system big data is faced with many risks and threats, mainly in the privacy of power system related data set. With the help of modern and intelligent technology, the value of power system data can be mined [12]. Although it can improve the data protection efficiency to a certain extent, there are still many information needs to be solved. Especially under the condition of network, the types and correlation degree of power system data are increasing, and the relationship between data is becoming more and more complex. The common sensitive data identification algorithm has been difficult to effectively match and adapt to the data protection requirements under the condition of informatization.

The traditional sensitive data recognition methods in power system have the problems of low recognition accuracy and slow recognition speed, which are difficult to effectively match the needs of large capacity and high complexity data recognition and processing. The pattern matching method is also easy to lead to high subjectivity in the data recognition process, and the recognition results of sensitive data have high differences. It can be seen that there are still many problems in the practical utilization of traditional sensitive data identification methods in power system, and it is difficult to effectively achieve the desired effect of sensitive data identification and processing.

3 Sensitive Data Identification Process in Power System

3.1 Protection Strategies of Sensitive Data

The protection strategy of sensitive data in power system includes data detection and corresponding protection. The detection rules include index file matching, accurate data matching and user-defined data matching. Response rules include auditing, blocking, and caching source files. By defining the data security level, the protection strategy is formulated [6]. It is suggested to distinguish illegal behaviors, establish protective measures, define the monitoring scope and issue the protection policy. In addition, the data terminal protection strategy is adopted to implement protection strategies and identify violations, which is to distinguish the content of violation, implement supervision measures, upload and record violations. Through transparent deployment, comprehensive coverage and flexible expansion, it implements the safe and reliable operation of file data, effectively prevents the leakage within the authority, strictly controls all leakage channels, and provides customized development services.

By integrating detection and defense into power system facilities, sensitive data is prevented from getting out of the control. By shelling sensitive data, only authorized users are allowed to access sensitive data. In addition, for initiative defense of unknown factors, it is necessary to block the external intrusion of multi-source through SQL injection detection and defense, to carry out decentralized management and label management of sensitive data and to simplify identity access. Sensitive data security administrators need to manage sensitive assets. Complex sensitive assets are created, classified, assigned, authorized and evaluated, which are further subdivided into the roles of creation, authorization and evaluation.

Through the establishment of a database access control strategy with separated authorities, a series of solutions such as security management of sensitive data, security audit, misoperation and intrusion prevention and recovery, terminal identification and multi-factor access of sensitive data database in power system are implemented to achieve the identification and comprehensive protection of sensitive data in power system.

3.2 Overall Sensitive Data Identification Process

The existing forms of power system sensitive data are mainly unstructured data represented by various source files and structured data represented by database files [3]. The protection process of power system sensitive data starts with the definition of sensitive data. The definition of sensitive data needs to be clear about the data content to be protected through IDM (Indexed Document Matching), EDM (Exact Data Matching) and other technology and system [4]. IDM technology is applied to unstructured data content, and EDM is applied to structured data content. If there is no sample file, data matching technology can be customized for unstructured and structured data, including keywords, regular expressions, file attributes, file tags, data identifiers, dictionary scripts, etc. IDM technology can implement intelligent matching of derived content, simple and convenient sample collection, automatic update of collected data, etc. [5].

EDM technology can carry out intelligent recognition, and DCM technology can realize the accurate matching of sensitive data and flexible configuration.

The process of sensitive data recognition in power system includes the establishment of data thesaurus, the extraction of sensitive features, the matching of sensitive features and the quality evaluation of sensitive data recognition in power system. Among them, improving the establishment of data thesaurus includes data preprocessing, vocabulary extraction and centralization, vocabulary deletion and data weighting. The frequency of data processing is directly related to its importance, and the construction of thesaurus is completed by calculating the vector weight. At the level of feature extraction of sensitive data, the sensitive features are extracted through the classification and recognition of thesaurus, especially the sensitive words and data are screened out, and a complete corpus of sensitive words is established.

After the data set model is established, it needs machine learning on the training set to implement the effective test and evaluation of the data set [7]. The contents of data set, training set and test set are shown in Table 2. For content-based power system sensitive data recognition, firstly, the contents of different document formats need to be extracted, and the known classified text library, sensitive text library and unknown classified text are taken as the input of preprocessed data. Secondly, by extracting the features of the data and calculating the weight of vector space, the data feature vector is formed. In addition, the similarity is calculated by cosine formula, the threshold is formed by statistical learning; the threshold is compared and analyzed to determine whether it is sensitive data, and the access control is carried out for sensitive data.

Table 2. The content of data set, training set and test set

Set types	Detailed contents
Data set	Training set, test set
Training set	Sensitive text library, classified text library
Sensitive text library	Sensitive data document Thesaurus

In addition, the process of power system sensitive data recognition includes data preprocessing and feature extraction, vector space weight calculation and feature vector generation [8]. Finally, the sensitivity of power system data is analyzed by judging the difference between cosine value and threshold value of data. The word segmentation results are obtained through the word segmentation interface, then the word selection, word frequency statistics, word length selection and word frequency selection are carried out, and the characteristic binary of key words and frequency is finally obtained.

3.3 Feature Extraction Method of Power System Sensitive Data

In the process of power system data text learning and recognition, in order to increase the recognition efficiency as much as possible, reduce the amount of data calculation and redundant information, the preprocessed data need to be reduced to the dimension of vector space to make its calculation simpler. Feature extraction of sensitive data is completed by processes of speech selection, word frequency statistics, word length selection and word frequency selection. At the part of speech level, redundancy is eliminated and other parts of speech are deleted [9]. At the level of word frequency statistics, according to the frequency of keywords, the word group, the frequency of phrase and the part of speech are formed. In addition, at the word length selection level, the length of each keyword is calculated. At the level of word frequency selection, the frequency of phrase occurrence is calculated.

With the help of TF-IDF equation, the weights of words are determined, so as to further determine the corresponding value. By calculating the frequency of a word in the text of power system data, it could define the information it contains, the type of document and the representativeness of the word [10]. Secondly, the similarity between two feature vectors in power system data is calculated by cosine formula. In addition, after calculating the cosine similarity of power system data, the results are compared with the threshold to determine the sensitivity of the data. With the help of processing and sensitive set cosine calculation, the sensitive data is defined, and the threshold value of unknown classification document is determined. Through the establishment of data sets, preprocessing and feature selection, calculation of feature vector, calculation of cosine value of known classification and sensitive data, the threshold value is finally determined [11]. The relationship between the number of sensitive data document libraries and error rate as well as initialization time are analyzed, so as to evaluate the recognition performance of sensitive data, and establish a fixed threshold determination mechanism.

3.4 Intelligent Matching Method of Power System Sensitive Data

The common methods of sensitive data recognition in power system include dictionary construction method, intelligent matching method and dictionary learning method. The dictionary construction method requires finding a more accurate root node, and its identification process includes the determination of root node and leaf nodes, the information transfer between root node and leaf nodes, and the setting of key dictionary. In addition, the dictionary learning method of sensitive data can set the keywords in the dictionary and add the keywords similar to those in the keyword dictionary.

After the collection of sensitive data in power system, the identification of data to be identified is carried out. The key words in the keyword dictionary are identified by row and column identification, and the data in the keyword data table is identified as sensitive data. Secondly, the sensitive data screened out from the power system are fuzzed or encrypted, and then the subsequent transmission process is carried out. In addition, the key words in the sensitive data of power system are matched, and the inclusion of the key words in the data to be identified is determined on account of the matching results. By keyword matching the leaf nodes on the tree path, it could judge whether the data to be identified is the corresponding keyword of the leaf node.

The use of intelligent data set algorithm can effectively identify the sensitive attributes in the data set. It is necessary to find out the appropriate privacy protection means to deal with the sensitive attributes in the power system, so as to effectively deal with a series of attacks and attacks such as link, background knowledge and aggregation attacks [13]. On the other hand, there is a complex relationship between the structured data features and the data in the power system, so it is needed to consider the relationship between the data features and the data from the perspective of data privacy identification, and finally find out the algorithm and scheme that can effectively meet the automatic recognition of the sensitive attributes of the structured data sets in the power system.

On account of the distance between entropy and maximum entropy of structured data attribute in power system, the pre-recognition of some sensitive attributes of power system data set is achieved by clustering algorithm. The association rules between the data sets of power system are established by intelligent algorithm, so as to sort out the correlation relationship of data attributes, so as to better judge the sensitivity of power system data [14]. According to the sensitive attribute characteristics of structured data in power system, an intelligent data sensitivity identification model is constructed, which can accurately identify the sensitive attribute features of structured data sets. The data sets recorded in power system are processed with full amount of data, and the data records are sampled evenly. Further processing according to the sampling results can effectively improve the efficiency of the recognition of the structural data sensitive attributes of power system.

The mathematical expectation of the self-info quantity of each message of the information source, also known as unconditional entropy, is expressed by H(x), as shown in Eq. (1). In general, H(x) is not equal to the average amount of information received by each message [15].

$$H(X) = E[I(x_i)] = \sum_{i=1}^{n} P(x_i)I(x_i) = -\sum_{i=1}^{n} P(x_i) \log P(x_i) \tag{1}$$

The entropy value of data attribute is positively related to its sensitive attribute. K-means algorithm is used to divide all data samples in each cluster subset into different categories. The K-means clustering algorithm uses the sum of squared error criterion function to evaluate the clustering performance, as shown in the formula (2), where X is the data set, and the data set of the power system only contains description attributes, not category attributes [16]. The cluster subsets of data are $X_1, X_2, X_3, ..., X_k$ and the number of samples in each cluster subset is $N_1, N_2, ..., N_k$ respectively. The mean representative points of each cluster subset are $m_1, m_2, ..., m_k$.

$$E = \sum_{i=1}^{k} \sum_{p \in X_i} \|p - m_i\|^2 \tag{2}$$

By setting the data sensitivity attribute of power system as different samples and clustering analysis, the empirical values of sensitivity of each data are set according to the above algorithm, and the sensitivity attributes of each data set can be effectively divided.

4   Identification System Model of Sensitive Data in Power System

4.1   Architecture of the System

The identification of sensitive data in power system adopts unified strategy, and uses intelligent content identification technology to discover, monitor and protect sensitive data in enterprise network, terminal, storage and application system. Among them, the regulatory level of sensitive data mainly includes web pages, instant messaging and other content. At the terminal supervision level, it includes network sharing and various mobile media. At the storage discovery level, it includes mail server, file server and database server. In addition, at the regulatory level of application system, including OA, ERP and other application systems using HTTP protocol [1]. The construction of sensitive data management platform of power system adopts the integrated management platform based on B/S architecture, which can be configured with user role-based access control and system management. Visualization of sensitive data distribution and security situation, real-time generation of leakage event logs and reports, can help users audit, manage and trace operations.

The functional architecture of power system sensitive data identification system includes several modules as shown in Fig. 4. The network monitoring module is responsible for monitoring all network links, analyzing the application protocol content, finding and auditing the communication data that violate the data security policy. In the aspect of network protection, real-time content recovery and scanning, real-time audit and blocking of HTTP protocol network data traffic are carried out. In addition, in the data discovery aspect, it scans the internal data, database and file server, and generate user sensitive information distribution map according to the scanning results.

By monitoring and automatically analyzing all outgoing data, the email violating the data security policy is immediately blocked and manually audited. In the aspect of terminal protection, it scans and discovers the distribution and improper storage of sensitive information in power system, monitors the behavior of sensitive information sending out and takes real-time protection measures. In the application and maintenance level of power system, it carries out content recovery, scanning, real-time audit and blocking for the access flow of OA, ERP and website application systems of relevant power entities.

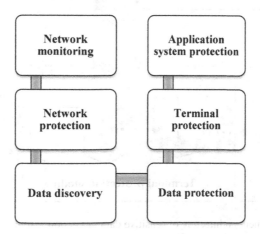

Fig. 4. Functional architecture of sensitive data identification system in power system

4.2 Operation Flow of the System

The operation process of power system sensitive data identification system includes four aspects: the start of sensitive data identification algorithm, the formulation of sensitive data protection strategy, the analysis of sensitive data flow and the identification of sensitive data. At the start level of sensitive data identification algorithm, it is mainly to initialize the content identification algorithm of documents, pictures and videos of each security module. In the aspect of making sensitive data protection strategy, it is necessary to make protection strategy combined with sensitive data and automatically send it to each security module. In addition, in the analysis aspect of sensitive data traffic, each security module analyzes the captured files or data content in real time according to the configured policies [2]. In the identification aspect of power system sensitive data, the protection strategy of hit configuration is adopted, and the targeted control measures of sensitive data are taken according to the defined response mode.

4.3 Deployment of the System

The logic deployment of power system sensitive data protection system includes management platform and terminal protection module represented by online client and offline client. Firstly, through the sensitive data management platform, the protection strategy of sensitive data is defined. Secondly, through the terminal protection module sensitive files are scanned and content fingerprint is generated and uploaded to management platform. In addition, through the terminal protection execution strategy, terminals upload the log to the management platform. The deployment architecture of power system sensitive data protection system is shown in Fig. 5.

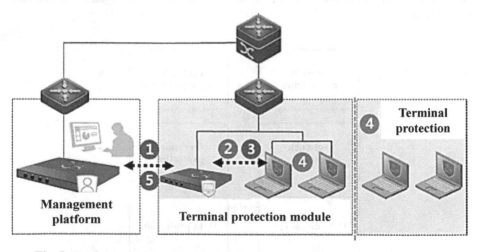

Fig. 5. Deployment architecture of sensitive data protection system in power system

4.4 Management of the System

There are many monitoring blind areas in the data of power system, so it is difficult to effectively grasp and track the whole process of data usage. The protection of sensitive data in power system has higher requirements on the information literacy and ability of relevant personnel, which requires relevant personnel to respond to the threat of sensitive events quickly. At present, the difficulties of sensitive data identification and protection in power system are mainly reflected in the following aspects: easily bypassed, unable to block in time, lack of monitoring, blind area of data supervision, difficult to effectively identify counterfeit applications and processing delay [17]. In view of the sensitivity of power system data, it is necessary to strengthen the basis of information security, especially the registration and protection of sensitive data, to clarify the independent management measures and establish the physical isolation and protection in many aspects as shown in Fig. 6.

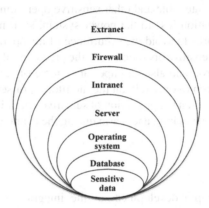

Fig. 6. Physical isolation and protection of sensitive data in power system

In addition, the ownership definition of power system sensitive data is a prerequisite for the protection of sensitive data. DBA's ability to access sensitive information have limitations [18]. Operation and maintenance users' unconscious or conscious access to sensitive data will lead to a variety of sensitive data attacks at network and application level.

5 Implementation of Sensitive Data Protection in Power System

The implementation process of power system sensitive data protection mainly includes prevention in advance, in-process control and post audit. In the prevention aspect, the access rules of sensitive data in power system are configured to achieve decentralized management. Then, it needs to specify the personnel and terminal equipment that can be authorized to access the data as well as the prohibition access software and so on [19]. Secondly, it needs to block the operation that does not conform to the data access rules of the power system, and timely warn in case of abnormal conditions, and further strengthen the authorization management. In addition, for the post audit process of sensitive data in power system, a rule-based audit and unified event search engine are established to implement personalized subscription and personalized report generation.

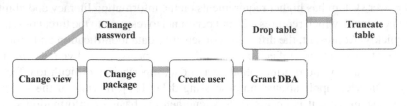

Fig. 7. The operation aspect of sensitive data processing in power system

In the operation aspect of power system sensitive data processing, we also need to carry out corresponding countermeasures in the dimensions as shown in Fig. 7. For example, drop table, truncate table and other sensitive operations will bring huge business damage and information loss to the power system, so it needs to strengthen the prevention countermeasures to avoid the occurrence of misoperation events. Secondly, for grant DBA and other sensitive operations, it is the precursor of power system database management out of control, and also an important source of sensitive data threat [20]. In addition, it is not enough to only rely on the monitoring of sensitive operations. It is necessary to further strengthen the protection of sensitive operations, so as to realize the prevention in advance, the blocking and alarm during the event, and the evaluation after the event.

6 Conclusion

In summary, with the rapid development of the integration of power system and power grid, the power transmission process in the power grid system integrates various resources and data such as power, data and information, which makes all kinds of sensitive data face the threat and risk of leakage in the transmission process. How to effectively identify the sensitive data in the power system has become an important matter. Through the risk analysis of sensitive data in power system, this paper studies the main problems of data security in power system. Through the research on the identification process of sensitive data in power system, the protection methods of sensitive data in power system are analyzed. Through the analysis of the architecture and function composition of power system sensitive data identification, the architecture, operation flow, deployment and management of power system sensitive data identification system are proposed.

In addition, through the analysis of the identification and protection scheme of the sensitive data of power system, this paper studies the protection implementation process of the sensitive data protection strategy in the power system.

Acknowledgement. This paper is supported by the science and technology project of State Grid Corporation of China: "Research and Application of Scenario-Driven Data Dynamic Authorization and Compliance Control Key Technology" (Grand No. 5700-202058481A-0-0-00).

References

1. Amin, S.U., Alsulaiman, M., Muhammad, G., et al.: Multilevel weighted feature fusion using convolutional neural networks for EEG motor imagery classification. IEEE Access **7**, 18940–18950 (2019)
2. Duan, Y.: Utilization of support vector machine in text classification. Comput. Digit. Eng. **40**(7), 87–88 (2012)
3. Qingyong, G.: Database encryption technology. Post Telecommun. Des. Technol. **7**, 58–60 (2017)
4. Weiwei, L., Tao, Z., Weimin, L., et al.: Research and implementation of sensitive data recognition method on account of text content. Comput. Eng. Des. **4**(34), 1202–1203 (2013)
5. Xiaohong, L.: Feature word extraction method in Chinese text classification. Comput. Eng. Des. **30**(17), 4127–4129 (2009)
6. Zin, L., Lv, H., Ming, L., et al.: A novel self-adaptive grid-partitioning noise optimization algorithm on account of differential privacy. Comput. Sci. Inf. Syst. **16**(3), 915–938 (2019)
7. Mehmood, A., Natgunanathan, I., Xiang, Y., et al.: Protection of big data privacy. IEEE Access **4**, 1821–1834 (2016)
8. Mendes, R., Vilela, J.P.: Privacy-preserving data mining: methods, metrics, and utilizations. IEEE Access **5**, 10562–10582 (2017)
9. Sasikala, S., Banu, N.: Privacy preserving data mining using piecewise vector quantization (PVQ). Int. J. Adv. Res. Comput. Sci. Technol. **2**(3), 302–306 (2014)
10. Schaub, F., Konings, B., Weber, M.: Context-adaptive privacy: leveraging context awareness to support privacy decision making. IEEE Pervasive Comput. **14**(1), 34–43 (2015)
11. Singh, B.C., Carminati, B., Ferrari, E.: Privacy-aware personal data storage (P-PDS): learning how to protect user privacy from external utilizations. IEEE Trans. Depend. Secure Comput. 1–14 (2019)
12. Sorber, L., Van Barel, M., De Lathauwer, L.: Structured data fusion. IEEE J. Select. Top. Signal Proc. **9**(4), 586–600 (2015)
13. Sweeney, L.: k-anonymity: a model for protecting privacy. Inter. J. Uncertain. Fuzziness Knowl. Based Syst. **10**(05), 557–570 (2002)
14. Yanlin, T., Honggeng, Y.: Research method of voltage sag fault frequency of sensitive load on account of maximum entropy principle. Electr. Meas. Instrument. **52**(18), 27–30 (2015)
15. Yi, W., Ning, Z., Chongqing, K., et al.: Power user behavior model: basic concepts and research framework. Acta Electro-Technics Sinica **34**(10), 2056–2068 (2019)
16. Xuetao, Y.: Research on sensitive data protection technology of wireless music service. Telecommun. Eng. Technol. Standard. **12**, 5–59 (2013)
17. Ying, J.W., Xin, H., Chen, G.E., et al.: Adaptive parameter optimization for real-time differential privacy streaming data publication. Comput. Sci. **46**(9), 99–105 (2019)
18. Qianhong, Z., Xuehua, C., Chuanguo, M., et al.: Research on computer terminal data security protection on account of network environment. Elect. Power Inf. **9**(11), 84–88 (2011)
19. Zhao, P., Wang, H.H., Tan, C.X.: Design and implementation of network isolation security audit system on account of firewall log. Comput. Util. Res. **7**, 114–116 (2007)
20. Kai, Z., Qianwen, G., Le, L., et al.: Rapid evaluation method for transient voltage disturbance tolerance of variable speed drive equipment. China Test **46**(07), 75–82 (2020)

Vehicle Road Privacy Recommendation System Equipped with Markov Chain

Xiangru Zhu, Yanfeng Shi$^{(\boxtimes)}$, and Yuan Tian

Nanjing Institute of Technology, Nanjing 211167, China
shiyf@njit.edu.cn

Abstract. Due to the development of in-vehicle network, location-based service has brought many conveniences to users. However, the user's behavior of constantly updating the location of the service provider will cause the private information to be exposed to the attacker, thus threatening the user's information security. Most of the current schemes ignore the differential protection of different road environments, which may lead to the abuse of privacy budget or be excluded by attackers according to actual environment analysis. We propose a method to protect the road privacy and meet the individual needs of users, and carry out the differentiated privacy protection based on road environment. First, we calculate the length of each road section, create a normalized matrix by a Markov model to describe the congestion degree of road sections, and filter the best route according to users' privacy preferences. Then, according to the congestion degree of the road section, the sensitive circle range is defined for each query position of the recommended route, and the acceptable deviation range of the user virtual position is superimposed to protect the differential privacy. Experimental results show that, compared with the current methods, the proposed scheme can reasonably protect users' privacy and obtain better service quality while satisfying users' preferences and considering the surrounding road environment.

Keywords: Personalized and differentiated privacy · Markov chain · Route prediction

1 Introduction

In today's information society, the continuous development of communication technology, data storage and cloud computing makes the collection, storage, analysis and transmission of data more and more convenient. At the same time, a lot of privacy protection problems have arisen. For example, in 2014, Yahoo's information disclosure incident involved 500 million e-mail accounts around the world. In the following December, the company discovered a large-scale hacker attack, which resulted in the theft of 1 billion user accounts, involving personal information of users, including names, emails, telephones, birthdays, etc. In 2018, a political data company illegally stole information from more than 50 million users on Facebook.

Y. Tian et al. (Eds.): ICBDS 2021, CCIS 1563, pp. 58–72, 2022.
https://doi.org/10.1007/978-981-19-0852-1_5

At present, there are still many loopholes in the protection of private information, and people's information is potentially threatened anytime and anywhere. With the development of in-vehicle network and navigation functions, users constantly update the location of the vehicle during driving, which leads attackers to guess its location information and attack. Therefore, the personalized location privacy protection in location based service becomes particularly important. For example, when the vehicle goes back and forth between two destinations, it constantly submits the geographic information location to the service provider, but such frequent interactive information will cause serious privacy leakage, and the attacker can invade the sensitive information of the user. Now, several travel software and navigation of the fire are also considering improving the protection of user information. For example, "Didi taxi" specially generates temporary numbers for passengers and drivers to ensure privacy. When "Gaode Map" provides navigation service, it will ask the user whether to allow the software to access the user's coordinate position. However, although all of the above are aimed at protecting users' privacy, in terms of road selection and users' differentiated needs, privacy protection and sensitivity are neglected when querying data. In particular, different sensitive attributes often contain different query locations. However, most privacy protection mechanisms can not answer sensitive technical queries through differentiated privacy, which makes it impossible to meet the privacy protection needs. Whether it is a short-term quick trip or a long-term travel trip, the important task of "reasonably protecting users' privacy while meeting users' personalized privacy needs, so as to obtain better service quality" is put forward.

In the paper, we create a road recommendation system. By considering routers installed at various intersections, we collect the user access density of this road section, and then judge the security level of privacy protection of this road section. During driving, we will allocate the noise required by different places in combination with the privacy budget, thus achieving the effect of protecting personal privacy. Then, combined with users' personalized needs, an optimal path with both travel efficiency and privacy protection is screened out. The first main goal of this work is to use routers at various intersections to obtain the access density between road sections, which can roughly reflect the congestion degree of this road section and the security degree of privacy protection. The second key point is to recommend the best travel route, which excludes dangerous road sections that are likely to reveal user information, and considers the user's personalized preferences for distance, time and privacy. The optimal route must be the statistical result obtained from the actual route traveled by others in the past. The work's significance is mainly to make up for the lack of protection for users' private information in the existing travel software, and to make diversified recommendations flexibly according to the actual situation. Through user-defined preference priority, the route is dynamically filtered. For example, if the user's destination is far away, it will take a bit more care with the driving distance, and if the destination is close, it will pay more attention to the degree of congestion. In addition, the user defines the privacy budget, which is flexible and dynamic, and can immediately change the road recommendation according to the user's personalized choice. The choice of which route completely depends on the user's demand for privacy protection and travel efficiency.

Given the starting and ending positions and the user's preferences, the system can check all existing routes and possible tracks covering the starting and ending positions. The route that is most used and not attacked will be defined as the best route. We use the access density at intersections to define the safety factor of the road sections. As a combination of different road sections, the optimal degree of a route can be determined by looking at historical recommendation data. Because everyone has a different definition of the best, we intend to use Markov chain model to solve the problem of finding the best route by combining trajectory segments.

At present, creating virtual location or space encryption to protect real location is the most common way to protect route privacy. Adding noise to increase regional density is a good method, which can play an effective role by superimposing it with the privacy budget allocation method, but this method still has some defects: different geographical locations and road environments are not considered, and whether the added noise is in line with the actual situation; Under the influence of spatial diversity, some attackers can eliminate some impossible virtual locations through geographical location-based analysis; It is known that when the allocation of privacy budget tends to be infinite, the area can be regarded as a safe area approximately, but the deviation between the real location and the virtual location is huge, and the availability of data is greatly reduced.

This paper contributes a recommendation tool that can balance the effectiveness of privacy budget allocation to deal with the above limitations. To ensure privacy and maximize efficiency, when adding noise to the real location, we can consider allocating privacy protection budget according to the surrounding environment. Test the vehicle density of access nodes. Too dense and crowded road sections can allocate a large amount of budget and improve data availability; For remote or less traffic sections, consider allocating less budget. However, too little budget allocation will lead to low system efficiency and loss of data availability, so the system will set the noise adding areas according to road conditions. It should be noted that only calculating the frequency of the vehicle system passing through a certain intersection is not enough to determine the safety degree of the road section. Because some road sections will prohibit large vehicles from entering, the traffic volume in the morning will be significantly larger than that at night, and some road sections are under construction recently, and the traffic volume will suddenly decrease or even be cleared. The basic goal is to use information based on data sets, and find long-term and short-term movement patterns. Our system can adjust the budget accordingly by using the long-term and short-term vehicle density of the above sections. We use a stochastic method called Markov chain to construct a transition matrix from raw data to show the short-term transition probability from one location to another. Then, using the initial state vector and transition matrix, the convergence probability can predict the long-term epidemic index of different locations, so as to capture the movement behavior between intersections and facilitate the search for the best path. Subsequently, the privacy budget of the route is defined as the sum of the privacy budget allocation of each road section of the route.

In order to achieve the above functions, we will meet the following challenges. First, we use the data set to form a transition matrix to display the vehicle density of the road section in a short time. We define the most frequent places as traffic jams. At this time, the original data needs a lot of preprocessing before it can be presented in a form that lays the foundation for the transformation matrix. The congestion degree of the road section needs to converge to a steady state. Therefore, Markov chain model is used to find the convergence probability of each position. By doing so, we provide a reasonable method to measure the long-term congestion degree of a route. After the completion of the above, these crowding degrees are transformed into security degrees, and combined with the constraints and preferences of users, privacy is protected to the maximum extent, and the congestion degree of the journey and route is minimized, thus forming the best route.

This paper mainly makes the following improvements to the most advanced solutions:

After preprocessing the data set, a transition matrix calculation algorithm is implemented. The data set collects various routes of vehicles traveling from different starting and ending points.

In order to improve the data's utility, by dividing the city into blocks, selecting typical road sections as the standard road conditions in the region, combining with a density index formula based on the steady-state convergence principle of Markov chain model, and giving an algorithm for predicting the long-term traffic density of different road sections in the city, this not only avoids the waste of real-time monitoring resources, but also realizes the consideration of time variation.

Set sensitive circle and protection circle for sensitive position, define user acceptable deviation based on geographical indistinguishability, and add salt and pepper noise.

2 Related Work

The privacy protection of the vehicle system is a highly related topic of the best route recommendation based on historical motion data. At present, the main research objectives are: location recommendation method, building privacy protection framework and model, location privacy protection, predicting users' movements or popular places, and collecting and querying customer information.

Recent research focuses on the combination of users' preference constraints and the pursuit of accurate and efficient recommendation. In order to better integrate user preferences, Li et al. [1] proposed an integration method to optimize recommendation performance by giving users confidence coefficient and creating convex loss function. In order not to sacrifice the accuracy of service, Wu et al. [2] put forward a framework of location privacy protection system, and built a model to express the constraints of coverage, and then the client returned the corresponding request results. In [3], by defining the sensitive area level, calculating the allocated privacy protection budget and screening the optimal path. The QUAD framework in [4] is proposed, which supports multiple modeling and seamless integration, and provides the probability representation of privacy risk under heterogeneous correlation. Literature [5] introduces the concept of edge nodes assisting vehicles, and proposes a basic privacy protection service usage framework deployed on edge nodes. Zhu et al. [6] proposed the privacy protection framework allows users to manage accuracy and privacy on the basis of every dynamic query.

At present, schemes of location privacy protection can be divided into virtual location protection [7–9], vehicle and rail privacy protection [10–12], cloud computing-based services [13, 14], and k-anonymous services [10, 15–18]. The PPCS method proposed by Sun et al. [7] considers the semantic information of virtual location and generates virtual location at the same time. Considering that service providers have not adopted the effective protection mechanism against false location submission, Mohammad Reza et al. [8] proposed PASPORT scheme to design a special scenario for mobile users to generate licenses to prove the authenticity of the location. PA-LBS was proposed by Ma et al. [9], which enables location service users to disclose their location information by scaling camouflage distance and location type. In addition to generating virtual positions, real trajectories are also focused on. Zhang et al. [11] integrated the constraints of the single position exposure risk and trajectory exposure risk, and proposed RcDT algorithm. Similarly, [12] defines three privacy measures based on different surrounding environments, which reflect the influence of road attributes on privacy protection. The DOA method in [13], through the combination of fog calculation and caching, the disadvantage of user overload in privacy protection method is solved. [14] also proposes PRF algorithm, which encrypts the location service data key and distributes the cloud server to protect the communication between them. K-anonymity is also a popular privacy protection method. The BUSA scheme in literature [10] uses k-anonymity to divide the track information queried by users into segments and send them to different agents for anonymity. Yang et al. [15] used compressed sensing technology to collect missing locations, then used the collected data to construct anonymous candidate sets, and finally used differential privacy mechanism to select anonymous locations. In [16], an IFTS method based on k-anonymity to build an edge clustering model is proposed. After preprocessing the original road, the weight is set as a comprehensive parameter about the trajectory distance and location type. Based on k-anonymity and DLP algorithm, Zheng et al. [17] dynamically determines the privacy protection intensity of different locations according to the user preference model, constructs anonymous areas, and requests the virtual location of vehicles. Fei et al. [18] proposed a two-layer privacy scheme, which grouped users and selected an agent to generate virtual location, and finally shared the results returned by service providers.

Markov chain is usually used to predict the random behavior of data, which is very popular in user trajectory prediction. The PSAI scheme proposed in [19] estimates the user's position by exploring the information of the user's sign-in trajectory and its social constraints. Similarly, an unsupervised association learning algorithm is proposed in [20], which estimates the correct mapping between users by hierarchical clustering and similarity matching according to the location change of mobile devices. In [21], a trajectory prediction model based on group travel mode is proposed, in which stopping points are extracted to construct cluster chain, and then two kinds of variable order Markov models are used to predict trajectory. Zhang et al. [22] used Markov structure to obtain the upper bound and lower bound of tracking level privacy leakage, and considered the time correlation between positions of the track. In [23], Markov chain is used to converge the popularity of road location, so as to present the short-term and long-term popularity index of the region. Contrary to the above prediction route, Zhang et al. [24] proposed a high-precision approximation algorithm to solve the essentially nonconvex optimization problem in order to prevent the user's position from being eavesdropped. SimHash technology is used by [25] and others to capture user behavior patterns and gather similarity preference users. In [26], combined with Laplace mechanism, it is the first attempt to apply differential privacy directly to query processing of optimal location selection. Liu et al. [27] also proposed LBSP method to construct a query outsourcing-oriented scheme, and used the Bloom filter of hash function to generate index to ensure the realization of query processing. [28] and [29] both propose to use spatial partition structure and differential privacy model to protect query accuracy and user information. Zou et al. [30] introduced the concept of blockchain, and the non-repudiation and non-tampering of information were realized by adopting decentralized structure and consistency method.

3   System Model

With regard to the recommendation system of road privacy protection in the vehicle-mounted network, its main goal is to collect real data of vehicle users under random behavior by using routers on the road, converge the normal congestion degree of each road section by combining Markov chain, and provide differentiated privacy protection according to different road environments. All road sections within the applicable scope of the system are provided as input together with user preferences, and the optimal route is screened based on user constraints. For the optimal route, according to the user's demand for privacy protection allocation, salt and pepper noise is used to blur the real position (Fig. 1).

The scene of the vehicle network recommendation system is as follows: the starting position of the vehicle user is S, the target position is Z, the current road section of the user at a certain intersection is A, the forward road section is B, the left road section is C, the right road section is D, and the sensitive position is set as the intersection of each large street. In this case, the navigation system will automatically calculate possible potential routes. The queries of users on all routes are regularly updated to the location-based service system. Frequent queries will lead to the leakage of users' privacy information when passing through sensitive locations, so the protection of users' privacy in sensitive locations is required. However, the current protection mechanism can't protect users' queries in sensitive locations by adopting more targeted differential privacy methods according to the differences of road surrounding environment.

So far, we have conceived a personalized recommendation scheme based on privacy budget allocation. The scheme can filter routes according to user preference priority, analyze the privacy requirements of different service request locations on routes, and provide differential privacy protection under privacy budget allocation, thus realizing consideration of different road conditions.

Vehicle users first set their own service requirements, including target location Z, privacy protection parameter ε and preference weights ω_1, ω_2, and the navigation system automatically plans m potential routes for users. For the selection of potential routes, we

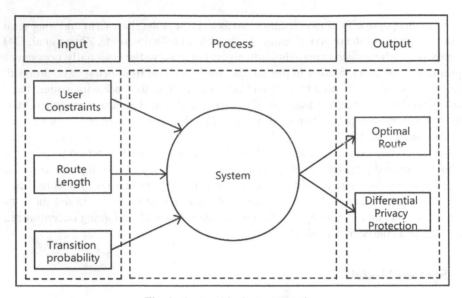

Fig. 1. System block representation.

choose the best route by calculating the route length and road congestion, and combining with the service needs of users.

Firstly, the system divides the road sections, gives the coordinates of the starting and ending points of each road section mapped on the navigation map, calculates the length of all road sections, and then obtains the distance of each potential route. In the second step, the system uses routers to collect road condition data to obtain the state transition probability of user vehicles in a certain road section, then creates a preliminary transition probability matrix according to the original data, and uses Markov model convergence matrix to find the steady state transition probability of each road section, which can reflect the long-term congestion degree of the road section, and then obtains the congestion coefficient of each potential route.

In the third step, m roads generate their own attribute sets, including the corresponding distance and congestion coefficient, and calculate the route utility according to the weight given by the user. The optimal route is constrained by the shortest distance and the minimum congestion coefficient at the same time, and the lowest score of utility computing result is the optimal route. Finally, the system determines the optimal route, and carries out differentiated privacy protection for each intersection on the route according to its congestion degree. For better service effect, we set a sensitive circle with radius R at the sensitive location. When the user's location enters the sensitive circle, the privacy is protected by adding Laplace noise to the protection circle with radius r, and the system sends the blurred virtual location to the service provider (Fig. 2).

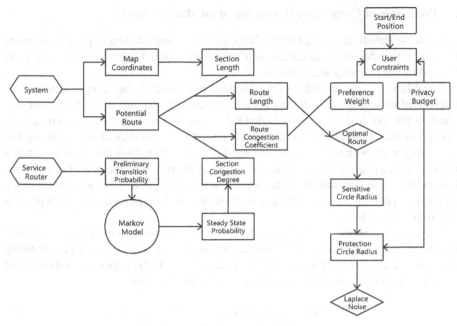

Fig. 2. Detailed system flow diagram.

3.1 Calculate the Potential Route Length

Because calculating the whole route directly involves complex problems such as radian and angle, the system judges the starting and ending points of each road section, maps it to the map to obtain coordinates, marks the road section number, divides the route into N straight lines for summation, and the system defaults the route to a two-dimensional environment, that is, does not consider the high and low latitudes of the road sections. After the user is given the target location, the system automatically generates m potential routes.

In this function, the first attribute express the length of k_{th} road segment with d_k:

$$d_k = \sqrt{(x_{k+1} - x_k)^2 + (y_{k+1} - y_k)^2} \tag{1}$$

The second attribute represents the length of K_{th} route with D_k:

$$D_K = \sum_{j=1}^{n} d_j (K \in (1, m)) \tag{2}$$

(x_k, y_k), (x_{k+1}, y_{k+1}) express the coordinates corresponding to the start and end points of k_{th} road sections, and the distance of K_{th} road section on the route is expressed d_j, and n is different for each route.

3.2 Prediction of Congestion Degree Based on Markov Model

Based on the statistical concept of Markov chain, this method aims to predict the long-term congestion degree of each road section and describe the behavior of vehicle users reflected by the real data we collected.

The Markov chain model, as an important stochastic dynamic system model, is widely used in the state transition of complex stochastic systems. A Markov process is a random process, and its property is that for a system state $X(t)$ with given time t, its next period state only depends on the current period state and transition probability, but has nothing to do with the previous periods state. P is a transition matrix, the elements of which are not negative and the sum is 1, which is expressed by the probability of each element, that is, the probability of the transition from the previous time position to the current time position. In short, Markov is characterized by a random transition process with discrete time and state.

The transition matrix X of Markov chain at time t is a matrix with $n \times n$, which contains the transition probability from one state to another. Particularly, given the ordering of the rows and columns of the matrix by the state space S, the transition probability of (i, j) element of the matrix P is given by the following formula,

$$p_{ij} = P(X_{n+1} = j | X_n = i), i, j = 1, 2, n = 0, 1, \ldots \tag{3}$$

Assuming that X_{t+1} is in state j, the probability of X_t being in state i is called one-step transition probability. Considering the general situation of roads, in order to improve work efficiency, we will not calculate the transition probabilities of all road sections, but take the form of dividing the service scope into blocks, and select typical road sections to calculate and regard them as the transition probabilities of all road sections in the region, thus ensuring reasonable transition and reducing workload. Through the router installed on the road, the system collects the transfer status of vehicles at a certain intersection, including stopping, advancing, turning left and turning right.

The multi-step transition probability can be calculated according to the one-step transition probability and Markov property, as follows:

$$P(X_{t+1} = 1) = P(X_{t+1} = 1 | X_t = 1)P(X_t = 1) + P(X_{t+1} = 1 | X_t = 2)P(X_t = 2) \tag{4}$$

$$P(X_{t+1} = 2) = P(X_{t+1} = 2 | X_t = 1)P(X_t = 1) + P(X_{t+1} = 2 | X_t = 2)P(X_t = 2) \tag{5}$$

For example, if the vehicle user is at the location l_1 at the time t, the probability of the user moving to the location l_2 will be at the location P_{12} of the transition matrix P.

The transition matrix shows the transition probability from one state to another in a short time. These probabilities converge to a steady-state matrix by repeated multiplication with the initial state vector. Let I be an arbitrarily distributed initial state vector,

$$I = [P(l_1)P(l_2)P(l_3) \ldots P(l_n)] \tag{6}$$

After constructing the transition matrix from the original data, we use the initial state vector and transition matrix to get the steady-state transition probability of the intersection when the probability converges $P_{n\to\infty}$, so as to predict the long-term congestion index of different road sections.

Assuming that the vehicle user drives to the current road section through the front intersection, stays in the state $A \to A$, continues to move forward in the state $A \to B$, turns left in the state $A \to C$, and turns right in the state $A \to D$, the four States in the other three directions are the same as above, then the congestion coefficient P_{all}^S of this road section can be expressed as,

$$P_{all}^S = P_Q + P_Z(Q, Z \in \{A, B, C, D\}) \tag{7}$$

This value can reflect the congestion degree of the road section, where Q is the user's entry direction, Z is the departure direction, P_A, P_B, P_C, and P_D is the steady-state transition probability of each direction converged by Markov chain, and further obtain the congestion coefficient of the route,

$$P_{all}^K = \sum_{k=1}^{n} P_{all}^{kS}(K \in (1, m)) \tag{8}$$

3.3 Screening the Optimal Route According to the User Preference Weight

The optimal driving route is mainly determined by two factors: first, give priority to the road closer to the destination; Second, priority will be given to roads with lower congestion. The attribute set that affects the user's choice is represented by $\{D_K, P_{all}^K\}$, and all routes that the user can choose are considered in m schemes. According to the attribute weights set by the user, the route utility index can be obtained:

$$\psi = \omega_1 D_K + \omega_2 P_{all}^K(K \in (1, m)) \tag{9}$$

Because the smaller D_K is, the shorter the distance is, and the smaller P_{all}^K is, the lower the congestion degree of the route is, so the smaller ψ the route means the higher the utility, ψ_{min} is the best route.

3.4 Differentiated Privacy Protection According to Road Conditions

In order to consider different road environments and allocate privacy budget more rationally, we decided to define the radius of sensitive circle at intersections according to the congestion degree of current road sections. Because the more vehicles on the road, the more difficult it is for attackers to infer the specific location of users, and the system will narrow the sensitive circle range. However, in the case of remote roads and few vehicles, the real location of users is easy to be exposed. At this time, we tend to expand the sensitive circle range and strengthen the privacy protection of this location.

The radiu of that sensitive circle is defined as follow,

$$R = 30 - \frac{P_\tau}{P_{\max}} \times 15 \tag{10}$$

P_τ is the current road congestion degree, and $P_{\max}$ is the extreme road congestion degree.

When the user's vehicle enters the sensitive circle, the system starts to protect the real position of the user by differential privacy, and defines the virtual random disturbance radius $r = Gamma(2, \frac{1}{\varepsilon})$ of the vehicle according to the geographical indiscernibility. At this time, the noise is indistinguishable from the vehicle position in this area.

Then, add salt and pepper noise to the protection circle, the system sends the processed error location to the location service system, and then the system completes the road recommendation and privacy protection service.

4 Experiment

In this part, we evaluate the performance of our proposed scheme by comparing with the existing privacy protection services, which include anonymity-based, data suppression-based and homomorphic encryption. SELECT SUM and SELECT AVG are anonymous-based frameworks to protect the privacy of participating entities. These frameworks protect privacy by modifying the original data set and limiting data query. SELECT SUM and SELECT AVG frameworks also use a variety of algorithms to achieve the security of aggregate queries. Given a certain configured threshold amount t, it ensures that each query is performed on a data set with at least t records. However, all the above schemes have some defects. Firstly, they are limited in scope and cannot handle large-scale areas. Secondly, they do not support dynamic preferences based on users. Thirdly, they lack consideration for different protected environments. On the other hand, our proposal covers all these restrictions.

In our experiment, the performance evaluation of our method is based on given hypothetical data. In the data set, there are about 100 road sections, and each intersection is sampled at an interval of 20–50 m.

We compare the quality of service loss of privacy protection with and without routing. As shown in the figure, compared with the method without routing, the system with routing has lower service loss and better quality (Fig. 3).

1) Under the condition of determining the privacy protection level, the system can ensure the lowest congestion degree of the route comprehensive road by selecting the best route, and the lower congestion degree means that a larger sensitive circle range will be allocated. Because the user's query position at the intersection needs to be updated regularly to the location service system, we need to add virtual noise to blur the position when the user's vehicle enters the sensitive circle, but according to the geographical indiscernibility, adding noise in the protection circle defined for the user will not be easily recognized by the attacker. In the edge range of the sensitive circle, some noise is in the protection circle and exceeds the sensitive circle range, which is the loss of service quality. With the continuous expansion of user privacy budget, the scope of the sensitive circle is also increasing, and the loss of service

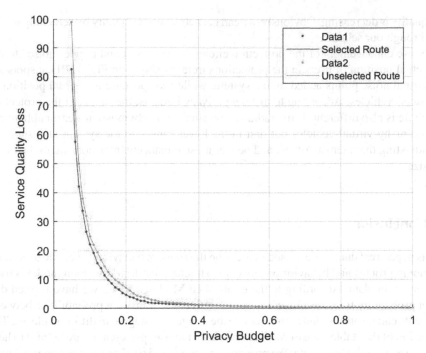

Fig. 3. Impact of route selection.

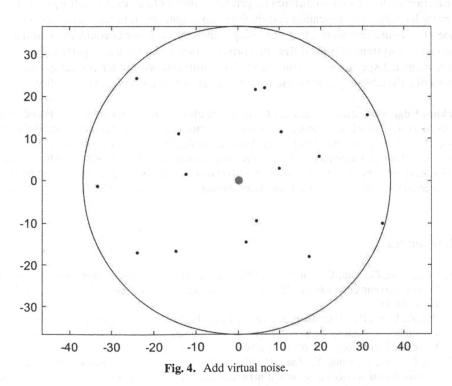

Fig. 4. Add virtual noise.

quality is decreasing. Obviously, we can get better service quality by screening routes through our scheme.

2) Noise enhancement of the protection circle: We add "salt and pepper noise" to the actual position of users in the protection circle, as shown in Fig. 4. Black spots are virtual noise points added by the system, while red spots are the actual position of users' vehicles. According to different privacy budgets, the radius of the protection circle is also different. If the radius is too small, it is obviously unreasonable to get too many virtual vehicles out first in the lower range, so the system also supports adjusting the intensity of salt and pepper noise enhancement according to the range size.

5 Conclusion

In this paper, real data sets are used to focus on the random behavior of vehicle users, and the moving routes and behavior patterns are extracted, and Markov chain model is used to analyze the data. According to the established Markov model, we have formed different probability transition matrixes, which reflect the transition probabilities between different road locations, and then calculate the congestion degree in different places. The prediction of the stable state of road environment and user preferences are helpful to help users screen out the best route. We propose a personalized road privacy recommendation protection system based on differential privacy, which obtains user constraints, such as current location, target location and preference weight, and returns the best route that meets the input constraints. Then, according to the surrounding environment of the query location, the system adds the differential privacy noise under the user's personalized privacy budget. Experimental results show that compared with other privacy protection protocols, the advantages of this scheme lie in better privacy and service quality.

Acknowledgement. This research was funded by the Philosophy and Social Science Foundation of the Jiangsu Higher Education Institutions of China "Research on Blockchain-based Intelligent Credit Information System and its Privacy Preservation Mechanism" (Grants No. 2021SJA0448), the Natural Science Foundation of Jiangsu Province (Grants No. BK20210928), the Higher Education Research Project of Nanjing Institute of Technology (Grants No. 2021ZC13), and Jiangsu province college students' practical innovation training program (Grants No. 202111276011Z).

References

1. Li, L., Liu, G., Yan, C., Jiang, C.: LORI: a learning-to-rank-based integration method of location recommendation. In: IEEE Transactions on Computational Social Systems, vol. 6, no. 3 (2019)
2. Wu, Z., Wang, R., Li, Q., Lian, X., Xu, G., Chen, E., Liu, X.: A location privacy-preserving system based on query range cover-up or location-based services. In: IEEE Transactions on Vehicular Technology, vol. 69, no. 5 (2020)
3. Xu, C., Luo, L., Ding, Y., Zhao, G., Yu, S.: Personalized location privacy protection for location-based services in vehicular networks. In: IEEE Wireless Communications Letters, vol. 9, no. 10 (2020)

4. Li, B., Zhu, H., Xie, M.: Quantifying location privacy risks under heterogeneous correlations. Digit. Obj. Ident. https://doi.org/10.1109/ACCESS.2021.3056152
5. Zhou, L., Yu, L., Du, S., Zhu, H., Chen, C.: Achieving differentially private location privacy in edge-assistant connected vehicles. IEEE Internet of Things J. **6**(3) (2019)
6. Zhu, X., Ayday, E., Vitenberg, R.: A privacy-preserving framework for outsourcing location-based services to the cloud. In: IEEE Transactions on Dependable and Secure Computing, vol. 18, no. 1 (2021)
7. Sun, G. et al.: Location privacy preservation for mobile users in location-based services. Digit. Obj. Ident. https://doi.org/10.1109/ACCESS.2019.2925571
8. Nosouhi, M.R., Sood, K., Yu, S., Grobler, M., Zhang, J.: PASPORT: a secure and private location proof generation and verification framework. In: IEEE Transactions on Computational Social Systems, vol. 7, no. 2 (2020)
9. Ma, C., Yan, Z., Chen, C.W.: SSPA-LBS: scalable and social-friendly privacy-aware location-based services. In: IEEE Transactions on Multimedia, vol. 21, no. 8 (2019)
10. Wu, H., LI, M., Zhang, H.: Enabling smart anonymity scheme for security collaborative enhancement in location-based services. Digit. Obj. Ident. https://doi.org/10.1109/ACCESS. 2019.2911107
11. Zhang, J., Wang, X., Yuan, Y., Ni, L.: RcDT: privacy preservation based on r-constrained dummy trajectory in mobile social network. Digit. Obj. Ident. https://doi.org/10.1109/ACC ESS.2019.2927140
12. He, X., Jin, R., Dai, H.: Leveraging spatial diversity for privacy-aware location-based services in mobile networks. In: IEEE Transactions on Information Forensics and Security, vol. 13, no. 6 (2018)
13. Albouq, S.S., et al.: A double obfuscation approach for protecting the privacy of iot location based applications. Digit. Obj. Ident. https://doi.org/10.1109/ACCESS.2020.3009200
14. Hu, Z., Liu, S., Chen, K.: Privacy-preserving location-based services query scheme against quantum attacks. In: IEEE Transactions on Dependable and Secure Computing, vol. 17, no. 5 (2020)
15. Yang, X., Gao, L., Zheng, J., Wei, W.: Location privacy preservation mechanism for location-based service with incomplete location data. Digit. Obj. Ident. https://doi.org/10.1109/ACC ESS.2020.2995504
16. Xu, J., Liu, L., Zhang, R., Xie, J., Duan, Q., Shi, L.: IFTS: a location privacy protection method based on initial and final trajectory segments. Digit. Obj. Ident. https://doi.org/10. 1109/ACCESS.2021.3052169
17. Zheng, Y., Luo, J., Zhong, T.: Service recommendation middleware based on location privacy protection in VANET. Digit. Obj. Ident. https://doi.org/10.1109/ACCESS.2020.2964422
18. Fei, F., Li, S., Dai, H., Hu, C., Dou, W., Ni, Q.: A K-anonymity based schema for location privacy preservation. In: IEEE Transactions on Sustainable Computing, vol. 4, no. 2 (2019)
19. Huang, C., Wang, D., Tao, J., Mann, B.: On physical-social-aware localness inference by exploring big data from location-based services. In: IEEE Transactions on Big Data, vol. 6, no. 4 (2020)
20. Zou, H., Zhou, Y., Yang, J., Spanos, C.J.: Unsupervised WiFi-enabled IoT device-user association for personalized location-based service. IEEE Internet of Things J. **6**(1) (2019)
21. Li, F., Li, Q., LI, Z., Huang, Z., Chang, X., Xia, J.: A personal location prediction method based on individual trajectory and group trajectory. Digit. Obj. Ident. https://doi.org/10.1109/ ACCESS.2019.2927888
22. Zhang, W., Li, M., Tandon, R., Li, H.: Online location trace privacy: an information theoretic approach. In: IEEE Transactions on Information Forensics and Security, vol. 14, no. 1 (2019)
23. Ahmad, S., Ullah, I., Mehmood, F., Fayaz, M., Kim, D.: A stochastic approach towards travel route optimization and recommendation based on users constraints using markov chain. Digit. Obj. Ident. https://doi.org/10.1109/ACCESS.2019.2926675

24. Zhang, T., Li, X., Zhang, Q.: location privacy protection: a power allocation approach. In: IEEE Transactions on Communications, vol. 67, no. 1 (2019)
25. Zhang, Q., Zhang, Y., Caizhong, L., Yan, C., Duan, Y., Wang, H.: sport location-based user clustering with privacy-preservation in wireless IoT-driven healthcare. Digit. Obj. Ident. https://doi.org/10.1109/ACCESS.2021.3051051
26. Park, S., Lee, J., Seog, P.: Maximum influential location selection with differentially private user locations. Dig. Obj. Ident. https://doi.org/10.1109/ACCESS.2020.2990706
27. Liu, Z., Wu, I., Ke, J., Qu, W., Wang, W., Wang, H.: Accountable outsourcing location-based services with privacy preservation. Digit. Obj. Ident. https://doi.org/10.1109/ACCESS.2019.2936582
28. Yadav, V.K., Verma, S., Venkatesan, S.: Efficient and secure location-based services scheme in VANET. In: IEEE Transactions on Vehicular Technology, vol. 69, no. 11 (2020)
29. Yan, Y., Gao, X., Mahmood, A., Feng, T., Xie, P.: Differential private spatial decomposition and location publishing based on unbalanced quadtree partition algorithm. Digit. Obj. Ident. https://doi.org/10.1109/ACCESS.2020.2999580
30. Zou, S., Xi, J., Wang, H., Xu, G.: CrowdBLPS: a blockchain-based location-privacy-preserving mobile crowd sensing system. In: IEEE Transactions on Industrial Informatics, vol. 16, no. 6 (2020)

Research on Power Security Early Warning System Based on Improved K-means Algorithm

XinLong Wang[1](✉), ChunXiao Song[2], and MingDai Yu[1]

[1] School of Computer Engineering, Nanjing Institute of Technology, Nanjing 211167, China
x00202180428@njit.edu.cn
[2] Postgraduate Department, Nanjing Institute of Technology, Nanjing 211167, China

Abstract. In response to the problem of data acquisition and massive alarm information screening and extraction in the traditional power grid security early warning system under the high-speed network environment, this paper integrates the improved K-means algorithm in the process of clustering analysis module processing alarm data, and analyzes the initial alarm data of intrusion detection system after feature processing and format conversion combined with Weka application platform, and finally obtains more efficient alarm information. The results of many experiments show that the power security early warning system based on the improved K-means clustering algorithm solves the problems existing in the traditional security system, which can largely avoid the problem of system omission and false alarm, and the overall performance of the power security early warning system has been greatly improved.

Keywords: Power safety · Data collection · Safety early warning · Cluster analysis

1 Introduction

Nowadays, we have entered the era of big data, with large data volume, high data density and multiple data types. In the face of increasingly complex network structures, threats and losses caused by network viruses and DDoS attacks are gradually increasing. The traditional security defense methods cannot meet the needs of current power system network security. Therefore, in order to ensure the maximum security of the system network, the power system threat detection and identification technology can be used to establish an intrusion detection system to realize network security early warning. Make it possible to improve the emergency response capability of the entire power system network, alleviate the harm caused by the attack.

Intrusion detection technology was first mentioned by Anderson in a report on computer security threats and surveillance to the US Air Force in 1980, and a simple definition was made [1]. Foreign research on intrusion detection started early, and many research teams have carried out early warning and intrusion detection technology research. There have been very rich research results and a large number of application practices. At

© Springer Nature Singapore Pte Ltd. 2022
Y. Tian et al. (Eds.): ICBDS 2021, CCIS 1563, pp. 73–89, 2022.
https://doi.org/10.1007/978-981-19-0852-1_6

present, data mining, computer immune technology and Agent technology have been gradually applied to intrusion detection in foreign countries.

In terms of architecture, the COAST team of Purdue University applied the concept of Agent to the intrusion detection process for the first time. Not only that, it also created a new research field of intrusion detection technology [2]. The literature [3] proposes a multi-user MIMO-OFDM system channel information full feedback scheme for virus intrusion detection in a multi-agent innovative network, which effectively improves the detection performance. However, with the increase of Agent users, the amount of system overhead increases rapidly, and it is difficult to practically apply. In the detection mechanism, there are researches on traditional artificial intelligence methods such as expert systems and pattern matching, as well as research based on artificial biological immune technology [4]. In the intrusion detection system, it mainly focuses on the integrity protection of data files and effective control of the virus. Artificial immunity can also be combined with machine learning algorithms to make the two complementary and improve the accuracy of intrusion detection. Tabatabaefar et al. combined the artificial immune system with the standard particle swarm algorithm and proposed an intrusion detection method [5] based on the artificial immune system. The detection accuracy of the system is improved by dynamically determining the antibody radius. In addition, in the study of early warning architecture, Kijewski gave people an information process for early warning and attack identification in a document. It introduces the flow [6] between attack analysis, early warning unit, detection generator, and knowledge base. The Wenke Lee research team of Columbia University first applied data mining to intrusion detection systems. The research team mainly applies data mining classification algorithms, sequence mining algorithms, and associated data mining algorithms to intrusion detection information systems. Data mining and detection [7] are carried out through data sources based on the network and the host. In the field of intrusion detection system combined with data mining, Eslamnezhad Mohsen et al. [8] proposed an intrusion detection method based on the MinMax K-means clustering algorithm. The clustering algorithm can greatly eliminate the sensitivity to randomly selecting the initial clustering center, so that high-quality clustering results can be obtained. Experiments show that the intrusion detection method is excellent in detection rate and false alarm rate. Al-Yaseen et al. [9] proposed a combination of improved K-means, SVM and ELM as a multi-level hybrid intrusion detection model. Through the final experimental results, it can be found that the proposed model can more accurately detect normal network behaviors and network attacks such as DOS and Probe.

China's research on intrusion detection technology started relatively late. The existing results mainly focus on the framework design and improvement of the intrusion detection system, and the establishment of simple linkage with the firewall, etc. There has not been a breakthrough in the detection algorithms and detection mechanisms used by the system. At present, in the aspect of intrusion anomaly detection, there are three core problems [10]: weak real-time performance of intrusion detection, high false alarm rate of intrusion detection, and weak ability of new types of intrusion detection. In the era of big data, these problems become more severe when dealing with massive security data. However, data mining technology has strong advantages in feature extraction or rule establishment for large amounts of data. Therefore, data mining technology can be used to analyze and process massive amounts of security data to detect attacks [11].

In the era of big data, the challenges faced by power system security are more severe. Power system network security early warning system is still an extremely important research topic in the field of power grid security. Security solutions under the background of traditional networks can no longer fully solve the power grid security problems under the current network scale. Therefore, it is necessary to use the latest developments in the network environment and research technology in the era of big data, integrated into the exploration and research of power grid security early warning system. In order to solve the problems faced by today's power system.

This article focuses on data acquisition and alarm information processing in many research directions of power security systems. The data mining algorithm of machine learning is combined with the processing of alarm data, and the data mining platform Weka is used as the basis for secondary development. Embed the improved K-means algorithm into the Weka platform to improve the accuracy and efficiency of clustering. On this basis, establish a power grid security early warning system that can efficiently respond to massive security early warning data. The power security early warning system based on the improved K-means algorithm proposed in this paper solves the problem that traditional power security systems face massive amounts of security data. At the same time, there are problems such as excessive flooding of alarm information, high system false alarm rate and high false alarm rate. Make the safety early warning system finally get more concise, efficient and accurate alarm information. In addition, the improved K-means algorithm based on density and distance proposed in this paper solves the problem of difficult evaluation and selection of the K value in the traditional K-means algorithm. Avoid the large fluctuations and inaccuracy of clustering results caused by random designation or empirical selection of initial clustering center points and K values in the process of traditional K-means clustering algorithm. Improved the stability and accuracy of clustering.

2 Principle Introduction

2.1 Principles of Data Mining Technology

Data mining is a process of extracting hidden, previously unknown and potentially valuable event information and knowledge from a large number of missing, noisy, fuzzy, repetitive and random data [12]. Data mining includes:

- The data source is real and massive. And it is noisy, incomplete, and needs to be preprocessed.
- The purpose of data mining is to explore information that is potentially valuable to users. From the massive data collection, we get hidden potentially valuable information that is not easy for people to find.

In addition, the process of data mining is a complex, a general term for comprehensive technical concepts that span multiple cross-disciplines. The whole process of machine learning methods, large-scale data set pattern calculation and discovery of the introduction of statistics can be attributed to the category of data mining [13].

Data mining is essentially the category of machine learning. In short, it is to explore the connection between massive data and information and summarize a certain potential rule or abstract a certain pattern. Then it can be applied to many aspects such as scientific research, decision-making, predictive analysis and so on. In recent years, data mining algorithms have been widely used in power grid research and engineering practice due to their fast calculation speed and strong generalization ability. Not only that, it also plays a huge role in the safety protection of the power system. One of the important applications of data mining is predictive analysis. Data mining algorithms can mine potential rules between data from large-scale and massive data [14]. The performance of intrusion detection can be greatly improved by combining intrusion detection technology with data mining technology or some algorithms in the data mining field. It can also make the intrusion detection system have real-time and intelligent advantages at the same time. Data mining technology can help extract public rules for various intrusion behaviors in intrusion detection. Or set a threshold to establish an abnormal behavior library as a criterion for distinguishing normal behavior from abnormal behavior. This thesis uses data mining technology to extract valuable feature rules from massive power grid security data and early warning information. It also uses the extracted feature rules as a behavior baseline to monitor the power grid system in real time. Identify threats to the system's access intrusion. Prevent it from continuing to invade.

For the grid risk early warning system based on the weka platform and improved K-means algorithm in this thesis, the data mining process is briefly divided into four steps, as shown (Fig. 1).

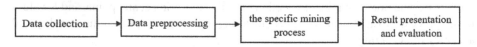

Fig. 1. Data mining process

- Data collection: Collect raw data according to specific business scenarios. For example, obtain the original data information from the log files of the security protection system, the web server logs, or the data traffic captured by the network packet capture tool. This thesis extracts the log data of the power security company's network security protection system.
- Data preprocessing: After the initial source data set is obtained, the original data needs to be preprocessed due to the inconsistency of data format, data redundancy and lack of data in the original data. That is to unify the processing of various missing values of the source data, and at the same time clean up useless data objects. Then standardize the data and unify the data format. Finally, perform data integration and unified storage of the data according to the business scenario. In this thesis, a relational database is selected to store the final data according to actual application scenarios.
- Specific mining process: Analyze the pre-processed data further and determine the way to further process the data. For example, according to the advantages and disadvantages

of machine learning models. Train each model. Then count the errors of the test data, select the model with the smallest error, and get the best model suitable for the required business scenario. Various data mining algorithms can be used. Such as decision tree, support vector machine, naive Bayes and other algorithms. Use data mining algorithms to get valuable result information from the data and output it. This thesis selects the K-means clustering algorithm to process the alarm data information in combination with the business scenario of the alarm data processing of the intrusion detection system. And finally get more valuable data information.

• Results display and evaluation: Comprehensive evaluation and analysis of the results obtained after completing the data mining process from a number of different perspectives. Record valuable laws or guidelines as prior knowledge for in-depth mining in the next step.

2.2 Weka Platform

Waikato Environment for Knowledge Analysis, referred to as Weka, is an open source software for data mining and machine learning developed by the University of Waikato in New Zealand [15]. Provides tools for data preprocessing, classification, clustering, association rules, regression and visualization. The software contains a set of data processing methods and algorithms for training machine learning models, which has strong compatibility and scalability. After years of development and improvement, the software platform has integrated almost all classic algorithms involved in data mining, and it has become one of the most complete open source data mining tools today.

ARFF file, a format for storing data in Weka and a text file. It describes a list of instances that share a set of attributes, that is, a two-dimensional table. Represents a relationship between attributes. The rows and columns of the table represent the instances and attributes of the data set, respectively. In addition, Weka also supports CSV format, XRFF format, and also supports database access via JDBC.

Weka has an easy-to-use graphical user interface that can combine many data preprocessing and subsequent processing methods. Explorer is the most commonly used component of Wek, with six functions: preprocessing, classification, clustering, association rules, attribute selection, and visualization. It also provides a visualization tool that allows the prediction of data sets and classifiers and clusters to be visualized in two dimensions. As shown in Fig. 2, the data set can be loaded from Explorer to browse its attribute characteristics and distribution. At the same time, it can not only perform operations such as classification and clustering on the data set, but also configure and execute clusters on the data set, which can be visualized in the pop-up data visualization tool.

This thesis is based on the data mining application Weka software for secondary development, embedding and integrating the improved K-means clustering algorithm into the Weka application platform. Use the Weka application platform to call Weka's original SimpleKmeans clustering algorithm and the improved K-means clustering in this article to process the same data set, and the performance of the two algorithms is compared and analyzed according to the final clustering results.

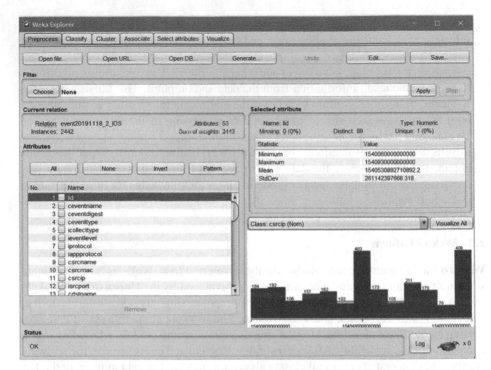

Fig. 2. Two-dimensional visualization forecast map

3   Improvement Based on K-means Algorithm

3.1   Overview of K-means Algorithm

The k-means algorithm is an unsupervised algorithm proposed by Macqueen in 1967 [16]. Because of its simple, fast and easy-to-understand characteristics, it is widely used in the field of data mining. The goal of k-means algorithm is to divide the sample data into multiple categories, so that the similarity of data points in each category is as large as possible, and the similarity of data points between different categories is as small as possible. The main research process of the K-means algorithm is to calculate the mean or centroid of the data points in each cluster. Think of it as the abstract center point of this cluster. According to the similarity between the data object and the abstract center, continuously update the position of the abstract cluster center and reduce the sum of squared error (SSE) of clusters through continuous iterative calculations. When the SSE no longer changes or the objective function converges, the clustering ends and the final clustering division is completed, as shown in Fig. 3.

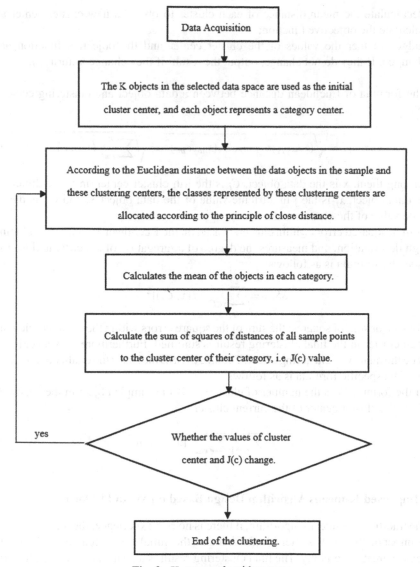

Fig. 3. K-means algorithm steps

The main steps of the algorithm are as follows:

1. According to certain established rules or experience, select K data objects as the initial centers, that is, as the initial cluster centers;
2. Calculate the Euclidean distance between each sample data and the center. According to the closest distance criterion, they are divided into the cluster corresponding to the closest cluster center;

3. Recalculate the mean distance of each cluster to obtain a new cluster center and calculate the objective function;
4. Judge whether the values of the cluster center and the objective function have changed. If they do not change, output the result; if they change, return (2).

The formula of Euclidean distance between a data object and clustering center in space is:

$$d(x, c_i) = \sqrt{(x_1 - c_{i1})^2 + \ldots + (x_m - c_{im})^2} = \sqrt{\sum_{j=1}^{m} (x_j - c_{ij})^2} \tag{1}$$

Among them, x is the data object, C_i is the i-th cluster center, m is the dimension of the data object, x_j is the j-th attribute value of the data object x, and C_{ij} is the j-th attribute value of the cluster center C_i.

Sum of squared errors within clusters: based on the Euclidean distance, it is obtained through deformation, and measures the degree of aggregation of the current cluster C_i. The specific formula is as follows:

$$SSE_i = \sum_{x \in C_i} |d(x, C_i)|^2 \tag{2}$$

Total error sum of squares: the sum of the square errors within the clusters calculated for each cluster in the final clustering result is summed. Furthermore, it is a statistic to evaluate the quality of clustering effect. The size of SSE indicates the quality of clustering results. The specific formula is as follows:

In the formula, k is the number of clusters, x is the sample object in the cluster C_i, and C_i is the cluster center of the current cluster

$$SSE = \sum_{i=1}^{k} \sum_{x \in c_i} |d(x, C_i)|^2 \tag{3}$$

3.2   Improved K-means Algorithm Design Based on Weka Platform

For the traditional K-means algorithm, if there is no rich experience, the manually specified number of clusters k is often blind; Choosing the initial cluster centers randomly will also cause great uncertainty. The final clustering result is also unstable. If the clustering center selection is not appropriate, it will directly increase the time complexity and space complexity of the algorithm. When faced with noise and outlier data, it is more likely to lead to the problem of falling into a local optimal solution.

This paper improves the traditional K-means clustering algorithm based on the design of density and distance, and integrates the core idea of the clustering algorithm based on density and distance. The traditional K-means algorithm is more sensitive to the selection of initial clustering centers. Randomly selecting the initial cluster centers will make the clustering results unstable. The initial center selected based on density is subjective [17]. The improved algorithm is not only based on the idea of density and distance, but also uses a weighted method to weigh the relationship between density and distance to select the ideal K cluster centers. The basic design idea of the algorithm is: In a sample data set with countless data points, first calculate the sample density and sample weight. Select the first $\sqrt{n}$ points with the highest sample density as sample U; First select the point with the highest density from the sample set as the first cluster center. Add to the cluster center point C. Then use the weight parameter to select the second, third…Kth cluster center from the sample U by comparing the size of the weight parameter.

Here first introduce the related concepts and formula definitions of the K-means algorithm based on density and distance improvement:

Suppose n sample data $X = \{x_1, x_2, x_n\}$ is the clustering data set, expressed as $x_i = \{x_{i1}, x_{i2}, ..., x_{im}\}$, $1 \leq i \leq n$. The dimension of the sample element is m, and the weight W $= (w_1, w_2, \cdots w_m)$ is defined, where $w_i, = (w_{i1}, w_{i2}, \cdots w_{im})$, $1 \leq i \leq n$, and the dimension of the sample element is m.

$$w_{id} = \frac{x_{id}}{P_d} \tag{4}$$

Among them, x_{id} represents the d-th component in the i-th sample data; $P_d = \frac{\sum_{i=1}^{n} x_{id}}{n}$ represents the average value of the dth component of each data object in the sample data; w reflects the overall distribution characteristics of the sample data.

Weighted Euclidean distance formula:

$$d_{w(x_i, x_j)} = \sqrt{\sum_{d=1}^{m} w_{id} \left(x_{id} - x_{jd}\right)^2} \tag{5}$$

Among them, $d_{w(x_i, x_j)}$ is the Euclidean distance calculated by dimensional weighting of sample x_i and sample x_j in the m-dimensional vector space. x_{id} and x_{jd} are the data values of the sample point x_i and sample point x_j in the vector space, respectively, and d is the dimension of the vector space.

The average Euclidean distance formula of all sample points:

$$avgd = \frac{\sum_{i=1}^{n-1} \sum_{j=i+1}^{n} d_{w(x_i, x_j)}}{C_n^2} \tag{6}$$

The density formula of sample point i in the data set is:

$$\rho_i = \sum_{j=1}^{n} f\left(avgd - d_{wij} avgd\right) \tag{7}$$

Among them, the function $f(x) = \begin{cases} 1, x \geq 0 \\ 0, x < 0 \end{cases}$, d_{wij} is $d_{w(x_i, x_j)}$.

The actual meaning of ρ_i is the number of sample points contained in a circle with the sample point x_i as the center and avgd as the radius. These points are classified into a cluster. The average distance m_i between the sample points of this cluster is defined by the formula:

$$m_i = \frac{\sum_{i=1}^{\rho_i} \sum_{j=i+1}^{\rho_i} d_{wij}}{C_{\rho_i}^2} \tag{8}$$

Define the distance d_{si} between clusters, which represents the minimum distance between sample x_i and another sample x_j with higher point density. Represents the dissimilarity between data points x_i and x_j. The larger the d_{si}, the farther the point is from the center of other larger clusters, that is, the more likely the point is to become the center of the cluster. The mathematical formula is as follows:

$$d_{si} = \text{min} d_{wij}, x_j \in D, \rho_j > \rho_i \tag{9}$$

Define the cluster effective value ratio as the ratio of the sample distance in the cluster to the sample distance between the clusters. The formula is:

$$h_i = \frac{d_{si}}{m_i} \tag{10}$$

The greater the d_{si}, the greater the distance between clusters, the greater the ratio h_i; the greater the m_i the greater the average distance within the cluster, which reflects to a certain extent that the distribution of points in the cluster is relatively loose, and the ratio h_i is smaller.

Define weight parameter f_i:

$$f_i = h_i.d_w\left(x_{i,}, C_{i-1}\right) \tag{11}$$

$d_w\left(x_{i,}, C_{i-1}\right)$ is the distance from x in the sample U to the last selected initial cluster center C_{i-1}. In the sample set, find the sample points to be selected. Calculate the distance from the previous center point. Then calculate the product of this distance and the effective value of the cluster, and finally select the point with the largest product. This point is the next cluster center to find. The initial cluster centers selected step by step according to f_i reduce the number of iterations of the algorithm.

The main steps of the improved K-means clustering algorithm based on distance and density are as follows:

Input: sample set X, containing n data sample objects.

Output: k clustering results that meet the requirements.

Step 1: Input the sample point set X, and calculate the average distance avgd of all sample points according to formulas (5) and (6).

Step 2: Draw a circle with any sample point as the center and R = avgd as the radius. The number of all sample points in the circle is taken as the density of the sample points.

Step 3: After calculating the density of all sample points, store the first $\sqrt{n}$ sample data into the data set U in descending order.

Step 4: Find the point with the largest weight parameter in the data set U as the second center point x_2 and add it to the center point set C. Then delete all points in U whose distance x_2 is less than avgd.

Step 5: Repeat the above process similarly, and select the cluster center according to the weight parameter. Until the data set U becomes an empty set, at this time $C = \{C_1, C_2, ..., k\}$, k initial cluster centers are obtained.

Step 6: Use the obtained initial cluster center and cluster number as input and perform a clustering operation on the given data set until the cluster center no longer changes.

Step 7: Output the final clustering result.

4　System Implementation

4.1　Cluster Analysis Module

After analyzing the core code of the improved K-means algorithm, the K-means algorithm based on density and distance is integrated and embedded into the Weka application platform. Use security data to test the clustering algorithm module, and use the SimpleKmeans algorithm that comes with the Weka platform to process the same security data set, and compare the performance of the two.

An alarm data record contains fields such as alarm type, source IP, source service port, destination service port, destination IP address, and receiving time. There are 2442 data records in total. The specific record content is shown in the Fig. 4.

lid	ceventdigest	csrcip	isrcport	cdstip	idstport	cdevip	loccurtime	lrecepttim	ccollectori
1.54015E+15	rsync服务远程缓冲	137.41.121.12!	40179	158.111.93.8:	873	249.111.155.1	1.57401E+12	1.57E+12	54.39.153.
1.54011E+15	rsync服务远程缓冲	137.41.121.12!	62197	158.111.93.8:	873	249.111.155.1	1.57401E+12	1.57E+12	54.39.153.
1.54012E+15	rsync服务远程缓冲	137.41.121.12!	62631	158.111.93.8:	873	249.111.155.1	1.57401E+12	1.57E+12	54.39.153.
1.54012E+15	rsync服务远程缓冲	137.41.121.12!	62626	158.111.93.8:	873	249.111.155.1	1.57401E+12	1.57E+12	54.39.153.
1.54016E+15	rsync服务远程缓冲	137.41.121.12!	41337	158.111.93.8:	873	249.111.155.1	1.57402E+12	1.57E+12	54.39.153.
1.54016E+15	rsync服务远程缓冲	137.41.121.12!	42429	158.111.93.8:	873	249.111.155.1	1.57402E+12	1.57E+12	54.39.153.
1.54015E+15	SHELLCODE x86 set	71.33.222.219	49787	221.148.187.	8001	249.111.155.1	1.57401E+12	1.57E+12	54.39.153.
1.54008E+15	rsync服务远程缓冲	137.41.121.12!	59541	158.111.93.8:	873	249.111.155.1	1.57401E+12	1.57E+12	54.39.153.
1.54009E+15	SHELLCODE x86 set	60.172.84.128	32938	221.148.187.	9001	249.111.155.1	1.57401E+12	1.57E+12	54.39.153.
1.54019E+15	rsync服务远程缓冲	137.41.121.12!	45513	158.111.93.8:	873	249.111.155.1	1.57402E+12	1.57E+12	54.39.153.
1.54019E+15	rsync服务远程缓冲	137.41.121.12!	44931	158.111.93.8:	873	249.111.155.1	1.57402E+12	1.57E+12	54.39.153.
1.54019E+15	rsync服务远程缓冲	137.41.121.12!	45191	158.111.93.8:	873	249.111.155.1	1.57402E+12	1.57E+12	54.39.153.
1.54019E+15	rsync服务远程缓冲	137.41.121.12!	45192	158.111.93.8:	873	249.111.155.1	1.57402E+12	1.57E+12	54.39.153.
1.54019E+15	rsync服务远程缓冲	137.41.121.12!	45196	158.111.93.8:	873	249.111.155.1	1.57402E+12	1.57E+12	54.39.153.
1.54019E+15	rsync服务远程缓冲	137.41.121.12!	45170	158.111.93.8:	873	249.111.155.1	1.57402E+12	1.57E+12	54.39.153.
1.54019E+15	rsync服务远程缓冲	137.41.121.12!	45179	158.111.93.8:	873	249.111.155.1	1.57402E+12	1.57E+12	54.39.153.
1.54019E+15	rsync服务远程缓冲	137.41.121.12!	45207	158.111.93.8:	873	249.111.155.1	1.57402E+12	1.57E+12	54.39.153.
1.54019E+15	rsync服务远程缓冲	137.41.121.12!	45201	158.111.93.8:	873	249.111.155.1	1.57402E+12	1.57E+12	54.39.153.
1.5402E+15	rsync服务远程缓冲	137.41.121.12!	45586	158.111.93.8:	873	249.111.155.1	1.57402E+12	1.57E+12	54.39.153.

Fig. 4. Alarm data record diagram

Here we use Weka's data preprocessing function to preprocess the primary alarm data file. Remove redundant and missing data and carry out standardized and standardized processing. The attribute distribution of the processed alarm data field is shown in Figs. 5, 6, 7, and 8. From the distribution of the field attributes of the graph, the overall distribution of the source IP, source service port, destination service port, destination IP address and other data in the intrusion alarm information can be roughly understood.

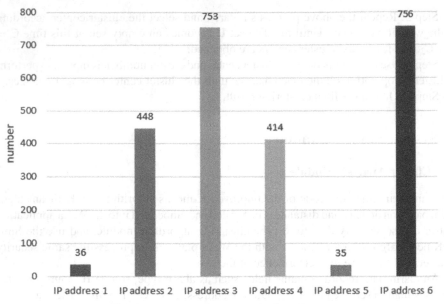

Fig. 5. Source IP address distribution diagram

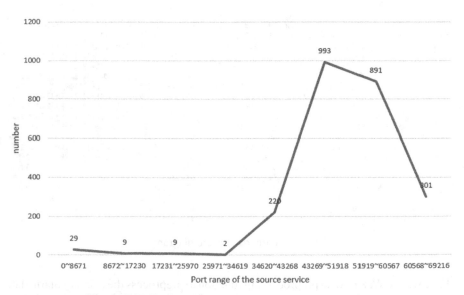

Fig. 6. Distribution diagram of source service port numbers

After the improved clustering algorithm based on density and distance analyzes and processes the primary alarm data, the final alarm data clustering information can be obtained. As shown in Fig. 9, the 2442 data records of the primary alarm data are finally grouped into 5 types, which greatly reduces the redundant alarm information and reduces the false alarm rate.

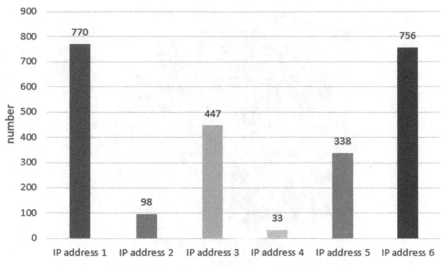

Fig. 7. Destination IP address distribution

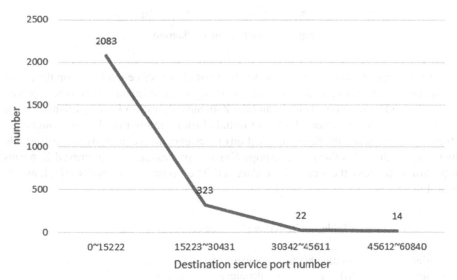

Fig. 8. Distribution diagram of destination service port numbers

4.2 Comparison of Cluster Analysis Modules

The SimpleKmeans that comes with the system needs to set the K value and the initial clustering center by itself. By setting different K values and initial clustering centers, multiple experiments are performed and the clustering effects of multiple experiments are compared. The experimental result with the smallest sum of squares of error is selected as the optimal solution. SimpleKmeans requires users to manually specify the K value and initial cluster centers based on experience or some established rules. Although simple

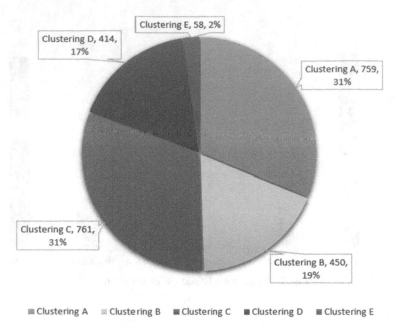

Fig. 9. Cluster summary diagram

and easy to implement, it cannot select the best initial cluster center based on the actual situation of the clustering object. On the contrary, the experiment needs to be repeated continuously. The time cost is high, and the K-means algorithm is very sensitive to the selected initial cluster centers. Different initial cluster centers may lead to completely different clustering results. Random selection of cluster centers can easily lead to unstable clustering results. This thesis uses SimpleKmeans processing and improved K-means algorithm to process the same alarm data set. The comparison results are shown in Table 1.

Table 1. Clustering algorithm comparison table

Clustering Algorithm	operation hours (ms)	Number of iterations	Clustering accuracy (%)	Sum of squared errors within clusters
Simple Kmeans	10	11	95.83%	163.478
K-means based on distance and density	5	6	97.56%	149.522

As can be seen from the comparison results of the clustering test in the above table, the improved K-means clustering algorithm based on distance and density embedded in the Weka platform in this paper has improved performance in many aspects than the traditional K-means algorithm. Not only the calculation time is shorter and the number of iterations is less, but the clustering effect is also better than the traditional K-means algorithm. Multiple experimental results are sufficient to show that the performance of the improved K-means clustering algorithm based on density and distance designed in this paper has been significantly improved.

4.3 Improvements to the Traditional Network Security Early Warning System

This article addresses the problem that traditional power grid security early warning systems are difficult to handle massive amounts of security data and the flood of warning information. In this paper, combined with the data mining software Weka platform, the traditional power grid security early warning system is difficult to deal with the problem of massive security data, the flood of alarm information and the alarm information output by the intrusion detection system. It is proposed to use the K-means clustering algorithm based on distance and density to process the initial alarm data, which can ultimately reduce the false alarm rate of the system. Compared with the traditional power grid security early warning system, this article mainly optimizes the system's data preprocessing and adds the alarm information cluster analysis module to improve the performance of the safety early warning system. The specific optimization and improvement contents are as follows:

Use data mining software Weka as the basic research platform. It also uses its integrated set of data processing methods and algorithms for training machine learning models. Preprocess the security data of the intrusion detection system. Remove missing values and redundant duplicate data. Standardize and standardize the initial data. Then increase the alarm information cluster analysis module to solve the problem of high false alarm rate.

In order to more conveniently solve the problem of redundancy and flooding of alarm information, the design of this paper adds a clustering analysis function module. It is proposed to use an improved K-means clustering algorithm based on distance and density to process the alarm data output by the system. After preprocessing the primary alarm data, the improved K-means algorithm is used in the process of processing the alarm data by the cluster analysis module. Solve the problems of the traditional K-means algorithm in the selection of the initial clustering center and K value, and improve the accuracy of clustering. The system will finally get more accurate and efficient alarm data, which greatly solves the problem of alarm data redundancy. And to a certain extent, it can reduce the false alarm rate of the early warning system and improve the performance of the power grid security early warning system.

5 Conclusion

With the rapid development of Internet technology and infrastructure, the power network system has also entered the era of large-scale data and large traffic. Not only brings more convenient management and control to the power network, but also brings a variety of network attacks and threats. Power system is the infrastructure of national economy, which is related to the economic development and people's livelihood of a country.

Therefore, the importance of ensuring the security of power grid is self-evident. The early warning technology is an important means to ensure the safe and stable operation of the power grid. In this paper, Weka basic research platform is used to design and improve the traditional power grid security early warning system. So that it can deal with massive security alarm data, and combined with data mining technology. The improved K-means algorithm is used to cluster the alarm information of intrusion detection system, which greatly reduces the problem of false alarm and missing alarm in the security early warning system.

Acknowledgments. This work is supported by the Innovation training program for college students of Nanjing Institute of Engineering under grant 202011276008Z.

References

1. Anderson, J.P.: Computer Security Threat Monitoring and SurveillanceR. James P. Anderson Co, Fort Washington (1980)
2. Jai, S.B., Jose, O.G.-F.: An Architecture for Intrusion Detection using Autonomous Agents. COAST Technical Report June 11 (1998)
3. Patcharamaneepakron, P., Armour, S., Doufexi, A.: Coordinated beamforming schemes based on modified signal-to-leakage-plus-noise ratio precoding designs. IET Commun. **9**(4), 558–567 (2015)
4. Qing, S.-H., Jiang, J.-C., Ma, H.-T., Wen, W.-P., Liu, X.-F.: Review on intrusion detection technology. J. Commun. **7**, 19–29 (2004)
5. Tabatabaefar, M., Miriestahbanati, M., Grégoire, J.C.: Network intrusion detection through artificial immune system. In: Systems Conference, pp. 1–6. IEEE (2017)
6. Kijewski, P.: ARAKIS-an early warning and attack identification system. In: The 16th Annual First Conference. s.n., Dudapest, Hungary (2004)
7. Lee, W., Stolfo, S.J., Mok, K.W.: A data mining framework for building intrusion detection models. In: Proceedings of the 1999 IEEE Symposium on Security and Privacy, pp. 120–132. IEEE (1999)
8. Eslamnezhad, M., Varjani, A.Y.: Intrusion detection based on MinMax K-means clustering. In: International Symposium on Telecommunications, pp. 804–808. IEEE (2014)
9. Al-Yaseen, W.L., Othman, Z.A., Nazri, M.Z.A.: Multi-level hybrid support vector machine and extreme learning machine based on modified K-means for intrusion detection system. Expert Syst. Appl. **67**, 296–303 (2017)
10. Zhang, C.-C.: Research and Application of Network Intrusion Detection System based on Data Mining, pp. 25–26. University (2006)
11. Jiang, Y.-Y., Cheng, S.: Intrusion detection based on data mining. Comput. Appl. Softw. **11**, 23–25 (2006)
12. Kantardzic, M.: Data Mining: Concepts, Models, Methods, and Algorithms. Wiley, Hoboken (2011)
13. Ma, B., Zhou, P., Zhang, J.-Y., Qing, S., Li, Y.: Data mining in big data era. China Sci. Technol. Inf. **23**, 117–118 (2014)
14. Liu, D.-W., Zhang, D.-X., Sun, H.-D., et al.: Matrix stabilizing situation in time and space data environment quantitative assessment and adaptive prevention and control system construction. Proc. CSEE **35**(2), 268–276 (2015)
15. Yuan, M.-Y.: Data Mining and Machine Learning, WEKA Application Technology and Practice. Tsinghua University Press, Beijing (2014)

16. Macqueen, J.: Some methods for classification and analysis of multi variate observations. In: Proceedings of Berkeley Symposium on Mathematical Statistics and Probability, pp. 281–297 (1967)
17. Yang, J.-C., Zhao, C.: A summary of research on K-means cluster algorithm. J. Comput. Eng. Appl. **55**(23), 7-14+63 (2019)

Research on Data Privacy Protection in Power Industry Control System

Xia Shangguan[1(✉)], Rongyan Cai[1], and Sheng Ye[2]

[1] State Grid Fujian Electric Power Co., Ltd., Fuzhou 350003, China
[2] State Grid Zhejiang Electric Power Co. Ltd., Hangzhou 310000, China

Abstract. Under the condition of network and information, the important data in the power Industrial Control System (ICS) is suffering more and more serious threat and destruction. It is necessary to further strengthen the protection of data privacy in the system, so as to effectively ensure the healthy and stable operation of the power ICS. On account of this, this paper first analyses the necessity of data privacy protection of power ICS, then studies the practical needs of data privacy protection of power ICS. In addition, data privacy protection technology and data privacy protection form of power ICS are analyzed. Finally, this paper gives the data privacy protection strategy for power industrial control network.

Keywords: Data privacy protection · Sensitive data · Power industry control system

1 Introduction

With the iterative progress and maturity of information technology, it has been widely and deeply studied and popularized in many fields, especially the utilization of intelligent technology in power industrial control system (ICS), which greatly accelerates the data privacy protection in power ICS. Electric power ICS is an important boost to enhance the efficiency of power supply system and ensures the stable development of all walks of life. ICS will produce a large number of structured and unstructured data in the operation process. How to mine the value of these data and how to protect the privacy of data has become the focus of current electric power ICS research. Under the condition of network and information, the important data in the power ICS is suffering more and more serious threat and destruction. It is necessary to further strengthen the protection of data privacy in the system, so as to effectively ensure the healthy and stable operation of the power ICS.

On the other hand, the data security and privacy threats faced by the power ICS will directly impact the normal operation of the whole power control network system. Only by systematically and comprehensively integrate data security in the power ICS, can it formulate scientific and reasonable data privacy protection measures to avoid the leakage of sensitive information and privacy data. According to the actual characteristics of data in power ICS, how to record and mine sensitive information such as data pattern, and protect privacy data effectively while publishing and analyzing data is a great test of data

© Springer Nature Singapore Pte Ltd. 2022
Y. Tian et al. (Eds.): ICBDS 2021, CCIS 1563, pp. 90–104, 2022.
https://doi.org/10.1007/978-981-19-0852-1_7

privacy protection level of power ICS. The current data privacy protection methods still have many shortcomings and problems, mainly in the lack of effective protection of data details, the need for special attack assumptions and background knowledge. Therefore, it is urgent to develop new technologies to effectively increase the data privacy protection level of power ICS.

With the continuous enhancement of the intelligent degree of power grid, the various data generated in the operation process has the typical characteristics of multiple sources and heterogeneous. Power ICS constructs a complex network mode, which is easy to cause inconvenience in the operation process, and further aggravates the data security risks. Intelligent power system is faced with the dual security threats of Internet and power grid ICS. It not only faces many kinds of data security threats, but also has high difficulty in data security defense, which brings great challenges to data privacy protection.

At present, the data privacy protection of power ICS mainly focuses on the static and dynamic level, and the rapid development of power network makes it difficult for the data protection system with physical isolation as the core mechanism to effectively adapt to and match the actual needs of data privacy protection and management under the condition of network. The following Table 1 shows the comparison between the traditional data privacy protection means and the data privacy protection requirements of power ICS under the condition of informatization.

Table 1. Situation and demand of data privacy protection in power ICS

Protection means	Management style	Features
Traditional means	Static, partial, correction after accidents	Low protection efficiency and mutual restriction of functions
Realistic needs	Dynamic data privacy protection system for the whole system	Active defense

In view of the practical needs of data privacy protection in power ICS under the condition of informatization, it is necessary to establish data privacy protection system consisting of a set of effective data privacy protection mechanisms including security, configuration and maintenance, so as to better meet the dynamic requirements of data privacy protection. At present, the data privacy protection in the power industry control system has several typical characteristics as shown in Fig. 1.

According to these typical characteristics, the data privacy protection means of the power industry control system are developed, which can effectively accelerate the power industry control network security, strengthen its active defense ability, and improve the security and stability of the system operation. Integrating active defense technology into the data privacy protection of power ICS can enhance the reliability of the system in the aspects of risk monitoring, control, prediction and protection of data privacy, which can effectively guarantee the privacy information security of related main units of power ICS.

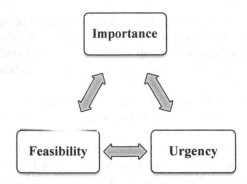

Fig. 1. The features of data privacy protection in the power industry control system

In addition, in the process of using the data in the power ICS, due to the inevitable existence of data sharing and other operations, there are some risks for data privacy leakage. When the data in the power ICS is attacked by distributed attack means, the situation will be worse, which makes the user's sensitive information face a serious threat. If the protection is improper, it will cause more serious damage to the interests of users. On account of this, according to the architecture characteristics of the power ICS, the in-depth protection and the security and privacy protection ability of the system are strengthened from several dimensions as shown in Fig. 2 below.

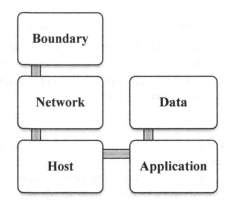

Fig. 2. Data privacy protection elements of power ICS

In a word, the privacy protection of data in power ICS should focus on the integrity, confidentiality and availability of data to ensure the security of key data. While ensuring the authenticity and accuracy of data, mutual trust should be established with users through the construction of privacy protection system. Therefore, the power ICS should strengthen the security protection of the power network data at the overall level and the system level to avoid exposing the data privacy in the unprotected information space, so as to effectively eliminate the data threat and attack risk. It can be seen that under the background of power ICS network complexity, deep coupling of power system, diversification of security and privacy evaluation indices, research on data privacy protection in power ICS has important practical value.

2 The Necessity of Data Privacy Protection in Power Industry Control System

2.1 Concept of Electric Power ICS

Electric power ICS is a business process management and control system which is composed of various automatic control components and process control components for real-time data collection and monitoring to ensure the automatic operation, process control and monitoring of electric power industrial infrastructure. As a kind of programmable logic controller, PLC in power ICS mainly controls various types of machinery or production process through digital or analog input/output. Additionally, as a relatively new intelligent control system, DCS (distributed control system) has been evolving and developing on the basis of centralized control system.

Data acquisition and monitoring control system as a computer-based DCS and power automation monitoring system, not only has a wide range of utilizations in the power system, but also can play an important role in the data acquisition and monitoring and control process of the power system.

As an important part of electric power ICS, RTU (remote terminal unit) is the core device of integrated automation system in electric power enterprise. It is usually composed of signal input/output module, microprocessor, wired/wireless communication module and power supply unit. It is controlled by microprocessor and supports network system. Through its own intelligent software system, RTU can be used to implement the functions of telemetry, remote control, remote signaling and remote adjustment of primary instruments in the production site of of power enterprises. The network architecture of power ICS is shown in Fig. 3 below. The strategic decision layer is used for engineering system, and the operation and management layer is used for system management and monitoring. Then, the production control layer is used for field detection and display, and the field control layer is used for protection and control of field equipment. Finally, the field execution layer is used for sensors and brakes including multiple input and output units.

2.2 Vulnerability in Power Industry Control System

With the increasing frequency of hackers invading the power industry control data acquisition and monitoring system, the network virus can collect intelligence data as well as stealing sensitive data by infecting the power industry control system. Due to power industry control system vulnerabilities, common intrusion will cause control system server and controller communication to varying degrees of interruption. At present, the power industry control system is faced with the threat of APT (advanced persistent threat) attacks, attacks using high-risk vulnerabilities in the control equipment, industrial network virus, equipment back door reserved from supply chain, wireless technology utilization risk and many other problems.

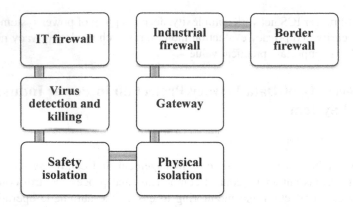

Fig. 3. Main protection means of electric power industrial control network

The main vulnerability in power industry control system include communication protocol vulnerability, operating system vulnerability, application software vulnerability, security policy and management process vulnerability, and antivirus software vulnerability [1]. The development of Internet of things make TCP/IP protocol and other general protocols more widely used in the power industry control network, and the problem of communication protocol vulnerability is also increasingly prominent. The operating system vulnerability of the power system is generated when the administrator does not patch the operating system after it is turned on, which may be a potential security hazard. In the aspect of application software vulnerability in power system, due to the variety of business processes, it is difficult to form a unified protection specification to deal with security problems [2]. In addition, when the application software is oriented to network utilizations, its corresponding ports must be opened, which may be an important attack channel.

The vulnerability of data security strategy and management process in power ICS is mainly due to the excessive pursuit of availability and the sacrifice of security, which leads to the lack of complete and effective security strategy and management process that poses a greater threat to the information security of power ICS. In order to ensure the availability of industrial control application software, many power ICS operation stations usually do not install anti-virus software. Even if the anti-virus software is installed, the virus database will not be updated regularly.

On the other hand, the existing protection means can not effectively defend against the escalating network attacks. The existing protection means on account of information network security in industrial control network mainly include several aspects as shown in Fig. 4 below. These defense systems and architectures can not effectively deal with the attack means in the industrial control network APT 2.0 era.

Through the analysis of the data privacy leakage events of industry control system in recent years, it is found that the related security events show an obvious growing trend. The attacks on key infrastructure such as power system are increasing year by year, and mainly concentrated in energy and other fields, while the data privacy events of energy industry represented by power industry occupy a large proportion. In the final analysis, these data security incidents of power system are caused by vulnerabilities of power industry control system, and the number of open vulnerabilities of power industry control system is still increasing.

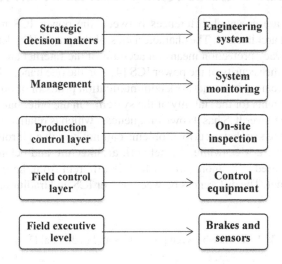

Fig. 4. Network architecture of power ICS

2.3   Evolution of Data Privacy Protection in Power ICS

The evolution of data privacy protection in power ICS has gone through several typical stages, such as emphasizing isolation, establishing defense in depth system, continuous protection system growing from the inside of power ICS, and strategy of taking attack as defense. Among them, in the stage of emphasizing isolation, physical isolation is mainly used, including gateway and one-way isolation [3]. This isolation is relatively fragile, and modern high-end persistent attacks are aimed at the isolation system. Secondly, in the construction stage of defense in depth system, most projects evolve into a simple stack of information security products, which cannot fully adapt to the characteristics of industrial network. In addition, in the construction stage of the continuous protection system growing inside the ICS, it is mainly through the innovation of the basic hardware to implement the low delay, high reliability, customizable continuous update, and accelerate the simplification of implementation and operation. In the stage of data privacy protection of power ICS, the security protection ability of data privacy protection technology is promoted by focusing on attack technology and experimental breakthrough.

3 The Practical Needs of Data Privacy Protection in Power Industry Control System

3.1 Typical Characteristics of Data Privacy Protection in Power ICS

First of all, there are essential differences between the power ICS network and the traditional Internet architecture. The characteristics of the power ICS determine that the traditional data privacy protection means on account of the Internet architecture cannot effectively protect the security of the power ICS [4]. On the one hand, a large number of private protocols are used in the network communication protocol of power ICS, which has higher requirements for the stability of the system. On the other hand, the operation environment of the power ICS has its own uniqueness, which is relatively backward, and the update cost is high so that security problems can not be solved through patches like the traditional Internet. Meanwhile, the network architecture and behavior stability of power ICS are required to be more strict, which is different from the frequent changes of traditional Internet. The differences between power ICS and traditional IT system are shown in Table 2.

Table 2. Difference between power ICS and traditional IT system

Items	ICS	Traditional IT system
Architecture	PLC, RTU, DCS, SCADA and sensors	Computer network formed by internet protocol
OS	VxWorks, uCLinux, winCE	General OS such as Windows, Linux and UNIX
Data exchange protocol	OPC, Modbus TCP, DNP3	TCP/IP protocol stack
System real time	High real-time requirements, cannot stop or restart	Lower real-time requirement, allow transmission delay
System upgrade	Poor compatibility and hard to upgrade software and hardware	Good compatibility, frequent software upgrades

It can be seen that the traditional network security technology is not suitable for the power industry control system since the traditional IT system requires more confidentiality than integrity and availability, while the power industry control system security requires more availability than integrity and confidentiality [5]. The differences between IT security requirements and power ICS security requirements are shown in Table 3.

Table 3. Differences between IT and power ICS security requirements

Items	ICS network	Traditional IT system
Firewalls	Format of exclusive agreement	TCP/IP protocol
Intrusion detection	False positives are not allowed	False positive rate
Vulnerability scanning	Patch repair difficult	Real time patch repair
Design intention	Usability	Confidentiality

3.2 The Practical Needs of Data Privacy Protection in Power Industry Control System

Power ICS has the typical characteristics of closeness, diversity, complexity and immutability [6]. Among them, closeness refers to the imperfection of security mechanism at the beginning of system design. Diversity refers to the existence of multiple data interfaces and the different protocol specifications. Complexity refers to special communication protocol or protocol. Immutability refers to the difficulty of upgrading the ICS program. By analyzing the defects of power industry control system software, it is found that the vulnerability of power industry control system software mainly involves input verification, password management, permission access, information authentication and system configuration. The typical data network architecture of power ICS is shown in Fig. 5 below.

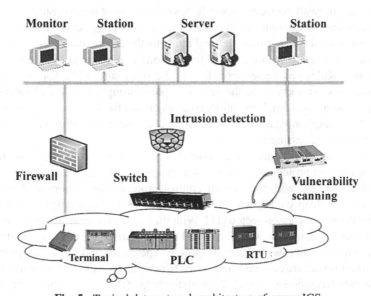

Fig. 5. Typical data network architecture of power ICS

Since the traditional IT security technology is not suitable for power industry control system, it is necessary to establish data privacy protection technology for power industry control system [7]. Aiming at the vulnerability of power ICS and the security of communication protocol, this paper studies the security protection technology of power ICS, and analyzes the security threats in power ICS, which is helpful to carry out the effective protection of data privacy in power ICS.

4 Data Privacy Protection Technology of Power ICS

4.1 The Objectives of Data Privacy Protection In Power ICS

In order to ensure the secure and stable operation of power industry control system, the data privacy protection of it should achieve the goals of communication control, area isolation and alarm tracking [8]. Among them, at the level of communication controllability, it is required to be able to visually observe, monitor and manage the communication data in the power ICS. It needs to ensure that only the power industrial control proprietary protocol data can pass through, and other communications are prohibited [9]. Secondly, at the target level of regional isolation, in order to prevent the global paralysis caused by the spread of local control network problems, network isolation should be deployed on the key data channels. In addition, in the aspect of alarm tracking, it is required to find the infection or other problems in the network in time, find out the fault point accurately, and record the alarm events to provide the basis for fault analysis.

4.2 Data Privacy Firewall for Power ICS

The data privacy firewall of electric power ICS is on account of access control technology to ensure the secure communication between areas of different security levels [10]. By setting access control rules, it manages and controls the information flow in and out of different security areas to ensure the effective use and management of resources within the legal scope. Rules can be set according to the black-and-white list, that is to say, only the data flow conforming to the rules can pass through, and any other data flow will be filtered as an abnormal operation, so as to ensure the legal use of power system resources. As to implementation of blacklist, it could set prohibition rules to prevent illegal clients from accessing resources.

In addition, the security area of the control system is divided through the regional control to isolate and protect the security area and protect the legitimate users to access the network resources. With the help of control protocol, the abnormal data flow of utilization layer is deeply analyzed, the OPC port is tracked dynamically, and the key registers and operations are protected [11]. With the help of the central management and control platform, industrial firewall distributed in the network can be configured to allow downloading and modifying the security policy. The alarm and log data uploaded by each industrial firewall are collected and stored to provide the basis for security audit and abnormal event correlation analysis [12]. With the help of the power industry firewall, the access control of the data flow between different nodes is carried out, the power industry communication protocol is deeply inspected so that the network behavior violating the security rules is given real-time alarm, and the abnormal events are uploaded to the abnormal event database.

4.3 Data Privacy Protection Module for Power ICS

The data privacy protection module of power ICS is mainly Modbus/TCP deep protection module, which has typical functions such as being able to arbitrarily connect to the computer in the network to change the I/O points or register values of the controller, reset, prohibit operation, download control logic operation, etc. [13]. The data privacy protection module can carry out data integrity detection, block the communication that does not meet the Modbus standard, and set the allowed Modbus function code, register and list. The architecture of data privacy protection module of power industry control system is shown in Fig. 6 below. Through in-depth inspection of power industry communication packets, it provides utilization layer protection whose security level is relatively higher than that of general firewall. Hence, it can effectively prevent the spread of virus to important controllers [14].

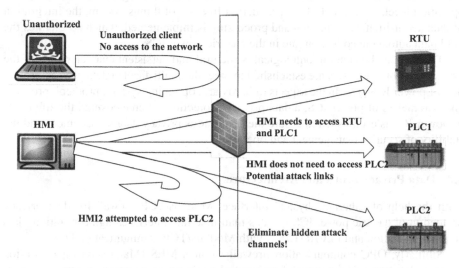

Fig. 6. Architecture of data privacy protection module in power ICS

In addition, the OPC (OLE for Process Control) protocol protection module of data privacy protection in power ICS only allows OPC standard format DCE/RPC access request and communication between specific client and server. The module only allows the client to use the specified port to communicate, and only allows TCP communication to occur in a specific OPC connection time [14]. Using dynamic tracking TCP port connection technology, it only open OPC required port and can minimize the attack surface, intercept non-OPC standard format DCE/RPC access request.

5 Data Privacy Protection Architecture of Power ICS

5.1 Privacy Data Fusion Structure

First of all, at the level of decision-making management, data warehouse technology is used to integrate the key data and operation data of the whole power system industry chain to implement data mining, monitoring, analysis, statistical query and visual display, so as to assist the management to carry out scientific decision-making and strategic management of privacy data protection. Secondly, in the operation and management level of power ICS, the ERP system is taken as the core to integrate the key data of various professional application systems and integrated management systems to form the operation and management data system of power system [15]. In addition, at the level of production and operation, an integrated and complete production and operation management platform is established with supply chain management. Finally, in the operation level, on account of the production Internet of things system, the integration of data acquisition, transmission and processing is implemented, which accelerates the field data automatic collection rate in the electric power ICS.

The genetic, behavioral, ontological, structural and persistent characteristics of the privacy data of power ICS are established to meet the multi-faceted data privacy protection of power ICS [16]. In the aspects of hardware, operating system, protocol, program and parameters of power ICS, a data privacy protection scheme covered the life cycle of power ICS is established to ensure the continuous privacy data management and the stability of security management and operation.

5.2 Data Privacy Protection Architecture

With the help of Ethernet physical interface, Modbus/TCP firewall for data privacy protection of electric power ICS isolates man-machine interface/engineer station, data acquisition station and PLC/RTU/SIS with Modbus/TCP communication [17].

Similarly, OPC communication firewall isolates MES (Manufacturing Execution System) data acquisition network from control network to protect communication security between OPC server and client, thus forming a multi-dimensional data privacy protection architecture of power ICS, including network isolation, OPC protection, advanced control station isolation, Modbus/TCP communication controller protection, ESD (Emergency Shutdown Device)/SIS (Safety Instrument System) protection and engineer station isolation [18]. The overall architecture of data privacy protection of power ICS is shown in Fig. 7.

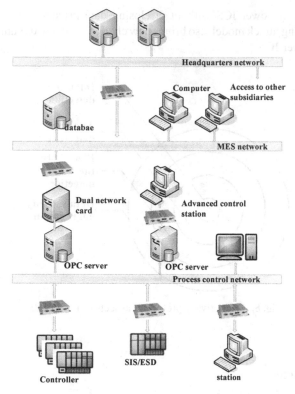

Fig. 7. The architecture of power ICS data privacy protection

6 Data Privacy Protection System for Power Industrial Control Network

6.1 Principle of the System

With the iterative progress of power industrial control network system technology, it has been widely used in all walks of life, but also further highlights the importance of power industrial control data privacy protection [19]. The data in power ICS often contains multi-dimensional privacy information, such as user's identity, track and behavior preference. If obtained by lawbreakers, it will greatly threaten the use and legitimate rights and interests of relevant users. Therefore, the data privacy protection of power industrial control network is not only to protect the interests of users, but also an important premise to ensure the stable and healthy development of power ICS [20]. In this context, it is urgent and necessary to carry out a comprehensive and systematic research on data privacy protection of power ICS.

At present, the research on data privacy protection of power industrial control network mainly focuses on several levels as shown in Fig. 8 below. Specifically, the level of data privacy protection mainly includes key technologies such as homomorphic encryption, shielding value, fragment combination and differential privacy protection. How to release and analyze data in power ICS without disclosing data privacy is the focus and the constantly changing attack model also brings new challenges to the dynamic data privacy protection of power ICS.

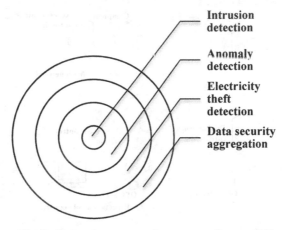

Fig. 8. Data privacy protection aspects of power ICS

6.2   System Design

Firstly, the structure design of data privacy protection system in power industrial control network includes presentation layer, business logic layer and persistence layer. The presentation layer is used to display the user interface, the business logic layer contains the business logic package, and the persistence layer contains the data access package. Its composition is shown in Fig. 9 below. Secondly, in the database collection design level of data privacy protection system, including user management module and data management module, the encrypted data is stored in the database during the whole operation of the system.

In addition, according to the characteristics of power industrial control network system, differential privacy protection aggregation algorithm is used to achieve differential privacy protection, which can significantly enhance the effect of privacy protection, and achieve the balance between data privacy protection and release and analysis necessary data of power ICS.

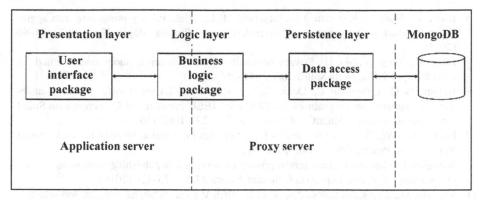

Fig. 9. Data privacy protection system in power industrial control network

7 Conclusion

In summary, power system is faced with the dual security threats of Internet and power grid ICS. Not only there are many kinds of data security threats, but also the data security defense is difficult, which brings great challenges to data privacy protection. This paper analyzes the necessity of data privacy protection in power ICS, studies the vulnerability of data privacy in power ICS and the evolution of data privacy protection in power ICS. Through the research on the practical needs of data privacy protection in power ICS, the typical characteristics of data privacy protection in power ICS are analyzed. Through the analysis of data privacy protection technology of power ICS, the architecture of data privacy protection and the associated system are proposed. The privacy technology, architecture and system in this paper can be used as a reference for security protection in power ICS.

Acknowledgement. This paper is supported by the science and technology project of State Grid Corporation of China: "Research and Application of Scenario-Driven Data Dynamic Authorization and Compliance Control Key Technology" (Grand No. 5700-202058481A-0-0-00).

References

1. Borges, F., Muhlhauser, M.: EPPP4SMS: efficient privacy-preserving protocol for smart metering systems and its simulation using real-world data. Smart Grid IEEE Trans. **5**(6), 2701–2708 (2014)
2. Choromanska, A., Choromanski, K., Jagannathan, G., et al.: Differentially-private learning of low dimensional manifolds. Theoret. Comput. Sci. **620**, 91–104 (2016)
3. Feng, D., Fangguo, Z.: Complete privacy protection system of smart meter. J. Cipher **1**(4), 400–409 (2014)
4. Westhoff, D., Girao, J., Acharya, M.: Concealed data aggregation for reverse multicast traffic in sensor networks: encryption, key distribution, and routing adaptation. IEEE Trans. Mob. Comput. **5**(10), 1417–1431 (2016)
5. Dwork, C.: Calibrating noise to sensitivity in private data analysis. Lect. Notes Comput. Sci. **3876**(8), 265–284 (2012)

6. Erkin, Z., Troncoso-Pastoriza, J.R., Lagendijk, R.L., et al.: Privacy-preserving data aggregation in smart metering systems: an overview. Signal Process. Magaz. IEEE **30**(2), 75–86 (2013)
7. Jiang, H., Zeng, G., Ma, H.: Privacy preserving greedy clustering anonymous method for table data publishing. Acta Sinica **28**(2), 341–351 (2017)
8. Kalogridis, G., Efthymiou, C., Denic, S.Z., et al.: Privacy for smart meters: towards undetectable appliance load signatures. In: 2010 First IEEE International Conference on Smart Grid Communications (SmartGridComm), pp. 232–237. IEEE (2010)
9. Li, W., You, W., Wang, X.: Review of power system information security research. Power Syst. Control Protect. **10**(39), 140–147 (2011)
10. Xiaoqian, L., Qianmu, L.: Differential privacy preserving data publishing method on account of clustering anonymization. Acta Commun. Sinica **37**(5), 125–129 (2016)
11. Mustafa, M., Zhang, N., Kalogridis, G., et al.: DESA: a decentralized, efficient and selective aggregation scheme in AMI. In: Innovative Smart Grid Technologies Conference (ISGT), 2014 IEEE PES, pp. 1–5. IEEE (2014)
12. Zhen, N., Qianmu, L., Yajuan, G.: Integrated prediction algorithm of anomaly monitoring for power big data log analysis platform. J. Nanjing Univ. Technol. **41**(5), 634–645 (2017)
13. Ruj, S., Nayak, A.: A decentralized security framework for data aggregation and access control in smart grids. Smart Grid IEEE Trans. **4**(1), 196–205 (2013)
14. Soria Comas, J., Domingo Ferrer, J., Snchez, D., et al.: Enhancing data utility in differential privacy via microaggregation-based k-anonymity. Int. J. Very Large Data Bases **23**(5), 771–794 (2014)
15. Ping, X., Tianqing, Z., Xiaofeng, W.: Differential privacy protection and its utilization. Acta Comput. Sinica **37**(1), 101–122 (2014)
16. Dong, X., Xian, L., Ziying, Z., et al.: Personalized privacy preserving algorithm for clustering mining. J. Harbin Eng. Univ. **39**(11), 51–57 (2018)
17. Jing, Y., Chao, W., Jianpei, Z.: Micro aggregation algorithm on account of sensitive attribute entropy. Acta Electron. Sin. **42**(7), 1327–1337 (2014)
18. Xiaojian, Z., Xiaofeng, M.: Differential privacy protection for data publishing and analysis. Acta Comput. Sinica **37**(4), 927–949 (2014)
19. Zhichu, Z., Jianghong, G., Haifeng, Z.: Efficient and secure data aggregation scheme for wireless sensor networks. Comput. Utiliz. **33**(S1), 137–140 (2013)
20. Ran, Z., Ji, S.: Review of foreign smart grid tech development practice. Electron. Qual. **9**, 24–29 (2016)

Recent Advances in Smart Meter: Data Analysis, Privacy Preservation and Applications

Ruixuan Dong, Shuyang Hao, Tian Hao Yang, Zhichao Tang, Yan Yan,
and Jianhua Chen[✉]

School of Electric Power Engineering, Nanjing Institute of Technology, Nanjing 211167,
Jiangsu, China
chjh@njit.edu.cn

Abstract. The widespread popularity of smart meters has promoted the transition from traditional grid into modern smart grid, which is aimed to meet the rapid-growing demand for higher quality service and take up the emergence of new challenges. How to analyze, transmit and make the most of massive smart meter data to enhance the efficiency and reliability is our priority. The purpose of this paper is to conduct a detailed review to summarize and evaluate the latest advances in smart meter data analysis, privacy preserving and residential energy management. We conclude the analysis of smart meter data, protecting techniques in the process of delivering and end-uses of smart meter data application according to the flowing direction of smart meter data. Compared with other review papers, we analyze the merits and drawbacks in corresponding situations and provide readers a more detailed eyesight to the research status in modern smart grid.

Keywords: Smart grids · Advanced meter infrastructure · Smart meter data · Data analysis · Energy management system · Privacy

1 Introduction

The electricity sector is confronted with critical challenges to satisfy the growing energy demand and address the constraint condition, such as higher reliability and quality of energy supply. All of these complications urge the advancement of energy efficiency [1] in the electricity sector. In this direction, traditional grids have been transformed into smart grids, which are characterized by a tight combination of developing Information and Communication Technologies (ICT) [2]. Meanwhile, because of automatic and adaptive learning features, Advanced Metering Infrastructure (AMI) is the basic building block of modern smart grids, which helps to collect [3], deliver, and analyze large quantities of data. Utilities across North America, Europe, Africa and Asia [4] have widely implemented Advanced Metering Infrastructure as a cost-effective way to boost their process of smart grids modernization.

The deployment of Advanced Metering Infrastructure, consisting of smart meters, communication technology, meter data management system, etc. [5], is regarded as a bridge between the residential households and energy providers. Smart meters are

© Springer Nature Singapore Pte Ltd. 2022
Y. Tian et al. (Eds.): ICBDS 2021, CCIS 1563, pp. 105–114, 2022.
https://doi.org/10.1007/978-981-19-0852-1_8

deployed to collect energy consumption and other parameters in real time. These time-based data are transmitted to the meter data management system through commonly available fixed networks and public networks. Then the smart meter data are recorded and analyzed to enable distribution grid operators to optimize electricity supply and distribution.

Unfortunately, sensitive smart meter data can reflect the resident's indoor activities and actual electricity duration [6–8], which may give rise to the leakage of customer's privacy. However, unlike traditional data privacy, smart meter data privacy should consider the complex structure of the electricity sector, the legacy of energy technologies based on the closed system and additional constraints at legal and regulatory aspects [2]. How to provide effective privacy protection against both malicious users and third parties is a priority to the current communication process.

In recent years, plenty of researches have proposed different solutions towards preserving privacy in smart grids and divided them into different categories. In security issues [9–13], Muhammad Rizwan Asghar and György Dán [9] conclude part of typical threats to the smart grid and categorize them according to specific security goals. In [10], considering application constraints like limited device computation capability guidelines on designing suitable security schemes in substation automation systems (SAS) are provided. In [12], security economics of electricity metering are discussed. In privacy-preserving challenges [14, 15] divides the privacy problems in smart grids into the problems metering for billing and metering for operations. [15] proposes a series of privacy-preserving protocols to data aggregation process more reliable in smart meter environment.

Meanwhile, Smart Home Energy Management System [16], which is equipped with distributed energy resources [17, 18] and energy storage system (rechargeable batteries) can utilize smart meter data. Considering users' preferences, real-time electricity price [19], actual demand and distributed energy resources, the system optimizes and arranges the schedule of electrical appliances and rechargeable batteries properly. Based on the real-time smart meter data, Home Energy Management Systems [19] have introduced different machine learning technologies with the purpose of designing an optimal energy management strategy to meet customers' personalized demand. Common methods and techniques include time series, clustering, deep learning, classification [20], online learning, and so on. The optimization of household operations is able to make demand side management more effective. In detail, customers can cut down their operation costs and lower peak demand. Moreover, the electricity network system will be more secure and reliable.

This paper is organized according to the smart meter data flowing direction, which concludes data analysis, protecting techniques in the process of delivering and its end use applications. The framework of this paper completely covers the three main components in AMI, providing a meta-analysis of the papers in this area. The main contributions of this review paper are summarized as follows:

- We organize this paper according to the flowing direction of smart meter data, including the analysis of data, privacy-preserving techniques and its end use applications.

- We take many emerging factors and future possible constraints into consideration, and present various models and applied algorithms according to different purposes and energy resources.
- We analyze the merits and drawbacks of presented papers in different scenarios and for customized purposes. This may provide readers a more overall and detailed eyesight to the research status in modern smart grid.

The remainder of the article is organized as follows. Section 2 conducts an overview of some related papers in privacy-preserving and data management. Section 3 introduces the significance of data analysis, composed of anomaly detection and load profiling. Section 4 clarifies the reasons for preserving data privacy and some representative methods used in privacy-preserving. Section 5 gives a detailed eyesight to smart meter data applications, including load forecasting and energy management system. Section 6 draws conclusions.

2 Related Work

There has been a significant amount of researches about the advanced metering infrastructure over decades, studying various methods and techniques to collect, protect, analyze and make the best of smart meter data. Early researches in residential demand modelling are restricted in certain region areas, ranging from local towns to specific cities. Such models can't be extended to most of the smart homes. Nowadays, owing to more and more advanced models, the trend of residential power demand all day, electricity consumption varying from morning to night and the fluctuations of loads can be evaluated more precisely through the load profile and machine learning.

The advancement of AMI and new optimization techniques results in the development of smart grids. More and more relevant survey papers have focused on the introduction and summary of the proposed algorithms in different possible scenarios, ignoring the comparison between different methods. On the basis of existing achievements, we conduct a brief overview of recent studies according to the different classifications of demand modelling and end-uses of smart meter data application in Table 1:

Table 1. Recent researches in residential demand modelling and applications of smart meter data

Review subject	References	Year
Top-down and bottom-up system models for residential power demand	[21–25]	2009, 2012, 2013, 2014, 2017
Demand forecasting for residential demand modelling	[26–30]	2011, 2014, 2016, 2017, 2018
Control systems with HEMS, distributed energy resources, and storage equipment in residential buildings	[31–36]	2011, 2014, 2015, 2016, 2018
Machine learning methods used in residential energy management	[37–40]	2010, 2014, 2020

3 Smart Meter Data Analysis

After collecting massive daily residential load profiles, the diversity in different customers' energy consumption patterns requires us to have a more accurate analysis of these useful smart meter data. We are eager to find out and distinguish the volatility and uncertainty of the load profiles. In the background of smart grids, making some essential analysis of smart meter data and pick up minor faults in massive data are indispensable preconditions of data application. The outcomes of data analysis help to make the best of these data in application part like load forecasting and demand response programs.

The analysis of smart meter data is composed by anomaly detection and load profiling. In the process of anomaly detection, different authors apply different techniques to ensure the reliability of collected data, which energy providers attach great importance to for accurate billing. In the load profiling section, it is possible to infer indoor individual appliances' operation based on the residential electrical load profile. By analyzing these data, energy providers are also capable of identifying the demand for the power of electricity consumers to guarantee demand response programs.

In [41], the author presents a blond dataset, in which energy measurements record the power consumption of offices at high sample rate. This paper deploys the longest continuous measurements to sample smart meter data at the same high rates and fully-labeled ground truth in physical level. Besides, some authors choose to use mathematical methods. In [42], the authors apply clustering techniques to establish an appropriate data grouping standard for analyzing different electrical load pattern data. This paper perfectly addressed the problem of accurately evaluating the performance of load profile and design a unique load pattern grouping method with the clustering algorithms. Moreover, with the introduction of machine learning methods, [43] presents a novel perspective of load profiling based on neural networks. The author uses a quantity of historical data points to train the network for the purpose of reducing the risk of over parametrization and overfitting.

4 Smart Meter Data Privacy

In recent years, with the continuous improvement of the Internet of Things technology, smart home related systems are constantly updated. Smart hardware provides services while synchronizing the data of cell phone users in real-time feedback. Most of them use non-intrusive load monitoring (NILM). The energy provider can determine the user's various electricity consumption information situation through the meter data. The system can reduce the corresponding cost and facilitate the use of users. However, there is a risk that the user's privacy and security will be compromised by the malicious use of the user's data.

Privacy protection processing is required to safeguard the user's data when it is necessary to be collected and when transmitting the data to access related services. This includes three components: smart meter identity information, smart meter real-time data and smart meter total electricity data. It is important not only to ensure that the energy provider receives accurate information about the user's use, but also to protect the information of the individual user.

4.1 Differential Privacy

A differential privacy approach is used so as to obtain data that cannot be used by third parties after processing. For example, data on the hourly electricity consumption of a resident during a year, the time and duration of power outages in the same year, etc. are processed to protect their location and possible identity information.

The basic idea of differential privacy is to first collect user data, then add noise to the original sample, and finally output the processed data to finally encrypt the data. Adding or removing any individual data record does not affect the query results on the data set too much.

The Laplacian mechanism achieves differential privacy protection by interfering with real output samples with the noise generated by the Laplacian distribution and is applicable to numerical output. So for the implementation of differential privacy, the Laplace mechanism is used. The increased noise level needs to be quantified in the face of different problems, and the quantification criteria are closely related to the sensitivity of the algorithm to satisfy differential privacy.

4.2 Energy Management Units with Smart Meter Data

The use of a suitable rechargeable battery to connect to the home user's side, while carrying a suitable charging and discharging algorithm. In this case, the rechargeable battery of limited capacity supplies the remaining load or to absorb the excess energy [44]. By charging and discharging the battery, the data measured by the smart meter can always be maintained in a constant unit. In conclusion, the rechargeable battery can be utilized to partially preserve the privacy of the information reserved in the home electricity load profile [45]. It can interfere with malicious third-party access to the actual energy use of the user by unusual means and mitigate privacy issues in and to a certain extent.

By acquiring power data from different users for developing battery privacy algorithms and working with energy management units (EMU), we can make purposeful use of rechargeable batteries. In this algorithm, the error between the demand for energy and the energy use data recorded by the smart meter can be maximized. At the same time, the utility, reliability, and privacy of this algorithm is evaluated based on the evaluation of the interaction information. In short, in order to maintain specific information. The rechargeable battery can be charged or discharged according to the user's energy demand [46]. The rechargeable battery storage can be utilized to a certain period of time to provide the entire energy demand required by the user without affecting the user's usage, without the need to pass the statistics of the smart meter.

5 Smart Meter Data Applications

In this part, we analyze two different end uses of applications: load forecasting and energy management system.

5.1 Load Forecasting

Short-term load forecasting (STLF) is the footstone of making operational schedule in power system. However, to meet the exponentially growing demand in the smart grid, short-term load forecasting (STLF) is confronted with different difficulties and constraints. Therefore, a large number of algorithms and techniques are introduced to enhance load forecasting safety and effectiveness.

To solve the problem of extensive data size needed in machine learning algorithms for load forecasting, parallel computing [47] is utilized to make great use of those available smart grid data. A novel hybrid deep-learning forecasting model for STLF based on different clusters [48] is proposed to improve the forecasting accuracy. It is shown that the training time can be notably reduced by clustering the distribution transformers. Compared to non-clustering models, the proposed model has better performance. Different from other prevalent methods, [49] presents an adaptive approach which selects the optimal algorithm according to the characteristic of historical data. The experimental results show that the in-depth analysis on the deviation is superior to traditional time-series methods in the terms of effectiveness.

5.2 Energy Management System

Energy management system plays a important role in modern smart grids, which is defined as the modifications of energy consumption pattern in households, aimed to achieve better efficiency and higher reliability. Confronted with customized demands and different family conditions, numerous methods are introduced and specific models are established to address the focused problems. Most models consist of three parts: energy providers, energy demand side and energy controller. Based on their residential models, authors take different factors into account and apply different techniques to solve their problems.

Models in Energy Management System. In [50] and [51], the entire demand management side is modeled and the load shifting technique is utilized to manage the load in residential areas, reducing the consumption of energy during peak time and releasing the burden in smart grids. In order to realize the future operational schedule evolving power distribution system, [52] proposed an Advanced Energy Management System (ADMS) model. It is defined as an integrated model composed of various subsystems. [53] takes distributed generators and household rechargeable batteries into account and models from individual users. [54] perfected the model in [53] and proposed an optimization model that considers the energy sharing between users, which is more in line with the development environment of the smart grids.

Efficient Techniques in Energy Management System. Taking many factors into consideration, such as privacy-preservation, system cost-saving and weather variability, latest machine learning methods are applied in the existing system model to balance these demands. Statistical techniques like Markov chains, Monte Carlo techniques and Probabilistic models have also successfully optimized the model and finally find out the best energy management strategy for consumers.

Dynamic Programming: In [55], an online optimization energy management strategy is designed to relax the Lyapunov optimization problem by online dynamic programming. Their system model effectively optimizes the balance between data privacy and system cost.

Convex Optimization: [56] studies the case that non-causal power demand profile and electricity prices are known. The authors solved a convex optimization problem between privacy and cost by using a low-complexity algorithm.

Statistical Techniques: Some papers apply Monte Carlo (MC) simulation [57] to cut down the sum of the expected electricity cost, which is called the scenario-based approach. In addition, [57] continues to analyze and address the privacy problems which could be triggered by high frequency measuring of smart meters. Aiming at the low-resolution data resources, [58] proposed trained probabilistic models to enrich those load data by using a Gaussian Process to figure out the features in those data and leveraging a Markov chain model to build the transition probability. This paper significantly recovered statistical properties of the instantaneous load uncertainty.

Pareto-optimal: Considering the operational costs and privacy-preserving demand from users, [59] proposed a utility-driven Demand-side management consisting of privacy leakage measure and optimal resolutions solved by achieving the Pareto-optimal trade-off privacy and energy cost.

6   Conclusion

In this paper, we have reviewed the recent advances in residential demand modellings and popular algorithms in the field of smart meter, including data analysis, privacy preserving and residential energy management. The models and techniques reviewed in this paper have presented rapid advances in modern smart grid. On account of numerous smart meter data, the deployment of AMI results in various end use applications like energy management system. Moreover, the development of machine learning, adaptive demand side modelling and the usage of advanced mathematical methods have boosted the efficiency and reliability of the proposed systems. We expect this review paper to provide readers a comprehensive and detailed eyesight to the research status in modern smart grid.

References

1. Momoh. Smart grid design for efficient and flexible power networks operation and control. In: 2009 IEEE/PES Power Systems Conference and Exposition, pp. 1–8. IEEE (2009)
2. Asghar, M.R.: Smart meter data privacy: a survey. IEEE Commun. Surv. Tutor. **19**(4), 2820–2835 (2017)
3. Preibusch, S.: Privacy behaviors after Snowden. Commun. ACM **58**(5), 48–55 (2015)
4. How many smart meters are installed in the United States, and who has them? https://www.eia.gov/tools/faqs/faq.php?id=108&t=3. Accessed 31 July 2017

5. Mohassel, R.R.: A survey on advanced metering infrastructure. Int. J. Electr. Power Energy Syst. **63**, 473–484 (2014)
6. McDaniel, P.: Security and privacy challenges in the smart grid. IEEE Secur. Priv. **7**(3), 75–77 (2009)
7. Molina-Markham, A.: Private memories of a smart meter. In: Proceedings of the ACM Workshop Embedded Sensors System Efficiency Building, Switzerland, pp. 61–66 (2010)
8. Kalogridis, G.: Elecprivacy: evaluating the privacy protection of electricity management algorithms. IEEE Trans. Smart Grid **2**(4), 750–758 (2011)
9. Komninos, N.: Survey in smart grid and smart home security: issues, challenges and countermeasures. IEEE Commun. Surv. Tutor. **16**(4), 1933–1954 (2014)
10. Lu, X.: Authentication and integrity in the smart grid: an empirical study in substation automation systems. Int. J. Distrib. Sens. Netw. **8**(6), 175262 (2012)
11. Khurana, H.: Smart-grid security issues. IEEE Secur. Priv. **8**(1), 81–85 (2010)
12. Anderson, R.J.: On the security economics of electricity metering. In: WEIS (June 2010)
13. Wang, W.: Cyber security in the smart grid: survey and challenges. Comput. Netw. **57**(5), 1344–1371 (2013)
14. Sharma, K.: Performance analysis of smart metering for smart grid: an overview. Renew. Sustain. Energy Rev. **49**, 720–735 (2015)
15. Finster, S.: Privacy-aware smart metering: a survey. IEEE Commun. Surv. Tutor. **16**(3), 1732–1745 (2014)
16. Nguyen, H.: Distributed demand side management with energy storage in smart grid. IEEE Trans. Parallel Distrib. Syst. **26**(12), 3346–3357 (2014)
17. Marsan, M.: Towards zero grid electricity networking: powering BSs with renewable energy sources. In: 2013 IEEE International Conference on Communications Workshops (ICC), pp. 596–601. IEEE (2013)
18. Borenstein, S.: Dynamic Pricing Advanced Metering and Demand Response in Electricity Markets. Center for the Study of Energy Markets (2002)
19. Han, J.: Green home energy management system through comparison of energy usage between the same kinds of home appliances. In: 2011 IEEE 15th International Symposium on Consumer Electronics (ISCE), pp. 1–4. IEEE (2011)
20. McArthur, S.: Multi-agent systems for power engineering applications—Part I: Concepts, approaches, and technical challenges. IEEE Trans. Power Syst. **22**(4), 1743–1752 (2007)
21. Swan, L.: Modeling of end-use energy consumption in the residential sector: a review of modeling techniques. Renew. Sustain. Energy Rev. **13**(8), 1819–1835 (2009)
22. Bucher, C.: Generation of domestic load profiles-an adaptive top-down approach. Proc. PMAPS **2012**, 10–14 (2012)
23. Prudenzi, A.: Analysis of residential standby power demand control through a psychological model of demand. In: 10th International Conference on Environment and Electrical Engineering, pp. 1–4. IEEE (2011)
24. Muratori, M.: A highly resolved modeling technique to simulate residential power demand. Appl. Energy **107**, 465–473 (2013)
25. Kavgic, M.: A review of bottom-up building stock models for energy consumption in the residential sector. Build. Environ. **45**(7), 1683–1697 (2010)
26. Suganthi, L.: Energy models for demand forecasting—a review. Renew. Sustain. Energy Rev. **16**(2), 1223–1240 (2012)
27. Davarzani, S.: A Novel Methodology for Predicting Potential Responsiveness in Residential Demand (2017)
28. Jazaeri, J.: Model predictive control of residential demand in low voltage network using ice storage. In: 2018 Australian & New Zealand Control Conference (ANZCC), pp. 51–55. IEEE (2018)

29. Barbato, A.: Forecasting the usage of household appliances through power meter sensors for demand management in the smart grid. In: 2011 IEEE International Conference on Smart Grid Communications (SmartGridComm), pp. 404–409. IEEE (2011)
30. Alzate, E.: A high-resolution smart home power demand model and future impact on load profile in Germany. In: 2014 IEEE International Conference on Power and Energy (PECon), pp. 53–58. IEEE (2014)
31. Shaikh, P.: A review on optimized control systems for building energy and comfort management of smart sustainable buildings. Renew. Sustain. Energy Rev. **34**, 409–429 (2014)
32. Vega, A.: Modeling for home electric energy management: a review. Renew. Sustain. Energy Rev. **52**, 948–959 (2015)
33. Fischer, D.: Model for electric load profiles with high time resolution for German households. Energy Build. **92**, 170–179 (2015)
34. Gottwalt, S.: Demand side management—a simulation of household behavior under variable prices. Energy Policy **39**(12), 8163–8174 (2011)
35. Muratori, M.: Impact of uncoordinated plug-in electric vehicle charging on residential power demand. Nat. Energy **3**(3), 193–201 (2018)
36. Ge, Y.: Domestic electricity load modelling by multiple Gaussian functions. Energy Build. **126**, 455–462 (2016)
37. Wu, Z.: Real-time scheduling of residential appliances via conditional risk-at-value. IEEE Trans. Smart Grid **5**(3), 1282–1291 (2014)
38. Chavali, P.: A distributed algorithm of appliance scheduling for home energy management system. IEEE Trans. Smart Grid **5**(1), 282–290 (2014)
39. McLoughlin, F.: The generation of domestic electricity load profiles through Markov chain modelling. Euro-Asian J. Sustain. Energy Dev. Policy **3**, 12 (2010)
40. You, Y.: Energy management strategy for smart meter privacy and cost saving. IEEE Trans. Inf. Forens. Secur. **16**, 1522–1537 (2020)
41. Kriechbaumer, T.: BLOND, a building-level office environment dataset of typical electrical appliances. Sci. Data **5**(1), 1–14 (2018)
42. Chicco, G.: Overview and performance assessment of the clustering methods for electrical load pattern grouping. Energy **42**(1), 68–80 (2012)
43. Sousa, J.C.: Load forecasting based on neural networks and load profiling. In: 2009 IEEE Bucharest PowerTech, pp. 1–8. IEEE (2009)
44. Salehkalaibar, S.: Hypothesis testing for privacy of smart meters with side information. IEEE Trans. Smart Grid **10**(2), 2059–2067 (2017)
45. Varodayan, D.: Smart meter privacy using a rechargeable battery: minimizing the rate of information leakage. In: 2011 IEEE International Conference on Acoustics, Speech and Signal Processing (ICASSP), pp. 1932–1935. IEEE (2011)
46. Kement, C.: Comparative analysis of load-shaping-based privacy preservation strategies in a smart grid. IEEE Trans. Indust. Inf. **13**(6), 3226–3235 (2017)
47. Zainab, A.: Distributed tree-based machine learning for short-term load forecasting with apache spark. IEEE Access **9**, 57372–57384 (2021)
48. Syed, D.: Deep learning-based short-term load forecasting approach in smart grid with clustering and consumption pattern recognition. IEEE Access **9**, 54992–55008 (2021)
49. Wang, Y.: Secondary forecasting based on deviation analysis for short-term load forecasting. IEEE Trans. Power Syst. **26**(2), 500–507 (2010)
50. Yadav, R.K.: A nature inspired strategy for demand side management in residential sector with smart grid environment. In: 9th International Conference System Modeling and Advancement in Research Trends (SMART), pp. 235–239. IEEE (2020)
51. Gaur, G., Mehta, N.: Demand side management in a smart grid environment. In: 2017 IEEE International Conference on Smart Grid and Smart Cities (ICSGSC). IEEE (2017)

52. Du, J., Lu, Y.: Model quality evaluation of advanced distribution management system based on smart grid architecture model. In: 2021 China International Conference on Electricity Distribution (CICED), pp. 688–691. IEEE (2021)

53. Souza, S.M.: Operation scheduling of prosumer with renewable energy sources and storage devices. In: 13th International Conference on the European Energy Market (EEM), pp. 1–5. IEEE (2016)

54. Mahmood, A.: Energy sharing and management for prosumers in smart grid with integration of storage system. In: 5th International Istanbul Smart Grid and Cities Congress and Fair (ICSG). IEEE (2017)

55. Yang, L.: Cost-effective and privacy-preserving energy management for smart meters. IEEE Trans. Smart Grid 6(1), 486–495 (2014)

56. Tan, O.: Privacy-cost trade-offs in demand-side management with storage. IEEE Trans. Inf. Forens. Secur. 12(6), 1458–1469 (2017)

57. Chen, Z.: Residential appliance DR energy management with electric privacy protection by online stochastic optimization. IEEE Trans. Smart Grid 4(4), 1861–1869 (2013)

58. Bu, F.: Enriching load data using micro-PMUs and smart meters. IEEE Trans. Smart Grid 12(6), 5084–5094 (2021)

59. Avula, R.R.: Design framework for privacy-aware demand-side management with realistic energy storage model. IEEE Trans. Smart Grid (99), 1 (2021)

Image Watermark Combining with Discrete Wavelet Transform and Singular Value Decomposition

Juncai Yao[✉] and Jing Shen

School of Computer Engineering, Nanjing Institute of Technology, Nanjing 211167, China

Abstract. In this paper, using the spectrum characteristics of discrete wavelet transform (DWT) and the features of image singular value decomposition (SVD), an image watermarking algorithm is proposed, which combined with the contrast sensitivity characteristics of human visual system (HVS). In the algorithm, the scrambled watermark is embedded into the singular value matrix of image with some intensity, and its inverse process is used to extract the watermark, by using HVS characteristics. The algorithm is verified by simulation, and tested by compression, shearing, Gaussian noise, and median filter attacks, and compared with 8 reported watermarking algorithms on the anti-attack performance. The results indicate that under the strong compression attack with a quality factor of 20%, the NC value of the extracted watermark can still reach 0.8467, and PSNR and SSIM of the watermarked image can reach 26.1793 dB and 0.8517, which has better robustness than the 8 existing watermarking algorithms. The comprehensive results indicate that the proposed algorithm can commendably balance the relationship among robustness, visual transparency and watermark embedding amount in the process of watermark embedding.

Keywords: Image watermark · Discrete wavelet transform · Normalized correlation coefficient

1 Introduction

With the rapid development of information and engineering technology, digital multimedia technology deeps into every corner of society, which makes people's life benefit a lot; However, at the same time, people can freely copy, tamper with and disseminate relevant information, especially in the current field of copyright protection and network communication, information security is under great threat, and there is an urgent need for an effective and practical digital anti-counterfeiting technology [1–3].

Digital watermarking is the superposition and embedding of some identification information (such as text, image and identifier) on the information carrier. It is required that the use value of the original information source cannot be affected, and digital watermarking cannot be detected and distinguished easily by human. And it can realize content authentication, copyright protection and information secret transmission through its hidden watermark information [2]. It is a very important research direction in information

© Springer Nature Singapore Pte Ltd. 2022
Y. Tian et al. (Eds.): ICBDS 2021, CCIS 1563, pp. 115–124, 2022.
https://doi.org/10.1007/978-981-19-0852-1_9

security technology. Currently, much research has been done on it at home and abroad, and many watermarking algorithms have been proposed [1–9], but it is far from meeting the requirements of the times, and many problems have not been solved, especially the digital watermarking technology combined with wavelet transform [3–6]. This technology mainly embeds the watermark information into the wavelet coefficients. Although its operation is simple, the watermark embedding amount is small and the anti-attack performance is poor [3–6]. For the watermarking technology combining with singular value decomposition (SVD), the current research shows that it has good robustness to some attacks, while the extracted watermark effect is relatively poor for compression, cutting and other attacks [6–9]. Based on these reasons, using the advantages of the two methods, according to the spectral coefficient characteristics of discrete wavelet transform (DWT) and the stability characteristics of image SVD matrix, an image watermarking algorithm combined with the contrast perception characteristics of human visual system (HVS) is proposed. In the algorithm, firstly, the original image is performed by the DWT transformation and SVD, to obtain the low-frequency sub-band coefficients of each sub block, and quantifies its singular values; then the watermark information is scrambled, and combined with the contrast sensitivity characteristics of HVS, in the singular value, the scrambled watermark is embedded to realize the watermark embedding; and finally, the inverse process is used to realize the watermark extraction. The simulation results show that the proposed algorithm has a good visual transparency and the effectiveness of watermark detection; and under the strong compression attack of 20% quality factor, the normalized correlation coefficient (NC) of the extracted watermark can still reach 0.8467, for the watermarked image, the peak signal-to-noise ratio (PSNR) reaches 26.17927 dB and the structural similarity index (SSIM) reaches 0.8517. Further, compares and analyzes its anti-attack performance with the separate watermarking algorithms based on the DWT and SVD, and the six other watermarking algorithms, which show that the proposed algorithm has an excellent anti-attack performance. The comprehensive results make known that the proposed algorithm can commendably balance the relationship among robustness, visual transparency, and amount embedded watermark, in the process of watermark embedding, which is an image watermarking algorithm with a good performance.

2   Watermark Scheme

2.1   Discrete Wavelet Transform

Wavelet transform (WT) is a time-frequency transform method that gradually refines the signal by scaling and translation operation. Its advantage is that it can fully highlight some characteristics of the problem through the transform, and can carry out multi-resolution analysis on the localization of time (or space) frequency [6]. According to the spectrum characteristics of DWT and the HVS contrast sensitivity characteristics [10, 11], if the watermark is embedded into the insensitive area of the observed image, the transparency of the image embedded watermark can be well guaranteed, and the embedding amount of watermark can be realized to the greatest extent [2, 6].

After the DWT primary transformation, an image is decomposed into 4 sub-images, as shown in Fig. 1. The sub-image (a), (b), (c) and (d) in Fig. 1 are the low-frequency component, horizontal detail, vertical detail, as well as high-frequency component of the original image, respectively. Accordingly, the low-frequency component is further decomposed into four sub-bands. If k is used to represent the series of decomposition, the total number of sub-bands is $3k + 1$ [9].

Fig. 1. Four sub-images after DWT primary transformation

2.2 Singular Value Decomposition

In linear algebra and decomposition method, SVD is a much important orthogonal matrix method. Often using SVD in image processing are mainly because: (1) image SVD can fully describe the relationship among image matrix elements, and reflects their internal characteristics, instead of the HVS characteristics; (2) Generally, the singular value is unchanged, and SVD is very stable; (3) After DWT decomposition, the low-frequency component includes main information of the original image, which is similar to the original image. Hence, their coefficient amplitude has a strong stability [4, 6–9]. Furthermore, in the watermarking combined with DWT, image SVD focus the low-frequency information in the transform domain on a few singular values of the matrix and their corresponding singular vectors, so as to better realize the transparency and robustness of the watermark image [4]. In image processing, Eq. (1) is used to SVD for image with the size of M × N [9].

$$A = U \times S \times V^{\mathrm{T}}, \quad A = \{a_{\mathrm{ij}}\}_{\mathrm{M \times N}} \tag{1}$$

Here, A represents the matrix of image, U and V denote respectively M × M and N × N unitary matrix, T represents transpose, S is M × N nonnegative diagonal matrix. As shown in Eq. (2), the values on the diagonal meet Eq. (3).

$$S = diag(\sigma_1, \sigma_1, \mathrm{L}, \sigma_r) \tag{2}$$

$$\sigma_1 \geq \sigma_1 \geq \cdots \geq \sigma_r \geq \sigma_{r+1} = \mathrm{L} = \sigma_m = 0 \tag{3}$$

Here, r is the rank of A, which is the number of non-zero singular values, then each σ_i value is determined and unique, which is the singular value of A. Therefore, Eq. (4) can be used to describe the SVD of A.

$$A = U \times S \times V^\mathrm{T} = \sum_{i=1}^{r} \sigma_i U_i V_i^T \tag{4}$$

2.3 Watermark Algorithm Design

The original image is written as I_0, the original watermark image is I_w, whose sizes are $I_0 = M \times N$, $I_w = m \times n$. Combining the advantages of DWT and SVD, the following watermarking algorithm (recorded as DWT-SVD) is proposed, which is described as follows.

(1) Using the Daubechies wavelet basis, the original image is transformed by DWT to obtain the low-frequency component, which is decomposed into sub-blocks with size of n × n;

(2) SVD is performed on all sub blocks, and the unitary matrices U and V, and the diagonal matrix S are obtained according to the above formula. S is the singular value matrix.

(3) To further improve the watermark security, the watermark information is first subjected to k iterative Arnold scrambling transform to obtain the watermark information I_w'. And k is as the key.

(4) The scrambled watermark is repeatedly embedded into the image singular value matrix S with some strength, and it is decomposed again by SVD to obtain U_1, V_1 and S_1. When embedding, the value after multiplying the intensity factor by I_w' shall not exceed the HVS threshold. When it is just equal to this threshold, it is the best embedding time, and the embedding amount reaches the maximum, otherwise the intensity factor will be changed. The HVS threshold is calculated by multiplying each element in the singular value matrix S of the image by the critical HVS contrast detection threshold [11, 12]. This process not only ensures the maximum embedding of watermark, but also realizes the invisibility of watermark (i.e. transparency) combined with HVS characteristics.

(5) Substituting U_1, V_1 and S_1 into Eq. (1), the processed image is the image embedded watermark in the transform domain, and the reconstructed watermark image is obtained by the inverse DWT, so as to realize the watermark embedding.

(6) The inverse process of watermark embedding is used to extract the watermark information, and the extracted watermark is record as Iw'. When extracting the watermark, the watermarked image and the original image are transformed by DWT, and C' and C are the wavelet coefficients of their transform respectively; then, according to the inverse process, the watermark is extracted by Eq. (5), and then the watermark is detected by Eq. (6) according to correlation [2, 9], i.e., when ρ is greater than a certain threshold, the watermark is considered to exist.

$$I'_w = \frac{C' - C}{\alpha} \tag{5}$$

$$\rho(I''_W, I_W) = \frac{\sum I''_{W_i} g I_{W_i}}{\sqrt{\sum (I''_{W_i})^2}} \tag{6}$$

3   Experimental Results

In order to verify the effectiveness of the proposed watermarking algorithm, Lena grayscale image with the size is 256 pixels × 256 pixels, is the original image, the "QQ" logo with 64 pixels × 64 pixels is used as the watermark information for simulation experiment. The results are shown in Fig. 2. From Fig. 2, subjectively, there is little difference between the watermarked image and the original image, and the extracted watermark is almost the same as the original watermark image, which indicates that the proposed watermark algorithm can better ensure the visual transparency of the watermark.

(a) Original image   (b) Original watermark   (c) Watermarked image   (d) Extracted watermark

Fig. 2. Simulation results of the proposed watermarking algorithm

To illustrate the advantages of the proposed algorithm, it is necessary to evaluate the quality of the watermarked image and the similarity between the extracted watermark and the original watermark. Among them, the quality of the watermarked image generally uses PSNR or SSIM to measure the difference between the embedded watermark image and the original image. Generally, the larger the PSNR and the closer the SSIM is to 1, the smaller the difference between the watermarked image and the original image, and the higher the quality of the watermarked image, the better the transparency. And when PSNR exceeds 30 dB, HVS can hardly distinguish the difference between the two images. The similarity between the extracted watermark and the original watermark is generally evaluated by the NC values, which is calculated as Eq. (7). Among them, the closer the NC is to 1, the closer the extracted watermark is to the raw watermark, indicating that the watermark effect is better [2, 3].

$$NC = \frac{\sum\limits_{i=1}^{H} \sum\limits_{j=1}^{W} W(i,j) \times W'(i,j)}{\sum\limits_{i=1}^{H} \sum\limits_{j=1}^{W} [W(i,j)]^2} \tag{7}$$

Where, $W(i,j)$ is the original watermark, $W'(i,j)$ is the extracted watermark, H and W represents the size of the watermark image.

According to the simulation experiment, the PSNR, SSIM and NC values are calculated, and the results are 38.5835 dB, 0.9917 and 0.9839 respectively. It shows that the watermarked image has a good visual transparency and the extracted watermark has a high effectiveness. At the same time, it also shows that the proposed watermarking algorithm is effective and feasible.

4   Testing and Discussion

4.1   Attack Testing

In the watermarking technology, the watermark also needs to have strong anti-attack performance, that is, robustness. To test the robustness of the proposed watermarking algorithm, the watermarked image is attacked by some artificial impairing, namely the compression with different compression quality factors QF (quality factor), shearing, Gaussian noise, and median filtering. And their PSNR, SSIM and NC values are calculated. The experimental results are shown in Fig. 3 and Table 1. Figure 3 shows the test results after JPEG compression attacks using different QFs.

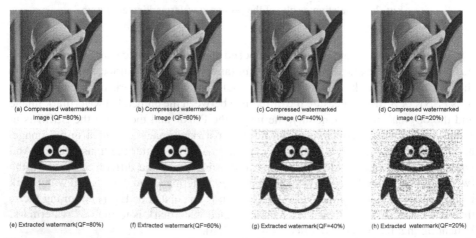

(a) Compressed watermarked image (QF=80%) (b) Compressed watermarked image (QF=60%) (c) Compressed watermarked image (QF=40%) (d) Compressed watermarked image (QF=20%)

(e) Extracted watermark(QF=80%) (f) Extracted watermark(QF=60%) (g) Extracted watermark(QF=40%) (h) Extracted watermark(QF=20%)

Fig. 3. The watermarked images after being attacked by compressing under the different QFs and the watermark extracted from them

Table 1. PSNR and SSIM evaluating the watermarked images after being attacked by 4 types and NC values of the extracted watermark

Attack form	JPEG compression				Shearing		Gaussian noise	Median filtering
Attack degree	QF = 20%	QF = 40%	QF = 60%	QF = 80%	middle 1/4	Upper left 1/4	0.1	[3 3]
PSNR/dB	26.1793	28.7317	32.0013	34.5459	19.9227	26.7619	27.0158	25.675
SSIM	0.8517	0.8999	0.9402	0.9881	0.8137	0.8859	0.8951	0.8556
NC	0.8467	0.8748	0.9243	0.9635	0.8471	0.8799	0.9577	0.9153

Analyzing the data in Fig. 3 and Table 1, from the test results of compression attack, it can be obtained that, subjectively, the watermarks extracted after different QF compression attacks are still relatively clear, especially when the QF reaches 20% strong compression, the extracted watermarks can still be clear and visible. And from the objective evaluation, meanwhile the NC value can still reach 0.8467. These results indicate that the extracted watermarks are effective and feasible. In the meantime, the watermarked image after compression attack basically does not have much distortion, and the PSNR and SSIM of the watermarked image reach 26.17927 dB and 0.8517, which ensures the visual transparency. From the test results of shearing, median filtering and Gaussian noise attack, the NC value of the extracted watermark can reach more than 0.81 after the attack, which ensures the effectiveness of the extracted watermark. The test results show that the proposed watermarking algorithm has a good anti-attack performance.

4.2 Discussion

In order to illustrate the advantages of the proposed watermarking algorithm, the anti-attack performance of the proposed watermarking algorithm (DWT-SVD) and other algorithms is compared and analyzed from two aspects.

(1) The watermarking algorithm based on DWT and the watermarking algorithm based on SVD are separately used for simulation, and the results are compared with the attack test results of the proposed DWT-SVD watermarking algorithm. In the simulation experiments, the watermarked image is tested by cutting (cutting 1/4 area in the middle), Gaussian noise and median filter, the watermark is extracted from the watermarked image after attack, the PSNR, SSIM, and NC value of the watermark are calculated. The comparison results are shown in Fig. 4.

The anti-attack performance of 3 watermarking algorithms (DWT, SVD and DWT-SVD) is compared and analyzed from Fig. 4. The results show that: (1) after being attacked by cutting, Gaussian noise and median filter, the PSNR and SSIM values of the watermarked image and the NC value of the extracted watermark using DWT-SVD algorithm are significantly larger than those of DWT and SVD. It shows that the watermark transparency effect and watermark extraction effect of the proposed algorithm are

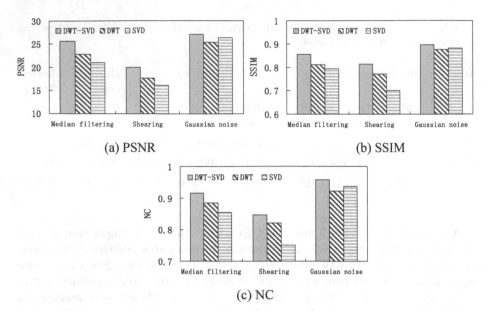

Fig. 4. Comparison of the anti-attack performance of 3 watermarking algorithms (namely DWT-SVD, DWT and SVD), (a) PSNR, (b) SSIM, (c) NC

significantly better than those of DWT and SVD. At the same time, it also shows that the anti-attack ability of the proposed algorithm is better than that of DWT and SVD. (2) For the shear attack, the PSNR, SSIM and NC values are increased more, and the effect of the proposed algorithm is improved more obviously, which shows that the proposed algorithm has a better anti-attack performance against the shear attack.

(2) The proposed watermarking algorithm DWT-SVD is compared with six water-marking algorithms in references [1, 9, 13–15] and [16]. The six watermarking algorithms: the digital watermarking algorithm based on visual saliency map [1], digital watermarking algorithm based on DWT and SVD [9], digital watermarking technology based on the interest region [13], digital watermarking embedding algorithm based on interest region [14], double watermarking algorithm by expanding single watermark [15], and robust watermarking algorithm based on visual threshold [16]. The comparison results are shown in Fig. 5.

From the comparison results in Fig. 5, it can be obtained, (1) for various attacks of different degrees, the anti-attack performance of the six watermarking algorithms in the references has their own strengths, weaknesses and great differences. But the anti-attack performance of the proposed watermarking algorithm can reach the best or second best of several methods for a variety of attacks. (2) For the attack of Gaussian noise, the NC value of watermark extracted by DWT-SVD algorithm is significantly higher than that of other algorithms, which shows that the anti-Gaussian noise attack of the proposed watermarking algorithm is better than the other six algorithms. The

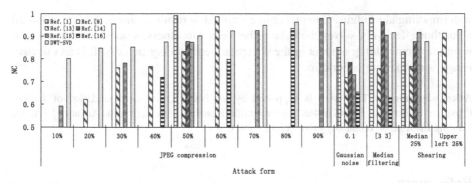

Fig. 5. Comparing of the anti-attack performance of proposed watermarking algorithm with the ones of 6 watermarking algorithms in the references

comprehensive comparison results show that the watermarking algorithm proposed in this paper has a good robustness.

The main reasons for the above results are as follows. (1) The proposed algorithm combines the advantages of DWT and SVD, which makes up for their shortcomings, and jointly improves the performance of the algorithm; (2) In the embedding process of the proposed algorithm, the HVS characteristics are combined, and the visual threshold is used as the limit of the embedding amount, which not only ensures the visual transparency, but also maximizes the embedding capacity. It increases the embedding amount and effectively improves the robustness of the watermark. Thus, the balance between visual transparency, robustness and watermark capacity in the process of watermark embedding is better solved.

5 Conclusion

In this paper, using the spectrum characteristics of DWT and SVD of image, an image watermark embedding and extraction algorithm combined with the HVS contrast perception characteristics is proposed, and is verified by simulation experiments. The results show that subjectively, the human cannot distinguish the difference between the watermarked image and the original image, as well as the extracted watermark and the original watermark; objectively, PSNR and SSIM of the watermark image are 38.5835 db and 0.9917 respectively, and the NC value of the extracted watermark is 0.9839. The simulation results indicate that the proposed algorithm has a good visual transparency and the effectiveness of watermark detection. The proposed algorithm has been tested by compression, shearing, Gaussian noise and median filter attacks, and is compared with the watermarking algorithms based on DWT, and watermarking algorithms based on SVD, and six watermarking algorithms proposed by predecessors in recent 5 years. The results show that the NC value of the proposed watermarking algorithm can still reach 0.8467 under the strong compression attack with QF of 20%; the PSNR and SSIM of the watermarked image reach 26.17927 db and 0.8517. The proposed watermarking algorithm has better robustness than the watermarking algorithms based on the single DWT, and watermarking algorithms based on the single SVD, as well as the previous six watermarking algorithms. Comprehensive simulation results indicate that the proposed algorithm effectively solves the balance between robustness, visual transparency and watermark embedding amount in the watermark embedding process. It is an effective image watermarking algorithm.

Acknowledgments. This work is supported by the Natural Science Foundation of Jiangsu Province, China (No. BK20201468), the Scientific Research Foundation for Advanced Talents, Nanjing Institute of Technology (No. YKJ201981).

References

1. Liu, X.X., Wang, X.H.: Digital watermarking algorithm based on saliency map. Opt. Techniq. **42**(3), 260–263 (2016)
2. Yao, J.C., Shen, J.: Image quality assessment based on the image contents visual perception. J. Electron. Imag. **30**(5), 053024 (2021)
3. Hao, K.L., Feng, G.R., Zhang, X.P.: Robust image watermarking based on generative adversarial network. China Commun. **17**(11), 131–140 (2020)
4. Ernawan, F., Ariatmanto, D., Firdaus, A.: An improved image watermarking by modifying selected DWT-DCT coefficients. IEEE Access **9**, 45474–45485 (2021)
5. Guo, Y., Li, B.Z., Goel, N.: Optimised blind image watermarking method based on firefly algorithm in DWT-QR transform domain. IET Image Proc. **11**(6), 406–415 (2017)
6. Imran, M., Harvey, B.A.: A blind adaptive color image watermarking scheme based on principal component analysis, singular value decomposition and human visual system. Radioengineering **26**(3), 823–834 (2017)
7. Agoyi, M., Elebi, E., Anbarjafari, G.: A watermarking algorithm based on chirp z-transform, discrete wavelet transform, and singular value decomposition. Signal Image Video Process. **9**(3), 735–745 (2015)
8. Wang, X.Y., Niu, P.P., Yang, H.Y., et al.: A blind watermark decoder in DTCWT domain using Weibull distribution-based vector HMT model. Acta Automat. Sin. **47**(12), 2857–2869 (2021)
9. Li, L., Bai, R., Lu, J.F., et al.: A watermarking scheme for color image using quaternion discrete Fourier transform and tensor decomposition. Appl. Sci. **11**(11), 5006 (2021)
10. Anis, K., Zied, K., Anis, S.: A reframed watermark extraction approach using the ABC algorithm. Chin. J. Electron. **30**(4), 736–742 (2021)
11. Yao, J.C., Liu, G.Z.: Bitrate-based no-reference video quality assessment combining the visual perception of video contents. IEEE Trans. Broadcast. **65**(3), 546–557 (2019)
12. Yao, J.C., Liu, G.Z.: Improved SSIM IQA of contrast distortion based on the contrast sensitivity characteristics of HVS. IET Image Proc. **12**(6), 872–879 (2018)
13. Xi, X.: The digital watermark based on the region of interest, Ph.D. Thesis, Shanghai Normal University (2008)
14. Yao, J.C., Shen, J.: Objective assessment of image quality based on image content contrast perception. Acta Phys. Sin. **69**(14), 148702 (2020)
15. Mahto, D.K., Singh, A.K.: A survey of color image watermarking: State-of-the-art and research directions. Comput. Electr. Eng. **93**(3), 107255 (2021)
16. Sun, J., Jiang, X.P., Liu, J., et al.: An anti-recompression video watermarking algorithm in bitstream domain. Tsinghua Sci. Technol. **26**(2), 154–162 (2021)

Research on Outsourced PSI Protocols for Privacy Preserving Data Sharing

Yanfeng Shi[1,2], Wenxiu Yang[1], Wanni Xu[1(✉)], and Qiong Li[2]

[1] School of Computer Engineering, Nanjing Institute of Technology, Nanjing 211167, China
[2] Beijing Key Laboratory of Security and Privacy in Intelligent Transportation, Beijing 100044, China

Abstract. Private set intersection (PSI), a basic privacy preserving technology for data sharing, is widely used in various practical applications such as educational system, anti-epidemic system and credit system. In traditional PSI solutions, two participants collaboratively calculate the intersection based on the plaintext sets they hold. In cloud computing scenario, cloud users would like to upload the encrypted data to the cloud rather than storing their own datasets locally, which needs to delegate cloud servers to execute PSI operations for data uses. Therefore, how to implement outsourced PSI computation is a hot topic of current research. In this paper, we mainly analyze the current researches focusing on the security and scalability of various existing out-sourced PSI protocols, including verifiable PSI, multi-party PSI, PSI-CA, quantum-based PSI, post-quantum-based PSI, fog-based PSI, blockchain-based PSI, attribute-based PSI, etc. Through the comparative analysis and summary of the existing schemes, we further discussed the future research direction.

Keywords: Private set intersection · Outsourced computing · Credit system · Fog computing

1 Introduction

Private set intersection (PSI) is a hot spot for privacy-preserving data analytics. PSI protocol enables all clients to compute the data sets intersection without disclosing effective message other than the intersection. It has a broad application, such as human genome computing, location-based detection, criminal investigation, educational resources sharing, social networks, homeland security, credit information system, anti-epidemic, etc.

The first PSI was introduced by Freedman et al. [1] in 2004. In the following years, re-searchers have designed many concrete PSI protocols. In cloud computing, it has been common for large enterprises and individuals to outsource data storage and computing. Therefore, how to design outsourced PSI protocols, making use of the powerful computing and storage capacity of cloud server, is a research hotspot. The main research directions for outsourced PSI include the following aspects:

© Springer Nature Singapore Pte Ltd. 2022
Y. Tian et al. (Eds.): ICBDS 2021, CCIS 1563, pp. 125–136, 2022.
https://doi.org/10.1007/978-981-19-0852-1_10

(1) Verifiable PSI: Although the cloud server can help the clients complete PSI computation, it is not completely trusted and may steal or tamper with privacy data. The malicious behaviors will do serious harm to enterprises. Therefore, it is necessary to study verifiable PSI [2], verifying the cloud server's honesty.

(2) Multi-party PSI: In the big data distributed scenario, it's necessary to study the PSI [3] that supports multiple parties to meet the needs of multi-party data sharing.

(3) PSI-CA: For some scenarios requiring high privacy requirements, traditional PSI will reveal a lot of information, such as part or even all of the data set. PSI-CA [4], as a variant of PSI, only returns the set intersection cardinality to meet the requirements of higher privacy.

(4) Anti-quantum PSI: With the development of quantum computers, how to design quantum PSI protocol [5] and post-quantum PSI protocol [6] to resist the attacks of quantum computer is a topic in the new era.

(5) Other PSI: To solve the problem of unacceptable delay or lack of mobility support in cloud computing, fog-based PSI [7] is studied; to solve the decentralization problem, blockchain-based PSI [8] is introduced; to simplify certificate management and solve the fine-grained authorization problem, identity-based PSI [9] and attribute-based PSI [10] are proposed, etc.

According to the above aspects, this paper intends to classify and summarize the research status of outsourcing PSI, compares and analyzes the security and performance of various solutions, and summarizes and prospects the existing problems and research trends of various PSI.

2 Preliminaries

2.1 PSI and PSI-CA

PSI [1] is an encryption protocol that enables all clients to calculate the data sets intersection without disclosing effective message. In the outsourced PSI protocol, it relies on the storage and computing capabilities of the cloud server.

PSI-CA (Private Set Intersection Cardinality) [4] means that it is sometimes necessary to only get the intersection cardinality, hiding the intersection content.

2.2 Adversary Model

The adversary models in PSI are divided into the following categories:

Semi-honest model (SH). In this model, each participant abides by the implementation process of the protocol, but it may infer other participants' information.

Malicious model (Mal). In this model, participants may not abide by the implementation process of the protocol. They might refuse to execute the protocol, modify the private input set information at will, and terminate prematurely protocol execution, etc. Some cryptographic protocols (bit commitment, zero-knowledge proof, etc.) can guarantee the correctness of computation results.

3   Protocol Classifications

3.1   Verifiable PSI

In 2014, Kamara et al. [2] introduced a verifiable delegated PSI with pseudo-random function (PRF). Although the protocol is efficient, it doesn't achieve storage outsourcing model.

In 2015, a verifiable delegated set intersection on outsourced encrypted data (VDSI) protocol is introduced by Zheng et al. [11], which is secure under malicious clouds. It is the first protocol that realizes intersection computing and storage outsourcing simultaneously. But this protocol will leak intersection contents to the cloud.

In 2016, Abadi et al. introduced VD-PSI protocol using the point-valued polynomial representation in [3]. The cloud must be authorized by all clients to use the data set, and the user can detect the cloud's tampering with the data. In addition, the verification cost is linear with the intersection cardinality.

In 2017, Oksuz et al. [12] designed a non-interactive, secure, effective and verifiable PSI protocol. The protocol does not allow malicious clouds to attack encrypted datasets. Specifically, users require the cloud to generate a proof related to the result of the computation. With the proof and the result, users can check whether the malicious cloud is executing an honest computation. If the cloud is malicious, verifiability tells the user about the malicious cloud server computing. And this verifiable computation is at most linearly related to the intersection cardinality. After that, Oliaiy et al. [13] used the El-Carnal cryptosystem to propose a verifiable and efficient VDSI protocol. Compared with [11], this protocol implements a pairing-free scheme and significantly reduces computational overhead.

In 2018, Wang et al. [7] introduced a scheme to outsource computing to fog server by using RSA cryptosystem, and verified its security in untrusted fog server. This protocol eliminates the computational overhead of Full Homomorphic Encryption and pairing operations for data owner.

In 2019, Qiu et al. [14] introduced two PPSI on large-scale data sets with Bloom filters. Their first scheme can be shown its security under the semi-honest adversary, and the enhanced PSI one can be proved its security and verifiability under the malicious model, which hides the intersection size. It also prevents the cloud from malicious tampering with the data set. These two protocols use a multi-round algorithm, which greatly improves the efficiency and takes only 15 s and 24 s to process 2 million datasets, respectively. Later, Jiang et al. [15] introduced a traceable solution based on ownership proof and committed Bloom Filter. The protocol supports probabilistic verification and reduces the computational complexity of verification, by checking a small part of random bits.

In 2020, Wang et al. [16] introduced the first VDPSI protocol that achieves counting operations and dynamic update. The difference between this protocol and previous ones is that it supports multi-subset and each subset will be marked by a classification tag. The cloud can only compute elements with a common tag during computation, which ensures the security of the data. The user verifies whether the result is correct through the verification algorithm.

In 2021, Debnath et al. [17] introduced an outsourced PSI (OPSI) with coupling zero-knowledge proofs and bloom filter. This protocol allows the client to perform multiple delegated PSI computations simultaneously by reusing the outsourced datasets on the cloud without preparing their datasets separately for each task and without revealing additional information to the cloud. Moreover, it can be shown secure against malicious adversary. With employing random permutations, this protocol can be enhanced to OPSI-CA. The protocol is the first non-interactive solution under the malicious model and can achieve a linear complexity overhead. Later, Li et al. [18] introduced PRISM to compute private set operations (intersection and union) with secret sharing, which supports large-scale datasets, and they experimented with 50 users using the TPC-H benchmark test, which took about 41 s on 5M data and approximately 7.3 min on 1B data and 2 database owners. In addition, Prism provides an oblivious result verification method to verify the behavior of public servers.

Table 1 compares the properties of existing verifiable PSI protocols. As shown that: There are few implementations in the malicious model, and they are basically proved safe under the semi-honest model. Moreover, constructing a protocol that supports both non-interactive and outsourced storage is still an open problem.

Table 1. Property summary for verifiable PSI protocols

Protocols	[2]	[11]	[3]	[12]	[14]	[16]	[17]
Non-interactive protocols	×	√	×	√	×	×	×
Outsourced storage	×	√	√	√	√	√	√
Hiding the intersection size	√	×	√	√	√	×	√
Multiple clients	√	√	√	×	×	×	×
Security model	Std	Std	Std	ROM	Std	ROM	Std
Adversary model	Mal	Mal	Mal	Mal	Mal	Mal	Mal
Computation complexity	O(v)	O(v)	O(v)	O(v)	O(L)	O(v)	O(v)
Communication complexity	O(v)	O(w)	O(v)	O(w)	O(L)	O(v)	O(v)
Verification complexity	O(kw)	O(w)	O(w)	O(w)	O(v)	O(a)	O(v)
Security assumptions	PRP	DL	AHE	VDDH	DE	q-SBDH	DDH

Note: v = Set Cardinality, w = Intersection Cardinality, k = Security parameter, L = The length of the bloom filter, a = All Set Cardinality

3.2 Multi-party PSI

In 2016, Abadi et al. [3] introduced VD-PSI that supports multiple clients along with delegating the set intersection's operations to the cloud, meanwhile this protocol can check the computation correctness. Zhang et al. [19] combined multiple keys based on Boneh et al. (CREPTO 2013) [20] to introduce two server-aided PSI protocols. Compared with previous server-aided protocols, where each party is required to encrypt private sets by using the same public-private key pair, this protocol supports multiple parties to use different keys for encryption with stronger security. Their first protocol is the server-assisted PSI, which hides and transmits the private sets through PRP functions and proxy re-encryption. However, the server may not comply with the protocol or leak privacy. The second enhanced protocol is proposed with socially rational parties, which assumes that all parties are characterized by rational and invariably select the strategy that gives them the most benefit, and give each party a reputation value. It will punish those who violate the PSI protocol and promote cooperation by increasing reputation.

In 2017, Abadi et al. [21] proposed two protocols for the use of private set intersection. The first O-PSI allows clients to independently store datasets with blinded polynomials form. But this protocol requires homomorphic encryption, which is inefficient. The second protocol mainly adapts hash table to achieve higher efficiency, without public key encryption. In addition, it continues to have most of ideal features of the first protocol.

In 2018, Zhang et al. [6] introduced a cloud outsourced multi-party PSI comparison protocol with homomorphic encryption and Bloom filters, which uses the NTRU proxy re-encryption algorithm and outsources a large number of complex computations to the cloud server, while users only need to do a small amount of operations. The complexity is linear, and the final comparison results can be obtained without leaking the users' privacy under a semi-honest model.

In 2019, Ghosh et al. [22] introduced a generalized solution for multi-party with Oblivious Linear Function Evaluation. Also, a protocol for multi-party computation in the fully malicious case is proposed, which improves efficiency by eliminating the costly zero-knowledge proofs and homomorphic threshold encryption. Later, [23] designed two multi-party PSI protocols. The first protocol leaked in the offline stage, and the second protocol was improved to reduce the leakage and with less overhead.

In 2020, Abadi et al. [24] introduced a delegated PSI which supports efficient extensible multi-party PSI and data updates. And the update operation has very low communication and computational complexity, which can exceed 800 updates for large datasets, and PSI computation is 2–2.5 times faster than existing protocols. In addition, Feather allows clients to securely and efficiently update outsourced private datasets without downloading the entire dataset. Ruan et al. [25] introduced an efficient PSI on the basis of homomorphic cryptography, point-value form of polynomials, and pseudo-random function. In this protocol, the complexity is linearly related to the dataset size. In addition, clients can outsource the dataset to the cloud regardless of any additional computation. Liu et al. [26] introduced a secure multi-party PSI-CA with quantum transformation, quantum measurement and quantum parallelism for the first time, and realizes multi-party data sharing without a third party. Mouchet et al. [27] presented a secure multi-party computation scheme with post-quantum RLWE. This scheme adapts Multiparty Homomorphic Encryption (MHE) and it is applicable to multi-party PSI computation in the cloud-aided setting.

Table 2 compares the properties of existing multi-party PSI protocols. As shown that: There are few implementations in the malicious model, and they are basically proved safe against semi-honest adversay. Moreover, constructing a protocol that supports both non-interactive and outsourced storage is still an open problem.

Table 2. Property summary for multi-party PSI protocols

Protocols	[3]	[19]	[21]	[6]	[24]	[25]
Non-interactive protocols	×	√	×	√	×	×
Outsourced storage	√	×	√	×	√	√
Hiding the intersection size	√	×	√	×	√	×
Computation integrity verification	√	×	×	×	×	×
Security model	Std	Std	Std	Std	Std	Std
Adversarial model	Mal	Mal	SH	SH	SH	SH
Computation complexity	O(v)	O(v)	O(v)	O(c + s)	O(v)	O(v)
Communication complexity	O(v)	O(v)	O(v)	O(c + s)	O(v)	O(v)
Security assumption	AHE	LWE	AHE	NTRU	PRF	HE

Note: v = Set Cardinality, c = Number of users, s = Number of servers

3.3 PSI-CA

Compared with the traditional PSI protocol, the cardinality of the set of participants is leaked. In 2011, Ateniese et al. [4] first proposed the concept of PSI-CA (Private Set Intersection Cardinality) to support the hidden client sets size. The protocol is a provably secure scheme based on RSA assumption. During the entire protocol process, the server did not obtain any information about the client's input sets and sets size.

In 2018, Tajima et al. [28] proposed two outsourced PSI-CA (OPSI-CA) with fully homomorphic encryption (FHE) and bloom filter. The first is a basic scheme, while the second is querier-friendly. The two protocols achieve the full delegation of PSI-CA computation which means clients do not involve in the stage of delegation at all, and the third-party queriers require the cloud server to perform PSI-CA computation. The protocols also achieve data storage outsourcing. The first basic protocol needs only a smaller number of additions and multiplications, however the communication and computation costs for retrieving the result for the querier are relatively large, while the computation and communication costs for the querier in the querier-friendly protocol smaller. In these two protocols, the cloud can directly perform join operations securely towards outsourced datasets, and the cloud cannot know the set intersection cardinality, which protects the privacy requirements for all parties. These are two PSI-CA schemes that firstly achieve outsourcing by adopting FHE.

In 2019, Qiu et al. [14] introduced two PPSI for large-scale datasets based on bloom filters, in which the second PSI protocol hides the intersection size from the cloud to prevent malicious tampering of the datasets by the cloud.

In 2020, Duong et al. [29] proposed a delegated PSI-CA based on oblivious distributed key PRF abstraction. It is also the first protocol allowing clients to delegate PSI-CA operations to cloud servers. The protocol's complexity has a linear relationship the smaller set size.

In 2021, Debnath et al. [17] proposed a delegated PSI protocol which ensures its security in the malicious environment. The protocol is based on the assumption of DDH,

Table 3. Property summary for PSI-CA protocols

Protocols	[28]	[14]	[29]	[17]
Security assumption	FHE	DE	OPRF	DDH
PSI-CA full delegation	$\checkmark$	$\times$	$\times$	$\times$
Multiple clients	$\times$	$\times$	$\times$	$\checkmark$
Security model	Std	Std	Std	Std
Adversarial model	SH	Mal	SH	Mal
Computation complexity	$O(\frac{L}{n} \cdot v)$	$O(L)$	$O(v)$	$O(v)$
Communication complexity	$O(\frac{L}{n} \cdot v)$	$O(L)$	$O(v)$	$O(v)$
Computation integrity verification	$\times$	$\checkmark$	$\times$	$\checkmark$
Non-interactive protocols	$\times$	$\times$	$\times$	$\times$

Note: L = The length of the bloom filter, n = Number of bloom filter slots, v = Set Cardinality

employing bloom filters, zero-knowledge proof (for discrete logarithms) and multiplicative homomorphic ELGamal encryption with a digital signature scheme to hide the size of intersection from the server and allow the client to verify the integrity of server's computation. This protocol is also the first non-interactive protocol that is secure under the malicious model and can achieve linear complexity cost.

Table 3 shows the properties of PSI-CA protocols. As shown that: Based on the analysis of the above specific protocols, there is currently no verifiable multi-party PSI-CA protocol that simultaneously supports full delegation of PSI-CA, and all of them require interaction between clients.

3.4 Quantum-Based PSI

In 2016, Shi [5] proposed the first unconditionally secure quantum PSI-CA protocol. This protocol's communication costs just $O(1)$, which can significantly reduce communication complexity. However, the protocol demands two additional set cardinality's assumptions, which may cause a limit to its wider application. In 2018, Shi [30] discarded the two additional assumptions about set cardinality in [5], and proposed a more practical quantum PSI-CA protocol without any restrictions. This protocol and [5] are not related to the sets' size, and are more fit for practical applications of large datasets. Since the existing technology cannot realize the quantum resources and measurements required by the quantum counting algorithm used in [5, 30], the protocols proposed in [5, 30] are only theoretical methods to approximate quantum PSI-CA.

In 2018, Shi [31] proposed unconditional quantum PSU-CA and PSI-CA protocols with aided non-colluding quantum clouds, which are able to compute |A ∪ B| together with |A ∩ B| simultaneously. Compared with [5, 31] discards the two additional set cardinality's assumptions, but has higher computation and communication complexity.

In 2019, Shi et al. [32] proposed a more feasible and practical quantum PSI-CA protocol than [5, 30, 31], which has lower communication complexity and higher security.

This protocol utilizes a non-colluding third party [31] to ensure the fairness. It uses single photon as a quantum resource, requiring only measurements and simple single-photon operators. Using current techniques, preparing the quantum resources required by [31, 32] and applying these quantum operators and measurements are feasible.

To solve multi-party data sharing, in 2020, Liu et al. [26] first introduced a secure multi-party PSI-CA based on quantum PSI-CA [5] and quantum counting [33, 34]. This protocol can support data sharing between multiple parties without a trusted third party. Zhang et al. [35] proposed a three-party quantum protocol that simultaneously solved the problems of PSU-CA and PSI-CA, in which any two or three parties can get the union and intersection cardinalities with the help of a semi-honest third party.

Table 4 shows the properties of the quantum-based PSI protocol. As shown that: Based on the analysis of the above specific protocols, the quantum-based PSI protocol currently only supports the computation of the set intersection cardinality, and the solution for computing the intersection content is yet to be studied.

3.5 Post-quantum-Based PSI

In 2018, Zhang et al. [6] firstly introduced the post-quantum multi-party PSI protocol with homomorphic encryption and bloom filters. This protocol applys NTRU to proxy re-encryption algorithms and outsource a large number of complicated computing to cloud servers. Clients only need do a few operations.

In 2020, Debnath et al. [36] firstly present the first post-quantum PSI-CA protocol with lattice based encryption and bloom filter. This protocol is based on the DLWE problem. The computation complexity of the protocol is linear with the size of the users' datasets, and only requires modular multiplications, which are very efficient. In addition, in order to prevent malicious clients from inputting forged datasets,

Debnath et al. extended PSI-CA to APSI-CA (authorized PSI-CA) by authorizing client data sets. This protocol is also the first APSI-CA protocol based on lattice based encryption. Mouchet et al. [27] present a multi-party homomorphic encryption (MHE) to implement multi-party PSI based on RLWE.

Table 5 shows the properties of the post-quantum-based PSI protocol. As shown that: Based on the analysis of the above specific protocols, The post-quantum-based PSI protocols all proved their security against the semi-honest adversary, but failed to achieve the security under the malicious model.

3.6 Other PSI

In 2018, in order to solve some inherent problems in cloud computing, Wang et al. [7] introduced a PSI protocol to outsource computation to the fog server by using RSA cryptosystem, and verified that it was secure in untrusted fog server, and the verification complexity was linear with the size of intersection. This protocol eliminates the computational overhead of Full Homomorphic Encryption and bilinear pairing, and reduces the computational burden of data owners.

In 2018, Kucuk et al. [8] combined blockchain with PSI to develop the BigBing platform, which uses the PSI-based protocol for data distribution. In 2021, Yang et al.

Table 4. Property summary for Quantum-based PSI protocols

Protocols	[5]	[30]	[31]	[32]	[26]	[35]
Quantum resources	$O(\log N)/O(\log)$-qubits entangled states	$O(\log N)/O(\log)$-qubits entangled states	$O(p)$ EPR pairs	$O(N\log N)$single photons	$O(\log N)/O(\log M)$-qubits entangled states	$O(\log N)/O(\log M)$-qubits entangled states
Quantum opeartors	$O(\log N)/O(\log M)$-qubits operators, QFTs and QFT^{-1} s	$O(\log N)/O(\log M)$-qubits operators, QFTs and QFT^{-1} s	$O(p)$ single-particle operators, I σ_x or σ_z	$O(N\log N)$ single-photon operators,I, σ_x or σ_z	$O(\log N)/O(\log M)$-qubits operators, QFTs and QFT^{-1} s	$O(\log N)/O(\log M)$-qubits operators, QFTs and QFT^{-1} s
Quantum measurements	$O(1)$ projective measurements in M-dimensional Hilbert space	$O(m)$ projective measurements in M-dimensional Hilbert space	$O(p)$ Bell-base measurements	$O(N\log N)$ single-photon projective measurements	$O(1)$ projective measurements in M-dimensional Hilbert space	$O(1)$ projective measurements in M-dimensional Hilbert space
Transmitted qubits	$O(\log N)$ qubits	$O(m\log N)$ qubits	$O(p)$qubits	$O(N\log N)$ qubits	$O(\log N)$ qubits	$O(\log N)$ Qubits
Computation complexity	$O(1)$	$O(m)$	$O(p)$	$O(N\log N)$	$O(1)$	$O(1)$
Communication complexity	$O(1)$	$O(m)$	$O(p)$	$O(N\log N)$	$O(1)$	$O(1)$
No additional cardinality assumptions	×	√	√	√	√	√
Support union operations	×	×	√	×	×	√

Table 5. Property summary for post-quantum-based PSI protocols

Protocols	[36]	[27]	[6]
Security assumtions	DLWE	RLWE	NTRU
Multiparty	√	√	√
Adversary Model	SH	SH	SH
Computation complexity	$O(t + q)$	$O(d)$	$O(S)$
Communication complexity	$O(t + q)$	$O(S)$	$O(S)$

Note: t = Server's set cardinality, q = Client's set cardinality, d = Polynomial degree, S = Number of participants

[37] combined the RSA blind signature based PSI protocol with the blockchain, and the PSI was executed by smart contract, which realized the attribute-based employee selection scheme and protected the data of all participants' privacy. This solution also achieves the tracing of the identity of malicious users.

In 2013, Qiu et al. [9] first proposed the identity-based symmetric PSI protocol (IBSPSI). It simplifies the certificate management. In 2020, Ali et al. [11] proposed an attribute-based PSI protocol (AB-PSI) which combined PSI and CP-ABE. In 2021, Shi et al. [38] introduced KP-ABSI which combined KP-ABE with PSI. The attribute-based PSI realizes fine-grained authorization. But in present, none of them can support the verification of computational correctness.

4   Discussion

In this work, we summarized the relevant research on outsourced PSI protocols. They can be applied in video analytics. Then we pointed out the problems requiring to be solved in the future.

Unfortunately, the current researches on PSI in blockchain, fog computing, post-quantum or attribute-based setting are still in its infancy. But with the increasing demand for video big data sharing and the development of quantum computers, PSI protocols for various architectures will become a new research hotspot fin the future.

Acknowledgement. This research was supported by the Higher Education Research Project of Nanjing Institute of Technology (Grants No. 2021ZC13), the Philosophy and Social Science Foundation of the Jiangsu Higher Education Institutions of China "Research on Blockchain-based Intelligent Credit Information System and its Privacy Preservation Mechanism" (Grants No. 2021SJA0448), the Natural Science Foundation of Jiangsu Province (Grants No. BK20210928), Beijing Tianrongxin Education Technology Co., Ltd, and Beijing Key Laboratory of Security and Privacy in Intelligent Transportation.

References

1. Abadi, A., Terzis, S., Dong, C.: VD-PSI: verifiable delegated private set intersection on outsourced private datasets. In: Grossklags, J., Preneel, B. (eds.) FC 2016. LNCS, vol. 9603, pp. 149–168. Springer, Heidelberg (2017). https://doi.org/10.1007/978-3-662-54970-4_9

2. Abadi, A., Terzis, S., Dong, C.: Feather: lightweight multi-party updatable delegated private set intersection (2020)
3. Abadi, A., Terzis, S., Metere, R., Dong, C.: Efficient delegated private set intersection on outsourced private datasets. IEEE Trans. Dependable Secure Comput. **16**(4), 608–624 (2017)
4. Ali, M., Mohajeri, J., Sadeghi, M.R., Liu, X.: Attribute-based fine-grained access control for outscored private set intersection computation. Inf. Sci. **536**, 222–243 (2020)
5. Ateniese, G., De Cristofaro, E., Tsudik, G.: (if) size matters: size-hiding private set intersection. In: Catalano, D., Fazio, N., Gennaro, R., Nicolosi, A. (eds.) PKC 2011. LNCS, vol. 6571, pp. 156–173. Springer, Heidelberg (2011). https://doi.org/10.1007/978-3-642-19379-8_10
6. Boneh, D., Lewi, K., Montgomery, H., Raghunathan, A.: Key homomorphic prfs and their applications. In: Canetti, R., Garay, J.A. (eds.) CRYPTO 2013. LNCS, vol. 8042, pp. 410–428. Springer, Heidelberg (2013). https://doi.org/10.1007/978-3-642-40041-4_23
7. Boyer, M., Brassard, G., Høyer, P., Tapp, A.: Tight bounds on quantum searching. Fortschritte der Physik: Prog. Phys. **46**(4–5), 493–505 (1998)
8. Debnath, S.K., Sakurai, K., Dey, K., Kundu, N.: Secure outsourced private set intersection with linear complexity. In: 2021 IEEE Conference on Dependable and Secure Computing (DSC), pp. 1–8. IEEE (2021)
9. Debnath, S.K., Stănică, P., Choudhury, T., Kundu, N.: Post-quantum protocol for computing set intersection cardinality with linear complexity. IET Inf. Secur. **14**(6), 661–669 (2020)
10. Duong, T., Phan, D.H., Trieu, N.: Catalic: delegated PSI cardinality with applications to contact tracing. In: Moriai, S., Wang, H. (eds.) ASIACRYPT 2020. LNCS, vol. 12493, pp. 870–899. Springer, Cham (2020). https://doi.org/10.1007/978-3-030-64840-4_29
11. Freedman, M.J., Nissim, K., Pinkas, B.: Efficient private matching and set intersection. In: Cachin, C., Camenisch, J.L. (eds.) Advances in Cryptology - EUROCRYPT 2004, pp. 1–19. Springer, Heidelberg (2004). https://doi.org/10.1007/978-3-540-24676-3_1
12. Ghosh, S., Nilges, T.: An algebraic approach to maliciously secure private set intersection. In: Ishai, Y., Rijmen, V. (eds.) EUROCRYPT 2019. LNCS, vol. 11478, pp. 154–185. Springer, Cham (2019). https://doi.org/10.1007/978-3-030-17659-4_6
13. Jiang, T., Yuan, X.: Traceable private set intersection in cloud computing. In: 2019 IEEE Conference on Dependable and Secure Computing (DSC), pp. 1–7. IEEE (2019)
14. Kamara, S., Mohassel, P., Raykova, M., Sadeghian, S.: Scaling private set intersection to billion-element sets. In: Christin, N., Safavi-Naini, R. (eds.) FC 2014. LNCS, vol. 8437, pp. 195–215. Springer, Heidelberg (2014). https://doi.org/10.1007/978-3-662-45472-5_13
15. Kucuk, Y., Patil, N., Shu, Z., Yan, G.: Bigbing: privacy-preserving cloud-based malware classification service. In: 2018 IEEE Symposium on Privacy-Aware Computing (PAC), pp. 43–54. IEEE (2018)
16. Li, Y., Ghosh, D., Gupta, P., Mehrotra, S., Panwar, N., Sharma, S.: Prism: private verifiable set computation over multi-owner outsourced databases. In: Proceedings of the 2021 International Conference on Management of Data, pp. 1116–1128 (2021)
17. Liu, B., Zhang, M., Shi, R.: Quantum secure multi-party private set intersection cardinality. Int. J. Theor. Phys. **59**(7), 1992–2007 (2020)
18. Mouchet, C., Troncoso-Pastoriza, J., Bossuat, J.P., Hubaux, J.P.: Multiparty homomorphic encryption from ring-learning-with-errors. Proc. Priv. Enhanc. Technol. **2021**(4), 291–311 (2021)
19. Nielsen, M.A., Chuang, I.L.: Quantum computation and quantum information. Phys. Today **54**(2), 60 (2001)
20. Oksuz, O., Leontiadis, I., Chen, S., Russell, A., Tang, Q., Wang, B.: Sevdsi: secure, efficient and verifiable data set intersection. Technical report, Cryptology ePrint Archive, Report 2017/215 (2017). http://ia.cr/2017/215

21. Oliaiy, M.M., Ameri, M.H., Mohajeri, J., Aref, M.R.: A verifiable delegated set intersection without pairing. In: 2017 Iranian Conference on Electrical Engineering (ICEE), pp. 2047–2051. IEEE (2017)
22. Qiliang, Y., Mingrui, Z., Yanwei, Z., Yong, Y.: Attribute-based worker selection scheme by using blockchain in decentralized crowdsourcing scenario. Chin. J. Electron. 30(2), 249–257 (2021)
23. Qiu, S., Dai, Z., Zha, D., Zhang, Z., Liu, Y.: PPSI: practical private set intersection over large scale datasets. In: 2019 IEEE SmartWorld, Ubiquitous Intelligence & Computing, Advanced & Trusted Computing, Scalable Computing & Communications, Cloud & Big Data Computing, Internet of People and Smart City Innovation (SmartWorld/SCALCOM/UIC/ATC/CBDCom/IOP/SCI), pp. 1249–1254. IEEE (2019)
24. Qiu, S., Liu, J., Shi, Y.: Identity-based symmetric private set intersection. In: 2013 International Conference on Social Computing, pp. 653–658. IEEE (2013)
25. Ruan, O., Huang, X., Mao, H.: An efficient private set intersection protocol for the cloud computing environments. In: 2020 IEEE 6th International Conference on Big Data Security on Cloud (BigDataSecurity), IEEE International Conference on High Performance and Smart Computing, (HPSC) and IEEE International Conference on Intelligent Data and Security (IDS), pp. 254–259. IEEE (2020)
26. Shi, R.H.: Efficient quantum protocol for private set intersection cardinality. IEEE Access 6, 73102–73109 (2018)
27. Shi, R.: Quantum private computation of cardinality of set intersection and union. Eur. Phys. J. D 72(12), 1–6 (2018)
28. Shi, R., Mu, Y., Zhong, H., Zhang, S., Cui, J.: Quantum private set intersection cardinality and its application to anonymous authentication. Inf. Sci. 370, 147–158 (2016)
29. Shi, R.H., Zhang, M.: A feasible quantum protocol for private set intersection cardinality. IEEE Access 7, 72105–72112 (2019)
30. Shi, Y., Qiu, S.: Delegated key-policy attribute-based set intersection over out-sourced encrypted data sets for CloudIoT. Secur. Commun. Netw. 2021 (2021)
31. Tajima, A., Sato, H., Yamana, H.: Outsourced private set intersection cardinality with fully homomorphic encryption. In: 2018 6th International Conference on Multimedia Computing and Systems (ICMCS), pp. 1–8. IEEE (2018)
32. Wang, Q., Zhou, F.C., Ma, T.M., Xu, Z.F.: Faster fog-aided private set intersectionwith integrity preserving. Front. Inf. Technol. Electron. Eng. 19(12), 1558–1568 (2018)
33. Wang, Q., Zhou, F., Xu, J., Peng, S.: Tag-based verifiable delegated set intersection over outsourced private datasets. IEEE Trans. Cloud Comput. (2020). https://doi.org/10.1109/TCC.2020.2968320
34. Zhang, C., Long, Y., Sun, Z., Li, Q., Huang, Q.: Three-party quantum private computation of cardinalities of set intersection and union based on GHZ states. Sci. Rep. 10(1), 1–10 (2020)
35. Zhang, E., Jin, G.: Cloud outsourcing multiparty private set intersection protocol based on homomorphic encryption and bloom filter. J. Comput. Appl. 38(8), 2256–2260 (2018)
36. Zhang, E., Li, F., Niu, B., Wang, Y.: Server-aided private set intersection based on reputation. Inf. Sci. 387, 180–194 (2017)
37. Zhang, E., Liu, F.H., Lai, Q., Jin, G., Li, Y.: Efficient multi-party private set inter-section against malicious adversaries. In: Proceedings of the 2019 ACM SIGSAC Conference on Cloud Computing Security Workshop, pp. 93–104 (2019)
38. Zheng, Q., Xu, S.: Verifiable delegated set intersection operations on outsourced encrypted data. In: 2015 IEEE International Conference on Cloud Engineering, pp. 175–184. IEEE (2015)

A Review on Traceable Attribute-Based Encryption

Yanfeng Shi[1,2], Wenhui Ni[1], Wanni Xu[1], Wenxiu Yang[1(✉)], Qiong Li[2], and Zekai Xue[1,3]

[1] Nanjing Institute of Technology, Nanjing 211167, China
yangwx2021@yeah.net
[2] Beijing Key Laboratory of Security and Privacy in Intelligent Transportation, Beijing 100044, China
[3] University of Oulu, Oulu, Finland

Abstract. Attribute-Based Encryption (ABE) is a kind of realization of fine-grained access to encrypted data of public key encryption method, but due to a variety of users can share the decryption key, the attribute of traditional encryption mechanism cannot track leaking key malicious users, so in recent years, people study new traceable attribute based encryption schemes, supporting tracing key holders. This article analyzes the strengths and weaknesses of traceable attribute base encryption schemes from various aspects and looks into the future research.

Keywords: Traceable attribute-based encryption · Revocation · Large universe · Multi-authority · Blockchain

1 Introduction

With the rapid and thriving development of science and network technology, computer network carries information transmission and sharing, such as anti-epidemic, educational resources, and credit system. And people are increasingly inseparable from the convenience and fast service brought to us by the network. However, while communicating on the Internet, numerous potential dangers will threaten users' information security, so privacy protection is imminent.

Sahai and Waters [18] first put forward the concept of Attribute-Based Encryption (ABE). Attribute-Based Encryption mechanism takes the attribute as the public key, and combines ciphertext, user's private key and attribute. Through access control policy, the processing overhead caused by access control greatly reduces data sharing fine-grained density. At present, ciphertext - policy attribute-based encryption (CP- ABE) and key-policy attribute-based encryption (KP-ABE) are the two main categories of attribute-based encryption. The user's private key cannot be separated from the attribute set in ciphertext- policy attribute-based encryption (CP-ABE). Also the ciphertext is closely related to the access policies defined by the cipher, so the cipher can flexibly decide which users can access the data. In key-policy attribute-based encryption, user's

© Springer Nature Singapore Pte Ltd. 2022
Y. Tian et al. (Eds.): ICBDS 2021, CCIS 1563, pp. 137–148, 2022.
https://doi.org/10.1007/978-981-19-0852-1_11

private key is relevant to the access policy that determines user's decryption capabilities, while ciphertext is related to the attribute.

For CP-ABE, the decryption key is relevant to the attribute set, the decryption key is defined on an attribute provided by multi-user. But this exposes the problem of not being able to track the occupant of the initial key. Since users with the same attribute set are likely to have the decryption permission, malicious users will share and disclose the decryption permission to a third party for economic benefit without being caught. Therefore, traceability attribute base encryption mechanism has been proposed in recent years. This mechanism was first proposed by Liu et al. [12] in 2012, which solved the problem that the owner of leaked key could not be traced for the first time. Its main research direction will be from white box, black box and blockchain in three aspects:

(1) White Box: In the study of white box, the large universe attribute in ABE has the flexibility to support the number of attributes [6, 15]; Besides traceable attributes, Wang et al. [8, 19] also conducted a comprehensive study on revocable attributes in t-ABE mechanism. Multiple permission centers [7, 29] also effectively solve the problem of security centers; Robert et al. [26] proposed dual encryption, which simultaneously implements data source tracing (security source) and user tracing (traitor tracing), etc.
(2) Black Box: Fu et al. [2] presented a new safe-proof traceable CP-ABE programme for handling black-box decoders.
(3) Blockchain: For purpose of protecting integrality and non-repudiation of the data, Wu et al. [21] adopts blockchain technology. Guo et al. [3] proposed blockchain technology to achieve the encrypted private data can be shared in the cloud in fine-grained form.

Also, for KP-ABE and Dual-ABE, the traceability is also researched in recent years.

2 Preliminaries

2.1 Traceable ABE

T-ABE is also separated into key-policy and ciphertext-policy. This scheme consists of five algorithm groups: Setup, Encrypt, KeyGen, Decrypt, Trace.

(1) Setup: The system creator performs Setup. The algorithm input security factor and all attributes, output master key and common parameters.
(2) Encrypt: Encryptor runs encrypt. The algorithm inputs public parameters, access structures, messages, encryption attributes, and outputs ciphertext.
(3) KenGen: Institutions execute KenGen. Algorithm input public parameter, master key, user attribute set, user ID, output private key.
(4) Decrypt: The user performs Decrypt. Algorithm input public parameters ciphertext, user's private key. Once the user's attribute information achieves the requirements, the output message M is displayed. Otherwise decryption fails, output orthogonal complement.
(5) Trace: Input the key to verify whether the key is normal. If the verification is successful, the ID of the user to which the key belongs can be known for tracking.

2.2 White Box and Black Box

T-ABE can be divided into white box T-ABE and black box T-ABE.

The object of white box tracking is the leaked key, and the malicious user is tracked according to the known key. The object of black box tracking is to decrypt the black box.

The black box tracking algorithm regards the decryption device as a decryption Oracle (providing ciphertext to the device and obtaining the plaintext from the device), which can track at least one malicious user involved in manufacturing the decryption device. If a black box device appears outside the system, the black box tracking algorithm can still find the original key owner who created and decrypted the black box when it promises to decrypt some policy related ciphertexts. The premise of white box tracking is that the decryption key and decryption algorithm are public, and the decryption key meets the specific lattice.

The scheme that can realize black box traceability also supports white box tracking. On the contrary, the scheme that supports white box tracking may not support black box tracking. The black box traceable scheme is more universal and has higher security.

2.3 Blockchain

Blockchain refers to a public ledger that is distributed and shareable, trusted through the consensus mechanism and can be checked by each participant. However, no centralized single user can control it. It can only be revised according to strict rules and open protocols. There are three properties as follows:

(1) Decentralization. In other words, there is no intermediary for each transaction recorded through the network. All transactions are direct transactions of the trader and are recorded in the client program of the trader's mobile phone or computer according to the transaction time. It can be seen from this that blockchain can bypass intermediaries to conduct transactions, so as to avoid the risk of intermediary transactions.

(2) Not tamperable and traceable. Each network transaction will have its occurrence time, so as to form a data block, which is encrypted by cryptographic technology. Blockchain is to linearly connect each data block according to the sequence of time. Due to the irreversibility and irreversibility of time, the blockchain has the characteristics of being tamperable. That is, all transactions of everyone are recorded. If there is fraud in a transaction link, we can accurately identify it through the block chain to realize the traceability of the transaction, so as to ensure the authenticity and reliability of the transaction.

(3) Information sharing and transparency. This mainly means that everyone in the network can see all transaction records and share the data ledger. Therefore, when there is a problem with the data of a block, it will not lead to the destruction of all transaction records and data assets. Therefore, based on these characteristics of blockchain, a certain trust mechanism can be established among network traders, which can simplify the transaction process and approval procedures and form a convenient, efficient and transparent working mechanism.

3   T-ABE Schemes

3.1   White Box CP-TABE

Liu et al. [12] firstly introduced a T-CP-ABE scheme in 2013, which realize the strategy represented by all monotonic access structure. This scheme adds traceability performance to the existing CP-ABE without compromising other performance. Later, more schemes for white box CP-TABE about large universe, revocation, multi-authorities, and so on.

Large Universe
In 2017, Liu et al. [11], put forward a system with both traceability and large universe. In addition to these two functional features, the proposed system solves the problem of user dynamic cancellation and is selectively proven safe in the standard model.

Ning et al. [15] put forward two functional white box CP-ABE systems with tracking properties on the basis of large universe in 2015. Both proposed schemes have two advantages: (1) There is no polynomial limit on the number of attributes; (2) It can track spiteful users who reveal decryption keys. Furthermore, other significant preponderance of the second scheme is the constant storage expenses of traitor tracking, making it available for the business application.

In 2020, G. Kumar et al. [6] proposed a white box traceable CP-ABE scheme with large universe properties. Property field value for technology is exponentially large and polynomial unbounded. What's more, the technology will track the identity of subscribers engaged in the spiteful activity. And any type of monotone tree access strategy can be shown as LSSS.

The main properties for schemes above can be shown as in Table 1.

Table 1. Property summary for white box T-ABE schemes over large universe

	[11]	[15]	[6]
Large universe	✓	✓	✓
Traceability	✓	✓	✓
Revocation	✓	×	×
Fine-grained access control	✓	✓	✓

Revocation
Wang et al. [19] realize a traceable CP-ABE system with user attribute revocation being realized and stored in the cloud in 2018, which has four advantages compared with other schemes. First, it has the ability to track down malicious users who leak critical information about the scheme. Besides, it has the abilities to realize attribute-level revocation to spiteful users. Third, it permits the updating of keys and ciphertext, thus achieving the effect of resisting user collusion attacks. Fourth, the computing burden can be reduced.

Furthermore, the project has been proved to be secure when it is hit under the access policy.

In 2018, Lian et al. [8] constructed a comprehensive traceability and revocable storage AUE (TRS - ABE) scheme to achieve access control under the cloud storage, which has characteristics of traceability and revocability as well as complete security. In addition, a recent cryptographic primitive called self-updating encryption (SUE) is introduced to implement the time updating mechanism. Finally, the scheme is completely safe under the hypothesis in the criterion model.

In 2019, Liu et al. [14] put forward a white box CP-ABE project that can be tracked and can be directly revoked by users. The value of leaf is used to track malicious users, add them to the revocation. The scheme is selectively safe under the hypothesis in the criterion model.

In 2020, Han et al. [4] realize a CP-ABE project to achieve revocation, white-box tracing, hidden policy application to solve the problem that plaintext access policy would leak sensitive information. The ciphertext is divided into different directions: one is associated with access policy of attribute values encryption. Another one is related to revocation message, which is created by binary trees relevant to subscriber. In the decryption key part, the leaf node value of the binary tree is used to track malicious users. The proposed scheme proved to be IND-CPA safe, efficient and promising.

In 2020, Zhang et al. [28] proposed a traceable MA-CP-ABE system that supports rapid access and accountability for spiteful users, and the scheme proved to be adaptive and safe. Moreover, Zhang et al. designed a MA-CP-ABE system with traceable and retractable based on proposed scheme, which can be used for efficient and secure cloud storage. In addition, when a spiteful user discloses own decryption key, the implemented project can check his identity and cancel his decryption authority.

Table 2. Property summary for revocable white box T-ABE schemes

	[14]	[4]	[29]	[11]	[19]	[7]	[8]	[20]	[16]	[5]
User revocation	√	√	√	√	√	√	√	√	√	√
Associated user revocation	×	×	×	×	×	×	×	√	×	×
Traceability	√	√	√	√	√	√	√	√	√	√
Ciphertext updating	√	√	√	×	×	√	√	×	×	√
Key updating	×	√	×	×	×	√	√	×	×	×

In 2020, Wang et al. [20] proposed a CP-ABE system to support association withdrawal and traceable function. The project adopts the identity directory technology to implement associated user or single-user revocation. To ensure the forward security of the revocation, the scheme uses ciphertext re-encryption technology. What's more there is no need to update the private key. Moreover, the scheme has the abilities to accurately track user identity by decrypting private key, also effectively address the trouble of malicious user key abusing. The solution is proven to be secure and trackable under the criterion model, effectively controlling computing and storage costs without compromising the functional advantages of the solution. It is applicable to actual scenarios such as tracing audit and user revocation.

In the cloud computing environment, cloud users could transfer decryption rights to unaccredited users for profit. To solve the problem of unrevocation when malicious users are caught, in 2021, Bouchaala et al. [1] proposed a traceable, accountable, revocable and keyless escrow CPABE solution (Track-CP ABE), which realize white box track and can be revocable directly. This solution mainly partitions the raw data after issuing to the cloud server. It affects a single slice in the case of user undo. At the same time, the scheme was formally proved to be secure using the Scyther tool.

The main properties for revocable white box TABE schemes above can be shown as in Table 2.

Multi-authority

In 2015, Jun et al. [29] proposed a white box trackable and revocable ABE on multiple permission attributes named TR-MABE, which can realize privacy protection without pulling-in additional special signatures. In electronic health systems, the scheme can effectively arrest other doctors from stealing the dignity of the patient and can be traced back to the doctor who leaked the key. Finally, the application of TR-MABE in electronic medical cloud computing system is effective and practical.

In the project delivered by dong Yang et al. [25] in 2017, the third party could not only directly track the dignity of the private key processor based on the leaked private key, but also publicly prove the validity of the user's identity. In addition, different permission centers together produce user private keys, which efficiently address the safety problems in the permission center. Besides, the solution is also applicable to cloud computing environments.

In 2017, Li et al. [7], to protect the confidentiality of shared data from untrusted third party, solve the single point of failure and solve the performance bottleneck of the authorization center and the key abuse of malicious users who reveal the private keys, an encryption scheme based on multiple permission attributes is proposed to support traceability and fine-grained revocation mechanism in social networks. Compared with traditional ABE, this scheme can achieve distributed access control, and also can realize complete fine-grained undo mechanism.

Table 3. Property summary for multi-authority white box T-ABE schemes

	[29]	[9]	[10]	[25]	[7]
Multi-authority	✓	✓	✓	✓	✓
Traceability	✓	✓	✓	✓	✓
Revocation	✓	×	×	×	✓
Outsourcing	×	×	✓	×	×
Policy update	×	✓	×	×	×

Generally, CP-ABE schemes have only one trusted authority. Different users may leak private keys so that they can gain additional benefits. Besides data owners need to change the access policies flexibly. In 2021, Ling et al. [9] constructed a multi-authority CP-ABE system. The solution achieve different permissions, traceability, and large property fields. It is proved that the design project is traceable security based on security model.

In 2021, Liu et al. [10] put forward a multi-authority ABE mechanism with traceability to prevent abuse of decryption authority. By outsourcing most of the decryption work to cloud servers, the solution significantly reduces the overhead of the equipment. In addition, the scheme implemented completely hidden strategy to guard the privacy of access strategy.

The main properties for multi-authority white box TABE schemes above can be shown as in Table 3.

Others

Due to the traceability CP-ABE scheme merely focuses on the primary user traceability, it is not fit for the two tier architecture in multi-domain environment. Hence, Yan et al. [23] proposed a white box traceability CP-ABE system capable of two-layer tracing in a multi-domain environment in 2019. At the domain level, the author mainly explains short signature technology is introduced to arrest attackers from counterfeiting trace parameters and achieving domain traceability. At the user level, linkable ring signature technology is used to provide users with a tracing method. The delivered project supports all monotonic access structure with complete security and low cost.

In 2020, Yan et al. [22] introduced a traceability ABE mechanism to prevent key delegation abuse in view of the fact that the traceability of ABE schemes based on traceability attributes is not enough to completely solve the key abuse problem. Attribute corresponding to the key components, the combination of all these components to complete the decryption, only a part of them cannot be decrypted, so as to obtain the real anti-key delegation abuse ability. Prevent the tracking parameters embedded in the user's private key from being forged, thereby achieving traceability to the user who leaked the user private key. It also supports key delegation abuse and user tracing, which enhances the security of the proposed scheme.

On behalf of solving the problem that most available ABE system with trait tracking seldom considers the importance of user attributes. In 2020, Yan et al. [24] designed a traceable weighted ABE project. The project uses a user private key composed of user's identity information to track down traitors. Besides, introducing the idea of weighted attribute, through property set segmentation algorithm converts property set to a weighted attribute set segmentation. By adopting a linear secret sharing scheme, the scheme is built to provide a fine-grained and flexible access control facility. This scheme can achieve the security against selected plaintext attack.

In 2019, Yu et al. [27] proposed an attribute-based encryption scheme based on an accountable ciphertext policy. This scheme has two institutions to issue the key for the user, but they can't in the absence of conspiring to decrypt any ciphertext. The Shared secret can be effectively track, if be to track the identity of the claim that he is innocent, the comptroller could expose audit who will be in charge of the shared secret.

3.2　White Box KP-TABE

In 2018, Qi et al. [16] delivered a KP-ABE system to realize revocability and traceability. This scheme can cancel subscriber attributes without renewing both system public key and user's private key, also the updating cost is low. Furthermore, the user dignity can be tracked on the basis of the decryption key to availably prevent anonymous user's key leakage. The system is based on the linear secret sharing scheme (LSSS). Compared with existing KP-ABE schemes, this scheme has obvious advantages, such as short public key length, low computational cost, and user identity traceability based on revocable attributes.

In attribute-based encryption, key distribution, data encryption and data decryption have high computational costs. In 2019, Gao et al. [5] put forward an ABE system that realize key attribute revocation and outsources key distribution and data decryption to cloud servers. The scheme uses hash function to verify the accuracy of outsourced calculation. In addition, the solution uses online/offline encryption to effectively protect user data privacy, reduce user computing workload, and improve the operation efficiency of the solution. And use tree access policies to provide more fine-grained access control. The re-encryption method implements fine-grained property revocation.

The main properties for white box KP-TABE schemes above can be shown as in Table 4.

Table 4. Property summary for white box KP-TABE schemes

	[16]	[5]
Policy model	KP	KP
Revocation	✓	✓
Verifiability	✓	×

3.3　White Box Dual-TABE

In 2021, Robert et al. [26] proposed an encryption and subset keyword search system (DT-DABE-SKS, short for DT) based on dual-traceable distributed attributes to realize both data source tracking (secure source), user tracking. A new concept of updated and transportable information lock encryption (UT-MLE) for dynamically encrypting file updates at block level is also introduced. In addition, it allows owners to transfer document proprietary to other system clients in a validated way through efficient computation.

3.4　Black Box TABE

CP-ABE

Due to the authorization authority can calculate and publish the private key of any user. To alleviate this problem, Fu et al. [2] realized the addition (Traceable-CP-ABE) scheme based on black-box traceable ciphertext policy attributes in 2015. A structure to implement the traceable CP-ABE system in the black box model is provided.

Qiao et al. [17] studied a new black-box traceable CP-ABE system that can track and expose malicious users who build decrypted black boxes in 2018. Owing to its relatively high scalability and productiveness, the scheme may be suitable for fog systems. The official define of mandatory traceability is given with a safety certificate, and the project is safe and mandatory traceability.

KP-ABE

In 2015, Liu et al. [13] studied the concept of traceability of key-policy ABE, and formalized the KP-ABE that supports full anti-collusion black box traceability. When constructing a decryption device, the attacker is permitted to access any quantity of keys he chooses, and provided such a decryption equipment. Black box tracking algorithm can find out decryption keys have been used to construct the equipment of one of the malicious users. The proposal proposes a structure that supports full anti-collusion black box traceability and high expressiveness (that is, any monotonic access structure). Besides, the structure is completely safe in standard model.

Table 5. Property summary for black box T-ABE schemes

	[2]	[17]	[13]
Policy model	CP	CP	KP
Black-box	✓	✓	✓

The main properties for black box TABE schemes above can be shown as in Table 5.

3.5 Blockchain-Based TABE

Blockchain technology could ensure data integrality and non-repudiation. In 2019, Wu et al. [21] put forward traceable ABE system with high efficiency and privacy protection. The scheme uses blockchain technology to ensure data integrality and non-repudiation, and uses pre-encryption technology to generate ciphertext quickly. When a key is used indiscriminately, you can query the origin of the abused key. And the scheme is safe and effective.

The decentralized and tamper-proof nature of blockchain makes it an emerging technology that protects the integrity of significant information stored on it. In 2021, Guo et al. [3] proposed an efficient traceable ABE (TABE-DAC) system about dynamic access control on account of blockchain. This TABE-DAC system realizes accountability traceability for spiteful users who reveal private keys. Furthermore this solution implements dynamic access control. And the scheme has been proved safe and reliable.

The main properties for blockchain-based T-ABE schemes above can be shown as in Table 6.

Table 6. Property summary for blockchain-based T-ABE schemes

	[3]	[21]
Blockchain	✓	✓
Traceability	✓	✓
Dynamic access control	✓	×
Pre-encryption technology	×	✓

4 Conclusions

This paper summarizes the domestic and foreign studies on T-ABE, and points out the shortcomings of this mechanism and prospects for future research.

It should be noted that there are few researches on KP - ABE in white box and related technologies in black box at present. At present, there are a lot of researches on support revocation and multi - authorization institutions, while the researches on fog calculation, key delegation abuse and weighting are still in their infancy. Much work remains to be done in the future, and we will continue to do so.

Acknowledgement. This research was funded by the Philosophy and Social Science Foundation of the Jiangsu Higher Education Institutes of China "Research on Blockchain-based Intelligent Credit Information System and its Privacy Preservation Mechanism" (Grants No. 2021SJA0448), the Natural Science Foundation of Jiangsu Province (Grants No. BK20210928), the Higher Education Research Project of Nanjing Institute of Technology (Grants No. 2021ZC13), Beijing Tianrongxin Education Technology Co., Ltd, and Beijing Key Laboratory of Security and Privacy in Intelligent Transportation.

References

1. Bouchaala, M., Ghazel, C., Saidane, L.A.: Trak-cpabe: a novel traceable, revocable and accountable ciphertext-policy attribute-based encryption scheme in cloud computing. J. Inf. Secur. Appl. **61**, 102914 (2021)
2. Fu, X., Nie, X., Li, F.: Black box traceable ciphertext policy attribute-based encryption scheme. Information **6**(3), 481–493 (2015)
3. Guo, L., Yang, X., Yau, W.C.: TABE-DAC: Efficient traceable attribute-based encryption scheme with dynamic access control based on blockchain. IEEE Access **9**, 8479–8490 (2021)
4. Han, D., Pan, N., Li, K.C.: A traceable and revocable ciphertext-policy attribute based encryption scheme based on privacy protection. IEEE Trans. Dependable Secure Comput. **19**(1), 316–327 (2022). https://doi.org/10.1109/TDSC.2020.2977646
5. Jiaxin, G., Jiameng, S., Jing, Q.: Traceable outsourcing attribute-based encryption with attribute revocation. J. Comput. Res. Dev. **56**(10), 2160 (2019)
6. Kumar, G.S.: Efficient data access control for cloud computing with large universe and traceable attribute-based encryption. Int. J. Fuzzy Syst. Appl. (IJFSA) **9**(4), 61–81 (2020)
7. Li, Y., Qi, F., Tang, Z.: Traceable and complete fine-grained revocable multi-authority attribute-based encryption scheme in social network. In: Wang, G., Atiquzzaman, M., Yan, Z., Choo, K.-K. (eds.) SpaCCS 2017. LNCS, vol. 10656, pp. 87–92. Springer, Cham (2017). https://doi.org/10.1007/978-3-319-72389-1_8

8. Lian, H., Wang, G., Wang, Q.: Fully secure traceable and revocable-storage attribute-based encryption with short update keys via subset difference method. In: 2018 Third International Conference on Security of Smart Cities, Industrial Control System and Communications (SSIC), pp. 1–8. IEEE (2018)
9. Ling, J., Chen, J., Chen, J., Gan, W.: Multiauthority attribute-based encryption with traceable and dynamic policy updating. Secur. Commun. Netw. **2021** (2021)
10. Liu, S., Yu, J., Hu, C., Li, M.: Traceable multiauthority attribute-based encryption with outsourced decryption and hidden policy for CIoT. Wirel. Commun. Mob. Comput. **2021** (2021)
11. Liu, Z., Wang, X., Cui, L., Jiang, Z.L., Zhang, C.: White-box traceable dynamic attribute based encryption. In: 2017 International Conference on Security, Pattern Analysis, and Cybernetics (SPAC), pp. 526–530. IEEE (2017)
12. Liu, Z., Cao, Z., Wong, D.S.: White-box traceable ciphertext-policy attribute-based encryption supporting any monotone access structures. IEEE Trans. Inf. Forensics Secur. **8**(1), 76–88 (2012)
13. Liu, Z., Cao, Z., Wong, D.S.: Fully collusion-resistant traceable key-policy attribute-based encryption with sub-linear size ciphertexts. In: Lin, D., Yung, M., Zhou, J. (eds.) Inscrypt 2014. LNCS, vol. 8957, pp. 403–423. Springer, Cham (2015). https://doi.org/10.1007/978-3-319-16745-9_22
14. Liu, Z., Duan, S., Zhou, P., Wang, B.: Traceable-then-revocable ciphertext-policy attribute-based encryption scheme. Futur. Gener. Comput. Syst. **93**, 903–913 (2019)
15. Ning, J., Dong, X., Cao, Z., Wei, L., Lin, X.: White-box traceable ciphertext-policy attribute-based encryption supporting flexible attributes. IEEE Trans. Inf. Forensics Secur. **10**(6), 1274–1288 (2015)
16. Qi, F., Li, Y., Tang, Z.: Revocable and traceable key-policy attribute-based encryption scheme. J. Commun. **39**(11), 63–69 (2018)
17. Qiao, H., Ren, J., Wang, Z., Ba, H., Zhou, H.: Compulsory traceable ciphertextpolicy attribute-based encryption against privilege abuse in fog computing. Futur. Gener. Comput. Syst. **88**, 107–116 (2018)
18. Sahai, A., Waters, B.: Fuzzy identity-based encryption. In: Cramer, R. (ed.) EUROCRYPT 2005. LNCS, vol. 3494, pp. 457–473. Springer, Heidelberg (2005). https://doi.org/10.1007/11426639_27
19. Wang, S., Guo, K., Zhang, Y.: Traceable ciphertext-policy attribute-based encryption scheme with attribute level user revocation for cloud storage. PLoS ONE **13**(9), e0203225 (2018)
20. Wang, X., Chi, Y., Zhang, Y.: Traceable ciphertext policy attribute-based encryption scheme with user revocation for cloud storage. In: 2020 International Conference on Computer Engineering and Application (ICCEA), pp. 91–95. IEEE (2020)
21. Wu, A., Zhang, Y., Zheng, X., Guo, R., Zhao, Q., Zheng, D.: Efficient and privacypreserving traceable attribute-based encryption in blockchain. Ann. Telecommun. **74**(7), 401–411 (2019)
22. Xixi, Y., Xu, H., Tao, L., Qing, Y., Jinxia, Y., Yongli, T.: Traceable attribute-based encryption scheme with key-delegation abuse resistance. J. Commun. **41**(4), 150 (2020)
23. Yan, X., He, X., Yu, J., Tang, Y.: White-box traceable ciphertext-policy attributebased encryption in multi-domain environment. IEEE Access **7**, 128298–128312 (2019)
24. Yan, X., Yuan, X., Zhang, Q., Tang, Y.: Traceable and weighted attribute-based encryption scheme in the cloud environment. IEEE Access **8**, 38285–38295 (2020)
25. Yang, X., Yang, P., An, F., Zhou, Q., Yang, M.: Traceable multi-authority attribute-based encryption scheme for cloud computing. In: 2017 14th International Computer Conference on Wavelet Active Media Technology and Information Processing (ICCWAMTIP), pp. 263–267. IEEE (2017)
26. Yang, Y., et al.: Dual traceable distributed attribute-based searchable encryption and ownership transfer. IEEE Trans. Cloud Comput. (2021)

27. Yu, G., Wang, Y., Cao, Z., Lin, J., Wang, X.: Traceable and undeniable ciphertextpolicy attribute-based encryption for cloud storage service. Int. J. Distrib. Sens. Netw. **15**(4), 1550147719841276 (2019)
28. Zhang, K., Li, Y., Song, Y., Lu, L., Zhang, T., Jiang, Q.: A traceable and revocable multi-authority attribute-based encryption scheme with fast access. Secur. Commun. Netw. **2020** (2020)
29. Zhou, J., Cao, Z., Dong, X., Lin, X.: TR-MABE: White-box traceable and revocable multi-authority attribute-based encryption and its applications to multi-level privacy-preserving e-healthcare cloud computing systems. In: 2015 IEEE Conference on Computer Communications (INFOCOM), pp. 2398–2406. IEEE (2015)

Trustworthy Collaborative Trajectory Privacy Scheme for Continuous LBS

Miada Murad[1]([✉]), Sarah Altwaijri[2], Johara Khabti[1], Ibtehal Baazeem[3], and Yuan Tian[4]

[1] King Saud University, Riyadh, Saudi Arabia
438204373@student.ksu.edu.sa, jkhabti@ksu.edu.sa
[2] Saudi Electronic University, Riyadh, Saudi Arabia
saltuwayjiri@seu.edu.sa
[3] King Abdulaziz City for Science and Technology, Riyadh, Saudi Arabia
ibaazeem@kacst.edu.sa
[4] Nanjing Institute of Technology University, Nanjing, China
ytian@njit.edu.cn

Abstract. With the high demand of using location-based services (LBSs) in our daily lives, the privacy protection of users' trajectories has become a significant concern. When users utilize LBSs, their location and trajectory information may expose their identities in continuous LBSs. Using the spatial and temporal correspondences on users' trajectories, adversaries can easily gather their private information. Using collaboration between users instead of location service providers (LSPs) reduces the chance of revealing private information to adversaries. However, there is an assumption of a trusting relationship between peers. In this paper, we propose the trustworthy collaborative query-trajectory privacy-preserving (TCQTPP) scheme, which anonymizes users' trajectories and resolves the untrustworthy relationship between users based on peer-to-region LBSs. Moreover, the TCQTPP scheme provides query content preservation based on a fake query concept in which we conceal the user's actual query among a set of queries. The results of several experiments with different conditions confirm that our proposed scheme can protect users' trajectory privacy successfully in a trustworthy and efficient manner.

Keywords: Continuous location-based services · Anonymity · Trajectory privacy protection · Fake queries · k-anonymization

1 Introduction

With the development of a wide variety of location detection technologies, such as GPS and RFID, location-based services (LBSs) provide ubiquitous services for mobile users. Examples of LBSs include transportation, emergency control, and local business searching. Since an LBS is provided for users based on their exact location information, a major threat regarding the user's location privacy has been raised [1, 2]. In general,

© Springer Nature Singapore Pte Ltd. 2022
Y. Tian et al. (Eds.): ICBDS 2021, CCIS 1563, pp. 149–170, 2022.
https://doi.org/10.1007/978-981-19-0852-1_12

spatial cloaking has been used to preserve users' privacy while they use an LBS; it blurs the exact user location into a cloaking area.

Three privacy metrics are used for LBSs: k-anonymity, the expected distance error, and differential privacy. To protect location privacy, k-anonymity is widely used [1] which "expands the precise position of the querier to an anonymity area including the other K-1 users, and the constructed area is used by the user to initiate the LBS request" [3]. The expected distance error measures the distance between the real location and the obfuscated location and improves privacy by increasing the distance between them to ensure that two locations. Each belongs to a different logical area. Finally, differential privacy requires the aggregate information of multiple users instead of a single user. It can be used with k-anonymity, where k is the number of locations that represent the information of multiple users [4].

In an LBS, users can query the location service provider (LSP) and obtain the search result in two ways: snapshot and continuous. In a snapshot query, the user requests a single point of interest (POI). By contrast, a continuous query comprises several requests along the user trajectory. Despite the beneficial services that an LBS provides, many problems related to user privacy and anonymity have emerged due to the possible subsequent malicious usage and analysis caused by the full control of users' locations [5].

Although abundant research has targeted these concerns in snapshot and continuous queries, the latter seems to require substantially more attention. In this request type, the relevance between the spatial and temporal information of the user's path can be used intuitively through the observation of a few sequential queries to identify a user's private data, such as a user identifier, home address, and recently visited locations [6, 7]. Accordingly, ensuring the protection of trajectory-based queries has become a major concern, with the main aim of preventing potential malicious usage of these continuous queries by eliminating any possible correlations and blurring the real paths of service users [7].

Figure 1 depicts the chance of schemes being subject to correlation attacks through the application of k-anonymity for privacy protection of user trajectory [5, 8]. The red circles represent a series of query points of the requester that are shown on his or her trajectory. The requester anonymizes the locations into k-anonymizing spatial regions. The attacker can then gather and analyze the accepted queries to identify the query issuer by learning the spatial and temporal correlations of the collected queries. By determining the time sequence of the collected queries, the attacker found one person present in all cloaking regions; thus he or she can reform the requester's trajectory.

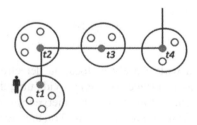

Fig. 1. Location correlation attack

One of the currently used approaches to preserving privacy is using a trusted third party (TTP) to act as an anonymizer. The drawback of this architecture is that a trusted anonymous server saves the location information of all users, which becomes an attractive target for attackers and a single point of failure [6]. Another approach used in LBS schemes is one that is decentralized or user-centric and depends on users to protect their privacy themselves instead of using a TTP. Different collaborative-based schemes have been proposed based on this concept [1, 9].

Based on the collaborative approach used in [6, 10], we propose a privacy-preserving collaborative scheme for continuous LBSs. However, instead of the user contacting one peer at a time, we allow the user to simultaneously contact multiple users arranged in multiple groups. These groups are created using a k-means clustering algorithm, which is an unsupervised learning algorithm used for dividing data iteratively into a number of disjointed k clusters defined by centroids. These centroids should be placed meticulously because different locations yield different results. The number of clusters (k) is an input parameter that is fixed a priori to partition the data set in order to minimize the total deviation of the data points from the cluster centers. Either the Euclidean (default) or Manhattan distance can be used in a k-means clustering algorithm [11].

Since k-means algorithms can form groups based on the Euclidean distance, which is the "ordinary" distance between two objects, k-means was used in this study to organize users into a number of distinct clusters so that each user is located precisely to one of the k clusters. These clusters represent regions in our case, with the set of locations in each region being close to each other.

Figure 2 illustrates how the proposed scheme protects the requester trajectory from hacker tracking by sending real and fake queries to different regions according to each hop along his or her way. In the following example, we set the hop distance threshold h, which is the distance between different users within the same region, to 2. At T1, the user receives a response to his or her request in one of the regions in Hop 2, and subsequently moves to this region. Subsequently, at T2, the user sends another query to all regions in the first hop; after receiving no answer, the user sends the query again to regions in Hop 2. When the user receives no reply to his or her request, the user prompts the LSP with the real and fake queries to move to the third location point. At T3, the user searches for the most recent destination found in the first hop with no need to contact the second hop. Finally, the user reaches the final destination at T4. Applying this peer-to-region sequence of steps protects the user's trajectory privacy.

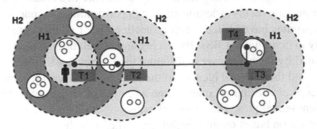

Fig. 2. The proposed scheme

We present the Trustworthy Collaborative Query Trajectory Privacy-Preserving (TCQTPP) scheme for enhancing location privacy in continuous LBSs. The major contributions of this scheme are summarized as follows:

1. We rely on users' collaboration to decentralize the method rather than using a TTP.
2. In our scheme, each user combines a number of fake queries with the real request. This helps to decrease the frequency of accessing the LSP and reduces the risk of a privacy leak.
3. We propose enhancing privacy through a peer-to-region fake query (PRFQ) algorithm that considers no trust to be among neighbors. Thus, many fake queries are included in each user's request to hide the main demand.
4. We intent to have a region for each group of users to reduce the expected requested area.
5. A cache region is applied to protect the collaborators' identities. The cache region combines all users' location information obtained from their previous requests, regardless of whether it is valuable.

The remainder of this paper is organized as follows: Section 2 reviews relevant studies that have shown the current state of privacy protection in continuous LBSs. Section 3 illustrates, in detail, the structure and an overview of the proposed system. In Sect. 4, we describe the scheme and adapted research methodology in detail. Finally, Sect. 5 presents an evaluation and discussion of the obtained results, and Sect. 6 summarizes the main outcomes of the paper and recommends future work.

2   Related Works

Because of the development of modern smart devices and positioning technologies, LBSs have become ubiquitous. In an LBS, the user must submit a query that includes the user's exact location and identity to the LSP; therefore, an adversary can expose the user's privacy. Consequently, considerable research has been conducted to reduce the potential threats while benefiting from an LBS, mainly involving identity and location privacy. The most widely used location privacy protection approach is k-anonymity, in which a TTP is responsible for maintaining all users' real locations and subsequently converts a service user's location to a cloaked region of a specified k number of users [5, 7]. However, although protecting the identity of the user in a cloaked region by using k-anonymity protection seems to demonstrate high performance in snapshot queries, and although many studies have utilized such protection [12, 13], this approach cannot be used adequately in continuous LBSs. By tracing and correlating a sequence of consecutive queries issued by the same user in different time series, an LSP can easily identify the query issuer and thus the real identity of the user [5, 7]. Several studies have targeted this major concern of continuous queries and attempted to hide users' real trajectories by using different techniques. The following subsections categorize selected studies of trajectory preservation based on their architecture (i.e., whether a TTP is used).

2.1 Trajectory Location-Based Service with a Trusted Server

Hwang, Hsueh, and Chung [5] addressed trajectory privacy protection by using a novel time-obfuscated algorithm. In this approach, a trusted anonymity server ensures secure communication between users by using a combination of r-anonymity, k-anonymity, and s-segment algorithms to confuse the LSP about the location and time. Ultimately, while the user is following the predefined path, the TTP uses a time obfuscation technique by sending random fake queries to the LSP, which disrupts the time sequence of the query and thus confuses the LSP.

Similarly, Ye et al. [7] applied the concept of fake queries to confuse the LSP in trajectory-based services, thereby preventing any potential violation of identity privacy. In this approach, the main concern of the TTP is to interrupt the possible relevance between query topics and the user's real identity and to dismiss the integrality of trajectories through the injection of several fake queries, thereby cloaking the real requests of the user in a continuous time series. Thus, instead of sending one user's query, his or her query is merged with the neighbors' requests and then sent as a single query.

Although the models proposed in previous research have successfully preserved privacy for continuous LBSs and protected user trajectory, the trusted anonymity server in centralized LBSs increases the vulnerability since it is more subject to attackers and might face a single point of failure [14]. Therefore, a decentralized or user-collaborative was introduced for improving LBS privacy, which replaces a TTP with the users themselves to protect their location privacy. Many relevant studies have used peer-to-peer (P2P) communication to eliminate the need for requesting services from the LSP by using particular techniques. Some of these techniques are presented in the following subsection.

2.2 Anonymity Using a Decentralized Approach (User Collaboration)

A previous study [9] used MobiCrowd, a user-centric scheme that stores each user's previously requested locations from the LBS server in a buffer that can be passed to collaborative neighbors. The results showed that MobiCrowd improved the location privacy for users by hiding an elevated fraction of queries. However, because of the used caching technique, this approach causes privacy concerns with the cold start and initial LBS requests. According to this insufficiency, in [15], the authors merged the characteristics of the TTP with user collaboration, leading to a semi-TTP. Numerous features were implemented to increase the efficiency of the result, such as order-preserving symmetric encryption, a catch mechanism, and a uniform grid.

A P2P spatial cloaking algorithm was proposed by Chow [16]. That study focused on generating a spatial cloaked region to cover groups of collaborated peers. The main concept of a P2P mechanism is that users forward their query to the service provider on behalf of specified k peers in the group. Therefore, the user cannot be distinguished from the k peers. In the same manner, another study [1] proposed a P2P spatial cloaking algorithm in which each mobile user can gather peer location information by using multi-hop routing. A historical location scheme was used to find k-1 peers and create a cloaked area that allowed the user to utilize the peer-cached location information.

Wang, Yang, and Zhang [10] applied the concept of creating a profile for each user according to their visited location area. Users obtain the location recommendation from their neighbors by taking advantage of the stored profile. The simplicity of neighbor selection in this study [10] influenced the quality of the result. To address this concern, Tao Peng in [17] extended his research by resolving the deficiency in the position data set preprocessing and neighbor selection mechanisms. To avoid the simplicity of neighbor selection, he used a density-based clustering algorithm to implement position data preprocessing.

Another peer communication approach was proposed by Tao Peng [6], which is a collaborative trajectory privacy-preserving scheme for continuous queries. It entails a multi-hop caching-aware cloaking algorithm to collect location information. If the user's requirement is satisfied by the gathered information, the user can send a fake query to obfuscate his or her real trajectory. Lastly, a study [18] proposed a deviation-based query exchange scheme, which obfuscates a user's trajectory in a mobile social network. It involves using a private matching algorithm based on the matrix confusion to find the best matching user. The best matching user is the user with the maximum location deviation.

Collaboration between users instead of LBSs reduces the chance of revealing private information to adversaries; however, the relationship between peers is assumed to be trusted. Additionally, by applying traditional k-anonymity, the attacker may reform the requester's trajectory based on spatial and temporal correlations. Moreover, query content is not always preserved. Consequently, in this paper, we propose a decentralized model in which users act as service providers by collaborating with each other in a trustworthy mode by maintaining a number of profiles. The proposed model is subsequently demonstrated, and a clustering algorithm is integrated into this scheme to enable collaboration with minimum communication and computation costs.

3   Problem Formulation

This section illustrates the architecture and the overview of the proposed TCQTPP scheme and describes its components.

3.1   System Architecture

The system architecture of the TCQTPP scheme consists of two layers: the region and user layer and the LSP layer (Fig. 3).

The first layer contains the LSP. LBS providers are online systems, such as Google Maps and Foursquare, that utilize location-based database servers containing information on some POIs, map data, and other location-based data. LSPs receive user queries and reply with location-based information for the requested service in the target area.

The second layer contains regions and users, which are described as follows:

Regions: Regions are clusters of users. Each region has a unique location that is the center for determining the hop distance. The hop in the proposed scheme represents a group of regions based on the distance between the user sending the query and the centroid of the regions around him or her.

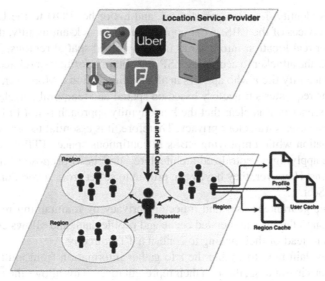

Fig. 3. System architecture

Users: Users are distributed over different regions. Users hold mobile devices with positioning functionality that states their location information. They can communicate with each other using local networks to create a collaboration group. Each user holds three data files in his or her mobile system: the user profile, user cache data, and region cache data.

a)-User profile: A user profile has information on the user's previously visited locations. It also contains his or her identity, POIs, types of interests (TOIs), his location coordinates, and timestamps. A timestamp presents the date on which the information was added, and it is deleted automatically after one year.

b)-User cache: User cache data are created from the replies of sent fake queries; thus, the fake queries in our case play another role that entails providing additional information to fill the user cache. Each added location contains a POI, TOI, its location coordinates, and timestamps. The user cache should contain the maximum number of saved locations from previously joined regions.

c)-Region cache: Each time a user joins a new region, he or she adds a randomly selected location from his or her cache and a randomly chosen location from the user profile. Each added location contains a POI, TOI, its location coordinates, and timestamps. Adding this information for each user hides the information associated with him or her, thus ensuring the privacy of the members even though they do not trust each other. The region cache is shared among all users in this region.

3.2 System Overview

While the requester, r, is seeking, for example, the nearest restaurant to where he or she is currently located, he or she sends a sequence of continuous queries (containing the requester's identity, location coordinates, and his or her POI) to the LSP in order to obtain the services of the LBS. After applying traditional k-anonymity, the requester blurs his or her real location into a series of anonymized spatial regions. This type of scheme enables the attacker to access the LSP and obtain information related to a certain user, and then identify the r who appears in all cloaking regions. Moreover, the attacker may reform the requester's trajectory based on spatial and temporal correlations. From the described scenario, it is clear that the k-anonymity approach is not fully applicable to preserving the user's trajectory privacy. Therefore, it is essential to protect the user's private information while employing LBSs in continuous space. TTP-based methods, which involve applying a centralized architecture, have been proposed for addressing privacy concerns. However, they have been proven to suffer from several drawbacks, as mentioned in Sect. 1.

Our scheme guarantees user and trajectory privacy by maintaining region-cached data, in addition to the user-associated cache and profile data, and allows collaboration between users instead of their having to contact a TTP directly.

First, we explain how to enable the r to gather information from multi-hop peers, which are regions in our case, through their representatives. This allows the r to fulfill his or her requirement locally, without contacting the LSP. Subsequently, we present how to combine location information that is randomly selected from each user's profile and cached data. The more users there are in a region, the larger the region cache becomes and, thus, the faster r receives the answer. After that, all users in each region share the same region cache data, and a representative user is randomly selected for each region.

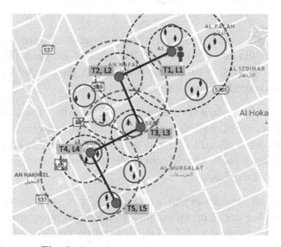

Fig. 4. Example of the proposed scheme.

An example of our proposal is shown in Fig. 4. The red circles on the trajectory indicate the footprints of the r. The blue circles indicate the regions and their users, and the two dotted circles show the hops. In this example, the hop threshold is set to 2. The green dotted circle represents the hop with the needed response. At the timestamp T1, the r is at location 1 (L1) and searching for L2. He or she broadcasts a request message to his or her first hop regions. If *r* finds the desired information from the representative of one of these regions, he or she moves to L2 at T2. Otherwise, he or she checks the next hop. He or she keeps doing that until maximum hop distance is reached. If *r* cannot find the required location, he or she joins the nearest region to form k-anonymity and thus can contact the LSP. After receiving a response from the LSP, *r* moves from L1 to the next location, which is L2 at T2. *r* repeats the same process until the final destination L5 is reached.

4   System Implementation

In the proposed TCQTPP scheme, each user holds three caches to store information: a user profile, which stores the real visited locations; a user cache, which saves responses to fake queries; and a region cache, which gathers information from the user cache and user profile. Each user profile and user cache are exclusive to that person alone. The region cache, on the other hand, is available to all users in a specified region. The region cache contains some user profile information as well as user caches of all users in the same region. The data are recorded in the following format: (POI, TOI, L(x,y), timestamp), where L(x,y) represents the x and y coordinates of the location, as shown in Table 1. In this section, we start by identifying the Peer-to-Region Fake Query Algorithm (PRFQ) and Region Cache Shuffled Generation Algorithm (RCSG) in A and B subsections. Later, we provide a construction of PRFQ and RCSG algorithms in subsection C.

Table 1. Summary of notation.

Notation	Meaning
Real	Real query
realResponse	Response to a real query
n-Fake	Number of fake queries sent {Fake1, Fake2, …, Faken}
h	Hop distance
H	Maximum hop distance
TimeThreshold	Freshness threshold
ID	Requester identity
POI	Point of interest
TOI	Type of interest
ProfThreshold	Number of randomly chosen locations from the user's profile
K	Number of regions
L(x,y)	x and y coordinates
Timestamp	Added time information
representative	User selected randomly from regionH

(*continued*)

Table 1. (*continued*)

Notation	Meaning
regionH	Region at h hop distance
r	Requester

4.1 Peer-to-Region Fake Query Algorithm

The PRFQ algorithm enables the requester to gather information from multi-hop regions through their representatives, which allows the service requester to fulfill his or her requirement locally without contacting the LSP. Algorithm 1 depicts the pseudo code for our PRFQ algorithm. We assume that the real query is Real, the number of fake queries is n-Fake, the maximum hop distance of peers is H, and the TimeThreshold specified by the user is TimeThreshold. The r uses the PRFQ algorithm and initializes the hop distance to 1 in line 3. The requester selects the region in the first hop distance region and selects a random user in regionH, as represented in lines 4 and 5. To request collaboration, the requester broadcasts a message containing five parameters: requesterID, Real, n-Fake, H, and TimeThreshold. The requester then listens to the network in line 6. A representative is a person who is willing to collaborate with r replies and shares valid data from his or her cache region. The shared data include the POI, TOI, L(x, y), and timestamp. When r receives a response from the region's representative, he or she stores the response in the answer list. Subsequently, in lines 8–14, r determines whether the realResponse is included in the gathered regionH. In line 9, r ascertains whether the realResponse is fresh and changes his or her location to the realResponseLocation. He or she also saves the realResponse with the current timestamp. In lines 15–27, r then determines whether the n-FakeResponse is included in the obtained regionH. However, the requester verifies the freshness of the n-FakeResponse. Moreover, r determines whether n-FakeResponse is duplicated and keeps the one with the fresher timestamp. Finally, he or she determines whether the user cache reached its maximum size and confirms the freshness of all data in the user cache and the freshness of the n-FakeResponse. Subsequently, r keeps the data with the latest timestamp. If r did not obtain realResponse data in the first hop, he or she searches for the second hop distance until a realResponse is received or the maximum threshold hop distance H is reached.

Algorithm 2 shows how a representative responds to a collaboration request that includes Real, n-Fake, and TimeThreshold. Upon receiving a request, the representative searches his or her region cache for Real and the n-Fake queries and replies with information containing the POI, TOI, L(x, y), and timestamp. Otherwise, the representative replies with an empty answer list.

4.2   Region Cache Shuffled Generation Algorithm

The RCSG algorithm combines randomly selected locations from each user profile in addition to their cached data. After running this algorithm, all users in each region share the same region cache data, and a representative user is randomly selected for each region.

Algorithm 3 illustrates how to create a region cache using the user cache, user profile, and randomSize as parameters. RandomSize is a number of randomly selected information from the user profile. Lines 3–5 show how to select information from the user profile. It shuffles the user profile and then randomly selects randomSize locations from the user profile. Lines 7–8 return the user cache. Finally, lines 10–11 merge the locations randomly selected from the user profile and user cache and save them in the region cache, which is the same for all users within a region.

Algorithm 1. Peer-to-Region Fake Query Requester.

```
input: Requester, Real, n-Fake, H, TimeThreshold
output: userProfile, userCachedData
1 function PRFQrequest (ID, Real, n-Fake, H, TimeThreshold )
2      while (h<H & real not found)
3      set h=1
4      select regions in hop distance h (regionH)
5      select random user in regionH
6      broadcast request to randomly selected representer in region
7         // algorithm 2 gives answer to algorithm1
8      if answer include real
9             if (reaResponse1.Timestamp < TimeThreshold )
10               userProfile<—userProfile U {realResponse}
11               Add currenttimeas timestamp for realResponse
12               Move user to real location in realResponse
13            end if
14      end if
15      if answer include n-FakeResponse
16            if (F-FakeResponse Timestamp < TimeThreshold )
17               if (F- FakeResponse in userCachedData)
18                  if ( n-FakeResponse .TimeStamp < old-n-Fake .TimeStamp)
19                     If (userCachedData < CachedDataMaxSize)
20                        userCachedData <—userCachedData U {n-FakeResponse}
21                     else (n- FakeResponse.Timestamp < userCachedData.Timestamp)
22                        Remove userCachedData with oldest timestamp
23                        userCachedData <—userCachedData U {n-FakeResponse}
24                  end if
25               end if
26            end if
27      end if
28      h=h+1
29      end while
30      return userProfile, userCachedData
31 end function
```

Algorithm 2. Peer-to-Region Fake Query Receiver.

```
input: Real, n-Fake, TimeThreshold
output: answer
1 function PRFQresponse (Real, n-Fake, TimeThreshold)
2     set answer<— {}
3     if (h=< H)
4         if representer.regionCashedRegion include real
5         answer <—answer U {realResponse}
6         end if
7         if representer.regionCashedRegion include n-Fake
8         answer <—answer U {n-FakeResponse}
9         end if
10    end if
11    return answer
12 end function
```

Algorithm 3. Peer-to-Region Fake Query Receiver

```
input: userCachedData, userProfile, randomSize
output: userCashedRegion
1 function RegionCacheShuffledGeneration (userCachedData, userProfile, randomSize)
2
3     shuffle userProfile
4     randomProfile<—select randomly randomSize from userProfile
5     userCashedRegion<—userCashedRegion U randomProfile
6
7     randomCachedData<—add userCachedData
8     userCashedRegion<—userCashedRegion U randomCachedData
9
10    userCashedRegion<—userCashedRegion U randomProfile U randomCachedData
11    return userCashedRegion
12 end function
```

4.3 Construction of PRFQ and RCSG Algorithms

First, the RPFQ is represented and explained generally, as shown in Fig. 6. Later, the idea of RCSG is described.

The following steps depict the main idea of RPFQ:

Step 1: First, we cluster the users into K regions, R, $R = \{R_1, R_2, ..., R_K\}$. Each region contains a number of users U_{ki}, $U = \{u_{11}, u_{12}, ..., u_{Ki}\}$ where u_{ki} is the ith user in region k, $1 \le k \le K$. This is clarified in Fig. 5.

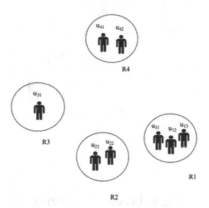

Fig. 5. Users clustered in regions.

Step 2: Fig. 6 shows the requester, r. At location $L(x1,y1)$, r is searching for $L(xd,yd)$. By using the PRFQ algorithm, r sends a query Q, where Q = {ID, real(POI, TOI), n-Fake(POI, TOI)}. r selects all regions, Ri, at distance h, then r picks a user randomly as a representative u_{ki} from all selected Ri. Afterward, Q is sent to all chosen representatives u_{ki}.

Step 3: All chosen representatives, u_{ki}, check their userCacheRegion CG_{ki} and respond with the founded (POI, TOI) as Answer. Answer $=$ {[n-FakeResponse, $L(x_f,y_f)$], [realRepsonse, $L(x_r,y_r)$]}.

Step 4: r checks the received Answers, if n-FakeResponse $\neq \emptyset$, then r checks the freshness as shown in Eq. (1). Hence, r adds n-FakeResponse to useCache UC_{ki}

$$\text{Freshness} = \text{CurrentTime} - \text{Timestamps} \leq \text{Threshold} \qquad (1)$$

Step 5: r checks the received Answers; if realResponse $\neq \emptyset$, then r checks the freshness as shown in Eq. (1). Hence, r adds realResponse to userProfile UP_{ki}. Then, r moves from $L(x_1,y_1)$ to $L(x_r,y_r)$. Furthermore, the realResponse timestamp is updated. However, if realResponse $= \emptyset$, r sends Q to all regions, R_i, at distance h + 1. If h + 1 > H. Then, the user makes k-anonymity and asks LBS.

For example, r broadcasts Q to u_{12} in R_1 and u_{21} in R_2 at $h_{1.1}$ hop distance. Since r did not get the desired answer, r sends Q to u_{31} in R_3 and u_{42} in R_4 at $h_{1.2}$. Finally, r receives the desired answer from u_{31} then he or she moves to $L(x_r,y_r)$. According to initializing the CG_{ki}, we use the RCSG algorithm. RCSG updates CG_{ki} by combining the locations randomly that are selected from each user's profile and cached data. The following shows how this algorithm works:

Step 1: Selects ProfThreshold from UP_{ki} and adds it to the CG_k for R_k. Moreover, adds UC_{ki} to the CG_k.

Step 2: CG_k is distributed to all users U_{ki} in R_k as CG_{ki}.

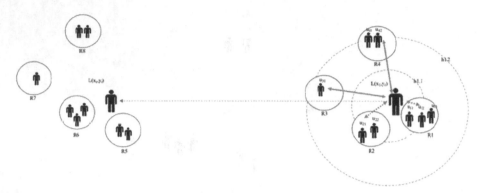

Fig. 6. Construction of PRFQ

5 Evaluation

This section presents a system analysis that entails using different parameters to evaluate the performance of the TCQTPP scheme. First, we show in details our experimental setup. Subsequently, we describe the different parameters, with different justifications, affecting the proposed system performance, analyze, and report the results.

5.1 Experiment Setup

We generated our own code using Eclipse Integrated Development Environment with the Java Development Kit 1.8. The experiments were conducted on a MacBook Pro with an Intel Core-i5 2.8 GHz, 8 GB 1600 MHz DDR3 and Mac OS X El Capitan. For simulation, we deployed the AnyLogic 8.3.3 [19] to model the scenario of our scheme. Figure 4 is a screen capture that illustrates a simulation experiment on part of a Riyadh map. We set several parameters in the analysis process. In our evaluation, various parameters were used for comparison. In each query, RP was set to 3–12, the value of K to 25–50, H_{Num} to 1–10, H to 80–100, h to 10–20, and TimeThreshold to 1–6 months.

Table 2 lists the parameters along with their descriptions, ranges, and default values. In our experiment, we assigned one user as the requester, r, selected a random real location (i.e., a restaurant), and implemented a random number of fake locations to obtain the average number of β.

Table 2. Notations used for evaluation

Notation	Description	Default value
K	Number of regions	50
H_{Num}	Number of hops	–
H	Maximum value of overall hop distance	100
h	Hop distance	10
RP	Number of randomly selection profile data	6
TimeThreshold	Maximum value of the validity of the location data	3 months
n-Fake	Maximum number of fake queries sent	4
userCacheSize	Size of the user cache	5
ß	Privacy degree	–

5.2 Privacy Degree

The main concept of the TCQTPP scheme is to meet the LBS requirement locally by user collaboration. The user collaboration obscures the user trajectory. A greater number of collaborations means more privacy and less information exposed to the LBS server. The success of our scheme depends on how much we are able to meet LBSs requests through collaboration. Thus, we compute privacy degree, β, by using Eq. (2) to show whether our scheme provides an effective privacy-preserving probability for the user:

$$\beta = \frac{\#query\ answered\ based\ on\ collaboration}{\#Total\ request} \tag{2}$$

Figure 7 shows the privacy degree with varying H and TimeThreshold. H changes from 50 to 200, and TimeThreshold varies from 3 to 12 months. A user has an improved β, which is an improved possibility of meeting the LBS requirement locally, when increasing H and TimeThreshold. When r requests greater H, more representatives can participate, and the coverage area is wider. Furthermore, when r requests a greater TimeThreshold, he or she has a higher probability of receiving a response with an old freshness timestamp. As Fig. 7 shows, the highest β resulted from H = 150 and 200 months and TimeThreshold = 12 months. There was a tradeoff between H and the computation cost. Moreover, there was a tradeoff between the TimeThreshold and the freshness of the information.

Figure 8 shows β with varying maximum numbers of fake queries and the userCacheSize. The n-Fake changes from 4 to 16, and userCacheSize varies from 2 to 8 months. A user has an improved β when increasing n-Fake and userCacheSize. When r requests greater numbers of n-Fake, he or she can collect more information from the query response, resulting in increased β. In addition, a user has an improved β when increasing the user cache size, which increases the amount of stored information, resulting in increased β. However, there is a tradeoff between n-Fake, userCacheSize, and computation cost.

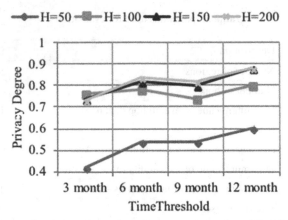

Fig. 7. Privacy degrees for the maximum hop distances ranging from 50, 100, 150, and 200, and the TimeThreshold ranging from 3, 6, 9, and 12 months.

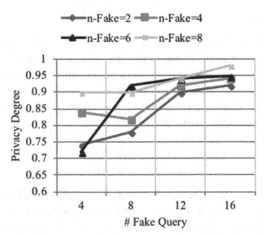

Fig. 8. Privacy degrees for the user cache sizes ranging from 2, 4, 6, and 8, and the maximum numbers of fake queries ranging from 4, 8, 12, and 16.

5.3   Confusion Degree

We used a confusion degree formula, Eq. (3), which is mentioned in [6], to evaluate the performance of the query. Each time r sends a query, he or she merges the real request with many fake requests. As the number of fake requests increases, the degree of confusion increases. For evaluation, the confusion degree is computed with varying H, TimeThreshold, and K.

$$Confusion\ degress = \frac{Num\ of\ Fake\ requests}{Overall\ requests} \qquad (3)$$

When r sends a query with a high TimeThreshold, the freshness is decreased, but the probability of the information being accepted as a response is increased. In general,

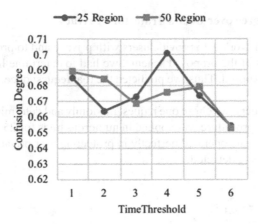

Fig. 9. Confusion degree vs. TimeThreshold, ranging 1–6.

a greater amount of available information may diminish the opportunity of revealing private information. Figure 9 shows how the TimeThreshold influences the degree of confusion, with two region values of 25 and 50. Here, the TimeThreshold ranges from 1 to 6 months. It is obvious that the best result was at TimeThreshold 4 when contending with 25 regions and TimeThreshold 1 when the region was set to 50. Conversely, there was no overall benefit from handling data that were available for 6 months.

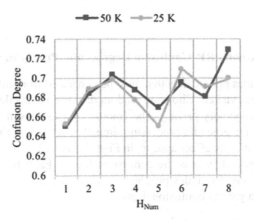

Fig. 10. Confusion degree vs. Number of hops, ranging 1–8.

The second comparison is between the confusion degree and H_{Num}. The evaluation involves estimating the performance of hiding the real data according to the number of hops. By raising the number of hops, more users are included in the collaboration. H_{Num} is set to 1–8 according to 25, and 50 K. Figure 10 depicts the blurring of a real request raised by increasing the number of requested users in diverse hops, especially for the large region.

5.4   Protection Degree over User's Trajectory Privacy

The main goal of our work is to provide users with privacy and to protect their data. To evaluate the features of the proposed scheme, we had to determine how easily a user's real request can be exposed. Thus, we predicted the real request once, each time the user sent a new query.

For each user's query, we chose one request randomly and determined whether it was the correct one. This procedure was applied in numerous hops for 25 regions. Figure 11 indicates that our scheme operated perfectly in protecting user privacy and guarded the real query against being detected.

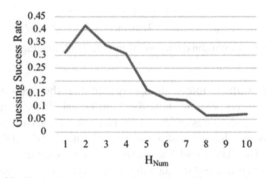

Fig. 11. Protection degree vs. the number of hops ranging 1–10.

5.5   Comparison Among RP, Confusion Degree, and Processing Time

A user's profile includes private data that must be concealed from others; it contains the places that the user has visited. Choosing random data from a profile each time is a way to preserve a user's trajectory privacy. The amount of data chosen from a profile's RP implies the confusion degree and processing time. The RP was set to values of 3, 6, 9, and 12, and the extent of its effect appears in Figs. 12 and 13.

Figure 12 presents RP versus the confusion degree. Each time we increased the data obtained randomly from the profile, r gained and utilized more information; subsequently, r had a greater confusion degree.

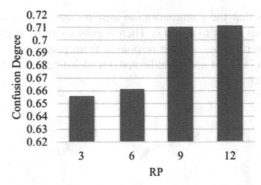

Fig. 12. Randomly chosen data from user profile ranging from 3, 6, 9, and 12 vs. confusion degree.

Figure 13 depicts RP versus the processing time. The processing time represents the overall time of the whole process until the user receives the final response. When we added more data from the users' profiles, r benefited. Therefore, the process took less time when we increased the RP value. However, having more data expanded the overall information and thus required more time for processing, as shown in RP 12 in Fig. 13.

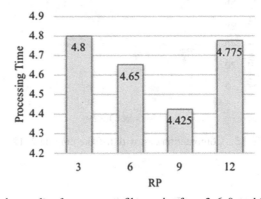

Fig. 13. Randomly chosen data from user profile ranging from 3, 6, 9, and 12 vs. processing time.

5.6 Communication Degree and Processing Time versus Number of Fake Queries

Figure 14 shows the processing time of the proposed scheme with different values of fake queries. The average processing time reached the lowest value when the n-Fake was 6, whereas it reached the highest point when F-query equaled 10. In general, the processing time was steady due to the parallel sending of queries for one or more regions in each H.

Figure 15 shows that the communication cost increases. It was almost the same when the F-query was equal to 2 and 6. Then it grows rapidly because r applied the PRFQ algorithm several times to gain responses from peers in the hop regions. The comparison between Figs. 14 and 15 indicated a tradeoff between the processing time and communication cost.

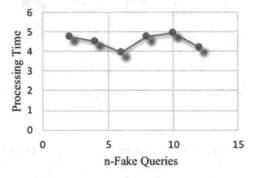

Fig. 14. Processing time with n-Fake ranging 2–12.

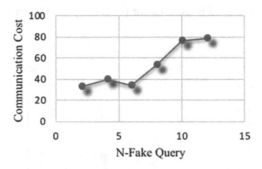

Fig. 15. Computation cost with n-Fake ranging 2–12.

5.7   Communication Degree and Processing Time versus Number of Fake Queries

Table 3 presents a comparison of our scheme with previous P2P collaboration schemes [6, 10]. First, our scheme is similar to the collaborative trajectory privacy-preserving (CTPP) scheme. It involves using a profile to store all previously visited locations; in addition, it ensures the trustworthy relationship between collaborating peers by encryption. On the other hand, our scheme ensures the trustworthy relation based on the cache region concept. The representative sends a response based on the cache region, which is common between all representatives. Second, our scheme is similar to the distributed collaborative recommendation location services (DCRLS) scheme. DCRLS is cache-aware trajectory privacy-preserving. Users use their cache and collaborate to answer LBS queries locally. Also, DCRL is fake query privacy-preserving; it preserves the query's privacy by sending multiple queries in different locations and times. In contrast to DCRLS, our scheme preserves query privacy by sending multiple fake queries with the main request.

Table 3. Comparison of the proposed scheme with previous works

	Query-privacy	Profile	Trajectory-privacy	K-anonymity	Trust-worthy
CTPP	✘	✔	✘	✔	✔
DCRLS	✔	✘	✔	✔	✘
Our scheme	✔	✔	✔	✔	✔

6 Conclusion

In this paper, a trustworthy collaborative trajectory and query privacy-preserving method are proposed. Using this approach in continuous LBSs, a TTP is eliminated, and the communication with the LSP is minimized through local fulfillment of LBS requests. Two algorithms are proposed: a PRFQ algorithm, which enables multi-hop peer collaboration, and an RCSG algorithm, which updates the region cache shared by all users using locations selected from each user's profile and cached data. Injecting a number of fake queries—which cloak the real requests of the user and contain different types of cached information—allows secure communication between users while they collaborate, even though they do not trust each other. This ensures the privacy of the trajectory and query. Ultimately, we evaluated the proposed scheme using a number of experiments within different parameters. After analyzing the findings, we proved the effectiveness of the proposed scheme. In the worst cases, when the user cannot obtain assistance from other users in a number of consecutive queries to eliminate any possible tracing while using k-anonymity, each time the user contacts the LSP, he or she must exchange his or her identity with one of the neighbors in the cloaking region and use this fake ID instead of the real one [18]. Moreover, to encourage users to actively participate in the formation of a k-anonymity set, a user's reputation concept [3] can be used, where users with a low reputation cannot obtain assistance from other users in their future requests.

References

1. Chow, C.-Y., Mokbel, M.F., Liu, X.: Spatial cloaking for anonymous location-based services in mobile peer-to-peer environments. GeoInformatica **15**(2), 351–380 (2011)
2. Chow, C.-Y., Mokbel, M.F.: Trajectory privacy in location-based services and data publication. SIGKDD Explor. Newsl. **13**(1), 19–29 (2011)
3. Li, X., Miao, M., Liu, H., Ma, J., Li, K.-C.: An incentive mechanism for K-anonymity in LBS privacy protection based on credit mechanism. Soft Comput. **21**(14), 3907–3917 (2017)
4. Peddinti, S.T., Saxena, N.: On the limitations of query obfuscation techniques for location privacy. In: The Proceedings of the 13th International Conference on Ubiquitous Computing (Beijing, China). ACM (2011)
5. Hwang, R., Hsueh, Y., Chung, H.: A novel time-obfuscated algorithm for trajectory privacy protection. IEEE Trans. Serv. Comput. **7**(2), 126–139 (2014)
6. Peng, T., Liu, Q., Meng, D., Wang, G.: Collaborative trajectory privacy preserving scheme in location-based services. Inf. Sci. **387**, 165–179 (2017)
7. Ye, A., Li, Y., Li, X.: A novel location privacy-preserving scheme based on l-queries for continuous LBS. Comput. Commun. **98**, 1–10 (2017)

8. Dewri, R., Ray, I., Whitley, D.: Query m-Invariance: Preventing Query Disclosures in Continuous Location-Based Services. City (2010)
9. Shokri, R., Theodorakopoulos, G., Papadimitratos, P., Kazemi, E., Hubaux, J.: Hiding in the mobile crowd: locationprivacy through collaboration. IEEE Trans. Dependable Secure Comput. **11**(3), 266–279 (2014)
10. Wang, P., Yang, J., Zhang, J.-P.: Protection of location privacy based on distributed collaborative recommendations. PLoS ONE **11**(9), e0163053 (2016)
11. Lei, Y., Yu, D., Din, Z., Yang, Y.: Interactive-means clustering method based on user behavior for different analysis target in medicine. Comput. Math. Methods Med. **2017** (2017)
12. Wang, J., Li, Y., Yang, D., Gao, H., Luo, G., Li, J.: achieving effective k-anonymity for query privacy in location-based services. IEEE Access **5**, 24580–24592 (2017)
13. Zheng, L., Yue, H., Li, Z., Pan, X., Wu, M., Yang, F.: k-anonymity location privacy algorithm based on clustering. IEEE Access **6**, 28328–28338 (2018)
14. Gupta, R., Rao, U.P., Kumar, M.: Perturbed Anonymization: Two Level Smart Privacy for LBS Mobile Users (2018)
15. Zhang, S., Choo, K.-K., Liu, Q., Wang, G.: Enhancing privacy through uniform grid and caching in location-based services. Future Gener. Comput. Syst. **86**, 881–892 (2018). https://doi.org/10.1016/j.future.2017.06.022
16. Chow, C.-Y., Mokbel, M.F., Liu, X.: A peer-to-peer spatial cloaking algorithm for anonymous location-based service. In: Proceedings of the Proceedings of the 14th Annual ACM International Symposium on Advances in Geographic Information Systems (Arlington, Virginia, USA). ACM (2006)
17. Wang, P., Yang, J., Zhang, J.: A strategy toward collaborative filter recommended location service for privacy protection. Sensors **18**(5), 1522 (2018)
18. Zhang, S., Wang, G., Liu, Q., Abawajy, J.H.: A trajectory privacy-preserving scheme based on query exchange in mobile social networks. Soft Comput. **22**(18), 6121–6133 (2017)
19. AnyLogic: AnyLogic: Multimethod Simulation Software. City (2018)

The Application of Beidou and Ultra-Broadband Positioning Technology in the Power Security Protection System

Yu-qing Yang[1]([✉]), Wei-wei Miao[2], and Zeng Zeng[2]

[1] NARI Group Corporation, State Grid Electric Power Research Institute, Nanjing, China
[2] State Grid Jiangsu Electric Power Co., Ltd., Nanjing, China

Abstract. In the Beidou positioning system, due to the obstruction of obstacles, the indoor is often unable to obtain positioning information. For this case, a scheme based on Beidou indoor and outdoor integration positioning is proposed. First, the algorithms of satellite localization and ultra wide band localization are studied, and a high-precision positioning algorithm compatible with both positioning modes is proposed. Seamless switching algorithm can realize positioning mode switching without affecting positioning accuracy. Based on the research of algorithm model of substation, determine the layout mode and positioning accuracy, and solve the problem of weak signal of indoor positioning. This scheme guarantees the positioning accuracy in the practical application environment, and it provides a theoretical basis for the positioning of people and equipment in the power system.

Keywords: Beidou satellite · Seamless positioning · Safety fence · Fusion algorithm · High-precision positioning

1 Introduction

With the smooth launch and networking of the third-generation Beidou satellite and the continuous development of the Beidou positioning and navigation software and hardware, the civil development of the Beidou system is advancing rapidly [1–4]. At present, the competitive environment and the product commercialization degree of the whole Beidou system application market need to be improved urgently, and the military and civil product system around the Beidou system also need to be mature [5]. The military and civilian product system around the Beidou system also needs to be mature, especially the mature development of the core products represented by the Beidou positioning and navigation chips. The large-scale application and industrial format of the power Beidou system will greatly promote the rapid development of the Beidou industry. As an important energy infrastructure, power grid is very closely related to the construction of national security and national defense [6, 7].

© Springer Nature Singapore Pte Ltd. 2022
Y. Tian et al. (Eds.): ICBDS 2021, CCIS 1563, pp. 171–182, 2022.
https://doi.org/10.1007/978-981-19-0852-1_13

Currently, positioning information is not available because the Beidou satellite is blocked by buildings and obstacles. As an important part of the grid, the stable operation of the substation directly affects the safety of the grid. In the process of indoor and outdoor transportation inspection of the substation, there are unclear operation path, unclear safety area and poor safety prevention in place, which will lead to the occurrence of dangerous accidents [8].

By making full use of Beidou indoor and outdoor seamless positioning technology, it can solve the problem of weak indoor positioning signal and achieve no perception of indoor and outdoor movement [9–11]. At the same time, the personnel inspection route can be effectively inspected, to ensure that each equipment is inspected in place.

2   Research on RTK High-Precision Positioning of Beidou

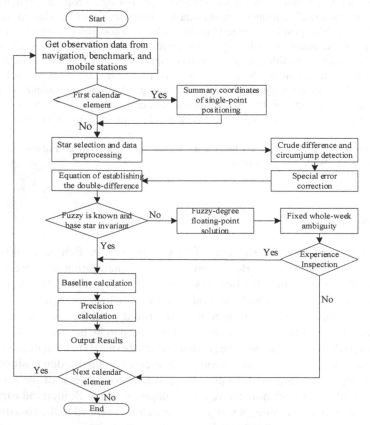

Fig. 1. Processing process for RTK data

The technology which most widely used in high precision positioning is Real Time Kinematic (RTK) [12]. RTK is based on relative positioning and requires coordination between reference stations and mobile stations. The specific workflow is as follows, the base station receives the observation data from the satellite, calculates the difference correction number, encodes the calculated correction number or the original observation data of the base station, and then transmits it to the mobile station. The mobile station obtains the correction number of the difference of the base station or the data and location data of the original observation, and codes it, calculates and displays the 3D coordinates of the user station in real time according to the principle of relative positioning [13, 14].

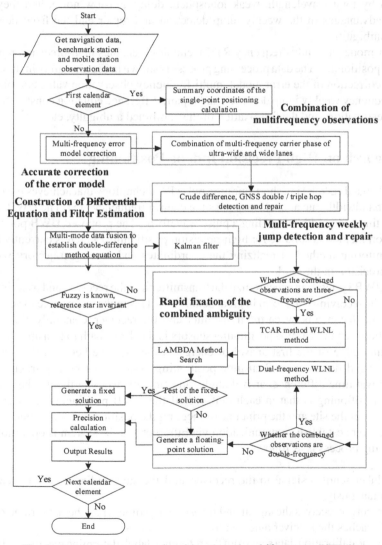

Fig. 2. Processing process of multimode and multifrequency RTK data

The process of data processing of RTK technology is shown in Fig. 1. At first, the flow station needs to determine its outline coordinates and determine the whole week ambiguity using high-speed data transmission error correction techniques. When the whole week ambiguity is determined, the whole week ambiguity of the previous calendar can be replaced as the known value when the base star is invariant and the satellite signal is not locked.

Multi-mode positioning has more available satellites than single Beidou positioning, forming a large number of redundant observation data. The correlation characteristics between data can reduce the interval of weekly fuzzy search and accelerate the fuzzy search. At the same time, the observation value of multi-frequency combination is characterized by long wavelength, weak ionosphere delay and low noise, and they have obvious advantages in the weekly jump detection and repair and the fixed degree of weekly ambiguity.

Multi-mode and multi-frequency RTK technology enables high-precision real-time dynamic positioning. The data processing process is shown in Fig. 2, mainly including the accurate correction of the error model, multi-frequency observation value combination, multi-frequency weekly jump detection and repair, difference equation construction and filtering estimation, and the fast fixation of the combined ambiguity, etc.

3   Research on High Precision Indoor Positioning

Ultra wide band (UWB) is a short-duration pulse RF technology that achieves the highest possible bandwidth rate at the lowest possible central frequency [15]. The UWB system achieves this bandwidth by sending a pulse waveform. The proposed UWB positioning application method is suitable for high-precision positioning, which is currently a real-time monitoring method of realizing the coordinates and moving trajectory with the highest precision in the world.

The UWB system can synchronize the transmitter and the receiver, and over time, can measure the receiving waveform in great detail [16]. This makes it possible to accurately measure the distance between the transmitter and the receiver. Generally, the shortest distance between the 2 UWB positioning sensors is the direct path to transmit the pulse. The leading edge of the first arrival of energy is the distance between the measured transmitter and the receiver. Real-time positioning systems can be constructed based on the arrival time difference, arrival angle, and time of two-way flight. The principle of UWB positioning is that in each unit, install the UWB positioning receiver at the four corners of the site and the principle of meeting the positioning requirements. These UWB receivers establish communication via Ethernet and the system is operational.

Working process is as follows

1) The label sends a signal to the receiver, and the surrounding receiver receives it simultaneously;
2) The receiver receives the signal and measures the time when the data frame of each label reaches the receiver antenna;
3) Using the calibration data sent from the reference label, determine the time difference between the labels reaching the different receivers. By using triangular positioning

technology and optimization algorithm, the label position is calculated combined with the configured receiver coordinates.

4 Study on the Seamless Connection Technology of High-Precision Indoor and Outdoor Positioning

To solve seamless switching, the indoor and outdoor positioning system combining Beidou and UWB is proposed [17–20]. It is realized by seamless positioning adaptive switching algorithm in indoor and outdoor environment. At the same time, increasing the threshold mechanism can effectively avoid the power consumption and operational resource waste caused by the repeated switching of the indoor and outdoor positioning system, so as to realize the seamless connection between the Beidou satellite positioning technology and the indoor UWB positioning technology. In the outdoor environment, the Beidou satellite positioning technology is used for positioning, switching to the integrated positioning mode of Beidou and UWB at the indoor and outdoor junction, and switching to the positioning mode of UWB after entering the indoor area. Seamless positioning switching model is shown in Fig. 3. Among them, AB1 is the auxiliary base station, RB1 is the base station in the indoor and outdoor overlapping positions, and MB1 and MB2 are the main base stations in two different indoor areas.

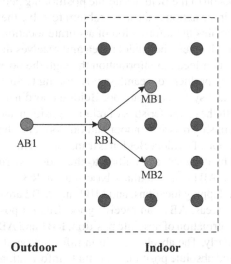

Outdoor   **Indoor**

Fig. 3. Switching model for seamless positioning

The steps to achieve seamless switching are shown below

1) Location sensing layer detects changes in transmission and receiving time of label to base station in real time. The sensing layer regularly reports the changes to the back-end switching module, while the Beidou terminal module detects the number of received satellite signals in real time;

2) The back-end processing module calculates the coordinate information of the detection position in real time according to the positioning algorithm, and feeds it back to the switching module at the back end;

3) Due to the certain delay of the satellite signal and the base station transmission signal at the indoor and outdoor overlap, the judgment of the instant data information is inaccurate. The switching module at the back end will simultaneously judge the detection number of satellite signals and the indoor positioning algorithm. When the back-end switching module detects the number of satellite signals in the window time is greater than or equal to 4, switch to the outdoor positioning mode. Open the Beidou positioning mode, close the indoor positioning mode of UWB, and calculate the position information of the latitude and longitude coordinates to realize the positioning. Outdoor location information cannot be positioned when the number of the satellite position is less than 4, therefore, the positioning mode of Beidou can switch to the positioning mode of indoor UWB, and complete the positioning according to the indoor positioning algorithm. The threshold is based on the number of satellite signals, i.e., 4 or more, when the threshold switches to the Beidou positioning mode automatically, and vice versa.

The unification of seamless positioning technology is a scalable model based on the research of the Beidou satellite positioning network, namely, the UWB indoor positioning network is the extension of the Beidou satellite positioning network, and the accurate acquisition of location information is the key problem to solve the seamless positioning system. The terminal obtains the information of accurate location coordinates from the indoor environment until it enters the outdoor area and receives the Beidou satellite signal, and obtains the outdoor location information through the positioning of the Beidou satellite. To solve the key problem of seamless positioning technology, the relationship between indoor coordinate system and outdoor Beidou coordinate system must be well handled. Combined with the characteristics of relative position and absolute position, in order to unify the relationship between indoor and outdoor coordinate system, the absolute coordinate information of outdoor Beidou is transformed into the relative coordinate relationship expressed by distance, and unified to the indoor starting point and relative base station coordinates. AB1 is the auxiliary base station, RB1 is the base station in the indoor and outdoor overlapping locations, and MB1 and MB2 are the main base stations in two different indoor areas. AB1 can receive good Beidou positioning information, obtaining coordinate information of absolute position. RB1 and AB1 remain on the same level and distance regularly. The absolute position information of RB1 can be obtained according to distance and absolute position coordinate information, and RB1 can realize monitoring and proofreading of position information. A confirmation mechanism for location synchronization information between MB1, MB2 and RB1 is established, as shown in Fig. 3.

5 Processing Software of Beidou and UWB

5.1 Research on the Software of Beidou and UWB

For seamless positioning post-processing software, the technical key is the seamless switching and conversion of Beidou positioning results and in-range UWB positioning results. In the two positioning modes, the positioning coordinates of the mobile end should be the same to ensure the consistency of the positioning results. Therefore, it is necessary to unify the coordinate system and time system of the two positioning modes, so that the whole monitoring range area is under a unified coordinate system, and ensure that the monitoring results do not occur wrong with the transformation of the positioning mode [21].

(1) The Unity of the Time

To realize the joint positioning, it is necessary to ensure the consistency of the Beidou time system and UWB base station time system. The Beidou time system is controlled by the atomic clock of the Beidou main control station, and the atomic clock on the monitoring station and the Beidou satellite are both synchronized with the main control station. Measure the clock difference of the satellite clock, then insert the clock difference message into the navigation message into the satellite, and release it to the user with the star calendar. UWB time system of various base stations can perform time synchronization by timing. There are inevitably small differences between them, such small differences in time that will cause greater errors to the positioning results, and therefore must be determined by exact comparison.

(2) Unity of the coordinate system

In the satellite positioning system, the GPS star calendar is given by the wgs-84 coordinate frame, while the Beidou satellite star calendar is given with the Chinese CGS2000 coordinate system as the coordinate frame.

The origin, scale, and axis pointing of the two coordinate systems are different, and the relationship can be described by the commonly used Bursa model.

Taking the Bursa model as an example, the coordinates in the CGS2000 coordinate system can be converted to the WGS-84 coordinate system by following formula [22]

$$
\begin{bmatrix} X^{WGS-84} \\ Y^{WGS-84} \\ Z^{WGS-84} \end{bmatrix} = \begin{bmatrix} X_0 \\ Y_0 \\ Z_0 \end{bmatrix} + (1+u) \begin{bmatrix} X^{CGS2000} \\ Y^{CGS2000} \\ Z^{CGS2000} \end{bmatrix} + \begin{bmatrix} 0 & \varepsilon_Z & -\varepsilon_Y \\ -\varepsilon_Z & 0 & \varepsilon_X \\ \varepsilon_Y & -\varepsilon_X & 0 \end{bmatrix} \begin{bmatrix} X^{CGS2000} \\ Y^{CGS2000} \\ Z^{CGS2000} \end{bmatrix}
$$

$$(1)$$

In the formula, X_0, Y_0, Z_0 is the translation parameter; u is the scale parameter; $\varepsilon_X, \varepsilon_Y, \varepsilon_Z$ is a rotation parameter. The above 7 parameters can be determined by common points with accurately known coordinates in both coordinate systems, and can be analyzed and tested according to the actual situation, eliminating the three, four, five, or six-parameter conversion model.

In the joint solution, it is necessary to unify with the Beidou coordinate system according to the coordinate system situation of the UWB base station. For example, the coordinates of UWB base station is the coordinate system of WGS-84, so the coordinate utilization formula of Beidou satellite in CGS2000 coordinate system should be converted into WGS-84 coordinates. The unified solution is then performed under the

WGS-84 coordinate system, and the resulting localization results belong to the WGS-84 coordinate system. Similarly, the same method can be used to convert the coordinates of the GPS satellite in the WGS-84 coordinate system into the CGS2000 coordinates, and then perform a unified solution under the CGS2000 coordinate system, and the resulting positioning results belong to the CGS2000 coordinate system (Fig. 4).

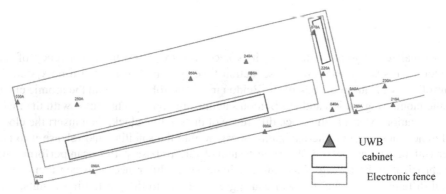

Fig. 4. Deployment diagram for the UWB

5.2   Platform Management Software

Under the software system of this platform, the real-time tracking and positioning of the patrol operation and maintenance personnel from indoor to outdoor in the substation can be realized [23]. At the same time, after the coordinate collection of some equipment and facilities with high risk coefficient within the system monitoring scope, monitoring the distance between inspection management personnel and equipment and facilities, defining safe operation space, a safe transportation inspection path area is set up to ensure the work safety of inspection operation and maintenance personnel.

In the two positioning modes, the positioning coordinates of the mobile end are the same, ensuring the consistency of the positioning results and the monitoring results are not wrong with the transformation of the positioning mode. Meanwhile, based on the special application scenarios and method of power system, the algorithm model in complex electromagnetic environment such as substation is studied. The algorithm model of the software is adjusted according to the data to ensure the positioning accuracy in the actual application environment.

The application framework and interface design of the whole platform management software are built, submenus of equipment management, path planning, electronic fence, cross-boundary alarm and other functions are developed. Moreover, each peripheral functions are designed and developed, as shown in Fig. 5 (Figs. 6, 7 and 8).

Fig. 5. The Software Interface

North-south displacement

Centimeter

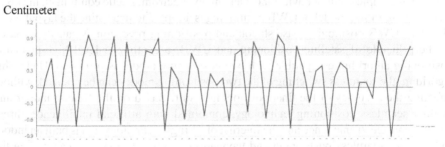

Fig. 6. North-south displacement

East-west displacement

Centimeter

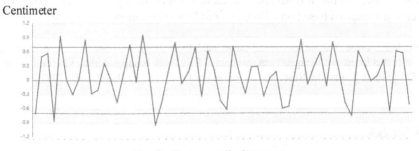

Fig. 7. East-west displacement

Displacement of the elevation direction

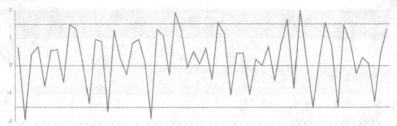

Fig. 8. Displacement of the elevation direction

6 Conclusion

This paper studies the Beidou outdoor high-precision positioning algorithm, completes the high-precision satellite positioning algorithm, and proposes the high-precision RTK algorithm model of the multi-system satellite positioning in a complex electromagnetic environment such as the power system. In addition, based on UWB indoor positioning algorithm, the optimization scheme for the layout of UWB base stations is proposed. In the case of complex indoor environment and many electromagnetic equipment, the high-precision algorithm model of UWB positioning is adopted to determine the layout mode of indoor UWB positioning base station and positioning precision. Meanwhile, based on the principle of satellite positioning and UWB, a centimeter-level high-precision positioning algorithm compatible with two positioning modes is proposed. Under this algorithm, the seamless switching of the two positioning modes can be realized, without affecting the accuracy of the final positioning result. Based on the Beidou indoor and outdoor seamless positioning technology, combined with artificial intelligence, three-dimensional electronic fence and the Internet of Things technology, it has built an indoor and outdoor seamless positioning and navigation system. The system can realize the functions of personnel operation path planning, danger area warning, authority control, behavior code control and historical responsibility tracking, and use the wearable equipment of the inspection personnel to give early warning of the potential dangers. With this system as the infrastructure, it can be used in other positioning and navigation application scenarios based on indoor and outdoor integration positioning.

Acknowledgments. The authors would like to thank the anonymous reviewers and editor for their comments that improved the quality of this paper. This work is supported by scientific project of State Grid Fujian Economic Research Institue under Grant NO. SGFJJ00GHJS2000044.

References

1. Bahl, P., Padmanabhan, V.N.: RADAR: an in-building RF-based user location and tracking system. In: INFOCOM 2000. Nineteenth Joint Conference of the IEEE Computer and Communications Societies, vol. 2, pp. 775–784 (2000)

2. Shaukat, M., Chitre, M.: Adaptive behaviors in multi-agent source localization using passive sensing. Adapt. Behav. **24**(6), 446–463 (2016)
3. Patil, N.A., Munson, J., Wood, D., Cole, A.: Blue Bot: asset tracking via robotic location crawling. Comput. Commun. **31**(6), 1067–1077 (2008)
4. Broumandan, A., Nielsen, J., Lachapelle, G.: Indoor GNSS signal acquisition performance using a synthetic antenna array. IEEE Trans. Aerosp. Electron. Syst. **47**(2), 1337–1350 (2011)
5. Rycroft, M.J.: Understanding GPS. Principles and applications. J. Atmos. Solar-Terr. Phys. **59**(5), 598–599 (2006)
6. Deng, Z., Yanpei, Y., Yuan, X., Wan, N., Yang, L.: Situation and development tendency of indoor positioning. China Commun. **10**(3), 42–55 (2013)
7. Jardak, N., Samama, N.: Indoor positioning based on GPS-repeaters: performance enhancement using an open code loop architecture. IEEE Trans. Aerosp. Electron. Syst. **45**(1), 347–359 (2009)
8. Alexandre, V.P., Samama, N.: Interference mitigation in a repeater and pseudolite indoor positioning system. IEEE J. Sel. Top. Signal Process. **3**(5), 810–820 (2009)
9. Ouyang, R.W., Wong, A.-S., Woo, K.T.: Indoor localization via discriminatively regularized least square classification. Int. J. Wireless Inf. Networks **18**(2), 57–72 (2011). https://doi.org/10.1007/s10776-011-0133-5
10. Tang Li, X., Yubin, Z., et al.: Research on K nearst neighbors algorithm under the indoor WLAN. Comput. Sci. B **36**(4), 54–55 (2009)
11. Ni, L.M., Liu, Y., Lau, Y.C., Patil, A.P.: LANDMARC: indoor location sensing using active RFID. Wireless Netw. **10**(6), 701–710 (2004)
12. Liebe, C.C., Murphy, N., Dorsky, L.: Three-axis sun sensor for attitude determination. IEEE Aerosp. Electron. Syst. Mag. **31**(6), 6–11 (2016)
13. Manandhar, D., Kawaguchi, S., Torimoto, H.: Results of IMES (indoor messaging system) implementation for seamless indoor navigation and social infrastructure platform. In: Proceedings of International Technical Meeting of the Satellite Division of the Institute of Navigation, vol. 7672, no. 6, pp. 1184–1191 (2010)
14. Dammann, A., Raulefs, R., Zhang, S.: On prospects of positioning in 5G. In: 2015 IEEE International Conference on Communication Workshop (ICCW), London, England, pp. 1207–1213 (2015)
15. Lee, J.-E., Lee, S.: Indoor initial positioning using single clock pseudolite system. In: 2010 IEEE International Conference on Information and Communication Technology Convergence (ICT), pp. 575–578. IEEE (2010)
16. Ward, A., Jones, A., Hopper, A.: A new location technique for the active office. IEEE Pers. Commun. **4**(5), 42–47 (1997)
17. Cui, Q., Zhang, X.: Research analysis of wireless localization with insufficient resources for next-generation mobile communication networks. Int. J. Commun. Syst. **26**(9), 1206–1226 (2013)
18. Wei, K., Wu, L.: Mobile location with NLOS identification and mitigation based on modified Kalman filtering. Sensors **11**(2), 1641 (2011)
19. Rui, X., Chen, W., Ying, X., Ji, S.: A new indoor positioning system architecture using GPS signals. Sensors **15**(5), 10074–10087 (2015)
20. Bu-lin, M., Fan, Y.: The design and implementation of WiFi localization GIS for mine. J. Xi'an Univ. Sci. Technol. **32**(3), 301–305 (2012)
21. Guanglong, Y., Yongping, K., Zhiming, Z., et al.: Indoor positioning system design and implementation of based on multimode fingerprint matching. Comput. Eng. Des. **34**(5), 1896–1901 (2013)

22. Mehmood, H., Tripathi, N., Tipdecho, T.: Seamless switching between GNSS and WLAN based indoor positioning system for ubiquitous positioning. Earth Sci. Inf. **8**(1), 221–231 (2014). https://doi.org/10.1007/s12145-014-0157-3
23. Guan, W., Deng, Z., Yu, Y., Ge, Y.: A NLOS mitigation method for CDMA2000 mobile location. In: 2010 2nd IEEE International Conference on Network Infrastructure and Digital Content, Beijing China, pp. 668–672 (2010)

Research on Navigation Algorithm Model of Virtual Tourism System Based on GIS

Jiayuan Wang[1](✉), Shengbin Yang[2], and Chong Cheng[1]

[1] Institute of Aviation Tourism, Sichuan Vocational College of Science and Technology, Chengdu 610000, China
[2] China Xi'an Satellite Control Center, Xi'an 710000, Shanxi, China

Abstract. In recent years, with the rapid development of economy, tourism has increasingly become an important part of people's life. Especially in recent years, thanks to the integration of modern information technology, virtual tourism is increasingly favored by the public. In a narrow sense, virtual tourism uses modern computer technology to model scenic spots or some cultural relics and community buildings with tourism value, and allows participants to experience the fun of tourism in a virtual environment with the help of information sensing equipment and objective carriers. This kind of tourism has the advantages of low cost, high efficiency and strong selectivity. However, in order to make consumers experience the fun of virtual tourism more conveniently and quickly, the research on this abstract network navigation algorithm has attracted more and more attention. Under this background, according to the virtual tourism intelligent selection system, this paper studies the navigation algorithm model in the virtual tourism system based on the Geographic Information System, and makes an empirical analysis with an example.

Keywords: Virtual tourism · Navigation algorithm · Geographic Information System

1 Introduction

1.1 Virtual Tourism

With the improvement of people's living standards, tourism has gradually become a national fashion and consumption hotspot. The analysis report of China's tourism industry shows that China's inbound tourism continues to show a good development momentum [1]. As early as the end of the 20th century, the long-term prediction report of the World Tourism Organization on World Tourism Development pointed out that China will become the largest host country of international tourism in the world by 2020.

The vigorous development of tourism is inseparable from the modern management of tourism resources [2]. However, the traditional way of managing tourism resources with paper map has been far from meeting the requirements of managers, because this way cannot update, manage and use the information effectively and timely, resulting in incomplete tourism information and weak real-time. At this time, the requirements of

© Springer Nature Singapore Pte Ltd. 2022
Y. Tian et al. (Eds.): ICBDS 2021, CCIS 1563, pp. 183–193, 2022.
https://doi.org/10.1007/978-981-19-0852-1_14

tourists' autonomy and personalization are becoming more and more obvious, and the traditional publicity and service methods cannot meet the increasing needs of tourists [3]. Informatization is the general trend of world economic and social development. It is a general trend to combine tourism with information technology and use information technology to improve tourism management and service level.

Tourism information system is a decision support system, which has various characteristics of information system [4]. In the tourism information system, the information stored and processed is mainly reflected in the spatial data related to tourism resources, a large number of attribute data and multimedia data related to tourism. The emergence of tourism information system is an embodiment of the combination of tourism and information technology.

1.2 Geographic Information System

Spatial data is an important part of human data. Since the birth of mankind, it has begun to explore and study the surrounding space, so as to obtain spatial data and seek the effective expression, storage, analysis and transmission of spatial data [5]. City is one of the main places for human production and life, and it is the concentrated embodiment of human civilization. With the rapid development of information technology, the collection and update speed of spatial data is also accelerating. The traditional spatial-temporal information expression based on map has been difficult to meet the needs of the current urban development process because of its disadvantages such as slow update speed, backward information transmission media and highly abstract expression.

With the development of informatization and the improvement of software and hardware facilities, urban informatization is gradually changing from "digital city" moving towards "smart city" [6], urban planning, construction and management are also more refined, standardized, scientific and intelligent [7]. With the development of economy and society and the improvement of urbanization rate, urban diseases such as environmental pollution, population expansion, traffic congestion and lack of resources are becoming more and more prominent. Understanding and analyzing urban space from a three-dimensional perspective is undoubtedly helpful to the treatment of urban diseases. Using 3D spatial data model to store, manage, analyze and assist decision-making of urban spatial information is increasingly becoming an inevitable way for government departments to carry out urban management. The 3D spatial data model is undoubtedly the basis for the expression, storage and analysis of urban spatial data. It is the core ability of 3D spatial data model to assist urban management. With the development and maturity of 3D reconstruction technology, more and more organizations begin to build 3D city models to meet their own needs. These 3D city models have been widely used in noise propagation simulation and distribution mapping [8], urban and communication planning [9, 10], and disaster management, indoor navigation [11] and real-time simulation training [12]. It can be seen that in these applications, the vast majority of 3D city models contain the geometric and semantic features of 3D spatial objects, and it is difficult to meet the application requirements simply relying on geometric and image models.

Digital city with GIS (Geographic Information System) as the core is the main source of urban informatization. One of the important signs is that after more than ten years of development, it is profoundly affecting people's daily production and life. People have lived in a dual urban structure composed of digital city and material city [13], especially three-dimensional GIS (3D GIS) However, 3D GIS is not only as simple as adding a spatial dimension to the traditional two-dimensional GIS, but also brings profound changes including the basic theory of data model, data acquisition, storage and management methods and spatial analysis methods.

2 Dynamic Optimal Path Algorithm Based on Navigation

The function selection system based on Virtual Tourism Floyd algorithm introduced in this paper aims to help customers explore the optimal path, so to make virtual tourism more convenient and efficient. In the design of system framework, the theory of road topology network relationship is also used. The system includes data layer, business layer and presentation layer [14]. The data layer forms an electronic map with the help of MapX, and constructs a road topology network relational structure database. The business layer mainly processes the data by modifying the optimized Floyd algorithm, so as to obtain the optimal path of virtual tourism. The presentation layer is an intuitive operation interface for customers, which can not only intelligently display the corresponding travel path, but also intuitively view the corresponding map information distribution. The functions of the intelligent selection system include the basic functions of map, the topological relationship of road network and the implementation of Floyd algorithm. The corresponding functional modules are shown in Fig. 1:

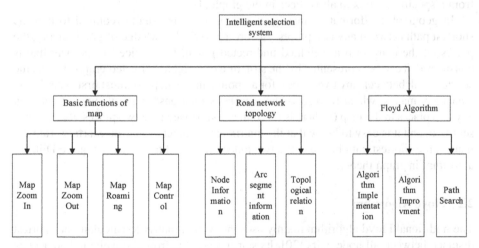

Fig. 1. Intelligent selection system function module

In Fig. 1, the basic function of the map is the basis of the system. In addition to the basic functions such as zooming in and out, it also has the functions of roaming and setting control, so as to ensure that the virtual tourism navigation effect is more intuitive and obvious. The road network topology relationship mainly constructs the association information between system points and lines, including node information, arc information and topology relationship. The formation of the road network topology relationship is the path for the system to obtain all node information in the tourism road layer, covering the broken chain and node matching in the road route. In addition. In order to better realize the function operation effect of the system and improve the calculation speed, the database of the function selection system can be updated in time to include the relevant information of road topology relationship in real time, so as to avoid repeated storage and reading of information during each construction of road network topology [15].

At present, many shortest path algorithms have been proposed at home and abroad, among which the well-known shortest path algorithms are Dijkstra algorithm [16], Floyd algorithm [17], heuristic search algorithm (A* algorithm) [18], two-way search algorithm and hierarchical search algorithm and so on. In these algorithms, the network is abstracted as a directed or undirected graph defined in graph theory, and the node adjacency matrix of the graph is used to record the association information between points. When traversing the graph to find the shortest path, the minimum of the target value is continuously determined based on the matrix until the final optimization path is obtained, these algorithms are introduced below.

2.1 Dijkstra Algorithm

Dijkstra algorithm is the shortest path algorithm proposed by E.W. Dijkstra in 1959, which is suitable for all arcs with non-negative weight. It is also recognized as the most classical algorithm for solving the shortest path problem. It can give the shortest path from a specified vertex to all vertices in the graph [19].

In geographic information management system, it is usually required to find the shortest path between any two places. According to the knowledge of graph theory, the points on the map form a weighted undirected graph. In practice, if one-way line is considered, it can be represented by the structure of weighted directed graph. To find the shortest path between any two places, for all points in the map, we must first establish an adjacency matrix, which represents the adjacency relationship and its weight between any two places in the map (if there is no connection between the two places, its weight is set to ∞, and it is easy to know that the matrix is a symmetric matrix. Starting from the matrix, the shortest path between the two places can be obtained by using the Dijkstra algorithm in graph theory.

2.2 Floyd Algorithm

The traditional Floyd algorithm mainly uses the weight matrix to calculate the shortest distance between all node pairs [20]. Its starting point is from the weighted adjacency matrix $D^{(0)}$, which aims to calculate the distance between any two nodes V_i and V_j. During the operation, all possible paths between any two nodes V_i and V_j shall be calculated first, and the shortest path shall be compared and filtered to replace $D^{(0)}$ and list $D^{(1)}$ iteratively. The elements in $D^{(1)}$ thus obtained represent the shortest path passed by any two points in the network. This shortest path may not be direct, but may also include the path passing through the middle, but in the end, it is the shortest path. Similarly, $D^{(2)}$, $D^{(3)} \ldots D^{(k)}$ can be obtained respectively, where $D^{(k)}$ is limited to the shortest path when the corresponding elements in the weighted neighbor matrix pass through $2^k - 1$ intermediate points at most or any two points do not pass through the intermediate points. By analogy, when $D^{(k+1)} = D^{(k)}$, the resulting $D^{(k)}$ indicates that the system has generated the shortest distance between each element node, so the matrix becomes the shortest distance matrix. The formulations corresponding to the above-mentioned Floyd algorithm are as follows:

Step1: Construct initial distance matrix $D^{(0)}$ and set:

$$D^{(0)} = \left(d_{ij}^{(0)}\right) \tag{1}$$

Step2: Build iterative matrix $D^{(k)}$ and set:

$$D^{(k)} = \left(d_{ij}^{(k)}\right) \tag{2}$$

Step3: If $D^{(k+1)} = D^{(k)}$, terminate the iteration, otherwise return to step 2 and go on.

Where in Eq. (1):

$$d_{ij}^{(0)} = \begin{cases} W_{ij}, & \text{if } i \text{ and } j \text{ are adjacent} \\ \infty, & \text{if } i \text{ and } j \text{ are not adjacent} \end{cases} \tag{3}$$

And in Eq. (2):

$$d_{ij}^{(k)} = \min\left(d_{ir}^{(k-1)} + d_{rj}^{(k-1)}, r = 1, 2, \ldots, n\right) \tag{4}$$

2.3 A* Algorithm

In the calculation, A* algorithm uses the self-owned information of the system state space and dynamically adjusts the search strategy with the help of a certain stock price function to obtain the corresponding optimal solution. It is a heuristic path planning algorithm. The evaluation function introduced by this algorithm is $f(j) = g(j) + h(j)$, where $g(j)$ represents the cost from the starting point of the system to the set point j, and $H(j)$ represents the lowest estimation function from the fixed-point J to the target point. If $H(j) = 0$, the A* algorithm is the same as the normal dijestra algorithm. In the path calculation, the minimum the vertex of $f(j)$ value is the priority search object of A* algorithm. When searching the shortest path, $H(j)$ is selected according to the path planning criteria formulated in advance. $H(j)$ is represented by the linear distance $d(j)$ from the current vertex j to the target vertex g, and $g(j)$ is represented by the actual distance $d(j)$ from the current vertex j to the target vertex g. The evaluation function obtained is: $f(x) = d^*(x) + d(x)$ [2].

2.4 Hasse Algorithm

Hasse algorithm is a method to calculate the shortest path of V_i and V_j at any two points in the system network. In recent years, Hasse algorithm has been gradually applied to the calculation of tourism path. Its calculation formula is:

$$d_{ij}^{(m)} = \min_k\left(d_{ik}^{(m-1)} + d_{kj}^{(m-1)}, i, j = 1, 2, \ldots, nm = 1, 2, \ldots, n-2\right) \tag{5}$$

Where $d_{ij}^{(m)}$ represents the shortest path between V_i and V_j in the system path obtained after m iterations; d represents the direct distance between V_i and V_j. If the arc between two points does not exist, then $d = 0$. If there are n fixed points in the system, $n - 1$ calculations should be carried out in the whole system path screening, so as to obtain the shortest distance and optimal path of the system path. If you want to calculate not only the shortest distance but also the shortest path, the subscript information should be retained in the operation process, the equation is as follows:

$$d_{sk} + d_{kj} = k_{skj} \tag{6}$$

2.5 Traceable Mountain Climbing Algorithm

The mountain climbing strategy based on heuristic search only selects the best child node for further expansion each time in the search process, and does not retain neither the brother node nor its parent node of the current node. Therefore, in the solution process, it only needs to search part of the state space, and cancels the open table, which reduces the overhead of dynamic maintenance. Therefore, the algorithm has low complexity, less memory space, high speed and high search efficiency. However, because the mountain climbing strategy does not save any historical records, it has no backtracking or other recovery mechanism. When encountering "multi peak", "basin", "ridge" and other problems, it is easy to fall into the local optimal value and finally cannot find the solution. The backtracking of mountain climbing strategy is an important guarantee to ensure that the search algorithm can find the solution.

3 The Optimization of Floyd Algorithm

To solve the problem of repeated calculation and relatively low efficiency of Floyd algorithm, an iterative matrix of $D^{(k)} = \left(d_{ij}^{(k)} \right)$ can be constructed. In this way, when calculating the shortest distance between V_i and V_j, the distance between the inserted node V_r can be compared first. If $d_{ir}^{(k-1)} \geq d_{ij}^{(k-1)}$ or $d_{rj}^{(k-1)} \geq d_{ij}^{(k-1)}$ is found, it can be concluded that the distance from node V_i to V_j through node V_r is not shorter than the original, Thus, you can directly enter the search of the next node without calculating $d_{ir}^{(k-1)} + d_{rj}^{(k-1)}$. In addition, a new sequence number matrix $A^{(k)} = \left(a_{ij}^{(k)} \right)$, $k = 0, 1, \ldots, n$ is constructed to record the insertion point of the k-th iteration. The improved Floyd algorithm is the core of the intelligent selection system. After these improvements and optimizations, the operation steps of Floyd algorithm are as follows:

Step1: Construct the initial distance matrix $D^{(0)} = \left(d_{ij}^{(0)} \right)$ and serial number matrix $A^{(0)} = \left(a_{ij}^{(0)} \right)$. Where:

$$d_{ij}^{(0)} = \begin{cases} W_{ij}, & \text{if } i \text{ and } j \text{ are adjacent} \\ \infty, & \text{if } i \text{ and } j \text{ are not adjacent} \end{cases} \tag{7}$$

$$a_{ij}^{(0)} = \begin{cases} 0, & \text{if } i \text{ and } j \text{ are adjacent} \\ \Phi, & \text{if } i \text{ and } j \text{ are not adjacent} \end{cases} \tag{8}$$

$d_{ij}^{(0)}$ represents the distance length of any two points V_i and V_j without passing through other nodes.

Step2: Construct serial number matrix $A^{(k)} = \left(a_{ij}^{(k)} \right)$ and iterative matrix $D^{(k)} = \left(d_{ij}^{(k)} \right)$. If $d_{ij}^{(k)} = d_{il}^{(k-1)} + d_{lj}^{(k-1)}$, and $d_{ij}^{(k)} < d_{ij}^{(k-1)}$, then record V_l, and $a_{ij}^{(k)} = \left\{ d_{il}^{(k-1)}, V_l, d_{lj}^{(k-1)} \right\}$, this indicates that after that iterative, the distance between V_i and V_j passing V_l will become shorter, otherwise if $d_{ij}^{(k)} = d_{ij}^{(k-1)}$. If $d_{ir}^{(k-1)} \geq d_{ij}^{(k-1)}$ or $d_{rj}^{(k-1)} \geq d_{ij}^{(k-1)}$, it indicates that after inserting node V_r, $d_{ij}^{(k-1)}$ will not become shorter, here we need not to calculate $d_{ir}^{(k-1)} + d_{rj}^{(k-1)}$.

Step3: if $D^{(k+1)} = D^{(k)}$, terminate the iteration, otherwise return Step2.

3.1 Algorithm Description

According to the design idea of the intelligent selection system, the application mode of the system is calculated with the network structure in Fig. 2.

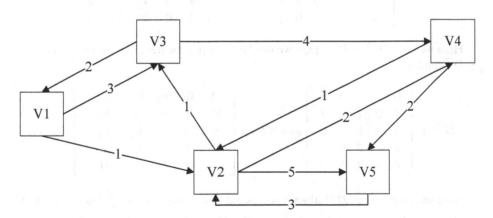

Fig. 2. Simulation of scenic spot network structure

It can be seen from Fig. 2 that the scenic spot network structure simulation system is a network structure without negative loop. The calculation steps of the optimal path by using the improved and optimized Floyd algorithm are as follows:

The initial distance matrix $D^{(0)}$ can be calculated as follows:

$$D^{(0)} = \begin{bmatrix} 0 & 1 & 3 & \infty & \infty \\ \infty & 0 & 1 & 2 & 5 \\ 2 & \infty & 0 & 4 & \infty \\ \infty & 1 & \infty & 0 & 2 \\ \infty & 3 & \infty & \infty & 0 \end{bmatrix} \tag{9}$$

The serial number matrix $A^{(0)}$ can be calculated as follows:

$$A^{(0)} = \begin{bmatrix} 0 & 0 & 0 & \Phi & \Phi \\ \Phi & 0 & 0 & 0 & 0 \\ 0 & \Phi & 0 & 0 & \Phi \\ \Phi & 0 & \Phi & 0 & 0 \\ \Phi & 0 & \Phi & \Phi & 0 \end{bmatrix} \tag{10}$$

$D^{(1)}$ and $A^{(1)}$ can be obtained according to the calculation steps of the optimized Floyd algorithm. Among them, for $d_{12}^{(1)}$, it is found that $d_{12}^{(0)}$ in $D^{(0)}$ is greater than or equal to other elements in the first line (except $d_{11}^{(0)}$), so the calculation step of $d_{1r}^{(0)} + d_{r2}^{(0)}$ can be omitted, but the direct result is $d_{12}^{(1)} = d_{12}^{(0)} = 1$, so that $a_{12}^{(1)} = a_{12}^{(0)}$ in $A^{(1)}$ remains unchanged. For $d_{13}^{(1)}$, it is found that only $d_{12}^{(0)}$ is less than $d_{13}^{(0)}$ (except $d_{11}^{(0)}$), so $d_{13}^{(1)} = \min\left(d_{13}^{(0)}, d_{12}^{(0)} + d_{23}^{(0)}\right) = \min(3, 1 + 1) = 2$, and $a_{13}^{(1)} = V_2$. Thus, the values of other elements in $D^{(1)}$ and $A^{(1)}$ can be obtained respectively and hence we have:

$$D^{(1)} = \begin{bmatrix} 0 & 1 & 2 & 3 & 6 \\ 3 & 0 & 1 & 2 & 4 \\ 2 & 3 & 0 & 4 & 6 \\ \infty & 1 & 2 & 0 & 2 \\ \infty & 3 & 4 & 5 & 0 \end{bmatrix} \text{ and } A^{(1)} = \begin{bmatrix} 0 & 0 & V_2 & V_2 & V_2 \\ V_3 & 0 & 0 & 0 & V_4 \\ 0 & V_1 & 0 & 0 & V_4 \\ \Phi & 0 & V_2 & 0 & 0 \\ \Phi & 0 & V_2 & V_2 & 0 \end{bmatrix} \tag{11}$$

Here we have $D^{(0)} \neq D^{(1)}$, then we need to continue the iteration. Similarly, we can get $D^{(2)}$ and $A^{(2)}$:

$$D^{(2)} = \begin{bmatrix} 0 & 1 & 2 & 3 & 5 \\ 3 & 0 & 1 & 2 & 4 \\ 2 & 3 & 0 & 4 & 6 \\ 4 & 1 & 2 & 0 & 2 \\ 6 & 3 & 4 & 5 & 0 \end{bmatrix} \text{ and } A^{(2)} = \begin{bmatrix} 0 & 0 & V_2 & V_2 & V_2, V_4 \\ V_3 & 0 & 0 & 0 & V_4 \\ 0 & V_1 & 0 & 0 & V_4 \\ V_2 & 0 & V_2 & 0 & 0 \\ V_2 & 0 & V_2 & V_2 & 0 \end{bmatrix} \tag{12}$$

Here we have $D^{(2)} \neq D^{(1)}$, then it is concluded that the value of $d_{ij}^{(2)}$ is the shortest path between the corresponding element nodes V_i and V_j, and $a_{ij}^{(2)}$ is the shortest path between the corresponding nodes V_i and V_j. For example, by querying the shortest path and the shortest path between nodes V_1 and V_5, the system can calculate that the shortest path between nodes V_1 and V_5 is 5 and the shortest path is $V_1 \rightarrow V_2 \rightarrow V_4 \rightarrow V_5$ according to the above calculation steps. After this result is obtained, the intelligent selection system can be intuitively presented to tourists in the map, and tourists can arrange virtual journey according to their actual needs.

4 Experiment and Results

The classical Dijkstra algorithm is a process of iterating to generate the shortest path according to the distance between the node and the starting point. It has great blindness in the search process and belongs to brute force search. The time complexity is $O(n^2)$, where n is the number of nodes of the road network model. Because the search process does not consider the direction and location of the end point, in the search process from the starting point, the probability of other nodes and target points being searched is the same. The search area can be approximately a circle with the starting point as the origin and the length of the starting point and the target point as the radius.

In the actual road network, the connection between the starting node and the target node basically represents the general direction of path navigation. Generally speaking, on both sides of the connection between the two nodes, a path from the starting node to the target node can be found. This algorithm drives each step of search towards the end through the setting of heuristic function. The search area can be approximately a rectangular area with the line from the starting point to the end point as the axis of symmetry (Table 1 and Fig. 3).

Table 1. Comprehensive performance comparison of algorithms

Path	#Passed nodes		#Visited nodes		Memory cost		Path length	
	D	BTC	D	BTC	D	BTC	D	BTC
1	2	2	296	1	5488	1000	143.56	142.56
2	4	4	740	13	5504	964	197.83	222.69
3	6	6	1776	168	5508	988	259.10	259.10
4	8	9	5624	562	5504	972	440.47	480.47
5	10	10	8584	749	5504	992	598.08	598.08
6	12	12	10804	1162	6268	984	835.74	835.74
7	14	14	9916	1355	6264	984	818.06	864.31
8	16	17	10804	2186	6280	1008	1256.24	1346.45
9	18	18	11320	2400	6288	1018	1327.11	1327.11

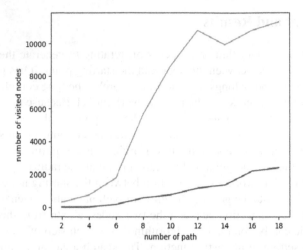

Fig. 3. Comparison of algorithm access nodes

5 Conclusion

This paper introduces the concept of and, their development status and future development trend. The related algorithms, their classification and construction methods and the future development direction are described in detail. Through the theoretical research of various spatial data analysis, this paper focuses on the concept of the shortest path. Then, by comparing the traditional shortest path algorithm, the corresponding representative algorithms are listed according to the three cases of the shortest path algorithm problem. Through empirical calculation, it can be found that the Floyd algorithm based on Virtual Tourism intelligent selection system is improved and optimized, which can effectively reduce the calculation time of traditional tourism path and provide tourists with efficient, intuitive and accurate navigation, which is conducive to the better development of virtual tourism and has important promoting significance for real tourism.

References

1. Yue, Y.: An efficient implementation of shortest path algorithm based on Dijkstra algorithm. J. Wuhan Tech. Univ. Surv. Mapp. **24**(3), 208–212 (1999)
2. Abdulrahman, A., Pilouk, M.: Spatial Data Modelling for 3D GIS. Springer, Heidelberg (2008). https://doi.org/10.1007/978-3-540-74167-1
3. Amirebrahimi, S., Rajabifard, A., Mendis, P., Ngo, T.: A data model for integrating GIS and BIM for assessment and 3D visualisation of flood damage to building. Locate **15**, 10–12 (2015)
4. Boada, I., Navazo, I., Scopigno, R.: Multiresolution volume visualization with a texture-based octree. Visual Comput. **17**(3), 185–197 (2001)
5. Chen, L.C., Wu, C.H., Shen, T.S., Chou, C.C.: The application of geometric network models and building information models in geospatial environments for fire-fighting simulations. Comput. Environ. Urban Syst. **45**, 1–12 (2014)

6. Zimmermann, T., Wirtz, H., Punal, O., et al.: Analyzing metropolitan-area networking within public transportation systems for smart city applications. In: International Conference on New Technologies. IEEE (2014)
7. Li, W., Zhao, Z.-K., Na, X.: Deep belief network based 3D models classification in building information modeling. Int. J. Online Eng. **11**(5), 57–63 (2015)
8. Devillers, O., Guigue, P.: Faster triangle-triangle intersection tests. Dissertation, INRIA (2002)
9. Chuck, E., Lee, J.-M., Jeong, Y.-S., et al.: Automatic rule-based checking of building designs. Autom. Constr. **18**(8), 1011–1033 (2009)
10. Funkhouser, T., et al.: A search engine for 3D models. ACM Trans. Graph. (TOG) **22**(1), 83–105 (2003)
11. Guttman, A.: R-trees: a dynamic index structure for spatial searching. ACM (1984)
12. Huang, G.-B., Zhu, Q.-Y., Siew, C.-K.: Extreme learning machine: theory and applications. Neurocomputing **70**(1–3), 489–501 (2006)
13. Choi, J., Choi, J., Cho, G., et al.: Development of open BIM-based code checking modules for the regulations of the fire and evacuation
14. Crane, K., Weischedel, C., Wardetzky, M.: Geodesics in heat: a new approach to computing distance based on heat flow. ACM Trans. Graph. **32**(5), 13–15 (2013)
15. Wang, J., Ying, S., Liu, Z., et al.: Route planning based on Floyd algorithm for intelligence transportation system. In: IEEE International Conference on Integration Technology, ICIT 2007. IEEE (2007)
16. Wei, D.: An optimized floyd algorithm for the shortest path problem. J. Networks **5**(12), 1496–1504 (2010)
17. Wei, D.: Implementation of route selection function based on improved Floyd algorithm. In: IEEE 2010 WASE International Conference on Information Engineering (ICIE), pp. 223–227 (2010)
18. Lin, S., Kernighan, B.W.: An effective heuristic algorithm for the traveling-salesman problem. Oper. Res. **21**(2), 498–516 (1973). https://doi.org/10.1287/opre.21.2.498
19. Hasan, B.S., Khamees, M.A., Mahmoud, A.: A heuristic genetic algorithm for the single source shortest path problem. In: IEEE/ACS International Conference on Computer Systems and Applications. IEEE (2007)
20. Khemlani, L.: Building product models: computer environments supporting design and construction. Autom. Constr. **11**(4), 495–496 (2002)

Financial Risk Analysis and Early Warning Research Based on Crowd Search Algorithm

Bian Tingting[⊠]

Dongying Vocational College, Dongying 257091, Shandong, China

Abstract. Nowadays, a broad consensus has been formed on the internationalization of corporate management. However, with the development of China's economy and society and the continuous expansion of the global investment market, more multinational companies and industries have entered our country, and Chinese companies will also face many uncertain operating factors, as well as increasingly fierce international competition. The development and future of the company will face very huge challenges. Make financial analysis and early warning before the financial crisis, and promptly notify the management, investors and other stakeholders of the problem, so that they can take timely measures to reduce the hidden dangers in financial risks, which has become the company's current urgent need for improvement the actual problem. This article focuses on the research of financial risk analysis and early warning based on crowd search algorithm, and understands financial risk analysis and early warning and related theories of crowd search algorithm on the basis of literature data, and then analyzes the financial risk analysis and early warning system of memory crowd search algorithm is designed and tested. The test results show that the comprehensive risk score of the experimental company in this paper is 0.349 in 2017. According to the company's 2018 financial data, the risk analysis of this paper is effective.

Keywords: SOA algorithm · Financial risk · Risk warning · Financial crisis

1 Inductions

The financial risks of enterprises are mainly formed through business activities, so they are highly related to business activities, and have the characteristics of great influence of the uncertainty of the external environment [1, 2], and therefore there is no method for companies to comprehensively and accurately predict operations and management. This makes a huge gap between the actual income of the enterprise and the predicted result [3, 4], and the combined effect of all the above uncertain factors will form the financial risk of the enterprise [5, 6]. Now that China's domestic financial market is increasingly open, Chinese domestic companies will also usher in an era where opportunities and challenges coexist. How to effectively prevent financial risks within the company in this uncertain market environment and ensure its smooth operation will be an urgent problem to be solved [7, 8].

For financial risk analysis and early warning research, some researchers have given a complete definition of corporate value and capital flow. In short, corporate financial

© Springer Nature Singapore Pte Ltd. 2022
Y. Tian et al. (Eds.): ICBDS 2021, CCIS 1563, pp. 194–202, 2022.
https://doi.org/10.1007/978-981-19-0852-1_15

risk refers to various internal and external factors that cannot be predicted and controlled during the company's business process, reducing its effectiveness and continuity. The interruption of changes in corporate value may deviate from the expected goal of the company's actual operating results, and have a negative impact on the company's survival, growth and profitability [9]. Some researchers believe that the specific causes of financial risks are not the same. These include external reasons for the business and necessary reasons for the business itself. In general, the main reasons are: first, the company's capital structure is unreasonable, second, the fixed asset investment decision-making is not scientific enough, third, financial managers do not understand financial risks, fourth is corporate finance, fifth, high credit sales gap, accounts receivable out of control [10]. To sum up, there are many researches on financial risk analysis and early warning, but the application research on deep learning in financial risk analysis and early warning needs to be studied in depth.

This paper conducts research on financial risk analysis and early warning based on crowd search algorithms, analyzes the classification of financial risks and the application of crowd search algorithms on the basis of literature data, and then designs a financial risk analysis and early warning system based on crowd search algorithms, and use examples to verify.

2 Financial Risk Analysis and Early Warning and Research on Crowd Search Algorithms

2.1 Financial Risk Classification

The categories of financial risks include three categories: legal and policy risks, financial risks and business risks. The procedure of financial risk analysis is shown in Fig. 1:

(1) Profit risk. As a profitable business, profitability is the most worrying issue for stakeholders, and profit risk is also the most worrying risk for stakeholders [11]. The profitability of a company is related to whether the company's market value can continue to grow, which is related to whether stakeholders can obtain the excess profits and interest they must obtain from their investment. Therefore, profitability is the most important factor affecting the company's stock price. When there is a problem with profitability, the company's market value fluctuates, which will adversely affect investors, fail to absorb good investments, and affect the company's steady growth.

(2) Debt repayment risk. The company's debt repayment risk mainly refers to whether there is sufficient cash flow to repay the debt after the debt matures. Corporate debt is divided into short-term debt and long-term debt [12]. Long-term borrowers can earn more profits through a small amount of business. After years of growth, there is an opportunity to convert debt into stocks and become shareholders to earn excess returns. The company also needs to maintain a good capital structure during the loan process. Not just because the company wants to use financial leverage to increase the rate of return, or because when the company is in danger of paying off its debts and cannot pay off its debts on time, creditors can apply to the court

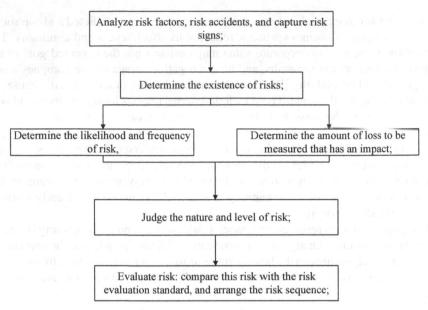

Fig. 1. Financial risk analysis procedures

for bankruptcy protection to protect their own interests. Debt service risk is usually measured by indicators such as current ratio, fast ratio, and asset-liability ratio.

(3) Operation is dangerous. Enterprises are faced with various operating risks in the process of production and operation. The biggest problem an enterprise faces in the course of its operation is the problem of cash flow. Customers have the problem of insufficient cash flow, and they often settle activities that occupy the company's funds in the form of accounts receivable or accounts receivable to improve the competitiveness of the industry. In daily business, operations and management need to support cash flow. The settlement method of accounts receivable is relatively risky. If the company does not manage the accounts receivable and invoices in accordance with the prescribed internal control system, the proportion of non-performing loans will increase, and the accounts receivable and bills will not be recovered, which will lead to interruption at the end of the company's capital chain.

(4) Development risks. The company's growth risk is whether the company's operating profit and operating profit will continue to grow in the long term. Whether a company can maintain the growth of operating income is an important indicator to measure the sustainable growth of a company's business. Whether a company has viable operating capabilities and good profitability are the growth risks it faces. Growth risks also depend on the fluctuations in the country's economy. As the country's economic situation improves, companies can track the country's development and gain more opportunities for growth. However, when the country's economy declines, the purchasing power of consumers will decline, and businesses will be hit hard by growth.

2.2 Application of Crowd Search Algorithm

With the advancement of science and technology, people expect that the requirements for information technology in human production and life will increase, and the progress of optimized computing will have a huge promotion significance for human progress. In real life, when a problem arises, the optimal solution can be found through the inertia of people's thoughts and actions. Intelligent behaviors generated during experience and social activities. SOA is mainly to study the intelligent behavior of human beings in the process of random search. These behaviors all involve reasoning, communication, collaboration, and cognitive learning, and combine search decision-making with evolutionary thinking, and then use the search team as the main research goal, and the individual's position is also used as a candidate solution for the optimization problem, and then used Human's reasoning method of search "experience gradient" and uncertainty respectively determines the search direction and search step length, and selects the final optimal solution based on this.

2.3 Crowd Search Algorithm

The ambiguous reasoning behavior of SOA refers to the ability of using fuzzy control systems to imitate the search action of intelligent humans and to link perception (ie objective function) with behavior (ie step length). The Gaussian membership function represented by the variable of the fuzzy search step is as follows:

$$u_A(x) = e^{-(x-u)/2\delta^2} \tag{1}$$

Here, the Gaussian membership variable is represented by u_A, the input variable is represented by x, and the membership function parameters are represented by u and δ respectively. If the output variable is greater than $[u - 38, u + 38]$, the value of participation less than 0.0111 will be negligible or not counted, so 0.0111 is set as the lower limit.

When using a linear membership function, the degree of participation is proportional to the order of the value in the function. That is, if the member value is the highest, it is in the best position. Currently the highest u is 1.0, and the lowest u is in the worst position. Currently, as shown in Eq. (2), the minimum participation rate is 0.0111,

$$u_{ij} = rand(u_i, 1) \tag{2}$$

Among them, u_i is the attribution degree of the objective function i j as the dimension in the search space, and u_{ij} is the attribution degree of the objective function i as the dimension in the search space j. The Rand function $(u_i, 1)$ is a real number distributed uniformly and randomly in $[u, 1]$.

3 Financial Risk Analysis and Early Warning System Based on Crowd Search Algorithm

3.1 Selection of Indicators

(1) Principles of index selection

1) Relevance. Different industries have different emphasis on different financial ratios, and different ratios have different names, reflecting the different financial risks of the company. Therefore, the choice of financial ratio needs to be based on the company's actual financial risks, which can reflect the characteristics of the industry and the company's specific conditions, and can provide a reliable reference value for the company's growth.
2) Comparability. The selected financial ratio should be able to reflect factors affecting financial risks and losses in a scientific and timely manner through horizontal or vertical comparison, and be more sensitive to economic changes.
3) Function. The choice of financial risk ratio must be accessible, functional, and truly reflect the company's financial status.
4) Content. Since financial risks are widely present in the company's various financial activities, the selection of financial risk early warning indicators should be as complete as possible and represent the company's overall financial status.

(2) Establishment of indicators

Combining the above analysis, choose financial indicators that can reflect the different financial status of the company's production and operation. This article selects five categories that can be used to measure the company's solvency, profitability, operating capacity, growth capacity and cash flow. 21 economic indicators were used as initial indicators.

Solvency ratio measures short-term solvency by selecting current ratio and high-speed ratio, and long-term solvency by selecting asset-liability ratio and net debt ratio.

For the rate of return, select the net sales rate, net assets ratio, return on net assets, and earnings per share.

In the performance indicators, select the account receivable turnover rate, inventory turnover rate, current asset turnover rate and total asset turnover rate.

The growth indicators select the growth rate of total assets, the growth rate of net profit, the growth rate of net cash flow from operating activities, and the growth rate of main business income.

3.2 Model Construction

Studies have shown that a BP neural network with only one hidden layer can infinitely approximate the continuous function of a closed space. Therefore, increasing the number of hidden layers will increase the difficulty of calculation, but will not affect the prediction research. Therefore, a 3-level BP neural network model will be selected in this article (the structure is shown in Fig. 1). The standard early warning system has nine variables, so the input layer has nine neurons. There is only one expected result, that is, the financial status of the company, so there is only one output neuron. Related research shows that the number of nodes in the middle layer is represented by the expression $n1 = n + m + a$, where n is the number of input neurons, m is the number of output neurons, and a is a parameter between 0 and 10. In this paper, n is 11. In order to satisfy the output value between 0 and 1, the transfer function of the middle layer adopts a tangent function, and the transfer function of the output layer adopts a logarithmic function.

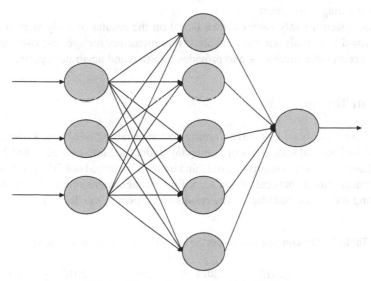

Fig. 2. BP neural network model structure

Before using the BP neural network to predict business status, the BP neural network must first be trained using training samples to create a BP neural network model. The selected 9 indicators are used as input samples, and the actual situation of listed companies is used as the target output sample. The output samples are divided into two groups according to the actual situation of the company, one group is critical and the other group is normal. A crisis enterprise is defined as 1, and a normal enterprise is defined as 0 (Fig. 2).

3.3 The Functional Design of the System

(1) Maintenance of system data

The data maintenance subsystem is the main data source of the system, which is filled with all the financial and other data required by the entire early warning system. The subsystem is mainly composed of four modules: parameter and basic data maintenance, index and model library maintenance, risk knowledge countermeasure maintenance, and financial statement data maintenance. The system provides users with different configurations, so that they can choose the method and method of early warning analysis according to the specific business conditions, and can flexibly adjust the time and method of alarm. The retention of financial statement data is mainly to maintain the company's three basic financial statements: balance sheet, income statement and cash flow statement. The system can import and export financial statements, integrate with other financial software systems, and directly use financial data for early warning analysis.

(2) Early warning analysis

The financial risk early warning analysis module is the core of the system and consists of two major modules: early warning analysis and indicator analysis.

(3) Alarm and diagnosis report

This subsystem mainly issues alarms based on the results of early warning analysis, uses crowd search algorithms to analyze risk measures for specific risks, provides appropriate preventive measures, and provides intuitive and accurate reports.

4 System Testing

According to the financial risk early warning system established above, a financial risk analysis of the financial statements of a company under the State-owned Assets Supervision and Administration Commission of China in 2018 is carried out. The total valuation of each financial statement is calculated according to four dimensions, and the company's annual rating scores are calculated. The results are shown in the Table 1.

Table 1. The company calculates the aggregate rating score for each year

	2013	2014	2015	2016	2017
Profitability	0.137	0.189	0.186	0.186	0.014
Solvency	0.259	0.297	0.267	0.267	0.191
Operating capacity	0.103	0.097	0.075	0.075	0.077
Development ability	0.229	0. 218	0.072	0.072	0.067
Overall ratings	0.728	0.801	0.6	0.6	0.349

It can be seen from Fig. 3 that from 2015 to 2016, the company's overall rating was 0.6, the company's financial risks were in a medium-warning state, the company's business activities were poor, some financial indicators were abnormal, the financial status was problematic, and the possibility of financial risks higher. The company's overall rating in 2017 was only 0.349. It is in a serious alert state in the financial early warning system, and the company faces higher risks. The company is in trouble, most of the financial indicators are obviously abnormal, the financial situation is deteriorating, and the possibility of financial risks is very high. According to 2018 data, the warnings in this article are effective.

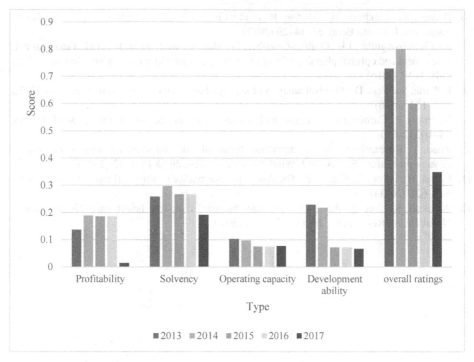

Fig. 3. The company calculates the aggregate rating score for each year

5   Conclusions

This paper studies the financial risk analysis and early warning based on the crowd search algorithm. After understanding the relevant theories, the financial risk analysis and early warning based on the crowd search algorithm is designed. Then use the system to conduct experimental tests. Through experiments, it is concluded that the comprehensive score of the experimental company in 2017 is only 0.349, which is in the position of serious warning in the financial early warning system. The company considers the risk of gluten to be greater. The warning in this article is effective.

References

1. Ca Rdoso, S.R., Barbosa-Povoa, A.P., Relvas, S.: Integrating financial risk measures into the design and planning of closed-loop supply chains. Comput. Chem. Eng. **85**, 105–123 (2016)
2. Wong, A., Carducci, B.: Do sensation seeking, control orientation, ambiguity, and dishonesty traits affect financial risk tolerance? Manag. Financ. **42**(1), 34–41 (2016)
3. Newall, P.: Downside financial risk is misunderstood. Judgm. Decis. Mak. **11**(5), 416–423 (2016)
4. Prades, J., Varghese, B., Reano, C., et al.: Multi-tenant virtual GPUs for optimising performance of a financial risk application. J. Parallel Distrib. Comput. **108**, 28–44 (2016)
5. Li, B., Arreola-Risa, A.: Financial risk, inventory decision and process improvement for a firm with random capacity. Eur. J. Oper. Res. **260**(1), 183–194 (2017)

6. Barnes, K., Mukherji, A., Mullen, P., et al.: Financial risk protection from social health insurance. J. Health Econ. **55**, 14–29 (2017)
7. Santibanez-Aguilar, J.E., Guillen-Gosálbez, G., Morales-Rodriguez, R., et al.: Financial risk assessment and optimal planning of biofuels supply chains under uncertainty. Bioenergy Res. **9**(4), 1–17 (2016)
8. Dellana, S., West, D.: Survival analysis of supply chain financial risk. J. Risk Finance **17**(2), 130–151 (2016)
9. Sadorsky, P.: Carbon price volatility and financial risk management. J. Energy Markets **7**(1), 83–102 (2016)
10. Zhao, Y.: Research on wireless distributed financial risk data stream mining based on dual privacy protection. EURASIP J. Wirel. Commun. Netw. **2020**(1), 1–12 (2020)
11. Crona, B., Folke, C., Galaz, V.: The Anthropocene reality of financial risk. One Earth **4**(5), 618–628 (2021)
12. Adhikari, S.R., et al.: Access to medicine; financial risk; free health care; Nepal; poor. J. Nepal Health Res. Counc. **16**(41), 372–377 (2019)

Design Guidance for Lightweight Object Detection Models

Rui Wang[1], Xueli Wang[1], Yunfang Chen[1], and Wei Zhang[1,2(✉)]

[1] School of Computer Science, Nanjing University of Posts and Telecommunications,
Nanjing 210023, Jiangsu, China
zhangw@njupt.edu.cn
[2] Jiangsu Key Laboratory of Big Data Security and Intelligent Processing, Nanjing
University of Posts and Telecommunications, Nanjing 210023, Jiangsu, China

Abstract. The lightweight target detection model is deployed in an environment with limited computing power and power consumption, which is widely used in many fields. Most of the current lightweight technologies only focus on a few steps of the model implementation and lack a global perspective. Therefore, this paper proposes a general lightweight model implementation framework, including network construction indicators, lightweight backbone network design, and model optimization. By analyzing the complexity indicator of network structure, the factors that affect network performance such as depth and width are summarized. On this basis, combine the One-Shot Aggregation (OSA) idea and Cross-Stage Partial Network (CSPNet) transformation to construct a general lightweight detection network CSPOSA. Further specific optimization strategies are proposed to prune the network structure and training process. For the network structure, the width and depth of the network are adjusted, the amount of parameters of the model is compressed. The training process is divided into the first, middle and last three stages to improve the detection performance of the model without adding extra computation. Taking embedded platform helmet detection as the experimental scene, the parameter amount of the realized model is 1/10 of the mainstream models YOLOv3 and YOLOv4, and the detection accuracy is similar, so it is more suitable for deployment on devices with limited computing power.

Keywords: Target detection · Lightweight model · Efficient convolutional layer · Model pruning · Finetuning

1 Introduction

As artificial intelligence technology advanced, a large number of target detection algorithms based on deep learning have emerged, which have been used in fields such as autonomous driving, industrial inspection, and robot vision. To improve the accuracy of the model, from shallow LeNet [10], Alexnet [9] to deep GoogleNet [17], etc., the number of network layers is gradually increasing. While

© Springer Nature Singapore Pte Ltd. 2022
Y. Tian et al. (Eds.): ICBDS 2021, CCIS 1563, pp. 203–217, 2022.
https://doi.org/10.1007/978-981-19-0852-1_16

the target detection effect is improved, it also brings a huge amount of parameters and longer reasoning time, which hamper these algorithms to be deployed in daily life scenarios. Therefore, researchers begin to focus on the lightweight of the model.

Lightweight target detection models need to make a trade-off between accuracy, parameter amount, and running speed, and strive to have better usability on embedded devices, mobile devices, and so on [13]. In the process of deploying the deep learning model and finally putting the network into use, the designed neural network is the key to the entire system. In other words, a model with a simple structure and high recognition accuracy is what we are looking for.

Lightweight target detection technology covers multiple aspects such as deep learning, model optimization, and data compression. However, these techniques only focus on a few points of model design and lack theoretical guidance and implementation framework throughout the whole process. In response to the above-mentioned problems and challenges, this paper proposes a general framework for implementing lightweight detection models for various specific applications. Our contributions are as follows:

• Propose four indicators for the construction of a lightweight object detection network: computing amount, memory access, memory access cost, and DRAM traffic, which help to network selection and modification.

• Combinene One-Shot aggregation (OSA) connection and Cross-Stage Partial Network (CSPNet) transformation to realize a general lightweight backbone network CSPOSA.

• Considering the specificity of the detection task, optimize the network structure of the model and the training process for the CSPOSA network.

2   Related Work

2.1   Target Detection Technology Based on Deep Learning

Traditional target detection algorithms mainly rely on manually extracted features to detect objects, which are difficult to meet the requirements of data processing performance, speed, and intelligence. With the vigorous development of deep learning, the target detection technology based on the convolutional neural network has surpassed traditional algorithms with the characteristics of simple and efficient network structure and gradually becomes the current mainstream algorithm. It can be divided into two main branches: two-stage detection and one-stage detection.

Two-stage detection divides the target detection problem into two stages: first, select region proposals from the input image, and then classify and regress them. The first two-stage object detection model is R-CNN [3] and one of the most representative models is Faster R-CNN [16] with region proposal network which improves efficiency. From R-CNN, SPPNet [5], Faster R-CNN to Mask R-CNN [4], these algorithms all adopt the basic idea of "region proposal + convolutional neural network + classification regression" to continuously improve the detection accuracy and speed. But in general, the real-time performance of these networks is poor, and it is difficult to meet actual needs. Therefore, the researchers put forward a new idea, namely one-stage detection.

The one-stage networks use one step to predict the position and category confidence of the target after generating the feature map in the backbone network and output the prediction result, which greatly improves the speed of the detection algorithm. SSD [12] and YOLO series networks are representative models of one-stage detectors. The detection accuracy of early one-stage networks such as YOLOv1 [14] is lower than that of the same period two-stage networks. With the introduction of new technologies such as anchor frame detection and feature fusion, the detection accuracy of current mainstream one-stage networks such as YOLOv3 [15], YOLOv4 [1], and has reached an advanced level. The one-stage detection not only meets the requirements of precision and real-time but also can easily replace the components of the network, which is more friendly to engineering applications.

2.2   Model Lightweight Technology

To ensure the real-time performance of the target detection model in practical applications, the network model is usually simplified and compressed to achieve lightweight goals. The existing technologies to realize model lightweight are mainly divided into four categories: pruning, network redesign, knowledge distillation, and quantitative acceleration.

The ideological basis of pruning is to find out and remove the redundant parts in the network structure, to reduce the loss of model accuracy while compressing the network size. A typical example is Li. H et al. [11] proposed the convolution kernel pruning with the smallest absolute value of weight cut off proportionally. However, the accuracy of this method decreases significantly, and it is necessary to train again on the original data set to restore accuracy, which increases the training cost.

Network redesign achieves compact models by designing a more efficient network with less accuracy loss. For example, Huang. R et al. [7] proposed the YOLOlite model, which simplifies the backbone network to a 7-layer shallow model, and achieves model lightweight on non-GPU devices. Network redesign relies on the designer's experience, and due to the different performance of the deployed equipment, different networks vary greatly.

Knowledge distillation exploits knowledge transferring between small model and large pre-trained model with high performance. Hinton. G et al. [6] use the pre-trained complex network with good performance to provide a soft target to guide the training process of the student network and obtain a student network with a much smaller size and enough accuracy.

Quantitative acceleration reduces the number of bits required to represent each weight to downscale models and speeds up forward inference. Krishnamoorthi. R [8] uses quantized weights and activation values during forwarding propagation and uses high-precision gradient descent during backpropagation. Because the quantization process reduces the accuracy of weights and activation values, models will suffer from accuracy loss after quantization.

3   Lightweight Network Construction and Model Optimization

The goal of the realized lightweight target detection model framework implemented is to help the model have sufficient detection accuracy while being used in actual detection tasks. This section first analyzes the indicators that restrict network construction, combines OSA connections and CSP ideas, and builds CSPOSA modules to reduce feature redundancy. Based on the general detection network, the network structure and training process are optimized to improve the model specificity of detection tasks. For the network structure, adjust the width and depth of the network, cut redundant parts, and compress the parameters of the model. As for the training process, it is divided into three stages, namely, the first, the middle, and the last, to improve the model's detection performance without adding additional computation.

3.1   Indicator Analysis of Lightweight Detection Model

The indicators for network construction can be summarized into two aspects: constraint conditions and network complexity. The constraint conditions include the performance of deployment equipment and the difficulty of detection tasks. The performance of the device mainly refers to its computing power and bandwidth. They determine the computing power and storage access capabilities of the device and restrict the complexity of the network structure. As for the difficulty of detection tasks, it is necessary to comprehensively consider factors such as the size of the target and its distribution density. The model should have enough feature extraction capabilities to avoid low detection accuracy.

Intuitively, the complexity of the network is mainly manifested in the smaller amount of parameters and shorter inference time, which represents the small scale and high operating speed of the network. However, by analyzing the calculation methods of network complexity, it can clarify which structural attributes of the network affect its performance, mainly including the following categories.

Computation Amount. Similar to the computing power of the device, the time complexity of the network is evaluated by the number of calculations. For the entire model, computation amount can be approximated as formula (1):

$$FLOPS \sim O(\sum_{l=1}^{d} M^2 \cdot K_l^2 \cdot C_{l-1} \cdot C_l) \tag{1}$$

M represents the size of the feature map obtained by performing the convolution operation on the input map for each convolution kernel in the convolution layer, K is the size of the convolution kernel, d is the number of convolution layers, and l represents the l-th convolution layer in the network structure, C_{l-1} and C_l are the number of input and output channels of the convolutional layer respectively. Compared with the convolution layer, the computation of the pooling layer, up-sampling layer, and other functional layers can be ignored, so the computation amount of the whole network can be approximated as the sum of the computation of all the convolution layers.

Memory Access Amount. Memory access amount is composed of the number of network parameters and the size of the feature map. These two parts represent the space complexity of the model.

Memory access amount can be approximated as formula (2):

$$Space \sim O(\sum_{l=1}^{d} K_l^2 \cdot C_{l-1} \cdot C_l + \sum_{l=1}^{d} M^2 \cdot C_l) \tag{2}$$

The first term of the formula is the approximation of the network parameters, and the second term is the approximation of the size of the feature map. K_l^2 is the amount of parameters contained in one channel of a convolution kernel, and C_{l-1} is the number of channels of a convolution kernel of the lth convolution. For a convolutional layer with C_l convolution kernels, the parameter amount is $K_l^2 \cdot C_{l-1} \cdot C_l$, and the volume of the feature map is $M^2 \cdot C_l$. Same as the computation amount, the memory access amount of the entire network structure can be approximated as the sum of the memory accesses of each convolutional layer.

According to formulas (1) and (2), since the number of convolutional layers is the depth of the network, the number of convolutional layer channels is the width of the network, and the feature map size is proportional to the resolution of the input image, so the factors that affect the network performance can be summarized as the depth, width, and resolution.

Memory Access Cost. Memory access cost (MAC) is the time cost of accessing the memory. During operation, the device needs to load the relevant data into the cache and then perform the calculation. This process does not increase the computation amount but affects the running speed of the model.

Take a convolutional layer with a convolution kernel size of 1×1 as an example, the number of input and output channels are set to c_1, c_2, and the width and height of the feature map are w, h, then the computation amount of this convolutional layer is $B = hwc_1c_2$. For 1×1 convolution, the image size is unchanged, and the size of the input and output feature maps are equal. MAC is shown in formula (3) :

$$MAC = hw(c_1 + c_2) + c_1c_2 \tag{3}$$

Putting the formula $B = hwc_1c_2$ into the mean inequality can derive formula (4), which shows that for this convolutional layer, MAC has a lower bound:

$$MAC \geq 2\sqrt{hwB} + \frac{B}{hw} \tag{4}$$

When $c_1 = c_2$, the MAC obtains the lower bound. This conclusion guides this paper to keep the number of input channels and output channels of the convolutional layer equal when designing the network structure of the model, so as to reduce the memory access cost and increase the speed of the network.

DRAM Flow. P. Chao et al. [2] put forward a viewpoint that reading weight parameters from dynamic random access memory (DRAM) causes more power consumption than network operations. Therefore, DRAM flow is an important indicator that affects network power consumption, and its unit is the sum of convolution input and output, as shown in formula (5):

$$CIO = \sum_l (C_{in}^{(l)} \cdot w_{in}^{(l)} \cdot h_{in}^{(l)} + C_{out}^{(l)} \cdot w_{out}^{(l)} \cdot h_{out}^{(l)}) \sim O(\sum_{l=1}^{d} M^2 \cdot (C_{in}^{(l)} + C_{out}^{(l)})) \tag{5}$$

CIO is the approximate value of the DRAM flow, which is the accumulation of the product of the number of input and output channels and the size of the feature map for each convolutional layer. The volume part of the feature map of the memory access amount is similar to that of the CIO and is affected by the depth, width, and resolution of the network.

3.2 Lightweight Detection Network Based on OSA Connection

The residual connection method linearly superposes inputs and nonlinear transformations of inputs. The dense connection method directly connects all convolutional layers, and the input of each convolutional layer is affected by the output of all previous convolutional layers in the module, to improve the information, which is an effective improvement of residual connection. However, dense connections also lead to feature redundancy and computational inefficiency. Therefore, the OSA connection proposed in this paper is improved based on the dense connection, with channel superimposition only at the end of the module, as shown in Fig. 1.

Since the OSA module also uses the superposition of all channels, it needs to add 1×1 point convolution to control the number of channels at the end. However, this method introduces more point convolutions and increases bandwidth consumption. To make the network structure lighter, we further introduces the network CSP transformation. The transformation is to divide the input of each module into two parts according to the channel. One part is input into the convolutional layer in the module, and the other part is superimposed with the output at the end of the module. CSPNet reduces the network width and makes the network lighter by truncating the gradient flow.

As shown in Fig. 2, the module connected by OSA is composed of k convolution layers. At the end of the module, the output of k convolution layers is superimposed on the input of the OSA module. Assuming that the number of

Fig. 1. OSA connection

channels of the input module is b, the input and output channels of each convolution layer are both g, then the total number of output channels of the module is (b + kg).

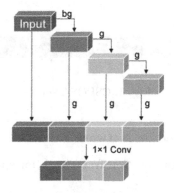

Fig. 2. OSA module

As shown in Fig. 3, if the OSA module is transformed, the number of channels of the input module is b/2. As the number of output channels of the module is twice the number of input channels, $b/2 + kg = 2b$. Formula (4) is applied to conclude that the number of input channels of each convolution layer is equal to the number of output channels, and $g = b/2$ is obtained. At this time, it can be concluded that the MAC of the module is optimal when $k = 3$.

As shown in Fig. 4, the final general lightweight detection network CSPOSA-Net is composed of 5 sets of CSPOSA modules stacked, including 5 downsampling. If the computing power of the deployed device is weak, the CSPOSA module can be appropriately simplified into a convolutional layer with a step size of 2. As the basic network before the next step of dedicated optimization, this network has a certain adjustment space and can flexibly respond to different deployment equipment.

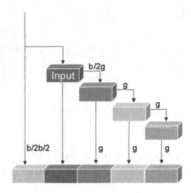

Fig. 3. CSPOSA module

Fig. 4. CSPOSANet

3.3 Optimization Based on Network Structure

Figure 5 shows a model optimization framework for specific detection applications.

Width Construction. The width of the network is the number of channels in each layer. A commonly used index to measure the importance of a channel is the scale factor of the batch normalization layer. The input of batch normalization is the input set $x : B = \{x_1, x_2, ..., x_m\}$ of a single training batch. The output is the normalized response $\{y_i = BN_{\gamma,\beta}(x_i)\}$ of the batch. Batch normalization is divided into four steps. The first two steps calculate the input mean μ_B and variance σ_B^2 of the batch.

$$\hat{x}_i = \frac{x_i - \mu_B}{\sqrt{\sigma_B^2 + \varepsilon}} \tag{6}$$

$$y_i = \gamma\hat{x}_i + \beta \equiv BN_{\gamma,\beta}(x_i)\} \tag{7}$$

The third step is as shown in formula (6). Use the mean and variance to normalize the training samples of this batch. ε is to avoid the tiny positive number with a denominator of 0. The fourth step, as shown in formula (7), introduces two learnable parameters, scale factor γ and offset factor β, and linearly transforms the normalized output. The size of γ indicates the channel's ability to transmit information. The channel with the stronger ability to transmit information is more important to the model.

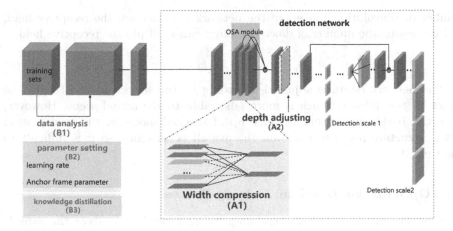

Fig. 5. Lightweight model optimization framework

The width pruning based on the scale factor is divided into two steps: sparse training and pruning. The purpose of sparse training is to make the distribution of scale factors sparse, enlarge the gap between different factors, and facilitate subsequent pruning.

$$L = \sum_{(x,y)} l(f(x, W), y) + \lambda \sum_{\gamma \in \Gamma} g(\gamma) \tag{8}$$

Formula (8) represents the objective function of sparse training, (x, y) represents the input and target values, The first term of the formula is the original objective function of the target detection model, the second term is the penalty function of the scale factor, and λ is used as the coefficient to balance the two terms. This paper chooses L1 regularization as the penalty function, namely $g(\gamma) = |\gamma|$. In addition, because L1 regularization is not smooth, sub-gradient descent is used as an optimization method.

Depth Adjustment. The depth of the model is determined by the number of layers of the network. This paper proposes a method to adjust the depth of the network based on detecting the receptive field of the input feature map of the head. As shown in Fig. 5, the area mapped by the pixels in the feature map of a certain layer of the network on the original input image is the receptive field of this layer. Because the target detection model sets a detection anchor frame on the area corresponding to each pixel of the detection head input feature map, the feature vector of the feature map is affected by the receptive field area.

The calculation method of the receptive field is shown in formula (9), which is mainly affected by the convolutional layer and the pooling layer of the backbone network. r_l represents the receptive field of layer l, s_l represents the step size, and k_l represents the size of the convolution kernel. For the pooled layer, the receptive field is r_l times that of the next layer. According to Formula (9), increasing the number of convolutional layers of the network can increase the receptive field, and increasing the number of down-sampling can multiply the receptive field.

$$r_{l-1} = s_l \times r_l + (k_l - s_l) \tag{9}$$

The network depth is adjusted according to the size characteristics of the target in the dataset, which is more adaptable to the actual scene. However, since the backbone network is made up of stacked modules, the modification of the structure needs to maintain the overall consistency, so it is difficult to fine-tune it.

3.4   Optimization Based on Training Process

Before Training. Before the training, we first need to analyze the sample dataset of the deployment scenario. When the source of the dataset is complex and the label quality is mediocre, the dataset should be cleaned and the incorrectly labeled labels should be modified or removed. After that, the characteristics of the dataset are analyzed from three aspects: image size, number of categories, and labeling frame.

For the image size, if there are many large-size images, the image needs to be segmented and preprocessed. Regarding the number of categories, pay attention to whether there is a serious imbalance between the categories in the dataset. For specific label frames, analyze the width and height distribution, aspect ratio distribution, and area distribution of each type of target.

Training in Progress. The optimization strategy applied in training is mainly the adjustment of hyperparameters. This paper mainly discusses the selection of the learning rate and the prior parameters of the anchor frame. The learning rate can be dynamically adjusted with the training process, and anchor frame parameters can refer to the k-means clustering results of labeled boxes.

Adjustment of Learning Rate. The learning rate is the step size in the gradient descent process. The current common learning rate adjustment strategy is to attenuate the learning rate to 1/10 of the previous one after a certain stage of training. The calculation method of the basic value of the learning rate is shown in formula (10), k represents the number of GPUs of the training platform, and s represents the number of images input in a training batch:

$$lr = k \times s \times 0.000125 \tag{10}$$

In addition, the learning rate can be warmed up. When the pre-training weights are not loaded, the parameter values of the model are randomly selected. If a larger initial value is directly selected, the model will have a larger shock. Therefore, it is necessary to use a small learning rate to "warm-up" the model, and then change the learning rate back to the basic value after the model is stable.

Anchor Frame Parameter Adjustment. As shown in Fig. 6, a set of anchor boxes of different sizes are set on each pixel of the feature map input in the detection head, and the problem of predicting the position and category of the target is transformed into the target judgment in the anchor box and the correction of the anchor box position. The size and proportion of the anchor frame are a set of pre-set parameters. Generally speaking, the pre-trained prior anchor frame parameters can achieve better training results, but in special detection scenarios, the prior parameters generated by K-Means on the data set are more targeted.

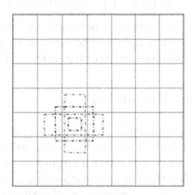

Fig. 6. A pixel on the feature map corresponds to a set of pre-set anchor frames

After the Training. The compression of the network structure will affect the accuracy of the model. Therefore, for models with severe accuracy loss after compression, using the model before compression as a teacher model for knowledge distillation can restore the accuracy to a certain extent and improve the lightness of the model.

The knowledge distillation of the image classification task uses the output of the softmax layer as the soft target, which only contains one dimension of category confidence. The output of the target detection task contains values in two dimensions of category and location regression. Therefore, the application of knowledge distillation in target detection needs to adjust the composition of the loss function, and calculate the loss function of category and location separately.

$$L_{cls} = \mu L_{hard}(P_s, Y) + (1 - \mu)L_{soft}(P_s, P_T) \tag{11}$$

Formula (11) expresses the loss function design of the confidence of the student model category: L_{hard} is the loss function of the confidence of the original category, which is the cross-entropy of the student model's prediction result of the category and the label value Y; L_{soft} is a soft loss function between the predicted values of the teacher model P_T and the student model P_s. μ is a hyperparameter used to balance the two items.

Since the regression direction, R_s provided by the teacher model may deviate from the true value Y, the L2 distance between the teacher model R_s and the student model R_T relative to the true value is calculated respectively. The soft loss function $L_b(R_s, R_T, Y)$ is defined as for formula (12):

$$L_b(R_s, R_T, Y) = \begin{cases} ||R_s - Y||_2^2, ||R_s - Y||_2^2 + m > ||R_T - Y||_2^2 \\ 0, else \end{cases} \quad (12)$$

The loss function of the bounding box regression of the student model is formula (13):

$$L_{reg} = L_{sL1}(R_s, Y) + \gamma L_b(R_s, R_T, Y) \quad (13)$$

According to the new loss function obtained by introducing the soft loss function, the student model is trained on the dataset under the guidance of the teacher model to further improve the accuracy of the student model.

4   Experiments and Results

In construction sites and factories, it is an integral part of smart security to monitor whether people entering the area are wearing hard hats as required. Since monitoring equipment usually needs faster inference speed and certain detection accuracy, this paper applies the implementation framework of the lightweight target detection model to such a scenario to realize the helmet detection model.

4.1   Experimental Environment and Data

The configuration of the training platform is a single CPU, Intel®Xeon®CPU E5-2678 v3@2.50 GHz, single GPU, NVIDIA GTX1080Ti, 11 GB video memory. The experiment only uses the CPU to complete the image detection, simulating the deployment environment without GPU.

This paper uses SHWD (Safe Helmet Wearing-Dataset) to train and test the detector. This dataset has a large scale and high labeling accuracy. SHWD mainly refers to the personnel wearing safety helmets in scenes such as construction sites and factories. The 7,581 images include 9,044 people wearing helmets and 111,514 people without them. The size distribution of helmet targets in the SHWD dataset is relatively uniform, which is close to the detection scene in daily life.

4.2   Evaluation Index

This paper uses four indexes to evaluate the performance of the model: mean Average Precision (mAP), inference time, frames per second (FPS), and model weight scale. mAP is a comprehensive index that combines precision and recall. In this paper, based on the Pascal VOC dataset standard, the IOU threshold is set to 0.5. The detection results with IOU > 0.5 are defined as true positives, and the remaining results are negative positives. Sort the confidence levels of the predicted values, and calculate the accuracy and recall rates in the prediction results whose confidence is higher than the given rank value. Different rank values will change the recall rate. Therefore, as in formula (14), choosing 11 different recall values is equivalent to selecting 11 different rank values, and we calculate the corresponding precision value. Then we could draw a precision-recall curve and the area under the curve is the average precision (AP) of the category. By averaging the AP values of all categories, we could obtain mAP value.

$$AP = \frac{1}{11} \sum_{r \in \{0, 0.1, \ldots, 1\}} p_{interp}(r) \tag{14}$$

The inference time represents the time required for the model to detect an image, and FPS represents the number of images that the model can process per second. The size of the parameter weight is the scale of the model and the memory consumption of the model when the deployment platform is running. The inference time and the number of parameters are an intuitive manifestation of the lightness of the model.

4.3 Model

Construct the lightweight detection network HD-OSA according to Chap. 3, and its network structure is shown in Fig. 7. This paper implements three detection models based on the HD-OSA network: (1) basic model is which is obtained by HD-OSA network training 100 batches on SHWD dataset. (2) Model HD-OSAprn after width compression. Applying the channel compression method proposed in Sect. 3.3, 300 batches of HD-OSA are trained on SHWD with a sparse ratio of 0.005, and then redundant channels are cropped at a compression ratio of 60% to improve the lightweight of the detection model. (3) Model HD-OSAdtl after knowledge distillation. Applying the knowledge distillation method proposed in Sect. 3.4, the model with an 80% compression ratio trimmed with a severe decrease in accuracy is used as the student model, and HD-OSA is used as the teacher model to restore the detection accuracy.

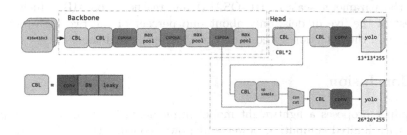

Fig. 7. Network structure of HD-OSA

4.4   Experiments and Results

We compared mAP, recall, weight scale, single-frame detection time, and FPS of HD-OSA, HD-OSAprn, HD-OSAdtl, and benchmark model YOLOv3, YOLOv4 on SHWD. The results are shown in Table 1.

Table 1. Performance comparison between HD-OSA and comparison model on SHWD dataset

Model	Recall	mAP	Weight scale	Single-frame detection time	FPS
HD-OSA	92.9	89.9	23.1	0.063	15.87
HD-OSAprn	80.4	76.2	6.81	0.046	21.74
HD-OSAdtl	82.1	77.4	2.63	0.046	21.74
YOLOv3	93.8	90.2	239.0	0.252	3.97
YOLOv4	94.5	91.8	243.1	0.417	2.40

It can be seen from Table 1 that the recall and mAP of HD-OSA are slightly lower than YOLOv3 and YOLOv4, but there is no significant drop. In this accuracy, the weight scale of HD-OSA is about 1/10 of YOLOv3 and YOLOv4, and the processing speed of a single image is about 4 times that of YOLOv3 and 6.6 times that of YOLOv4, effectively improves the usability of the detection model.

HD-OSAprn further reduces the weight scale to 6.81 MB, and FPS is 21.74, reaching the speed of quasi-real-time detection. However, compared with HD-OSA, its mAP dropped by 13.7%, and its recall dropped to 80.4%. This shows that the width compression has a more obvious impact on the detection accuracy of the model.

HD-OSAdtl performs knowledge distillation on the model compressed with 80% pruning rate with serious loss of accuracy, so that mAP and recall are slightly higher than HD-OSAprn. Although the mAP is still lower than HD-OSA, the parameter scale of HD-OSAdtl has reached 2.63 MB, which is the smallest of the five models, only about one percent of the two high-precision models, and the detection speed is also reached quasi-real-time.

5   Conclusion

This paper proposes a lightweight model implementation framework for platforms with limited computing power and power consumption. The model was applied to the detection of safety helmets, and the lightweight detection networks HD-OSA, HD-OSAprn, and HD-OSAdtl were constructed. Compared with the YOLOv3 and YOLOv4, the accuracy of HD-OSA is similar to the former two, the parameters are 1/10 of the former two, and the inference speed is 4 times and 6.6 times that of them respectively. HD-OSAdtl compresses the parameters to

1% of the mainstream model under the premise of a 12% reduction inaccuracy, and is close to quasi-real-time processing. Therefore, we believe that the proposed model is lighter, faster, and more suitable for deployment in lightweight real-time inspection models than the reference model.

Acknowledgement. This work is supported by National Key R&D Program of China (No. 2019YFB2101700).

References

1. Bochkovskiy, A., Wang, C., Liao, H.M.: Yolov4: optimal speed and accuracy of object detection. arXiv preprint arXiv:2004.10934 (2020)
2. Chao, P., Kao, C., Ruan, Y., et al.: HardNet: a low memory traffic network, pp. 3552–3561 (2019)
3. Girshick, R., Donahue, J., Darrell, T., et al.: Region-based convolutional networks for accurate object detection and segmentation. IEEE Trans. Pattern Anal. Mach. Intell. **38**(1), 142–158 (2015)
4. He, K., Gkioxari, G., Dollár, P., et al.: Mask R-CNN, pp. 2961–2969 (2017)
5. He, K., Zhang, X., Ren, S., et al.: Spatial pyramid pooling in deep convolutional networks for visual recognition. IEEE Trans. Pattern Anal. Mach. Intell. **37**(9), 1904–1916 (2015)
6. Hinton, G., Vinyals, O., Dean, J.: Distilling the knowledge in a neural network. arXiv preprint arXiv:1503.02531 (2015)
7. Huang, R., Pedoeem, J., Chen, C.: YOLO-LITE: a real-time object detection algorithm optimized for non-GPU computers, pp. 2503–2510 (2018)
8. Krishnamoorthi, R.: Quantizing deep convolutional networks for efficient inference: a whitepaper. arXiv preprint arXiv:1806.08342 (2018)
9. Krizhevsky, A., Sutskever, I., Hinton, G.: ImageNet classification with deep convolutional neural networks. In: Advances in Neural Information Processing Systems, pp. 1097–1105 (2012)
10. LeCun, Y.: Lenet-5, convolutional neural networks **20**(5), 14 (2015). http://yann.lecun.com/exdb/lenet
11. Li, H., Kadav, A., Durdanovic, I., et al.: Pruning filters for efficient convnets. arXiv preprint arXiv:1608.08710 (2016)
12. Liu, W., Anguelov, D., Erhan, D., et al.: SSD: single shot multibox detector, pp. 21–37 (2016)
13. Plastiras, G., Kyrkou, C., Theocharides, T.: EdgeNet: balancing accuracy and performance for edge-based convolutional neural network object detectors. In: Proceedings of the 13th International Conference on Distributed Smart Cameras, pp. 1–6 (2019)
14. Redmon, J., Divvala, S., Girshick, R., et al.: You only look once: unified, real-time object detection, pp. 779–788 (2016)
15. Redmon, J., Farhadi, A.: Yolov3: an incremental improvement. arXiv preprint arXiv:1804.02767 (2018)
16. Ren, S., He, K., Girshick, R., et al.: Faster R-CNN: towards real-time object detection with region proposal networks. In: Advances in Neural Information Processing Systems, vol. 28, pp. 91–99 (2015)
17. Szegedy, C., Liu, W., Jia, Y., et al.: Going deeper with convolutions. In: Proceedings of the IEEE Conference on Computer Vision and Pattern Recognition, pp. 1–9 (2015)

Application of Digital Twin in the Security Protection of the Internet of Things in Power System

Yu Chen[✉], Ziqian Zhang, and Ning Tang

NARI Group Corporation/State Grid Electric Power Research Institute, Nanjing, China

Abstract. This paper provides an overview of DT and PSDT, and explores the potential applications of PSDT. For power digital twin, its purpose is to promote the effective use of data flow, with virtual deduction means, combined with real-time situation perception, to get a full understanding of the power system, and then can play an auxiliary role in the formulation of regulatory decisions. Different from the current simulation software, PSDT has the features of data-driven, real-time interaction and closed-loop feedback. This paper analyzes the background and purpose of PSDT from the perspective of engineering and scientific science, and expounds the ideas and characteristics of construction, and further designs the implementation framework of PSDT. Finally, the application status and prospects of PSDT in many fields of power systems are clarified. The research results of this paper promote the development of dt technology and the application of data science in engineering.

Keywords: Digital twin · PSDT · Power system · Power flow calculation · Data-driven

1 Introduction

Power system is by far the largest, most complex, financial and technology-intensive synthetic composite system of all industrial systems in the world, and is one of the most important achievements in the history of human engineering science [1–3]. The nonlinear, high-dimensional, hierarchical, distributed and other characteristics of power system are the difficult problems of power system cognition. In recent years, the power system is open, flat, decentralized and boundary fuzzy. This will further increase the complexity of the power system cognition [4, 5].

Correct cognition of power system is a prerequisite for power grid operation management and scheduling control. Cognition mainly involves timely and accurate perception of the current state of the system and deduce the possible development trend of the system [6]. The cognitive difficulty of modern power system is that, first of all, the entities in the system are diversified and have high asymmetry, and each entity has a strong nonlinear, uncertainty and concealment. Secondly, the system itself and its operating environment are complex and are in a state of constant evolution. The information is inaccurate, the

© Springer Nature Singapore Pte Ltd. 2022
Y. Tian et al. (Eds.): ICBDS 2021, CCIS 1563, pp. 218–229, 2022.
https://doi.org/10.1007/978-981-19-0852-1_17

update of the network topology of the distribution network may be delayed, the line impedance parameters are vulnerable to the climate environment, and the measurement data will also be defects, such as missing, abnormal and unsynchronous. Digital Twin is an integrated, multidisciplinary, and Simulation processes of multi-physical quantities, multi-scale, and multi-probabilities. Digital Twin is compatible with the current popular technologies of intelligent sensors, 5G communications, cloud platform, big data analysis and artificial intelligence [7]. The purpose of the digital twin is to design the virtual body model in the digital space and establish the mapping relationship between the physical entity of the digital virtual body by fully mining the benefits brought by the massive data resources.

Digital twin of power systems (PSDT) is an emerging product under the increasing complexity of power model, data blowout trend and the development and improvement of DT technology [8, 9]. Compared to focusing on information-physics systems for manipulating real-time entities or classic model-driven simulation software, PSDT focuses more on data-driven real-time situational perception. In addition, DT will introduce the concept of people in the future and eventually build interactive systems in real physical space and virtual digital space, which is also a research direction of DT [10].

Based on the data flow carried by the power Internet of Things, this paper focuses on the data utilization methodology from two engineering and scientific perspectives, and answers the scientific question of how to extract the value of the power data flow. This paper combines the thinking, cognition and practice of PSDT and analyzes the connotation and extension of the basic knowledge of PSDT.

2 Construction Background of the PSDT

2.1 Cognitive Approach of Classical Power Systems

As mentioned in the introduction, the modern power system is by far the most complex man-made system in the world, and its stable operation is related to the national economy and even people's livelihood [11]. Correct cognition of the power system is an important means to ensure the operation of the stable system. Inadequate situation awareness is also one of the root causes of the power outage.

Such methods mainly take physical models as the main driving force (model-based), supplemented by low-dimensional statistics, belonging to the first three stages of the scientific paradigm, cannot avoid its inherent drawbacks [12]. First, for complex systems and their behavior, it is difficult to establish physical models that satisfy the solution speed and accuracy constraints, especially for (intertwined) systems strongly interwoven with the units or factors under its jurisdiction. Secondly, the utilization and effect of the data are subject to the built physical mode. The dimensions of the model will limit the upper limit on the number of utilization of variables, the accuracy of the model affects the accuracy of the cognitive results, and the personalization of the model causes the difficulty of information selection. Thirdly, it is difficult to analyze and deal with the uncertainty, and the error transfer mechanism and the error accumulation effect between the various subphysical models are difficult to describe and evaluate, so that the characterization effect of the extracted final characteristics cannot be guaranteed. The above drawbacks can seriously affect its engineering application and may even cause serious wrong decisions.

2.2 Digital Twinning Technology

The architecture of cable distribution technology based on digital twinning is in Fig. 1, which has five parts, real cable management point, twin cable management point, cable twin data, data service platform, cable control system. The real cable material management point refers to the physical entity space composed of assembly cable, personnel and so on, carrier of digital twin. Twin cable material management point is the mapping of physical entities in digital space, including models and rules, and is the driving force of digital twins. Cable twinning data is a collection of simulation data of real cable material management point and twin cable material management point, and is the core of digital twinning. The data service platform mainly includes the field bus for data transmission, the data interface, the intelligent gateway and the noise reduction algorithm program for information processing. By identifying and processing the multi-source heterogeneous information of the real distribution point and the twin distribution point, the real-time and effective information is finally transmitted to the database, and the twin data that forms the cable material management point is the engine of the digital twin. The cable control system is the brain of digital twin, which is used to judge and predict the real-time distribution state by positioning and simulation technology.

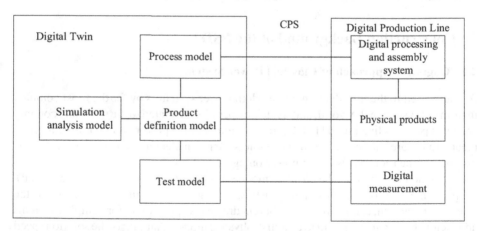

Fig. 1. Digital twinning and digital production line

Digital twin describe the model of each specific link connected by digital thread. Digital thread runs through the entire product life cycle, especially seamless integration from product design, production [14], operations and maintenance. Digital twin is more like the concept of smart products, which emphasizes feedback from product operations to product design. Digital twin is the digital shadow of physical products. Through the integration with external sensors, it reflects all the characteristics of objects from micro to macro, and shows the evolution process of product life cycle. And, of course, not just products, systems that produce products and systems that are in use and maintenance need to be as needed.

3 Frame Design of the PSDT

DT is shown in Fig. 2, when acting on a power system, which is data-driven as the kernel and gathers traditional model-driven and expert systems. Compared with the simulation of the classical physics mechanism such as Matpower [8], PSCAD, the establishment of the electric power twin system PSDT is less dependent on the physical system and is more flexible. PSDT relies mainly on history, real-time data, and matching high-dimensional statistical analysis, machine deep learning and other tools. PSDT can correct the comparison with the real value, and other active behavior to ensure the consistency of the virtual system.

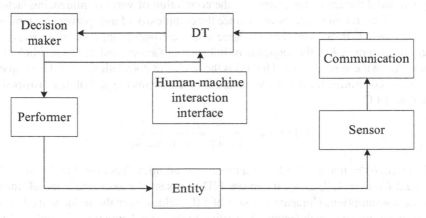

Fig. 2. Schematic diagram of the digital twin in the power system

For the above purposes, PSDT should have three features: data driven, closed-loop feedback and real-time interaction. Data drive makes PSDT more applicable to today's complex power systems. We can build a physical system model based on the obtained data and analyze the system. Model-driven mode requires preprocessing of large amounts of information. For example, the topology of the grid and Jacobian matrix can do the tide Flow calculation, and the model driving mechanism lacks an effective mechanism to deal with the evaluation and transmission of inherent errors and uncertainties of assumptions, simplification and the system. The data-driven mode can effectively avoid the above problems, and can achieve the model and interwoven problem decoupling to some extent. Closed-loop feedback enables the data model of PSDT to achieve adaptive update and optimization by actively learning massive data after the operation, and the learning effect improves with the increase of data. And real-time interaction and linkage data-driven and closed-loop feedback, further improved PSDT real-time situational awareness and super real-time virtual testing, so that it can accurately control the system in normal operation or even emergency situations unified situation and quickly simulate feasible optimized decision schemes to achieve the class twin effect than Apollo. In terms of data input and pre-processing, the data of PSDT is still of electrical quantity such as voltage, power, and its data sources can be from the synchronous phase amount measurement device PMU or voltage transformer PT and current transformer ct, etc. This part mainly describes the treatment of constraints and uncertainties. Some constraints existing in the power system can be defined by normalization or preset domain.

4 Operating Mechanism of Digital Twins in Power Systems

4.1 Power Prediction Model Based on Digital Twin

User electricity consumption is related to holidays, weather and other factors, and the same factors have different degrees of influence between different users. This paper uses the maximum influence factor to analyze the correlation between user electricity consumption and different factors. Organize the correlation of various influencing factors, remove weak correlation factors, and reduce the complexity of user power consumption prediction model. In the correlation degree statistical operation, a is the sequence of power consumption, b is the sequence of influencing factors, and the largest influence factor between the variables a and b reflects the degree of correlation. Let C be a sequential dual set, containing the a and b variables. $C|_E$ represents the probability distribution of the data set C.

$$\text{FID}(C) = \max_{ab < B(|C|)} \frac{I * (C, a, b)}{\log_2 \min\{a.b\}}$$

$I * (C, a, b) = \max_E I(C|_E)$, F is a monotonic addition function, $F(n) = o(n)$. For individual $C_k (k = 1, 2, ..., n)$, it can use FID to assess the associated size of impact and user consumption. Compare the size of FID values, sort the influencing factors, and group strong and weak factors. According to the actual situation, a number of top influencing factors are selected to construct the training sample set to train the prediction model of user electricity consumption. An integrated model for C, X training trees on datasets with l training samples and j user power features uses the k sub-functional phase superposition to obtain the final output.

$$\hat{b} = \varphi(a_i) = \sum_{k=1}^{k} f_k(a_i), \quad f_k \in M$$

$$M = \{f(a) = wq(a)\}(q : R^j \longrightarrow Y), w \in R^Y$$

M is the space of the decision tree; q is the structure of the tree; Y is the corresponding number of leaf nodes. Each M corresponds to a tree structure q and a leaf junction point w. The score of the leaf i is indicated by w_i. Use the decision rule of the tree to classify it to the corresponding leaf node, while combining the score and addition of the corresponding leaf node as the final power consumption prediction value. To obtain the corresponding function clusters in the decision tree model, the following target functions can be minimized.

$$\begin{cases} N(\varphi) = \sum_i n(\widehat{b_i}, b_i) + \sum_k \Omega(M_k) \\ \Omega(M) = \gamma Y + \frac{1}{2}\lambda \|a\|^2 \end{cases}$$

In the formula, N is a differentiable convex loss function, the difference between power consumption prediction and target value; Ω is a threshold function, controlling the complexity of the decision tree model.

4.2 Process for the Model

The following explains the operation process from the three working mechanism of the overall power situation in the key equipment area of the power Internet of Things and the low-voltage power supply fault perception, and the specific steps is shown below.

Step1, mass data of power generation, transmission, substation, distribution and power consumption in ubiquitous power Internet of Things is collected through high-performance data collection equipment.

Step 2, organize the real-time data of the power grid equipment according to the collected real-time data of the power grid equipment and the historical data of the power grid equipment service cloud platform. Quality comparison is used to compare the historical data of the algorithm to the service platform. Determine whether the grid equipment in operation meets the quality requirements according to the specification data of the grid equipment service cloud platform.

Step 3, if the quality requirements are not met, interact with the matching grid equipment twin model and find 3D maintenance instructions in the ubiquitous power IoT experience library.

Step 4, the 3D maintenance guidance connects and communicates with the relevant maintenance operation guidance through the actual equipment maintenance service, and builds a digital twin model based on high fidelity. It simulates the maintenance process of the power grid equipment to improve the accuracy of maintenance.

Step 5, interiterate the repaired grid equipment data for acquisition and matching twin model and jump to step 3.

Step 6, if the quality requirements are met, the simulation data such as axial fatigue wear, torsional vibration and thermal stress generated by the digital twin model, and the fusion data obtained through multidimensional data processing and fusion, are exchanged to realize the prediction of the power grid risk part.

Step 7, comparing and interact with the current desired state defined by the digital twin model of ubiquitous power IoT, evaluate the current ubiquitous power IoT operation state, and realize iterative optimization of fault diagnosis, prediction and health management technologies of ubiquitous power IoT systems.

Step 8, according to the obtained user file data, process real-time electricity data and historical data, and statistics all relevant influencing factors.

Step 9, when the load problem occurs in the overall area, it interacts with the matching power twin model, three-dimensional maintenance instructions are found in the ubiquitous power Internet of Things experience library, and the power supply adjustment process is simulated on the digital twin model to improve the accuracy of maintenance.

Step 10, jump the adjusted power data with the matching twin model to step 9.

Step 11, when there is no load problem in the overall area, it iterates with the simulation data such as axial fatigue wear, torsional vibration and thermal stress produced by the digital twin model, so as to realize the prediction of the risk part of the power network.

Step 12, comparing and interact with the current desired state defined by the digital twin model of ubiquitous power IoT, evaluate the current ubiquitous power IoT operation state, and realize iterative optimization of fault diagnosis, prediction and health management technologies of ubiquitous power IoT systems.

Step 13, according to the collected real-time data of the low voltage power supply area and other influencing factors, as well as the historical data of the low voltage power supply service cloud platform, the fault wave recording data is reviewed by connecting the digital double knowledge database and the experience database.

5   DT Implementation and Case Analysis

In this section, the measured data has obtained 2 results through the flow equation and data drive, and the reliability of the PSDT analysis is verified by analysis of both. On the other hand, when the mechanism model is insufficient, the data-driven model can still provide a more reasonable result. In this process, it is reflected that PSDT and traditional power methods can be well combined well, and the two will provide the dispatchers with more reliable and more comprehensive information through mutual verification and supplement.

5.1   Calculation of the Power Flow

Power flow calculation is the basis of power system operation planning and the first step of steady state and transient analysis. Classical power flow calculation systems such as Matpower follow the regular design of the ontology system, as shown in Fig. 3

Power flow calculation first needs to know the topology and parameters of the network, then divide them into 3 nodes according to the attributes of the node, and then list the equations and solve the n system state variables by Niuola method and so on.

The core steps are as follows.

1) Active and reactive power of the node i

$$
\begin{cases}
P_i = U_i \sum_j U_j (G_{ij} \cos \theta_{ij} + B_{ij} \sin \theta_{ij}) - U_i^2 g_i \\
Q_i = U_i \sum_j U_j (G_{ij} \sin \theta_{ij} - B_{ij} \cos \theta_{ij}) + U_i^2 b_i
\end{cases}
$$

Where, $Y_{ij} = G_{ij} + jB_{ij}$ is the derivative matrix parameter and $y_{ij} = g_i + jb_i$ is the pair-ground derivative of the node i.

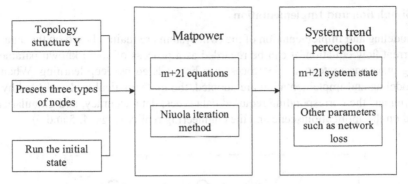

Fig. 3. Conventional model

2) Based on (1), the Jacobian matrix j is

$$
\begin{cases}
H_{ij} = \frac{\partial P_i}{\partial \theta_j} = U_i U_j (G_{ij} \sin \theta_{ij} - B_{ij} \cos \theta_{ij}) - \delta_{ij} Q_i + \delta_{ij} U_i^2 b_i \\
N_{ij} = \frac{\partial P_i}{\partial U_j} U_j = U_i U_j (G_{ij} \cos \theta_{ij} + B_{ij} \sin \theta_{ij}) + \delta_{ij} P_i - \delta_{ij} U_i^2 g_i \\
K_{ij} = \frac{\partial Q_i}{\partial \theta_j} = U_i U_j (-G_{ij} \cos \theta_{ij} - B_{ij} \sin \theta_{ij}) + \delta_{ij} P_i + \delta_{ij} U_i^2 g_i \\
L_{ij} = \frac{\partial Q_i}{\partial U_j} U_j = U_i U_j (G_{ij} \sin \theta_{ij} - B_{ij} \cos \theta_{ij}) + \delta_{ij} Q_i + \delta_{ij} U_i^2 b_i
\end{cases}
$$

3) Based on (2), the solution is solved iteratively by the oxlar method

$$
\Delta y := \begin{bmatrix} \Delta P_1 \\ \cdots \\ \Delta P_m \\ \Delta P_{m+1} \\ \cdots \\ \Delta P_{n-1} \\ \Delta Q_{m+1} \\ \cdots \\ \Delta Q_{n-1} \end{bmatrix} = \begin{bmatrix} H_{m\times m} & H_{m\times m} & H_{m\times m} \\ H_{m\times m} & H_{m\times m} & H_{m\times m} \\ H_{m\times m} & H_{m\times m} & H_{m\times m} \end{bmatrix} \begin{bmatrix} \Delta \theta_1 \\ \cdots \\ \Delta \theta_m \\ \Delta \theta_{m+1} \\ \cdots \\ \Delta \theta_{n-1} \\ \Delta U_{m+1} / U_{m+1} \\ \cdots \\ \Delta U_{n-1} / U_{n-1} \end{bmatrix} =: \Delta x
$$

In classical model-driven modes, the power flow computing problem and the Jacobian matrix evaluation problems are intertwined. Jacobi matrix evaluation is part of the current flow calculation, and requires the current flow, the Jacobian matrix must be obtained. Moreover, the lack of errors, error transfer of various parameters and error accumulation lacks effective description or analysis means, which makes it difficult to control the final evaluation effect.

5.2 Simulation and Implementation

The modeling and implementation of the twin system are mainly based on the data. For the current flow equation, it can be regarded as a process of some known parameters solving other parameters, so the process can be modeled by deep learning. When the DT modeling and implementation are adopted, the mathematical tools selected by DT modeling and the corresponding required data types, data accuracy, and granularity all depend on the application scene and the engineering reality (Figs. 4, 5 and 6).

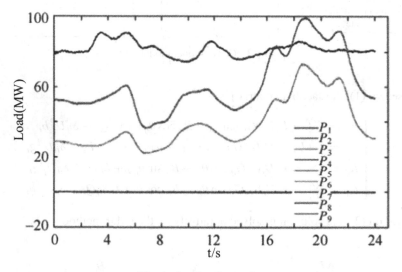

Fig. 4. Load active setting

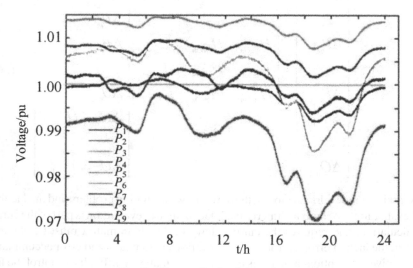

Fig. 5. The amplitude of the voltage

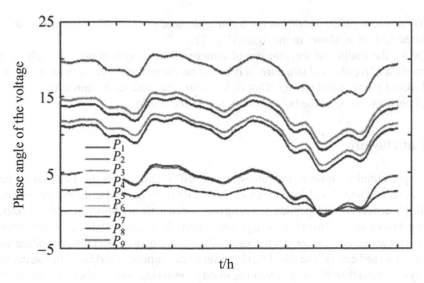

Fig. 6. Phase angle of the voltage

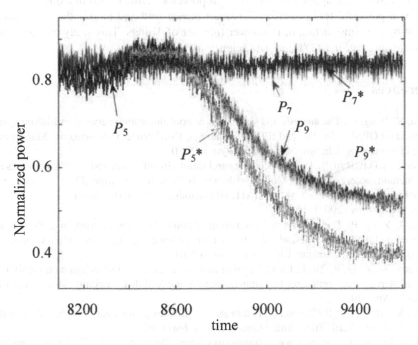

Fig. 7. Normalized power

Similarly, the voltage amplitude and phase angle can be normalized, the 5-layer ann network is established, and the number of neurons in each layer is [14 50 50 50 14], Use

1–8400 moment (0: 00-21: 00) as the training set and 8401–9600 moment (21: 00-24: 00) as the test set as shown in the figure (Fig. 7).

Unlike the traditional way, the establishment of the dt system does not rely on the information of topological structure. It is based on the artificial neural network through two links of training and testing. That is, the historical data set is trained to establish a neural network and uses the built network to test the results.

6 Conclusion

This paper initially explores the framework of PSDT, and details the data-driven, real-time interaction and closed-loop feedback. When PSDT is applied to the power system, it has simple access and independent learning compared to the traditional simulation mode, making it more suitable to the modern power system. In addition, PSDT is closely related to big data analysis to better tap the value of massive data, especially in dealing with uncertainties and errors. The data level is easier to decoupling interleaved problems than the physical model level, such as treating trend monitoring and Jacobian matrix evaluation as two independent problems, and this performance further enhances the engineering utility of PSDT. The application of PSDT in power systems is still in exploring times, PSDT is a powerful tool to realize the smart power grid and realize the data benefits brought by the construction of the power Internet of Things. This study on PSDT also drives the application of DT and data science in engineering.

References

1. Jia, Y., Peng, Z.: The analysis and simulation of communication network in Iridium system based on OPNET. In: The 2nd IEEE International Conference on Information Management and Engineering, Chengdu, China, 16–18 April 2010
2. Connors, D.P., Ryu, B., Dao, S.: Modeling and simulation of broadband satellite networks Part I: medium access control for QoS provisioning. IEEE Commun. Mag. 37(3), 72–79 (1999)
3. Mahafza, B.R., Elsherbeni, A.Z.: MATLAB Simulations for Radar Systems Design. A CRC Press Company (2004)
4. Yu, J., Zong, P.: The analysis and simulation of communication network in iridium system based on OPNET. In: The 2nd IEEE International Conference on Information Management and Engineering, Chengdu, China, 16–18 April 2010
5. Wang, X., Zong, P., Yu, J.: Link analyzing and simulation of TDRSS based on OPNET. In: The International Conference on Communications and Mobile Computing, Shenzhen, China, 12–14 April 2010
6. He, X., Ai, Q., Qiu, R.C., et al.: A big data architecture design for smart grids based on random matrix theory. IEEE Trans. Smart Grid 8(2), 674–686 (2015)
7. Gray, J.: Jim gray on escience: a transformed scientific method. In: The Fourth Paradigm: Data-Intensive Scientific Discovery, pp. xvii–xxxi (2009)
8. Hong, T., Chen, C., Huang, J., et al.: Guest editorial big data analytics for grid modernization. IEEE Trans. Smart Grid 7(5), 2395–2396 (2016)
9. Burges, C., Shaked, T., Renshaw, E., et al.: Learning to rank using gradient descent. In: Proceedings of the 22nd International Conference on Machine learning (ICML-05), pp. 89–96 (2005)

10. Yuan, Y., Ardakanian, O., Low, S., et al.: On the inverse power flow problem. arXiv preprint arXiv:1610.06631 (2016)
11. Chen, Y.C., Wang, J., Domínguez-García, A.D., et al.: Measurement-based estimation of the power flow Jacobian matrix. IEEE Trans. Smart Grid 7(5), 2507–2515 (2015)
12. Kelly, J., Knottenbelt, W.: Neural nilm:deep neural networks applied to energy disaggregation. In: Proceedings of the 2nd ACM International Conference on Embedded Systems for Energy-Efficient Built Environments, pp. 55–64. ACM (2015)
13. Xu, S., Qiu, C., Zhang, D., et al.: A deep learning approach for fault type identification of transmission line. In: Proceedings of the CSEE, vol. 39, no. 1, pp. 65–74 (2019)
14. Boschert, S., Rosen, R.: Digital twin—the simulation aspect. In: Hehenberger, P., Bradley, D. (eds.) Mechatronic Futures, pp. 59–74. Springer, Cham (2016). https://doi.org/10.1007/978-3-319-32156-1_5

Research on Blockchain Security Risk Analysis and Coping Strategies

Guohong Yu[1], Chenggong Ni[2], and Tianquan Liu[3(✉)]

[1] College of Artificial Intelligence, Suzhou Chien-Shiung Institute of Technology,
Suzhou 215400, China
[2] College of Smart Agriculture, Suzhou Polytechnic Institute of Agriculture,
Suzhou 215008, China
[3] College of Internet of Things Engineering, Jiangsu Vocational College of Information
Technology, Wuxi 214153, China
liutq@jsit.edu.cn

Abstract. With the development of blockchain, and its security issues have attracted the attention of more and more researchers. Currently, the related research is still in its infancy. This paper first reviews the basic technology and development of blockchain, summarized and introduced the blockchain structure. In terms of blockchain security, we analyze and summarizes the domestic and foreign literatures in recent years, and divide blockchain security issues into three aspects: protocol security, privacy security and system security, and the problems of blockchain security in these three aspects are analyzed. At present, protocol security research mainly focuses on the encryption mechanism of blockchain technology and smart contract vulnerabilities; Privacy security research covering mainly the potential security issues facing blockchain applications; The system security research mainly includes the classification of attack methods on blockchain. Then, we summarized the defense strategies to deal with the above security issues and analyzed the shortcomings and problems. Finally, based on the current research status of blockchain, we point out two future research directions.

Keywords: Blockchain security · Protocol security · Privacy security · System security

1 Introduction

1.1 Overview of Blockchain

Blockchain is a distributed storage technology used to store transaction information in Bitcoin. Each block contains a unique ID, the ID of the previous block, transaction information and a timestamp, etc. Blockchain solved the ancient Byzantine General problem by proposing a decentralized trust mechanism [1]. Blockchain technology was first described in the paper "Bitcoin: A peer-to-peer electronic cash system" published by Nakamoto in 2008 [2]. Blockchain is a current research hotspot in the field of computing, which is characterized by decentralization, data immutability, autonomy, and privacy [3].

© Springer Nature Singapore Pte Ltd. 2022
Y. Tian et al. (Eds.): ICBDS 2021, CCIS 1563, pp. 230–242, 2022.
https://doi.org/10.1007/978-981-19-0852-1_18

Blockchain technology is essentially a distributed system of records jointly maintained by nodes on a system that is self-trusting and tamper-evident. Each node can store the received transaction information in the form of a Merkle tree [4] through a specific hash function and pack it into a time-stamped data block that is linked to the system to form a new block through a decentralized consensus mechanism. All blocks are interconnected in a chain-like structure, hence the name blockchain. Blockchain is the technical infrastructure for building trust in the Internet society, and provide foundational support for the next generation of Internet technologies including anonymous online payments, money transfers, and other transactions.

Blockchain is not a single technological innovation, but the result of a deep integration of various technologies such as P2P network technology, cryptography, Merkle trees, consensus mechanism, and smart contract, which enable the management of transactions through transparent and trusted rules. As shown in Fig. 1, blockchain technology mainly includes the following features.

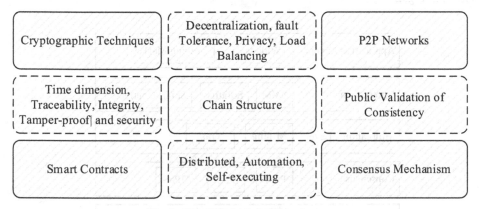

Fig. 1. Blockchain technology features

1.2 Development of Blockchain

Blockchain is an emerging technology system developed on the basis of Bitcoin technology [5], which adds smart contracts, cryptography and other computer technologies to the original technical architecture of Bitcoin, with better programmability and data privacy protection. Its development history can be roughly divided into three stages [6].

Blockchain 1.0, the era of programmable currency, has laid the theoretical foundation of blockchain technology and formed a relatively perfect technical system, and the application scenario is mainly in the field of digital finance, and the classic application is Bitcoin.

Blockchain 2.0, the era of programmable applications, gives blockchain better programmability and compatibility through the introduction of new consensus algorithms, smart contracts and other technologies. The application scenario extends from financial services to games, healthcare, education and other fields, and the representative application is Ether.

Blockchain 3.0, the era of programmable society, the integration of blockchain applications in various industries and the formation of a blockchain ecosystem based on the real society. From the industry integration in 2.0 era, it has changed to social integration [7]. And realize information sharing, such as healthcare, digital intellectual property, Internet of Things, etc.

1.3 Architecture of Blockchain

Nakamoto divides the blockchain system into data layer, network layer, consensus layer and incentive layer. The Ministry of Industry and Information Technology of China [8] divided the blockchain architecture in blockchain 2.0 stage into data layer, network layer, consensus layer, incentive layer and smart contract layer. Yuan Yong etc. [9] researchers divided the blockchain into data layer, network layer, consensus layer, incentive layer, contract layer and application layer. In this paper, we use the blockchain architecture as shown in Fig. 2.

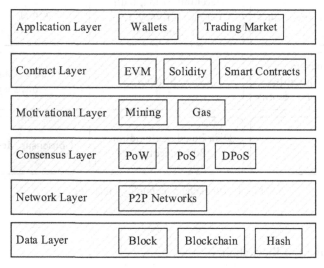

Fig. 2. Blockchain structure

2   The Security Trend of Blockchain

This section will analyze the security issues facing blockchain from three aspects: protocol security, privacy security and system security. The classification of security issues faced by blockchain and the corresponding attack methods are summarized in Table 1.

Table 1. Blockchain security issues classification.

Security issues	The corresponding attack methods
Protocol security	Encryption mechanism, smart contract vulnerability
Privacy security	Identity privacy, transaction privacy
System security	51% Attack, other attacks

2.1 Protocol Security

The main protocol security issues facing blockchain technology are cryptographic mechanisms and smart contract vulnerabilities.

(1) Encryption Mechanism

Private Key Security Issues. In blockchain systems, the private key is the user identity credential. Mayer et al. found a vulnerability in the ECDSA (Elliptic Curve Digital Signature Algorithm) scheme, where Bitcoin and Ether run on a specific curve-secp256k1-and only generate private and public keys, meaning that all parameters are public and could potentially leak information, and an attacker could use the vulnerability to replicate the user's private key, which is difficult to recover once the user's private key is stolen [10]. In [11], a study by Stanford University showed that the addition and multiplication operations in the elliptic encryption algorithm differed significantly in time and performance overhead, and thus secp256k1 was evaluated as an insecure encryption algorithm. Schmidt etc. [12] found that an attacker can use a temporary private key to attack the user and steal the user's signed private key. Courtois et al. proposed a class of ECDSA attacks with bad random numbers, where each of two user signatures can compute the private key of the other signer if the same random number is used in the ECDSA scheme [13].

Cryptographic Algorithm Security Issues. The security of blockchain depends on the strength of cryptographic encryption algorithms. Most blockchain operations use hash algorithms in cryptography, which are currently very secure in theory, but there are still security risks. In [14], Horalek's team analyzed the use of rainbow tables to break the hash function, where the attacker uses the generated rainbow tables to collide with the hash function to obtain the password. Hash length extension attacks are also a class of methods used by attackers to break hash functions, and length extension attacks are attacks against certain cryptographic hash functions that are allowed to contain additional information when the length of the message and key are known [15]. In addition, quantum computing has been a threat to the security of traditional cryptography. In the future, quantum computing is likely to succeed in breaking asymmetric cryptographic algorithms such as ECDSA and DSA (Digital Signature Algorithm).

(2) Smart Contract Vulnerability

Smart contracts are stored on the blockchain and are scripts that can be run automatically on each distributed network node. As long as the terms of the contract are met, the transaction will be carried out automatically without third party supervision [16]. A smart contract is a computer protocol designed to disseminate, validate, or enforce a contract in an informational manner, and is essentially a code program that necessarily and inevitably has incomplete considerations leading to vulnerabilities [17]. As the current smart contract vulnerability prevention measures for blockchain systems such as ethereum are not good enough, contract developers with average security awareness are likely to develop smart contracts that contain fatal vulnerabilities. Huang Kaifeng etc. [18] analyzed and summarized the smart contract security issues. Menglin Fu etc. [19] studied the smart contract vulnerability analysis tool. the contract analyzer Oyente proposed by Luu etc. [20] found four potential smart contract security vulnerabilities. They analyzed 19,366 ethereum smart contracts and found that 8,833 contracts were vulnerable. Currently, there is no uniform specification for the design and implementation of smart contracts. Smart contracts are a cooperative way of interaction between multiple people, and if the contract is not standardized, it can easily lead to misunderstanding of contract behavior by different people, which can lead to a large number of security problems. Due to the mandatory automatic execution of smart contracts, some researches have used smart contracts to achieve access control to resources.

2.2 Privacy Security

This subsection analyzes the privacy security issues facing blockchain in terms of both identity privacy and transaction privacy.

(1) Identity Privacy

Although blockchain technology is considered to have anonymity, it is very difficult to achieve complete anonymity, and most blockchain systems suffer from the security problem of insufficient anonymity. Each node in the blockchain is connected to each other through a P2P network, and Koshy et al. identified three anomalous relay patterns in P2P networks where an attacker can use the bitcoin address to find the corresponding user IP address [21]. Users' transaction behavior may also leak personal information, Androulaki etc. [22] summarized six transaction behaviors that may leak personal information and conducted an experiment in a university by using Bitcoin as a transaction currency and found that by clustering analysis of transaction behaviors, the personal data of 40% of users can be approximated Attackers may also compromise or block decentralized anonymity protocols through witch attacks [23] (using a single nodes to falsify multiple identities and thus attack the system, disrupting the system's redundancy mechanism) to compromise or block decentralized anonymity protocols, creating the risk of compromising the user's true identity [24].

(2) Transaction Privacy

In addition to the potential compromise of user identity privacy, attackers may also steal users' transaction privacy through attacks on users. In [25], Fleder etc. suggest that attackers may combine external information sources with techniques such as information flow analysis to analyze typical user behavior, spending and query habits, bitcoin flows between multiple accounts of the same user, and other relevant statistics to steal users' transaction privacy.

2.3 System Security

System security is the root of blockchain security, and this subsection mainly describes the attacks faced by blockchain system security are 51% attack and other attacks. The Summary of blockchain system security is summarized in Table 2.

Table 2. Summary of blockchain system security.

	Type	Items	Main attack targets	Difficulty
System security	51% attack	Double spending attack	PoW, PoS	High
		History-revision attack	PoW, PoS, DPoS	High
		Shot selling attack	PoS	High
		Selfish mining attack	PoW	High
	Other attacks	Nothing at stake attack	PoS	Low
		Pre-computation attack	PoS	Low
		Long range attack	PoS	Medium

(1) 51% Attack

So what is the 51% arithmetic attack problem? 51% arithmetic attack, also known as Majority attack, refers to the recalculation of already confirmed blocks after controlling more than 50% of the arithmetic power in the network, destroying the decentralized nature of the blockchain, while leaving the network under the risk of several attacks, such as double flowering, random forking, etc. When the mining pool arithmetic power is too large, it is possible to tamper with blockchain data if a malicious organization holds 51% of the arithmetic power of the entire blockchain network [26]. In August 2016, Krypton and Shift, two ethereum-based projects, were subject to a 51% attack. In 2018, the Blockchain.com website reported that the total computing power of the top 5 mining pools already exceeded 70% of the network's computing power. If these mining pools cooperate with each other, a 51% attack can be easily achieved. For the Proof of Stake algorithm, a 51% attack can be launched if the total number of coins owned by a miner exceeds 50% of the network. Once a 51% attack occurs, nodes other than the attacker will not recognize the chain generated by the attacker, and the coins in the entire network may become worthless. Therefore, from the point of view of the attacker's interest, it is difficult for a 51% attack to happen in reality.

(2) Other Attacks

Nothing at Stake Attack [27]. This is an attack against the PoS consensus mechanism, in which an attacker can use equity to maximize the benefits of multiple forks when a fork is created in the blockchain. Since the attacker does not need to consume as much arithmetic power as in the PoW system, he only needs to vote on the equity to maximize the benefit, which is also known as the disinterested problem of "no cost to do evil, infinite benefit", which in a disguised way encourages the creation of blockchain forks.

"Smart" miners tend to adopt the best strategy of "mining on every fork at the same time" in order to get the most profit, which will lead to too many forks in the blockchain, and no longer the only chain. This will lead to too many forks in the blockchain, which will no longer be the only chain. The network nodes will not be able to reach consensus, which will lead to double-spend attacks and the proliferation of illegal transactions.

Pre-computation Attack [28]. In the hybrid consensus mechanism "PoW+PoS", the difficulty of the current block depends on the parameters of the previous block (e.g., hash value). The attacker can calculate and choose a parameter that is most favorable for him to generate the next block by random trial-and-error method when generating the block. In this way, the attacker has a greater advantage to be rewarded with the next block.

Long Range Attack [29]. In PoS system, the block generation speed is much faster than PoW, so the attacker may try to rewrite the blockchain ledger to achieve the purpose of token double spending. This attack is similar to the long-range 51% attack in PoW, but the difference is that in the long-range attack, the attacker may forge a new blockchain master chain without consuming a lot of computing power, and the cost of the attack is lower, so it poses a greater security threat.

3   Blockchain Security Defense Strategies

This section discusses the defense strategies in terms of protocol security, privacy security, and system security challenges, respectively.

3.1   Protocol Security Defense Strategies

(1) Research on Encryption Mechanism
To address the cryptographic mechanism security issue, Gennaro et al. proposed an ECDSA-based threshold signature algorithm to protect Bitcoin wallets [30], where the threshold wallet technique means that the key is partitioned and only the signature authorization can be obtained if the threshold is exceeded. Specifically, the key is divided into n copies, each copy is kept by a node, and when the threshold is t, the key information is available only when no less than t nodes participate in the transaction. Gennaro proposes an optimized threshold DSA algorithm based on the ECDSA key algorithm used in the Bitcoin system, which improves the rate of signature while ensuring the security of the private key.

Generally speaking, the common standard cryptographic algorithms used in blockchain are secure at present, but these algorithms also have certain security risks. Therefore, the following countermeasures can be taken: first, adopt the cryptographic algorithms that are secure at the present stage when designing, and at the same time pay attention to the progress of cryptographic research on anti-quantum attacks and give priority to their use when they mature; second, refer to the way Bitcoin handles public key addresses to reduce the potential risk caused by public key leakage.

(2) Research on Smart Contract Vulnerability

In addition, developers and users of smart contracts can summarize known vulnerabilities in smart contracts and develop formal verification tools for smart contracts to prevent such attacks. Luu etc. proposed a symbolic execution tool called Oyente to detect smart contract vulnerabilities. Oyente uses symbolic execution techniques to analyze the bytecode generated by smart contract compilation and track the execution of the bytecode in the Ethernet virtual machine. Since Ethernet stores bytecode in its own blockchain, Oyente can be used to detect deployed contracts. Oyente takes Ethernet bytecode and global state as input, and the core module consists of four parts: a control flow graph builder, a detector, a core analyzer and a verifier. Tsankov etc. [31] proposed a lightweight and scalable detector for Ethernet smart contracts called Security, it can explicitly indicate whether a contract is secure or not. Pierrot etc. [32] proposed a formal verification framework for smart contracts that uses a program for program verification in the functional language F*, or decompiles an Ethernet Virtual Machine Bytecode program into a program in F*. Town Crier (TC) is an authenticated data input system proposed by Zhang F et al. for off-chain data interaction [33]. Since the smart contracts deployed on the blockchain cannot access the network directly and cannot obtain data directly through https, TC can act as a bridge between https data sources and smart contracts.

Currently, smart contract security analysis tools Oyente, Security and Town Crier have all been put into use.

3.2 Privacy Security Defense Strategies

Due to the public nature of blockchain, the privacy of users may be at risk. This section introduces two privacy protection techniques for blockchain: peer-to-peer hybrid protocols, ring signatures, and non-interactive zero-knowledge proofs.

(1) Research on Identity Privacy

Ring signatures as a digital signature can generate anonymous and valid signatures from a set of possible signers and do not need to inform the actual signature generator [34]. User A chooses a group of participants containing himself and forms a ring, each participant has a public key, User A signs the message with his private key and all the public keys of the ring members, the verifier can know that one of the participant groups has signed the message, but does not know who the actual signer is, so the ring signature provides complete anonymity to the signer. One of the modified versions of ring signatures is the traceable ring signature. This type of ring signature detects whether two signatures are generated by the same user, and each traceable ring signature has a token T containing the public key and specific option tags for each member. User A signs with his private key and the token T, and the verifier also uses T to verify the generated signature, not just the public key.

(2) Research on Transaction Privacy

Peer-to-peer hybrid protocol: Users can obfuscate their transaction traces through peer-to-peer hybrid protocols, where users broadcast their transaction information at the same time, and mix the funds of unrelated anonymous customers through hybrid protocols to complete synthetic transactions without any trusted third party, and since the customers are mutually anonymous, it is difficult for an attacker to get the user's information through the transactions Since the customers are mutually anonymous, it is difficult for an attacker to get the user's information through the results Privacy [35].

Non-interactive zero-knowledge proofs: A zero-knowledge proof is a cryptographic method that aims to prove a given proposition without revealing any additional information. Non-interactive zero-knowledge proofs are an extension of zero-knowledge proofs in which no interaction between the seeker and the prover is required. Sasson etc. [36] propose Zerocoin, a digital currency that applies non-interactive zero-knowledge proofs to achieve both anonymous transactions and transaction privacy security, Zerocash uses zero-knowledge succinct non-interactive knowledge arguments (zk-SNARKs) and a commitment scheme to hide the original address of the transaction and allow the currency value to be assigned in the commitment scheme and zero-knowledge proofs to make the monetary value publicly verifiable. The sender of a transaction encrypts the transaction amount and other metadata using the receiver's public key, which does not reveal the transaction amount or the destination address. Zerocash achieves a high level of anonymity and protects transaction privacy, but requires high computational resources.

3.3 System Security Defense Strategies

This section will analyze two blockchain security techniques for system security issues: SmartPool and countermeasures against other attacks.

(1) Research on 51% Attack

In [37], Luu etc. proposed SmartPool, an ethereum-based smart contract mining pool, which aims to provide efficient and distributed mining services. SmartPool is executed as follows: First, the miner constructs a block template before mining, i.e., the address of the pool contract is used as the Coinbase address. Then, the miner starts mining shares. Once enough shares are mined, the miner starts to build an extended Merkle tree (for secure and efficient proofs) and submits the shares to the pool. After the pool receives the shares, the miner starts to submit the ShareProof proof. Finally, the pool issues a reward based on the verification of the ShareProof proof. The claimList in the pool contract is used to store the shares submitted by users, and the verClaimList is used to store the verification of proofs. Miners who fail to validate do not receive any revenue.

(2) Research on Other Attacks

In a disinterested attack scenario, the Casper mechanism penalizes most malicious behavior and raises the cost of creating a malicious fork, making disinterested attacks unprofitable for the attacker. If a miner wants to participate in mining, he must pledge a certain amount of Ether as a deposit to guarantee that he is mining on the longest chain. If the block is confirmed to be on the chain, the miner recovers his deposit and receives a reward. If other miners try to mine on multiple branch chains to perform disinterested attacks, they will forfeit their deposits on multiple branch chains, a concept called slasher protocol [38], which means that if a miner signs two commitments at the same time on the same tier of the fork, the miner will lose the block reward or even forfeit the deposit. In a precomputation attack scenario, the key for an attacker to determine the computational difficulty of the next block by precomputation is the correlation between the previous block hash and the computational difficulty of the next block in the block generation algorithm. Therefore, in order to prevent precomputation attacks in PoS systems, the block generation algorithm should be reformulated. First, we can consider breaking the connection between the computational difficulty of the current blockchain and the hash value of the previous block, so that the attacker cannot control the computational difficulty of the subsequent block through precomputation; second, we can also consider adding new computational elements, so that the hash value of the previous block is no longer the only factor to determine the computational difficulty of the next block. In the long-range attack scenario, the blockchain network cannot prevent the attacker from forging a new blockchain master chain, but it can prevent the long-range attack by limiting the acceptance of the chain by the whole network nodes by increasing the authentication and reputation value comparison in a way similar to BlockQuick.

4   Future Research

By sorting out and analyzing related researches and combining with the background of blockchain technology development, this subsection analyzes the future trends of blockchain security research field from two aspects. This subsection proposes two future trends of blockchain security research.

A. Blockchain Technology and Artificial Intelligence
Blockchain technology provides data for artificial intelligence, which can be written, traceable and untamperable under consensus mechanism. With blockchain technology, this super data ledger can be established with little cost and without worrying about the security of data. Blockchain technology enables almost barrier-free value exchange, artificial intelligence has the ability to analyze massive amounts of data at high speed, and their combination will produce a whole new paradigm. For example, digital copyright, driverless, etc. Its data security should also get our high enough attention.

B. Blockchain Technology and Electronic Privacy
As blockchain technology becomes increasingly popular and widespread, the number of applications built on blockchain is gradually increasing, and the number of users and assets involved is also increasing, and the ensuing difficulty and risk of privacy protection will also increase.

The value and application of blockchain in information security and privacy protection, protecting privacy is precisely one of the main features of blockchain technology that attracts users. Blockchain privacy protection technology can certainly provide security for the privacy of ordinary people, but some unscrupulous people use blockchain to carry out illegal acts, causing users' privacy or property to be threatened. It is conceivable that strengthening the regulation and review of blockchain technology and improving electronic privacy are important safeguards for the application of blockchain technology. To conclude, blockchain technology plays an important role in electronic privacy protection.

5 Summary

The research on blockchain security is gradually increasing, but its overall is still in its initial stage. In this paper, after researching a large number of blockchain security papers, we first introduce the development history of blockchain and the current system structure. Then, we elaborate the blockchain security posture with the themes of protocol security, privacy security, and system security. Through in-depth analysis of the security problems faced by blockchain and the shortcomings of existing research work, we fundamentally point out the strategies to mitigate or solve the corresponding blockchain security, lay the foundation of blockchain security defense system, and build a relatively complete blockchain security defense system. Finally, the research direction of blockchain security is prospected, and the future hot research directions such as the combination of blockchain technology and big data security under artificial intelligence, blockchain and electronic privacy protection are pointed out.

Acknowledgement. This paper is supported by the 13th Five-Year Plan for Education Science of Jiangsu Provincial in 2020 (Grant No. D/2020/03/10), Soft Science Research Program Projects of Taicang City (Grant No. 202001).

References

1. Ye, C.C., Li, G.Q., Cai, H.M., et al.: Security detection model of blockchain. Ruan Jian Xue Bao/J. Softw. **29**(5), 348–1359 (2018)
2. Nakamoto, S.: Bitcoin: a peer-to-peer electronic cash system (2020). https://bitcoin.org/bitcoin.pdf
3. Dagher, G.G., Mohler, J., Milojkovic, M., et al.: Ancile: privacy-preserving framework for access control and interoperability of electronic health records using blockchain technology. Sustain. Cities Soc. **39**, 1–43 (2018)
4. He, K., Shi, J., Huang, C., Hu, X.: Blockchain based data integrity verification for cloud storage with T-merkle tree. In: Qiu, M. (ed.) ICA3PP 2020. LNCS, vol. 12454, pp. 65–80. Springer, Cham (2020). https://doi.org/10.1007/978-3-030-60248-2_5
5. Huang, J.F., Liu, J.: Survey on blockchain research. J. Beijing Univ. Posts Telecommun. **41**(2), 1–8 (2018)
6. He, H.W., Yan, A., Chen, Z.H.: A survey of smart contract technology and application based on blockchain. J. Comput. Res. Dev. **55**(11), 2452–2466 (2018)
7. Tian, G.H., Hu, Y.H., Chen, X.F.: Research progress on attack and defense techniques in block-chain system. Ruan Jian Xue Bao/J. Softw. **32**(5), 1495–1525 (2021)
8. Ministry of Industry and Information Technology. China Blockchain Technology and Application Development White Paper (2016)
9. Yuan, Y., Wang, F.Y.: Blockchain: the state of the art and future trends. Acta Automatica Sinica **42**(4), 481–494 (2016)
10. Mayer, H.: ECDSA security in bitcoin and ethereum: a research survey. CoinFaabrik **28**, 126 (2016)
11. University Stanford: Pertinent Side Channel Attacks on Elliptic Curve Cryptographic Systems. Stanford University, Stanford (2011)
12. Schmidt, J.M., Medwed, M.A.: Fault attack on ECDSA. In: 2009 Workshop on Fault Diagnosis and Tolerance in Cryptography, Lusanne, Switzerland, pp. 93–99. IEEE (2009)

13. Nicolas, T.C., Pinar, E., Filippo, V.: Private key recovery combination attacks: on extreme fragility of popular bitcoin key management, wallet and cold storage solutions in presence of poor RNG events. IACR Cryptol. ePrint Arch, 848 (2014)
14. Horalek, J., Holik, F., Horak, O., et al.: Analysis of the use of rainbow tables to break hash. J. Intell. Fuzzy Syst. **32**(2), 1523–1534 (2017)
15. Coron, J.S., Dodis, Y., Malinaud, C., Puniya, P.: Merkle-Damgård revisited: how to construct a hash function. In: Shoup, V. (eds.) CRYPTO 2005. LNCS, vol. 3621, pp. 430–448. Springer, Heidelberg (2005). https://doi.org/10.1007/11535218_26
16. Liu, A.D., Du, X.H., Wang, N., Li, S.Z.: Research progress of blockchain technology and its application in information security. Ruan Jian Xue Bao/J. Softw. **29**(7), 2092–2115 (2018)
17. Chen, T., Li, X., Luo, X., et al.: Under-optimized smart contracts devour your money. In: 24th International Conference on Software Analysis, Evolution and Reengineering (SANER), Klagenfurt, Austria, pp. 442–44. IEEE (2017)
18. Kaifeng, H., Shengli, S.J.: The security research of blockchain smart contract. J. Inf. Secur. Res. **5**(3), 192–206 (2019)
19. Menglin, F., Lifa, W., Zheng, H., et al.: Research on smart contracts vulnerability mining technique. J. Comput. Appl. **39**(7), 1959–1966 (2019)
20. Luu, L., Chu, D., Olickel, H., et al.: Making smart contracts smarter. In: 2016 ACM SIGSAC Conference on Computer and Communications Security, Vienna Austria, pp. 254–269. ACM (2016)
21. Koshy, P., Koshy, D., McDaniel, P.: An analysis of anonymity in bitcoin using P2P network traffic. In: Christin, N., Safavi-Naini, R. (eds.) FC 2014. LNCS, vol. 8437, pp. 469–485. Springer, Heidelberg (2014). https://doi.org/10.1007/978-3-662-45472-5_30
22. Androulaki, E., Karame, G.O., Roeschlin, M., Scherer, T., Capkun, S.: Evaluating user privacy in bitcoin. In: Sadeghi, A.-R. (ed.) FC 2013. LNCS, vol. 7859, pp. 34–51. Springer, Heidelberg (2013). https://doi.org/10.1007/978-3-642-39884-1_4
23. Douceur, J.R.: The sybil attack. In: Druschel, P., Kaashoek, F., Rowstron, A. (eds.) IPTPS 2002. LNCS, vol. 2429, pp. 251–260. Springer, Heidelberg (2002). https://doi.org/10.1007/3-540-45748-8_24
24. Bissias, G.,Ozisik, A.P., Levine, B.N., et al.: Sybil-resistant mixing for bitcoin. In: 13th Workshop on Privacy in the Electronic Society, Scottsdale, AZ, USA, pp. 149–158. IEEE (2014)
25. Fleder, M., Kester, M.S., Pillai, S.: Bitcoin transaction graph analysis. arXiv preprint arXiv: 1502.01657 (2015)
26. Miller, A., Ahmed, E.K., Katz, J., et al.: Nonoutsourceable scratch-off puzzles to discourage bitcoin mining coalitions. In: 22th ACM SIGSAC Conference on Computer and Communications Security, Denver, CO, USA, pp, 680–691. ACM (2015)
27. Houy, N.: It Will Cost You Nothing to 'Kill' a Proof-of-Stake Crypto-Currency (2014). https://papers.ssrn.com/sol3/papers.cfm?abstract_id=2393940
28. CryptoWiki. Proof-of-Work System (2020). http://cryptowiki.net/index.php?title=Proof-of-work_system
29. KwonJ. Tendermint: Consensus without mining (2014). https://pdfs.semanticscholar.org/df62/a45f50aac8890453b6991ea115e996c1646e.pdf
30. Gennaro, R., Goldfeder, S., Narayanan, A.: Threshold-optimal DSA/ECDSA signatures and an application to bitcoin wallet security. In: Manulis, M., Sadeghi, A.R., Schneider, S. (eds.) ACNS 2016. LNCS, vol. 9696, pp. 156–174. Springer, Cham (2016). https://doi.org/10.1007/978-3-319-39555-5_9
31. Tsankov, P., Dan, A., Drachsler-Cohen, D., et al.: Securify: practical security analysis of smart contracts. In: 2018 ACM SIGSAC Conference on Computer and Communications Security, CCS 2018, Toronto Canada, pp. 67–82. ACM (2018)

32. Pierrot, C., Wesolowski, B.: Malleability of the blockchain's entropy. Cryptogr. Commun. **10**(1), 211–233 (2018)
33. Zhang, F., Cecchetti, E., Croman, K., et al.: Town crier: an authenticated data feed for smart contracts. In: 2016 ACM SIGSAC Conference on Computer and Communications Security, Vienna Austria, pp. 270–282. ACM (2016)
34. Rivest, R.L., Shamir, A., Tauman, Y.: How to leak a secret. In: Boyd, C. (ed.) ASIACRYPT 2001. LNCS, vol. 2248, pp. 552–565. Springer, Heidelberg (2001). https://doi.org/10.1007/3-540-45682-1_32
35. Conti, M., Kumar, E.S., Lal, C., et al.: A survey on security and privacy issues of bitcoin. IEEE Commun. Surv. Tutor. **20**(4), 3416–3452 (2018)
36. Sasson, E.B., Chiesa, A., Garman, C., et al.: Zerocash: decentralized anonymous payments from bitcoin. In: 2014 IEEE Symposium on Security and Privacy, San Jose, CA, pp. 459–474. IEEE (2014)
37. Luu, L., Velner, Y., Teutsch, J., et al.: Smartpool: practical decentralized pooled mining. In: 26th USENIX Security Symposium, Vancouver, BC, Canada, pp. 1409–1426. IEEE (2017)
38. Hu, Y., Chen, H.M., Delbruck, T.: Slasher: stadium racer car for event camera end-to-end learning autonomous driving experiments. In: 1st IEEE International Conference on Artificial Intelligence Circuits and Systems, Hsinchu, Taiwan, China, pp. 29–33. IEEE (2019)

Towards Convergence of Blockchain and Self-sovereign Identity for Privacy-Preserving Secure Federated Learning

Rakib Ul Haque[1,3] , A. S. M. Touhidul Hasan[2,3,4(✉)] , Apubra Daria[3] ,
Qiang Qu[4] , and Qingshan Jiang[4(✉)]

[1] School of Computer Science and Technology, University of Chinese Academy
of Sciences, Shijingshan District, Beijing 100049, China
rakibulhaqueraj@mails.ucas.ac.cn
[2] Department of Computer Science and Engineering, University of Asia Pacific,
Dhaka 1205, Bangladesh
touhid@uap-bd.edu
[3] Institute of Automation Research and Engineering, Dhaka 1205, Bangladesh
apubra@iar-e.com
[4] Shenzhen Key Laboratory for High Performance Data Mining, Shenzhen Institute
of Advanced Technology, Chinese Academy of Sciences, Shenzhen 518055, China
{qiang.qu,qs.jiang}@siat.ac.cn

Abstract. More and more researchers are eager to train their Machine
Learning (ML) model by the distributed dataset in a federated manner.
However, there are numerous privacy and security concerns in federated
learning, i.e., adversarial attacks, authentication, and model inversion
attacks. In this paper, we integrate self-sovereign identity for privacy-
preserving secure federated learning. The proposed framework represents
identity management and authentication scheme for edge devices, which
are participated in FL. It guarantees participants' privacy, where users'
private data are not shared with the centralized training module. The
trust triangle and Blockchain ensure the authenticity of the distributed
federated learning, where data privacy is handled with Differential Privacy. Result analysis is done based on measured score and time complexity. In terms of accuracy, BCWD, HDD, and DD achieve 94.69%, 81.05%
and 78.00%, respectively on standard ML, whereas 94.45%, 80.59% and
76.43% on ϵ DP-based FL with privacy budget, $\epsilon = 3$. For the time complexity measurement, the total number of transactions employed in the
system is 1000. Transactions time and their verification took 3323.15 s.
Moreover, the proposed system shows robust performance in both cases.

Keywords: Self-sovereign identity (SSI) · Blockchain · Federated
learning · Privacy · Differential privacy

This research work is supported by the Key-Area Research and Development Program
of Guangdong Province under Grant No. 2019B010137002, and National Key Research
and Development Program under Grant NO. 2020YFA0909100.

Y. Tian et al. (Eds.): ICBDS 2021, CCIS 1563, pp. 243–255, 2022.
https://doi.org/10.1007/978-981-19-0852-1_19

1   Introduction

Internet of Things (IoT) [1] has become the subset of edge intelligence endeavors as the demand for seamless real-time remote services is at its peak. Data owners/providers collect sensor enabled data for analysis from IoT devices. These data are pre-processed for training various machine learning (ML) [2–5] models in distinct manners such as federated learning (FL) [6], reinforcement learning (RL) [7], and so on.

One of the most popular methods for training an ML model is FL. Rather than aggregating the original data to a centralized Cloud for training, FL allows the data shared on the client edge devices and trains a distributed model on the server by aggregating locally calculated updates. As a result, FL was considered as a mitigator of many systemic privacy risks and costs resulting from conventional ML methods but that's not the case exactly [6].

FL has various concerns, such as privacy concerns and adversarial attacks. Though FL retains raw data private in edge devices, it distributes additional information (model parameters). This additional information also reveals sensitive information to the central server. In general cases, all participants are considered trustworthy, but this is not true for the real world. Adversaries in the act of participants may cause adversarial attacks. An adversarial attacker has intentionally designed inputs to cause the model to make a mistake. So, authentication and verification of each participant are necessary [8].

In order to solve the above-mentioned concerns, this study proposes a unified and novel on-chain self-sovereign identity (SSI) [9] and differential privacy-based framework indicated as secure SSI-FL. This framework authenticates the government-issued identity of an individual through zero-knowledge proof. Differential privacy (DP) [10] is used for making sure data privacy. All intermediate data are recorded in the Blockchain [11], neither party can deny their past transactions. The main contributions are as follows.

- To the best of our knowledge, this is the first attempt to combine SSI, FL, and DP.
- DP is employed for protecting the privacy of the data set of data providers.
- Blockchain is employed so that participants cannot deny their previous transactions.

The rest of the article is structured as follows. Related works and Preliminaries are analyzed in Sect. 2 and 3, respectively. System model are delineated in Sect. 4. Section 5 illustrates the experiment and performance evaluation. Finally, Sect. 6 concludes this article.

2   Related Works

This section will discuss related works and their limitations.

Coelho [12] proposed a secure, decentralized, and shared repository of certified personal attributes. Liu [13] presented an SSI platform that advances the notion of the design pattern as a service. The authors implemented a prototype and evaluated it for feasibility and scalability. Li [14] discussed the unique characteristics and challenges of federated learning. Li [15] aimed to review prevailing applications in industrial engineering to guide for the future landing application. The author also identified six research fronts to address FL literature. Xu [16] reviewed federated learning technologies in the biomedical space. In particular, the authors summarized the general solutions to the statistical challenges, system challenges, and privacy issues in federated learning, and point out the implications and potentials in healthcare.

All of the previous work does not combine SSI and FL. Some works only focus on identity management through SSI [12,13] and others [14–16] focus on the only FL but all of them has the following limitations:

- None of the previous work focuses on the authenticity of persons in the case of FL.
- None of the previous work uses an immutable ledger for intermediate data sharing.
- None of the previous work fulfills the requirement of an ideal protected, privacy-preserving FL schema.

This study proposes secure SSI-FL, where SSI is implemented for decentralized lightweight authentication. DP is implemented for protecting the privacy of the data of data owners. Blockchain is implemented for recording all the intermediate transactions.

3   Preliminaries

All the required preliminaries and threat models are discussed in this section.

3.1   Self-sovereign Identity

Self-sovereign identity is an innovative design for digital identity on the internet. It can act as an identity layer for the internet. The main goal is to find a way to prove an entity's identity to the apps, services, and websites. This results to build entrusted connections to obtain or preserve private information. SSI has seven basic building blocks. They are Verifiable credentials or digital credentials, The trust triangle (issuers, holders, and verifiers), Digital wallets, Digital agents, Decentralized identifiers (DIDs), Blockchains, or other verifiable data registries and Governance frameworks or trust frameworks [17].

Summarization of each building block is described below:

- The digital equivalent of the physical credentials is Verifiable credentials, which are carried by people in their wallets in order to prove their identities.
- The trust triangle consists of three roles, such as Issuers, holders, and verifiers. The issuer issues the credential, the holder holds it in a wallet and the verifier verifies it when the holder presents it. Figure 1 shows an overview of trust triangle.

- The digital equivalent of physical wallets is Digital wallets, which can be held by any modern computing device such as smartphone, laptop, etc. for holding verifiable.
- Software modules or apps that empower individuals to utilize digital wallets are known as Digital agents. It can substitute verifiable credentials, securely communicate, manage connections, and present credentials with other digital agents.
- A digital address powered by cryptography, which does not has the requirement of a centralized registration authority is known as Decentralized identifiers (DIDs).
- Verifiable data registries and Blockchains are shared, databases, which are secured by cryptography can labor as a root of trustworthiness for DIDs and public keys. It can achieve that without being directed to any attack or single points of failure.
- The assortment of jurisdictions for managing SSI infrastructure, which will allow interoperable digital trust ecosystems of any volume is indicated as Governance frameworks.

3.2   Differential Privacy

Perturbation is added with raw data for preserving data privacy. The perturbation must be randomized. The core concept of DP is explained in [18]. The $\epsilon-$ DP is defined in Definition 1.

Definition 1. $\epsilon-$ *DP can be achieved by a randomized function V if all datasets d_1 and d_2 varying on at most unit component, and all $U \subseteq Range(V)$,*

$$Pr[V(d_1) \in U] \leq e^{\epsilon} \times Pr[V(d_2) \in U]$$

3.3   Federated Learning

Federated learning is one kind of distributed machine learning approach where the global model on the server continuously learns from the client edge device. The client-side edge device interacts with the user and most of the time edge device learns from the user's personal information and preferences. The edge model learns from these user data and to keep the user data private, only the client model's weights are sent to the server model [6]. There is various kind of FL. They are Centralized, Decentralized, and Heterogeneous federated learning.

3.4   Threat Model

All participants in the secure SSI-FL are curious but honest adversaries, which means participants are honest in following the protocols but try to infer other data and also may try to apply adversarial attack. None of them trust each other. The threat model considered for this study is listed below:

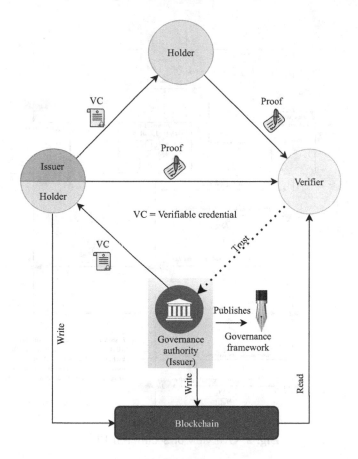

Fig. 1. Core roles in the trust triangle for verifiable credential

- Adversaries may try to apply adversarial attacks, which will decrease the performance of the ML model.
- Adversaries may apply Model Inversion Attack. They can get success in retrieving the training data points only if it has access to the machine learning model.
- Adversaries may apply Membership Inference Attack, where the foe assumes that the prediction result will be different on the data points on which it is trained versus on the data points on which it is not trained.
- Two or more participants may try to learn the private data of other participants.

3.5 Security Goals

The Secure SSI-FL satisfies the following requirements.

- Privacy of all participants must be preserved.

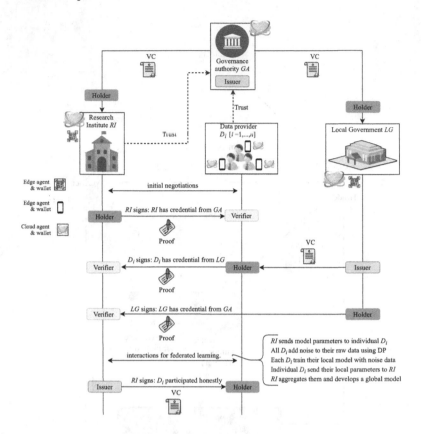

Fig. 2. Overview of Secure SSI-FL

- Participant will not be able to get the private dataset of other participants.
- Any adversarial attack can be traced back to the attacker.
- Model inversion attack will not be successful.
- Membership inference attack will not be successful.

4   System Model

This section discusses the system model, and security analysis of Secure SSI-FL. Figure 2 shows the overview of the entire system.

In this scenario, the entities are Research Institute (RI), Data Provider (D_i), Governance Authority (GA), and Local Government (LG). RI wants to train its ML model in a federated manner. D_i finds that information from the website or invitation of RI. D_i, who is interested, has enough amount of dataset and has adequate power to train an ML model in their edge device will connect with LG for VC. Note that, LG and RI already has their VC from GA.

RI and D_i want to form a secure private connection in order to participate in FL and they do not meet in person. RI and D_i don't have a pre-established trust relationship. VC (ID credentials) issued from LG are understood and accepted by RI for the verification of D_i. On the other hand, RI will use VC issued by GA for their authentication to D_i.

4.1 D_i Connect to LG

The connection between D_i and LG's cloud agent is formed through the scanning of a QR code on LG's website. LG installed the SSI plug-in, which is configured with the QR code. Edge agent app of D_i allows receiving the invitation for connection. DID document, the key pair, and peer DID are generated by edge agent of D_i for the relationship request message, when D_i presses Yes. Further, send it to D_i's cloud agent to dispatch it to cloud agent of LG. LG receives the connection request and approves it. DID document, key pair, and peer DID are generated by the cloud agent of LG for the response message of connection. It is again sent back via the edge agent of D_i. Finally, storage is done of connection completion.

4.2 D_i Requests a VC from LG

Edge agent of D_i prove its identity to the LG. D_i meets the policies of LG for allocating a fresh VC. LG dispatches the credential to the edge agent of D_i and store it in the wallet of D_i. Connection is done in between them according to the scenario Sect. 4.1.

4.3 RI Requests a VC from D_i

The RI requests proof of D_i's VC, which is issued from LG. VC's QR code requesting proof is scanned by D_i. Edge agent of D_i prompts it to endorse sending the proof. When D_i agrees and yields the proof, the private key is signed for the connection. D_i sends the proof to the cloud agent RI. The cloud agent of RI confirms the evidence by examining the LR's DID on a public Blockchain (Ethereum) and recovering the DID record with the public key. If the proof verifies, D_i is permitted to participate in FL with RI. Each D_i also authenticate RI as per scenario Sect. 4.3.

4.4 RI & D_i Participant in FL

After establishing a secure connection, RI sends ML model ($k-$ nearest neighbor $k-$nn) parameters (centroids (c_x, c_y), nearest distance k) to individual D_i. All D_i add noise to their raw data ($data_{raw}$) using DP. Each D_i train their local model with noisy data. Individual D_i send their local parameters to RI. RI aggregates them and develops a global model. Note that all data sharing is done cryptographically.

4.5 Trust Triangle of SSI-FL

The trust triangle of SSI-FL has been discussed in Fig. 2. RI and D_i both trust GA. RI and LG are verified by GA. In other words, both of them have VC from GA. GA is the issuer and RI and LG are the holders. Issuer writes the DID in the public Blockchain. D_i need VC from LG in order to join in FL with RI. So, LG is the issuer, and each D_i is a holder. This VC will be verified by RI so RI is the verifier. This process is done based on zero-knowledge proof. Again RI is authenticated by each D_i in a similar manner.

4.6 Security Analysis

Proposition 1. *(Security of Secure SSI-FL). Secure SSI-FL in Fig. 2 can ensure the privacy of participants and their dataset against curious but honest adversaries. It is also secured from adversarial, model inversion, and membership inference attacks, where participants are curious but honest adversaries.*

*Proof (**Proof of Proposition** 1).* In Secure SSI-FL GA, LG, RI, and D_i^n , four entities are involved. The view of each entity are as follows:
The view of GA:

$$view_{GA}^{SSI-FL} = \Big(VC \in \{[DID]_{RI}, [DID]_{LG}\} \Big)$$

GA stays at the top of the pyramid. GA only publishes VC to LG and RI, where GA write the DID's of VC in the public Blockchain. So, GA is not related to any kinds of attacks.
The view of LG:

$$view_{LG}^{SSI-FL} = \Big(VC \in \{[DID]_{D_i^n}\} \Big)$$

LG only publishes VC to D_i^n, where LG write the DID's of VC in the public Blockchain. So, LG is not related to any kinds of attacks.
The view of RI:

$$view_{RI}^{SSI-FL} = \Big((c_x, c_y), k, ([[VC]] \in \{D_i^n, LG\}), (c_x', c_y')_i^n \Big)$$

RI has it's model parameters { (c_x, c_y), k }. It also has the proof $[[VC]]$ of D_i^n and LG's VC. RI verifies their VC using zero-knowledge proof. So, without the public DID of D_i^n and LG all private information is secret. Now RI also have all the local model parameters $(c_x', c_y')_i^n)$ from n number of data providers. RI may try to infer the raw data of D_i^n from these local model parameters but it's not possible because all D_i^n has added noise with their raw data before training their local model. So, RI will not succeed with any Model inversion attack or Membership inference attack.
The view of individual D_i:

$$view_{D_i}^{SSI-FL} = \Big((c_x, c_y), k, [[VC]]_{RI}, (c_x', c_y')_i \Big)$$

Each D_i can have the initial model parameters (c_x, c_y) of RI but none of them will have the local model parameters of other D_i. D_i may try to perform an adversarial attack but that D_i can be traced out because the hash of all intermediate transactions is recorded in the public Blockchain.

Finally, all data shared in the secure SSI-FL channels encrypted end to end cryptographically as a result eavesdropping and other middle man attacks are ineffective. There secure SSI-FL is secure in the curious but honest scenario. ■

5   Experiment and Performance Evaluation

This segment represents the performance analysis of the proposed framework.

5.1   Testbed

FL Service Machine Configuration: MacBook Pro with memory (Ram: 16 GB 2667 MHz DDR4, Processor: 2.3 GHz 8-Core Intel Core i9 GPU: Intel UHD Graphics 630 1536 MB. k−nn implemented in the Browser: Google Chrome; Language: Python 3; Platform: Google's Collaboratory, where the system is concurrently laboring as RI and n number of D_i. SSI Service Machine Configuration: Memory 66 GB. Processor: Intel(R) Xeon(R) W-2135 CPU @ 3.70 GHz (Core 6). GPU: Attached GPUs : 4. Product Name : NVIDIA GeForce RTX 2080 Ti. SSI Performance Test Machine: Memory 16 GB 2667 MHz DDR4. Processor: 2.3 GHz 8-Core Intel Core i9. GPU: Intel UHD Graphics 630 1536 MB

5.2   Dataset

Health Datasets from UCI repository, namely Breast Cancer Wisconsin Data Set (BCWD)[1,] Heart Disease Data Set (HDD)[2], Diabetes Data Set (DD)[3]. Statistics of the dataset is represented in Table 1. For training 80% and for testing 20% data set are utilized. For this study, the number of data providers is 10, which means $(D_{i=1}^{n=10})$.

Table 1. Statistics of datasets.

Measures	Datasets		
	BCWD	HDD	DD
Instances	699	303	768
Attributes	9	13	9

[1] https://archive.ics.uci.edu/ml/datasets/Breast+Cancer+Wisconsin+(Diagnostic).
[2] https://archive.ics.uci.edu/ml/datasets/heart+disease.
[3] https://archive.ics.uci.edu/ml/datasets/diabetes.

5.3   Score Evaluation Metric

For the evaluation of ML methods of secure SSI-FL, three metric are used, i.e., accuracy in Eq. 1, precision in Eq. 2, recall in Eq. 3 [19, 20].

$$accuracy = \frac{T_N + T_P}{T_P + T_N + F_P + F_N} \tag{1}$$

$$precision = \frac{T_P}{T_P + F_P} \tag{2}$$

$$recall = \frac{T_P}{T_P + F_N} \tag{3}$$

Here, relevant classes, irrelevant class, relevant but mislabeled and the number mislabeled but irrelevant are represented as T_P, F_P, F_N and T_N, respectively.

5.4   Scalability Evaluation Metric

Three metrics are used, namely total verification time in Eq. 4, total transaction time in Eq. 5, average latency in Eq. 6, and average throughput in Eq. 7 by the number of transactions. These metrics are described below verification start time (V_S), verification decision time (V_D), transaction deployment time (T_D), and transaction end time (T_E).

$$total\ verification\ time = \sum_{i=1}^{N}(V_D - V_S) \tag{4}$$

$$total\ transaction\ time = \sum_{i=1}^{N}(T_E - T_D) \tag{5}$$

$$latency = T_E - T_D$$

$$average\ latency = \frac{\sum_{i=1}^{N}(T_E - T_D)}{N} \tag{6}$$

$$throughput = \frac{1}{average\ latency}$$

$$average\ throughput = \frac{throughput}{N} \tag{7}$$

Table 2. Performance of secure SSI-FL $(k - nn, t = 8)$.

Measures	Dataset	FL	FL with ϵ-DP	
		Standard	$\epsilon = 0$	$\epsilon = 3$
Accuracy	BCWD	94.69%	92.48%	94.45%
	HDD	81.05%	75.09%	80.59%
	DD	78.00%	70.43%	76.43%
Precision	BCWD	94.45%	85.48%	93.49%
	HDD	81.58%	74.55%	80.57%
	DD	75.90%	69.12%	74.56%
Recall	BCWD	94.55%	88.34%	94.67%
	HDD	82.58%	75.34%	81.33%
	DD	74.97%	68.43%	73.95%

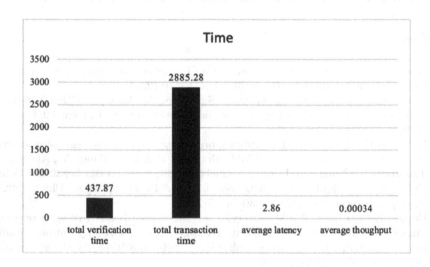

Fig. 3. Scalability analysis for one thousand transactions

5.5   Result Evaluation

This section discusses the proposed system's measured scores and scalability. Table 2 shows the measured scores of the proposed system. For the proposed system, this study considers privacy budget $\epsilon \in \{0, 3\}$. Performance analysis shows that the proposed system achieves approximately similar accuracy in comparison to standard FL. In terms of accuracy, BCWD, HDD, and DD achieve 94.69%, 81.05% and 78.00%, respectively on standard ML, whereas 94.45%, 80.59% and 76.43% on ϵ DP-based FL with privacy budget $= 3$.

For this study total number of transactions is 1000. Figure 3 shows the scalability analysis of the secure SSI-FL. X-axis holding time in seconds (s) and Y-axis represent the scalability measure. They are total transaction time, total verification time, average time, and average throughput. The total transaction took 2885.28 s but their verification took just 437.87 s. Moreover, the proposed system shows robust performance in case of time complexity.

6   Conclusion

This study aims to combine SSI and FL in order to develop a secure, privacy-preserving model. SSI is employed for authentication of the entities, Blockchain labor an immutable record of transactions and DP makes sure the data privacy. Several properties of SSI such as trust triangle, governance framework are described and security analysis is also done. $k-$nn is employed in a federated manner, where all participants are honest but curious adversaries. Performance analysis is done based on accuracy and time complexity. Based on the results in Table 2 and Fig. 3, it is clear that the proposed system is robust and realistic.

References

1. Lee, I., Lee, K.: The Internet of Things (IoT): applications, investments, and challenges for enterprises. Bus. Horiz. **58**(4), 431–440 (2015)
2. Akter, S., Shamrat, F.M., Chakraborty, S., Karim, A., Azam, S.: COVID-19 detection using deep learning algorithm on chest X-ray images. Biology **10**(11), 1174 (2021)
3. Haque, R.U., Hasan, A.S.M.T.: Privacy-preserving multivariant regression analysis over blockchain-based encrypted IoMT data. In: Maleh, Y., Baddi, Y., Alazab, M., Tawalbeh, L., Romdhani, I. (eds.) Artificial Intelligence and Blockchain for Future Cybersecurity Applications. SBD, vol. 90, pp. 45–59. Springer, Cham (2021). https://doi.org/10.1007/978-3-030-74575-2_3
4. Haque, R.U., Hasan, A.S.M.: Overview of Blockchain-Based Privacy Preserving Machine Learning for IoMT, Big Data Intelligence for Smart Applications, Studies in Computational Intelligence, eBook ISBN 978-3-030-87954-9 (2022). https://doi.org/10.1007/978-3-030-87954-9
5. Akter, S., et al.: Comprehensive performance assessment of deep learning models in early prediction and risk identification of chronic kidney disease. IEEE Access **9**, 165184–165206 (2021)
6. Bonawitz, K., et al.: Towards federated learning at scale: system design. arXiv preprint arXiv:1902.01046 (2019)
7. Wang, H., et al.: Optimizing federated learning on non-IID data with reinforcement learning. In: IEEE INFOCOM 2020-IEEE Conference on Computer Communications. IEEE (2020)
8. Bhagoji, A.N., et al. :Analyzing federated learning through an adversarial lens. In: International Conference on Machine Learning. PMLR (2019)
9. Tobin, A., Reed, D.: The inevitable rise of self-sovereign identity. In: The Sovrin Foundation, 29 September 2016
10. Dwork, C.: Differential privacy: a survey of results. In: Agrawal, M., Du, D., Duan, Z., Li, A. (eds.) TAMC 2008. LNCS, vol. 4978, pp. 1–19. Springer, Heidelberg (2008). https://doi.org/10.1007/978-3-540-79228-4_1
11. Nofer, M., et al.: Blockchain. Bus. Inf. Syst. Eng. **59**(3), 183–187 (2017)

12. Coelho, P., Zúquete, A., Gomes, H.: Federation of attribute providers for user self-sovereign identity. J. Inf. Syst. Eng. Manage. **3**(4), 32 (2018)
13. Liu, Y., et al.: Design pattern as a service for Blockchain-based self-sovereign identity. IEEE Softw. **37**(5), 30–36 (2020)
14. Li, T., et al.: Federated learning: challenges, methods, and future directions. IEEE Signal Process. Mag. **37**(3), 50–60 (2020)
15. Li, L., et al.: A review of applications in federated learning. Comput. Ind. Eng. **149**, 106854 (2020)
16. Xu, J., et al.: Federated learning for healthcare informatics. J. Healthcare Inform. Res. **5**(1), 1–19 (2021)
17. Preukschat, A., Reed, D.: Self-sovereign Identity: Decentralized Digital Identity and Verifiable Credential. Manning Publications, 8 June 2021. ISBN-10: 1617296597, ISBN-13: 978–1617296598
18. Dwork, C.: Differential privacy. In: Bugliesi, M., Preneel, B., Sassone, V., Wegener, I. (eds.) ICALP 2006. LNCS, vol. 4052, pp. 1–12. Springer, Heidelberg (2006). https://doi.org/10.1007/11787006_1
19. Rasool, A., Tao, R., Kamyab, M., Hayat, S.: GAWA-a feature selection method for hybrid sentiment classification. IEEE Access **8**, 191850–191861 (2020). https://doi.org/10.1109/ACCESS.2020.3030642
20. Rasool, A., Jiang, Q., Qu, Q., Ji, C.: WRS: a novel word-embedding method for real-time sentiment with integrated LSTM-CNN model. In: 2021 IEEE International Conference on Real-time Computing and Robotics (RCAR), pp. 590–595. IEEE, July 2021

Research on Load Forecasting Method Considering Data Feature Analysis Based on Bi-LSTM Network

Zhihua Ding[1], Yijie Wu[2(✉)], Peng Jia[2], Jiaxing Li[2], and Sijia Zhou[2]

[1] State Grid Fujian Electric Power Company, Fuzhou 350000, Fujian, China
[2] School of Electric Power Engineering, Nanjing Institute of Technology, Nanjing 211167, Jiangsu, China

Abstract. The accuracy of power load forecasting is sensitive to various characteristic factors. For the massive historical load data, how to mine the correlation between different attributes in the characteristic data set is the key to improve the accuracy of load forecasting. In this paper, a load forecasting method based on Bi-LSTM network considering data feature analysis is proposed. Firstly, the attribute correlation feature analysis of massive historical load data is realized by using random forest algorithm, and the features with strong correlation with load are selected as the input of the model; Secondly, Bi-LSTM network with good data fitting accuracy is used for load forecasting modeling. Finally, the actual load data of a city is used for simulation analysis. The simulation results show that this method has more advantages in accuracy than traditional forecasting methods, which verifies the effectiveness and practicability of this method.

Keywords: Multidimensional characteristics · Load forecasting · Random forest · Bi-LSTM · Feature selection

1 Introduction

Realizing the dynamic balance between power supply and power load is the premise of stable and economic operation of power system. Predicting power load in advance and reasonably arranging power supply are of great significance to power supply departments. Load has strong volatility and nonlinearity, and with the development of data acquisition system, load information presents multi characteristics, which increases the difficulty of prediction. Therefore, mining the internal relationship between load and characteristic factors and reducing the dimension of input variables is of great significance to accurately predict load.

Load forecasting mainly includes traditional forecasting method and neural network method [1, 2]. The traditional forecasting method is mainly represented by time series method and trend extrapolation method. In reference [3], aiming at the problem of poor accuracy of short-term load forecasting, the cumulative autoregressive dynamic average is improved by using the transfer function. The simulation results show that the improved model improves the forecasting accuracy. With the wide application of artificial neural

© Springer Nature Singapore Pte Ltd. 2022
Y. Tian et al. (Eds.): ICBDS 2021, CCIS 1563, pp. 256–268, 2022.
https://doi.org/10.1007/978-981-19-0852-1_20

network in image recognition, speech recognition and other fields, it has strong adaptive ability for massive and nonlinear data. The ability of autonomous learning and high fitting performance are the characteristics that the traditional prediction method does not have. Reference [4] proposed a load forecasting model combining particle swarm optimization algorithm and error back propagation neural network, which can effectively improve the convergence speed and prediction accuracy of BP network. Literature [5] uses long short term memory network to predict the power load of a single energy user, and the load forecasting accuracy is greatly improved compared with the traditional forecasting model. The above literature makes an in-depth study on load forecasting under the influence of single feature, which effectively reduces the prediction error. However, the above methods cannot effectively deal with high-dimensional time series information, which takes a long time for model training and has low prediction accuracy.

To solve the above problems, a load forecasting method based on Bi-LSTM [6] network considering data feature analysis is proposed. Firstly, the feature selection algorithm based on random forest is used to screen the input features with strong correlation with load, so as to reduce the dimension of input prediction model data; Secondly, Bi-LSTM network is constructed to predict the load data after feature selection; Finally, the actual load data of a city is used for simulation analysis. The simulation results show that this method has more advantages in accuracy than the traditional forecasting method.

2 Feature Selection Based on Random Forest

The random forest (RF) [7] algorithm was proposed by Breiman in 2001. He combined bagging method with cart decision tree to form a new integrated classification algorithm. Random forest, in short, is a forest composed of many randomly formed decision trees. In the formation process of each decision tree, the sample set is generated by putting back and random sampling, and each decision tree is different. After a random decision tree is obtained, when a new sample is input, each decision tree in the forest will make a classification judgment, and finally get the unique result according to the principle of minority obeying majority. Its schematic diagram is shown in Fig. 1.

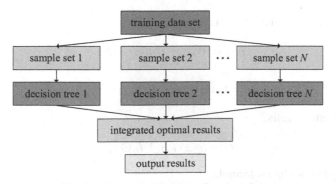

Fig. 1. Schematic diagram of random forest

Suppose that the training set has m samples, and M samples are taken back to obtain the sampling set. The samples not taken are called out of bag data. In the process of generating random forest by splitting regression tree, the splitting variables are selected according to the criterion of minimum variance. The regression tree grows in the optimal direction to form a random forest containing N trees, and the purpose of feature selection can be achieved by calculating the data error outside the bag. The specific steps are as follows:

Step 1: calculate the out of pocket data error of each decision tree Ei_{OOB1}.

Step 2: only introduce noise interference into column j (the j-th load characteristic) of out of bag data, and recalculate the error value of out of bag data.

Step 3: if the random forest has n decision trees, the calculation formula of the j-th feature importance score is as follows:

$$J_{import} = \frac{1}{N} \sum_{i=1}^{N} (Ei_{OOB2} - Ei_{OOB1}) \tag{1}$$

Step 4: calculate the importance scores of all features and arrange them in descending order to screen the features with strong correlation with load.

3   Bi-LSTM Network Model

The long-short-term memory [8] network is an improved time cycle neural network. It adds three gating units for controlling information transmission: forgetting gate, input gate and output gate to the structure of the recurrent neural network [9], which effectively solves the gradient disappearance or explosion defect of the recurrent neural network in processing the long-term sequence. Its unit structure is shown in Fig. 2. Among them, the forgetting gate retains useful information while avoiding the backward transmission of useless information at the last moment. The function of the input gate and output gate is to read data and transfer the processed data to the next moment.

Calculation formula of forgetting door:

$$f_t = \sigma \left(W_f x_t + U_f h_{t-1} + b_f \right) \tag{2}$$

Enter the door calculation formula:

$$i_t = \sigma (W_i x_t + U_i h_{t-1} + b_i) \tag{3}$$

$$\widetilde{c}_t = Tanh(W_c x_t + U_c h_{t-1} + b_c) \tag{4}$$

Update memory cells:

$$c_t = f_t \odot c_{t-1} + i_t \odot \widetilde{c}_t \tag{5}$$

Output gate calculation formula:

$$o_t = \sigma (W_o x_t + U_o h_{t-1} + b_o) \tag{6}$$

$$h_t = o_t \odot \tanh(c_t) \tag{7}$$

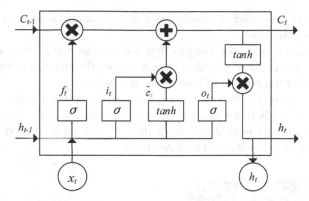

Fig. 2. Structure diagram of LSTM unit

In the above formula, W_f, W_i, W_o, W_c are the weights of three gates and cell state respectively, b_f, b_i, b_c, b_o are the corresponding offset vectors, $\tilde{c}_t$ is the input state of the memory unit, x_t, h_t are the input and output of the hidden layer respectively at time t, σ is the sigmoid function, and $\odot$ represent the multiplication of vector elements.

The input structure of Bi-LSTM network is shown in Fig. 3. The input needs to pass through two LSTM networks in opposite directions, and the output result is the splicing of the two LSTM networks. Therefore, the output of load forecasting model based on Bi-LSTM network contains the information of time series in the forward and reverse directions, and shares the weight to reduce the risk of under fitting while having strong expression ability.

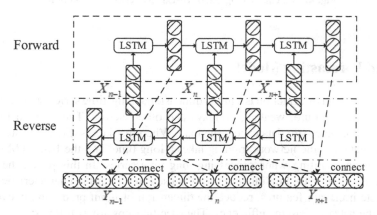

Fig. 3. Bi-LSTM structure diagram

The steps of building Bi-LSTM network are as follows:

1): pre experiment. In order to improve the generalization ability of the model, the pre experiment is used to determine the super parameters of the model, and the data is divided into training set and test set. The training set is used as the training data of the pre experiment model, and the test set is used as the data to verify the performance of the model, so as to determine the number of selected features, neural network iteration cycle and training step size.

2): training neural networks. The loss function is set as root mean square error, and the gradient descent method is used to correct the weight matrix and bias term in the network until the preset number of iterations is reached.

3): load forecasting. Use the input matrix to obtain the output matrix at the next time, including the load prediction value and the new input matrix. Take this output matrix as the latter input matrix to continue the prediction until the prediction at all times is completed. The prediction diagram is shown in Fig. 4.

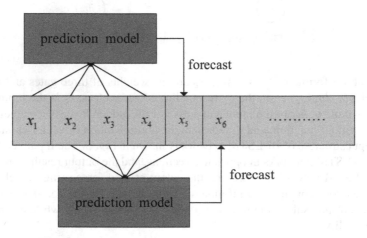

Fig. 4. Schematic diagram of Bi-LSTM network prediction

4 Load Forecasting Model

The essence of load information is a multi-dimensional long-time series, which is mainly affected by temperature, weather, holidays and other factors. The original load data contains 12 characteristic data except the load. When the data is directly input into the Bi-LSTM network, the network training takes a long time, and the Bi-LSTM network is prone to under fitting when processing long time series. In this paper, the feature selection algorithm based on random forest is used to screen the characteristic data of load, delete irrelevant features, reduce the dimension of input prediction network and improve the network training efficiency. The specific steps are as follows:

Step 1: enter a load dataset. The load data set constitutes the input vector.

Step 2: data preprocessing. In the process of data acquisition, due to objective factors such as equipment failure and abnormal signal, lost and abnormal bad data will be formed. If the original data set containing bad data is directly analyzed, it will cause large errors. Therefore, it is necessary to preprocess the original data set.

Firstly, the $3\ \sigma$ criterion is used to distinguish the outliers of the data set. The essence of the $3\ \sigma$ criterion is to compare whether the difference between all values and the average value exceeds 3 times the standard deviation σ. Let the original load data be $x_1, x_2, \cdots\cdots, x_n$, according to Eq. (8), the standard error σ is calculated. If the residual error of a certain load value x_i meets $|v_i| > 3\sigma$, x_i can be determined as an abnormal value.

$$\sigma = \left[\frac{1}{n-1} \sum_{i=1}^{n} v_i^2 \right]^{1/2} = \left\{ \left[\sum_{i=1}^{n} x_i^2 - (\sum_{i=1}^{n} x_i)^2 / n \right] / (n-1) \right\}^{1/2} \tag{8}$$

After the distinguished abnormal value is deleted, the missing value is filled by K-Nearest Neighbors (KNN) algorithm. The filling steps of KNN algorithm are as follows:

1) Initialize the load data to form a complete data matrix;

2) Calculate the Euclidean distance w between the missing data and all data in the complete data matrix $d_i(x_i, y) = \sqrt{(x_i - y)^T (x_i - y)}$;

3) The smallest K data in Euclidean distance are selected as the K nearest neighbors of missing data;

4) Calculate the weight of the nearest neighbor of missing data: $w_i = D_i / S_i$, $D_i = 1/d_i$, $S_i = \sum_{i=1}^{k} D_i$;

5) Fill in the missing data: $y^{\sim} = \sum_{i=1}^{k} w_i a_i$, and a_i is the value of the nearest neighbor;

6) Repeat 2)–5) to fill in all missing values.

In order to eliminate the influence of different dimensions of data on the prediction accuracy of the model, the data are often normalized or Z-score standardized. When the data are relatively concentrated, the processed results are close and tend to zero easily. The latter avoids this problem, makes the standardized data in the standard normal distribution, and highlights the influence of different characteristics on the load prediction results, It is helpful to improve the effect of feature selection. Therefore, Z-score [10] is used to standardize the original data, and its formula is shown in Eq. (9).

$$x^{\wedge} = \frac{x - a(x)}{s_{td}} \tag{9}$$

Where: x is the original value, $x^{\wedge}$ is the standardized value, $a(x)$ is the average value of the corresponding characteristics of x, and s_{td} is the standard deviation of all characteristic numbers corresponding to x.

Step 3: feature selection based on random forest. The number and maximum depth of decision trees are the main parameters affecting the performance of random forest. Grid search algorithm [11] is used to determine that the number of decision trees is 110 and the maximum depth is 20. Take the standardized data as the input of random forest, calculate the importance scores of all features and arrange them in descending order, and select the feature vector with strong correlation with load.

Step 4: load forecasting based on Bi-LSTM network. The data after feature selection is input into Bi-LSTM network for training. After model training, the test set data is predicted. The flow chart of load forecasting based on random forest and Bi-LSTM network is as follows (Fig. 5):

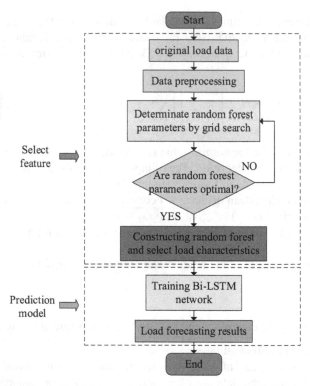

Fig. 5. Flow chart of load forecasting based on RF and Bi-LSTM fusion network

5 Example Analysis

In order to scientifically verify the method proposed in this paper and compare it with the traditional method, the example data selects the power load data of a city for 10 months, the sampling frequency is 15 min, including 28276 samples, the data of the first 8 months is the training set, and the data of the last 2 months is the test set. The load data includes 13 load influencing factors such as daily temperature, time, holidays, etc. the column vectors formed by them are arranged according to the time acquisition order to form a characteristic matrix as the original data set. The specific characteristics are shown in Table 1.

Table 1. Load characteristic description.

Feature category	Characteristic expression
Weather factors	maximum temperature, minimum temperature
Date factor	year, month, day, hour, minute, weekdays, week, holidays
Load factor	average load, maximum load, minimum load

5.1 Prediction Model Evaluation Index

In order to quantify the prediction results, some indicators need to be proposed to measure the prediction error. In this paper, the common root mean square error and average absolute error are used as the model evaluation indicators. The root mean square error and average absolute error can well reflect the prediction accuracy of the model. The smaller the error difference, the better the model performance. The formula is as follows:

$$E_{rmse} = \sqrt{\frac{1}{n}\sum_{i=1}^{n}\left(x_i - x_i^*\right)^2} \tag{10}$$

$$E_{mae} = \frac{1}{n}\sum_{i=1}^{n}\left|x_i - x_i^*\right| \tag{11}$$

Where x_i is the actual value, and x_i^* is the predicted value.

5.2 Feature Selection

Firstly, standardize the load data, take the actual load as the label value, and the other 13 characteristic data affecting the load as the input variables, use the random forest algorithm for training, and visualize the importance score of each feature. The visualization results are shown in Fig. 6. Figure 6 shows the characteristics of the top 8 importance scores. Due to the influence of day and night work and rest rules, the load values during the day and night are significantly different. The time of the day has a great impact on the load, and the importance score ranks first.

Build a two-layer Bi-LSTM network, set the number of iterations to 50, take the first 8 digits of the feature importance score as the input variable, and successively delete the features with the smallest feature importance score, so as to obtain the load forecasting results of different feature inputs. By calculating the root mean square error and average absolute error, take the corresponding feature vector when both are small as the input of the model, The prediction errors of different input eigenvectors are shown in Fig. 7. As can be seen from Fig. 7, the features in the top 6 of the importance score are selected to form the feature vector and used as the input of the prediction network. At this time, the expression of sequence information is the richest and the load forecasting accuracy is the highest.

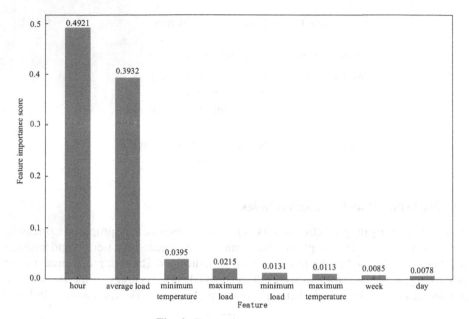

Fig. 6. Feature importance score

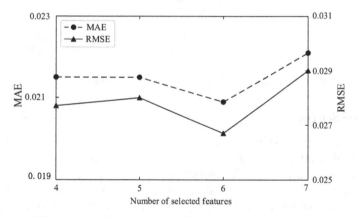

Fig. 7. Prediction results of different characteristic numbers

5.3 Determining Network Super-Parameters

When constructing LSTM neural network, selecting appropriate network super parameters has a great impact on obtaining high prediction accuracy and improving training efficiency. In order to obtain high load forecasting accuracy, different parameters will be selected for training to study the impact of different parameters on the forecasting performance and efficiency of LSTM network.

This paper mainly studies the impact of the number of iterations and time step on the network performance. The optimal eigenvector obtained in the previous section is used as the input. The prediction results are shown in Table 2.

Table 2. Prediction results under different parameters

Epochs	Time step	MAE	RMSE
10	10	0.0282	0.0344
10	20	0.0235	0.0301
10	30	0.0288	0.0357
50	20	0.0204	0.0262
100	20	0.0213	0.0275

As can be seen from Table 2, when the time step is 20, the prediction accuracy is the highest. If the step continues to increase, the gradient of the network disappears and the prediction error increases; When the number of iterations is 50, the fitting degree of the network is the best. Increasing or reducing the number of iterations will lead to over fitting and under fitting of the model. Therefore, the time step of neural network is set to 20 and the number of iterations is set to 50.

5.4 Analysis of Prediction Results

Build the model according to the parameters determined in the previous sections, and compare the built model (RF-BiLSTM) with LSTM and Bi-LSTM networks. The comparison of test set prediction error results is shown in Table 3.

Table 3. Test set prediction error

Prediction model	MAE	RMSE	Training time/s
LSTM network	0.0357	0.0456	308
Bi-LSTM network	0.0255	0.0328	506
RF-BiLSTM network	0.0204	0.0263	464

When processing multi-dimensional long time series, LSTM network is prone to problems such as gradient disappearance, and the prediction error is higher than the other two models; Bi-LSTM network is composed of two LSTM networks, which can better deal with long-time series. Compared with LSTM network, Mae and RMSE are reduced by 0.0102 and 0.0128 respectively; RF-BiLSTM network adopts the feature selection algorithm based on random forest to select the feature quantity with strong correlation with load, reduce the dimension of input quantity, improve the model training efficiency and improve the prediction accuracy. Compared with Bi-LSTM, MAE and RMSE are reduced by 20% and 18% respectively, and the training time is shortened by 42 s.

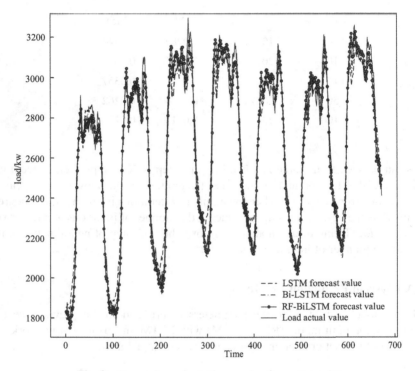

Fig. 8. Comparison chart of seven day forecast results

Figures 8 and 9 are the comparison diagrams of seven day and one-day load forecasting respectively. It can be seen from Fig. 8 that the load has a certain weekly cycle law, and RF-BiLSTM can better fit this change law. As can be seen from Fig. 9, compared with other models, the load predicted value at each time sampling point of RF-BiLSTM is closer to the actual value. The load fluctuation verifies the accuracy of feature screening. The working hours are from 8 a.m. to 6 p.m. every day. The factory is in normal production and the load rises; From 7 p.m. to 7 p.m. the next day, the workers rest, the factory stops production and the load drops. Therefore, the hour has the greatest impact on the load. To sum up, when predicting multi characteristic loads, the prediction accuracy of RF-BiLSTM is improved compared with LSTM and Bi-LSTM.

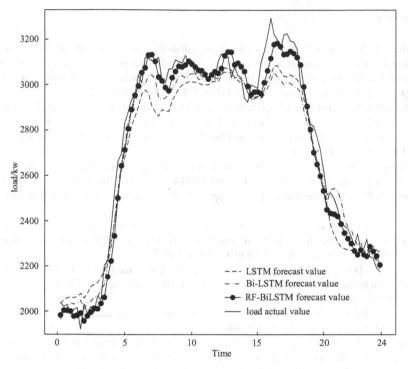

Fig. 9. Comparison chart of one day forecast results

6 Conclusion

Aiming at the influence of multiple characteristic factors on power load forecasting in power system, this paper proposes an ultra-short-term load forecasting method based on feature selection for bi-directional Bi-LSTM networks. The feature selection algorithm based on random forest is used to screen the input features with strong correlation with load, and the Bi-LSTM network is constructed to predict the load data after feature selection. Compared with the traditional forecasting methods, it has the following advantages: (1) Screening the characteristic data affecting load can fully mine the nonlinear relationship between load and influencing factors, increase a priori knowledge and improve the training efficiency of neural network, especially for feature sensitive power load forecasting. (2) Bi-LSTM network is used to build the prediction model. Bi-LSTM network has strong expression ability for continuous long-time series, and its prediction accuracy is improved compared with LSTM network. The method proposed in this paper is mainly to predict the single load value at the time sampling point. The amount of information is limited, so it is impossible to predict the interval. In the future, the distribution or interval prediction will be further studied in order to better guide the actual production.

References

1. Khatoon, S., Ibraheem, A., Singh, K., et al.: Analysis and comparison of various methods available for load forecasting: an overview. In: 2014 Innovative Applications of Computational Intelligence on Power Energy and Controls with their impact on Humanity (CIPECH), pp. 243–247 (2014).https://doi.org/10.1109/CIPECH.2014.7019112
2. Mustapha, M., Mustafa, M.W., Khalid, S.N., et al.: Classification of electricity load forecasting based on the factors influencing the load consumption and methods used: an-overview. IEEE Conf. Energy Convers. (CENCON) **2015**, 442–447 (2015). https://doi.org/10.1109/CENCON.2015.7409585
3. Zhang, L., Xu, L.: Forecasting of fluctuations and turning points of power demand in China based on the maximum entropy method and ARMA model. In: 2010 5th International Conference on Critical Infrastructure (CRIS), pp. 1–6 (2010). https://doi.org/10.1109/CRIS.2010.5617508
4. He, Y., Xu, Q.: Short-term power load forecasting based on self-adapting PSO-BP neural network model. In: Fourth International Conference on Computational and Information Sciences, pp. 1096–1099 (2012).https://doi.org/10.1109/ICCIS.2012.279
5. Kong, W., Dong, Z.Y., Jia, Y., et al.: Short-term residential load forecasting based on LSTM recurrent neural network. IEEE Trans. Smart Grid **10**(1), 841–851 (2019). https://doi.org/10.1109/TSG.2017.2753802
6. İnce, M.: BiLSTM and dynamic fuzzy AHP-GA method for procedural game level generation. Neural Comput. Appl. (2021) (Prepublish)
7. Zhang, J., Zhi, M., Zhang, Y.: Combined generalized additive model and Random Forest to evaluate the influence of environmental factors on phytoplankton biomass in a large eutrophic lake. Ecol. Indicators **130**, 108082 (2021)
8. Wang, M., Oczak, M., Mona, L., et al.: A PCA-based frame selection method for applying CNN and LSTM to classify postural behaviour in sows. Comput. Electron. Agric. **189**, 106351 (2021)
9. Noor, S.T., Asad, S.T., Khan, M.M., et al.: Predicting the risk of depression based on ECG using RNN. Comput. Intell. Neurosci. **2021**, 1–12 (2021)
10. Zhu, L., Li, M., Metawa, N.: Financial risk evaluation Z-score model for intelligent IoT-based enterprises. Inf. Process. Manage. **58**(6), 102692 (2021)
11. Gamze, E.E., Sinem, B.K., Mahmut, Y.: Grid Search optimised artificial neural network for open stope stability prediction. Int. J. Mining Reclam. Environ. **35**(8), 600–617 (2021)

Research on Cloud Computing Security Technology of Power System

Hongzhang Xiong[✉], Jie Cheng, YanJin Wang, Xiaokun Yang, and Kuo Wang

State Grid Jibei Marketing Service Center (Fund Intensive Control Center and Metrology Center), Beijing 100045, China

Abstract. The integrated function of cloud computing technology can effectively guarantee the security of power system data, and lay a solid foundation for the healthy and stable development of power system. At present, the application of cloud computing security technology in the power system is still in the primary stage, and there is a large space for improvement in both the application depth and the strategy level. On account of this, this paper first analyzes the overall security requirements of power system and the concept and connotation of cloud computing security technology in power system. Then it proposes the security structure target of power system. Finally, this paper analyses and studies the power system architecture of cloud computing security and applied technologies of cloud computing security.

Keywords: Cloud computing · Security · Sensitive data · Power system

1 Introduction

With the development and popularization of computer technology, it has been widely and deeply researched and popularized in many fields, especially the application of computer intelligence technology represented by cloud computing in power system security, which greatly improves the security and development of power system. Cloud computing, as an intelligent computing method integrating IT facilities and network expansion, systematically integrates several computing methods as shown in Fig. 1. The computing form has less hardware, installation software and site requirements, which can significantly reduce the cost and investment, greatly saving the storage and computing resources of power system. On the other hand, cloud computing can bring timely and stable software system services to power system, and make the whole system achieve remarkable results in architecture construction, planning and design, development and other aspects.

With the deep application of smart grid in all walks of life, it produces a large number of data in the process of operation, but also produces and processes some more critical and sensitive information, which puts forward higher requirements for the security of the power system. The data and information of power system not only contains important potential value, but also plays an important supporting role in the healthy and stable development of the whole system. The use of cloud computing technology can effectively

© Springer Nature Singapore Pte Ltd. 2022
Y. Tian et al. (Eds.): ICBDS 2021, CCIS 1563, pp. 269–283, 2022.
https://doi.org/10.1007/978-981-19-0852-1_21

protect the security of power system, expand the boundary and dimension of system security protection, and accelerate the effective operation, transmission and processing of power system data. Generally, the current application of cloud computer security technology in the power system is still not sophisticated enough, and there is much room for enhancement in both the in-depth application and the application strategy.

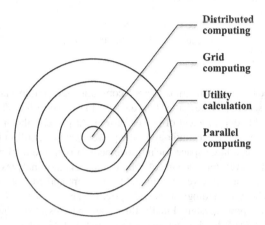

Fig. 1. Computing means of cloud computing technology integration

With the continuous development of power system intelligence and informatization, the data generated in the operation process is not only huge, but also has high value. On the other hand, the information reform of power system puts forward higher challenges and requirements for data and information security. How to effectively protect the data security of power system, especially the privacy of key sensitive data, has become the key to the design of power system. The overall architecture of the power system involves data collection, data calculation, data storage, data integration, data analysis and many other links. Using the cloud computing architecture, it could carry out the security analysis of the power system in many links as shown in Fig. 2, and provide stronger technical support for its security protection by integrating the computing capacity and storage resources. Using cloud computing security technology, combined with the characteristics of power system architecture, the security architecture and key technologies of power system cloud computing system are established, which can ensure the security of power system architecture from the design level and application mode dimension.

At present, the emergence of security threats and network attacks in the power industry makes the data security of the power system increasingly threatened, which seriously impacts the normal operation of the power system. Power system as a pillar industry, if there are security incidents, will often bring greater adverse effects and produce huge losses. One of the core of power information system security protection is the protection of large-scale data sets. In addition, the security of the power system provides a key support for the stable and reliable development of the power industry. With the integration of cloud computing technology, it can effectively guarantee the security of the data of the power system, and lay a solid foundation for the healthy and stable development of the power system. By using the power information system

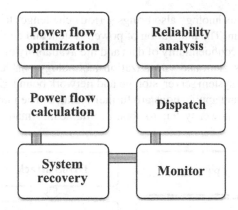

Fig. 2. Power system security analysis elements of cloud computing

security analysis and integrating cloud computing environment, the data is integrated and processed, the security analysis model of power information system is constructed, and the effectiveness of the cloud computing security algorithm is verified.

With the strengthening of power system interconnection and the expanding structure of power system scale, the security assurance, security evaluation and security control of power system become more and more difficult. In this context, the centralized power system computing has been difficult to effectively meet the security needs of the power system. It is necessary to integrate all the computing resources of the power system with the help of cloud computing technology, integrate and analyze all the information, and establish a power system security analysis platform on account of cloud computing, which helps to effectively solve the challenges of the power system in the information security level. The application of cloud computing security technology in the security analysis of power system is mainly to analyze the anticipated accidents, and carry out warning in advance, so as to effectively prevent the occurrence of security accidents.

In a word, under the background of increasingly complex power system architecture and diversified data formats, aiming at the urgent practical needs of power system security, we need to further optimize the cloud computing security algorithm to meet the calculation, data and analysis process of power system. In view of the fact that the existing computing power and security protection architecture has been difficult to effectively adapt to and match the security needs of power system, it has important practical value to carry out the research on cloud computing security technology of power system.

2 Security Requirements of Power System

2.1 Security Situation of Power System

With the deepening application of information technology in power system, power system business is increasingly dependent on modern information technology. In this context, the security attacks against the power system have gradually risen to the national level. Secondly, the power system security incidents occur from time to time, which makes the power business continuity pressure continues to grow. In addition, the rapidly changing information technology also brings serious challenges to the existing security system of power system. The integration of power system and cloud computing significantly ameliorates the confidentiality of data and the availability of applications [1]. The integration of power system and virtualization technology enables the reconstruction and isolation of power system server, storage and network boundaries. With the integration of mobility, data and applications are further isolated. The introduction of big data technology enables the power system to obtain valuable information from massive data.

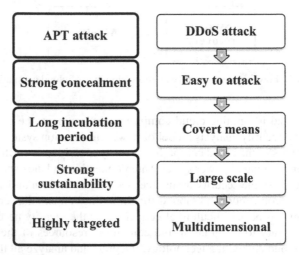

Fig. 3. Typical characteristics of APT attack and DDoS attack

At present, the security threats of power system mainly include APT attack and DDoS attack. Among them, APT attack mainly aims at stealing confidential information of power system, destroying power system and power infrastructure; However, DDoS attack is aimed at the failure of power system to provide normal services. Typical characteristics of APT attack and DDoS attack are shown in Fig. 3. In general, the practice of security attacks against the power system is more profitable and politicized, and the attack is more targeted.

2.2 Security Requirements of Power System

At present, the integration of power system and information network makes the integration of power system and information network in the level of facilities and architecture continue to deepen. The continuous strengthening of the intelligent degree of the power system information network effectively enhances the information perception of the power system. With the help of information technology, the efficiency of business and process of power system has been continuously grown, and the office efficiency and customer experience have been continuously optimized. On the other hand, with the increasing information level of power system, the greater the information security challenges it faces, the higher the demand for the security of the power system. The security requirements of power system firstly focus on the continuity of power business and the security management of power information. Secondly, the power system needs to establish an emergency response mechanism for security incidents, implement personnel management from the perspective of power system security, and support the protection of equipment and system operating environment.

In addition, the practical needs of power system security are mainly reflected in the access control, staff security awareness, audit and accountability, security assessment and certification, configuration management and other aspects. Among them, in the aspect of access control, it is mainly to ensure that information and network assets are not illegally accessed. In the aspect of improving the safety awareness of employees, it is mainly through training to enhance the safety awareness and capability of employees. Secondly, at the level of audit and accountability, it is mainly through periodic review and evaluation to ensure clear responsibilities in the dimension of system security [2]. At the level of security assessment and certification, with the help of periodic security state assessment, the security management of the assets allocated by the power system is carried out. Power system security risk assessment is an important part of security management, especially for the integrity of power system data to meet the security needs of power system at the system and network architecture level.

2.3 Power System Security Threat Model

The security threats of power system mainly include destruction, theft, abuse, and eavesdropping and communication interruption [3]. Among them, in the dimension of power system destruction, it mainly destroys the information and network resources of power system. The main dimension of stealing is illegal acquisition of information assets. Power system abuse refers to the abuse of information and other network resources. Secondly, eavesdropping mainly attacks the confidentiality of power system data and illegally accesses power system information assets. In addition, by attacking e power system network, communication interruption accelerates the power system business interruption and makes the power network invalid or unavailable. The common countermeasures against the security threats of power system are shown in Table 1.

Table 1. Common countermeasures for power system security threats

Security dimension	Security threats				
	Destruction	Tampering	Embezzlement	Information leakage	Service interruption
Access control	×	×	×	×	
Identity authentication			×	×	

(continued)

Table 1. (*continued*)

Security dimension	Security threats				
	Destruction	Tampering	Embezzlement	Information leakage	Service interruption
Non-repudiation	×	×	×	×	×
Confidentiality			×	×	
Communication security			×	×	
Data integrity	×	×			
Effectiveness	×				×
Privacy				×	

3   Security Strategy of Power System Cloud Computing

The cloud computing of power system has the characteristics of data and service outsourcing, virtualization, multi-tenant and cross domain sharing, which not only brings high convenience and efficiency to the data processing of power system, but also brings unprecedented security challenges. The security threat of power system cloud computing service has always existed. Security and privacy issues have become one of the main obstacles to the popularization of cloud computing technology in power system. The security technology of cloud computing in power system is more dependent on the network and server, which inevitably faces the problem of server data privacy, especially in the network environment [8]. Since power system users have great doubts about the security and confidentiality of cloud servers, the data of power system related entities cannot be efficiently transferred to the cloud computing environment, which makes the application of cloud computing in power system have many problems.

The security structure of power system architecture involves all stages of power system, including the definition, strategy, process and technology of power system security and the security implementation and maintenance phase, guiding the development of comprehensive security policy, the selection of different security technologies, and assisting the management of security policy [9]. In addition, the security structure objectives of the power system mainly focus on the dimensions as shown in Fig. 4. In the business level, through access control, legitimate personnel and devices can access the management business data provided by the network element and communication link, or access the business management data on the storage device. At the level of identity authentication, it authenticates the individuals and devices to access business management data.

At the non-repudiation level, the behavior of individuals and devices accessing power business management data is recorded as access evidence. By protecting the power business management data from illegal access and browsing, the confidentiality of power data is guaranteed [10]. By ensuring that the business management data stream is not illegally intercepted and diverted, the security of power data is guaranteed. By protecting

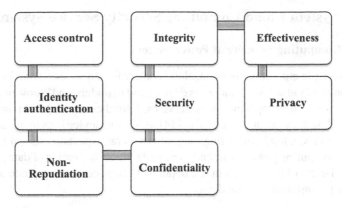

Fig. 4. Security structure objective of power system architecture

the business management data from being illegally modified, created and received, the integrity of power data is guaranteed. By ensuring the validity of the accessed power business management data, the network element will not provide the relevant information of power business management activities to illegal users. The goal of security structure of power system is to prevent leakage, privilege and attack from data security practice, power security consulting and service, power security solutions and products, and to carry out overall security planning, hierarchical protection construction, risk assessment and corresponding permeability test.

The power system security system should be developed from the system organization, strategy, personnel, power system asset classification and protection, physical security, business continuity, operation and maintenance management, application development, compliance and technical support, so as to ensure the business domain requirements of the main body of the power system and meet the data security of the power system. The power system security organization should be established in the levels including system, process, technical support and so on, and the power system security system should be constructed to implement the security strategies [11]. In addition, the cloud computing security architecture of power system should follow the security management framework where management is the core, prevention first, technical means is the support, legal deterrence is the supplement, in order to build an information security system as a whole. On the basis of risk management, security, efficiency and cost should be balanced.

The security of power system needs top-level attention to ensure investment, full participation and special management. In order to ensure the security of power system business as the purpose and starting point, it is necessary to enhance the awareness and responsibility of information security [12]. By paying equal attention to security management and technology, power companies need to strengthen the construction of information security, and accelerate the implementation of power system cloud computing security.

4 Power System Cloud Computing Security Service System

4.1 Cloud Computing Security of Power System

As a highly scalable computing method, cloud computing provides resources to users in the form of on-demand services, and users do not need to understand, know or control the technical infrastructure supporting these services. Cloud computing data and software are in the cloud, so they are not afraid of loss [4]. After the device logs in, it can carry out computing services. Cloud computing integrates several aspects as shown in Fig. 5 to distribute the computing power to the end users and reduce the burden of data processing, so that the end users of power system can obtain sufficient computing processing power only with simple input and output devices.

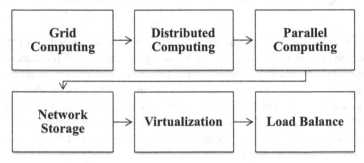

Fig. 5. Technology of cloud computing integration

Cloud computing security technology has the typical characteristics of super large scale, virtualization, high reliability, universality, high scalability and on-demand service [5]. Cloud computing security technology can ensure the high reliability of service by applying data multi-copy fault tolerance and computing node isomorphism interchangeability, and the use of cloud computing is more reliable than using local computer.

Compared with traditional computing represented by distributed computing, cloud computing has significant cost advantages, as shown in Fig. 6. In addition, cloud computing security technology is a homogeneous resource, a single organization, mainly charged by data processing, and targeted at cloud service consumers [6]. It provides a unified login interface and access to set service levels for cloud service consumption on account of the status of cloud service resources and consumer demand, and manages cloud consumer status and requests.

The security problems of power system cloud computing mainly include malicious use, data loss/data leakage, malicious industry insiders, account service or traffic hijacking, potential risks of sharing technology, unsafe API and unknown risk prediction [13]. Due to the characteristics of power system cloud computing, it is inevitable to face several problems as shown in Table 2. In fact, traditional security technologies, such as encryption, security authentication, access control policy, cannot completely solve the privacy security problem of cloud computing. For the security protection of power

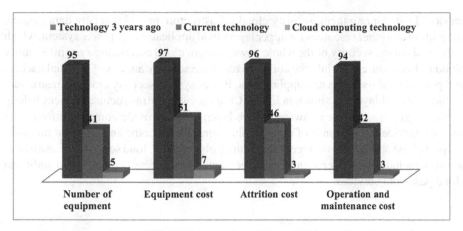

Fig. 6. Cost advantage of cloud computing compared with traditional computing

system cloud computing, we need to establish a complete system from multiple levels and dimensions. For example, the multi-dimensional privacy security model of power system, fully homomorphic encryption algorithm, dynamic service authorization protocol, virtual machine isolation and virus protection strategy and other aspects could be set up to provide a comprehensive technical guarantee for power system cloud computing security.

Table 2. Cloud computing security of power system

Characteristics of cloud computing	Security threats
Data outsourcing	Privacy leakage, Code stolen
Service outsourcing	Privacy leakage, Code stolen
Cross domain sharing	Difficult to establish, manage and maintain trust relationship
Multi-tenancy	Service authorization and access control become more complex
Virtualization	Cooperative attack becomes easier and more covert

It can be seen that the privacy security and content security of cloud computing environment are the key issues of power system cloud computing technology research. It can not only guarantee the convenient use of cloud computing services for the relevant institutions of power system, but also effectively accelerate the sustainable and in-depth development of cloud computing.

4.2 Power System Cloud Computing Security Service System

Power system cloud computing security service system includes power system security cloud infrastructure, cloud security infrastructure services and cloud security utilization services [14]. Among them, security cloud infrastructure provides secure data storage, computing and other resources for upper layer cloud applications of power system, which is the basis of the security of the whole power system cloud computing system. Security cloud infrastructure is mainly the ability to resist the security attacks of external hackers and protect their own data and applications. Power system security cloud infrastructure includes several layers as shown in Fig. 7. Cloud security infrastructure services belong to the cloud infrastructure software service layer, which provide common information security services for all kinds of cloud applications, and become an important means to support cloud applications to meet user security objectives. Cloud security infrastructure services include cloud user identity management, cloud access control, cloud audit and cloud password services.

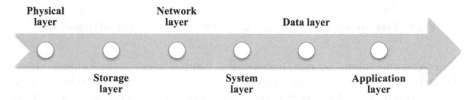

Fig. 7. Power system security cloud infrastructure

Cloud user identity management is mainly to carry out the creation, cancellation and authentication of power system user identity. In the cloud environment, it is convenient to share identity information and authentication services, so as to reduce the operation cost caused by repeated authentication. Cloud identity joint management is carried out on the premise of ensuring the privacy of users' digital identity, which is more challenging to ensure the security management of the whole life cycle of power system [15]. The authentication process on account of federated identity also has higher security requirements in the cloud computing environment. It is necessary to establish an effective access control model represented by role-based, attribute based and mandatory/autonomous access.

In addition, to carry out the power system cloud audit not only helps to protect the user's security management and proof ability, but also helps to clarify the security responsibility of the power system. Therefore, we need to carry out objective audit services on account of the third party to ensure that cloud service providers meet various compliance requirements. Furthermore, with the help of data encryption and decryption operation, it simplifies the design and implementation of cryptographic module for users, and also makes the use of cryptographic technology more centralized, standardized, and easier to manage.

Power system cloud computing security services include DDoS attack protection cloud service, botnet detection and monitoring cloud service, cloud web filtering and antivirus utilization, content security cloud service, security event monitoring and early warning cloud service, cloud spam filtering, prevention and control, etc. [16]. In the technical framework of cloud security services, data collection includes customers, partners, power system R & D center, samples, submission, web mining, automatic submission and behavior analysis.

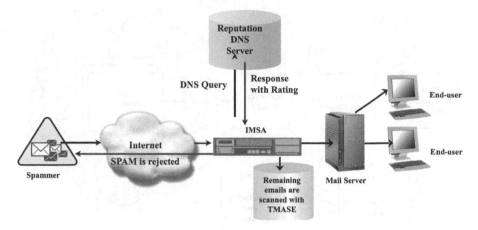

Fig. 8. Application architecture of e-mail reputation technology in power system

Through the use of file reputation technology, it can continuously update in real time in the cloud, and implement the protection deployment [17]. Among them, the application architecture of e-mail reputation technology is shown in Fig. 8, which can isolate and save network resources before spam reaches the gateway.

5   Key Technologies of Power System Cloud Computing Security Service System

5.1   The Architecture of Cloud Computing Security Technology

The overall architecture of cloud computing security technology includes operation and maintenance management, to ensure the standardization of operation and maintenance work, to maintain the large-scale system in the cloud architecture by means of automation, to improve the efficiency and quality of operation and maintenance management, and to ameliorate the response speed of security service demand [7]. With the help of unified monitoring and management, the software, hardware and utilization systems in the cloud architecture are monitored and managed in an all-round way. In addition, in the cloud computing security management level, through the server security management, data security management and network security management, the power system server security reinforcement, data storage encryption, power data transmission encryption, power data backup, intrusion prevention and security domain management are realized. The cloud computing security architecture is shown in Fig. 9.

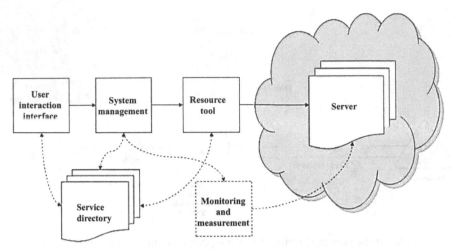

Fig. 9. Cloud computing security architecture

5.2 Trusted Access Control and Cipher-Text Processing

In order to implement the access control of data objects with the help of non-traditional access control means in power system, the data access control on account of cryptography is mainly used. For example, access control on account of hierarchical key generation and distribution policy, KP-ABE using key rules, or CP-ABE using cipher-text rules [18]. The data access control strategy also includes proxy re-encryption method, key embedded access control tree method and so on. In addition, at the level of power system cipher-text processing, security index and cipher-text scanning are mainly used for retrieval. The power system cipher-text processing is mainly concentrated in the level of secret homomorphic encryption, so as to ensure that the power data in the process of converting into cipher-text, is avoided the loss of characteristics.

5.3 Data Privacy Protection

Due to the large scale of power system data, in order to ensure the continuity of its data in the verification process, we need to use the knowledge proof protocol and probability analysis to judge the integrity of remote data in power system. Typical verification and judgment methods include POR (Proofs of Retrievability), PDP (Provable Data Possession, PDI (Provable Data Integrity) and so on. At the level of power system data privacy protection, differential privacy protection can be used to prevent unauthorized privacy data leakage and automatic de-encryption of calculation results in map reduce [19]. In addition, the client based privacy management implements the effective utilization of power system sensitive information in the cloud through the establishment of a customer-centered trust model. The power data privacy processing technology represented by k-anonymity and graph anonymity can effectively establish massive power system data privacy protection solutions.

5.4 Virtual Security Technology

Power system virtual technology is a key component of its cloud computing. With the help of cloud architecture, the security and isolation of cloud computing can be effectively unified. For example, with the help of VR technology, different data resource management such as data isolation execution, data perception core allocation and cache partition can be realized, so as to effectively guarantee the balance between data operation performance and security isolation. Secondly, the image file corresponding application is implemented through the resource management framework of cloud architecture to ensure its integrity and security sharing mechanism [20]. In addition, with the help of image file management system, the security detection and repair of image files are implemented. In power system resource access across multiple domains, each domain has its own access control policy. In resource sharing and protection, it is necessary to formulate a common data access control policy for shared resources and ensure the security of the policy.

5.5 Trusted Cloud Computing

The integration of trusted computing into power system cloud computing can further enhances the credibility of cloud services. For example, with the help of TCCP (Trusted Cloud Computing Platform), a closed data processing environment can be established to ensure the confidentiality of power system data in the virtual environment. Secondly, through the test of IaaS service security, the reliable software and hardware data platform is established to ensure the reliability of power system data processing. In addition, with the help of the security inspection of service data, it is also necessary to effectively solve the confidentiality and integrity of outsourcing data, realize the effective association between each inspection module, and avoid the disclosure of sensitive data in the process of functional operation of key data of power system.

6 Conclusion

In summary, the data and information of power system contains important potential value, and plays an important supporting role in the healthy and stable development of the whole system. Cloud computing technology can effectively protect the security of power system, expand the boundary and dimension of system security protection, and accelerate the effective operation, transmission and processing of power system data. On account of the analysis of the overall security requirements of power system, this paper studies the security situation, security requirements and threat model of power system. Through the research on the concept of power system cloud computing security technology, this paper analyzes the characteristics, advantages and overall architecture of cloud computing security technology. Through the analysis of the security structure goal of power system, the framework of power system security assurance system is proposed.

In addition, through the analysis of cloud computing security and its key technologies of power system, this paper studies the cloud computing security of power system, power system cloud computing security service system and security service architecture. This paper also analyzes the key technologies of power system cloud computing security, such as trusted access control and cipher-text processing, data privacy protection, virtual security and controllable cloud computing.

Acknowledgement. This paper is supported by the science and technology project of State Grid Corporation of China: "Research and Application of Scenario-Driven Data Dynamic Authorization and Compliance Control Key Technology" (Grand No. 5700-202058481A-0-0-00).

References

1. Agarwal, A., Jain, S.: Efficient optimal algorithm of task scheduling in cloud computing environment. Int. J. Comput. Trends Tech **9**(7), 81–83 (2014)
2. Fu, T.: Discussion on resource pool construction of power grid enterprise information system on account of cloud computing. Electron. World **24**, 7 (2014)
3. Huang, C.: Discussion on data security technology of power information system on account of cloud computing. Sci. Technol. Innov. **17**(33), 27–28 (2015)
4. Fei, L., Qi, H., Yuan, J., et al.: Realization of graphic browsing service for GIS platform of power transmission and distribution. Power Syst. Autom. **41**(11), 99–105 (2017)
5. Liu, X., Ma, L., Yu, H.: Research on data security technology of power information system in cloud computing environment. Info Comput. Theor. Ed. **12**, 23–24 (2016)
6. Luo, X., Duan, X.: Research on multi graph display and hierarchical management in power system software. Power Autom. Equipment **22**(6), 16–19 (2012)
7. Maguluri, S.T.: Optimal resource allocation algorithms for cloud computing Dissertations Theses-Gradworks, (5), pp. 634–645 (2015)
8. Ni, J., Han, Q.: Design of data recovery system for power information system on account of Oracle database. Electr. Utilizations **12**, 74–76 (2016)
9. Qiao, L., Hu, N., Tong, D., et al.: Design of power grid integrated information system on account of GIS technology. Electron. Des. Eng. **24**(15), 88–92 (2016)
10. Qu, C., Diao, Y., Bo, X., et al.: Database caching model of power information system on account of multi prediction tree combination algorithm. Electr. Measure. Instrum. **51**(6), 70–75 (2014)
11. Su, Z.: Infrastructure and key technologies of power data center on account of cloud computing. East China Sci. Technol. Acad. Ed. **7**, 187 (2014)
12. Wang, B., Liu, Z.: Remote file synchronization optimization model on account of Rsync. Comput. Modernization **4**, 10–13 (2015)
13. Wang, X., Yan, J., Zeng, Q.: Intelligent task scheduling algorithm for multi-level optimization in cloud computing. Control. Eng. **24**(5), 1008–1012 (2017)
14. Wang, Y., Chang, F.: Utilization and analysis of cloud computing technology in power system. Comput. Knowl. Technol. **7**, 101–122 (2015)
15. Wu, K., Liu, W., Li, Y., et al.: Power big data analysis technology and utilization on account of cloud computing. China Electr. Power **48**(2), 111–116 (2015)
16. Xie, F., Ding, Y.: Data security protection technology in the process of information system management and control. Netw. Secur. Technol. Utilization **8**, 65 (2015)
17. Jie, Y., Tian, N., Yi, Y.: Utilization effect of smart grid information platform on account of cloud computing. Electron. Technol. Softw. Eng. **22**, 189–190 (2014)
18. Yang, Y., Jiang, X., Wu, S.: Exploring the security problems and Countermeasures of power information system. Info Commun. **190**(10), 284–285 (2018)

19. Chun, Z., Jing, C.: Cloud environment service classification algorithm on account of data mining technology. Laser J. **36**(3), 84–87 (2015)
20. Zhou, H.: Research on information security of power system. China Hi Tech Zone **14**, 233 (2018)

Research on Optimization of Fuzzing Test of Unknown Protocol Based on Message Type
Black Box Testing

WeiQing Fang[1] ⓘ, Peng Li[1,2](✉) ⓘ, YuJie Zhang[1] ⓘ, and Yang Chen[1] ⓘ

[1] School of Computer Science, Nanjing University of Posts
and Telecommunications, Nanjing 210023, China
lipeng@njupt.edu.cn
[2] Institute of Network Security and Trusted Computing, Nanjing 210023, China

Abstract. In recent years, due to the large number of unknown protocols, it is necessary to study the security of unknown protocols. IFuzzing is a universal method that can be used to study unknown protocols. In unknown protocol fuzzy test, the test object in reality often tend to be in a state of isolation, in most cases only black box testing is used, and black box testing can get feedback information is very little, which makes the black box testing of unknown protocol is often a violent test method, and it is difficult to optimize. In view of the above situation, this paper proposes a method to optimize fuzzy testing by analyzing the message of unknown protocol and combining the concept of path testing to build the message type time series tree (MTTS-Tree). Experiments show that this approach makes black-box testing of unknown protocols more strategic.

Keywords: Unknown protocol · Fuzzy testing · Black box testing · Path testing

1 Introduction

The research on fuzzing optimization of unknown protocols is generally devoted to three aspects. One is to optimize the generation of test cases based on the analysis of the protocol format and semantics, and to optimize the generation of test cases through the message format of the unknown protocol and the semantics of the message fields; the second is to improve the efficiency of test data generation and the effectiveness of test data generation. Especially, efficiency is very important in fuzzy testing; the third is to enhance the ability of vulnerability mining, locate and analyze the abnormality of the target program in time during the test process [1].

However, in reality, fuzzy testing objects of unknown protocols are often non-cooperative objects, so that fuzzy testing for unknown protocols is usually a black-box testing situation. Because it is difficult to get feedback from test objects, and it is impossible to directly study the running logic inside the test. It is impossible to study the test object directly, which makes it difficult to optimize fuzzy testing for unknown protocols. Therefore, it is necessary and practical to make full use of the network traffic that can be captured and study its law to optimize the process of fuzzy testing.

© Springer Nature Singapore Pte Ltd. 2022
Y. Tian et al. (Eds.): ICBDS 2021, CCIS 1563, pp. 284–298, 2022.
https://doi.org/10.1007/978-981-19-0852-1_22

In addition, there is a lack of research on the correlation between test cases in fuzzy test optimization protocol. The status of a test object changes after receiving various types of packets. The transition relationship between states can be represented by the state machine of the protocol. What causes the test object to trigger an abnormal state is also related to the transition between states, that is, to the state machine transition path. A sample diagram of a protocol state machine is shown in Fig. 1. Different types of packets cause the sending status to migrate.

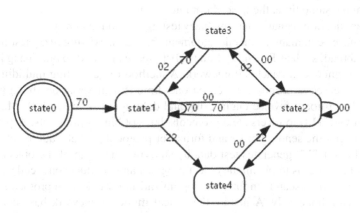

Fig. 1. Sample diagram of the state machine for the protocol

However, it is difficult to infer the protocol state machine. In this paper we propose a method to study the association rules between all kinds of messages in the message sequence instead of directly studying the protocol state machine. The fuzzy test optimization of unknown protocol is carried out by constructing time series tree of message type.

2   Related Work

According to the statistics of the Center for Global Security, the traffic of unknown protocols in the backbone network has reached as high as 45%. Currently, unknown protocols are widely used in various kinds of networks, such as the data interaction of industrial equipment in the industrial control network [2], and the data interaction of various application layers in other kinds of networks. Security is also difficult to know because of the varied designs of unknown protocol structures. The original intention of the design protocol is to make the data communication more orderly, efficient and secure. However, due to the inevitable defects in the design, there may be some high-risk vulnerabilities that endanger the security of the entire network system [3]. Therefore, it is very necessary to dig out the security holes of the protocol and improve the protocol design in time [4].

Generally speaking, the methods for mining security vulnerabilities of protocols mainly include dynamic analysis [5], vulnerability feature analysis [6], model testing [7] and fuzzy testing. Among of them, fuzzy testing is a method that injects a large amount of random or semi-random data into the target, monitors the operation of the target at the same time [8], and records the abnormal behavior of the target at the same time to further study its potential vulnerabilities. It is often used to study the robustness of the program. The clear advantage of fuzzy test method is that it does not need to have strong mining skills, and does not need to carry out in-depth analysis of the target program, at the same time, the false alarm rate is low.

In the application scenario of using fuzzy testing method to mine protocol vulnerabilities, there have been many further developments based on existing fuzzy testing tools at home and abroad, such as Peach [9], Sulley [10], Spike [11] and so on. Zhang [12] et al. made improvements on Peach's framework. A method of generating multidimensional variation test cases is proposed based on one-dimensional variation strategy. LZfuzz [13] used the protocol reverse engineering and debugging framework PaiMei [15] on the basis of GPF [14] to reverse text protocols, but not binary protocols. Asp-fuzz [16] directly changed the sending order and format of protocol packets, but the effect is not good. IOTFuzzer [17] generates test data by studying the logic of the object program using data, but it needs to obtain the object program and conduct some code analysis.

In recent years, research on fuzzy test optimization for unknown protocols has been carried out simultaneously. A mature theoretical model framework has been formed, such as the integrated sequence allocator algorithm proposed by Zhang et al. [18] under the guidance of protocol inverse generation of a certain protocol format, the complete automatic protocol fuzzy testing framework is used to generate test cases by multidimensional mutation and to conduct active detection to locate anomalies. Shen et al. [19] used the model learning method based on automata theory and the protocol state fuzzy testing technology to carry out black box test analysis on OpenVPN system, providing a new idea for testing protocol security from the aspect of vulnerability mining.

3   Description of Algorithm

In order to introduce the multi-policy black box testing algorithm based on packet time series tree more clearly. This section will explain some of the concepts and logic of the algorithm. This paper introduces the algorithm and the purpose of message type time series tree by illustrating the method.

3.1   Related Notion

- Message Type
    There are various types of packets in a session flow, among which the packets sent to the test object can be divided into several limited types by clustering algorithm. Such as A, B, C... represent various types of packets, as shown in Fig. 2.

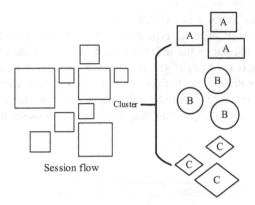

Fig. 2. Clustering of messages

- Test Period

    The packet in the session flow can be vaguely regarded as a sequence of packet types, as shown in Fig. 3. To generate a message type time series tree that guides the order in which test cases are sent. In this article, the sequence of message types is divided by the size of the test cycle. The advantage is that the depth and breadth of the tree can be limited. The test period is the number of packet types in the packet sequence. The effect of segmentation is shown in Fig. 4. A sliding window is used to divide the data, and the step size of the sliding window is 1.

Fig. 3. Message sequence

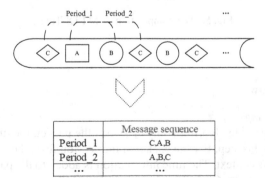

Fig. 4. Message sequence segmentation by slide windows

● Message Type Time Series Tree (MTTS-Tree)

The composition of message type time series tree is shown in Fig. 5. The tree consists of two parts: one is the index list used to retrieve the message time series tree, and the other is the body of the constructed message type sequence tree. The components of a node in a tree include the name of the node (for example, C1) and the number of the node (:2). An index table consists of the name of a leaf node and a pointer to that node. The algorithm of constructs such a message time series tree is described below.

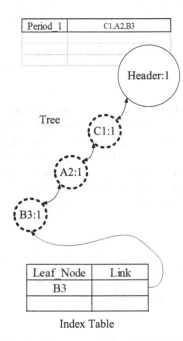

Fig. 5. The composition of MTTS-Tree

3.2 Algorithm Flow

1) Data pre-processing

Because the clustering algorithm only classifies the packet, the time information of the packet is lost in this step. For the packet in the session flow, the time information is critical to analyze its context. The time information is added to the packet type for each test cycle, as shown in Fig. 6.

	Message sequence
Period_1	C,A,B
Period_2	C,B,A
Period_3	A,C,B

	Message sequence
Period_1	C1,A2,B3
Period_2	C1,B2,A3
Period_3	A1,C2,B3

Fig. 6. Data pre-processing

2) Initialization

The algorithm generates an empty index list and a body tree with only head nodes, as shown in Fig. 7.

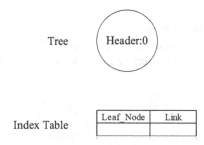

Fig. 7. Initialization of the Tree

3) Insert the first test period sequence

Insert the first test cycle sequence and update the message type time series tree (as shown in Fig. 8). Starting from the first node, add 1 to the count of the head node, and then retrieve whether a node named C1 already exists among the children nodes of the head node: If so, add 1 to the count of the node; If not, create a new node, insert the new node into the children nodes of the head node, and set its count to 1; Insert A2 to retrieve C1, insert B3 to retrieve A2, same as above.

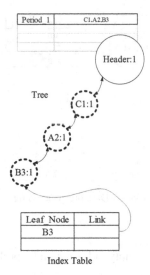

Fig. 8. Insert period _1

4) Insert the next test period sequence

Insert the next test cycle sequence tree and update the message time series tree (as shown in Fig. 9). The method of inserting the node is the same as in Step 2.

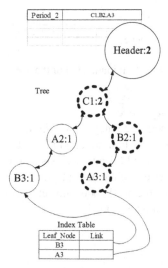

Fig. 9. Insert period _2

5) Loop through the previous step

Loop through the previous step until the sequence ends. The final generation of the example use case is shown in Fig. 10.

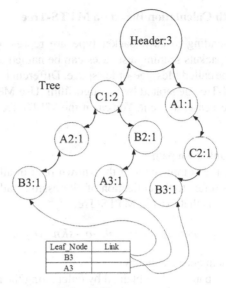

Fig. 10. Final generation

The pseudo-code of the algorithm is shown in Table 1 below:

Table 1. The pseudo-code of the algorithm

Algorithm : MTTS-Tree
Input : Message_sequence
Output :MTTS-Tree
1. Init_Tree()
2. If(Message_sequence!=null):
Read_First_sequence(Message_sequence)
Insert(sequence)
Update_IndexTable()
3. While(Read_next_sequence!=null):
Insert(sequence)
Update_IndexTable()
4. Return MTTS-Tree
5. End

3.3 The Policy in Path Calculation Based on MTTS-Tree

The test cases corresponding to each packet type are represented as A-sample, B-sample..., the order of packets sending test cases can be named as Message-order, and all possible orders can be called Message-order-space. Different types of Message-order can be mined in MTTS-Tree generated by the algorithm. Use Message-Order to guide the order in which the test cases are sent. You can mine MTTS-Tree to generate different types of paths.

- Fuzzy test based on unknown path
    As shown in (1), the complement of the known path in all possible paths is the unknown path. m-o-s refers to the collection of all possible paths. Known path refers to the collection of paths that exist in MTTS-Tree.

$$unknown\,path \;=\; Cm\!-\!o\!-\!sKnown\,path \tag{1}$$

- Fuzzy test based on sequence frequency
    The frequency of a path can be obtained by calculating the ratio of the number of last nodes of the path to the number of head nodes. The calculation formula is shown in (2), where FN.count indicates the number of last nodes in the path, and Header.count indicates the number of head nodes.

$$Frequency \;=\; FN.count \,/\, Header.count \tag{2}$$

3.4 Optimization of Test Path

In the process of fuzz testing, there are often repeated test paths on the test path, and these repeated test paths can be removed by analyzing and calculating the subtree.

Take Fig. 11 below as an example. The test path included in the subtree in the figure. In order to remove the repeated test path, we use the breadth first search algorithm (BFS) to remove the repeated path. The optimized result is shown in Fig. 12.

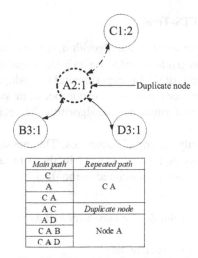

Main path	Repeated path
C	
A	C A
C A	
A C	Duplicate node
A D	
C A B	Node A
C A D	

Fig. 11. The path before optimized

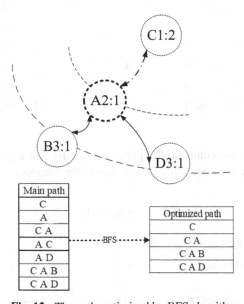

Main path
C
A
C A
A C
A D
C A B
C A D

Optimized path
C
C A
C A B
C A D

Fig. 12. The path optimized by BFS algorithm

4   Experiment and Analysis

The process of fuzzing test objects generally takes a lot of time, so the algorithm proposed in this paper does not take a lot of time as long as it consumes time. Compared with time consumption, more attention should be paid to the consumption of memory space. This section will analyze the performance of the algorithm proposed in this article from two levels of experiment and theoretical calculation.

4.1 Experimental of MTTS-Tree

Before analyzing the performance of the algorithm, a brief introduction to the experimental data in this article is given. In order to verify the time consumption and memory space consumption of the algorithm, the experimental part adopts the method of controlling variables, and the sequence length and the number of message types are controlled respectively to analyze the performance of the algorithm. The experimental data is shown in Table 2.

The data are all randomly generated sequences. The message type in the table represents the number of message types contained in the data, and the sequence length represents the number of messages contained in the data.

Table 2. The introduction of data

Data number	The introduction of data		
	Data name	Message type	Sequence length
a	Msg-3-5000	3	5000
b	Msg-3-10000	3	10000
c	Msg-3-15000	3	15000
d	Msg-4-5000	4	5000
e	Msg-5-5000	5	5000
f	Msg-6-5000	6	5000

After running the algorithm in this paper repeatedly, the experimental results are shown in Table 3. The units are milliseconds and MByte respectively.

Table 3. Experimental results

Data number	The introduction of data		
	Data name	Run time (ms)	Memory consumption (MB)
A	Msg-3-5000	612	6.4
B	Msg-3-10000	834	6.8
C	Msg-3-15000	1035	6.5
d	Msg-4-5000	734	10.4
E	Msg-5-5000	962	12.2
F	Msg-6-5000	843	20.3

- *Time complexity T(n)*

   Time complexity consists of two parts. One part is the insertion operation O((f + f^2)*n) on the tree, and the other part is the update operation O(n/f) on the index table. The formula is as (3).

$$T(n) = O((f + f^2) * n) + O(n/f) \tag{3}$$

   f = message type, n = sequence length in (3).

- *Space complexity S(n)*

   Space complexity consists of two parts. One part is the memory space O(n/f) of the tree, and the other part is the memory space O(n/f) of the index table. The formula is as (4).

$$S(n) = O(f^f) + O(n/f) \tag{4}$$

   f = message type, n = sequence length in (4).

   From the results of experimental analysis and theoretical analysis, the algorithm performance is proportional to the message type and sequence length in terms of running time, and in actual situations n >> f, so the time performance is more affected by the sequence length. The memory space consumption is less affected by the sequence length, and with the increase of the message type, the memory consumption of the algorithm is greatly increased by the influence of the message type.

4.2 Fuzzy Test Case Generation Experiment

The experiment uses boofuzz as the experimental platform. The feasibility of the algorithm is analyzed by comparing the number of generated fuzz test cases before and after optimization. Figure 12 above is the path diagram executed in the experiment.

   There are four types of messages in the experiment, and the optimized path is shown in Figs. 12 and 13 is the field format of different types of messages defined in the experiment, in which green indicates the fields that need to be mutated. The length of the variant bytes of each type of message is the same. The experiment separately studied the number of test cases generated when the max string mutation byte length is from 256 bytes to 1024 bytes, and the span is 256 bytes. Figure 14 is the result of this experiment. After optimizing the test path, the number of generated test cases is greatly reduced.

   From the experimental results, this experiment can show that after the algorithm simplifies the test path, the experimental use cases are greatly reduced, which reduces the time spent on testing.

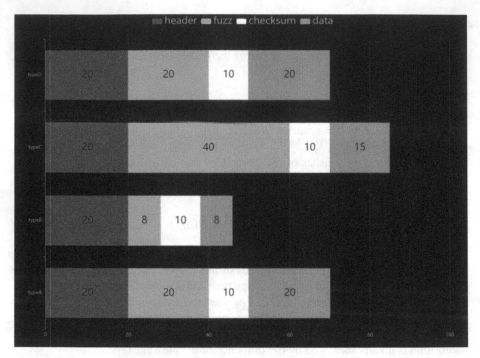

Fig. 13. Field format of different types of messages

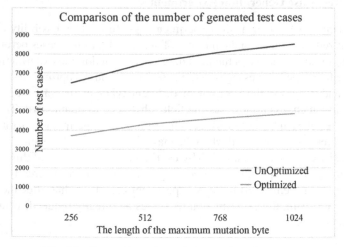

Fig. 14. Comparison chart of the number of test cases

Acknowledgment. The subject is sponsored by the National Natural Science Foundation of P. R. China (No. 61872196, No. 61872194, and No. 61902196), Scientific and Technological Support Project of Jiangsu Province (No. BE2019740, No. BK20200753, and No. 20KJB520001), Major Natural Science Research Projects in Colleges and Universities of Jiangsu Province (No.

18KJA520008), Six Talent Peaks Project of Jiangsu Province (RJFW-111), Postgraduate Research and Practice Innovation Program of Jiangsu Province (No. SJKY19_0761, No. SJKY19_0759, No. KYCX20_0759).

I would like to thank Nanjing University of Posts and Telecommunications for the help provided in this research, and also for the support provided by Computer Academy. In addition, this research is also inseparable from the help of every reference author mentioned in the article.

References

1. Zhang, X., Li, Z.: Survey of fuzz testing technology. Comput. Sci. **43**(05), 1–8 (2016)
2. Paes, R., Mazur, D.C., Venne, B.K., Ostrzenski, J.: A guide to securing industrial control networks: integrating IT and OT systems. IEEE Ind. Appl. Mag. **26**, 47–53 (2020)
3. Goo, Y., Shim, K., Lee, M., Kim, M.: Protocol specification extraction based on contiguous sequential pattern algorithm. IEEE Access **7**, 36057–36074 (2019)
4. Khan, Z., Aalsalem, Y.M., Khan, K.: Five acts of consumer behavior: a potential security and privacy threat to Internet of Things. In: 2018 IEEE International Conference on Consumer Electronics (ICCE), pp. 1–3 (2018)
5. Kim, S., Ryou, J.: Source code analysis for static prediction of dynamic memory usage. In: International Conference on Platform Technology and Service (PlatCon), pp. 1–4 (2019)
6. Zolanvari, M., Teixeira, M.A., Gupta, L., Khan, K.M., Jain, R.: Machine learning-based network vulnerability analysis of industrial Internet of Things. IEEE Internet Things J. **6**, 6822–6834 (2019)
7. Li, Z., Zhang, J., Liao, X., Ma, J.: Survey of software vulnerability detection techniques. Jisuanji Xuebao/Chin. J. Comput. **38**, 717–732 (2015)
8. Sutton, M., Greene, A., Amini, P.: Fuzzing: Brute Force Vulnerability Discovery. Addison-Wesley Professional, Massachusetts (2007)
9. Wang, H., Wen, Q., Zhang, Z.: Improvement of peach platform to support GUI-based protocol state modeling. In: 2013 IEEE International Conference on Green Computing and Communications and IEEE Internet of Things and IEEE Cyber, Physical and Social Computing, pp. 1094–1097 (2013)
10. Lee, H., Shin, S., Chio, K., Chung, K., Park, S., Chio, J.: Detecting the vulnerability of software with cyclic behavior using Sulley. In: 2011 7th International Conference on Advanced Information Management and Service (ICIPM), pp. 83–88 (2011)
11. Aitel, D.: The advantages of block-based protocol analysis for security testing. Immunity Inc. (2002)
12. Zhang, L., Liang, J., Liu, L., Jiang, Z., Liu, J.: Improvement of the sample mutation strategy based on fuzzing framework peach. In: International Conference on Artificial Intelligence and Big Data, pp. 33–37 (2018)
13. Bratus, S., Hansen, A., Shubina, A.: LZfuzz: A Fast Compression-based Fuzzer for Poorly Documented Protocols. Darmouth College, Hanover (2008)
14. DeMott, J., Enbody, R., Punch, F.: Revolutionizing the Field of Grey-Box Attack Surface Testing with J. Clerk Maxwell, A Treatise on Electricity and Magnetism, 3rd edn., vol. 2, pp.68–73. Clarendon, Oxford (1892)
15. Amini, P.: PaiMei - reverse engineering framework. In: Reverse Engineering Conference, Benevento, Italy, pp. 21–49 (2006)
16. Kitagawa, T., Hanaoka, M., Kono, K.: AspFuzz: a state-aware protocol fuzzer based on application-layer protocols. In: The IEEE symposium on Computers and Communications, Riccione, Italy, pp. 202–208 (2010)

17. Chen, J., Diao, W., Zhao, Q., Zuo, C., Zhang, K.: IoTFuzzer: discovering memory corruptions in IoT through app-based fuzzing. In: Network and Distributed System Security Symposium, San Diego, California, USA, pp. 1–15 (2018)
18. Zhang, W., Zhang, L., Mao, J., Xu, Z., Zhang, Y.: An automated method of unknown protocol fuzzing test. Jisuanji Xuebao/Chin. J. Comput. **43**, 653–667 (2020)
19. Shen, Y., Gu, C., Chen, X., Zhang, X., Lu, Z.: Vulnerability analysis of OpenVPN system based on model learning. Ruan Jian Xue Bao/J. Softw. **30**, 3750–3764 (2019)

Risk Prediction of Diabetic Readmission Based on Cost Sensitive Convolutional Neural Network

Bin Fan[1], Zuoling Xie[2], Haitao Cheng[1], and Peng Li[1,3(✉)]

[1] School of Computer Science, Nanjing University of Posts
and Telecommunications, Nanjing 210023, China
lipeng@njupt.edu.cn
[2] Zhongda Hospital Southeast University, Nanjing 210009, China
[3] Institute of Network Security and Trusted Computing, Nanjing 210023, China

Abstract. Diabetes is a chronic disease that nearly affects people of all ages. Some scholars find that the potential risk of diabetes can be effectively predicted by modeling the readmission data. However, a large number of data missing and data imbalance problems exist in diabetes medical data. Traditional machine learning approaches employ feature extraction and classification prediction. However, the huge problems caused by imbalances in medical data and the different costs of category labels and misclassification errors are not fully taken into account. In this paper, we propose a Cost Sensitive Convolutional Neural Network (CSCNN) model for the imbalanced diabetes dataset. We combined convolutional neural networks (CNN) and cost sensitive loss function to deal with data imbalance, and conducted sufficient experiments on the diabetes readmission dataset. Compared with other methods, our model has achieved good results in all aspects of indicators. In experiments, the F3 score of the model reaches 0.584 and the sensitivity reaches 0.782. We find that our proposed model can effectively classify the inpatient data of unbalanced diabetes and solve imbalance and skewness problems effectively.

Keywords: Readmission risk · Skew data · Convolutional Neural Network ·
Cost sensitive

1 Introduction

Diabetes is a common chronic disease, which will not only lead to the instability of blood sugar, but also lead to a series of complications, even life-threatening in serious cases. Over time, the disease causes severe damage to the heart, blood vessels, eyes, kidneys and nerves. There are three types of diabetes: type 1, type 2 and gestational diabetes. Type 2 diabetes is the most common form and usually affects adults. However, over the past 20 years type 2 diabetes has become more common in children and adolescents as more young people become obese or overweight.

According to the ninth edition of IDF (International Diabetes Federation) Diabetes Atlas, approximately 463 million adults between the ages of 20 and 79 worldwide have

© Springer Nature Singapore Pte Ltd. 2022
Y. Tian et al. (Eds.): ICBDS 2021, CCIS 1563, pp. 299–311, 2022.
https://doi.org/10.1007/978-981-19-0852-1_23

diabetes (1 in 11 is diabetic) in 2019. Nearly 4.2 million people died from diabetes or its complications in 2019, equivalent to one death every eight seconds.

Diabetes has greatly affected people's physical and mental health worldwide, so it is particularly important to assist the diagnosis of diabetes through medical technology. For an inpatient with diabetes, it makes a lot of sense to study the risk of readmission. Readmission means to be admitted within a specified period of time after the first admission, such as 30 days or 90 days, etc. Taking readmission rate as an "alternative indicator" of hospital service quality and as the most accurate predictor of hospital mortality has been widely accepted by scholars. The machine learning method is used to establish a model to predict whether the body indicators of diabetic patients have reached the discharge standard during hospitalization, which can reduce the risk of readmission.

Data mining techniques can be used to predict a diabetic's risk of readmission. Some prediction algorithms have been used to predict the risk of diabetes. Sneha and Gangil [1] used Naive Bayes (NB) to focus on using prediction models to select features related to early detection of diabetes for prediction, and the results showed that the highest accuracy of the model reached 82.30%. Chen [2] suggest a hybrid forecast model to better detect type 2 diabetes. However, these algorithms have some shortcomings that make them unsuitable for the existing imbalanced medical datasets:

(1) The skewed distribution of diabetic datasets is not considered. In real medical admission dataset, data samples of the normal condition are abundant while data samples of the abnormal are relatively scarce. The unbalanced distribution of data will cause the classifier to pay more attention to the majority of classes and ignore the minority classes.
(2) The misclassification costs of different categories are not considered. In practical scenarios, the cost loss of misdiagnosing a patient as healthy differs from that of a healthy person as a patient.

In this paper, a diabetic readmission risk prediction model based on cost sensitive convolutional neural network (CSCNN) is proposed, which can tackle the problem of the imbalance of the dataset and get a better prediction effect on recall score and F3 score.

The data set in this paper is from UCI machine learning library, which records the clinical nursing records of diabetes patients in 130 American hospitals during the decade from 1999 to 2008. For details of the data, please refer to literature [3].

We adopted CSCNN to monitor the readmission risk of diabetic patients and did a lot of experiments to prove the validity of the model. The experimental results show that, compared with the existing prediction algorithms, our prediction algorithm based on CSCNN achieves a better performance in the unbalanced diabetes dataset by comparing the recall rate, ROC curve and other evaluation criteria. Our main work in this paper is as follows:

(1) For unbalanced diabetes data set, a cost-sensitive method is proposed to solve the problem of data imbalance.
(2) Combined with convolution neural network to predict diabetes readmission data, we have good experimental results. The recall score of CSCNN model in the test

set reaches 0.782, and the F3 score reaches 0.582. Compared with other diabetes prediction algorithms, the model has a better classification effect on imbalanced data.

The rest of this article includes: Sect. 2 introduces the related work. Section 3 describes cost sensitive convolutional neural network model. In Sect. 4, we investigate the experiment on diabetes data set and get the best effect. In Sect. 5, we conclude the article with the summary and possible future studies.

2 Related Work

The related work mainly includes two parts: imbalanced data and diabetes prediction.

2.1 Imbalanced Data

In many practical applications, skewed data is a very common phenomenon in which one category has more samples than the other. Many algorithms focus more on the classification of major samples, while ignoring or wrongly classifying a small number of samples, which tend to be rare but very important samples [4]. The main methods to deal with unbalanced data classification include sampling-based approach and cost-sensitive learning-based approach.

Data sampling approach has attracted much attention in data mining related to data imbalance problem. Data sampling is mainly divided into over-sampling and under-sampling. Over-sampling attempts to balance the dataset by adding samples to the dataset, while under-sampling tries to eliminate most samples from the dataset to overcome the problem of unbalanced category distribution. Chawla et al. [5] suggested an oversampling method, SMOTE, which oversampled the minority classes by creating the resultant minority class instances. Seiffert et al. [6] combined random undersampling (RUS) with Adaboost algorithm to propose a new hybrid sampling algorithm, RUSBoost, which randomly deleted majority class instances to form balanced data.

Cost sensitive learning [7] is a new approach in the field of machine learning. It mainly considers how to train classifiers when different classification errors lead to different penalties. It can design classifiers based on different types of misclassification costs and overall misclassification cost minimization, which can solve the problem of data imbalance to some extent. Haishuai Wang et al. [8] used electronic medical record data to embed the features obtained by the neural network into the multi-layer perceptron (MLP) for prediction, and trained MLP in the prediction process using cost-sensitive formulas. Fahimeh Ghobadi et al. [9] developed a credit card fraud detection model based on cost sensitive methods, which greatly improve the accuracy of prediction.

Due to the addition of new data or deletion of original data, sampling technology has a great influence on the original real data, resulting in a large error in classification results and a large probability of over-fitting. For instance, under-sampling may lead to loss of important information. Cost sensitive learning approaches solve the problem of data imbalance by assigning different weights to different categories. The advantage of such methods is that the prediction model can be directly improved without manipulating the original data, and the classification results can take into account different loss costs, which is often better than the over-sampling techniques [10]. Therefore, in our paper, we choose the cost sensitive method to solve the classification of unbalanced data.

2.2 Diabetes Prediction

Kamble et al. [11] used a limited Boltzmann machine (RBM) in the Indian Horse diabetes data set to predict and diagnose diabetes, and a decision tree model was proposed to diagnose type 1 or type 2 diabetes. Swapna et al. [12] proposed a deep learning approach to diagnose diabetes based on electrocardiogram (ECG) signal data. The method used support vector machine (SVM) for classification and achieves an accuracy of 95.7% on ECG datasets. Sisodia et al. [13] used a variety of machine learning algorithms to process and predict PIDD dataset. Among these algorithms, naive Bayes was the best and achieved accuracy of 76.3%. Han et al. [14] improved KNN and Logistic algorithms and conducted experiments on PIDD diabetes data. The algorithm selected the value of initial seed points through experiments to predict and diagnose diabetes, and its prediction accuracy improved 3.04% compared with other model.

3 Cost Sensitive Convolutional Neural Network Model

3.1 Cost Sensitive

Cost Sensitive Learning (CSL) is a learning algorithm for classification weight modification. Based on the original standard cost loss function, the algorithm adds constraints and weight conditions, consider misclassification costs and minimize the total cost through continuous iteration. The obvious characteristic of cost sensitivity is that the cost of misdiagnosis is different. In the readmission test of diabetes in this paper, the loss caused by misdiagnosis of a serious diabetic patient as a healthy person is far greater than that caused by misdiagnosis of a healthy person as a diabetic. The costs caused by these two types of misdiagnosis are different.

Using the cost matrix, the cost sensitive problem can be transformed into an optimization problem, and the function value can reach the minimum value through the back propagation of the loss function. The expected cost loss of dividing instance x into class j (through classifiers) Loss(x, v) can be defined as:

$$\text{Loss(x, v)} = \sum_j P(u|x) \cos t(u, v) \tag{1}$$

Where Loss(x, v) represents the expected loss of classification of sample x as class v, $P(u|x)$ represents the posterior probability that the sample belongs to class u, and $\cos t(u, v)$ represents the misclassification cost of classification of class u as class v.

In particular, when $\cos t(u, v) = 1$, for any u and v, cost sensitive learning will degenerate into the traditional classification learning algorithm which pursues the lowest classification error rate.

3.2 Convolutional Neural Network

CNN is a feedforward neural network. The connection of layers is inspired by the animal visual cortex. The structure of CNN mainly includes convolutional layer, pooling layer and fully connected layer. The layers are used to accomplish feature learning and classification tasks. In this paper, one-dimensional CNN is used to extract the characteristics of diabetes hospitalization data.

3.3 Cost Sensitive Convolutional Neural Network Model

In this paper, a serious problem in the diabetes dataset is the imbalance of data. After data preprocessing, data imbalance will greatly affect the prediction effect. Among 87910 data samples in the training set, 10924 samples will be readmitted in a short time, and 86986 samples will not be readmitted, of which the imbalance ratio is 7.96. In order to solve the problem caused by imbalanced data, we build CSCNN model as shown in Fig. 1 to analyze and predict the readmission of patients.

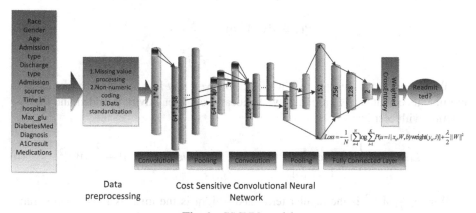

Fig. 1. CSCNN-model

After standardization, the diabetes hospitalization data will be sent to the convolutional neural network model, which is constructed with convolutional layer, pooling layer and full connection layer. After convolutional layer, dropout operation can be added to effectively suppress overfitting. According to relevant literature [16], ReLU activation function often achieves better results. So for the activation function of each layer, we use the linear rectifying function (ReLU), which can be defined as

$$\text{ReLU}:g(\xi) = \max(0, \zeta) \tag{2}$$

In the one-dimensional convolution in this paper, with the above formula, it is assumed that the length of the input sequence is X, the weight of the convolution kernel is W_{ij}^l, then the function can be expressed as follows:

$$X_j^l = \text{ReLU}(\sum_{i \in N_j} X_i^{l-1} * W_{ij}^l + b_j^l) \tag{3}$$

Where: X_i^{l-1} is the i th feature of the layer $l-1$; W_{ij}^l is the convolution weight matrix between the i th feature of layer $l-1$ and the j th feature of the layer l; b_i^l is the bias of the j th characteristic of the layer l; ReLU(.) is the activation function mentioned above.

The addition of dropout after the convolutional layer can effectively suppress overfitting, and the pooling layer after the dropout is used to compress the convolutional layer information and prevent overfitting. There are max-pooling and mean-pooling methods. In previous academic studies, max-pooling has better performance in feature extraction. Therefore, max-pooling is chosen in our model which can be defined as:

$$P_j^l = \max\left\{x_{j*k:(j+1)*k}^{l-1}\right\} \tag{4}$$

In Eq. 4, p_j^l is the output value of the jth neuron of layer l. max() is the aggregation function to calculate the maximum value in the target region. $x_{(j*k:(j+1)*k)}^{(l-1)}$ is the jth area of layer $l-1$, the length of the neuron segment in this region is k. After fully connect layer, we use softmax to probabilistic the output of neural network. x_o is the last output layer, then the estimate of probability of class i given x can be formulated as follows:

$$P(y = i|x, W, b) = \frac{e^{x_o}}{\sum\limits_{k=1}^{K} e^{x_o}} \tag{5}$$

Traditional cross entropy loss function, however, pay less attention to rare cases in an imbalanced dataset. Consequently, the idea of cost sensitivity is added and the loss function with cost is:

$$Loss = -\frac{1}{N}[\sum_{n=1}^{N} \log \sum_{i=1}^{K} P(u = i|x_n, W, b)\text{weight}(y_n, i)] + \frac{\lambda}{2}||W||^2 \tag{6}$$

Where, $\frac{\lambda}{2}||W||^2$ is the regular term, and weight is the misclassification cost ratio. The misclassification cost ratio is an adjustable parameter, and the classification effect of this model on imbalanced data under different misclassification costs can be observed. We compare the original loss function and the loss function with the weights of 2 to 14 respectively, and compare the classification effect.

4 Experiments

4.1 Data Set

The dataset is loaded from UCI, which records the clinical nursing records of diabetes patients in 130 American hospitals during the decade from 1999 to 2008. More details are listed in literature [3]. There are 10,766 data and 55 attribute columns, including label variables of '<30', '>30' and 'NO'. They represent that a patient will be readmitted within 30 days after discharge, readmitted over 30 days and no longer admitted, respectively. The label variables of patients who will be readmitted within 30 days are set as 1 (positive cases), and those who are not readmitted after 30 days were set as

0 (negative cases). The readmission record label can be used to determine whether the patient is likely to be readmitted within a short period of time, thus determining the effect of this treatment. The description of some key attributes is shown in literature [3]. The dataset includes attributes of the number of patients, race, gender, age, type of admission, length of stay, resident medical specialty, number of laboratory tests, Hb1A1c test results, diagnosis, number of medications, number of diabetes medications, number of outpatient visits, number of inpatients, and number of emergency visits in the year prior to hospitalization.

Due to the common incompleteness of medical data, the corresponding data volume has a large number of missing. According to the attribute description, the following aspects are considered: The missing rates of some attributes are high, such as the missing rate of body weight reaches 96.86%, the payment method code reaches 39.56%, and the missing rate of medical doctors' specialty is 49.08%. The missing rate has a serious impact on the classification performance. So, these attributes are deleted. In addition, the features of 'encounter_ID' and 'patient_nbr' have little effect on our data training, so the attributes are deleted. In raw medical data, the physician makes three diagnoses of the inpatient, and the attributes 'diag_1', 'diag_2', and 'diag_3' represent these diagnoses. After data cleaning of relevant characteristics, the corresponding characteristics are sorted out according to the International Statistical Classification of Diseases (ICD) (Table 1).

Table 1. The diagnose classification description

Group name	ICD-9 codes	Percent
Circulatory	390–459,785	30.66%
Respiratory	460–519,786	13.6%
Digestive	520–579,787	9.3%
Diabetes	250.xx	8.2%
Injury	800–999	6.7%
Musculoskeletal	710–739	5.8%
Genitourinary	580–629,788	4.90%
Other	Other	20.84%

In addition, for the characteristics of non-numeric types, one-hot encoding is adopted in this paper, so that data can be input into the neural network. In this paper, 75% of the samples are used as the training set and 25% as the test set. Among all the samples, there are only 10924 positive cases, accounting for 11.1%, and 88.9% negative cases. We can easily observe in Table 2 that the imbalance problem in this dataset is very serious. In machine learning classification models, in order to accelerate model convergence and effectively improve accuracy, data normalization is usually carried out, so that features of different dimensions are on the same numerical order, and the influence of features with large variance is reduced to make model classification more accurate. Z-score normalization (also known as zero-mean normalization, as shown in Formula 7) will normalize the data to mean value of 0 and variance of 1, which is more conducive to data model convergence.

$$\frac{x - mean(x)}{std(x)} \tag{7}$$

After data processing, the diabetes dataset contains 98052 pieces of information, including 70 characteristic variables in addition to label variables.

Table 2. Sample segmentation

Sample set	Amount	Percentage
Total	97910	100%
Positive	10924	11.1%
Negative	86986	88.9%
Training set	73432	75%
Testing set	24478	25%

4.2 Model Evaluation Criteria

Confusion matrix is a matrix that is classified according to whether the predicted results match the real data, and is often used to measure the degree of classification accuracy of classifiers (Table 3).

Table 3. Confusion matrix

True	Predict	
	Not readmitted	Readmitted
Not readmitted	TN(cost(0,0))	FP(cost(0,1))
Readmitted	FN(cost(1,0))	TP(cost(1,1))

In this paper, positive refers to the patients who will be readmitted in a short period of time. The indicators of their body do not meet the discharge criteria and the patients exist as the minority. Negative refers to the patients who will not be readmitted. These patients exist as the majority. At present, the main classification evaluation criteria are Accuracy, Precision, Recall and F-score. In medical diagnosis, a positive class recall rate is usually referred to as Sensitivity, and a negative class recall rate is called Specificity. F-measure is commonly used in F1, and it is usually defined as follows:

$$Accuracy = \frac{TP + TN}{TP + TN + FP + FN} \tag{8}$$

$$Sensitivity = \frac{TP}{TP + FN} = Recall \qquad (9)$$

$$Specificity = \frac{TN}{TN + FP} \qquad (10)$$

$$F_\beta = \frac{(1 + \beta^2) \times \text{Precision} \times \text{Recall}}{\beta^2 \times \text{Pr } ecision + \text{Recall}} \qquad (11)$$

$$G - mean = \sqrt{Sensitivity \times Specificity} \qquad (12)$$

For F_β, when $\beta = 1$, it is the standard F1 score; When $\beta > 1$, the recall rate has a greater impact; When $\beta < 1$ the sensitivity rate has a greater impact.

TN and TP are the correct categories of prediction, which will not lead to loss. The main causes of loss are misjudgment of positive cases as negative cases (FN) and misjudgment of negative cases as positive cases (FP). However, in the medical diagnosis scenario discussed in this paper, misdiagnosing sick people as healthy will do more damage to patients. Therefore, in this case, the model should pay more attention to the sensitivity of the model rather than the accuracy rate. Thus, we select F_β as the main criteria to evaluate the classifier, and take $\beta = 3$.

In general, the misclassification cost of cost sensitive problems can be expressed as a cost matrix. According to the cost matrix parameter, different costs are assigned to false positive and false negative. Normally, there are: cost $(0, 0) = $ cost $(1, 1) = 0$, and cost $(1, 0) > $ cost $(0, 1)$. According to the confusion matrix and the cost matrix, the Total Misclassification Cost (TMC) can be obtained:

$$TMC = cost(1, 0) \times FN + \cos t(0, 1) \times FP \qquad (13)$$

As can be seen from Eq. 13, compared with FP, FN has higher misclassification cost and greater impact. In order to minimize the total misclassification cost, FN should be as small as possible. In addition, because it is impossible to know the specific quantitative value of cost (1,0) and cost (0,1), we select the proportion of the positive and negative as the cost, and take TMC as the auxiliary reference criteria. Since the numerical ratio of positive samples and negative samples in this data set is close to 1:8, this paper chooses $cost(1, 0) = 8$, $cost(0, 1) = 1$, and TMC can be expressed as:

$$TMC = 8 \times FN + FP \qquad (14)$$

In order to consider the performance of classifier quantitatively, AUC is proposed as the average standard. AUC (Area Under Curve) represents the area under the ROC curve. The larger the area is, the better the performance of the classifier is. The ROC can maintain a good stability in the imbalanced positive and negative class sample distribution.

4.3 Experimental Results

In the traditional CNN classification, the penalty weight of FN and FP is the same, we find that the imbalance has a huge impact on the classification effect. We select

75% as training set and 25% as test set, batch size is set to 32 and epoch is set to 40. In this experiment, Random Gradient Descent (SGD) was selected as the optimization algorithm, and the learning rate was set to 0.001. The specific parameters of the model are shown as followed (Table 4):

Table 4. Parameters of CSCNN

Layer	Parameters
Input	40 * 1
convolution1	64 * 1
pooling1	2
convolution2	128 * 3
pooling2	2
fully connected1	128 * 9, 256
fully connected2	256, 128
Output	128 * 2

Among the 97,910 data, 1 sample (positive) was 10924, and 0 sample (negative) was 86986. It is found that due to the imbalance of data, the ratio of sample 1 to sample 0 is close to 1:8, which greatly affects the classification effect. After epoch0, the accuracy rate ((TP + TN)/(FN + FP + TP + TN)) reached 89%. However, in fact, in the test set, the probability of sample 0 in the total test set was 89%. Although the test set has reached a high accuracy rate, the F3 value and recall value in the test set are both 0. Actually, all patients are judged to be normal and minority class is ignored, which greatly increases the risk of readmission. To tackle the problem of imbalanced data prediction, we use different weights to improve the cross-entropy loss function, and take the best effect after multiple iterations. The experimental results of F3, sensitivity, g-mean, are shown in Fig. 2. The experimental results TMC are shown in Fig. 3.

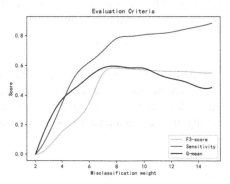

Fig. 2. Evaluation criteria

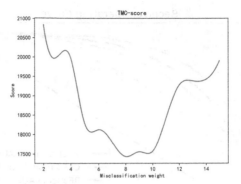

Fig. 3. TMC-score

It can be seen from the Fig. 2 that with the increasing of misclassification weight, the F3 score is increasing. When the weight reaches 8, the score begins to decline slightly; The value of Sensitivity is increasing because it has been expanding the weight of minority proportion, but the growth rate slows down when the weight is 8; the G-mean score reaches the maximum when the weight is 8, and Sensitivity and Specificity achieve a good balance effect. But after 8, G-mean has a slow downward trend. The recall rate of the positive category is increasing, but with the increase of the recall rate, Specificity will gradually decline, leading to a slight decline in the G-mean score.

TMC-score can be clearly seen to reach the minimum at the weight of 8, which shows that the cost loss is the minimum and the classification effect is the best.

Considering the experimental results, the experiment reaches the best effect when the weight is 8, which is the imbalance ratio of positive and negative samples in the initial data. In this case, the CSCNN network model can achieve the best results in F3, sensitivity, g-mean, cost and AUC. When the weight is 8, F3 is 0.584, sensitivity is 0.782, g-mean is 0.596, AUC reaches 0.792 and TMC descends to 17434. Therefore, CSCNN model can effectively solve the problem of data imbalance in the risk prediction of diabetes readmission.

In order to verify the effect of the model, other models are selected for comparative experiments. We choose Weighted Logistic Regression (CS_LR), Weighted Random Forest (CS_RF), Weighted Cart Decision Tree (CS_Cart) and non-cost sensitive ordinary CNN model for model experiment comparison. We select the weight of 8 for training test and the results are shown in Table 5, AUC comparison curve is shown in Fig. 4.

Table 5. Comparison experiment

	CNN	CS_SVM	CS_LR	CS_RF	CS_CART	CSCNN
F3	0	0.415	0.482	0.431	0.421	0.584
Sensitivity	0	0.505	0.648	0.533	0.511	0.782
G-mean	0	0.584	0.587	0.569	0.589	0.596
AUC	0.574	0.643	0.673	0.724	0.749	0.782

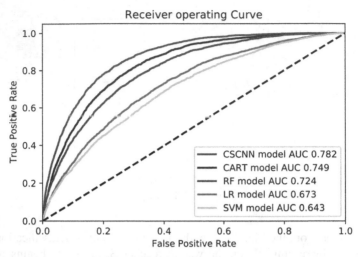

Fig. 4. AUC comparison chart

From Fig. 4 and Table 5, it can be clearly seen that CSCNN model has better classification effect in various experimental indicators compared with various weighted supervised algorithms dealing with imbalances. At the same time, through logical regression, it can be seen that cost sensitive classifiers have better classification effect compared with over-sampling and under sampling methods.

5 Conclusion

In practical application, data classification is faced with many imbalance problems, especially in the medical field, the readmission patients often only account for a small proportion of patients, which will cause great difficulties to the traditional classification learning methods. In this paper, a model called CSCNN is proposed to detect readmission of diabetic patients. In order to solve the training bias caused by unbalanced data, we modify the loss function of softmax and select the best misclassification cost weight. After many experiments and modifications, the test score of this model achieves a good result: F3 is 0.584, Sensitivity is 0.782, G-mean is 0.596 and AUC is 0.792. Compared with other machine learning prediction methods, CSCNN model has a better effect in the readmission prediction of diabetic patients, and can effectively solve the problem of data imbalance.

Acknowledgement. The subject is sponsored by the National Natural Science Foundation of P. R. China (No. 61872196, No. 61872194, No. 61902196, No. 62102194 and No. 62102196), Scientific and Technological Support Project of Jiangsu Province (No. BE2019740, No. BK20200753 and No. 20KJB520001), Major Natural Science Research Projects in Colleges and Universities of Jiangsu Province (No. 18KJA520008), Six Talent Peaks Project of Jiangsu Province (No. RJFW-111), Postgraduate Research and Practice Innovation Program of Jiangsu Province (No. KYCX19_0909, No. KYCX19_0911, No. KYCX20_0759, No. KYCX21_0787, No. KYCX21_0788 and No. KYCX21_0799).

References

1. Sneha, N., Gangil, T.: Analysis of diabetes mellitus for early prediction using optimal features selection. J. Big Data **6**(1), 1–19 (2019). https://doi.org/10.1186/s40537-019-0175-6
2. Chen, W., Chen, S., Zhang, H.: A hybrid prediction model for Type 2 Diabetes using K-means and decision tree. In: 2017 8th IEEE International Conference on Software Engineering and Service Science (ICSESS) (2017)
3. Strack, B., et al.: Impact of HbA1c measurement on hospital readmission rates: analysis of 70,000 clinical database patient records. Biomed. Res. Int. **2014**, 1–11 (2014)
4. Longadge, R., Dongre, S.: Class imbalance problem in data mining review (2013)
5. Chawla, N.V., Bowyer, K.W., Hall, L.O.: SMOTE: synthetic minority over-sampling technique. J. Artif. Intell. Res. **16**, 321–357 (2002)
6. Seiffert, C., Khoshgoftaar, T.M., Van Hulse, J., Napolitano, A.: RUSBoost: a hybrid approach to alleviating class imbalance. IEEE Trans. Syst. Man Cybern. Part A Syst. Hum. **40**, 185–197 (2010)
7. Elkan, C.: The foundations of cost-sensitive learning. In: Proceedings of the Seventeenth International Joint Conference on Artificial Intelligence (2001)
8. Wang, H., Cui, Z., Chen, Y., Avidan, M., Abdallah, A.B., Kronzer, A.: Predicting hospital readmission via cost-sensitive deep learning. IEEE/ACM Trans. Comput. Biol. Bioinf. **15**, 1968–1978 (2018)
9. Ghobadi, F., Rohani, M.: Cost sensitive modeling of credit card fraud using neural network strategy, pp. 1–5. IEEE (2016)
10. Nathalie, J., Shaju, S.: The class imbalance problem: a systematic study. Intell. Data Anal. **6**(5), 429–449 (2002)
11. Kamble, T., Patil, S.T.: Diabetes detection using deep learning approach. Int. J. Innov. Res. Sci. Technol. **2**(12), 342–349 (2016)
12. Swapna, G., Vinayakumar, R., Soman, K.P.: Diabetes detection using deep learning algorithms. ICT Express **4**, 243–246 (2018)
13. Sisodia, D., Sisodia, D.S.: Prediction of diabetes using classification algorithms. Procedia Comput. Sci. **132**, 1578–1585 (2018)
14. Wu, H., Yang, S., Huang, Z., He, J., Wang, X.: Type 2 diabetes mellitus prediction model based on data mining. Inform. Med. Unlocked **10**, 100–107 (2018)
15. Fuqua, D., Razzaghi, T.: A cost-sensitive convolution neural network learning for control chart pattern recognition. Expert Syst. Appl. **150**, 113275 (2020)

A Survey on Content-Based Encrypted Image Retrieval in Cloud Computing

Meng Zhang, Ying Cai$^{(\boxtimes)}$, Yu Zhang, Xin Li, and Yanfang Fan

Department of Computer Science and Technology,
Beijing Information Science and Technology University, Beijing 100101, China
ycai@bistu.edu.cn

Abstract. With the wide popularization of intelligent devices and digital imaging technology, the types and volumes of images are growing rapidly. The resource constrained data owners outsource the local data to cloud servers, where data can be stored, shared and retrieved. However, the image data may contain the user's sensitive information, which may be exposed to the semi-trusted cloud providers and external attackers, resulting in the privacy leakage of users. Among numerous methods to solve the content-based image retrieval (CBIR) with privacy protection in cloud computing (e.g., access control, digital watermark, encryption), we mainly study the content-based encrypted image retrieval (CBEIR), which is more effective because it operates directly on the data itself. In CBEIR, some operations (e.g., feature extraction, index building) consume quite a few computing resources. In this paper, according to the trade-off of user resources, we divide the existing schemes into two categories: feature-based CBEIR schemes and image-based CBEIR schemes. For each category, its system model and common encrypted algorithms are introduced in detail. And other factors affecting these two schemes are summarized, including feature selection, feature similarity measurement methods and appropriate index structure. Finally, the future research directions are discussed and prospected.

Keywords: Cloud computing security · Image encryption · Image retrieval · Privacy protection

1 Introduction

With the popularity of the Internet, mobile devices with cameras and digital image technology, large image databases in various fields are growing explosively. According to Facebook [1], nearly 300 million images are uploaded every day. For such generous images, people's demand for efficient storage and effective retrieval is increasing. Cloud computing attracts more and more resource constrained

This work was supported in part by the National Natural Science Foundation of China under Grant 61672106, and in part by the Natural Science Foundation of Beijing, China under Grant L192023 and in part by the project of Scientific research fund of Beijing Information Science and Technology University of under 5029923412.

users because of its storage resources and rich computing. However, the image data may contain the user's sensitive information (e.g., location, interest [36]), and there are a lot of malicious users on the Internet [30], and the "honest but curious" cloud service providers are semi-trusted [31], people feel anxious about the privacy and security of uploaded images.

In the existing schemes, privacy-preserving CBIR is mainly designed through access control technology, digital watermark technology, encrypted technology. Among these methods, access control technology prevents image searchers from unauthorized access to image data on the cloud by designing effective access control strategies. Digital watermark technology embeds specific digital signals into digital images to protect the copyright or integrity of images. Image encryption technology encrypts images or image features to protect the image privacy in the process of image retrieval. These technologies can protect the privacy of images to a certain extent. Here we mainly study the CBEIR to protect image privacy. Because encrypted technology directly protects the data itself [7,8,15,47], it is more effective than other methods.

In CBEIR, due to certain operations (such as feature extraction, indexing) will consume a large amount of computing resources, the existing solution is divided into two categories: image-based CBEIR schemes and features based CBEIR schemes. In the feature-based CBEIR schemes, it encrypts images using standard encryption methods. The key point is that the similarity between images can still be measured using encrypted image features. This type of encryption schemes are usually very complicated. In the image-based CBEIR schemes, It is necessary to devise an image encryption algorithm that makes the extraction feature still effective. However, the security and accuracy of existing scenarios need to be further improved. The Quality of Service (QoS) of the scheme may be reduced after encryption. The current schemes are the balance of retrieval efficiency, security and accuracy. [16,17,37] directly distribute the key to the user, resulting in the risk of image key leakage. [16,37] sacrifice accuracy to improve efficiency, while [17,33,38] bring a lot of overhead to improve security.

The rest of this article is arranged as follows. Section 2 and Sect. 3 represent the feature-based CBEIR schemes and the image-based CBEIR schemes respectively, including the system model and the encryption algorithms. Later on, the detailed description of other factors are introduced in Sect. 4. Finally, we summarize the work in Sect. 5.

2   Design of the Feature-Based CBEIR Schemes

2.1   System Model

In the feature-based encryption scheme, there are three types of entities: image owner, image user and cloud server. The cooperation among the three entities is illustrated in Fig. 1.

1) Image owner: the image owner extracts the images feature vectors, encrypts the images and the extracted feature vectors with the key, and constructs

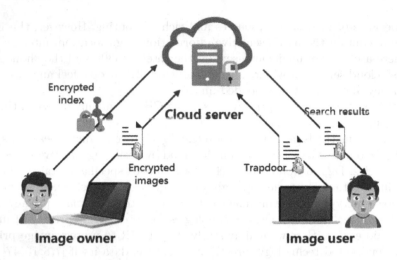

Fig. 1. Feature-based CBEIR architecture.

a secure searchable index. Finally, the encrypted images, the encrypted feature vectors and the secure index are uploaded to the cloud server. In some scenarios, the image owner also undertakes the task of making access policies.

2) Image user: legitimate users authorized to retrieve images. The image user executes the feature extraction algorithm to extract the feature vector of the query image, then encrypts the vector, and uploads the ciphertext to the cloud server as the query trap. After receiving the query results, the key shared by the image owner is used for decryption.

3) Cloud server: the cloud server stores the encrypted images, encrypted feature vectors and security index, processes the retrieval request from the image searcher, and performs the retrieval task according to the access policy. Finally, the cloud server searches the similarity vector on the index and returns the sorted first few similar images to the image user.

2.2 Feature-Based Encryption Algorithms

Asymmetric Scalar-Product-Preserving Encryption. Since many encryption methods only support privacy protection and they can't perform operations similar to query and retrieval after encryption. Therefore, Wong et al. [39] proposed a secure inner product algorithm based on the research of k-nearest neighbor computation, also known as Asymmetric Scalar-Product-Preserving Encryption (ASPE) algorithm. The data vector and query vector encrypted by ASPE algorithm can ensure that the inner product value of ciphertext is consistent with that of plaintext, so k-nearest neighbor query in ciphertext domain can be realized. In order to further improve the confidentiality of the vector, Li et al. [24] split the encrypted data vector and the query vector, then, they need two reversible random matrices to encrypt the data vector and the inverse matrix to encrypt the query vector. Huang et al. [20] first converted the high-dimensional image descriptor into compressed binary coding, and then the confidentiality of the image is guaranteed by ASPE. Hu et al. [18] proposed a faster scheme than linear search. They constructed a tree index.

ASPE can effectively encrypt plaintext and determine the similarity between ciphertexts, but it is not a practical method because it assumes that users are completely trusted in the real world and may have the problem of key leakage. Therefore, Li et al. [22] proposed a new CBIR scheme based on the attack of data owners, cloud servers and users from the perspective of homomorphic encryption and ASPE. The scheme can perform addition and multiplication in the encrypted domain to solve the problem of key leakage. In order to avoid key transmission, Zhu et al. [49] proposed an improved ASPE algorithm to ensure the accuracy of calculation while image users do not have all the encryption keys, but the scheme does not support image retrieval.

Comparative Encryption. Comparative encryption algorithm [13] is proposed for the first time, which solves the disadvantage of directly comparing the order of a single number in order preserving encryption. It is a request based compared encryption scheme, which requires users to provide ciphertext labels to compare ciphertext data. However, the length of the ciphertext obtained by the original comparative encryption algorithm is longer, which is not suitable for practical application. Therefore, Furukawa et al. [14] proposed a new comparative encryption scheme based on the original scheme to reduce the length of ciphertext to a certain extent.

Locally Sensitive Hash Function. Local Sensitive Hash (LSH) [17] uses hash function to encrypt image features. Hash function is a kind of compression mapping, and it can't be recovered from the hash value, or even the unique input value can't be determined from the same hash value. Good unidirectionality ensures feature security. The standard hash function maps the feature vectors to different hash buckets. The data points with non-uniform distribution are nearly uniform in the bucket, and the nearest neighbor relationship of the feature vectors is not preserved. However, retrieval needs to compare the similarity of feature vectors. In order to achieve effective retrieval, the nearest neighbor relationship between feature vectors must be maintained in the hash value of features. Therefore, LSH that can maintain the close neighbor relationship of data is widely used.

LSH is a common fast nearest neighbor search method, which makes the adjacent feature vectors in the original space still adjacent with high probability in the projection space, while the adjacent feature vectors in the original space have little probability in the projection space. Reference [27] implements ciphertext image retrieval based on minHash algorithm. Abduljabbar et al. [2] improved the proficiency and efficiency of the system by using LSH to build searchable index. Xia et al. [37] also proposed a privacy protection scheme with high retrieval efficiency, which was designed on the basis of LSH. However, the accuracy of MPGE-7 feature descriptor extracted by this scheme is low.

The comparisons of the above algorithms are shown in Table 1.

Table 1. Comparisons of feature-based encryption algorithms

	ASPE	Comparative encryption	LSH
Typical scenarios	Suitable for multi-user scenarios	Query operation involving sequence information	Cloud sever is allowed to calculate the distance between any query record and the record in the database
Advantages	Ensure the confidentiality of vector data and hide the associated information of data	Low computational and retrieval overhead	The good unidirectionality ensures the feature security and greatly improves the retrieval efficiency
Disadvantages	There is no guarantee that the query users are honest	The security is not high, and frequent interaction between entities is required	A specific hash function needs to be designed to improve the collision probability

3   Design of the Image-Based CBEIR Schemes

3.1   System Model

In the image-based encryption scheme, there are three types of entities: image owner, image user and cloud server. The cooperation among the three entities is illustrated in Fig. 2.

1) Image owner: the local resources of the image owner are limited, so they only need to encrypt the images, and then outsource the encrypted images to the cloud server.
2) Image user: the image user uses the same encryption method as the image owner to encrypt the images, and uploads images to the cloud server as a query trap. After receiving the query results, use the key shared by the image owner to decrypt.
3) Cloud server: according to the protocol made by the image owner, the cloud server extracts the feature vectors of the uploaded encrypted images and constructs the searchable index. The cloud server extracts feature vectors of the image uploaded by the user, then similar images are retrieved in the index, and the first k similar images are returned to image searcher.

3.2   Image-Based Encryption Algorithms

Homomorphic Encryption. Homomorphic encryption technology can be divided into partial homomorphic encryption and full homomorphic encryption. Zhang et al. [21] introduced a large-scale cloud image search system to protect

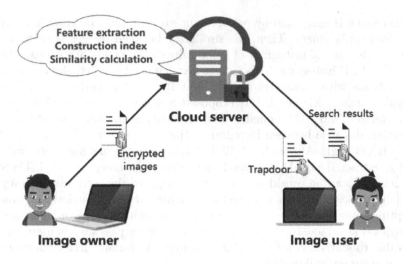

Fig. 2. Image-based CBEIR architecture.

privacy. The core of the system is to use multi-level homomorphic encryption protocol to calculate the distance between feature vectors. Zhu et al. [48] proposed a kNN query system scheme, which makes use of the additive homomorphism of Paillier encryption system, so that there is no need to share the key between image users. In order to improve the search accuracy, Hsu et al. [17] proposed a privacy preserving image search scheme based on homomorphic encryption, which has high search overhead. This is because compared with feature randomization, homomorphic encryption will produce more time-consuming operations [26]. Xu et al. [44] presented a method of using a partially encrypted image retrieval method. But, [44] maybe cause information leakage. Bellafkira et al. [5] proposed a privacy protection CBIR scheme using homomorphic cryptosystem. Using the image encrypted by Paillier algorithm, the wavelet coefficients of the image can be calculated directly. Then, the similarity between the images is measured by L1 distance. The disadvantages of the scheme are that the encryption time is too long and the image owner owns all the decryption keys. In another work [6], Bellafkira et al. dealt with similarity calculation by introducing a trusted server. But a new problem has arisen: the possibility of collusion between the two servers.

Other Methods. Cheng et al. [46] proposed a CBIR scheme for privacy protection, which is specially devised for JPEG images. Firstly, the paper parses the bit stream of file and obtains the coefficient value pair and run length pair. In order to improve the retrieval accuracy, Cheng et al. [9] cancelled the arrangement of DCT coefficient blocks, which would interfere with the visual information of the image, and only shuffled the DCT coefficients. Finally, Markov model is used to extract image features. These information can be used to collect information in images. Ferreira et al. [11,12] proposed an image encryption scheme, in which the pixel value is encrypted by replacement and the pixel position is encrypted by random replacement. Then, the similarity between images is calculated by hamming distance of histogram of color values. Xia et al. [40] is characterized by a global LBP histogram. This feature has achieved good results in face recognition scheme with privacy protection, but it does not perform well in image retrieval. Further, Xia et al. [41] proposed a scheme to extract features from spatial domain and DCT domain. The similarity is measured by stitching the Manhattan distance between histograms. However, the search accuracy of this scheme is not high. Although [11,12,17,23,37] scheme has high retrieval accuracy, the extracted global histogram is not suitable for image retrieval. Therefore, these schemes can be considered to further improve the retrieval accuracy. Xia et al. [43] proposed a privacy protection scheme with high retrieval accuracy by encrypting images through replacement and substitution. In order to improve the retrieval accuracy. In this scheme, a single letter password is used, but it is vulnerable to statistical attacks. If it is changed to a multi letter password, the retrieval accuracy will decline.

The comparisons of the above algorithms are shown in Table 2.

Table 2. Comparisons of image-based encryption algorithms

	Homomorphic encryption	Other methods
Typical scenarios	High security requirements	Specific scenarios
Advantages	High security, ciphertext addition and multiplication are equivalent to plaintext	The retrieval accuracy is not high, and the security of encryption algorithm needs authentication
Disadvantages	High computational complexity and ciphertext expansion	There is a lot of room for improvement

4 Other Factors

4.1 Selection of Image Feature

As a kind of multimedia data, images have the characteristics of rich information content. The comparison of image similarity is usually achieved through the comparison of image features. Image features are data that can represent the whole or local visual information of an image. According to the way of feature extraction and generation, it can be divided into three levels: shallow, medium and deep.

1) Shallow features encode and aggregate the pixel matrix, which contains many global and local features. Global image features can represent the features of the whole image, and are used to describe the color and shape of the image or object. The idea of local feature extraction is similar, that is, the image is divided into local regions, and then the gradient of the local region is calculated to obtain the gradient histogram. Table 3 compares some common global features with local features.

Table 3. Shallow feature comparisons

Image feature	Feature type	Extraction algorithm	Advantages	Existing problems
Global features	Color histogram, texture, shape and spatial relationship	Local binary pattern, directional gradient histogram	Simple calculation, intuitive representation, high performance of feature extraction and similarity measurement	The feature dimension is high, the amount of calculation is large, and the description image is usually vague, which makes the retrieval accuracy not high
Local features	Corner feature and spot feature	SIFT, HOG, SURF	The correlation between features is small, and it is robust to image transformations such as illumination, rotation, and viewpoint changes. Contain rich image information, describe the image more accurately	There are few feature points, and the feature of the target with smooth edges cannot be accurately extracted

2) Middle level features encode and aggregate local features on the basis of shallow image features. Bag of Words (BoW) [35] is the most typical method. The model clusters local features. The representative point of each class is regarded as a visual word, and all visual words constitute a dictionary. Given an image, all local features are matched with visual words, and the frequency of matching visual words is counted. The normalized histogram is the BoW feature. So middle level feature can describe the local block better.

3) Deep features refer to high semantic image features obtained through deep learning. Such as CNN features. Deep network has semantic abstract receptive field. The low-level features of the network reflect the image texture, middle-level features can better depict the local block, and high-level features reflect the image target. It realizes the semantic progression from the detail texture to the local block and then to the specific object.

Shallow features and middle features are hand-designed image features, so the extraction mode is fixed and the feature description ability is limited. If deep features want to obtain high semantic features of plaintext image, they need to go through complex calculation. If the features are extracted directly from the encrypted images, homomorphic encryption algorithm can be used to solve the problem, but it will further increase the computational complexity. So we can choose the appropriate image features according to the design requirements of different schemes.

4.2   Similarity Measurement Methods

Different similarity measurement methods are selected according to different encryption methods and index construction methods. The current similarity measurement methods include Euclidean distance, Hamming distance, Jacquard similarity, EMD distance, histogram intersection, KL divergence, JS divergence and so on. Next, several common measurement methods are introduced.

1) Euclidean distance is the most commonly used distance measurement formula [29], which is used to measure the absolute distance between points in space.

$$D(x, y) = (\sum_{i=1}^{n} \mid x_i - y_i \mid^p)^{\frac{1}{p}}, p = 2 \tag{1}$$

Euclidean distance is a special case of Minkowski Distance, namely p = 2, which is called L2 distance for short. If p = 1, the above formula becomes Manhattan distance, which is called L1 distance for short. The Euclidean distance is used for ciphertext image retrieval in literature [45].
2) Hamming distance is often used in information measurement, which represents the number of numerical differences in the same position of binary code.

$$H(x, y) = \sum_{i=1}^{n} \mid x_i - y_i \mid, x_i, y_i \in \{0, 1\} \tag{2}$$

For example, the values of 100111 and 010100 are different in positions 1, 2, 5, 6, so the Hamming distance between them is 4. When two binary codes XOR the same random sequences get encrypted binary sequences, the Hamming distance between ciphertext sequences is still equal to the Hamming distance between plaintext sequences. In addition, the ciphertext Hamming distance is still equal to the plaintext Hamming distance by scrambling the values at different positions of the binary sequence. Based on the above characteristics, the Hamming distance is used to retrieve the ciphertext image in literature [28].
3) Jaccard similarity is used to measure the similarity between two sets.

$$J(x, y) = \frac{\mid x \cap y \mid}{\mid x \cup y \mid} \tag{3}$$

Here, the elements of x and y are symbols or boolean values, so we can't measure the specific numerical value, we can only get the result whether they are equal or not. In Ref. [25], Jaccard similarity is used for ciphertext image retrieval.

4.3 Selection of Index Structure

As the number of images increases dramatically and the wide popularity of network, the real-time requirements of image retrieval are increasing gradually. Linear retrieval is no longer applicable for high-dimensional image data sets. In CBIR, the existing index technology is divided into three categories, namely hash index, inverted index and tree index.

1) To solve the problem of nearest neighbors search, Indyk et al. [27] first proposed the concept of LSH in their main memory algorithm. It is first proposed based on strict mathematical description, which can map similar data into the same bucket. The core idea is to construct a set of hash functions to make the closer points collide with high probability, while the farther points collide with low probability. However, the most basic LSH function has the advantage of being fast and simple only if the input vector points are located in Hamming space. Under this condition, Deter et al. [10] proposed LSH based on p-stable distribution, and proved that it can calculate the L1 distance between data. Sadowski et al. [32] proposed SimHash algorithm to detect the similarity between data by calculating the angle cosine between data. To further improve the retrieval accuracy and efficiency of LSH, the sum function is introduced into the hash function, which requires a lot of storage space and improves the computational complexity. Therefore, in practical application, large capacity database needs more storage space, which affects the retrieval performance of the system. In the field of image retrieval, LSH has always been an effective retrieval mechanism [42]. In addition, it can also be used for the nearest neighbor matching to speed up the retrieval speed of the scheme.

2) Inverted index in image retrieval is an image index method based on visual bag of words [25]. In CBIR, it is necessary to train the image content into visual words in advance, and comprehensively index all visual words in the image dataset through the index file. In 2003, Sivic et al. [35] first proposed an inverted index based on visual words, which uses text description to complete the object matching process in video. Jegou et al. [19] proposed an inverted index for user nearest neighbor search based on asymmetric distance calculation. This scheme needs a lot of clustering operations, which seriously affects the final search time. Babenko et al. [3] constructed the inverted index of kxk, and took the index closest to the query feature as the final search result.

3) The traditional tree index structures (e.g., B-tree, red black tree) are created for the data with dimension less than 10. For high-dimensional data, the most commonly used are KD tree and R-tree. KD tree will spend more time in the retrieval process to find the optimal solution, which makes the retrieval performance of the scheme decline greatly. Generally speaking, when the data dimension increases to a certain extent, KD tree index is equivalent to linear retrieval in retrieval efficiency. On this basis, a KD tree with logarithmic retrieval complexity is proposed. However, this index structure is still only effective for low dimensional data. Beis et al. [4] proposed a similar retrieval method based on KD tree, which improves the retrieval performance

by introducing stop mechanism in the scheme. Slipa et al. [34] improved the overall retrieval speed by introducing multiple KD trees. In addition, for R-Tree index family, its index structure has high retrieval efficiency for low dimensional data, but it also has the problem of "dimension disaster" for high dimensional data.

5   Conclusion

CBEIR provides solutions to the privacy problems in the outsourcing storage and retrieval of image data. Encryption technology is the main solution to achieve image data privacy protection, but efficiency and accuracy are also very important in image retrieval. For efficiency, designing efficient index is one of the key factors to solve this problem. For accuracy, the selection of image features is crucial. Therefore, how to achieve effective and even efficient large-scale image retrieval under the premise of privacy protection is a challenge for image retrieval with privacy protection in the future. At present, most of the researches on privacy in image retrieval design are to solve the untrusted problem of cloud server. For the untrusted image retriever, access control is the main way to restrict. However, it does not rule out the possibility that the image retriever will maliciously distribute the key and the images. The malicious distribution of images can be restricted by watermark technology. The key leakage problem can be solved by homomorphic encryption, but a large number of calculations will increase the burden of the client. Therefore, it is an urgent need to design a lightweight image encryption algorithm for data retrieval to reduce the computation of the client with limited resources.

References

1. The Top 20 Valuable Facebook Statistics-Updated, September 2018. https://zephoria.com/top-15-valuable-facebook-statistics/
2. Abduljabbar, Z.A., Hai, J., Ibrahim, A., Hussien, Z.A., Zou, D.: Privacy-preserving image retrieval in IoT-cloud. In: 2016 IEEE Trustcom/BigDataSE/I SPA (2017)
3. Babenko, A., Lempitsky, V.: The inverted multi-index. IEEE Trans. Pattern Anal. Mach. Intell. **37**(6), 1247–1260 (2015)
4. Beis, J.S., Lowe, D.G.: Shape indexing using approximate nearest-neighbour search in high-dimensional spaces. In: Conference on Computer Vision & Pattern Recognition (1997)
5. Bellafqira, R., Coatrieux, G., Bouslimi, D., Quellec, G.: Content-based image retrieval in homomorphic encryption domain. In: Annual International Conference of the IEEE Engineering in Medicine and Biology Society (EMBC), p. 2944 (2015)
6. Bellafqira, R., Coatrieux, G., Bouslimi, D., Quellec, G.: An end to end secure CBIR over encrypted medical database. In: Engineering in Medicine & Biology Society (2016)
7. Cai, Y., Zhang, S., Xia, H., Fan, Y., Zhang, H.: A privacy-preserving scheme for interactive messaging over online social networks. IEEE Internet Things J. **7**(2020), 6817–6827 (2020)

8. Cai, Y., Zhang, H., Fang, Y.: A conditional privacy protection scheme based on ring signcryption for vehicular ad hoc networks. IEEE Internet Things J. **8**, 647–656 (2020)
9. Cheng, H., Zhang, X., Yu, J., Li, F.: Markov process-based retrieval for encrypted JPEG images. EURASIP J. Inf. Secur. **2016**(1), 1–9 (2015). https://doi.org/10.1186/s13635-015-0028-6
10. Datar, M.: Locality-sensitive hashing scheme based on p-stable distributions. In: Proceedings of the 20th ACM Symposium on Computational Geometry (2004)
11. Ferreira, B., Rodrigues, J., Leitao, J., Domingos, H.: Practical privacy-preserving content-based retrieval in cloud image repositories. IEEE Trans. Cloud Comput. **7**(3), 784–798 (2019)
12. Ferreira, B., Rodrigues, J., Leito, J., Domingos, H.: Privacy-preserving content-based image retrieval in the cloud. IEEE (2014)
13. Furukawa, J.: Request-based comparable encryption. In: Crampton, J., Jajodia, S., Mayes, K. (eds.) ESORICS 2013. LNCS, vol. 8134, pp. 129–146. Springer, Heidelberg (2013). https://doi.org/10.1007/978-3-642-40203-6_8
14. Furukawa, J.: Short comparable encryption. In: Gritzalis, D., Kiayias, A., Askoxylakis, I. (eds.) CANS 2014. LNCS, vol. 8813, pp. 337–352. Springer, Cham (2014). https://doi.org/10.1007/978-3-319-12280-9_22
15. Gong, Y., Ying, C., Guo, Y., Fang, Y.: A privacy-preserving scheme for incentive-based demand response in the smart grid. IEEE Trans. Smart Grid **7**, 1304–1313 (2017)
16. Guo, C., Su, S., Choo, K.K.R., Tang, X.: A fast nearest neighbor search scheme over outsourced encrypted medical images. IEEE Trans. Ind. Inform. **17**(1), 514–523 (2018)
17. Hsu, C.Y., Lu, C.S., Pei, S.C.: Image feature extraction in encrypted domain with privacy-preserving sift. IEEE Trans. Image Process. **21**(11), 4593–4607 (2012)
18. Hu, H., Xu, J., Ren, C., Choi, B.: Processing private queries over untrusted data cloud through privacy homomorphism. In: 2011 IEEE 27th International Conference on Data Engineering, pp. 601–612 (2011)
19. Jégou, H., Douze, M., Schmid, C.: Product quantization for nearest neighbor search. IEEE Trans. Pattern Anal. Mach. Intell. **33**(1), 117–128 (2010)
20. Huang, K., Xu, M., Fu, S., Wang, D.: Efficient privacy-preserving content-based image retrieval in the cloud. In: Cui, B., Zhang, N., Xu, J., Lian, X., Liu, D. (eds.) WAIM 2016. LNCS, vol. 9659, pp. 28–39. Springer, Cham (2016). https://doi.org/10.1007/978-3-319-39958-4_3
21. Lan, Z., Jung, T., Feng, P., Liu, K., Liu, Y.: PIC: enable large-scale privacy preserving content-based image search on cloud. In: International Conference on Parallel Processing (2015)
22. Li, J.S., Liu, I.H., Tsai, C.J., Su, Z.Y., Liu, C.G.: Secure content-based image retrieval in the cloud with key confidentiality. IEEE Access **8**, 114940–114952 (2020)
23. Li, M., Zhang, M., Qian, W., Chow, S., Lit, C.: InstantCryptoGram: secure image retrieval service. In: IEEE INFOCOM 2018 - IEEE Conference on Computer Communications (2018)
24. Li, Y., Ma, J., Miao, Y., Wang, Y., Choo, K.: Traceable and controllable encrypted cloud image search in multi-user settings. IEEE Trans. Cloud Comput. **PP**(99), 1 (2020)

25. Lu, W., Swaminathan, A., Varna, A.L., Min, W.: Enabling search over encrypted multimedia databases. In: Media Forensics and Security I, Part of the IS&T-SPIE Electronic Imaging Symposium, Proceedings, San Jose, CA, USA, 19 January 2009 (2009)
26. Lu, W., Varna, A.L., Min, W.: Confidentiality-preserving image search: a comparative study between homomorphic encryption and distance-preserving randomization. IEEE Access **2**(2), 125–141 (2014)
27. Lu, W., Varna, A.L., Swaminathan, A., Wu, M.: Secure image retrieval through feature protection. In: 2009 IEEE International Conference on Acoustics, Speech and Signal Processing, pp. 1533–1536 (2009)
28. Lu, W., Varna, A.L., Swaminathan, A., Wu, M.: Secure image retrieval through feature protection. In: 2009 IEEE International Conference on Acoustics, Speech and Signal Processing (2009)
29. Parhizkar, R.: Euclidean distance matrices: properties, algorithms and applications. IEEE Signal Process. Mag. **32**(6), 12–30 (2015)
30. Ren, K., Cong, W., Qian, W.: Security challenges for the public cloud. IEEE Internet Comput. **16**(1), 69–73 (2012)
31. Rushe, D.: Google: don't expect privacy when sending to Gmail (2016)
32. Sadowski, G.C.: SimHash: hash-based similarity detection (2007)
33. Shen, M., Cheng, G., Zhu, L., Du, X., Hu, J.: Content-based multi-source encrypted image retrieval in clouds with privacy preservation. Future Gener. Comput. Syst. **109**, 621–632 (2020). p. S0167739X17321969
34. Silpa-Anan, C., Hartley, R.: Optimised KD-trees for fast image descriptor matching. In: IEEE Conference on Computer Vision & Pattern Recognition (2008)
35. Sivic, J.: Video Google: a text retrieval approach to object matching in videos. In: Proceedings of IEEE International Conference on Computer Vision, vol. 2 (2003)
36. Smith, M., Szongott, C., Henne, B., Voigt, G.V.: Big data privacy issues in public social media. In: IEEE International Conference on Digital Ecosystems Technologies (2012)
37. Sun, X., Xiong, N.N., Xia, Z., Vasilakos, A.V.: EPCBIR: an efficient and privacy-preserving content-based image retrieval scheme in cloud computing. Inf. Sci. Int. J. **387**, 195–204 (2017)
38. Wang, X., Ma, J., Liu, X., Miao, Y.: Search in my way: practical outsourced image retrieval framework supporting unshared key. In: IEEE INFOCOM 2019 - IEEE Conference on Computer Communications (2019)
39. Wong, W.K., Cheung, W.L., Kao, B., Mamoulis, N.: Secure kNN computation on encrypted databases. In: ACM SIGMOD International Conference on Management of Data (2009)
40. Xia, Z., Jiang, L., Ma, X., Yang, W., Ji, P., Xiong, N.: A privacy-preserving outsourcing scheme for image local binary pattern in secure industrial Internet of Things. IEEE Trans. Ind. Inform. **16**, 629–638 (2019)
41. Xia, Z., Lu, L., Qin, T., Shim, H.J., Chen, X., Jeon, B.: A privacy-preserving image retrieval based on AC-coefficients and color histograms in cloud environment. Comput. Mater. Continua **58**(1), 27–43 (2019)
42. Xia, Z., Wang, X., Zhang, L., Qin, Z., Sun, X., Ren, K.: A privacy-preserving and copy-deterrence content-based image retrieval scheme in cloud computing. IEEE Trans. Inf. Forensics Secur. **11**(11), 2594–2608 (2017)
43. Xia, Z., Jiang, L., Liu, D., Lu, L., Jeon, B.: BOEW: a content-based image retrieval scheme using bag-of-encrypted-words in cloud computing. IEEE Trans. Serv. Comput. **15**, 202–214 (2019)

44. Xu, Y., Gong, J., Xiong, L., Xu, Z., Wang, J., Shi, Y.Q.: A privacy-preserving content-based image retrieval method in cloud environment. J. Vis. Commun. Image Represent. **43**, 164–172 (2017)
45. Yan, Z., Li, Z., Peng, Y., Jing, Z.: A secure image retrieval method based on homomorphic encryption for cloud computing. In: International Conference on Digital Signal Processing (2014)
46. Zhang, Y., Xinpeng, J., Cheng, H.: Encrypted JPEG image retrieval using block-wise feature comparison. J. Vis. Commun. Image Represent. **40**, 111–117 (2016)
47. Zhang, S., Cai, Y., Xia, H.: A privacy-preserving interactive messaging scheme based on users credibility over online social networks (2017)
48. Zhu, Y., Huang, Z., Takagi, T.: Secure and controllable k-NN query over encrypted cloud data with key confidentiality. J. Parallel Distrib. Comput. **89**(C), 1–12 (2016)
49. Zhu, Y., Wang, Z., Zhang, Y.: Secure k-NN query on encrypted cloud data with limited key-disclosure and offline data owner. In: Bailey, J., Khan, L., Washio, T., Dobbie, G., Huang, J.Z., Wang, R. (eds.) PAKDD 2016. LNCS (LNAI), vol. 9652, pp. 401–414. Springer, Cham (2016). https://doi.org/10.1007/978-3-319-31750-2_32

Big Data

Methodology-Driven Characteristics of Scientific Research Collaboration Networks in the Field of Economic Management: Mining and Analysis Based on Big Data

Hao Xu[1,2](✉) [iD], Shihui Chen[1] [iD], Mengxue Yi[1], Ke Feng[1] [iD], Xi Ding[1] [iD], Yilin Liu[1] [iD], and Yiyang Chen[3] [iD]

[1] Nanjing Institute of Technology, Nanjing 211167, China
[2] Nanjing University, Nanjing 210023, China
[3] University of St. Andrews, St. Andrews KY16 9AJ, UK

Abstract. Objective: Research takes the methodological knowledge in the full text of academic literature as a knowledge production element, and divides it into four categories: Theory &Method, Data, Model, and Tool & Software. Identify the complex network characteristics of scientific research collaboration in economic management field driven by it, in order to achieve efficient promotion of knowledge production. **Methods:** Develop a crawler by python, and uses CNKI as data source to obtain the full text data of 5,564 papers (about 50,076,000 characters) from 2000 to 2019 in "Management World", then combines the TF-IDF, fusion rules and manual annotation to extract 6946 records of methodological knowledge data and its subsidiary information. The relationship were visualized by Gephi, and characteristics are analyzed. **Results/Conclusions:** The overall collaboration network and scientific research institutions driven by Theory &Method are the most complexity and multi-mode (complete and continuous development model are included), while it has a cohesive collaborative subnet. Methodological knowledge-driven scientific research collaboration networks have different characteristics: Theory & Method driven has the highest complexity, a long duration, and much more mature in economics and management field. The network formed by institutions has a low density, means a cross-institutional, large-scale collaboration model has not yet been formed, which may be restricted by geographical factors and research topics. Among the four types of methodological knowledge, the Theory &Method and Data type drive the research collaboration of institutions more obviously. **Limitations:** The types and numbers of data sources in this study need to be expanded, and the extraction of specific methodological knowledge for the full text of academic literature needs to be further expanded by relying on machine learning and other methods.

Keywords: Data retrieval and knowledge mining · Scientific research collaboration · Methodological knowledge driven · Characteristics of scientific research collaboration network

© Springer Nature Singapore Pte Ltd. 2022
Y. Tian et al. (Eds.): ICBDS 2021, CCIS 1563, pp. 329–347, 2022.
https://doi.org/10.1007/978-981-19-0852-1_25

1 Introduction

In the era of big science, many scientific researches can no longer be carried out by one person alone, and often require many scientific researchers with diverse knowledge structures and complementary advantages to cooperate and complete together [1]. There are also studies showing that major scientific and technological achievements that have won the Nobel Prize in Science are usually completed by an interdisciplinary team. In the process of multi-dimensional collaboration of scientific researchers and joint knowledge production, an intangible network of relationships, scientific research collaboration network, has been formed. Cloud computing, internet of Things, artificial intelligence and other technologies are developing rapidly today with the explosive growth of data. The speed of knowledge update iteration is much faster than before, and the knowledge update cycle is getting shorter and shorter, which puts forward higher requirements for the accuracy, traceability and timeliness of knowledge production achievements. In the process of domain knowledge production, because methodological knowledge can guarantee the accuracy and authority of knowledge production results, the academic community pays more and more attention to the academic contributions of methodological knowledge producers [2]. Methodological knowledge has become one of the important knowledge production factors, which drives the scientific research collaboration in the process of knowledge production.

Academic literature is the final result of creators' creation, coding, and processing of knowledge units such as their thoughts and opinions. The formation process of empirical literature can be regarded as the process of using research methods to solve research problems. Usually, a certain research tool or method or even a certain instrument or reagent (collectively referred to as methodological knowledge in this research) is used to assist experiments, analyze data, statistical analysis, and process images [3]. The development of the literature open access movement and intelligent information extraction oriented to the full text of academic literature make it possible to go deep into the full text of academic literature and to mine the methodological knowledge adopted by it. Many scholars in the field have explored. Wang Fang [4] used content analysis methods to identify methodological knowledge in the research field of information science in our country, and analyzed the subject distribution characteristics of methodological knowledge in this field from the perspective of mixed application of methodological knowledge. Wang Yuzhuo [5] identified the core algorithms in the field of natural language processing based on manual labeling and machine learning, and gave their time distribution characteristics. Can the methodology knowledge used in the field of economic management research be further subdivided? What kind of complex network characteristics does methodological knowledge exist as a factor of knowledge production in the process of driving collaboration between scholars and institutions? The in-depth analysis of these issues will help to grasp the research direction and research topics of researchers in a timely manner, promote knowledge exchange between scholars, and assist the knowledge production process in the subject area. This will promote the efficient and high-quality realization of scientific research goals by scientific researchers, and ensure the accuracy and authority of the knowledge production process [6].

In this context, this research takes the field of economic management as the research object, and based on the full-text data published in the authoritative journal "Management

World" in the field of economics and management collected by CNKI, to identify the methodological knowledge used in the process of knowledge production. The article is developed from the two levels of the academic research collaboration network and the research institution collaboration network, identifying the characteristics of the complex network driven by methodological knowledge, and exploring the knowledge exchange mode in the field of economic management research.

2 Related Research

This research takes the field of economic management as the research object, and builds a full-text database of academic literature based on the full-text data of academic literature published in the authoritative economic management journal "Management World" included in CNKI. Relying on big data-oriented data mining and analysis methods to identify methodological knowledge in the full text of academic literature, and then to identify methodological knowledge-driven scientific research collaboration network characteristics. Related research fields involve two aspects: research on the influencing factors of scientific research collaboration networks and the characteristics of scientific research collaboration networks in subject areas.

2.1 Research Status of Influencing Factors of Scientific Research Collaboration Network

Scientific research collaboration is a social network formed by scientific researchers in the process of scientific research collaboration. Many scholars have discussed it from the perspectives of factors such as the influencing factors of scientific research collaboration and the characteristics of scientific research collaboration networks. Ye Guanghui et al. [7] conducted a systematic survey on the current situation of cross-regional scientific research cooperation, and proposed a cross-regional scientific research collaboration model analysis framework. The study found that the strength of scientific research collaboration between cities will slowly decrease as the geographic distance between cities increases, showing a weak negative correlation. This confirms the rationality of the conclusion that the intensity of scientific research collaboration between cities in the same region is greater than that between cities across regions. In his analysis of the proximity of scientific research collaborations between American cities, Yu Zhongjie [8] pointed out that with the development of science and technology, the communication methods between scholars and institutions have become more diversified, and the hindrance of geographical factors to scientific research collaborations is gradually weakening. Factors such as economy, strength, and technology are playing an increasingly important role in scientific research collaboration among scholars and institutions. Disciplinary factors also have a certain impact on scientific research collaboration. Wang Xianwen et al. [9] pointed out that the similarity of disciplines also has a certain impact on the collaboration of institutional papers. The disciplines with strong professional nature can transcend the limitations of geography, such as geology, astronomy, oceanography, meteorology, etc. Since there are not many domestic scientific research institutions engaged in these disciplines, it is easier for these disciplines to form a sub-network of discipline cooperation compared with disciplines such as machinery, chemical engineering, and electronics. This kind of cross-regional scientific research cooperation dominated by disciplinary advantages is more conducive to the output and transformation of disciplinary frontier achievements [10]. In addition to scientific research collaboration within subject areas, some major scientific research projects that require the application of knowledge in multiple fields are also promoting interdisciplinary scientific research collaboration. Multidisciplinary research enables researchers from different disciplines to inspire each other, which makes it easier to generate new ideas and perspectives and promote knowledge production [11]. In addition, when Wang Chunlei [12] studied the influencing factors of university teachers' scientific research cooperation, he found that institutional factors have become the main obstacle for university teachers to carry out scientific research cooperation. In order to prevent the phenomenon of "academic free-riding", the management department denied the achievements of academic cooperation other than the first author. This imperfect title review system and scientific research reward system have reduced the willingness of scholars to carry out scientific research cooperation. To a certain extent, the incentive scientific research policy has become an important factor in inducing scientific research personnel to cooperate. Through reading the literature, many scholars have analyzed the influencing factors of scientific research collaboration from the perspectives of geographical proximity, disciplinary relationships, and the pros and cons of institutional and policy factors. However, there are few researches that regard methodological knowledge as an influencing factor of scientific research collaboration. Starting from the methodological knowledge, the author will study the complex network characteristics of the methodological knowledge as a knowledge production factor in the process of driving knowledge production, and then promote the interdisciplinary flow, iteration and update of the methodological knowledge.

2.2 Research Status of the Characteristics of Scientific Research Collaboration Networks in Subject Fields

When the scientific research collaboration relationship between scholars and institutions develops to a certain scale, a scientific research collaboration network will be formed. Identifying its structure and characteristics can promptly grasp the scientific research direction and research topics of scientific researchers, promote knowledge exchange between scientific researchers, and strengthen exchanges and cooperation between scientific researchers. In the end, it can promote scientific research personnel to achieve scientific research goals and knowledge production with high efficiency and high quality [6]. Xu Hao et al. [13] took the Chinese literature in the field of acoustics in our country as an example, based on CiteSpace's analysis of the research hotspots and research collaboration network models in the field of acoustics in our country since the 20th century. The overall scientific research collaboration model in the field of acoustics presents three types of continuous development subnets, complete subnets, and dual-core subnets. He revealed the characteristics and reasons for the formation of each subnet. Li Gang et al. [1] constructed the co-author network, co-word network and author keyword coupling network model in the field of oncology research. Using methods such as centrality analysis and cohesive subgroup analysis in social network analysis methods, he revealed the characteristics of the overall network and individual networks, thereby discovering the relationship between the members of the scientific research team, the research theme of the scientific research team, and the team. Gao Xia et al. [14] used the patent database of the State Intellectual Property Office, selected our country's Information and Communication Technology (ICT) industry as the research object, and used complex network analysis methods to study the dynamic mechanism and network structure evolution characteristics of the formation of our country's ICT industry-university-research cooperative innovation network. Wang Jiaxin et al. [15] used the authors of Wuhan University and Nanjing University in the field of library and information research and the number of articles as the research object, established a directed cooperation network between the author and the first author, and calculated the structure of cooperation between the two institutions. Wang used Pajek, a social network analysis software, to visualize the cooperation network relationship, and to analyze the characteristics of the tripartite relationship group. Then identified the structural characteristics and differences of the internal cooperation network of the two institutions, and tapped the cooperation potential, which can provide reference for enhancing the cooperation and communication between the authors. Based on previous studies, this research uses Gephi software to construct a visual network based on the perspective of complex network analysis and uses Gephi statistical algorithms to study the sub-network structure of scientific research collaboration networks to reveal its network characteristics.

Studies at home and abroad have shown that scientific research collaboration is one of the main modes of knowledge production, and it is one of the main driving forces for innovative results. As an important knowledge production tool, methodological knowledge plays a pivotal role in the process of generating innovative results. However, the current domestic and international research on scientific research collaboration networks is rarely carried out from the perspective of methodological knowledge-driven. This research is expanded from this perspective, taking the field of economic management research as the research object, and identifying the author's collaboration network and its institution collaboration network in the process of driving knowledge production in this field by methodological knowledge.

3 Research Tools and Data Sources

This work uses the full-text data of 5,564 papers (about 50,076,000 Chinese characters) collected from journal of "Management World" in the field of economics and management from 2000 to 2019 as the initial data source. With the help of predecessors' research experience [16], uses content analysis methods and rules to identify the methodological knowledge used in papers. And merge synonymous terms from the perspective of semantics, and identify 6,946 data on methodological knowledge. Based on this, the methodological knowledge in the field of economics and management research is divided into data, method and theory, model, and tool software through expert consultation. Category 4 categories, the definitions, examples, basis and acquisition methods given are shown in Table 1. Use Python to process the data, import the processed data set into the complex network analysis software Gephi [17] to draw various scientific research collaboration networks, and conduct research on the characteristics and related indicators of scientific research subnets.

Table 1. Definitions and examples of four types of methodological knowledge

No.	Categories	Definition	Examples	Relevant basis	Method of obtaining
1	Data	Including but not limited to various data set information, databases, statistical yearbooks, data materials and data websites, etc.	Census micro-database, CSMAR database, Wind database, China Statistical Yearbook, Customs Statistical Yearbook, etc.	Data sources in the research process	Manual & rule base
2	Theory & Method	Including but not limited to all kinds of data processing analysis and testing methods and functions, subject research theories, general methods, etc.	Stepwise regression, least squares, F test, Granger causality test, Hausman test, CD production function, impulse response function, Maslow's hierarchy of needs theory, etc.	Theoretical support and data analysis basis in the research process	Manual & rule based
3	Model	Including but not limited to various theoretical research models, data analysis models, etc.	Structural inflation model, economic endogenous growth model, panel data model, Probit model, etc.	Play an auxiliary analysis role in the research process	Manual & rule base
4	Tool & Software	Including but not limited to various research tools, modeling and analysis software, etc.	SPSS software, STATA software, UCINET software, Yongyou software, SmartPLS software, Matlab software, Lisrel software, etc.	Software tools to aid research	Manual & rule base

4 Methodological Knowledge-Driven Characteristics of Collaboration Network

Scientific research also increasingly requires mutual cooperation among scientific research members. The scientific research work in the "academic network" exchanges, communicates, consults, and collaborates in the tangible and intangible academic social networks, forming a special relationship network. In the process of joint knowledge production, a scientific research collaboration network is formed [18]. Analyzing the scientific research collaboration network, the occurrence and development characteristics of the research collaboration network are conducive to exploring the status of knowledge exchange among scholars and the mode of scientific research collaboration. Different methodological knowledge forms a scientific research collaboration network with different characteristics, which reflects the influence of methodological types on scientific research collaboration. The author regarded a total of 5,564 articles published in the 20-year period 2000–2019 of the journal "Management World", and firstly build an overall scientific research collaboration network from the two dimensions of scholars and scientific research institutions, and then conducted a more in-depth study on the characteristics of the scientific research collaboration network under the four categories of methodological knowledge. In addition, the author also revealed that different types of methodological knowledge, as factors of production, drive scientific research collaboration in the process of knowledge production.

4.1 Network Analysis of Scholars' Scientific Research Collaboration

Because there is a lot of collaborations between scholars and the collaboration is only one time, and the collaboration of the collaboration network has not yet been formed, relevant studies have shown that such phenomena can be regarded as "Academic Encounters". In addition, considering that the focus of this research is on the core of methodological knowledge-driven the discovery of the scientific research collaboration network, so this study selects the collaboration relationship where the number of scientific research collaborations is greater than twice. It should be noted in this study that the scientific research collaboration network is considered as a process of knowledge exchange, and the direction of knowledge exchange should be undirected. Therefore, "edge" rather than "arc" should be used to express this kind of relationship. When an academic document is completed by multiple authors in collaboration, the two-dimensional group of authors' cooperative pairs is constructed to express this type of relationship.

The process of constructing author's collaborative pair for one paper can be described as:

(1) In the process of forming for one academic document driven by methodological knowledge, if there are n authors $n \geq 2$ who have completed the work together, then the author relationship can be expressed as $\{A_1, A_2, A_3, \ldots \ldots A_n\}$;

(2) Total amount of two-dimensional author groups for one paper (such as $\{A_1, A_2\}$) for $\{A_1, A_2, A_3, \ldots \ldots A_n\}$ is $C_n^2 = \frac{n!}{2! * (n-2)!}$;

(3) All authors in a certain field are recorded as $\{B_1, B_2, B_3, \ldots \ldots B_n\}$, and the relationship between authors in the field of scientific research cooperation can be

revealed in the form of a matrix (Fig. 1). In Fig. 1, data on the diagonal is the number of collaborations between authors, denoted as W (W_{B12} is the cooprerate times of B_1 and B_2, and $W_{B12} = W_{B12}$), In addition, the authors of the field have no cooperative relationship with themselves, so the data of the diagonal is 0.

	B_1	B_2	B_3	$\cdots$	B_n
B_1	0	W_{B21}	W_{B31}	$\cdots$	W_{Bn1}
B_2	W_{B12}	0	W_{B32}	$\cdots$	W_{Bn2}
B_3	W_{B13}	W_{B23}	0	$\cdots$	W_{Bn3}
$\vdots$	$\vdots$	$\vdots$	$\vdots$	0	$\vdots$
B_n	W_{B1n}	W_{B2n}	W_{B3n}	$\cdots$	0

Fig. 1. Two-dimensional matrix for author cooperation network

(4) Import the formed matrix and its weight data into the information visualization software Gephi, and the network setting layout is Fruchterman Reingold.

The above data calculation process can be automated with the help of python programming. The data analysis language is used to import the processed data set into the complex network analysis software Gephi. With scholars as nodes and the collaborative relationship between scholars as edges, an undirected graph of the overall scientific research collaboration network of scholars is drawn. 427 nodes and 451 edges are formed. The result is shown in Fig. 2. The size of the node represents the number of nodes connected to it (that is, the size of the degree), and the thickness of the edge represents the weight of cooperation between scholars.

Network $G = \{V, E\}$, V stands for node and E stands for edge, N stands for the amount of node, E_i is the number of edges of node i. Average weighting degree of network graph (AWD) could be calculate by formula 1, and the graph density (D) is formula 2.

$$AWD = \frac{\sum_{i=1}^{n} E_i}{N}, \tag{1}$$

$$D = \frac{2 * \sum_{i=1}^{n} E_i}{N * N - N}, \tag{2}$$

The average weighting degree of the undirected graph of the overall scientific research collaboration network driven by methodological knowledge in Fig. 2 is 4.852, and which was calculated as in formula 1. It can be seen from formula 1 that the higher the average weighting degree, the greater the number of connected nodes in the graph, or the greater the weight of the connected edges. The distribution of node degrees is shown in Fig. 3, which shows the number of nodes corresponding to different degrees. The larger the degree, the more nodes are connected to it, indicating that the node is more important, reflecting the author's importance in the scientific research collaboration network. The graph density of the undirected graph of the scholar's overall scientific research collaboration network is 0.005. The higher the density, the closer the nodes in the graph are connected, and the more complex the author's collaborative network relationship.

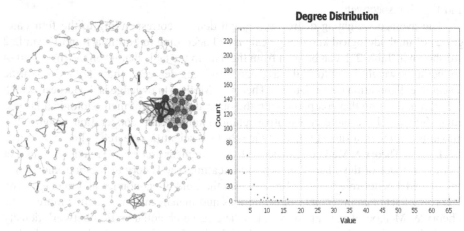

Fig. 2. Undirected graph of the overall collaboration network

Fig. 3. Distribution diagram of node degree for Fig. 2. *Note: The abscissa is the node degree, and the ordinate is the number of nodes corresponding to each value.*

With reference to previous research results [19], we found that the methodological knowledge-driven scientific research collaboration network presents a dual-core model network, a complete model network, and a continuous development model network. Among them, the dual-core mode has and only two scholars directly cooperate with each other; the complete mode means that the number of internal nodes in the network is greater than 2 and the out-degree value of any node is equal to the in-degree value, and any node can become the central node of the network. It is a relatively stable network structure, but the greater the number of network nodes, the smaller the possibility of forming a complete complex network; the sustainable development model has a lot of internal nodes in the network, a complex structure, and multiple subnets. The characteristics of a long time to form and the knowledge-driven methodology of scientific research collaboration How Net has the above three modes show that the knowledge-driven methodology of scientific research collaboration network has the characteristics of a complex network and has a certain sub-network structure.

Further analyze Fig. 2, we find that in the analysis of the scientific research collaboration network from the four methodological knowledge categories, the author's collaboration relationship driven by Theory & Method knowledge accounts for the largest proportion, about 60%. From the form of expression, the Theory & Method knowledge driven scientific research collaboration network is more consistent with the overall network form, as shown in Fig. 4. As Tool & Software knowledge accounts for about 6% of all methodological knowledge, and the amount is small, the structure of the formed scholars' scientific research cooperation network is simple, and only four two-way cooperative relations are formed, which is a "dual core" model, as shown in Fig. 5. Compared with the methodological knowledge of Theory & Method, although the model and data methodological knowledge form a network diagram of scholars' scientific research collaboration, the number of nodes is small. Although individual nodes present the characteristics of a complete model network, the overall structure is loose and the cooperative relationship between scholars is loose. Sparse, as shown in Fig. 6 and Fig. 7, respectively.

The average weighting degree and graph density corresponding to the four categories of methodological knowledge calculated according to Formula 1 and Formula 2 are shown in Table 2. It can be seen from the data in the table that when the threshold of cooperation weight is set to 2, the average weighting degree of the scholars' scientific research collaboration network under Theory & Method knowledge is the largest, which is 5.223, indicating that compared with the other three types of methodological knowledge, Scholars have more cooperative relations and greater cooperation weight. The maximum number of subnet nodes of the scholar's scientific research collaboration network under Theory & Method knowledge is 23, which far exceeds the maximum number of subnet nodes of the other three types, indicating that Theory & Method knowledge has played a better role in related research in the field of economics and management. The role of scholars in the field of economics and management research is more in the Theory & Method of mutual cooperation. The research collaboration network density of scholars under tool and software methodological knowledge is the largest, which is 0.143, indicating that the cooperation between scholars under this type of methodological knowledge is relatively close; while the research collaboration network density of scholars under methodological knowledge is the smallest, which is 0.007. It shows that although it has more nodes, the relationship between nodes is less, the network structure is relatively loose, and multiple close scientific research collaboration networks have not yet been formed.

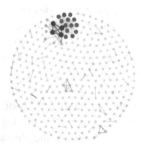

Fig. 4. Collaboration network: driven by Theory & Method

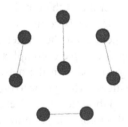

Fig. 5. Collaboration network: driven by Tool & Software

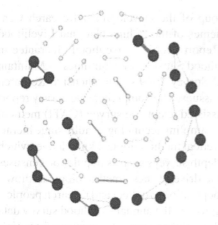

Fig. 6. Collaboration network: driven by Model

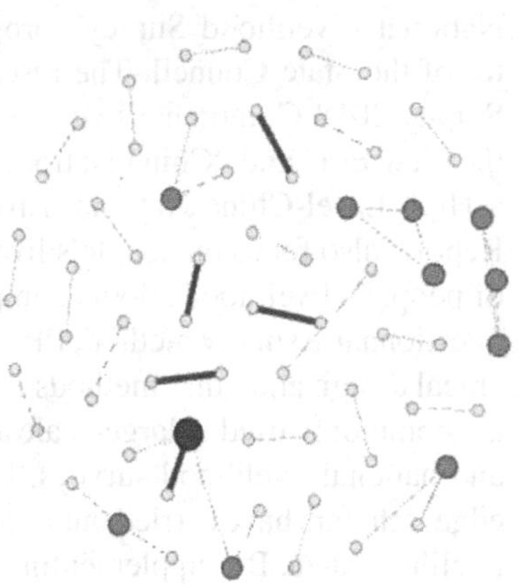

Fig. 7. Collaboration network: driven by Data

Table 2. Statistics of scholars' scientific research collaboration network graphs driven by different types

Indicator name	Theory & Method	Tool & Software	Model	Data
Average weighting	5.223	2	3.043	2.531
Network density	0.007	0.143	0.02	0.019
Maximum number of subnet nodes	23	2	3	4

Combined with methodological knowledge-driven research results, it is found that:

(1) From the perspective of the number of sub-networks formed by each mode under different methodological knowledge types, the collaboration mode is mostly a dual-core mode, indicating that a large-scale collaborative communication network for scholars in the field of economics and management has not yet formed, which may be due to the different academics of scientific researchers in the field of economics and management. The limitations of resources, background, research direction, geographical location and other factors indicate that the cooperation between scholars needs to break down the barriers, and the breadth of scientific research cooperation needs to be strengthened.

(2) Among the scholars' scientific research collaboration network formed under methodological knowledge, Zhang Junkuo, Ye Xingqing, Ge Yanfeng, Jin San-lin and Zhu Xianqiang have formed a typical complete model scientific research collaboration network with a relatively stable network structure, as shown in Fig. 8. After further inquiries, it was found that the five persons are researchers of the Development Research Center of the State Council, and both belong to the "China

National Livelihood Survey" project group of the Development Research Center of the State Council. The research themes of the "China National Livelihood Survey 2018 Comprehensive Research Report-People's Livelihood Guarantee in the New Era" and "China National Livelihood Satisfaction Continues to Maintain a High Level-China National Livelihood Survey 2019 Comprehensive Research Report" also focus on people's livelihood issues. The comprehensive survey report of people's livelihood adopts computer-assisted telephone survey (CATI) method, questionnaire survey method, PPS system sampling technology, multi-stage hierarchical design and other methods and theoretical methodological knowledge, which are commonly used in large-scale and in-depth surveys such as population censuses and national livelihood surveys. Under the drive of these methodological knowledge, scholars have carried out in-depth cooperation to collect and research people's livelihood data. By supplementing and improving the annual livelihood survey data and comparative analysis, it is concluded that three years The themes of people's livelihood development are "People's livelihood development under the background of economic stabilization", "People's livelihood security in the new era" and "Chinese people's livelihood satisfaction continues to be maintained at a high level". A series of reports on people's livelihood have been completed and related fields have been promoted. The scholars have conducted more in-depth communication and exchanges, thereby accelerating the production process and iterative update of knowledge.

(3) The four nodes of Li Lan, Pan Jiancheng, Peng Siqing, and Hao Dahai are the largest in the scholars' scientific research collaboration network formed under Theory & Method methodology knowledge, indicating that there are more scholars connected to them; the thicker the edge representing the collaborative relationship, it indicates the four-person cooperation has the highest weight. The four-person-centered network drives the surrounding cooperation network, forming a scientific research collaboration network under the sustainable development model, as shown in Fig. 9. The cooperative relationship between the four people can be traced back to 2007. In the past ten years, Li Lan, Pan Jiancheng, Peng Siqing and Hao Dahai focused on the theme of "Questionnaire Follow-up Survey of Chinese Enterprise Operators" and mainly used questionnaire survey methods to carry out the survey., Relevant research combined with the survey data of the Chinese Entrepreneur Survey System over the years, since 2007, a number of survey research reports on Chinese enterprises and Chinese entrepreneurs have been published, revealing the development and operation status and existing problems of Chinese enterprises over the years, providing Chinese entrepreneurs It provided effective advice for the growth and development of the company, and gradually expanded the scale of the scientific research collaboration network over a long period of time. The collaboration network centered on Li Lan, Pan Jiancheng, Peng Siqing and Hao Dahai drove Fan Gang, Yu Mingqin, Yu Mingqin, Li Qiang, Cong Liang, Wang Keliang, Yu Ping, Hao Yufeng, Yang Yuanwei, Gong Sen, Li Yanbin, Sheng Yunlai, Yu Wu, Zhang Tai, Dong Bo, Han Xiulan, Lu Jiangyong, Zheng Mingshen, Zhong Weiguo, Wang Yunfeng and others, this A subnet has 23 nodes, showing the characteristics of a large number of internal nodes in the network and a long time of formation, forming a relatively complex network structure, which is the core scientific research subnet

in the field of economic management research in China, showing good cooperation continuity. Present a sustainable development model.

(4) There are four two-way cooperation relationships in the scholars' scientific research collaboration network formed under the knowledge of Tool & Software methodology, all of which are dual-core models. The software and tools involved in the formed scientific research collaboration network include SPSS software, HLM software, Lisrel software, AMOS, and Matlab software. SPSS is a data analysis software used for statistical analysis operations, data mining, predictive analysis and decision support Tasks and so on. HLM is a professional hierarchical linear model analysis software that can process multi-level data and perform linear and nonlinear hierarchical model analysis. It is widely used in the fields of social science and behavioral science. Lisrel and AMOS are structural equation modeling and statistical analysis software, commonly used with dimensionality reduction analysis and linear regression analysis. Jiang Han and Jin Zhanming jointly published two articles in 2008. Using Lisrel8.70 as the main analysis tool, the structural equation modeling method was used to test the related hypotheses of the proposed conceptual model. First, the empirical research was conducted from the perspective of relationship strength. The choice of strategic mode has an impact on corporate relationship governance behavior, and then based on the perspective of inter-firm interdependence, the empirical study of the impact of the strength of inter-firm relationships on the relationship value mechanism increases the depth of research and reflects the knowledge of Tool & Software methodology as knowledge production The elements in the process can continuously drive scientific research collaboration in the field, so as to complete the continuous iteration and update of knowledge.

(5) Methodological knowledge with different characteristics has different usage methods, applicable scenarios, application steps, etc. Scholars usually choose methodological knowledge based on their knowledge background and familiarity with software tools when conducting scientific research. However, after research, it is found that the research collaboration subnet formed by Wang Haizhong, Yu Chunling and Zhao Ping is more representative of the research collaboration network of scholars formed under the knowledge of model methodology and Tool & Software methodology. At the same time, the three of them formed the research collaboration network is also reflected to a certain extent by scholars under the methodological knowledge. The research results mostly focus on consumer ethnocentrism [20], target market segmentation [21], brand equity [22] and other topics. The research team appropriately used structural equation modeling, SPSS software, K-Maens clustering method and factor analysis and other types of methodological knowledge to carry out empirical research in different forms and sufficient arguments for different research topics, and then proposed "Consumer-based brand equity is composed of four dimensions of company capability association, brand awareness, quality recognition, and brand resonance. It is a three-level ladder that can explain the output of the brand in the product market" and other innovative conclusions. It can be explained that the mixed application of multiple types of methodological knowledge [4] can promote knowledge production, strengthen the ability of scholars to collaborate in scientific research, and then promote the generation of innovative results.

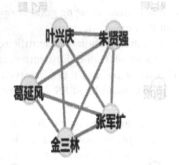

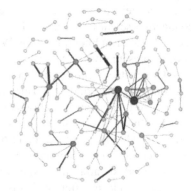

Fig. 8. Complete model driven by Theory & Method (subnet and example)

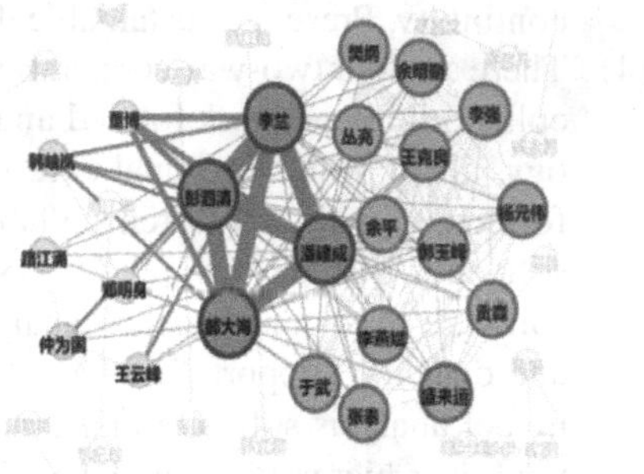

Fig. 9. Sustainable development model driven by Theory & Method (subnet and example)

4.2 Institutional Research Collaboration Network Research

The authors of the literature also have institutional attributes, and research on the characteristics of the scientific research collaboration network of scientific research institutions will help to reveal the characteristics of methodological knowledge in driving the process of institutional cooperation.

The data processing process of the institutional cooperation network relies on Python. After the initial data is formed, it is imported into the information visualization software GEPHI. The methodological knowledge-driven scientific research cooperation network formed is shown in Fig. 10, and in which:

Fig. 10. Theory & Method-driven collaboration network diagram of scientific research institutions

(1) In the overall network between various institutions, there is a scientific research collaboration network that exhibits the characteristics of a dual-core model. The cooperative subnets established by cooperative institutions show a relatively obvious modularity phenomenon: These are the sub-networks formed by Beijing Outstanding Entrepreneur Growth Research Foundation, China Entrepreneur Survey

System, National Bureau of Statistics, China Economic Prosperity Monitoring Center, School of Social and Demography, Renmin University of China, and Public Administration Office of the Development Research Center of the State Council. And the sub-networks formed by the International Business School of University of International Business and Economics, Tsinghua University School of Economics and Management, Southwest Jiaotong University School of Economics and Management, Southwestern University of Finance and Economics, and Southwestern University of Finance and Economics. Scientific research resources and strength are more prominent, but a large-scale, in-depth collaborative methodological knowledge-driven scientific research collaboration network has not yet formed (Fig. 11).

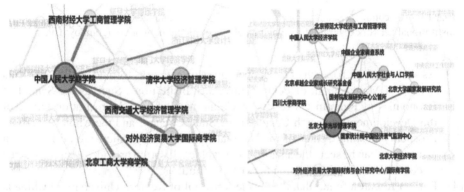

Fig. 11. Subnet centered on Guanghua College of Peking University

Fig. 12. Subnet centered on Renmin University of China Business School

(2) From the perspective of the scientific research collaboration network formed by various methodological knowledge, the research collaboration network situation driven by methodological knowledge is similar to the overall network structure, and the research collaboration network under the three categories of data, model and Tool & Software is further Research and analysis found that the scientific research collaboration network formed by institutions in the field of economic management research under the category of Tool & Software has not formed an obvious model structure; In the scientific research collaboration network formed under the data and model categories, there are more obvious collaboration networks with complete model characteristics, as shown in Fig. 13 and Fig. 14, The research collaboration sub-network composed of the School of Politics and Public Affairs Management of Sun Yat-sen University, the Public Management Research Center of Sun Yat-sen University, the Institute of Transformation and Open Economics of Sun Yat-sen University, and Lingnan College of Sun Yat-sen University all have complete model characteristics.

(3) In terms of geographic factors, the four types of methodological knowledge-driven scientific research collaboration networks geographically related to different places.

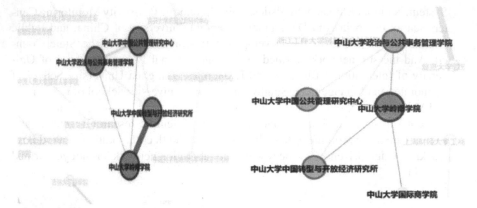

Fig. 13. The complete structure of institutional network diagram driven by model

Fig. 14. Complete structure in the institutional network diagram by data

As shown in Fig. 10, each of the cooperative sub-networks formed by the Guanghua School of Management of Peking University Institutions. Such as the School of Economics of Renmin University of China, the Public Administration Office of the Development Research Center of the State Council, and the China Economic Prosperity Testing Center of the National Bureau of Statistics, are all located in Beijing. As can be seen, the adjacent geographical location provides a certain degree of convenience for cooperation between institutions.

(4) Further research found that the business School of Renmin University of China is the central hub. Driving the School of Business Administration of Southwestern University of Finance and Economics, School of Economics and Management of Tsinghua University, School of Economics and Management of Southwest Jiao Tong University, School of International Business of University of International Business and Economics, and Beijing Technology and Business University. In the cooperation sub-network formed by the business school, in addition to the regional cooperation between some institutions in the same city, there has also been a "Beijing – Sichuan" cross-regional exchange and cooperation, as shown in Fig. 12. From the geographical point of view, the cooperation of the above-mentioned institutions is not restricted by the geographical position. From the point of view of the type of institutions, the cooperative institutions are all economic and management colleges; from the point of view of the subject content, there is also a more obvious presence in the subject content of the research. The crossovers are all areas of economics and management disciplines, and in their research process, the methodological knowledge used is mostly methodological knowledge. The methodological knowledge flow generated during the cooperation process will help to enhance the knowledge reserve of various institutions, thereby driving the scientific research collaboration network Formation. It can be seen that the relationship between disciplines is also an important force to promote institutional cooperation [14].

(5) In Fig. 10, the Guanghua School of Management of Peking University and the School of Business of Renmin University of China, which are at the core of the scientific research collaboration network in Fig. 10, have conducted four cooperation. Of which the Theory & Method category accounted for 73.33%, and the Tool & Software category and model category each accounted for Compared with 6.67%, the data category accounted for 13.33%. It can be seen that the two research institutions have a more comprehensive process of methodological knowledge-driven scientific research collaboration, of which the Theory & Method category has the largest driving effect; Shanghai University of Finance and Economics School of Management and Shanghai University of Finance and Economics Accounting The cooperation with the Institute of Finance is relatively close. The two institutions have cooperated 12 times in total. Among the methodological knowledge they adopted, the methodological knowledge and the data methodology each accounted for 35.71%, the model category accounted for 25.00%, and the Tool & Software category accounted for the proportion 3.57%, it can be seen that the methodological knowledge of Theory & Method and data has a greater driving effect in the cooperation between the two institutions. Between Chinese Family Business Research Center, Zhongshan University School of Management and Sun Yat-sen also has close ties, which, Li Chinese New Year is to promote cooperation between the two institutions the core authors, the prominent display of the driving role of theoretical knowledge of class methodology.

5 Conclusion

This research takes the field of economic management research as the research object, and selects the 20-year full-text data of the authoritative journal "Management World" in this research field as the basic data source. The research used big data mining and analysis methods, with the help of two research tools, the programming language Python and the information visualization tool GEPHI, to study the various characteristics of the methodological knowledge-driven scientific research collaboration network and the institutional collaboration network. In the actual research process, based on the reality of the complex application of methodological knowledge, the research used the opinions of experts in the field to divide the methodological knowledge into four categories: Theory & Method, Model, Data and Tool & Software, respectively revealed the characteristics of the scientific research collaboration network that drives the knowledge production in the economic management research field. The results of the study indicated: (1) The methodological knowledge-driven overall scientific research collaboration network of scholars and scientific research institutions presents multi-modal characteristics and has a typical scientific research sub-network. Among them, methodological knowledge-driven research in the field of economics and management has formed two typical models that are conducive to the dissemination and sharing of knowledge, namely, the complete model and the sustainable development model. (2) Belong to the State Council Development Research Center, "Chinese People's Livelihood Survey" research group, Zhang Junkuo, Ye Xingqing, Ge Yanfeng, Jin Sanlin and Zhu Xianqiang formed a complete model research collaboration network. The core cooperation sub-network formed by Li Lan, Pan Jiancheng, Peng Siqing and Hao Dahai has the characteristics of long formation time and close cooperation, and has driven a series of scholars in a relatively long period of time, and has good continuity. The research sub-networks formed by the overall scientific research collaboration network of the institution are mostly one-point-driven multi-point relationships, the form is relatively simple, and the sub-networks not connected to each other. Typically, the Guanghua School of Peking University and the Business School of Renmin University of China form them, Research subnet. (3) Although the scientific research collaboration network formed by scholars and scientific research institutions under the methodology category shows certain pattern characteristics, the overall structure is relatively loose and the characteristics are not easy to identify.

This research has certain limitations. In terms of data sources, only 20 years of data from the journal "Management World" selected in the field of economics and management research, which indicates that although there are certain limitations in the types of journals in the research field, such limitations are caused. The fundamental reason is that this research uses content analysis methods to identify methodological knowledge in academic literature, and divided into 4 categories. This process mainly relies on manual methods. This process is heavy and has different standard systems. In future research will combine the identification rules of the content analysis method of this research, use full-text analysis, intelligent information processing and other technologies to automatically identify the methodological knowledge in the full-text of academic literature, and gradually realize the field-oriented methodology-driven scientific research based on the full-text data of academic literature. Build a knowledge base, and then identify the characteristics of the methodological knowledge-driven scientific research collaboration network under the support of big data, give better play to the guarantee role of the methodological knowledge in the process of driving knowledge production, promote the exchange and sharing of knowledge across disciplines, and promote innovation the generation of sexual results.

Acknowledgements. The research was supported by Jiangsu Provincial Social Science Foundation Youth Project: Research on the recommendation strategy of electronic literature resources integrating online academic social information (No. 21TQC003); the University Philosophy and Social Science Research Project of Jiangsu province (No. 2019SJA2274); Innovation Fund General Project I of Nanjing Institute of Technology (No. CKJB202003); Major Project of Philosophy and Social Science Research in Universities of Jiangsu Provincial Department of Education (No. CKJA201706); National College Student Practice Innovation Training Program Project of Nanjing Institute of Technology (No. 202011276021Z).

References

1. Li, G., Li, C., Li, X.: Research on the discovery of scientific research teams based on social network analysis. Libr. Inf. Serv. **58**(07), 63–70, 82 (2014)
2. Pan, X.: Research on automatic extraction of software entities and academic influence. Nanjing University (2016)
3. Xu, H., Zhu, X., Zhang, C., et al.: Analysis and design of methodological knowledge extraction system for full text of academic documents. Data Anal. Knowl. Disc. **3**(10), 29–36 (2019)

4. Wang, F., Zhu, N., Zhai, Y.: The application of hybrid methods in China's information science research and the analysis of their field distribution. J. Inf. **36**(11), 1119–1129 (2017)
5. Wang, Y., Zhang, C.: Using the full-text content of academic articles to identify and evaluate algorithm entities in the domain of natural language processing. J. Informetr. **14**, 101091 (2020)
6. Wang, Z.: Research on the application of social network analysis methods in scientific research collaboration networks. Dalian University of Technology (2006)
7. Ye, G., Xia, L.: Analysis of cross-regional scientific research collaboration model. J. Libr. Sci. China **45**(03), 79–95 (2019)
8. Yeh, Yu, Z., Qian, L.: Multidimensional effects of proximity between the US cities of research collaboration. Inf. Theory Pract. **43**(11), 86–91 + 27 (2020)
9. Wen, W., Ding, K., Zhu, Z.: Scientific cooperation network of China's major research institutions in the analysis - based on Web of Science study. Res. Sci. **28**(12), 1806–1812 (2010)
10. Chai, Y., Liu, C., Wang, X.: The construction and characteristic analysis of China's university scientific research cooperation network —— based on the data of "211" universities. Libr. Inf. Serv. **59**(02), 82–88 (2015)
11. Zhao, R., Wen, F.: Research collaboration and knowledge exchange. Libr. Inf. Serv. **55**(20), 6–10, 27 (2011)
12. Wang, C.: Research on the influencing factors of university teachers' scientific research cooperation: taking Guangxi as an example. Sci. Technol. Prog. Policy **29**(21), 145–149 (2012)
13. Xu, H., Huang, C., Jin, W., et al.: Research hotspots in subject areas and pattern recognition of scientific research collaborations —— taking Chinese literature in the field of acoustics in China as an example. Jiangsu Sci. Technol. Inf. **37**(19), 13–16 (2020)
14. Gao, X., Chen, K.: Complex network analysis of the evolution characteristics of cooperative innovation network structure. Sci. Res. Manage. **36**(06), 28–36 (2015)
15. Wang, J., Hou, H., Fu, H., et al.: Author cooperation network structure and group differences in the tripartite relationship analysis. Libr. Inf. Serv. **62**(09), 102–111 (2018)
16. Wang, F., Shi, H., Ji, X.: Application of theory in information science research in China: based on the content analysis of "Journal of Information." J. Inf. **34**(06), 581–591 (2015)
17. Gephi. https://gephi.org/
18. Li, L.: Research on the research collaboration network —— based on the perspective of social network theory. Huazhong Agricultural University, Hubei (2011). https://doi.org/10.7666/d.y2003857
19. Peng, X., Zhu, Q., Shen, C.: Analysis of author cooperation in the field of social computing based on social network analysis. J. Inf. **32**(03), 93–100 (2013)
20. Wang, H., Yu, C., Zhao, P.: The duality of consumer ethnocentrism and its market strategic significance. Manage. World **02**, 96–107 (2005)
21. Wang, H., Zhao, P.: Research on market segmentation based on consumer ethnocentrism. Manage. World (05), 88–96, 156 (2004)
22. Wang, Y., Yu, C., Zhao, P.: The relationship between the consumer model of brand equity and the product market output model. Manage. World **01**, 106–119 (2006)

Smart Hotel Management Under the Background of Big Data

Junyi Xu[✉]

Gingko College of Hospitality Management, Chengdu 611047, Sichuan, China

Abstract. Traditional hotel management and service quality are easily affected by service personnel, and various procedures are cumbersome. Smart hotel management under the control of big data information can effectively improve the quality of hotel stays. The installation of smart guest room control systems has become a major trend. Based on this, this paper designs an intelligent hotel management system, which realizes the informatization and intelligence of hotel management. The smart home system developed in this paper has been promoted to many hotels, showing good market value. At the same time, this paper also proposes a collaborative filtering algorithm based on the comprehensive similarity of users, and builds a personalized movie recommendation system based on this, and realizes the display of the movie recommendation system to make smart hotel management more personalized. Experimental results show that our smart hotel management system and personalized movie recommendation system have the characteristics of high stability, and intelligence. They are easy to maintain and manage, and can effectively reduce operating costs and improve service quality.

Keywords: Smart hotel management · Big data · Personalized movie recommendation

1 Introduction

With the development of society, traditional hotel management is often difficult to accurately obtain customer needs and cannot provide services in a timely and effective manner. With the advent of the Internet era, the application of big data in hotel management will also play its important role. Smart hotel management has gradually entered people's lives and has had a profound impact on the development of the hotel industry.

A smart hotel means that the hotel has a complete set of intelligent systems, supported by cloud computing, Internet of Things, and big data technologies, based on related platforms and software, providing intelligent software and hardware technologies to empower traditional hotel models, and building smart terminals with data collection. Create a smart hotel format with intelligent big data operation system and digital management service process [1]. Smart hotel management integrates and optimizes hotel customer information on the basis of big data, and develops convenient and efficient service plans with good experience and strong personalization. Specifically, smart hotels use big data technology to mine and analyze user behavior preferences, build consumer

© Springer Nature Singapore Pte Ltd. 2022
Y. Tian et al. (Eds.): ICBDS 2021, CCIS 1563, pp. 348–359, 2022.
https://doi.org/10.1007/978-981-19-0852-1_26

portraits, classify different customer characteristics and provide matching services and products, which is conducive to maximizing the value of user data. Not only allows consumers to get better accommodation care, but also improves user experience and hotel repurchase rates. Smart hotel management relies on big data to provide sufficient beneficial resources, and carry out effective mining, analysis and application, so that the hotel management industry can be further developed.

The existing smart hotel management system uses the customer terminal placed in the room to complete the reservation of various services without having to go to the front desk for processing, which improves the consumer's experience of staying in the hotel, but the function is still very single. All devices cannot be remotely controlled by the mobile terminal, and remote monitoring cannot be performed when the system fails. There is no delay when the light is turned on and off, and intelligent light brightness adjustment can not be realized [2, 3]. In addition, the client terminal has been activated for a long time and cannot be linked with the room card or other objects that can achieve identity verification. There is no multi-personalized recommendation for the room.

In smart hotel management, recommendation systems have become the most commonly used part of Web sites such as e-commerce and online movies. The personalized recommendation algorithm is the foundation of the entire recommendation system. The recommendation technology in the recommendation system is mainly collaborative filtering recommendation technology. As a recommendation algorithm with a wide range of applications and a high degree of popularity, collaborative filtering algorithm has a lot of research on collaborative filtering algorithm at home and abroad. The personalized recommendation system PKOAKS and Reaferral Web [4] are user-based collaborative filtering systems, and the item-based collaborative filtering algorithm [5] also adopts the idea of collaborative filtering.

Aiming at the problem of data sparseness that affects the recommendation effect of collaborative filtering algorithms, Dempster [6] and Thiessoii et al. [7] proposed to use clustering technology to solve the problem of data sparseness, clustering users according to their interests, and after clustering is completed, Regard users in the same category as the user's neighbors, and then use the neighbor's hobbies to predict the hobbies and interests of the target user. Although this method can solve the problem of data sparseness to a certain extent, this method has no effect on the noise in the data set. The data is more sensitive and susceptible to noise interference and influence. In some cases, the effect is not ideal. Massa et al. [8] used trust value to replace the similarity between users for scoring prediction, reducing the dependence on scoring data, and reducing the impact of sparsity on recommendation results.

Based on the above, we first designed an intelligent hotel management software system, the system includes the main controller module, LED power control module, intelligent power control module, air conditioning control module, human body sensor module and doorbell touch module. Then, this paper proposes a collaborative filtering algorithm based on the user's comprehensive similarity, and builds a personalized movie recommendation system based on this, and realizes the display of the movie recommendation system. The algorithm divides the similarity of users and introduces the characteristics of users into the similarity calculation, so that the similarity between users does not only depend on the user's rating data, even for newly registered users, there are still ways to calculate the new registration. The similarity between users and other users, then the user-based collaborative filtering algorithm can solve the "cold start" problem and reduce the impact of data sparsity on the recommendation quality to a certain extent.

2 Smart Hotel Management System Design

2.1 Smart Hotel Management System Overall Plan

The smart hotel management system requires that all home appliances in the guest room, such as TVs, air conditioners, electric curtains, smart door locks, lights, etc., can be controlled through a smart touch panel, and the smart system of each room needs to be connected to the hotel server through Ethernet technology. At the same time, the intelligent control system of each guest room supports WeChat applet and mobile phone APP for remote control. The mobile phone can remotely open-door locks, open or close window curtains, and turn on or off-air conditioning through APP. The guest room's intelligent system also supports a personalized movie recommendation system.

The smart hotel management system mainly includes: main controller, bedside touch panel, air conditioner touch panel, doorbell touch panel, human infrared sensor, smart light driver, smart door lock, smart curtain and strong current controller. The whole system is interconnected through RS485 bus or Zigbee wireless technology communication.

2.2 Smart Hotel Management Software System

Design Ideas of Smart Hotel Management Software System. According to the communication baud rate, the specific time for the main controller to access a module is calculated, and the calculation time is from the main controller sending out the inquiry signal to the main controller receiving the response information of the corresponding module. The slowest response time of each module of the smart hotel guest room management and control system is calibrated, and the main controller confirms the specific time slice of the access task according to this time. The main controller accesses the fixed IP address of the guest room Ethernet through the TCP/TP protocol, records the IP address, and sets the IP address as its own fixed IP address. In the future, the server will control the smart hotel guest control system through this address. After the main controller receives the wireless networking application requested by the customer, it communicates with the wireless ZigBee module through the serial port, and finally realizes the networking of the motherboard and the wireless door lock of the guest room. The smart hotel guest room management and control system communicates with the back-end server through the Ethernet interface to realize the function of APP remotely controlling the guest room management and control system. The main controller synchronizes the time with the server regularly through the Ethernet interface, and sends the time to the air conditioning control module regularly through the RS485 bus, and sends the time to the smart door lock through the ZigBee wireless communication module to ensure the door lock and smart air conditioner The control module and the network time are the same.

Smart Hotel Management Software System Process. The Cortex-M3 chip is used as the main controller, which has strong data processing capabilities. The Cortex-M3 chip accesses the data sent and received by uart through DMA, and responds to the bus in time. When a device is hung up or there is a missing code, the main controller will ask the module again, when the module responds correctly, the main controller will count the packet loss rate of the module, if the module has not responded yet, the module is marked as damaged.

Smart hotel guest room management and control system control equipment includes electric curtains, air conditioning systems, TV sets, LED power control modules, smart touch doorbell modules, smart human body induction modules, smart bedside control modules, and high-power control modules. All devices are connected together via RS485 bus, which is based on Modbus protocol. The main controller sends query commands to all sub-modules one by one, and all sub-modules are set to receive mode. After receiving data, first compare and confirm whether the main controller is asking itself. If the addresses match, within 3.5 bytes of time Return relevant data to the main controller, and the main controller controls other related equipment according to the data [9–11].

When the main controller asks which module and the module does not respond correctly within the confirmation time, the main controller will take the initiative to issue another query command. If the corresponding module does not respond correctly, the main controller will Record the situation that the module does not reply, print it through the debugging port, and count the packet loss rate of the system.

The main controller inquiries about the program flow chart of all sub-modules, as shown in Fig. 1. After the smart hotel guest control system is powered on, all states are initialized. The main controller will inquire the state of each module in the system according to the addresses of different modules. When which module is inquired, the module will respond and report the response information to the main. The main controller determines how the system will act according to this information.

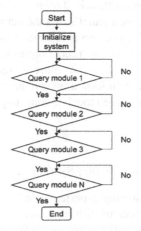

Fig. 1. Flow chart of main controller query

When the bedside control module receives the control instruction sent by the person, it saves the action information, and when the main controller inquires it, it will report the information to the main controller. The main controller judges the information, and controls the system to perform corresponding actions based on the information, such as opening the electric curtain, the program flow is shown in Fig. 2.

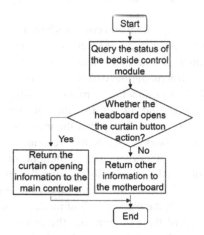

Fig. 2. Flow chart about the opening of electric curtains

The doorbell touch module has three functions, the do not disturb indicator light, the please clean indicator light, and the doorbell reminder touch button. When someone outside the door presses the doorbell button, the Dingdong doorbell in the guest room will ring twice. When the please clean or do not disturb button of the bedside control module in the guest room is pressed, the corresponding indicator light on the doorbell touch panel Light up. The program flow is shown in Fig. 3. When the doorbell touch button is pressed, the doorbell touch panel saves the action information, and when the main controller queries it, the information is reported to the main controller. The main controller judges the information, and the relay outputs a strong electric pulse signal to make the doorbell ring twice. When the main controller receives the information sent by the bedside control module, and the information is related to the doorbell touch module, the main controller controls the doorbell touch module to perform corresponding actions according to the information.

2.3 Smart Hotel Management Software System

In order to enhance the guest's staying experience and the overall service quality of the hotel, according to the preferences of different users, establish a personalized movie recommendation system. A personalized recommendation system is particularly important for information data filtering. It can record information based on the user's past behavior when the user does not have a clear goal or is faced with a large amount of complex data. Analyze the user's preference needs and personal preferences, discover

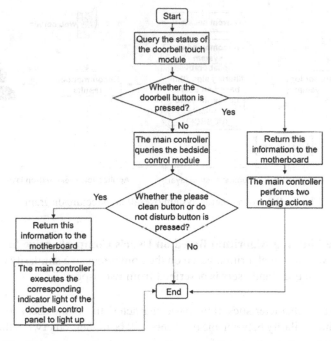

Fig. 3. The flow chart of the main controller controlling the doorbell control module

the user's interest in the complex data, and actively recommend it to the user. The use of the recommendation system not only saves users a lot of time, but also improves user recognition and enhances user experience and stickiness. In response to this, this paper proposes a collaborative filtering algorithm based on user comprehensive similarity, and builds a personalized movie recommendation system.

The Overall Design of A Personalized Movie Recommendation System for Smart Hotel Guest Rooms. In order to provide users with personalized movie recommendation services more effectively, we divide the personalized recommendation system into two levels: data storage layer, logical system layer, and application display layer. Each layer can refine more functional modules, with storage and computing functions. The independence of each unit is very high. If a unit is changed and upgraded in the future, it will not affect other units. The overall architecture diagram is shown in Fig. 4.

The main function of the data storage layer is to store a large amount of user behavior record data. The main responsibility of the logical system layer is to realize the logical operation of the recommendation system. The function of the application display layer is to display the final recommendation result to the user. This article provides customers with a collaborative filtering algorithm based on user comprehensive similarity. The recommendation system obtains the user's past behavior record data through database, memory or file reading, and then the user can select the recommendation strategy that he wants to use, and finally generates a recommendation list for the user.

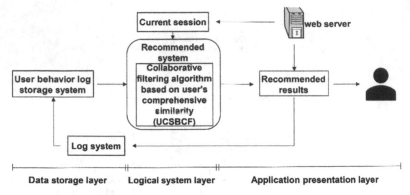

Fig. 4. Recommendation system overall architecture diagram

Collaborative Filtering Algorithm Based on User's Comprehensive Similarity. In the collaborative filtering algorithm based on the comprehensive similarity of users, the similarity between users and users is described from two aspects:

(1) User and user characteristics. If the basic characteristics of the user and the user are similar, the similarity between the two users will be higher; otherwise, the similarity will be lower.
(2) Users and user ratings. The score can directly reflect the user's preferences, and the similarity of two user scores means that the user's preferences for the item are more similar.

Therefore, this paper uses two aspects of rating similarity and feature similarity to measure user similarity. User similarity is calculated by weighting feature similarity and rating similarity, and its calculation formula is as shown in formula (1):

$$sim(i,j) = \lambda sim_f(i,j) + (1 - \lambda)sim_r(i,j) \tag{1}$$

Here, $sim(i,j)$ represents the comprehensive similarity of users i and j, $sim_f(i,j)$ represents feature similarity between users i and j, $sim_r(i,j)$ indicates the similarity of ratings of users i and j, λ is the weight of feature similarity, between 0–1. The recommendation process based on the user's comprehensive similarity algorithm is shown in Fig. 5.

User Feature Similarity. In various systems, basic user information generally includes age, gender, and occupation. For example, movie sites can obtain the gender, age and occupation of all users. Taking into account the problem of the data set, in the standard data set Movielens, the user's information mainly has four aspects, namely age, gender, occupation and zipcode. There are only three aspects of information that can truly characterize the user's characteristics, age, gender and occupation. There are 21 kinds of occupations for users. Because there are many and messy occupational information, there are also many occupation-related classifications at home and abroad. It is also very difficult to effectively use this part of information. So far, no good solutions have been

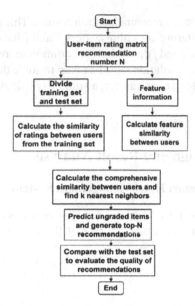

Fig. 5. Recommendation process based on user's comprehensive similarity algorithm

found, so the article Only the user's age and gender information are introduced into the similarity of user characteristics. The algorithm divides the user's feature similarity into two basic parts, namely gender similarity and age similarity. Since these two human factors have basically the same influence on users' interest preferences, the weight of the information is 50%, So the calculation formula of feature similarity is as formula (2):

$$sim_f(i,j) = \frac{1}{2}\left[sim_g(i,j) + sim_a(i,j)\right] \tag{2}$$

Here, $sim_g(i,j)$ is the gender similarity, $sim_a(i,j)$ is the age similarity.
Define the gender similarity $sim_g(i,j)$ of users i and j as:

$$sim_g(i,j) = \begin{cases} 1 & i \; and \; j \; have \; the \; same \; gender \\ 0 & otherwise \end{cases} \tag{3}$$

Define the age similarity $sim_a(i,j)$ of users i and j as:

$$sim_a(i,j) = \begin{cases} 1 & |A_i - A_j| \le 5 \\ \frac{5}{|A_i-A_j|} & otherwise \end{cases} \tag{4}$$

Here, A_i is the age of user i.

User Rating Similarity. Lu et al. [12] proposed the transfer of similarity based on the transferability of trust relationships, and used the transfer of similarity to reduce the impact of data sparseness on the recommendation results. This situation often occurs in user-based collaborative filtering algorithms: users i and j have a high similarity with the third user k, but because i and j do not have a common score, the similarity between i and j cannot be calculated. A solution must be taken to solve the problem. To solve this problem, using the principle of trust transfer, a similarity calculation based on common neighbors is proposed.

3   Experimental Design and Result Analysis

3.1   Overall Results of Smart Hotel Management System

The equipment has been used in a large number of sites and is currently operating well. We have made statistics on the occupancy rate of the four hotels, and the results are shown in Fig. 6.

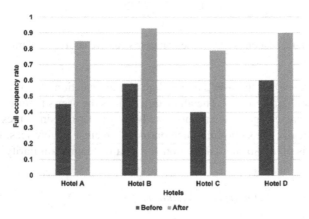

Fig. 6. The occupancy rate of four hotels before and after using the smart hotel management system

Figure 6 shows that the occupancy rate of the hotel rooms currently installed with this system has increased by approximately 0.38. From the above data, the social value brought by the system is considerable, so there is a large market waiting for us to explore.

3.2   Experimental Design and Result Analysis of Personalized Movie Recommendation System for Smart Hotel Guest Rooms

Experimental Design of Collaborative Filtering Algorithm Based on User Comprehensive Similarity

Dataset. The experiment uses the MovieLens data set provided by the School of Computer Science and Engineering at the University of Minnesota in the United States, which is a data set specifically used to study collaborative filtering algorithms. The MovieLens data set provides basic information of 943 users, including age, gender, occupation and zip code. Among them, the user's occupation involves 21 types, including students, writers, salespeople, programmers, retirees, etc.; information on 1682 movies, Including movie name, release date, genre and other information. There are more than ten types of movies, such as action movies, adventure movies, romantic dramas, etc.; among them, there are 100,000 score records, and these scores come from all users, and any one Users have rated at least 20 movies. The scores are divided into 5 levels, with values of 1, 2, 3, 4, and 5. The score indicates the degree of preference. The lower the score, the lower the preference for Chengdu. The data set is randomly divided into 5 parts, using the 5-fold crossover method, one of which is selected in turn as the test set, and the remaining 4 parts are used as the training set to generate recommendation predictions and then measure the quality of recommendation.

Quality Evaluation. We use one of the most commonly used indicators Mean Absolute Error (MAE) for measuring recommended accuracy. The mean absolute error is the average of the absolute values of the deviations of all single predicted values from the arithmetic mean, and can be define as

$$MAE = \frac{1}{n} \sum_{i=1}^{n} |P_{i,c} - R_{i,,c}| \tag{5}$$

Here, $P_{i,c}$ represents predicted rating, n is number of predicted items.

After the average absolute error is obtained, the smaller the value of the average absolute error, the better the recommended effect.

Experimental Results of Collaborative Filtering Algorithm Based on User's Comprehensive Similarity. According to the division of the data set, the experiment is carried out 10, 20, 30, 40 and 50 times, each time using 4 of the data set (80%) as the training set, and the remaining 1 (20%) as the test set. Experiment result takes the average of 5 tests. The number of inner neighbors $k = 80$, outer neighbors $M = 30$, and $\lambda = 0.2$ are empirically selected in this experiment. We compare the proposed collaborative filtering algorithm based on user comprehensive similarity with the traditional user-based collaborative filtering algorithm (UBCF) and the collaborative filtering algorithm based on common nearest neighbor (CNBCF), and the result of average absolute error of the three under different numbers of external neighbors is shown in Fig. 7.

It can be seen from Fig. 7 that the recommendation accuracy of the collaborative filtering algorithm is the highest among the three algorithms, while the user-based collaborative filtering algorithm has the lowest accuracy. In summary, the collaborative filtering algorithm based on user comprehensive similarity is better than others.

Experimental Design of Personalized Movie Recommendation System for Smart Hotel Guest Room. It is stipulated that when the user rating is greater than or equal to 3, the user is considered to like the movie. In the experiment, 15 users were randomly selected from the system as experimental subjects, and the recommended list length was 20, and the recommendation accuracy and recall rate of the recommendation system were calculated. Generally, for the recommendation performance test of the recommendation system, the evaluation index of the commonly used recommendation system includes the accuracy rate, the recall rate, and the coverage rate.

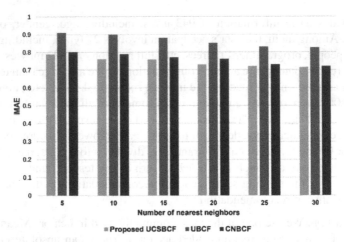

Fig. 7. Comparison results of the average absolute error of the three algorithms under different numbers of external neighbors

(1) Accuracy. Accuracy refers to the length of the total list of items recommended by the user. It can be defined as

$$P = \frac{N_u}{L} \tag{6}$$

Here, L represents the length of the recommendation list, N_u represents the number of movies that the user u likes in the recommendation list.

(2) Recall. It can be defined as

$$R = \frac{M}{N} \tag{7}$$

Here, M represents the number of movies the user likes in the recommendation list, and N represents the total number of movies watched by the user.

Analysis of Experimental Results of Personalized Movie Recommendation System for Smart Hotel Guest Rooms

From the results in Table 1, the recommendation system based on the user's comprehensive similarity of collaborative filtering algorithm has improved accuracy and recall rate compared with the other two algorithms, and the hybrid recommendation effect is better than the user-based collaborative filtering algorithm.

Table 1. Recommendation system recommends accuracy and recall results

Measures	Algorithms		
	UCSBCF	UBCF	CNBCF
Accuracy	0.8566	0.5434	0.7643
Recall	0.7556	0.4532	0.6875

4   Conclusion

In order to solve the shortcomings of traditional hotel management, this article designed a smart system suitable for use in the hotel management. The equipment has been used in a large number of sites and is currently operating well.

Aiming at the data sparse problem of traditional movie recommendation systems in smart hotel management, this chapter proposes a collaborative filtering algorithm based on user comprehensive similarity. The experimental results show that the collaborative filtering algorithm based on user comprehensive similarity has good recommendation quality in the case of sparse data.

References

1. Pan, H., Cai, R., Gu, T.: Smart hotel construction and image recognition—taking Nanjing as an example. Northern Econ. **11**, 74–75 (2014)
2. Liu, S.: High-Brightness LED Lighting and Switching Power Supply. China Electric Power Press, Beijing (2009)
3. Chen, H., Cui, L., Xie, K.: Comparative research on the architecture and implementation methods of the Internet of Things. J. Comput. **01**, 168–188 (2013)
4. Bennett, K.P., Fayyad, U.M., Geiger, D.: Density-based indexing for approximate nearest neighbor queries. In: Proceedings of 5th International Conference on Knowledge Discovery and Data Mining (KDD99), pp. 233–243. ACM Press (1999)
5. Stawar, B., Karypis, J., Konstan, J., Riedl, J.: Item-based collaborative filtering recommendation algorithms. In: Proceedings of the 10th International World Wide Web Conference, pp. 285–295 (2001)
6. Dempster, A., Laird, N., Rubin, D.: Maximum likelihood from incomplete data via the EM algorithm. J. Roy. Stat. Soc. **39**(1), 1–38 (1977)
7. Thiesson, B., Meek, C., Chickering, M., et al.: Learning mixtures of DAG models. In: Proceedings of the Fourteenth Conference on Uncertainty in Artificial Intelligence, pp. 504–513 (1998)
8. Massa, P., Avesani, P.: Trust-aware recommender systems. In: Proceedings of the 2007 ACM Conference on Recommender Systems (2007)
9. Rao, J.: Application of MODBUS communication protocol in automatic monitoring of water level. Electron. Technol. Softw. Eng. (2016)
10. Jiang, C., Wang, H., Ling, Z., Lu, W.: Modbus/TCP multi-layer access control filtering technology. Autom. Instrum. **37**, 76–80 (2016)
11. Hou, G., Gao, J., Xu, K., Wu, Y.: Design and realization of electric power dispatching based on remote monitoring technology. Electron. Des. Eng. (2016)
12. Lu, Z.: Research on collaborative filtering recommendation strategy based on trust relationship. Electron. Des. Eng. (2017)

Power Grid Missing Data Filling Method Based on Historical Data Mining Assisted Multi-dimensional Scenario Analysis

Guangyu Chen[1], Zhengyang Zhu[1]([✉]), Li Yang[2], Gang Lin[3], Yujiao Yun[1], and Peng Jiang[1]

[1] School of Electric Power Engineering, Nanjing Institute of Technology, Nanjing 211167, Jiangsu, China
[2] State Grid Fujian Electric Power Company, Fujian 350000, China
[3] State Grid Fujian Electric Power Company, Quanzhou Power Supply Company, Fujian 362000, China

Abstract. In recent years, power grid data missing which caused by manual operation error and equipment failure often occurs, bringing difficulties to power grid big data analysis. In order to solve the problem that the accuracy of grid data filling is insufficient, a method of grid missing data filling based on historical data mining assisted multi-dimensional scenario analysis is proposed. Firstly, the highly correlated attribute data are selected as the reference basis for missing attribute data filling through the Fluctuation cross-correlation Analysis (FCCA), and the correlation degree is further quantified by combining weights. Secondly, based on load scenario analysis, the similarity between data sources is measured by Dynamic Time Warping (DTW). Finally, combined with DTW and combined weight, the date which has the most similar data was found, and use the same time period data of it to fill the missing data. The simulation results show that the proposed data filling method has higher accuracy.

Keywords: Missing data filling strategy · Fluctuation cross-correlation analysis · Entropy weight analysis · Scenario analysis · Dynamic time warping distance

1 Introduction

In the era of big data, smart power grid is a development direction of China's power industry. The ultimate goal of smart power grid is to monitor the production and power consumption process of the whole power grid in real time to ensure the reliability of power grid operation. Data missing is an unavoidable problem in smart grid. There are various reasons for data loss, such as the failure of equipment to collect data during the collection process, or the loss of data during the uploading process due to communication failure. In addition to device reasons, human operations may also result in data missing [1, 2]. Missing data will reduce sample information and increase the complexity of statistical analysis. If not processed or improperly processed, meaningful information cannot be extracted, or even error information can be extracted [3]. Therefore, how to

© Springer Nature Singapore Pte Ltd. 2022
Y. Tian et al. (Eds.): ICBDS 2021, CCIS 1563, pp. 360–371, 2022.
https://doi.org/10.1007/978-981-19-0852-1_27

correctly and efficiently process missing data and restore complete data becomes the key to data analysis [4, 5].

There are two main methods to deal with missing data: delete method and fill method. For the data set with missing data, the deletion method directly deletes the incomplete data set, but it also loses the opportunity to find meaningful implied information, resulting in huge loss. The filling method is to select an appropriate value to replace the missing part of the data set, so as to form a complete data set. This kind of method needs to ensure the accuracy of filling data and avoid distortion as far as possible. Literature [6] mentions three main types of data missing: (1) missing completely at random (MCAR), where missing data do not depend on observed data. (2) missing at random (MAR), where missing data only depends on the observed instance data. (3) missing not at random (MNAR), where the missing data depends on the unobserved data. Literature [7] uses the K-NN algorithm to speculate the class label of the test set through the labels of K nearest neighbors of it. K-NN involves two problems: the number of neighbors K and distance measurement D. If the number of neighbors is small, outliers may affect the result, while a large number of neighbors may suffer from irrelevant data [8–10]. Literature [11] proposes a machine learning framework containing two learning models, corresponding to two conditions of missing data. The framework designs a spatio-temporal correlation method for feature entire missing condition and a feature correlation method for feature partial missing condition, in order to fill the missing data.

Based on the correlation between attribute in the power grid, we propose a missing data filling method based on historical data mining assisted multi-dimensional scenario analysis. Firstly, the Fluctuation Cross-Correlation Analysis (FCCA) was used to select the attribute data with strong correlation as the reference basis for filling the missing attribute data and the Entropy Weight Method (EWM) was used to match the selected strong correlation attributes with corresponding combination weights to further quantify the correlation degree between attributes. Secondly, on the basis of load scenario analysis, Dynamic Time Warping (DTW) is used to measure the data similarity of each attribute between the missing date and the historical data, combined with the combination weights, the date with the most comprehensively similar data is found, and use the same time period data of it to fill the missing data. The case analysis uses a grid load data set which is randomly deleted one or several data, and the accuracy of the proposed algorithm is compared with the Expectation-Maximum (EM) algorithm. The results show that the proposed method can effectively fill the missing data of the grid.

2 The Framework of Grid Missing Data Filling Based on Historical Data Analysis

Existing missing data filling methods mostly operate from the perspective of one dimension, which only consider the missing data attribute itself, and they did not take advantage of the historical data, also ignoring the correlation between different data attributes. Based on the situation above, we propose a missing data filling method based on historical data from the correlation analysis of various attributes. Firstly, the correlation degree between each attribute and the attribute with missing data is calculated by using the Fluctuation Cross-Correlation Analysis algorithm, with a threshold in order to extract the strongly correlated attribute, and the combined weight of each attribute is calculated to quantify the correlation degree between attributes. Secondly, the selection range of historical data is narrowed and the selection process is optimized through the load scenario analysis. Thirdly, the similarity between the data was calculated by Dynamic Time Warping distance, and the comprehensive similarity of the data was calculated with DTW and combination weights. The data at the same time of the date which has the highest comprehensive similarity was selected to replace the missing data. The main process of filling the missing data of power grid based on historical data analysis is shown in the figure below (Fig. 1).

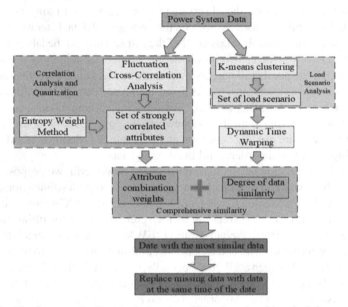

Fig. 1. The framework of grid missing data filling based on historical data analysis

3   Multi-attribute Correlation Analysis Based on Fluctuation Cross-Correlation Algorithm

3.1   Correlation Analysis Based on Fluctuation Cross-Correlation Coefficient

In order to extend the Fluctuation Analysis algorithm to study the correlation of two time variables, the Fluctuation cross-correlation Analysis (FCCA) algorithm was proposed. The fluctuation cross-correlation coefficient represents the change of the difference between the values of two time series with the change of time difference. In the Detrended Cross-Correlation Analysis (DCCA) algorithm, the trend of the observed values at a particular time point t is only affected by other observed values in the same interval. Because DCCA is fitted in subsection intervals, the observed values outside this interval do not affect the observed values at this point t. However, the FCCA algorithm extends the range of time axis and considers this problem in a deeper time width, without partitioning and looking for the degree of interaction between observed values in the series in its entirety [12].

Take a time sequence of active power variables $\{P_{xi}, i = 1, 2, ..., N\}$ and a time sequence of voltage variables $\{U_{yi}, i = 1, 2, ..., N\}$ with equal time span range as an example. First, calculate the fluctuation outline of the two time series respectively.

$$
\begin{aligned}
\Delta P_x(l) &= \sum_{i=1}^{l} (\Gamma_{xi} - \overline{P_x}), l = 1, 2, \cdots, N \\
\Delta U_y(l) &= \sum_{i=1}^{l} (U_{yi} - \overline{U_y}), l = 1, 2, \cdots, N
\end{aligned}
\tag{1}
$$

Where l is the length of sampling step. $\Delta P_x(l)$ and $\Delta U_y(l)$ are the fluctuation outline of P_{xi} and U_{yi} in the sampling step l respectively; $\overline{P_x}$ and $\overline{U_y}$ are the mean of P_x and U_y respectively; N is the length of time sequence.

Calculate the forward difference which represents the autocorrelation of P_x and U_y respectively:

$$
\begin{aligned}
\Delta P_x(l, l_0) &= P_x(l_0 + l) - P_x(l_0), l_0 = 1, 2, \cdots, N - l \\
\Delta U_y(l, l_0) &= U_y(l_0 + l) - U_y(l_0), l_0 = 1, 2, \cdots, N - l
\end{aligned}
\tag{2}
$$

Where $l = 1, 2, ..., N - 1$. For each sampling step, there are $l_0 = N - l$ difference. $\Delta P_x(l, l_0)$ and $\Delta U_y(l, l_0)$ is the forward difference of P_x and U_y at l_0 in the sampling step l respectively.

Calculate the covariance of P_x and U_y:

$$
C_{xy}(l) = \sqrt{\left[\Delta P_x(l, l_0) - \overline{\Delta P_x(l, l_0)}\right] \times \left[\Delta U_y(l, l_0) - \overline{\Delta U_y(l, l_0)}\right]}
\tag{3}
$$

$$
\begin{aligned}
\overline{\Delta P_x(l, l_0)} &= \frac{1}{N-l} \sum_{l_0}^{N-l} \Delta P_x(l, l_0) \\
\overline{\Delta U_y(l, l_0)} &= \frac{1}{N-l} \sum_{l_0}^{N-l} \Delta U_y(l, l_0)
\end{aligned}
\tag{4}
$$

Where $C_{xy}(l)$ is the covariance of P_x and U_y. When there are some correlation between P_x and U_y, $C_{xy}(l)$ satisfies a power law distribution $C_{xy}(l) \sim m^{h_{xy}}$, where h_{xy} fluctuation cross-correlation coefficient of P_x and U_y, which represents the correlation degree. By fitting the power law distribution, h_{xy} is obtained. When $h_{xy} = 0$, P_x and U_y are irrelevant; When $h_{xy} > 0$, P_x and U_y have positive correlation; When $h_{xy} < 0$, P_x and U_y have negative correlation. The bigger h_{xy} is, the correlation degree of P_x and U_y is higher. When using FCCA coefficient to represent the correlation between voltage, current, active power and reactive power, the bigger h_{xy} is, the correlation degree of two attributes is higher.

3.2 Combination Weight Calculation of Multi-dimensional Correlation Attribute Based on Entropy Weight Analysis

In order to avoid attribute data which have low correlation influencing the filling results, the threshold of is set up. If the fluctuation cross-correlation coefficient of the attribute with missing data and another attribute is lower than the threshold, the reference value of this attribute is low and this attribute should be abandoned; if the coefficient is greater than the set threshold, the reference value of this attribute is high and this attribute should be reserved. After the screen progress, the remaining M attributes are called *Know* attributes, which are numbered from 1 to M, and the attribute with missing data is called *Unknow* attribute.

In power grid data, the correlation between *Know* attribute data and *Unknow* attribute data is different, so the reference and utilization value of them are different. Therefore, the combined weights of *Unknow* attributes need to be calculated to ensure reasonable utilization of historical data [13]. The larger the fluctuation cross-correlation coefficient is, the stronger the correlation between *Know* attribute and *Unknow* attribute is, and so this *Know* attribute should have a higher weight.

Calculate the combination weight w_j between each *Know* attribute j and *Unknow* attribute:

$$w_j = \frac{c_j}{\sum_{j=1}^{M} c_j}$$
$$\sum_{j=1}^{M} w_j = 1$$

(5)

Where M is the amount of *Know* attribute. $j = 1, 2, \cdots, M$, c_j is the fluctuation cross-correlation coefficient of *Know* attribute j and *Unknow* attribute.

4 Comprehensive Data Similarity Calculation Based on Load Scenario Analysis

4.1 Load Scenario Division Based on K-means Clustering

The filling of missing data needs to traverse all the longitudinal historical data of the node containing missing data, i.e. at a different date but the same time period of the historical data. If the historical data set is too big, the computational cost is correspondingly expensive. It has become another key of our research that how to reduce historical data samples, which reduces the amount of calculation to improve efficiency.

K-means clustering algorithm, which measure data similarity by Euclidean distance, uses error sum of squares criterion as clustering criterion [14]. The 4 steps of clustering progress are as follow:

(1) Initializing: confirm the amount of clusters k and the initial cluster centers;
(2) Cluster division: calculate the distance between N samples and k cluster centers and distribute N samples to the nearest cluster center, and form k clusters;
(3) Solve the cluster center: calculate the mean value of all objects of each cluster, which is used for new cluster centers of k clusters;
(4) Convergence judgment: when the new cluster centers have little difference with the old one, or the difference is smaller than a threshold, the convergence of algorithm is stable, clustering progress is over.

The steps of load scene division based on K-means clustering are as follows: First, using the load active power value as the reference, the active power curves of each load with sampling interval of 15min are drawn and clustered, which can be divided into three categories in total: Working days, regular rest days and special holidays. Second, calculate the distance between load curve of the date containing *Unknow* attribute and three cluster centers, and finally classify it into the closest cluster, so as to find H dates of the same scenario for the date containing *Unknow* attribute in the historical data of power grid. The dates with *Unknow* attributes are called missing dates, and the found H dates are called similar dates. The following figure shows the scenario analysis flow of the missing date (Fig. 2).

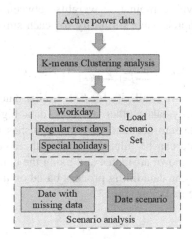

Fig. 2. The scenario analysis flow of the missing date

4.2 Comprehensive Similarity Calculation of Historical Data Based on Dynamic Time Warping

For the calculation of comprehensive similarity of historical data, the time period of *Unknow* attribute data in the missing date is determined first, and then the same time period of each similar date is selected accordingly. Dynamic Time Warping (DTW) was used to measure the similarity between the *know* attribute data of missing dates and those data of similar dates.

Dynamic Time Warping (DTW) distance pairs different time elements of two time sequences through dynamic time planning, and finds the most appropriate correspondence between the two time sequences. By minimizing the distance between two time sequences, the algorithm can well measure the overall shape similarity between time sequences [15].

Since the dynamic time warping distance is used to measure the similarity degree of two time sequences, and the data missing occurs at a certain time, in order to preserve the integrity of data and symmetry of calculation, we set the time when the missing attribute data occurs as time t_n, and take n time points forward and backward from t_n, i.e. $t_{n+1}, t_{n+2}, \cdots, t_{2n}$ and $t_{n-1}, t_{n-2}, \cdots, t_0$, so the time period $(t_0, \cdots, t_{2n})$ which contain the missing attribute data is formed, with $2n + 1$ time points total. Denote M *Know* attributes as $A_1, A_2, \cdots, A_M$ and *Unknow* attribute as A_0.

Denote *Know* attribute data $A_1, A_2, \cdots, A_M$ at $t_0, t_1, t_2, \cdots, t_{2n}$ in h-th similar date as $D_{(1,h)}, D_{(2,h)}, \cdots D_{(M,h)}$, $D_{(j,h)} = \sum_{g=0}^{2n} d_{(j,h,g)}$, $d_{(j,h,g)}$ represents data of *Know* attribute A_j at time t_g in h-th similar date, $j = 1, 2, \cdots, M$, $h = 1, 2, \cdots, H$, $g = 0, 1, 2, \cdots, 2n$.

Measure the similarity $S_{(j,h)}$ between $D_{(j,h)}$ (data of *Know* attribute A_j at time $t_0, t_1, t_2, \cdots, t_{2n}$ in h-th similar date) and $D_{(j,p)}$ (data of *Know* attribute A_j at time $t_0, t_1, t_2, \cdots, t_{2n}$ in missing date) with Dynamic Time Warping distance, where p means missing date. Combined with combination weights between each *Know* attribute and *Unknow* attribute, the comprehensive similarity for each similar date is calculated by Eq. (6).

$$C_h = \sum_{j=1}^{M} \sum_{h=1}^{H} w_j \times S_{(j,h)} \tag{6}$$

Where C_h is the comprehensive similarity for h-th similar date.

Comprehensive similarity takes other attribute data highly associated with the attribute with missing data into account, and distinguishes the importance of other attributes. The missing data can be filled by finding the date with the highest comprehensive similarity of unknown attributes and using the data at the same time of the most similar date. The missing data filling process based on the dynamic time-bending distance is shown in the figure below (Fig. 3).

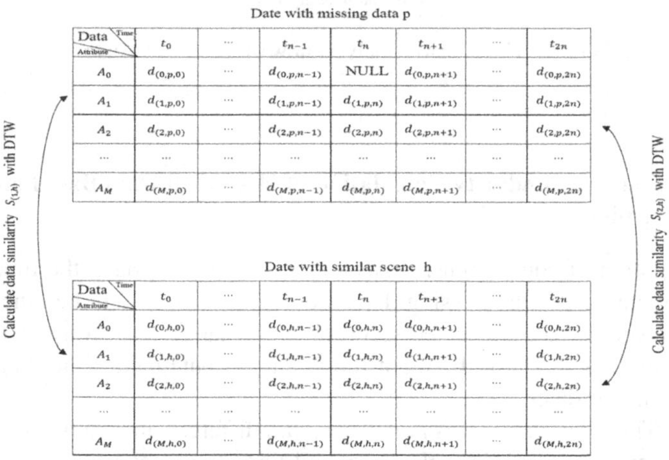

Fig. 3. Diagram of missing data filling

5 Case Experiment and Analysis

5.1 Case Background Introduction

In order to verify the validity and rationality of the method proposed in this paper, the actual data of a regional power grid for about 200 days was taken as the experimental object. The sampling interval of load data was 15min. The monitoring values included active power, reactive power, low-voltage side current, power factor and outlet side voltage, and the missing data filling object was the value of outlet side voltage. The computer used in the experiment included CPU: AMD Ryzen 5 3500X six core processor, 16 GB RAM, and MatlabR2020a software.

5.2 The Comparison Between FCCA and Pearson Correlation Analysis

Firstly, the fluctuation cross-correlation coefficients between voltage and current, voltage and active power, voltage and reactive power, voltage and power factor is calculated by fluctuation cross-correlation analysis algorithm. Meanwhile, Pearson correlation coefficients of those parameter pairs above were calculated and compared as well. The results of the two algorithms are shown as the Table 1 below.

Table 1. The calculation results of FCCA and Pearson algorithm

Attribute pair	Pearson correlation coefficient	Fluctuation cross-correlation coefficient
Voltage-Current	0.22	0.68
Voltage-Active power	0.32	0.66
Voltage-Reactive power	0.30	0.85
Voltage-Power factor	0.18	0.47

According to the results of Pearson algorithm, voltage and current, voltage and active power, voltage and reactive power, voltage and power factor are all weakly correlated, which does not match practical experience. In contrast, the fluctuation cross-correlation analysis algorithm is based on the fluctuation analysis and mainly compares the development of the change trend between the two variables. According to the results, the current, active power and reactive power all have high correlation with voltage. We set the threshold of the number of fluctuation correlations as 0.6, so the 'power factor' attribute is abandoned. The combination weight results of current, active power and reactive power are shown in the Table 2 below.

Table 2. The calculation results of combination weight

Attribute	Combination weight
Current	0.31
Active power	0.30
Reactive power	0.39

5.3 Clustering Analysis of Load Curves

The K-means clustering algorithm is used to conduct clustering analysis on the samples. Due to the relatively small number of samples and scenarios, set the number of clustering centers $k = 3$, the load curves can be divided into three scenarios: working days, regular rest days and special holidays. The distribution of load curves before clustering is shown in the figure below (See Fig. 4). The distribution of load curves after clustering is shown in the figure below (See Fig. 5).

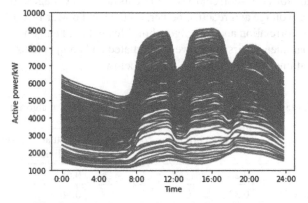

Fig. 4. Load curves distribution before clustering

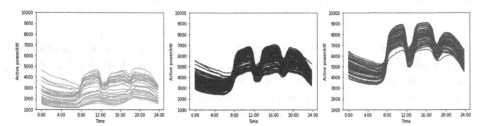

Fig. 5. Load curves distribution after clustering, from left to right: special holidays, regular rest days and working days

According to the cluster result, 'working days' scenario includes 106 days, 'regular rest days' scenario includes 68 days, 'special holidays' scenario includes 27 days. As we can see, the difference between clusters is obvious, and the curve trend within the cluster is basically consistent.

5.4 Comprehensive Similarity Calculation of Historical Data

Firstly, a voltage data is randomly deleted. After searching, the deleted voltage data was collected at 12:45 on August 12, and the load active power curve on August 12 is retrieved. Through the above cluster analysis, it is found that the load scenario on August 12 belongs to the first type of load scenario, i.e. working days. Therefore, all

106 daily load curves under the 'working days' scenario were retrieved to participate in the comprehensive similarity calculation. The partial results of calculating dynamic time bending distance and comprehensive similarity are shown in the Table 3 below.

Table 3. The calculation results of DTW and comprehensive similarity

Date	DTW (active power)	DTW (reactive power)	DTW (current)	Comprehensive similarity
July 24	3.2193	6.1305	2.4901	4.13075
July 2	3.5670	6.2966	2.3150	4.2434
June 19	3.1398	7.1904	2.2488	4.4471
May 31	5.8232	9.5362	3.1642	6.44698
June 9	6.9957	10.2949	3.5835	7.61126
...	...	...	...	...

We find the date with the largest comprehensive similarity by sorting the comprehensive similarity, which is July 24, and the data collected at 12:45 on July 24 was finally selected to fill the original missing data.

5.5 Performance Comparison of Different Filling Methods

In order to verify the effectiveness of the proposed method, a random deletion method was adopted. Firstly, only one voltage data was deleted, and the other data were reserved. The traditional Expectation Maximization Algorithm (EM) was selected for comparative analysis under this situation. Compare the accuracy of the proposed method and the EM algorithm, the result shows that the proposed method is relative better in missing data filling accuracy than the EM algorithm. The result of experiment is shown in the figure below (Fig. 6).

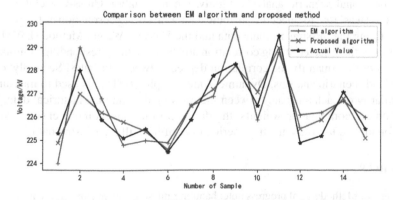

Fig. 6. Comparison of EM algorithm and proposed method

Continuously increase the proportion of deleted voltage data to 1%, 3%, 5%, 10%, 20%, 25%, and 30% of the voltage data set. Filling accuracy was used to evaluate the filling results under different voltages and other relative missing degrees. The evaluation method of filling accuracy δ was as follows: $\delta = \frac{n_r}{n} \times 100\%$, where n_r is the number of qualified estimates, n is the number of missing data.

In order to ensure the reliability of the experimental results, five calculations were made under different situation, and the average value of the five calculations was taken as the final experimental result. The final results show that with the continuous improvement of data missing rate, the accuracy of proposed filling method gradually decreases, but there is still a certain improvement compared with EM algorithm (See Fig. 7). Therefore, this method has a good filling effect when there are only a few or low proportion of data missing.

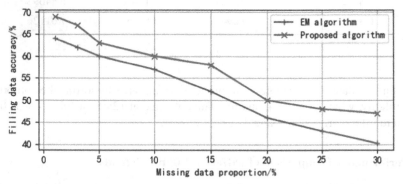

Fig. 7. Comparison of filling accuracy between EM algorithm and the proposed method under different data missing rates

6 Conclusion

We propose a missing data filling method based on historical data mining assisted multi-dimensional scenario analysis. Firstly, the Fluctuation Cross-Correlation Analysis (FCCA) was used to select the attribute data with strong correlation as the reference basis for filling the missing attribute data and the Entropy Weight Method (EWM) was used to match the selected strong correlation attributes with corresponding combination weights to further quantify the correlation degree between attributes. Secondly, on the basis of load scenario analysis, Dynamic Time Warping (DTW) is used to measure the data similarity of each attribute between the missing date and the historical data, combined with the combination weights, the date with the most comprehensively similar data is found, and use the same time period data of it to fill the missing data.

References

1. Zhang, N.: Methodolgical progress note: handling missing data in clinical research. J. Hosp. Med. **14**(4), 237–239 (2020)

2. Zhao, Y.: Statistical inference for missing data mechanisms. Stat. Med. **39**(1), 4325–4333 (2020)
3. Venugopalan, J., Chanani, N., et al.: Novel data imputation for multiple types of missing data in intensive care units. J. Biomed. Health Inf. **23**(3), 1243–1250 (2019)
4. Mahmud, M.S., Huang, J.Z., et al.: A survey of data partitioning and sampling methods to support big data analysis. Big Data Min. Anal. **3**(2), 85–101 (2020)
5. Markovsky, I.: A missing data approach to data-driven filtering and control. IEEE Trans. Autom. Control **62**(4), 1972–1978 (2017)
6. Panda, B.S., Adhikari, R.K.: A method for classification of missing values using data mining techniques. In: International Conference on Computer Science, Engineering and Applications (ICCSEA), pp. 1–5. IEEE (2020)
7. Xiao, J.L.: SVM and KNN ensemble learning for traffic incident detection. Physica A **517**, 29–35 (2019)
8. Zhang, S., Li, X., Zong, M., Zhu, X., Wang, R.: Efficient kNN classification with different numbers of nearest neighbors. IEEE Trans. Neural Netw. Learn. Syst. **29**(5), 1774–1785 (2018)
9. Marchang, N., Tripathi, R.: KNN-ST: exploiting spatio-temporal correlation for missing data inference in environmental crowd sensing. IEEE Sens. J. **21**(4), 3429–3436 (2021)
10. Purwar, A., Singh, S.K.: Hybrid prediction model with missing value imputation for medical data. Expert Syst. Appl. **42**(13), 5621–5631 (2015)
11. Sun, C., Chen, Y., et al.: Imputation of missing data from offshore wind farms using spatio-temporal correlation and feature correlation. Energy **229**(1), 161–173 (2021)
12. Huawei, H., Ning, S., et al.: Alarm root-cause identification for petrochemical process system based on fluctuation correlation analysis. In: Chinese Control and Decision Conference (CCDC), pp. 373–376 (2019)
13. Lu, C., Li, L., et al.: Application of combination weighting method to weight calculation in performance evaluation of ICT. In: 15th International Conference on Advanced Learning Technologies, pp. 258–259. IEEE (2015)
14. Wang, X., Jiao, Y., et al.: Estimation of clusters number and initial centers of k-means algorithm using watershed method. In: 14th International Symposium on Distributed Computing and Applications for Business Engineering and Science (DCABES), pp. 505–508 (2015)
15. Hong, J.Y., Park, S.H., et al.: Segmented dynamic time warping based signal pattern classification. In: International Conference on Computational Science and Engineering (CSE) and International Conference on Embedded and Ubiquitous Computing (EUC), pp. 263–265. IEEE (2019)

The Training Mode of Experimental Talents in Colleges and Universities Based on Big Data

Yunhai Zhao[✉]

Shaanxi Radio and Television University, Xi'an 710119, China

Abstract. As the main position of talent training, university laboratories bear the educational responsibility of carrying out practical activities. In order to better play the educational role of laboratories, analyze the status quo of laboratory management and innovative talent training in colleges and universities, and propose a big data-based experimental talent training model in colleges and universities based on the main problems, in order to provide reference for college educators and managers and reference. Specifically, we first perform statistics on traditional talent training models from different perspectives, then reduce the collected data through big data reduction methods, and then use machine learning-related models to analyze the obtained data, and finally get the corresponding conclusion.

Keywords: Talent training · Big data · Machine learning

1 Introduction

For a long time, university laboratories have been the core base for the application of innovative technologies. Strengthening university laboratory management and talent training can not only improve the overall educational management quality of universities, but also provide an important source of strength for technology accumulation [1]. Therefore, in-depth analysis of the current situation of university laboratory management, using innovative management concepts and methods to strengthen the training of talents, continuously improving the management level and talent training quality of universities, creating a more free and relaxed experimental environment, and providing a solid foundation for talent training [2–4].

Under the background of the comprehensive implementation of education reform, the main contradictions in the practice of university laboratory management have become increasingly prominent. While fully committed to satisfying learning needs, the construction of scientific research functions of the laboratory is ignored, resulting in the failure of university laboratories to meet teaching and Two aspects of scientific research needs. One of the reasons is that in order to give full play to its role, university laboratories have a more reasonable operation mode, and various scientific research projects are selected as the main scientific research objects every year, which puts forward higher requirements for the functions of the laboratory itself. Requirements, need to have equipment and instruments for scientific research. Second, with the rapid development of education, the number of students in China's universities has increased in recent years, and

Y. Tian et al. (Eds.): ICBDS 2021, CCIS 1563, pp. 372–379, 2022.
https://doi.org/10.1007/978-981-19-0852-1_28

the society's demand for applied talents has also increased. As a result, university laboratories have to expand their scale and use new experimental teaching methods to train Students' hands-on and practical ability to meet the needs of educational development. However, in reality, the education and teaching funds of major universities in our country are limited, and they cannot take into account a large number of teaching courses while undertaking scientific research projects. This results in certain difficulties in the management and operation of university laboratories, which affects their use in a new environment. Innovation and development.

In the era of big data, the processing of data and the analysis of the density of knowledge contained in it cannot obtain accurate results only by relying on traditional sampling analysis [5]. Therefore, in this process, it is necessary to combine statistical theory and rationally apply statistical thinking to break the correctness. The tradition of relying on a small number of data samples uses statistical tools to perform statistical analysis on all data information, and further studies the valuable information embodied in the data. In terms of data processing, big data requires people to properly handle a large amount of messy data [5]. Do not pursue the accuracy of the data excessively, but analyze the changes of the data through statistical tools to provide a certain reference value for related decision-making. Big data processing does not have strict requirements for data accuracy. Data with errors is more conducive to discovering hidden laws and helping to understand the overall situation. More complex and disordered data can better reflect the real situation.

Data analysis refers to the classification and statistics of a large amount of data in the era of big data, followed by analysis through relevant information technology, and through induction and summary, the valuable data is extracted, and these data and unprocessed data are analyzed. Big data uses statistical tools to perform statistical analysis of data [6, 7]. There is a clear difference between valuable information mining and traditional sampling analysis. It uses more statistical thinking to get rid of the traditional dependence on data samples, and the application is more. A wide range of ways to collect and process data and information. For most of the data, the effective value it contains is reflected in the data analysis, so we must pay attention to the accumulation of data and refine the data processing process. In the era of big data, the fluidity of data is relatively strong, and the amount of data will accumulate over time. Data must be streamlined and regenerated to increase the value of valuable data and connect closely connected data. Carry out effective integration, even if problems are discovered and dealt with.

In order to solve the appeal problem, this paper designs a personalized recommendation system architecture that can handle the education field through the research of recommendation systems and key technologies in a big data environment, and realizes a personalized recommendation system based on educational resources. In this architecture, based on the content and collaborative hybrid recommendation algorithm, we study a flexible, reliable, high-performance product personalized recommendation system architecture, which can store and process data, and can recommend in real time, and study personalized recommendation engines. Data preprocessing, data mining, model construction and design.

2 Traditional Talent Training Model

In terms of talent training, classroom teaching, practical teaching, and second classroom are the three pillars of data science and big data technology, which are equally important, as shown in Fig. 1.

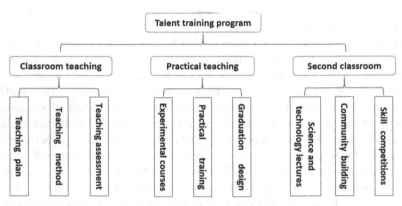

Fig. 1. Schematic diagram of talent training program

In classroom teaching, the efficiency of classroom teaching is mainly improved through measures such as the formulation of teaching plans, the integration of multiple teaching methods, and the regular assessment of teaching effects. In the practical teaching, in addition to experimental course teaching and graduation design, in order to meet the needs of the era of big data, actively promote students to enter the banking, insurance, securities and other fields of enterprises for internships, and cultivate students' hands-on ability and practical working ability. In addition, attach importance to the training role of the second classroom, create various opportunities for students to participate in scientific research lectures by domestic and foreign big data experts, participate in the construction of innovation studios, participate in computer audits, basic computer knowledge, "Internet +" , "Blue Bridge Cup" Wait for the information technology talent contest. Let the profession adapt to the actual jobs of big data companies as soon as possible, and shorten the distance between school talent training and the employment of big data-related companies.

3 Design of Intelligent Teaching System Based on Big Data Analysis Technology

Designing intelligent teaching of big data analysis technology with multi-layer system structure system, the overall function structure of the system is shown in Fig. 2.

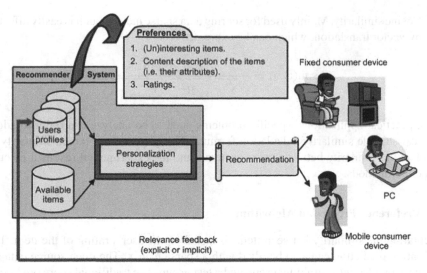

Fig. 2. Big data recommendation module structure

3.1   Collaborative Filtering Recommendation Algorithm

The main process of implementing the item-based collaborative filtering recommendation (IBCF) algorithm: firstly calculate the similarity between items; secondly, obtain the predicted score through the user_item score matrix and the similarity of the items; finally, select the most interesting items through the sorting method Generate a recommendation list for users [8]. Measuring the similarity between different vectors is usually calculated by using the "distance" between the vectors. Suppose the similarity between items a and b is sim(a, b), and the measurement methods are mainly as follows:

(1) Euclidean distance. Since the sum of squares is an important expression in the linear rule, Euclidean distance similarity is used in most scenarios, expressed as:

$$sim(a, b) = \sqrt{\sum_{i \in U_{ab}} (a_i - b_i)^2} \qquad (1)$$

Among them, U_{ab} represents the set of users who have rated items a and b, and a_i represents the rating of user i on item a.

(2) Pearson similarity. Firstly, the outliers are preprocessed, and then the distance between users is calculated by the number product. Because the calculation is relatively complicated, it can only be applied to scenes with scores. The scores of different dimensions have a better effect when measuring similarity, which can be expressed as:

$$sim(a, b) = \frac{\sum_{n \in N_{ab}} \left(r_{u,a} - \overline{r_a}\right)\left(r_{u,b} - \overline{r_b}\right)}{\sqrt{\sum_{n \in N_{ab}} \left(r_{u,a} - \overline{r_a}\right)^2}\sqrt{\sum_{n \in N_{ab}} \left(r_{u,b} - \overline{r_b}\right)^2}} \qquad (2)$$

(3) Cosine similarity. Mainly used for scoring data sparse matrix, but it is easily affected by vector translation, which can be expressed as:

$$\text{sim}(a, b) = \frac{\sum_{n\in N_{ab}} R_{u,a} R_{u,b}}{\sqrt{\sum_{n\in N_{ab}} R_{u,a}^2} \sqrt{\sum_{n\in N_{ab}} R_{u,b}^2}} \tag{3}$$

In practical applications, specific problems need to be analyzed in order to adopt the most suitable similarity calculation formula. This paper uses Pearson similarity to calculate the similarity between users or items, and the experimental results are better than other methods.

3.2 Preference Prediction Algorithm

Calculating the similarity between items is based on the user's rating of the item. The final rating prediction can also be filled with a sparse matrix. The open source data set is usually divided into a training group and a test group. The traditional score prediction algorithm is as follows:

1) The user-based neighborhood algorithm is to correlate the predicted scores of the items of the users with the highest similarity with the target users, and construct the final scores of the target users, which can be expressed as:

$$\hat{r}_{ui} = \bar{r}_u + \frac{\sum_{v\in c(u,k)\cap T(i)} S_{uv}(r_{vi} - \bar{r}_v)}{\sum_{v\in c(u,k)\cap T(i)} |S_{uv}|} \tag{4}$$

where c(u, k) represents the k sets closest to user preferences, T(i) represents the set of user behavior data on the ith item, rvi represents the rating of user v on the ith item, and rv represents user v's The average score of the item, Suv indicates the similarity between users can be calculated by Eq. (2);
2) The item-based neighborhood algorithm is to correlate the predicted scores of users with similar interests in the collection of items with the highest similarity between the products, and construct the final score of the target user, which can be expressed as:

$$\hat{r}_{ui} = \bar{r}_i + \frac{\sum_{j\in c(i,k)\cap T(u)} S_{ij}(r_{uj} - \bar{r}_j)}{\sum_{v\in c(i,k)\cap T(u)} |S_{ij}|} \tag{5}$$

Where c(i, k) represents the sum of items with the highest value similar to i, T(u) represents the sum of user u behavior data items, ri represents the average value of item i, and S_{ij} represents the similarity between items.

3.3 Enhanced Matrix ERM

Use the eigenvalues that characterize the user's willingness to buy to establish the purchasing intention scoring matrix Spif. Suppose the ranking of product i in the user's purchase willingness score is RankScore (i.e. rsi). After normalizing and standardizing the rsi value, it is substituted into the penalty factor weighting formula, and finally the weight is substituted into the enhanced similarity formula to obtain the enhanced matrix Predict score.

Min-max standardization: Express the original data in a linear manner, and specify the data result in [0, 1]. Perform a linear transformation on the sequence x1, x2, ... , xn:

$$y_i = \frac{x_i - \min_{1 \le j \le n} x_j}{\max_{1 \le j \le n} x_j - \min_{1 \le j \le n} x_j} \tag{6}$$

In this paper, the linear relationship of the variables X or Y in the scoring matrix cannot be clearly reflected. After data conversion, the new penalty factor weighting formula is obtained as:

$$W_{pf-i} = \frac{1}{lg(2 + rs_i - \beta)} \tag{7}$$

Where β is the penalty coefficient.

Let S_e be the ERM prediction score, and its value is the weight of the purchase willingness score matrix S_{pif} and the weight W_{pf-i}, then divided by the sum of the weights. This algorithm is mainly aimed at the long-tail effect caused by the low-ranking products with purchase intention, which are not recommended in time. Because the head subject matter will be consumed by more and more users, and the long tail subject matter with better quality and the user's willingness to buy will not get enough attention due to less user attention behavior and insufficient self-descriptive information. S_e can be expressed as:

$$S_e = \frac{\sum_{i \in I_c} S_{pif} \times W_{pf-i}}{\sum_{i \in I_c} W_{pf-i}} \tag{8}$$

4 Experiment

In order to verify the practical application effect of the design system, the recommendation system based on the knowledge graph is used as the control group, the recommendation system based on big data designed in this paper is used as the experimental group, and all the curriculum ideological and political teaching resource data of the school are input into two respectively Compare in the system.

In the course of the experiment, this paper selects 5 volunteers as system users to test the two systems respectively, so that they can choose the curriculum ideological and political teaching resources with higher preference during the test process, and use the clocks of the two systems. The chip compares the server response time of the respective systems and calculates the user's preference for recommended resources, as shown in Table 1.

Table 1. Experimental results of two recommendation systems

User name	Experimental group system		Control system	
	Response time/ms	User preference	Response time/ms	User preference
User 1	15.63	0.98	52.63	0.52
User 2	17.26	0.96	51.23	0.53
User 3	12.63	0.92	54.02	0.45
User 4	11.52	0.91	53.02	0.56
User 5	16.42	0.97	50.26	0.51

It can be seen from Table 1 that compared with the control group system, the experimental group system has a shorter server response time when recommending courses ideological and political teaching resources for users, which is only 13.24 ms. In addition, from the perspective of user preference, the user preference of the experimental group system recommended resources is above 0.90, while the user preference of the control system recommended resources are all around 0.50. It can be seen that the experimental group's system recommends resources when, Server response time is shorter, and user preference is higher. The main reason for this phenomenon is that the design system automatically filters out the curriculum ideological and political teaching resources that do not meet the requirements, and adds more operating conditions in the system design process, so as to realize the good recommendation of the curriculum ideological and political teaching resources. In summary, the curriculum ideological and political teaching resource recommendation system designed by this article using big data technology can shorten the response time of the system server on the basis of fully satisfying user preferences, and provide users with more accurate recommendation services.

Figure 3 indicates the performances as a function of the number of observed customers and of the size n of the given subsets. It can be seen from the experimental results that as the embedded dimension of knowledge graph representation learning increases, the root mean square error of the algorithm in this paper first shows a downward trend. When the embedding dimension is 150 dimensions, the RMSE value is the lowest. As the

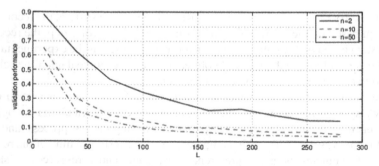

Fig. 3. Performances comparison

dimension increases, the RMSE value increases. The increase in the embedding dimension of the algorithm can better express the deep features between users and items, the model is more fitting, and the recommendation effect is better; but when the embedding dimension increases to a certain extent, the characteristics of users and items in the training set are too detailed. Makes the algorithm over-fitting, and the prediction effect becomes worse.

5 Conclusion

In a brand-new educational environment, the main goal of college education and teaching is to provide society and enterprises with more innovative talents through various practical activities. University laboratories are the main place to cultivate students' innovative ability and undertake the important task of talent cultivation. In order to further optimize the effectiveness of laboratory management practices in colleges and universities, the training of innovative talents should be the main goal in the work, and management concepts and methods should be constantly updated to build the laboratory into a university practice base to provide a more solid guarantee for talent training. This paper designs a new curriculum ideological and political teaching resource recommendation system based on big data technology, and proves the feasibility and advantages of the design system through comparative experiments. However, due to limited research capabilities, the design system of this article still has some shortcomings, such as the inability to prevent users from repeatedly uploading the same curriculum ideological and political teaching resources, resulting in repeated storage of resource data.

References

1. Katz, A., Karvonen, O., Di Caro, A., et al.: SHARP joint action–strengthening international health regulations and preparedness in the EU. Eur. J. Public Health **30**(Suppl._5), ckaa166–606 (2020)
2. Seale, A.C., Hutchison, C., Fernandes, S., et al.: Supporting surveillance capacity for antimicrobial resistance: laboratory capacity strengthening for drug resistant infections in low and middle income countries. Wellcome Open Res. **2** (2017)
3. Falfushynska, H.I., Buyak, B.B., Tereshchuk, H.V., et al.: Strengthening of e-learning at the leading Ukrainian pedagogical universities in the time of COVID-19 pandemic. In: CEUR Workshop Proceedings (2021)
4. Bassi, A., John, O., Praveen, D., et al.: Current status and future directions of mHealth interventions for health system strengthening in India: systematic review. JMIR mHealth uHealth **6**(10), e11440 (2018)
5. Cheng, Y., Chen, K., Sun, H., et al.: Data and knowledge mining with big data towards smart production. J. Ind. Inf. Integr. **9**, 1–13 (2018)
6. Hariri, R.H., Fredericks, E.M., Bowers, K.M.: Uncertainty in big data analytics: survey, opportunities, and challenges. J. Big Data **6**(1), 1–16 (2019)
7. Li, K., Li, G.: Approximate query processing: what is new and where to go? Data Sci. Eng. **3**(4), 379–397 (2018)
8. Yue, W., Wang, Z., Liu, W., et al.: An optimally weighted user-and item-based collaborative filtering approach to predicting baseline data for Friedreich's Ataxia patients. Neurocomputing **419**, 287–294 (2021)

Research on Anomaly Detection of Smart Meter Based on Big Data Mining

Haowei Tang[1], Jing Shen[2], Congying Yao[1], and Juncai Yao[2(✉)]

[1] School of Electrical Engineering, Nanjing Institute of Technology, Nanjing 211167, China
[2] School of Computer Engineering, Nanjing Institute of Technology, Nanjing 211167, China

Abstract. With the development of smart grids and the widespread application of advanced measurement systems, power companies have obtained super-large power data, and the use of these data will bring huge benefits to the development of the power grid. Therefore, this paper analyzes the development status of electric power big data and the processing methods of data analysis, proposes a smart meter anomaly detection framework, and explains the advantages of the detection algorithm to provide a data mining solution for the development of electric power big data.

Keywords: Big data · Smart meter · Data analysis · Abnormal detection

1 Introduction

In recent years, with the development of big data and artificial intelligence technology, the State Grid Corporation of China has installed a large number of smart sensing devices and used remote communication technology to collect real-time data from smart meters, power distribution automation, digital protection devices and other smart devices6 [1]. For collecting large amounts of data, how to analyze and mine the hidden information has become a shortcut and challenge for the current traditional power grid to transform into a smart grid. With the widespread increase in the use of electric energy, the amount of user data has increased geometrically. Therefore, it is necessary to develop an efficient and practical data analysis method based on the characteristics of power data. Through the results of data analysis, it is necessary for the daily maintenance, fault repair, and repair of the power system. Provide reliable advice on user management and other aspects. In recent years, data analysis has developed rapidly in the power industry, such as user classification, load forecasting, reliability analysis, etc. These developments are mainly due to the collection of real-time information by smart meters [2]. This article mainly analyzes the development status of electric power big data, discusses the analysis method of the measurement data of smart meters, and conducts case analysis based on the data.

2 Power Big Data

2.1 Development Status

Big data is the large scale of data involved, and conventional tools cannot be used to manage, process, and sort out information that is helpful for decision-making in a short period of time. The five characteristics of big data are massive, high-speed, diverse, low-value density, and authenticity. New processing models are needed to have stronger decision-making, insight, and process optimization capabilities to adapt to massive, high growth rates and diverse information assets. The strategic significance of big data is not to master huge data information, but to professionally process these meaningful data. Therefore, the ability to process data is a key link to realize the value of data [3].

With the development of informatization, many domestic and foreign companies have issued white papers on smart grid big data, and have preliminary prospects for the development of power big data. State Grid's development of smart grids includes research on the state assessment of power transmission and transformation equipment based on big data analysis, research on the implementation of big data monitoring technology for transmission lines, and big data analysis technology for smart power distribution terminals, covering the entire generation, transmission, transformation, and transformation of electricity. All-round development of power distribution. The State Grid Corporation of China uses data analysis methods such as AMI (advanced metering infrastructure) to conduct specific research on power grid line loss analysis, power theft early warning, time-of-use step price, user energy consumption analysis, and power load forecasting. At the same time, the China Electric Power Research Institute is also conducting research on power big data technology and strategy, conducting power big data application demand analysis, developing a power big data platform, and carrying out big data energy efficiency analysis and demand response.

At present, the information acquisition system of the power grid company has been relatively complete, combining the acquisition system with cloud computing, storage, and processing systems [4]. The data collected by the intelligent electricity meter is transmitted via the Internet, and at the same time, a suitable communication gateway is selected for transmission. After the data is buffered and processed, it is sent to the processing system for analysis and processing. The server queries the results from the data processing system according to the client's request. The cloud computing platform can also be used to process and store data [5, 6]. Build a power database and store it synchronously with the cloud database. The electric power data acquisition and processing flow is shown in Fig. 1.

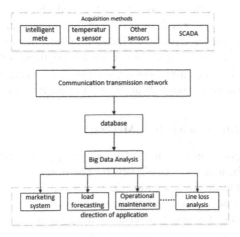

Fig. 1. Electric power data acquisition and processing flow

2.2 Smart Meter Data

With the installation of a large number of power grid automation equipment, the data volume of power companies has grown rapidly. Taking a provincial power company as an example, each power user used to collect electricity meter data once a month, 12 times a year, but the current smart electricity meter collects data per hour per day, increasing the data volume by 720 times. With each household's electricity meter generating 5 KB of data per day, which is 150 KB per month, when the number of smart meter users in a city reaches 2 million, the database will add 10 GB of data per day. Therefore, it is necessary to adopt appropriate data analysis methods to process in time, and tap potential information to feed back to the power system [7, 8]. At the same time, in addition to smart meters, there are also remote terminals, switches, circuit breakers, monitoring equipment in GIS (geographic information system), and DMS (distribution management system) all generate a lot of data.

3 Data Analysis Method

3.1 Big Data Analysis

Compared with traditional data analysis, the data collection objects used for big data analysis are different. First of all, the traditional model mostly obtains part of the data for analysis through sampling. Big data can analyze all the massive data collected, and the data source for analysis is transformed from sampled data to all data. The data analyzed has evolved from traditional incomplete data to full-system observation data. This main advanced measurement system is widely used in the power industry, so that data that cannot be observed in the traditional power grid can be obtained through equipment and then used for analysis. Secondly, the data source for analysis has expanded from traditional single-domain data to cross-domain data. Big data can combine data from different domains for analysis. For data fusion in the power field and other fields, such as fusing historical load data with meteorological data, and performing data analysis such as load forecasting. Moreover, traditional data analysis is more concerned about the causal relationship between the data source and the analysis result. In big data analysis, the data source and the analysis result are no longer just causal relationships, and reliable results can also be analyzed and predicted based on related data sources. For example, in the analysis of users' electricity consumption behavior, there is no causal relationship between the load data between users, but there must be a correlation between them. At this time, the big data analysis method can be used to get the results of concern.

3.2 Electric Power Big Data Analysis Method

At present, there are about three methods for analyzing power data: descriptive analysis, predictive analysis, and normative analysis. The descriptive analysis method is to perform pattern recognition based on historical data and power grid data, analyze and restore the historical state of the equipment; for example, use the recognition to process the historical data of the smart meter to analyze the detection of electricity theft.

Predictive analysis method is to use past data to mine potential laws and provide forward-looking predictions for the power grid, which can help power grid operation planning and equipment maintenance; for example, the use of historical operating data analysis of transformers to achieve fault warning and equipment service life probability prediction; also, predictable the impact of tiered electricity prices on load and forecast user demand. The normative analysis method is to provide the optimal plan for the operation of the grid under certain prerequisites; to provide the plan for the power generation dispatching and distributed generation regulation [5].

Power data analysis methods can also be classified according to different objects of collected data. At present, the common ones are divided into the following three categories: user data analysis methods, including electricity meter data analysis, demand response analysis, user classification, etc.; Asset optimization data analysis methods, including regional management, transformer management, etc.; grid optimization data analysis methods, including quality management, advanced distribution management, power outage management, advanced transmission management, etc. It is worth mentioning that this classification does not have a unified standard in the industry. It has many different names, but most of its functions can be understood from the name, such as failure data analysis methods, distributed energy data analysis methods, etc.

Due to the application of big data analysis methods, many new data analysis methods and applications have been produced in the field of power transmission and distribution. Including data collection, data management, data visualization, data analysis, data integration and platform architecture. For transmission systems, these applications are embodied in power grid dynamic parameter identification, adaptive transmission line protection, dynamic modeling, power detection, etc. For the power distribution system, there are power theft analysis, electric vehicle charging detection, fault prediction, distribution network status evaluation, distributed energy management, etc.

4 Anomaly Detection Method

Abnormal use of electricity can cause huge losses, so power companies must attach great importance to it. There are many factors that cause abnormal electricity usage, including severe weather conditions, animal contact, equipment failure, and electricity theft. With the large-scale application of smart meters, monitoring power consumption through fine-grained time intervals provides a new and effective way for power companies to monitor abnormal power consumption in the network. Some abnormal electricity consumption in the entire distribution network may be reflected in the data collected by smart meters. The big data collected by smart meters can realize data mining for the identification of electricity consumption in different cities and the classification of abnormal electricity users. Task. This paper constructs an anomaly detection framework through four steps: feature extraction, feature classification, training classification, and judgment results.

4.1 Feature Extraction

After collecting the data of the electric smart meter obtained in real time, it needs to be processed first to extract the characteristics that can reflect the essence of the data. The commonly used method is to process the data through the clustering algorithm. Currently, clustering-based methods have been widely used and have shown promising results in many applications, from image segmentation, handwriting recognition, document clustering, topic modeling to information retrieval [9].

In this paper, K-means++ clustering algorithm is used to evaluate the data set to obtain the data characteristics. Based on the K-means algorithm, the K-means++ algorithm optimizes the error caused by the initial clustering center selection. The implementation steps are as follows:

1) Randomly select a sample point from the data set as the first initial cluster center;
2) Calculate the shortest distance between each sample and the current existing cluster center. The distance function is defined as formula (1); then calculate the probability of each sample point being selected as the next cluster center. The farther the distance, the greater the probability Big.

$$d_{ij} = 1 - IoU_{ij} \tag{1}$$

Here, is the intersection ratio between the marked boxes as the distance parameter, and j is the marked box.
3) Repeat the second step until K cluster centers are selected.

4.2 Genetic Evolution Algorithm (GP)

The electricity usage feature recognition algorithm creates feature variables suitable for abnormal electricity usage detection based on the data features in the data set. For example, it is possible to generate feature variables suitable for abnormal electricity use detection by combining existing data features or applying various transformations to the features. Due to the large amount of data collected by smart meters, the number of combinations of data features can grow very rapidly, so machine learning algorithms are required to optimize the combinations of all data features.

In this paper, genetic evolution algorithm (GP) is used to optimize the feature combination of collected electricity consumption data. GP provides a method to automatically create new feature variables by applying a set of defined functions on the original data features. Figure 2 shows the basic flow of the GP algorithm. In Fig. 2, the GP algorithm first creates a set of random data feature combination variables. These variables can be implemented by applying some preset data feature combinations to the user data collected by the smart meter. Then quantify the detectability in each of these newly created feature variables (individuals). Then, the algorithm will create a new generation of data feature combination variables by applying genetic operations. The created new generation of feature combination variables have high fitness values. The generation method of the new generation data feature combination variable is: copy the feature combination variable selected in the previous generation, and randomly combine the intersection of the two selected feature variables.

4.3 Classifier

The role of the classifier: the conventional task is to use a given category, known training data to learn classification rules and classifiers, and then classify (or predict) the

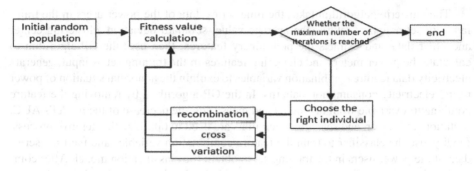

Fig. 2. GP algorithm flow

unknown data. Logistics regression, (Support Vector Machine) SVM, etc. are often used to solve binary classification problems. For multi-class classification problems, such as recognizing handwritten numbers, it requires 10 categories. Logistic regression or SVM can also be used.

For the classification of power data, SVM, KNN, etc. are usually used. The basic idea is to find a dividing hyperplane in the sample space based on the training set to separate different types of samples. In theory, there will be countless hyperplanes. Due to limitations or noise factors in the training set, samples outside the training set may be closer to the segmentation boundary of the classification.

4.4 Anomaly Detection Framework

Figure 3 shows the detection framework of abnormal electricity use structure. The framework mainly consists of three parts, the K-means algorithm for clustering, the GP algorithm for data feature combination, and the classifier for classification.

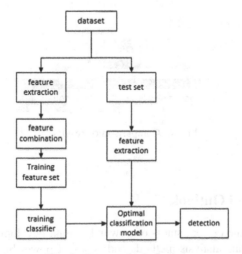

Fig. 3. Data analysis flow chart

The clustering algorithm takes the time series data of the power users in the training data set as input, returns the average value, standard deviation, clustering center and other data, and extracts the preliminary features; then uses the GP algorithm to calculate the power meters and clustering features in the training set as input, generate electricity data feature combination variables to explain the abnormal situation of power users' electricity consumption patterns. In the GP algorithm, by removing the feature combination variable from the model and measuring the decrease of the model's AUC, mutation, crossover, and selection operations are used to optimize the iterative process. Finally, use the classifier to train the feature combination variables and the time series data of the power users in the training set to obtain the classification model. After completing the training of the model, the abnormal behavior detection of real-time data can be performed.

5   Case Analysis

The research data in this article comes from a data set collected by public smart meters on the Internet, including data records of 1,000 households' electricity consumption. Electricity data is recorded on the phone every 30 min, which constitutes a record, including household number, electricity meter data, collection time, date, etc. Use MATLAB to simulate and process and analyze data. The known abnormal state types include four types of power theft, transformer out-of-step, power meter circuit failure, and transmission error.

Through the comparison of the training network detection model and the traditional collection of information results, the two comparison results are shown in Fig. 4. It can be seen that the detection results of the anomaly detection framework in this paper are significantly higher than the traditional methods in the four types of failures. The effectiveness of the detection method in this paper.

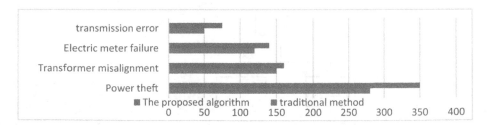

Fig. 4. Comparison of results

6   Conclusion and Outlook

This paper analyzes the current status of power big data development in smart grids, briefly explains the data analysis methods and types of power big data, and proposes an anomaly detection framework suitable for smart meter data collection based on clustering algorithms and evolution. The genetic algorithm realizes the cluster analysis of power users and the mining of power consumption data characteristics, and then uses the gradient boosting algorithm to optimize the classification. Through the abnormal detection method, abnormal power consumption detection can be effectively realized, the degree of automation can be improved, and the potential information of power big data can be fully excavated, so as to provide a feasible solution for the development of power big data.

Acknowledgments. This work is supported by the National Natural Science Foundation of China (No. 61301237), the Natural Science Foundation of Jiangsu Province, China (No. BK20201468) and the Scientific Research Foundation for Advanced Talents, Nanjing Institute of Technology (No. YKJ201981).

References

1. Bao, J.R., Jin, Y., Xiong, L.: Discussion on the method and application of electric energy big data collection based on big data cloud platform. China New Commun. **23**(14), 101–102 (2021)
2. Jin, W.: Application of smart meter in smart grid. Electrotechnical (18), 53–54+62 (2020)
3. Luan, W.P., Yu, Y.X., Wang, B.: AMI data analysis method. Chin. Soc. Electr. Eng. **35**(1), 29–36 (2015)
4. Yao, J.C., Liu, G.Z.: Bitrate-based no-reference video quality assessment combining the visual perception of video contents. IEEE Trans. Broadcast. **65**(3), 546–557 (2019)
5. Liu, X.H., Gao, J.C., Wang, S.L., et al.: Smart grid abnormal power consumption detection frame-work. Autom. Technol. Appl. **39**(12), 124–128+160 (2020)
6. Yao, J.C., Shen, J.: Image quality assessment based on the image contents visual perception. J. Electr. Imaging **30**(5), 053024 (2021)
7. Liu, Y., Zhang, J.Y., Fan, H.Y., Lei, S.B., et al.: Analysis and diagnosis of remote error of smart meter based on electric power big data. Single Chip Microcomput. Embed. Syst. Appl. **21**(09), 46–49+54 (2021)
8. Yao, J.C., Shen, J.: Objective assessment of image quality based on image content contrast perception. Acta Physica Sinica **69**(14), 148702 (2020)
9. Yao, J.C., Liu, G.Z.: Improved SSIM IQA of contrast distortion based on the contrast sensitivity characteristics of HVS. IET Image Proc. **12**(6), 872–879 (2018)

Using Big Data Technology to Analyze the Application of Calligraphy Art in Modern Digital Media

Jianlong Jiang and Kun Huang^(✉)

Anhui Xinhua University, Hefei 230088, Anhui, China

Abstract. Chinese characters are an unavoidable information carrier for carrying and disseminating Chinese culture. At the same time, calligraphy, as an unavoidable important part of art, has a broader space for development. The purpose of this article is to use big data technology to study the application of calligraphy art in modern digital media. It mainly introduces the research and application background of calligraphy art in modern digital media, and analyzes the application status of Chinese calligraphy art platforms based on big data. Starting from big data and modern digital media, with the help of the Internet and big data analysis platforms, it can realize user behavior data. Collection, visual display. Analyze the visits of calligraphy art websites and the source of user visits of calligraphy art websites respectively. The experimental results show that the direct access rate of calligraphy art websites and the access rate of direct search for "calligraphy art" related keywords are both close together. At the level of 65%, the application effect of the art of description method in modern digital media is better.

Keywords: Big data technology · Calligraphy art · Digital media · Application analysis

1 Introduction

With the development and wide application of new media and multimedia technology, as well as the continuous update and expansion of big data technology, the development of calligraphy art undoubtedly has greater potential [1]. The art of calligraphy has changed from the single-layer media in the past to more diversified dynamic interactive media [2]. Dynamic things make it easier for readers to remember and increase readers' sense of participation [3, 4]. While we pay attention to the art of calligraphy as a source of information, we must also pay attention to the development of new technologies and artistic expressions [5]. Exploring and studying the application of calligraphy in new media, making it a carrier of Chinese cultural dissemination and dissemination, and playing the most powerful role in the modern digital media environment is the inevitable development of Chinese calligraphy [6].

Different from traditional calligraphy, digital Chinese calligraphy is created and presented using digital technology in a human-computer interaction environment [7].

© Springer Nature Singapore Pte Ltd. 2022
Y. Tian et al. (Eds.): ICBDS 2021, CCIS 1563, pp. 388–396, 2022.
https://doi.org/10.1007/978-981-19-0852-1_30

Zhang J provided the latest introduction to digital calligraphy research. After analyzing the research background and goals of digital calligraphy, they put forward the most important topics of digital calligraphy: calligraphy tool modeling, calligraphy image analysis and processing, calligraphy morphology analysis and synthesis. Each research topic is accompanied by the latest introduction and current trends of the topic. Finally, they discussed important issues related to the further development of digital calligraphy [8]. Fei C proposed a robot calligraphy system. First, the human arm gestures are used to establish a font database of basic Chinese strokes and English letters, and then use the created database and human gestures to write Chinese characters and English words. A 3D motion sensing input device was deployed to capture the human arm trajectory for building font database and training classifier integration. 26 human gestures are used to write English letters, and 5 gestures are used to generate 5 basic strokes for writing Chinese characters [9]. Using big data technology to analyze the application of calligraphy art in modern digital media can promote the development of calligraphy art.

The innovation of this article: For the first time, it analyzes the influence of Chinese Internet social networking platforms on calligraphy art. It has enriched global research in this field, especially the related research on calligraphy. This is the first time we have discussed the application of calligraphy-related information on modern digital media platforms; we have successfully applied some big data technologies to collect calligraphy information on social media and the Internet, and quantified the factors affecting the popularity of calligraphy. Research and analysis provide reference for thinking; Research has found that modern digital media maintain a high degree of coverage of calligraphy art. The higher intensity and continuity of information contributes to the widespread dissemination of the art of calligraphy.

2 Using Big Data Technology to Analyze the Research of Calligraphy Art in Modern Digital Media

2.1 Characteristics of Big Data

The foundation of big data is a huge data system and a mathematical model of hundreds of millions of data analysis [10]. It immediately rejected "sample analysis" and "random search", which is a data analysis method that uses partial generalization. The use of big data analysis can truly realize the ideal "sample is the whole" analysis system [11, 12]. Like Google's flu forecast, it analyzes billions of Internet search files in the United States. It analyzes the entire database rather than a random sample. This analysis method not only improves the accuracy of the analysis, but can even predict the flu situation in a specific city.

Big data is often a record of behavior that we usually don't care about. It may just be the moment the computer is turned on, or it may be the name of a specific movie entered in the search bar, or it may be just clicking and fast forwarding the video. All these behaviors that are ignored by people are constantly being transmitted through the powerful network transmission system. Sampling big data with storage system.

In the era of big data, the value of data has changed from the most basic use to possible future uses, completely changing the way people use data. The development of technology allows people to use all the data received, but the substantial increase in the amount of data will inevitably lead to inaccurate results, and some incorrect data will also enter a huge database. People relax the wrong model and have more data. Big data usually speaks for itself. The whole society is used to this kind of thinking. This takes a lot of time. When we expand the data, we must be prepared for chaos.

2.2 The Art of Calligraphy in Modern Digital Media

Multimedia networks have become a new way to spread calligraphy, bringing calligraphy into the information age. Multimedia network is synonymous with modern information system. It is a method and operator that uses computer and network technology to process and distribute a large amount of text, audio, video and other data at the same time. It has the advantages of large amount of information, fast speed, and strong communication skills. The development and dissemination of multimedia networks and the promotion of calligraphy websites have greatly promoted the dissemination and exchange of calligraphy information.

One is the accumulation of rich and powerful electronic media. There are many pictures of classic calligraphy works of the past dynasties, electronic calligraphy dictionaries, calligraphy techniques of past dynasties, modern teachers, and writing videos on the websites of modern calligraphy teachers. There are many online. Its content and flexibility are unmatched by tradition. With the development of multimedia networks, calligraphy has become a treasure trove of art for the whole people, not only as a source of information used by a small number of elites and people with higher education in the past.

The second is to open a quick and interactive calligraphy message channel. The network has the characteristics of publishing, deployment, and interaction. With the development of multimedia networks, information has moved from closed to open, free from time and geographical constraints. Report and publish the latest developments in the book world in time for calligraphy lovers. The integration of graphic, text, video and multimedia networks makes traffic content complete, rich, intuitive, and transparent, and gets rid of the "page" constraints of traditional media. For example, for a large-scale national calligraphy exhibition, the Internet can provide a comprehensive and intuitive list of participating artists, works photos, opening ceremony scenes, and many details of the exhibition hall for the first time.

The third is the calligraphy writing comment on freedom and equality of creation. On the Internet, public IDs can be virtual and have no meaning in terms of vision, status, authority, and knowledge. Whether you are experts, experts or the general public, you can publish articles freely and evenly on the same platform. Thoughts and thoughts. Netizens can post their own projects so that others can comment at any time. Many of them can get feedback from well-known teachers and artists. You can also click to view the calligraphy or comment posted by other people.

2.3 The Influence of Digital Media on the Art of Calligraphy

First, it has gathered a rich and large collection of electronic calligraphy resources. The Internet has a large number of pictures of classic calligraphy works of the past, electronic calligraphy dictionaries, calligraphy theories of past dynasties, as well as videos of on-site writing and teaching by modern and contemporary calligraphy masters. Its comprehensiveness and convenience are unmatched by traditional media. With the development of network multimedia, calligraphy is no longer just a resource occupied by a small number of elites and upper-class people in the past, but has realized the sharing of public resources and has become a treasure house of art resources for the public. Owning network multimedia is like owning a huge library and museum. This provides convenience for the study of calligraphy techniques and the study of calligraphy theory.

The second is to open up a quick and interactive calligraphy message channel. The network has the characteristics of publicity, timeliness and interactivity. With the development of network multimedia, information has changed from closed to open, and there is no longer a time and geographical boundary. Calligraphy Network reports and releases the latest news of the book world for calligraphy lovers in a timely manner. The coverage is wide and free, and the integration of network multimedia graphics, text, and video makes the report content more comprehensive, rich, intuitive and intuitive. Vividness breaks the limitation of traditional media "page". For example, a report on a major national calligraphy exhibition, the Internet can provide a comprehensive and intuitive report on the list of exhibited authors, works pictures, opening ceremony scenes and many details of the exhibition hall situation in the first time, making the audience feel like "visiting the scene". Advantages that traditional media do not have. In addition, as Mr. Liu Zongchao said: "Calligraphy art information dissemination has a two-way or even multi-directional interactive function". The number of participants in online reports is wide and interactive. "Pair-to-many" has become the "many-to-many" of network media, forming "non-linear" communication, which can better enable the general audience to provide comprehensive and timely feedback messages, and better enable the public to participate in various calligraphy activities. The popularization of calligraphy network has also strengthened the communication of calligraphy information between regions, which is conducive to better understanding of external calligraphy information in remote counties and cities, publicizing local calligraphy characteristics, and carrying out calligraphy activities, so that regional calligraphy can better communicate with the outside world.

The third is to build a free and equal platform for calligraphy speech. In the Internet, everyone's identity can be virtual, and generation, status, class, and knowledge are not of practical significance. Whether experts, scholars or ordinary people, they can publish their own freely and equally on the same platform without barriers. Opinions and opinions. Netizens can upload their own works for others to comment at any time. Many of them can get comments from masters and famous artists. They can also click to watch the calligraphy works uploaded by others and post criticisms on posts. The true view. Many calligraphy networks also set up online activities for famous artists, and famous artists interact with netizens on-site through the Internet. There are even famous artists who are in their sixties who have directly registered a calligraphy online account or log in to QQ to communicate with young calligraphy lovers. All kinds of equal and free exchanges have narrowed the distance between calligraphy elites and ordinary fans. The public can better understand famous artists directly, and famous artists can better hear the truth and accept the most extensive and direct criticism from the general public.

The Internet of free speech has given birth to many popular "Internet critics", such as "Wild Fox Zen" and "Natural Nerds". They represent the voices of the "grassroots" and often speak ridiculously and outspoken the book world.

3   Using Big Data Technology to Analyze the Investigation and Research of Calligraphy Art in Modern Digital Media

3.1   Data Collection

The Chinese Calligraphy Art website actually contains four websites with different domain names. One is the calligraphy forum website itself, whose main purpose is to discuss the art of calligraphy; the other is a calligraphy culture mall that mainly exchanges and sells calligraphy and calligraphy works and stationery; the third is a Chinese painting circle forum with Chinese painting as the main exchange content; the fourth is the engraving The calligraphy and painting forum for the main exchange content. The latter two, the Chinese Painting Circle Forum and the Calligraphy and Painting Forum, are new websites developed independently from the original calligraphy website, aiming to segment users. The main object of this article is the Chinese calligraphy art website itself. Due to the limited space of the text page, the timetable for statistical data is not easy to be very long. Considering the start date, the main data collection time is two months.

3.2   Data Preprocessing

When the collection center collects a user's sensitive message value, it needs to be sent to the data server. In order to prevent any data server from trying to analyze user data and exposing its privacy (such as internal attacks), we have set up multiple data servers to η user information. (Integer) is divided into three integers, λ, μ, ν, then as shown in formula 1.

$$\eta = \lambda + \mu + \nu \tag{1}$$

If the analysis and query is the correlation value coefficient of a measurement of user attributes with another measurement under some interference of the measurement, corresponding to the semi-partial correlation protocol, the semi-partial correlation coefficient is calculated as shown in formula 2:

$$r_{Y(X.A)} = \frac{(r_{XY} - r_{YA}r_{XA})}{\sqrt{1 - r_{XA}^2}} \tag{2}$$

4   Using Big Data Technology to Analyze the Analysis and Research of Calligraphy Art in Modern Digital Media.

4.1   Analysis of the Number of Visits to the Calligraphy Art Website

The number of visits to a website is an important indicator to measure whether a website is welcomed by users. The following intercepted daily visits data of the first two months are shown in Table 1.

Table 1. Daily visits data

Date	Maximum number of views (ten thousand)	Minimum number of views (ten thousand)
January 1	4.56	0.75
January 10	7.53	1.67
January 20	5.87	1.2
January 30	6.44	1.33
February 1	4.21	0.66
February 10	3.1	0.34
February 20	4.11	0.58

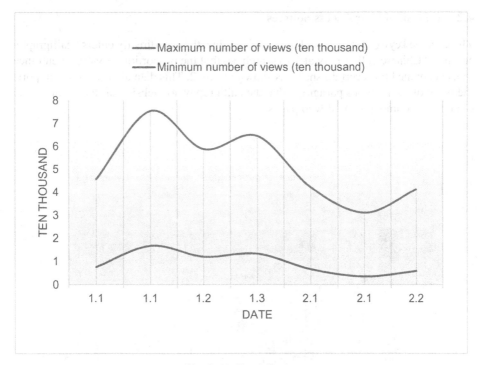

Fig. 1. Daily visits data

The traffic statistics chart is shown in Fig. 1. The number of daily visits to the calligraphy website in the first two months was the highest on January 10 and the lowest on February 10. The average number of visits is the lowest. From a statistical point of view, in addition to the lowest traffic on February 10, network congestion may be caused by server maintenance (because the traffic resumed quickly on February 17 the next day), the total traffic was one month higher than that in February. The reason for this phenomenon may be that February is the Spring Festival, and major art colleges are closed, resulting in a decrease in the number of visitors. From the perspective of user visit depth, January 10, which has the largest daily visit volume, has also become the day with the highest user visit depth value. The average daily user visit depth in January is also higher than that in February. The reasons can be summarized as follows: First, the dispute over the authenticity of Su Shi's "Kung Fu Iron" in January is constantly fermenting, and the competition for incentives in the domestic and international art market continues. Check out the calligraphy website on January 10, which was the most visited day in the past two months. The day before was the day when the relevant expert research report was officially released. The second is the last sprint period before January. Students are preparing for the college entrance examinations of major art colleges. There will be more visits in January than in February. In addition, it is due to the decrease in network time used by users during the Spring Festival holiday.

4.2   Analysis of User Access Sources

Through the keyword statistics of the search engine, the user directly enters "calligraphy art" and "Chinese calligraphy art" to search, so that the proportion of website entrance links accounted for a certain share, as shown in Fig. 2. This data also strongly supports the point of the previous paragraph that the calligraphy art website has a certain degree of popularity among related web pages.

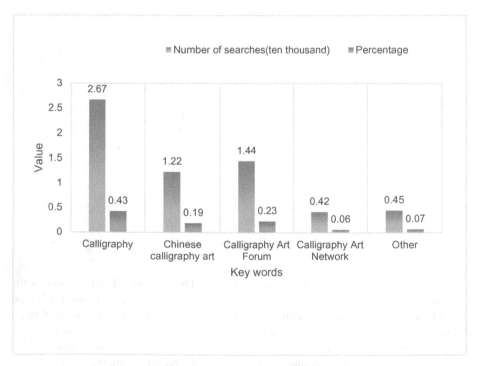

Fig. 2. Search keyword statistics

Comprehensive analysis of user resources, the instant access rate of calligraphy websites, and the access rate of instant search keywords "calligraphy" related keywords has approached 65%. The proportion of this user source is relatively high. The reasons are nothing more than one is that the calligraphy website is very well-known, and the other is that the traffic through other related advertisements and other forms of external links is relatively small. When promoting private labels, the artistic method of description may need to be strengthened.

The main audience of calligraphy websites is still concentrated in middle-aged men. This is also in line with our expectations of the analysis results. After all, the popularity and popularity of traditional culture represented by Chinese calligraphy among the younger generation cannot be compared with that of middle-aged people.

5 Conclusions

With the popularization of modern digital media, calligraphy, one of the foundations of traditional culture, has been greatly influenced. Modern media promoted the spread of calligraphy, created a new ecosystem for the development of calligraphy, and had a great impact on the aesthetics of traditional calligraphy. The development and progress of calligraphy is the focus of diversity. This article focuses on "Calligraphy and Modern Digital Media". Modern digital media refers to the emerging media represented by computer networks in the current era. This article uses big data technology to analyze and research the application of calligraphy in modern digital media and form its own point of view. Look for the development of calligraphy in the context of modern culture.

Acknowledgements. Outside the school sketch practical training teaching team (Excellent offline course project of Teaching Quality Project of Anhui Education Department, Item number: 2018jxtd163).

References

1. Hernandez, S.: Case study: digitising cleveland museum of art history one negative at a time. J. Dig. Media Manag. **6**(4), 327–338 (2018)
2. Wang, Z., Lian, J., Song, C., et al.: CSRS: a Chinese seal recognition system with multi-task learning and automatic background generation. IEEE Access **PP**(99), 1 (2019)
3. Hung, C.C.: A study on a content-based image retrieval technique for Chinese paintings. Electron. Libr. **36**(1), 172–188 (2018)
4. McDonald, J.M., et al. Moving to the cloud: the state of the art for cloud-based production pipelines. J. Dig. Media Manag. **6**(3), 215–230 (2018)
5. Lai, W.S., Lin, Y.B., Hsiao, C.Y., et al.: FrameTalk: human and picture frame interaction through the IoT technology. Mob. Netw. Appl. **24**(5), 1475–1485 (2019)
6. Sayre, L.: The art of hip-hop in digital media. Writ. Waves **1**(1), 17 (2019)
7. Silva, D.A.E., Camargogrillo, S.V.D.: New paths for science: a contrastive discourse analysis of modifications in popularizing science through digital media. Bakhtiniana Revista de Estudos do Discurso **14**(1), 54–81 (2019)
8. Zhang, J.: A survey of digital calligraphy. Scientia Sinica Informationis **49**(2), 143–158 (2019)

9. Fei, C., Huang, Y., Xin, Z., et al.: A robot calligraphy system: From simple to complex writing by human gestures. Eng. Appl. Artif. Intell. **59**, 1–14 (2017)
10. Moreno, L.: Museums and digital era: preserving art through databases. Collect. Build. **38**(4), 89–93 (2019)
11. Horáková, J.: Listening to art on a seabed. Musicol. Brun. **52**(1), 155–168 (2017)
12. Khakzand, M., Babaei, S.: Developing a new method for the architectural design process: an experimental study using found-object art in the design studio. Des. J. **21**(2), 209–225 (2018)

Research on Resource Allocation of Multi-beam Satellite Based on Big Data Under Rain Fading

Zhang Ming[⊠]

NARI Group Corporation, State Grid Electric Power Research Institute, Nanjing, China

Abstract. Aiming at the adverse effect of rain decay on satellite communication in high frequency band, adaptive FEC coding is used to reduce the amount of information transmitted, a method of adaptive channel allocation under rain failure is proposed. The modified method can ensure the transmission of useful information by increasing the number of channels and meet the requirements of the system for bit error rate, and effectively utilize the limited satellite channel resources. The simulation results show that the algorithm can effectively guarantee the stability of the useful information transmission on the basis of the error rate requirement of the system.

Keywords: Rain attenuation · Resource allocation · Bit error rate · Adaptive coding · Communication link

1 Introduction

The rapid development of wireless communication will provide users with global multimedia services, including multi-party conference, remote teaching, online multi-machine game, etc. [1–3]. Because of the inherent advantages of satellite communication, such as broadcast communication and the ability of wide coverage, satellite communication will be the most ideal choice for remote and wide range communication. Satellite communication is the only option, especially for users in areas where there is no ground network and users who are far away from each other. The transmission power and propagation delay of LEO satellites are small, so they have many advantages over high-orbit satellites in providing global real-time communication for small handheld mobile terminals, so they can provide direct communication for low-power handheld terminals [4]. Moreover, the ground coverage of LEO satellites is multi-cell cellular coverage, which can provide more capacity than high-orbit satellites. Satellite communication is an open communication system, its communication links are vulnerable to external conditions, especially the effect of rain. In high-band communication, the rain seriously affects the quality of communication [5].

We note that the research on channel allocation methods is based on the ideal communication environment in the literature, and the impact of emergencies on the channel is not taken into account [6–8]. In this paper, a channel allocation method applied under rain fading is proposed. The simulation results show that the new method can effectively mitigate the effect of rain fading, and ensure the quality of communication.

© Springer Nature Singapore Pte Ltd. 2022
Y. Tian et al. (Eds.): ICBDS 2021, CCIS 1563, pp. 397–408, 2022.
https://doi.org/10.1007/978-981-19-0852-1_31

2 Theoretical Analysis

In a LEO satellite communication system with multiple point beams, the projection area of each point beam on the ground is a cell [9]. Suppose each cell has C channels, under the condition of the coexistence of voice service and data service, according to the different state of each service, it is divided into new voice call, voice switching call, new data call and data switching call.

Their arrival rates obey the Poisson distribution with the parameter of λ_{nv}, λ_{hv}, λ_{nd}, λ_{hd} respectively, and the service time obeys the negative exponential distribution. $1/\mu_d$ and $1/\mu$ are the average service times for data traffic and voice traffic, respectively. Different types of calls have different requirements for delay, and the priority of voice is higher than that of data traffic. Therefore, there are C channels, the data traffic can only use K of them, while the remaining $C\text{-}K$ channels only serve the voice service, which ensures the priority of the voice service.

2.1 System Model

In the event of rainfall, in order to alleviate the influence of rain fading on communication quality, a variety of coding methods, such as Forward Error Correction (FEC) are adopted [10] (Fig. 1).

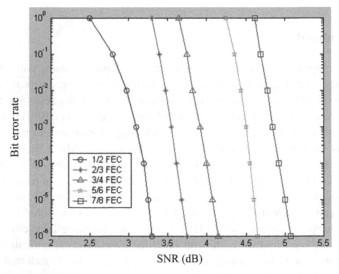

Fig. 1. Bit error rate versus SNR for various FEC schemes

Different coding methods are suitable for different rain fading, Because of the different requirements of voice and data services for bit error rate (BER), the choice of coding method is also different. In order to ensure the transmission rate of useful information, different coding modes require compensation of different channel bandwidths. Q (t) is the proportion of channel bandwidth compensation for data traffic. B_v is the bandwidth occupied by voice service, B_d is the bandwidth occupied by data service, and the bandwidth occupied by rain fading is as follows.

$$B_v = (1 + P(t))B_{sv}$$
$$B_d = (1 + Q(t))B_{sd} \tag{1}$$

B_{sv} is the bandwidth occupied by voice service in sunny world, and B_{sd} is the bandwidth occupied by data service in sunny world. The voice service can use all c channels in the cell, and the data service can only occupy k channels, which ensures that even if a large number of data services arrive in the cell, there are still C channels available for voice services, and the high priority of voice services is guaranteed.

On sunny days, when the number of idle channels is less than C, the voice service can access the cell, and when the number of idle channels is less than K, the data service can access the cell, as follows

$$B_{sv} \le C - (iB_{sv} + jB_{sd})$$
$$B_{sd} \le K - (iB_{sv} + jB_{sd}) \tag{2}$$

Where i, j is the number of voice and data services currently used in the cell. In the case of rainy days, expressed as follows.

$$\left(1 + P_{(i+1)}(t)\right)B_{sv} \le C - \sum_{k=1}^{i}(1 + P_k(t))B_{sv} - \sum_{k=1}^{i}(1 + Q_k(t))B_{sd}$$
$$\left(1 + Q_{(j+1)}(t)\right)B_{sd} \le K - \sum_{k=1}^{i}(1 + P_k(t))B_{sv} - \sum_{k=1}^{i}(1 + Q_k(t))B_{sd} \tag{3}$$

2.2 Mathematical Analysis

After the minimum requirements of bit error rate (BER) is given, the compensation ratio of channel at each time is given, and the number of voice and data services that can be accommodated in the cell on a sunny day is [11]

$$m = [C/B_{sv}]$$
$$n = [K/B_{sd}] \tag{4}$$

S is the state space of the channel occupied by the traffic in the cell

$$S = \{(i, j)| + aj \le m, 0 \le j \le n\} \tag{5}$$

Where a is the ratio of the channel occupied by the data service to the bandwidth occupied by the voice service.

The two-dimensional Markov process is shown in Fig. 2.

$q(i, j; i', j')$ represents the probability of transition from state (i, j) to state (i', j'), in which, in the case of a rainy day, the probability is

$$q(i, j; i - 1, j) = i\mu_v(0 \le i \le m, 0 \le j \le n)$$
$$q(i, j; i + 1, j) = (\lambda_{nv} + \lambda_{hd})\pi_v(i, j; i + 1, j)(0 \le i \le m, 0 \le j \le n)$$

$q(i,j; i, j-1) = i\mu_d (0 \le i \le m, 0 \le j \le n)$

$q(i,j; i, j+1) = (\lambda_{nv} + \lambda_{hd})\pi_d(i,j; i, j+1)(0 \le i \le m, 0 \le j \le n)$

$\pi_v(i,j; i+1, j) = \Pr\{(1 + P_{i+1}(t))B_{sv}$

$$\le C - (\sum_{k=1}^{i}(1 + P_k(t))B_{sv} - \sum_{k=1}^{i}(1 + Q_k(t))B_{sd})$$

$\pi_d(i,j; i, j+1) = \Pr\{(1 + Q_{i+1}(t))B_{sd}$

$$\le K - \sum_{k=1}^{i}(1 + P_k(t))B_{sv} - \sum_{k=1}^{i}(1 + Q_k(t))B_{sd}$$

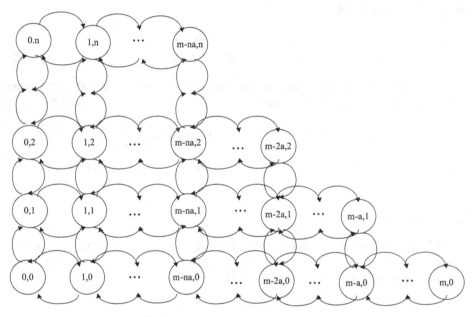

Fig. 2. Two-dimensional Markov chain

Because the new call and the handover call have the same priority, the failure rate of switching is the same as the blocking rate of new call.

The blocking rate of new call (failure rate of handover) of the voice service is

$$P_{Bv} = \sum_{i=0}^{m-an}\sum_{j=0}^{n}p(i,j)[1 - \pi_v(i,j; i+1, j)]$$

$$+ \sum_{k=1}^{n}\sum_{i=m-a(n-k)+1}^{m-a(n-k)}\sum_{j=0}^{n-k}p(i,j)[1 - \pi_v(i,j; i+1, j)] \tag{6}$$

The blocking rate of new call (failure rate of handover) of the data service is

$$P_{Bd} = \sum_{i=0}^{m-an} \sum_{j=0}^{n} p(i,j)[1 - \pi_d(i,j;i,j+1)]$$

$$+ \sum_{k-1}^{n} \sum_{\substack{i=m \\ -k+1)+1}}^{m-a(n-k)} \sum_{j-0}^{n-k} p(i,j)[1 - \pi_d(i,j;i,j+1)] \tag{7}$$

Where $p(i,j)$ is the probability of state transition p in sunny day.

$$P(i,j) = P(0,0) \cdot \frac{(\lambda_{nv} + \lambda_{hv})^i}{i!\mu_v^i} \cdot \frac{(\lambda_{nd} + \lambda_{hd})^j}{j!\mu_d^i}, \quad 0 \le j \le n, \ i+aj \le m$$

$$P(0,0) = [\sum_{\substack{0 \le j \le n \\ i+aj \le m}} \frac{(\lambda_{nv} + \lambda_{hv})^i}{i!\mu_v^i} \cdot \frac{(\lambda_{nd} + \lambda_{hd})^j}{j!\mu_d^j}]^{-1}$$

$$= [\sum_{j=0}^{n} \frac{(\lambda_{nd} + \lambda_{hd})^j}{j!\mu_d^j} \sum_{i=0}^{m-aj} \frac{(\lambda_{nv} + \lambda_{hv})^i}{i!\mu_v^i}]^{-1} \tag{8}$$

2.3 Calculation of Communication Link

$P(t)$ and $Q(t)$ are the ratio of channel bandwidth compensation for voice and data services. Their values depend on the coding method selected in the current state, and the choice of coding mode depends on the signal-to-noise ratio of the current link. Rain fading is the main factor affecting signal-to-noise ratio (SNR), so the value of $P(t)$ and $Q(t)$ mainly depends on rain fading [12].

$$A_{th} = (E_b / N_0)_{CS} - (E_b / N_0)_{th} \tag{9}$$

A_{th} is the maximum value of rain fading that can be sustained right now. $(E_b/N_0)_{CS}$ is the signal-to-noise ratio (SNR) on a sunny day. $(E_b/N_0)_{th}$ is the minimum channel ratio that reaches the threshold of bit error rate.

Because the rain fading changes over time, the call duration is T_s, and the rain fading is

$$A_{(t_0+T_s)} = (E_b / N_0)_{CS(t_0+T_s)} - (E_b / N_0)_{(t_0+T_s)} \tag{10}$$

The rain fading at the beginning of the communication is

$$A_{t_0} = (E_b / N_0)_{CS} - (E_b/N_0)_{t_0} \tag{11}$$

In reference 4, the relationship between the values of rain fading at two times is given

$$f_{A_{t_0}A_{(t_0+T_s)}}(A_{t_0}, A_{(t_0+T_s)}, T_s) =$$

$$\frac{1}{2\pi S_a^2 A_{t_0} A_{(t_0+T_s)}} \exp[-\frac{1}{2}Q(A_{t_0}, A_{(t_0+T_s)}, T_s)] \tag{12}$$

$$Q(A_{t_0}, A_{(t_0+T_s)}, T_s)] = \frac{1}{1-r_A}\{\frac{(\ln A_{t_0} - \ln A_m)^2}{S_a^2}$$

$$-\frac{2r_A(\ln A_{t_0} - \ln A_m)(\ln A_{(t_0+T_s)} - \ln A_m)}{S_a^2}$$

$$+\frac{(\ln A_{(t_0+T_s)} - \ln A_m)^2}{S_a^2}\} \tag{13}$$

The calculation methods of A_m, r_A, S_a have been given in reference 4.
The signal-to-noise ratio of the link is

$$\frac{E_b}{N_0} = P_t + G_t + L_p + L_m + G_c + G_r$$

$$- 10\log(B) - 10\log(KT) - A \tag{14}$$

Where Pt is transmit power, Gt is the gain of transmit antenna, LP is free space path loss, Lm is other miscellaneous loss, Gc is coding gain, Gr is receiving antenna gain, B is bandwidth, K is Boltzmann constant, T is noise temperature, A is rain fading. Except that the value of rain fading is unpredictable, all other parameters are predictable.

Bit error rate is

$$P_b = \frac{1}{2}e^{-\frac{E_b}{N_0}} \tag{15}$$

3 Simulation Results

3.1 Setting of Simulation Parameters

The simulation model is Iridium system. The model establishment of Iridium system has been completed in previous research, and the simulation parameters used are shown in Table 1.

The maximum bit error rate (BER) that voice service can bear is 10^{-3}, and the maximum bit error rate (BER) that data service can bear is 10^{-5}. The $P(t)$ (or $Q(t)$) of 1/2 FEC, 2/3 FEC, 3/4f FEC, 5/6 FEC and 7/8 FEC are 1, 2, 3, 5, 7, respectively. Because the voice service has a higher priority than the data service, the data service can only use 80% of the channel in the total bandwidth.

The terminals are distributed in Nanjing area. The average rainfall in Nanjing is 60 mm/h, and Nanjing is 8.9 m above sea level.

Both the uplink and the downlink use the access mode of MF-TDMA. The total bandwidth of the Iridium system is 10.5 M, where the structures of TDMA and FDMA

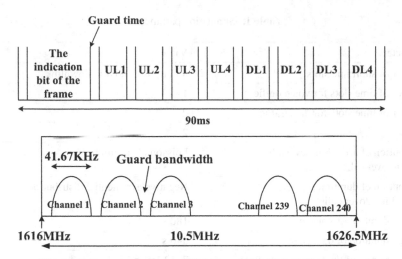

Fig. 3. Schematic diagram of TDMA and FDMA in Iridium system

are shown in the following figure. In the figure, UL1, UL2, UL3, UL4 are uplink slots and DL1, DL2, DL3, DL4 are downlink slots. The method of resource allocation in the uplink and the downlink is the same, so only the resource allocation of the uplink is discussed in the simulation (Fig. 3).

Each iridium star has 48 beams, each beam has 240/48 = 5 frequencies, because the frequency reuse factor is 12, so each beam has 240/12 = 20 frequencies. The available uplink has 4 time slots and the downlink has 4 time slots, so the number of available channels in each beam is 20 × 4 = 80. The distribution of the entire resource can be represented by a two-dimensional array, as shown in the following figure (Fig. 4).

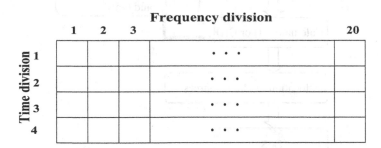

Fig. 4. Schematic diagram of channel allocation

The process of bandwidth adjustment is shown in the following (Fig. 5).

Table 1. Simulation parameters

Parameter	Value
Number of subframe slots	4 in uplink and 4 in downlink
Number of time slots for voice traffic	1
Number of time slots for data traffic	2
Data	2
Distribution of arrival of new calls and handover calls	Poisson distribution
Distribution of duration of new and handover calls	Negative exponential distribution
Average duration of voice calls	180 s
Average duration of data calls	540 s
The arrival rate of the voice data traffic	7–12 Ireland

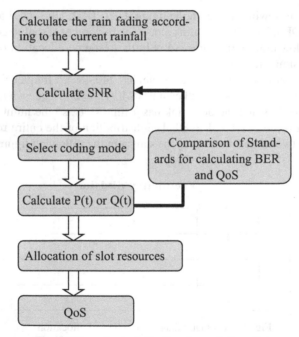

Fig. 5. Flow chart of adaptive channel allocation

As can be seen from Figs. 6 and 7, the blocking rate of new call and failure rate of handover increase with the increase of traffic and frequency. The blocking rate of new call and failure rate of handover for voice service are smaller than that of data service, because voice service has higher priority than data service. In Fig. 8, the channel utilization increases with the increase of traffic, and the channel utilization decreases with the increase of frequency. The higher the frequency, the greater the rain fading. In order to ensure the transmission of useful information, the number of channels is increased dynamically, which leads to the increase of failure for new calls, the increase of switching failure for handover calls, and the decrease of channel utilization.

As can be seen from Figs. 9 and 10, since the number of allocated channels for voice and data services is not affected by channel occupation time on sunny days, therefore the blocking rate of new call and switching failure rate are constant. In the case of rainy days, due to the rain fading, the dynamic change of signal-to-noise ratio (SNR) leads to the change of bit error rate (BER). In order to meet the requirement of the system for bit error rate, adaptive coding is adopted. In order to increase the amount of transmission of useful information, the number of channels must be dynamically increased, and the blocking rate of new call and switching failure rate increase with the increase of bit error rate. Because the rain fading increases with the increase of channel occupation time, the longer the average duration of voice and data traffic is, the greater the rain fading is, and the more channels are increased, so the greater the blocking rate of new call and the switching failure rate.

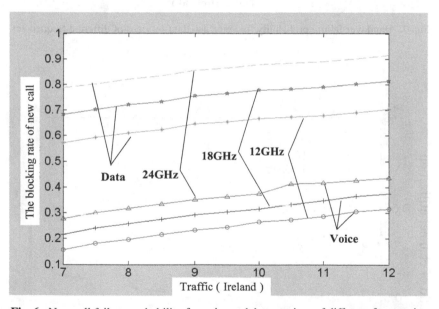

Fig. 6. New call failure probability for voice and data services of different frequencies

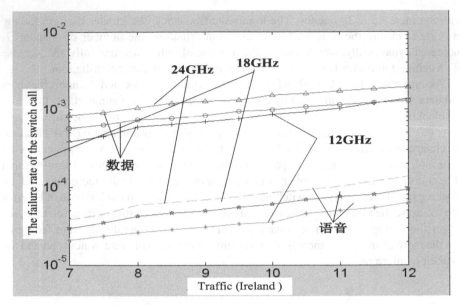

Fig. 7. Handover failure probability for voice and data services of different frequencies

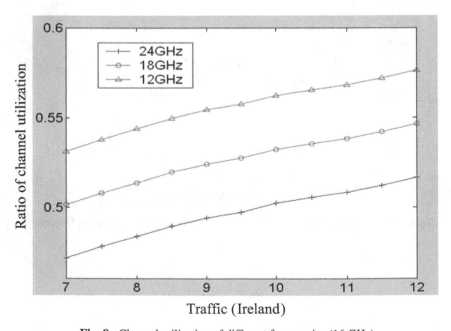

Fig. 8. Channel utilization of different frequencies (16 GHz)

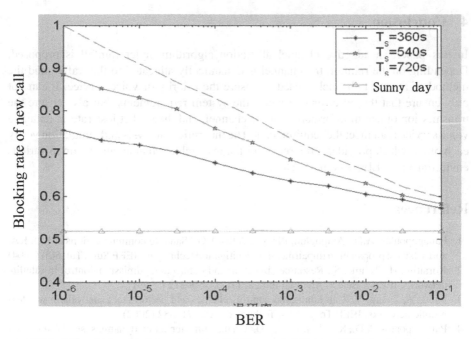

Fig. 9. The relationship between new call failure probability and BER for data services

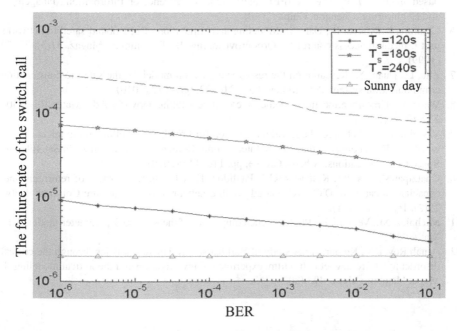

Fig. 10. The relationship between handover failure probability and BER for voice services

4 Conclusion

In this paper, an adaptive channel allocation algorithm under rainfall is proposed. Depending on the rainfall, the channel is dynamically allocated to the traffic, and the method of reserved channel is used to ensure the priority of voice service. It can not only ensure that the bit error rate meets the system requirements, but also ensure the transmission of useful information in the channel, and the packet loss rate of data and voice services can meet the requirements. The theoretical analysis and simulation verify each other, which provides a reference for the research of channel allocation in various environments in LEO satellite system.

References

1. Panagopoulos, A.D., Arapoglou, PD-M., Cottis, P.G.: Satellite communications at KU, KA, and V bands: propagation impairments and mitigation techniques. IEEE Surv. Tut. **6**(3) (2004)
2. Koraitim, H., Tohmé, S.: Resource allocation and connection admission control in satellite networks. IEEE J. Select. Areas Commun. **17**(2), 360–372 (1999)
3. Fang, Y., Zhang, Y.: Call admission control schemes and performance analysis in wireless mobile networks. IEEE Trans. Veh. Technol. **51**(2), 371–382 (2002)
4. Panagopoulos, A.D., Kanellopoulos, J.D.: On the rain attenuation dynamics: spatial-temporal analysis of rainfall rate and fade duration statistics. Int. J. Sat. Commun. Netw. **21**(6), 595–611 (2003)
5. Jia, Y., Peng, Z.: The analysis and simulation of communication network in Iridium system based on OPNET. In: The 2nd IEEE International Conference on Information Management and Engineering, Chengdu, China (2010)
6. Connors, D.P., Ryu, B., Dao, S.: Modeling and simulation of broadband satellite networks part i: medium access control for QoS provisioning. IEEE Commun. Magaz. **37**(3), 72–79 (1999)
7. Zhu, L., Duan, Y.: Research on the resource allocation model for the satellite constellation communication system. Adv. Mater. Res. **121–122**, 669–677 (2010)
8. Wang, L.: Timeslot allocation scheme for cognitive satellite networks.Adv. Mater. Res. 230–232:40–43 (2011)
9. Vassaki, S.: Market-based bandwidth allocation for broadband satellite communication networks. In: Proceedings of the Second International Conference on Advances in Satellite and Space Communications, Athens, Greece, pp. 110–115 (2010)
10. Chatziparaskevas, P.1, Koltsidas, G.1, Pavlidou, F.-N.1.: On the fairness of return channel capacity allocation in DVB-RCS-based satellite networks. Int. J. Satellite Commun. Netw. **29**(2), 163–184 (2011)
11. Michałek, M., Ventura, E.: Phylogenetic complexity of the Kimura 3-parameter model. Adv. Math. (2019)
12. Arnab Roy, P.S., Kumar, A.: A study of Barkhausen avalanche statistics through the critical disorder in a ferromagnetic thin film: experimental investigation and theoretical modeling. J. Magn. Magnetic Mater. **493** (2020)

Blockchain and Internet of Things

A Cryptocurrency Price Prediction Model Based on Twitter Sentiment Indicators

Zi Ye[1], Weichen Liu[2], Qiang Qu[1], Qingshan Jiang[1(✉)], and Yi Pan[1]

[1] Shenzhen Institute of Advanced Technology, Chinese Academy of Sciences,
Shenzhen 518055, China
{zi.ye,qiang,qs.jiang,yi.pan}@siat.ac.cn
[2] Guangdong University of Technology, GuangZhou 510006, China
liuweichen@mail2.gdut.edu.cn

Abstract. The cryptocurrency becoming increasingly expensive, price prediction methods have also been widely studied. As an application of big data in finance, the sentiment tendency of related topics on social platforms is an important indicator of cryptocurrency price prediction methods and has attracted broad attention. However, the accuracy of the existing macro-sentiment indicator calculation methods should be further improved. Aiming at the problem that the accuracy of price prediction is not significantly improved by applying the existing macro-sentiment indicators, this paper proposes three new public sentiment indicators based on small granularity. Correlational analysis between the indicators and price data is conducted in the paper as well. By analyzing the degree of sentiment tendency of each comment, the accuracy of the three public sentiment indicators is improved. Specifically, this paper quantifies public sentiment indicators by taking into account the degree of emotional bias of each tweet, which makes sentiment indicators with small granularity. Compared with previous methods, the value prediction accuracies of cryptocurrencies have been improved under three deep learning frameworks LSTM, CNN, and GRU with the use of small granularity sentiment indicators.

Keywords: Cryptocurrency · Big data · Price prediction · Sentiment analysis · Twitter media

1 Introduction

In recent years, cryptocurrencies have received widespread attention due to innovative features, simplicity, transparency and increasing popularity. Since Nakamoto [1] first summarized Bitcoin in a paper, the price of Bitcoin has grown surprisingly. Some investors think of Bitcoin as currency, while Selgin, Baeck and Elbeck [2] believe that Bitcoin ought to be regarded as a speculative commodity rather than a currency.

This research work is supported by the National Key Research and Development Program under Grant NO. 2020YFA0909100.

Unlike the prices of fiat currencies issued by banks and crude oil futures on the traditional trading market, the prices of virtual currencies are much more susceptible to public emotion. News and posts on social media often lead to volatility in the cryptocurrency market. For example, Tesla CEO Elon Musk's remarks on social media often lead to dramatic price fluctuations in the cryptocurrency market represented by Bitcoin and Dogecoin. Compared to the traditional stock market, the cryptocurrency market is still an emerging market. Traditional news media do not cover news timely, making social media like Twitter a source of information for cryptocurrency investors. Twitter not only provides real-time updates of information about cryptocurrencies, but is also a great source of sentiment analysis.

Existing study results include the web-based search data of Choi and Varian [3] and Ettredge et al. [4]. In particular, Choi and Varian's Google Trends data can be used to predict several macroeconomic statistics, including car sales and unemployment rate. Jethin Abraham et al. [5] predicted the prices of Bitcoin and Ethereum based on the number of relevant tweets on the Twitter. Toni Pano and Rasha Kashef [6] predicted the price of Bitcoin by analyzing the sentiment trend of tweets on the Twitter platform during the COVID-19 pandemic. In fact, Werner Antweiler et al. proposed a method to describe the sentiment trend of Internet comments in 2004 [7]. Three parameters can describe the overall sentiment trend of Internet comments.

However, the existing study has two main limitations. The first is that few types of cryptocurrencies have been predicted so far, and the price changes of a single cryptocurrency often cannot represent changes in the overall trend of the cryptocurrency market. The second limitation is that the current work is not accurate in describing the sentiment trend of single comment.

The relevant text data comes from the Twitter, which shows the sentiment trend of cryptocurrency investors. This article selects five representative cryptocurrencies in the cryptocurrency market as analysis objects. Such a choice can not only reflect the price change trend in the cryptocurrency market, but also will not introduce noise due to the price fluctuation of single cryptocurrency. VADER dictionary is used in this paper to generate the composite score of tweets. Based on scores, we optimize the method of quantifying market sentiment indicators proposed in [7], and applied composite scores to the calculations of indicators to make the granularity of market sentiment index smaller.

2   Related Work

Study based on sentiment method usually uses Loughran & McDonald financial corpus, Harvard IV-4 psychological corpus [8] and Valence Aware Dictionary and sEntiment Reasoner (VADER) [9] dictionary for sentiment analysis. Most of the studies on the impact of sentiment trends on the financial market are based on regression models or Granger causality tests. The regression model or test results are used to analyze the predictive ability of Twitter sentiment tendencies in financial markets [8,10]. The work of Kraaijeveld et al. [11] shows that Twitter sentiment, as well as message volume can forecast price fluctuations of multiple cryptocurrencies, and Twitter robot accounts may spread misinformation about cryptocurrency. In the work of stock price prediction based on news and price data by Li and Pan [12] work, the news data are pre-processed with VADER to generate composite sentiment scores. Also in the work of Mohapatr [13] to predict cryptocurrency price, they use the VADER sentiment analysis algorithm to assign each tweet a composite sentiment score based on the degree of sentiment trend.

In recent years, many scholars have tried to find the potential qualitative relationship between Bitcoin price and many factors. They mainly use econometric error correction model (ECM) [14], vector autoregressive model (VAR) [15] and other method. The traditional time series model for cryptocurrency price prediction includes Holt-Winters exponential smoothing [16], ARIMA [17], GARCH [18] and their variants. In the cryptocurrency price prediction task, ARIMA performs greatly under the condition of a short forecast time (2 d), and the forecast error under the condition of a longer forecast time (9 d) is relatively large. Machine learning and deep learning methods have advantages in analyzing nonlinear multivariate data and have less negative impact by the noise contained in data. By using classic machine learning models such as SVM, Bayesian Networks, and Multilayer Perceptron [19–21] good results were achieved on the task of predicting cryptocurrency prices and stock market prices. In [22], a combination of factors including bitcoin's trading information and external factors such as macroeconomic variables are considered to influence the price of cryptocurrencies. Andrew Burnie [23] shows that in the cryptocurrency market, the prices of various cryptocurrencies will also affect each other. Olivia Angela et al. [24] confirmed that the price of digital cryptocurrency is affected in many ways, including the impact of the EUR/USD. More importantly, Olivia Angela et al.found that Bitcoin and 2 altcoins (Litecoin and Monero) significantly affect the price of Ethereum. At the same time, the study of Darko Stosic et al. [25] found that the collective behavior of the digital cryptocurrency market is different from other financial markets. The minimum spanning tree of cryptocurrency cross correlations reveals distinct community structures that are surprisingly stable. Deep learning methods, as the special machine learning strategy, made major breakthroughs in the fields of computer vision, speech recognition, and natural language processing and often used for time series prediction. Indera et al. [26] use price data set to build a non-linear autoregressive model based on a multilayer perceptron in the price prediction of Bitcoin. The Stacked Noise Reduction Autoencoder was implemented to predict one day later Bitcoin price. Indera et al. use some benchmark methods for comparison, such as Back Propagation Neural Network and Support Vector Regression. These benchmark methods are widely regarded as the best performing machine learning methods and are very popular in the field of prediction[27]. [28] shows that GRU and LSTM are better than the traditional Machine learning model. The GRU model with cyclic dropout significantly improves the accuracy of predicting Bitcoin prices.

3   Methodology

The proposed methodology is given in Fig. 1. The details are given in subsections.

3.1 Data Acquisition

The data acquisition of this study can be divided into two parts. The first part is the crawling of Twitter text data, and the second part is the crawling of the historical prices of five digital currencies. We registered a Twitter developer account and successfully applied for access key and token to have authority access the data interface provided by Twitter. Twitter's API was developed under the constraints of REST architecture(Representational State Transfer) [29]. It transmits a representation of the State of the resource to the requester or endpoint when a developer makes a client request through the RESTful API. In order to improve the efficiency of collecting tweets, Twitter's stream API can be combined with Tweepy [30] to collect tweet data for sentiment analysis. JSON-formatted objects are obtained when using the Twitter data interface [31]. After the information returned by API is extracted, it is converted to CSV format for subsequent data cleaning. In the study, high-dimensional Big Data of tweets about five cryptocurrencies – BTC, DOGE, XRP, LTC, ETH – were retrieved and crawled from January 1, 2021 to June 30, 2021.

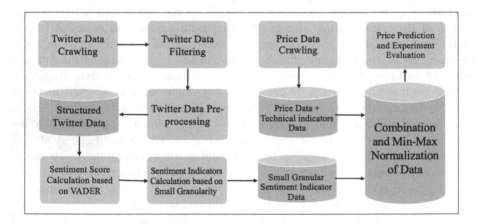

Fig. 1. The proposed architecture

3.2 Twitter Data Pre-procressing

After crawling from Twitter and obtaining the text data, advertising and promotional tweets are filtered. The process will be shown in the Evaluation section. As stated in the literature [32], each tweet contains a lot of words that are irrelevant to its sentiment. Therefore, it is suggested to conduct the pre-processing techniques on the unstructured tweets to attain the highest accuracy of sentiment. Important data pre-processing steps are as follows:

1) Emoji and Emoticons: We introduce the *EMOT* library to help us convert Emoji and Emoticons into emotional vocabulary.

2) Format "@user": We remove these format data by *Regex Search*.
3) Stop-word: We import *StopWords* from the *NLTK* library and write a function to remove stop words.
4) Tokenization: Tokenization means dividing the text into words or sentences. We use *LingPipeTokenizer* in this process.
5) Stemming: The main method of stemming reduction is to convert words into stems, such as "animals" to "animal", and "attractively" to "attract". We use *PorterAlgorithm* in this process.
6) Lemmatization: Lemmatization mainly refers to changing the word into its original form by means of transformation, for example, "drove" was treated as "drive" and "driving" was treated as "drive". *WordNetLemmatizer* is used to lemmatization process.

3.3 Sentiment Score Calculation Based on VADER

For the filtered and preprocessed tweets, sentiment analysis is used to analyze the textual data, aiming at identify the emotional trends of tweets about cryptocurrencies. Sentiment analysis is to extract and measure subjective emotions or opinions expressed in a text, and to achieve this goal in a variety of ways. Based on the attributes of data in this study, the VADER is chosen as the sentiment analysis tool with the generation of a set of sentiment scores. VADER is a sentiment analysis model based on dictionaries and rules [33], proposed by Gilbert and Hutto in 2014. Compared with traditional sentiment analysis methods [9,34,35], VADER has the advantages that it is specially designed for analyzing emotions expressed in social media.

3.4 Sentiment Indicators Calculation Based on Small Granularity

Antweiler and Frank [7] proposed three indicators to measure market sentiment trends based on the results of text analysis in 2004. As a method of measuring stock market changes based on Internet message board messages, these parameters represent different aspects of market sentiment. We made a simple adjustments to two of the three indicators to fit the data we have. Rather than using discrete label shape values as a representation of sentiment bias, we use more accurate the degree of emotional bias of each tweet.

The first indicator to measure the trend of market sentiment is the amount of related comments, which indicates the attention of a topic. This is exactly what Antweiler and Frank proposed before. The calculation methods is as following Eq. 1:

$$Comt_t = M_t^{Pos} + M_t^{Neu} + M_t^{Neg} \tag{1}$$

where $Comt_t$ is the evaluation volume of related topics in the tth time interval, and M_t^{Neg} is the number of tweets that have negative views on a specific topic on the Twitter platform in the tth time interval. The calculation method of $Comt_t$ is given in Algorithm 1.

Algorithm 1. Calculate $Comt_t$

Input: $D(t)$:Comments of the tth time interval
        $M_t^{Pos} \leftarrow 0$ Initial amount of positive tweets
        $M_t^{Neu} \leftarrow 0$ Initial amount of neural tweets
        $M_t^{Neg} \leftarrow 0$ Initial amount of negative tweets
  while $D(t)$ not empty **do**
    if $C_t > 0.05$ **then**
      $M_t^{Pos} \leftarrow M_t^{Pos} + 1$;
    else
      $PASS$;
    end if
    if $C_t < -0.05$ **then**
      $M_t^{Neg} \leftarrow M_t^{Neg} + 1$;
    else
      $M_t^{Neu} \leftarrow M_t^{Neu} + 1$;
    end if
    $Comt_t = M_t^{Pos} + M_t^{Neu} + M_t^{Neg}$;
  end while

The two improved indicators are as follows. The Small Granular Sentiment Bullish Index (SGSBI) represents the macro sentiment trend of related tweets on the platform, and its calculation method is shown below. The value of SGSBI represents the trend of positive macro sentiment corresponding to the comments of the digital currency. The higher the SGSBI value is, the more people have confidence in its price rise; the smaller the SGSBI value, it means that few people are confident of its price rise. The specific calculation method is as following Eq. 2:

$$SGSBI_t = \frac{\sum C_t^{Pos} + \sum C_t^{Neg}}{\sum M_t^{Pos} + \sum M_t^{Neg}} \tag{2}$$

where $SGSBI_t$ represents the small granular sentiment bullish index in the tth time interval. We use the VADER sentiment dictionary to perform sentiment analysis on each comment and output a sentiment score value. Vader can not only say that the sentiment tendency of comments is divided into positive,negative and neutral, but can also express the degree of positive,negative and neutral attitudes with a value of -1 to 1, thereby making the sentiment bias of each tweet more precise. The $\sum C_t^{Pos}$ is to sum up the sentiment scores of all tweets with positive sentiment in the tth time interval. The $\sum C_t^{Neg}$ is to sum up the sentiment scores of all tweets with negative sentiment in the tth time interval. The calculation method of $SGSBI_t$ is given in Algorithm 2.

The Small Granular Sentimental Divergence Index (SGSDI) represents the differences in the opinions of different users of the platform. The larger the value is, the greater the difference in the views of the market among investors is; the smaller the value is, the smaller the difference in the views of the market among investors is. The readers' understanding of market trends tends to be consistent. The method of calculating the sentiment divergence index is as following Eq. 3:

$$SGSDI_t = \frac{\sum_{i \in D(t)} (C_i - SGSBI_t)^2}{\sum M_t^{Pos} + \sum M_t^{Neg}} \tag{3}$$

where $SGSDI_t$ is the sentiment divergence index in the tth time interval. $D(t)$ is the collection of all relevant comments in the t time interval; C_i is the sentiment score value of a single tweet, and the value range is (0, 1). The calculation method of $SGSDI_t$ has been given in Eq. 2. The calculation method of $SGSDI_t$ is given in Algorithm 3.

Algorithm 2. Calculate $SGSBI_t$

Input: C_i :Compound value list of the tth time interval
       $D(t)$:Comments of the tth time interval
       $SGSBI_t$ Sentiment bullish index of the tth time interval
       $SGSDI_t \leftarrow 0$:Initial SDI value
       $\sum C_t^{Pos} \leftarrow 0$ Initial positive compound value sum
       $\sum C_t^{Neg} \leftarrow 0$ Initial negative compound value sum
while $D(t)$ not empty **do**
   if $C_t > 0.05$ **then**
      $\sum C_t^{Pos} \leftarrow \sum C_t^{Pos} + C_t$;
   else
      $PASS$;
   end if
   if $C_t < -0.05$ **then**
      $\sum C_t^{Neg} \leftarrow \sum C_t^{Neg} + C_t$;
   else
      $PASS$;
   end if
   $SGSBI_t \leftarrow \frac{\sum C_t^{Pos} + \sum C_t^{Neg}}{\sum M_t^{Pos} + \sum M_t^{Neg}}$;
end while

Algorithm 3. Calculate $SGSDI_t$

Input: C_t :Compound value list of the tth time interval
       $SGSBI_t \leftarrow 0$ Initial SGSBI value
       $\sum C_t^{Pos} \leftarrow 0$ Initial positive compound value sum
       $\sum C_t^{Neg} \leftarrow 0$ Initial negative compound value sum
while C_t not empty **do**
   if $C_t > 0.05$ **then**
      $\sum C_t^{Pos} \leftarrow \sum C_t^{Pos} + C_t$;
   else
      $PASS$;
   end if
   if $C_t < -0.05$ **then**
      $\sum C_t^{Neg} \leftarrow \sum C_t^{Neg} + C_t$;
   else
      $PASS$;
   end if
   $SGSDI_t \leftarrow \frac{\sum_{i \in D(t)} (C_i - SGSBI_t)^2}{\sum M_t^{Pos} + \sum M_t^{Neg}}$;
end while

3.5   Digital Currency Price Prediction Method

The dataset of Big Data for experiments are complex and diverse, with different units and ranges. They are normalized for prediction models to ensure stable weights and partiality. Without data normalization, the models will perform poorly. The $MinMaxScaler$ package is used in this normalization process. $MinMaxScaler$ normalization linearly transforms the original data, mapping from the original range interval $[x_{min}, x_{max}]$ to the new range interval $[x'_{min},$

x'_{max}]. The normalization preserves the relationship between the original data values. In our study, we choose [x'_{min}, x'_{max}] as [0, 1]. The formula is presented as following Eq. 4:

$$X_{\text{scaled}} = \frac{(x - x_{\min})}{(x_{\max} - x_{\min})}(x'_{\max} - x'_{\min}) + x'_{\min} \tag{4}$$

We use LSTM (Long Short Term Memory) to predict the price of cryptocurrencies. First proposed by Hochreiter & schmidhub [36] in 1997, LSTM is a neural network with the ability to remember long-term and short-term information. As an improved RNN model, LSTM can solve the gradient dispersion problem of RNN models and can handle long-distance dependence. The LSTM model can store important past information in the unit state and delete the information that needs to be forgotten. Its memory unit is composed of three parts: forgetting gate, input gate and output gate [37]. The schematic diagram of LSTM structure is shown in Fig. 2.

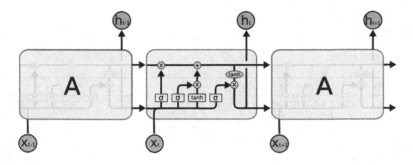

Fig. 2. LSTM Basic Architecture [38]

The first step of LSTM is to decide what information will be abandoned from the cell state, where the decision is controlled by a sigmoid layer called the "forget gate". f_t (forget gate) observes h_{t-1} (output vector) and x_t (input vector), and outputs a number between 0 and 1 for each element in the cell state C_{t-1}. 1 means keeping this information completely, 0 means discarding this information completely. The calculation formula for f_t is as following Eq. 5 [38] :

$$f_t = \sigma(W_{fx}X_t + W_{fh}h_{t-1} + b_f) \tag{5}$$

The input gate is used to calculate the current information that needs to be saved. It is mainly divided into two parts. The first part is the value range of i_t, which is from 0 to 1. 1 means all reserved, 0 means all discarded. The second part (c_t) represents new information. The cell creates a new memory by combining these two parts. The calculation formulas for i_t and c_t are as following Eqs. 6 and 7 [38]:

$$i_t = \sigma(W_{ix}X_t + W_{ih}h_{t-1} + b_i) \tag{6}$$

$$\tilde{c}_t = tanh(W_{cx}X_t + W_{ch}h_{t-1} + b_c) \tag{7}$$

Then the old cell state c_{t-1} updates to the new state C_t with the formula in Eq. 8.

$$C_t = f_t c_{t-1} + i_t \tilde{c}_t \tag{8}$$

Finally, the output gate is used to calculate the information to be output, and the output is the hidden layer state h_t. In the formula, h_t represents the state information C_t at the current moment, and it is the output in certain proportion.

3.6 Performance Evaluation

Many models are conducted to compare the performances of price value prediction. To comprehensively evaluate the performance of the models, one widely-used indicator is adopted in the experiments, which is Mean Absolute Percentage Error (MAPE). MAPE reflects the extent to which the predicted value deviates from the real value. The indicator is defined as Eq. 9.

$$MAPE = \frac{100\%}{N} \sum_{i=1}^{N} |\frac{y_i - \hat{y}_i}{y_i}| \tag{9}$$

where y_i is the ith true value and $\hat{y}_i$ is the ith predicted value, N is the amount of data in the experiments. The smaller the MAPE value, the larger the accuracy of the prediction.

4 Results Evaluation

4.1 Data Description

Through the above Twitter crawler steps, we retrieved and crawled over 7 million English tweets related to five cryptocurrencies from January 1, 2021 to June 30, 2021 on Twitter, which constitute the cryptocurrency-related data set of Big Data used in the experiment of this paper. The cryptocurrencies are BTC, DOGE, XRP, LTC, and ETH. The tweet data includes the timestamp of the tweet, text data, the number of likes and comments. Due to the existence of automated Bot accounts on Twitter, the data contains a large number of advertisements or spams, which would not only reduce the efficiency of this study, but also lead to deviations in the understanding and calculation of the overall sentiment trend of relevant topics. Fortunately, Twitter provides an easy and effective approach to filter such data with the use of "$" sign plus the name of the search theme. The original data and the filtered data distributions are shown in Tables 1 and 2. After applying the data pre-processing techniques mentioned in methodology chapter, we get structured textual data. The cleaned data distribution is shown in the Table 3.

Table 1. The distribution of the original tweets of the five cryptocurrencies

Month	BTC	DOGE	ETH	LTC	XRP
Jan	45595	8830	46427	96260	37654
Feb	55790	23210	55494	126540	39941
Mar	53675	45445	93566	126020	219024
Apr	151395	93455	143359	207945	478535
May	473395	1328755	913654	208445	367208
Jun	1218265	454165	727801	137235	226589

Table 2. The distribution of the filtered tweets of the five cryptocurrencies

Month	BTC	DOGE	ETH	LTC	XRP
Jan	14967	3143	13121	24842	13074
Feb	13870	5666	13688	32420	9317
Mar	14222	11473	23891	30245	48236
Apr	36575	21877	35108	49907	172231
May	113351	270901	223507	50027	89121
Jun	351489	113451	17618	25784	58312

Table 3. The distribution of the cleaned tweets of the five cryptocurrencies

Month	BTC	DOGE	ETH	LTC	XRP
Jan	9139	1786	9434	19452	5895
Feb	11558	4722	11407	27308	7681
Mar	11935	9189	19095	25204	40197
Apr	30479	18231	29257	41589	92026
May	94459	225751	186256	41689	70617
Jun	201653	92853	148488	21487	43594

As shown in Table 4, sources of models' inputs can be divided into three parts: besides transaction data and sentiment indicators, technical indicators are considered as well. Four technical indicators: moving average convergence and divergence (MACD), relative strength index (RSI), money flow index (MFI) and on balance volume (OBV) are chosen.

Table 4. Parameters and indicators used in the model

Transaction information	Technical indicators	Proposal sentiment indicators
Open price	MACD	Modified Sentiment Bullish Indicator
Close price	RSI	Modified Sentiment Diffusion Indicator
Highest price	MFI	Total Sentiment values
Lowest price	OBV	
Trading Volume		

4.2 Correlational Analysis

In order to intuitively observe the relationship between tweets amount change and cryptocurrency price change, we draw five graphs of changes in cryptocurrency price with the changes in the number of related tweets, as shown in Fig. 3(a-e).

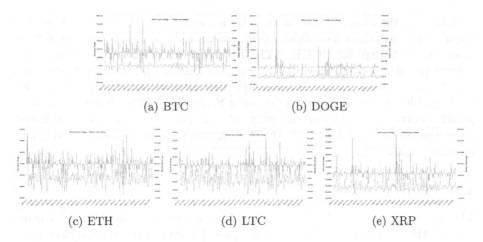

(a) BTC   (b) DOGE

(c) ETH   (d) LTC   (e) XRP

Fig. 3. Price changes with the comment number changes of the five cryptocurrencies

Figure 3(a-e) reveal an obvious relation between price change and the comment amount change, and the trend of price changes and the trend of comment number change are consistent to some extent. It remains unclear to which degree of correlation between them due to the frequent fluctuation. As mentioned in related work, previous work shows that sentiment indicators have a significant impact on price changes. They can be considered in price value prediction with high accuracy. In this study, we focus on the proposed granular market sentiment indicators and explore the accuracy of prediction with the use of small granular market sentiment indicators.

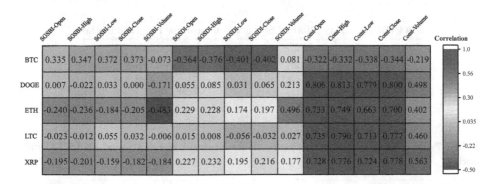

Fig. 4. Heat diagram of correlation between Small Granular Sentiment Indicators and Price Data

Figure 4 is the heat diagram of the correlation between each of the small granular sentiment indicators and each of the price data. The closer the color is to red and the darker the color is, the stronger the positive correlation between variables is; the closer the color is to green and the darker the color is, the stronger the negative correlation between variables is. It can be seen intuitively from the heat map: for DOGE, ETH, LTC and XRP, Comment Amount has a great positive correlation with opening price, closing price, highest price and lowest price, and Comment Amount has a moderate positive correlation with trading volume. For BTC, Small Granular Sentiment Bullish Index has a weak positive correlation with opening price, closing price, highest price and lowest price and Small Granular Sentiment Bullish Index has a medium negative correlation with trading volume.

4.3 Price Prediction

Three neural networks, BP, GRU and LSTM, are used to predict bitcoin's closing price of the same data set. We are using past 3 d data to predict the close price of the next day.

Table 5. Distribution of cleaned tweets of five cryptocurrencies based on BP network

MAPE%	Category	Normal Sentiment indicators	Proposed method
BP	BTC	7.22%	6.46%
	DOGE	6.52%	5.23%
	ETH	3.78%	3.22%
	LTC	5.81%	5.01%
	XRP	4.12%	3.86%

Table 6. Distribution of cleaned tweets of five cryptocurrencies based on GRU network

MAPE%	Category	Normal Sentiment indicators	Proposed method
GRU	BTC	6.72%	6.12%
	DOGE	5.92%	4.77%
	ETH	3.18%	2.62%
	LTC	5.01%	4.12%
	XRP	3.20%	3.06%

Table 7. Distribution of cleaned tweets of five cryptocurrencies based on LSTM network

MAPE%	Category	Normal Sentiment indicators	Proposed method
LSTM	BTC	5.98%	5.20%
	DOGE	5.02%	4.10%
	ETH	2.77%	2.30%
	LTC	4.23%	3.80%
	XRP	2.92%	2.70%

As shown in tables 5, 6 and 7, the present study confirms the finding that proposed small granular market sentiment indicators are effective in improving the accuracy of value prediction. Experimental results that if sentiment indicators are added, the price prediction accuracy of crytocurrencies other than Bitcoin will be higher prove the conclusion of heat map that the price data of crytocurrencies other than Bitcoin are more easily affected by public opinion. Another promising finding is that the BP neural network has the worst performance among the three models, and LSTM has more advantages in the value prediction of XRP, ETH and DOGE than GRU, while GRU performs better in value prediction of LTC and BTC.

5 Conclusion

The contribution of this paper is to propose a public sentiment indicator based on small granularity. By predicting the price of five cryptocurrencies in the next day on three deep learning frameworks, the effectiveness of the indicator is verified. Compared with the traditional public sentiment indicators under the same framework, the average loss percentage of our method is reduced by 0.65%. Based on the proposed sentiment indicators, correlational analysis between the indicators and price data is conducted. It is observed from the heat map that cryptocurrencies other than Bitcoin are more susceptible to public sentiment. The price prediction of cryptocurrencies other than Bitcoin are more sufficient when public sentiment is taken into account.

In the future, we will try to build sentiment indicators that better reflect sentiment trends on social platforms based on our knowledge of financial and sentiment analytics, and expand the sources of comment data to meet the generalization capabilities of the emerging social platforms such as streaming media.

References

1. Nakamoto, S.: Bitcoin: a peer-to-peer electronic cash system. Decentralized Business Rev. 21260 (2008)
2. Urquhart, A.: The inefficiency of bitcoin. Econ. Lett. **148**, 80–82 (2016)
3. Choi, H., Varian, H.: Predicting the present with google trends. Econ. Record **88**, 2–9 (2012)
4. Ettredge, M., Gerdes, J., Karuga, G.: Using web-based search data to predict macroeconomic statistics. Commun. ACM **48**(11), 87–92 (2005)
5. Abraham, J., Higdon, D., Nelson, J., Ibarra, J.: Cryptocurrency price prediction using tweet volumes and sentiment analysis. SMU Data Sci. Rev. **1**(3), 1 (2018)
6. Pano, T., Kashef, R.: A complete vader-based sentiment analysis of bitcoin (BTC) tweets during the era of covid-19. Big Data Cogn. Comput. **4**(4), 33 (2020)
7. Antweiler, W., Frank, M. Z.: Is all that talk just noise? the information content of internet stock message boards. J. Finance, **59**(3), 1259–1294 (2004)
8. Mao, H., Counts, S., Bollen, J.: Predicting financial markets: comparing survey, news, twitter and search engine data. arXiv preprint arXiv:1112.1051 (2011)

9. Kamyab, M., Rasool, A., Tao, R., Hayat, S.: Gawa-a feature selection method for hybrid sentiment classification. In: IEEE Access, pp. 191850–191861 (2020). https://doi.org/10.1109/ACCESS.2020.3030642

10. Bollen, J., Mao, H., Zeng, X.: Twitter mood predicts the stock market. J. Comput. Sci. **2**(1), 1–8 (2011)

11. Kraaijeveld, O., De Smedt, J.: The predictive power of public twitter sentiment for forecasting cryptocurrency prices. J. Int. Financial Markets Instit. Money **65**, 101188 (2020)

12. Li, Y., Pan, Y.: A novel ensemble deep learning model for stock prediction based on stock prices and news. Int. J. Data Sci. Anal. (2021). https://doi.org/10.1007/s41060-021-00279-9

13. Mohapatra, S., Ahmed, N., Alencar, P.: Kryptooracle: a real-time cryptocurrency price prediction platform using twitter sentiments. In: 2019 IEEE International Conference on Big Data (Big Data), pp. 5544–5551. IEEE (2019)

14. Li, X., Wang, C. A.: The technology and economic determinants of cryptocurrency exchange rates: the case of bitcoin. Decision Support Syst. **95**, 49–60 (2017)

15. Demir, E., Gozgor, G., Lau, C.K.M., Vigne, S. A.: Does economic policy uncertainty predict the bitcoin returns? an empirical investigation. Finance Res. Lett. **26**, 145–149 (2018)

16. Ahmar, A.S., Rahman, A., Mulbar, U.: α-sutte indicator: a new method for time series forecasting. J. Phys. Conf. Series,**1040**, 012018. IOP Publishing (2018)

17. Bakar, N.A., Rosbi, S.: Autoregressive integrated moving average (arima) model for forecasting cryptocurrency exchange rate in high volatility environment: a new insight of bitcoin transaction. Int. J. Adv. Eng. Res. Sci. **4**(11), 130–137 (2017)

18. Katsiampa, P.: Volatility estimation for bitcoin: a comparison of garch models. Econ. Lett. **158**, 3–6 (2017)

19. Rezaei, H., Faaljou, H., Mansourfar, G.: Stock price prediction using deep learning and frequency decomposition. Expert Syst. Appl. **169**, 114332 (2021)

20. Mallqui, D.C.A., Fernandes, R.A.S.: Predicting the direction, maximum, minimum and closing prices of daily bitcoin exchange rate using machine learning techniques. Appl. Soft Comput. **75**, 596–606 (2019)

21. Matkovskyy, R., Jalan, A.: From financial markets to bitcoin markets: a fresh look at the contagion effect. Finance Res. Lett. **31**, 93–97 (2019)

22. Li, Y., Dai, W.: Bitcoin price forecasting method based on cnn-lstm hybrid neural network model. J. Eng. **2020**(13), 344–347 (2020)

23. Burnie, A.: Exploring the interconnectedness of cryptocurrencies using correlation networks. arXiv preprint arXiv:1806.06632 (2018)

24. Angela, O., Sun, Y.: Factors affecting cryptocurrency prices: evidence from ethereum. In: 2020 International Conference on Information Management and Technology (ICIMTech), pp. 318–323. IEEE (2020)

25. Stosic, D., Stosic, D., Ludermir, T.B., Stosic, T.: Collective behavior of cryptocurrency price changes. Physic. A Statist. Mech. Appl. **507**, 499–509 (2018)

26. Indera, N.I., Yassin, I.M., Zabidi, A., Rizman, Z.I.: Non-linear autoregressive with exogeneous input (narx) bitcoin price prediction model using pso-optimized parameters and moving average technical indicators. J. Fundamental Appl. Sci. **9**(3S), 791–808 (2017)

27. Ozbayoglu, A.M., Gudelek, M.U., Sezer, O.B.: Financial time series forecasting with deep learning: a systematic literature review: 2005–2019. Appl. Soft Comput. **90**, 106181 (2020)

28. Dutta, A., Kumar, S., Basu, M.: A gated recurrent unit approach to bitcoin price prediction. J. Risk Finan. Manage. **13**(2), 23 (2020)

29. Roy, T.: Fielding: architectural styles and the design of network-based software architectures. University of California, Irvine (2000)
30. Tweepy documentation (2021). docs.tweepy.org/en/stable/
31. Ecma International. Ecmascript® 2021 language specification (2021). www.ecma-international.org/publications-and-standards/standards/ecma-262/
32. Rasool, A., Tao, R., Marjan, K., Naveed, T.: Twitter sentiment analysis: a case study for apparel brands. J. Phys. Conf. Series, **1176**, 022015. IOP Publishing (2019)
33. Agarwal, A., Xie, B., Vovsha, I., Rambow, O., Passonneau, R.J.: Sentiment analysis of twitter data. In: Proceedings of the Workshop on Languages in Social Media, LSM'11. Citeseer (2011)
34. Hutto, C., Gilbert, E.: Vader: a parsimonious rule-based model for sentiment analysis of social media text. In: Proceedings of the International AAAI Conference on Web and Social Media, Vol. 8 (2014)
35. Kirli, A., Orhan, Z.: A novel ensemble deep learning model for stock prediction based on stock prices and news. arXiv preprint arXiv:2007.12620 (2020)
36. Hochreiter, S.: Ja1 4 rgen schmidhuber."long short-term memory". Neural Comput. **9**(8) (1997)
37. Selvin, S., Vinayakumar, R., Gopalakrishnan, E.A., Menon, V.K., Soman, K.P.: Stock price prediction using lstm, rnn and cnn-sliding window model. In: 2017 International Conference on Advances in Computing, Communications and Informatics (icacci), pp. 1643–1647. IEEE (2017)
38. Colah, R.: Understanding lstm networks (2015). colah.github.io/posts/2015-08-Understanding-LSTMs/

A Survey on Task Scheduling Schemes in Mobile Edge Computing

Mengxin Jia[✉], Yanfang Fan, and Ying Cai

School of Computer, Beijing Information Science & Technology University, Beijing, China
jiamengxin@bistu.edu.cn

Abstract. Mobile Edge Computing (MEC) extends the capabilities of cloud computing to the network edge. By bringing the edge server closer to the mobile device, transmission latency and energy consumption are reduced. It also mitigates the risk of privacy breaches during the transmission of data over long distances. However, with the proliferation of applications on mobile devices, the amount of tasks that need to be processed is enormous. Edge servers have limited resources, and tasks with high resource requirements may occupy the server for a long time if priority is not set for the tasks. This will lead to a large number of tasks that cannot be completed. Consequently, some flexible task scheduling strategies are needed to improve task completion and resource utilization. In this paper, we consider the scheduling schemes for dependent and non-dependent tasks in single-server and multi-server scenarios, respectively. At the end, we summarize our work and describe the challenges ahead.

Keywords: Mobile Edge Computing · Task scheduling · Independent tasks · Dependent tasks

1 Introduction

Advances in Internet of Things (IoT) and wireless technology has laid the foundation for the emergence of applications on mobile devices. Examples include augmented reality, face recognition, medical detection [1], etc. Most of these applications are computationally intensive live latency sensitive and require large amounts of computational and storage resources, which places high demands on the capabilities of mobile devices [2]. Due to the limited computing power of mobile devices, they cannot handle heavy tasks locally. So the tasks are offloaded to remote cloud servers with high computing power. However, because the cloud server is located far from the mobile device, remote offloading will result in unpredictable transmission delays [3, 4]. To cope with this problem, the European Telecommunications Standards Institute (ETSI) proposed Mobile Edge Computing (MEC) in 2014 [5]. In MEC, servers are deployed at the edge of the network closer to the mobile device while providing the capabilities of cloud computing [6]. MEC reduces the end-to-end latency in mobile service delivery by reducing the distance between mobile devices and servers, which in turn improves the mobile devices' experience. More importantly, the possibility of illegal program intrusion during transmission is reduced, and the risk of data privacy leakage from mobile devices is also reduced.

© Springer Nature Singapore Pte Ltd. 2022
Y. Tian et al. (Eds.): ICBDS 2021, CCIS 1563, pp. 426–439, 2022.
https://doi.org/10.1007/978-981-19-0852-1_33

However, the resources of edge servers are not sufficient compared to cloud servers [7]. Numerous tasks may pile up in the server at a certain moment, and there will be a resource constraint, which leads to a higher task failure rate due to the tasks competing for resources. Therefore, it is necessary to set a processing order for tasks, that is, to set a priority for tasks. The priority setting takes into account the different attributes of the tasks. When the goal is to minimize latency, the priority is divided according to the latency tolerance of the task. When the goal is to handle more tasks, the division can be based on the size of the tasks. Furthermore, it may also be divided according to the importance of the task, since some tasks are not allowed to fail. To process tasks more efficiently, a task scheduling strategy that considers priority is needed. Designing the best task scheduling strategy is a challenge because tasks have many different characteristics [8]. In this paper, we summarize and classify the articles related to task scheduling in MEC. We divide the task scheduling scenarios into single-server and multi-server. And we classify tasks into independent tasks and dependent tasks based on whether they are related to each other.

The remainder of the paper is structured as follows. First, we briefly discuss the related concepts of task scheduling in Sect. 2. Second, we review and summarize existing related works in Sect. 3. Finally, we conclude the survey and describe the challenges ahead in Sect. 4 and Sect. 5.

2 Introduction to Task Scheduling in MEC

2.1 Concept of Task Scheduling

The essence of task scheduling is a mapping process [9]. It maps the tasks offloaded by the mobile device to the corresponding server for execution under certain constraints based on the resources required for the tasks in the network environment and the server load status, and then the server returns the processing results [10]. In order to rationalize the use of resources, tasks are usually sequenced and prioritized according to some rules. Priority is set so that tasks are executed sequentially, which allows for fair scheduling of tasks and mitigates the failure of multiple tasks competing for resources.

2.2 Process of Task Scheduling

Task scheduling consists of mapping tasks to the server and sequencing the tasks waiting to be processed. The specific operations in the server are divided into the following steps:

1) Tasks are deposited in the queue: Tasks are first stored in a buffer or queue where they wait to be scheduled for CPU execution.
2) Prioritization: Tasks are prioritized according to their characteristics, such as latency tolerance, dependency, etc., to determine the urgency of the task.
3) Task sending: Tasks are sent from the buffer or queue to a different server or left on the current server.
4) Task execution: Tasks are processed in the server.
5) Results returned: Server return results to mobile devices.

2.3 Optimization Goals

In existing studies of task scheduling strategies, common optimization objectives are latency, energy consumption, user quality of experience, and system overhead.

1) Minimize latency: Latency is the time it takes for a mobile device to go from submitting a task to receiving the return result [11]. There are various latency optimizations in specific studies. If the task is executed locally, only the execution time is optimized. If the task is offloaded to the server, the time between the task request and the result return is optimized. Most optimization goals are to minimize latency.
2) Minimize energy consumption: Energy consumption can occur during the work of mobile devices or servers. If the energy consumption exceeds the acceptable range of the equipment, it will lead to a reduction in the computing power of mobile devices and servers, so reducing energy consumption is also one of the optimization objectives in recent years' research [12].
3) Maximize the quality of experience (QoE): Quality of user experience describes the user feedback after the decision execution is completed and represents the user's evaluation of the environment and services. There are many metrics to describe QoE, such as communication cost, reputation [13, 14], a quantitative method that describes the subjective perception of users.
4) Minimize system cost: System cost is the time and resources spent by the whole system to perform the tasks of mobile devices, and most of the research at this stage is to minimize the system cost.

3 MEC Task Scheduling Schemes

There are two problems that need to be solved for task scheduling: 1) Which server should be scheduled to handle the offloaded tasks. 2) In what order each edge server should handle the offloaded tasks. Therefore, the scheduling scheme is divided into single-server scheduling and multi-server scheduling depend on whether there is a cooperative relationship between the servers. In single-server scenario, only the order of execution of all tasks that are scheduled to the server needs to be considered. In multi-server scenario, the number of tasks on each server may vary. To avoid wasting resources, tasks can be scheduled on other servers to achieve load balancing.

Tasks are classified into independent and dependent tasks based on whether they are related to each other or not. Independent tasks are tasks that are not related to each other. The state of a task does not have an impact on other tasks. Dependent tasks are those tasks that have a non-negligible association between multiple tasks. The start or end of the one task affects the start or end of other tasks. Usually, a task contains multiple subtasks, and the subtasks are dependent on each other. For example, in an in-vehicle augmented reality application, a model of the vehicle's surroundings can only be built after the vehicle has been tracked. Perspective transformation and merging processes can be performed only after the vehicle has been identified. In the authentication process [15], for both face recognition and fingerprint recognition, information needs to be collected first, then features are extracted, and then the comparison task is uploaded to the server for processing. The server returns the authentication result, and the authentication process can be completed.

A directed acyclic graph is often used to represent the dependencies between tasks. Directed means that the edges connecting two nodes have directions, and acyclic means that going along a directed edge from a node is not possible to return to this node. The direction of the edges represents the inheritance relationship between tasks and the execution order of tasks.

3.1 Single-Server Scheduling

Single-server scheduling means that all tasks are processed on only one server. Therefore, only the order of task execution on a single server needs to be considered. In existing research, the priority of tasks can be classified according to the characteristics of tasks such as size, dependency, latency tolerance, and importance [16]. The smaller the task or the lower the latency tolerance or the lower the importance, the higher the priority of the task. Some scholars consider the above-mentioned characteristics of tasks for prioritization. In this paper, tasks are classified into two categories based on whether they have dependencies or not: independent tasks and dependent tasks.

Independent Tasks. Wang et al. [17] considered the different sensitivity of on-board tasks to latency. Therefore, a joint offloading decision and task scheduling (JTSRA) algorithm was proposed. In the single-server case, task processing blocks, management blocks, and resource blocks were set up in the server to minimize task and settlement delays. This scheme was able to reduce the probability of task interruptions. Chen et al. [18] studied the problem of task scheduling and energy management considering latency tolerance in a single server in a renewable energy smart grid and proposed an algorithm that exploited latency flexibility and time-varying prices. The objective was to minimize the total cost of extracting energy from the external grid under a latency constraint. Zhang et al. [19] proposed an actor-critic based deep reinforcement learning (ADRL) that considered different latency sensitivities and did not allow tasks to migrate between ESs when they were offloaded to an edge server. The goal was to minimize the total cost of the task within the latency constraint. Yang et al. [20] considered a multi-user and multi-server MEC architecture, and jointly considered the task offloading and scheduling problem. The authors specified that only one server can be selected for each task and studied the scheduling order of multiple tasks on a single server with the goal of minimizing the task execution latency under the completion deadline constraint. Zhan et al. [21] studied the task scheduling problem of weighing task latency and energy consumption in a highway scenario. Li et al. [22] studied computational resource scheduling in autonomous driving problems by transforming the starting point into a multi-armed bandit problem, designing a stochastic scheduling scheme based on Whittle metrics, and then determining the metrics using deep reinforcement learning. The focus in the paper was on the scheduling of computational tasks in one processor, as scaling to multiple processors was straightforward. Simulation results showed that the scheme can adapt to the mobility of vehicles and improved the task data transfer speed. Liu et al. [23] considered both mobile devices, cloud and network collaboration and proposed a custom optimization framework and simulated annealing-based single-objective optimization and tri-objective optimization algorithms to solve the task scheduling problem, where the scheduling algorithm assigned tasks to cloud servers and left the rest to be executed locally. Samanta et al. [24] proposed a heuristic task scheduling algorithm using the service competition time and quality of service of the tasks to determine the priority, which required estimating the latency optimal demand of the device tasks. Liu et al. [25] solved the dual time-scale optimization problem of task scheduling for MEC systems by using a Markov decision process approach, considering the task queue state, local as well as edge server states. In the paper, a one-dimensional search algorithm was proposed to find the best scheduling policy, which can achieve shorter average execution latency.

Dependent Tasks. Yang et al. [26] considered a model with sequentially dependent subtasks in MEC and jointly optimized multi-user task partitioning on cloud servers and scheduling on servers. Simulation results showed that this scheme had better performance than existing list scheduling algorithms in terms of application latency. Zhang et al. [27] proposed an online joint task scheduling algorithm based on a deep deterministic policy gradient considering features such as container constraints and task dependencies. The objective is to maximize the system utility and at the same time minimize the system cost. Shu et al. [28] studied the problem of fine-grained task offloading in low-power IoT systems. Task dependencies and heterogeneous resources on the edge server were considered. Only one server can be selected at a time for each task. A lightweight but efficient offloading scheme was proposed for multi-user edge systems. The scheme effectively reduced the end-to-end task execution time and improved the resource utilization of the edge servers. Zhang et al. [29] argued that the scheduling method needs to consider execution time and execution energy simultaneously. So a data-dependent task rescheduling algorithm was proposed. The experimental results showed that the algorithm performs better in terms of scheduling length and energy consumption under both homogeneous and heterogeneous resources. Żotkiewicz et al. [30] proposed a minimum-dependency energy-efficient DAG scheduling. Both deadlines and dependencies of tasks were considered. The scheme outperformed other methods in terms of energy efficiency. Wang et al. [31] argued that the dependency between data was not considered in the scheme to improve the efficiency of parallel operations. A dependency-aware network adaptive scheduler was designed. Experimental results showed that the scheduler not only significantly improved the performance of dependent jobs, but was also friendly to non-dependent jobs. Komarasamy et al. [32] argued that in cloud computing, random submission of job tasks made scheduling difficult. Proposed the Adaptive Deadline for Cloud Computing Job Scheduling (A2DJS) algorithm. The algorithm considered task dependencies and priorities and was able to alleviate the time span of jobs and improved the processor utilization (Table 1).

3.2 Multi-server Scheduling

Multi-server scheduling means that tasks are scheduled between multiple servers and can share the resources of multiple servers. For example, when the current server does not have enough resources to handle the task, some of the tasks can be scheduled to other servers with more resources to achieve load balancing.

Table 1. Single-server scheduling literature.

	Considered Factors	Algorithm	Optimization objective
[17]	·Latency tolerance	·MDP(Markov Decision Processes) ·RL(Reinforcement learning)	Minimize task latency
[18]	·Latency tolerance	·Joint task scheduling and energy selling algorithm	Minimize end-user cost
[19]	·Latency tolerance	·RL	Minimize task total cost
[20]	·Latency tolerance	·Search method ·Heuristic algorithms	Minimize task latency
[21]	·Backup servers provide arithmetic power	·MDP ·DRL(deep reinforcement learning)	Minimize cost between task latency and energy consumption
[22]	·Vehicle mobility	·Whittle metric	Minimize vehicle travel distance
[23]	·Collaboration of mobile devices	·Simulated annealing	Minimize task energy consumption
[24]	·Service contention time and quality of service for tasks	·Optimal latency estimation engine	Minimize service latency
[25]	·Buffer queuing status ·Transfer units status	·One-dimensional search algorithm	Minimize average task latency
[26]	·Task dependency	·Heuristics for offline ·Algorithms for online	Minimize average task latency
[27]	·Container constraints ·Task dependency	·Online joint task scheduling algorithm based on deep deterministic policy gradients	Maximize system utility
[28]	·Task dependency	·Distributed consensus algorithms for low-power IoT devices	Minimize average task latency
[29]	·Heterogeneous resources ·Execution time ·Execution energy ·Earliest task completion time	·Data-dependent task rescheduling algorithms	Shut down inefficient resources
[30]	·Task deadlines ·Task dependency	·Minimum dependency energy efficient DAG scheduling	Minimize task energy consumption
[31]	·Data dependency	·Dependency-aware network adaptive scheduler	Smooth network traffic to improve utilization
[32]	·Task dependency ·Task prioritization	·Adaptive Deadline (A2DJS) algorithm	Minimize the time span of jobs

Independent Tasks. Zhu et al. [33] considered user mobility, which affected the movement of tasks between servers. In this paper, the scheduling problem on multiple servers was defined as a minimum energy consumption problem subject to task deadlines. Fan et al. [34] studied scheduling tasks from clouds, small clouds and mobile devices. The problem of user mobility and task movement on the server was considered. The problem was considered as a 0–1 backpack problem and solved using an improved ant colony algorithm that can predict the user's location. Meng et al. [35] considered network bandwidth and computational resource management and proposed an online algorithm that greedily scheduled new arrivals and considered replacing the ongoing task with a new task if the deadline for the new arrival was short. Zhu et al. [36] proposed a two-stage planning approach to alleviate the resource competition problem among users and thus reduce the offloading delay. In the scheduling phase, the authors scheduled the task to the next service area after the vehicle left the current service area to ensure the proper connection between the vehicle task and the processing node. Lin et al. [37] proposed a distributed application-aware scheduling algorithm that considered the impact of multiple scheduling of task types so that multiple edge servers can be load balanced and reduced the energy consumption during task scheduling. Tan et al. [38] developed an energy-aware strategy and proposed an iterative critical path-based algorithm that considered the deadline constraints of tasks in a fog computing environment. The paper specified that each server can only process one task and to schedule tasks during multiple services. The objective was to minimize the energy consumed by scheduling. Dai et al. [39] considered scheduling in a cloud computing environment as an NP-hard problem and proposed a scheduling algorithm with multiple QoE constraints by considering time consumption, security and reliability in the policy. Zhang et al. [40] proposed a two-stage task scheduling cost optimization algorithm. On the basis of the objective that the goal was to minimize the cost of the edge computing system, a suitable edge server was selected to handle the tasks because the cost of each edge server to handle the tasks was different. Sun et al. [41] studied the joint offloading and task scheduling problem in an in-vehicle edge computing environment. Tasks were scheduled to the next server as the vehicle moves. In this paper, a combination of uniparental genetic algorithm and heuristic rules is used to obtain the optimal solution while reducing the time complexity. Li et al. [42] proposed a task partitioning and scheduling algorithm (TPSA) to determine the workload assignment. Second, an artificial intelligence (AI)-based collaborative computing approach was developed to determine task offloading, computation, and result delivery policies for vehicles.

When mobile devices are vehicles, some studies consider the idle resources on the vehicles and let the moving or parked vehicles act as processing nodes for the tasks. Chen et al. [43] proposed a hybrid dynamic scheduling scheme (HDSS) for the task scheduling problem in a heterogeneous MEC environment, which had the ability to dynamically optimize task scheduling in a variable system environment, utilizing the idle resources on the vehicle and scheduling tasks to achieve task latency minimization. Wang et al. [44] divided the vehicles on the road into service demand vehicles as well as service providing vehicles, clustered the service providing vehicles into a cluster, and proposed an online task scheduling algorithm based on imitation learning with the goal of minimizing the system energy consumption while satisfying the task latency constraints. Ma et al. [45] considered the idle resources on parked vehicles and let parking vehicle assist the edge server to handle the task of offloading. The article designed a scheduling algorithm and a local scheduling strategy. Simulation results showed that the method can improve the performance of offloading scheduling. Joe et al. [46] considered vehicles as edge computing resources to build collaborative distributed computing architecture. A collaborative task offloading and output transfer mechanism was proposed. The scheme was able to guarantee application-level driving experience while reducing perceptual response time. Huang et al. [47] solved a resource scheduling optimization problem in a vehicle edge computing environment using the Stackelberg game approach considering the free computational resources on the vehicles. The optimization goal is to minimize the overhead of the user device. Simulation results show that the algorithm is able to reduce the service cost of the user as a way to serve more vehicles.

Dependent Tasks. Scheduling dependent tasks in a multi-server environment requires complete scheduling of related tasks: if a task is scheduled to a server, all tasks have dependent relationships should be scheduled to the same server. This is because later tasks can start only when the current task has been completed, and tasks are inextricably related to each other. If tasks are scheduled separately, the requirement of dependency is violated.

Al-Habob et al. [48] considered tasks consisting of interdependent subtasks scheduled to a set of servers in parallel and in sequence and proposed two scheduling algorithms, based on a genetic algorithm and a conflict graph model, with the goal of minimizing the offloading latency and the probability of failure, respectively. Lee et al. [49] proposed a dependency-aware task assignment algorithm in a distributed edge computing environment, which was a heuristic algorithm with low complexity, considering the collaborative processing of tasks using multiple edge clouds. Liu et al. [50] considered that the dependencies among the on-board tasks in MEC affected the execution order of the tasks, and by considering the dependencies and completion time constraints of the tasks.Hu et al. [51] proposed a cluster scheduler which considered both task dependency and heterogeneous resource requirements. And a new scheduling framework Spear was proposed which aimed to minimize the completion time of complex jobs. Liu et al. [52] argued that previous scheduling efforts could not simultaneously achieve low response times and high resource utilization. Considering task dependencies and resource requirements in the scheduling algorithm. Experimental results showed that the method outperformed other methods (Table 2).

Table 2. Multi-server scheduling literature.

	Considered Factors	Algorithm	Optimization objective
[33]	·User mobility	·localized partially rational task plan construction algorithm ·LoPRTC for multiple MDs	Minimize energy consumption of MDs and MEC servers
[34]	·Task mobility ·User mobility	·Improved ant colony algorithms for predicting user location	Improved QoE for end users
[35]	·Network bandwidth ·Resource management	·Online algorithms	Maximize number of deadlines

(*continued*)

Table 2. (*continued*)

	Considered Factors	Algorithm	Optimization objective
[36]	·Multi-tenant resource contention	·Two-phase planning approach	Minimize average service latency
[37]	·Impact of multiple scheduling of task types	·Distributed application-aware scheduling algorithms	Minimize task energy consumption
[38]	·Task Deadline	·Critical path based iterative algorithm	Minimize task energy consume
[39]	·Time consumption, overhead ·Security ·Reliability	·Multiple QoS-constrained scheduling algorithms	Maximize user quality of service
[40]	·Consider the costs incurred by edge servers	·Two-phase task scheduling cost optimization algorithm	Minimize system costs
[41]	·Vehicle mobility	·Combination of uniparental genetic algorithms and heuristic rules	Maximize system offloading utility
[42]	·Collaboration between edge servers	·Task division and scheduling algorithms ·Artificial intelligence (AI)-based collaborative computing methods	Minimize service costs
[43]	·Vehicle idle resources	·Hybrid dynamic scheduling scheme	Minimize task latency
[44]	·Vehicle idle resources	·Online task scheduling algorithm	Minimize system energy consumption
[45]	·Resources for parking	·Scheduling algorithms ·Local task scheduling strategies	Predictive models to generate time-dependent predictions
[46]	·Vehicle idle resources	·Collaborative task offload and output transfer mechanisms	Reduce perceived response time
[47]	·Resources for parking	·Stackelberg game approach formulates a resource scheduling optimization problem	Minimize user cost
[48]	·Task dependency	·Algorithms based on genetic algorithms and conflict graph models	Minimize offloading delay and failure probability
[49]	·Multiple edge clouds to collaborate on tasks	·Dependency-aware task allocation algorithms	Minimize task latency
[50]	·Task dependency	·Multi-application multi-task scheduling algorithms	Minimize average task latency

(*continued*)

Table 2. (*continued*)

	Considered Factors	Algorithm	Optimization objective
[51]	·Task dependency ·Heterogeneous resources	·Scheduling framework Spear	Minimize complex jobs' latency
[52]	·Task dependency ·Resource requirements	·Dependency awareness and resource efficient scheduling	Minimize application computation time

4 Open Challenges

1) QoE optimization. As the amount of mobile devices in MEC environments grows, feedback from mobile devices on scheduling results becomes increasingly important [53]. In previous studies, scheduling dependent tasks rarely considers QoE. Since interdependent tasks must be processed on the same server, the waiting time of the latter tasks affects QoE and should be considered.
2) Task failure rate optimization: Due to the dynamic nature of resources on servers and and mobile devices, it is difficult to meet the demands of tasks in real time, which can easily lead to high task failure rates. Failure of task scheduling is inevitable, so a more comprehensive scheduling strategy should be developed to ensure task completion rate and reduce the failure rate as much as possible.
3) Security. In a mobile edge computing environment, the transmission of data is exposed to unpredictable security threats. For example, the handing over of data from mobile devices to servers and the transmission of data between multiple servers may lead to privacy leakage of mobile terminals. While less work is done to consider security issues in existing task scheduling, more attention should be paid to security issues during task transmission.
4) Low-priority task optimization: Low-priority tasks are not dominant in the queue, especially when new tasks are added with higher priority. This may result in low-priority tasks being kept in a waiting state. Therefore, when developing a scheduling strategy, consider the waiting time of tasks and let tasks with long waiting time be processed first as much as possible [54]. Few task-dependent ones have been considered in existing studies, so a more comprehensive scheduling strategy should be designed.

5 Summary

In the mobile edge computing environment, resources are limited, it is very necessary to arrange the order of tasks in order to allocate computational resources reasonably. This paper focuses on task scheduling in MEC, first introducing the development of mobile edge computing, and then describing the meaning, process, and the main optimization objectives of task scheduling. Then the scheduling of independent and dependent tasks in single-server and multi-server environments are summarized respectively. Finally, existing challenges are further discussed. We hope it will motivate researchers better understanding and working on task scheduling in the edge computing environment.

Acknowledgement. This work is supported by Qin Xin Talents Cultivation Program, Beijing Information Science & Technology University (No. QXTCP C202111).

References

1. Gaikwad, P.P., Gabhane, J.P., Golait, S.S.: A survey based on smart homes system using Internet-of-Things. In Proc. Int. Conf. Comput. Power Energy Inf. Commun. (ICCPEIC), Chennai, India, pp. 0330–0335
2. Soyata, T., Muraleedharan, R., Funai, C., Kwon, M., Heinzelman, W.: Cloud-vision: real-time face recognition using a mobile-cloudlet-cloud acceleration architecture. In: Proc. IEEE Symp. Comput. Commun. (ISCC), pp. 59–66 (2012)
3. Shi, W., Cao, J., Zhang, Q., Li, Y., Xu, L.: Edge computing: vision and challenges. J. IEEE Internet Things **3**(5), 637–646 (2016)
4. Roman, R., Lopez, J., Mambo, M.: Mobile edge computing, fog et al.: a survey and analysis of security threats and challenges. Future Gener. Comput. Syst. **78**, 680–698 (2018)
5. ETSI. Mobile-Edge Computing–Introductory Technical White Paper. https://portal.etsi.org/Portals/0/TBpages/MEC/Docs/Mobileedge_Computing_Introductory_Technical_White_Paper_V1%2018-09-14.pdf
6. Ai, Y., Peng, M., Zhang, K.: Edge computing technologies for Internet of Things: a primer. Digital Commun. Netw. **4**(2), 77–86 (2018)
7. Shaw, S.B., Singh. A.K.: A survey on scheduling and load balancing techniques in cloud computing environment. In: 2014 International Conference on Computer and Communication Technology (ICCCT), pp. 87–95 (2014)
8. Fang, X., et al.: Job scheduling to minimize total completion time on multiple edge servers. IEEE Trans. Netw. Sci. Eng. **7**(4), 2245–2255 (2020)
9. Gupta, A., Garg, R.: Workflow scheduling in heterogeneous computing systems: a survey. In: 2017 International Conference on Computing and Communication Technologies for Smart Nation (IC3TSN), pp. 319–326 (2017)
10. Wu, H.: Research of Task Scheduling Algorithm in the Cloud Environment. Nanjing University of Posts and Telecommunications, Nanjing (2013)
11. Yousefpour, A., Ishigaki, G., Gour, R., Jue, J.P.: On reducing IoT service delay via fog offloading. IEEE Internet of Things J. **5**(2), 998–1010 (2018)
12. Mach, M., Becvar, Z.: Mobile edge computing: a survey on architecture and computation offloading. J. IEEE Commun. Surv. Tutor. **19**(3), 1628–1656 (2017)
13. Cao, Y., Chen, Y.: QoE-based node selection strategy for edge computing enabled Internet-of-Vehicles (EC-IoV). In: 2017 IEEE Visual Communications and Image Processing (VCIP), pp. 1–4 (2017)
14. Itu, T.P.: Methods for subjective determination of transmission quality. J. ITU-T Recommend. p. 800 (1996)
15. Wang, M., Ma, T., Wu, T., Chang, C., Yang, F., Wang, H.: Dependency-aware dynamic task scheduling in mobile-edge computing. In: 2020 16th International Conference on Mobility, Sensing and Networking (MSN), pp. 785–790 (2020)
16. Liao, J.X., Wu, X.W.: Resource allocation and task scheduling scheme in priority-based hierarchical edge computing system. In: 2020 19th International Symposium on Distributed Computing and Applications for Business Engineering and Science (DCABES), pp. 46–49 (2020)
17. Wang, G., Xu, F., Zhao, C.: Multi-access edge computing based vehicular network: joint task scheduling and resource allocation strategy. In: 2020 IEEE International Conference on Communications Workshops (ICC Workshops), Dublin, Ireland, pp. 1–6 (2020)

18. Chen, S., Shroff, N.B., Sinha, P.: Heterogeneous delay tolerant task scheduling and energy management in the smart grid with renewable energy. J. IEEE J. Select. Areas Commun. **31**(7), 1258–1267 (2013)
19. Zhang, T., Chiang, Y.-H., Borcea, C.: Learning-based offloading of tasks with diverse delay sensitivities for mobile edge computing. In: 2019 IEEE Global Communications Conference (GLOBECOM), pp. 1–6 (2019)
20. Yang, T., Chai, R., Zhang, L.: Latency optimization-based joint task offloading and scheduling for multi-user MEC system. In: 2020 29th Wireless and Optical Communications Conference (WOCC), pp. 1–6 (2020)
21. Zhan, W., et al.: Deep-reinforcement-learning-based offloading scheduling for vehicular edge computing. IEEE Internet of Things J. **7**(6), 5449–5465 (2020). https://doi.org/10.1109/JIOT. 2020.2978830
22. Li, M., Gao, J., Zhao, L., Shen, X.: Adaptive computing scheduling for edge-assisted autonomous driving. J. IEEE Trans. Veh. Technol. **70**(6), 5318–5331 (2021)
23. Liu, H., et al.: A holistic optimization framework for mobile cloud task scheduling. IEEE Trans. Sustain. Comput. **4**(2), 217–230 (2019)
24. Samanta, A., Chang, Z., Han, Z.: Latency-oblivious distributed task scheduling for mobile edge computing. In: 2018 IEEE Global Communications Conference (GLOBECOM), pp. 1–7 (2018)
25. Liu, J., Mao, Y., Zhang, J., Letaief, K.B.: Delay-optimal computation task scheduling for mobile-edge computing systems. In: IEEE International Symposium on Information Theory (ISIT) (2016)
26. Yang, L., Cao, J., Cheng, H., Ji, Y.: Multi-user computation partitioning for latency sensitive mobile cloud applications. IEEE Trans. Comput. **64**(8), 2253–2266 (2015). https://doi.org/ 10.1109/TC.2014.2366735
27. Zhang, F., Tang, Z., Lou, J., Jia, W.: Online joint scheduling of delay-sensitive and computation-oriented tasks in edge computing. In: 2019 15th International Conference on Mobile Ad-Hoc and Sensor Networks (MSN), pp. 303–308 (2019)
28. Shu, C., Zhao, Z., Han, Y., Min, G., Duan, H.: Multi-user offloading for edge computing networks: a dependency-aware and latency-optimal approach. J. IEEE Internet of Things J. **7**(3), 1678–1689 (2020)
29. Xiaoqing, Z., Yajie, H., Chunlin, A.: Data-dependent tasks re-scheduling energy efficient algorithm. In: 2018 IEEE 4th International Conference on Computer and Communications (ICCC), pp. 2542–2546 (2018)
30. Zotkiewicz, M., Guzek, M., Kliazovich, D., Bouvry, P.: Minimum dependencies energy-efficient scheduling in data centers. J. IEEE Trans. Parall. Distrib. Syst. **27**(12), 3561–3574 (2016)
31. Wang, S., Chen, W., Zhou, X., Zhang, L., Wang, Y.: Dependency-aware network adaptive scheduling of data-intensive parallel jobs. IEEE Trans. Parall. Distrib. Syst. **30**(3), 515–529 (2019)
32. Komarasamy, D., Muthuswamy, V.: Adaptive deadline based dependent job scheduling algorithm in cloud computing. In: 2015 Seventh International Conference on Advanced Computing (ICoAC), pp. 1–5 (2015)
33. Zhu, T., Shi, T., Li, J., Cai, Z., Zhou, X.: Task scheduling in deadline-aware mobile edge computing systems. J. IEEE Internet of Things J. **6**(3), 4854–4866 (2019)
34. Fan, J., Liu, J., Chen, J., Yang, J.: LPDC: mobility-and deadline-aware task scheduling in tiered IoT. In: 2018 IEEE 4th International Conference on Computer and Communications (ICCC), pp. 857–863 (2018)
35. Meng, J., Tan, H., Xu, C., Cao, W., Liu, L., Li, B.: Dedas: online task dispatching and scheduling with bandwidth constraint in edge computing. In: IEEE INFOCOM 2019 - IEEE Conference on Computer Communications, pp. 2287–2295 (2019)

36. Zhu, C., Pastor, G., Xiao, Y., Li, Y., Yla-Jaaski, A.: Fog following me: latency and quality balanced task allocation in vehicular fog computing. In: Proc. 15th Annu. IEEE Int. Conf. Sensing Commun. Netw. (SECON), pp. 1–9 (2018)
37. Lin, L., Li, P., Xiong, J., Lin, M.: Distributed and application-aware task scheduling in edge-clouds. In: 2018 14th International Conference on Mobile Ad-Hoc and Sensor Networks (MSN), pp. 165–170 (2018)
38. Tan, H., Chen, W, Qin, L., Zhu, J., Huang, H.: Energy-aware and deadline-constrained task scheduling in fog computing systems. In: 2020 15th International Conference on Computer Science & Education (ICCSE), pp. 663–668 (2020)
39. Dai, Y., Lou, Y., Lu, X.: A task scheduling algorithm based on genetic algorithm and ant colony optimization algorithm with multi-QoS constraints in cloud computing. In: 2015 7th International Conference on Intelligent Human-Machine Systems and Cybernetics, pp. 428–431 (2015)
40. Zhang, Y., Chen, X., Chen, Y., Li, Z., Huang, J.: Cost efficient scheduling for delay-sensitive tasks in edge computing system. In: 2018 IEEE International Conference on Services Computing (SCC), pp. 73–80 (2018)
41. Sun, J., Gu, Q., Zheng, T., Dong, P., Valera, A., Qin, Y.: Joint optimization of computation offloading and task scheduling in vehicular edge computing networks. J. IEEE Access **8**, 10466–10477 (2020)
42. Li, M., Gao, J., Zhao, L., Shen, X.: Deep reinforcement learning for collaborative edge computing in vehicular networks. J. IEEE Trans. Cognitive Commun. Netw. **6**(4), 1122–1135 (2020)
43. Chen, X., Thomas, N., Zhan, T., Ding, J.: A hybrid task scheduling scheme for heterogeneous vehicular edge systems. J. IEEE Access **7**, 117088–117099 (2019)
44. Wang, X., Ning, Z., Guo, S., Wang, L.: Imitation learning enabled task scheduling for online vehicular edge computing. J. IEEE Trans. Mob. Comput. **21**(2), 598–611 (2022)
45. Ma, C., Zhu, J., Liu, M., Zhao, H., Liu, N., Zou, X.: Parking edge computing: parked-vehicle-assisted task offloading for urban VANETs. J. IEEE Internet of Things J. **8**(11), 9344–9358 (2021)
46. Qiao, G., Leng, S., Zhang, K., He, Y.: Collaborative task offloading in vehicular edge multi-access networks. IEEE Commun. Mag. **56**(8), 48–54 (2018). https://doi.org/10.1109/MCOM. 2018.1701130
47. Huang, X., Yu, R., Liu, J., Shu, L.: Parked vehicle edge computing: exploiting opportunistic resources for distributed mobile applications. J. IEEE Access **6**, 66649–66663 (2018)
48. Al-Habob, A.A., Dobre, O.A., Armada, A.G., Muhaidat, S.: Task scheduling for mobile edge computing using genetic algorithm and conflict graphs. J. IEEE Trans. Veh. Technol. **69**(8), 8805–8819 (2020)
49. Lee, J., Kim, J., Pack, S., Ko, H.: Dependency-aware task allocation algorithm for distributed edge computing. In: 2019 IEEE 17th International Conference on Industrial Informatics (INDIN), pp. 1511–1514 (2019)
50. Liu, Y., et al.: Dependency-aware task scheduling in vehicular edge computing. IEEE Internet of Things J. **7**(6), 4961–4971 (2020)
51. Hu, Z., Tu, J., Li, B.: Spear: optimized dependency-aware task scheduling with deep reinforcement learning. In: 2019 IEEE 39th International Conference on Distributed Computing Systems (ICDCS) (2019)
52. Liu, J., Shen, H.: Dependency-aware and resource-efficient scheduling for heterogeneous jobs in clouds. In: 2016 IEEE International Conference on Cloud Computing Technology and Science (CloudCom), pp. 110–117 (2016)

53. Meriam, E., Tabbane, N.: A survey on cloud computing scheduling algorithms. In: 2016 Global Summit on Computer & Information Technology (GSCIT), pp. 42–47 (2016)
54. Kumari, S., Kapoor, R.K., Singh, S.: A survey on different techniques for information resource scheduling in cloud computing. In: 2015 International Conference on Computational Intelligence and Communication Networks (CICN), pp. 736–740 (2015)

Research on Dynamic Simulation Modeling
of Chemical Industry Based on Edge Algorithm

Liu Pengpeng(⊠)

Dongying Vocational Institute, Dongying 257091, Shandong, China

Abstract. Chemical dynamic simulation modeling plays an important role in process system engineering and process operation analysis. The establishment of a general dynamic simulation modeling platform for chemical process can greatly shorten the research cycle of chemical process and further improve the production efficiency of chemical process. However, the development of such systems is often accompanied by complex data calculation and transmission requirements, which is greatly limited in practical application scenarios. In order to solve this problem, a chemical dynamic simulation modeling method based on edge algorithm is proposed in this paper. As a decentralized computing architecture, edge computing moves the computing of applications, data and services from the central node of the network to the edge node of the network logic for processing, that is, the large services originally handled by the central node are decomposed, cut into smaller and easier to manage parts, and distributed to the edge node for processing. This method is closer to the user terminal device, which can speed up the data processing and transmission speed, reduce the delay, and meet more the needs of chemical dynamic simulation modeling in practical application scenarios. The experimental part shows the examples of chemical dynamic simulation modeling based on edge algorithm, which verifies the effectiveness of the method proposed in this paper.

Keywords: Edge compute · Chemical dynamic simulation model · Decentralized computing

1 Introduction

1.1 The Simulation Model of Chemical Industry

At present, with the high requirements for product quality, the upgrading of production environment safety and the strict supervision of surrounding environmental protection, dynamic modeling and simulation has become more and more important in process system engineering and process operation analysis. However, dynamic modeling and simulation is a time-consuming and requires a lot of manpower and material resources. It has high requirements for developers. They not only need high-level system experts, but also need to skillfully use computers to realize the designed simulation. Although there is many professional chemical process simulation software at this stage, with rich module library and algorithm library, it can simulate most processes. However, with the introduction of new devices, we spend a lot of money and are also limited by

© Springer Nature Singapore Pte Ltd. 2022
Y. Tian et al. (Eds.): ICBDS 2021, CCIS 1563, pp. 440–451, 2022.
https://doi.org/10.1007/978-981-19-0852-1_34

the update speed of the software [1]. In addition, for the simulator, complex code or non-intuitive modeling rules will affect the effect of modeling. Therefore, according to their own resources, the establishment of a general chemical process dynamic simulation modeling platform is a way to solve the above problems. Through the graphical interface, drag and drop modules from the module library, use the connection between modules to establish the connection between each module, so as to build the whole chemical unit, and then simulate the whole process, which is the content of this paper. Through the above platform to give the simulator an intuitive feeling, liberate from the heavy modeling and coding, and turn their attention to simulation analysis and optimization. From steady-state simulation to dynamic simulation.

The earliest process simulation system is the flexible flowsheet developed by Kellogg Company in 1958. It is used for the process simulation of large-scale synthetic ammonia and has achieved good results [2]. Subsequently, a number of specialized process simulation software emerged, such as Aspen, pro-ii, HYSIM, etc. China's development is relatively late compared with foreign countries. It was the first large-scale hydrocarbon separation simulation system launched by the fifth Design Institute of the former Ministry of chemical industry in 1977. Subsequently, domestic process simulation software has also made great progress, but the main development efforts are concentrated in scientific research institutes, universities and large petrochemical enterprises [3]. Because of the relativity and temporality of steady-state simulation, it cannot well describe the changes or sudden factors such as fluctuation, interference and accidents in process industry, so dynamic simulation is developed. Dynamic simulation can study the dynamic characteristics of the process, and get the correct design scheme, excellent control strategy and better operating conditions from the variation law of process parameters with time. The representative dynamic simulation software includes speed up and dynamics of Aspen tech. Dynamics simulation software integrates steady-state and dynamic simulation [4].

1.2 The Mathematical Model

With the emergence of intelligent methods, some such methods are also used while establishing mathematical models. The representative methods are artificial neural network [5], support vector machine [5], fuzzy theory [5] and so on:

Because the existing computing architecture is difficult to meet the needs of low delay and high data volume when building chemical dynamic simulation modeling system, edge computing is proposed as a supplement to the existing computing modes such as cloud computing. Edge computing is to set up computing/storage nodes near the user terminal to meet the needs of mobile users. It can effectively alleviate the pressure in cloud center and network transmission and improve the real-time performance of data processing. At present, computing and task scheduling, architecture, security and other issues in edge computing are hot research directions in the field. Emerging technologies such as software defined network [6], blockchain [7], machine learning [8] have also been applied to edge computing, and edge computing is also used in medical [9], smart city [10], virtual reality [11] Good progress has been made in smart industry [12], driverless [13], environmental monitoring [14].

After several years of development, many people have also made many contributions in different fields of edge computing, providing strong support for the follow-up development. Literature [15] summarizes the background, concept, development status, core technology and problems of edge computing. Considering the resources required for effective technology transmission and processing, document [16] proposed a new architecture of cloud edge coupling, which dynamically manages the complete analysis pipeline of IOT equipment through the edge layer, so as to generate large data sets to achieve the ultimate goal. Literature [17] designed a lightweight scheduler, which uses deep neural network to realize the automatic allocation of data center and mobile devices, and realizes the data exchange between cloud center and edge nodes in this way. The above work is to discuss the collaboration and interaction between cloud edge devices, but does not pay attention to the interaction and task allocation between edge devices.

In order to solve the problems of large amount of data calculation, long calculation time and high demand for data transmission in chemical dynamic simulation modeling, this paper proposes a new modeling method combined with edge computing. This method transfers the computing node from the system center to the computing node at each terminal position of the modeling system, and uses a distributed method to deal with the computing problem, and each computing node saves its own data, which saves the time loss in data transmission and improves the work efficiency of the modeling system. At the same time, in order to solve the difficulty of task scheduling in edge computing, a new task scheduling algorithm based on improved ant colony algorithm is proposed, which jointly completes the construction of chemical dynamic simulation modeling system.

2   Method

2.1   Edge Computing and Task Scheduling

The research of edge computing is still in the primary stage. People in different application fields have their own understanding of its definition, but its essence has been determined: store and process data at the edge of the network close to the data source, and cooperate with the cloud to provide users with low latency and efficient services. Task scheduling is a very important link to realize edge computing [14]. An excellent scheduling algorithm can make full use of the computing and storage resources on the device, minimize data transmission and maximize application execution performance, and create better service effect for users in limited resources.

The typical task scheduling scenario of edge computing is shown in Fig. 1. It can be described as n independent tasks assigned to m edge nodes with different computing capabilities, and N is usually greater than m. The computing resources of each edge node are very different, and the requirements of task n will also show different states. According to the optimization objectives to be achieved, the matching relationship between tasks and edge nodes is established to achieve the optimal task allocation.

Problem Definition

The number of tasks received by an edge node at a certain time is n and it is represented as $T_N = \{t_{n_1}, t_{n_2}, \ldots, t_{n_n}\}$, The resource requirements of task i are described as $(d_{cpu_i}, d_{gpu_i}, d_{mem_i})$, where d_{cpu_i} indicates the CPU requirements of the task, d_{gpu_i} stands for the GPU requirements of the task, d_{mem_i} indicates the memory requirements of the task. The node should allocate all the tasks to the edge network reasonable. The number

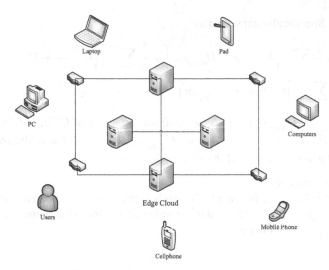

Fig. 1. Edge network allocation model

of computing nodes that can be allocated in the edge network is m, and can be represented as $P_M = \{p_{m_1}, p_{m_2}, \ldots, p_{m_n}\}$, The resources available in node j are described as $(r_{cpu_j}, r_{gpu_j}, r_{mem_j})$, where $r_{cpu_j}, r_{gpu_j}, r_{mem_j}$ indicates the available CPU, GPU and memory of the node respectively.

The allocation relationship between task T_N and the node P_M can be represented as matrix A:

$$A = \begin{bmatrix} a_{11} & a_{12} & \ldots & a_{1n} \\ a_{21} & a_{22} & \ldots & a_{2n} \\ \vdots & \vdots & \ddots & \vdots \\ a_{m1} & a_{m2} & \ldots & a_{mn} \end{bmatrix} \tag{1}$$

Where a_{ij} denotes task T_i and node P_j's correspondence, $a_{ij} \in \{0, 1\}$, $i \in \{0, 1, \ldots, n\}, j \in \{0, 1, \ldots, n\}$, $a_{ij} = 1$ indicates that task I is assigned to node j.

Multi Objective Optimal Edge Computing Task Scheduling Based on Improved Ant Colony Algorithm

Based on the labeled ant colony algorithm, this paper optimizes and improves the initialization and update of pheromone and the setting of heuristic factors, so as to achieve the target task and meet the requirements of edge computing environment.

Definition of the Problem Solution.

In this paper, the load imbalance degree is used to measure the load balance of the edge node. The value is between 0 and 1. The smaller the value is, the more uniform the load distribution of the tasks of the edge node is and the higher the overall performance of the system is. Specifically expressed as:

$$N = \frac{1}{n}\sum_{i=1}^{n}\left|U_{no_i}^{CPU} - U_{avge_i}^{CPU}\right| + \frac{1}{n}\sum_{i=1}^{n}\left|U_{no_i}^{GPU} - U_{avge_i}^{GPU}\right|$$
$$+ \frac{1}{n}\sum_{i=1}^{n}\left|U_{no_i}^{MEM} - U_{avge_i}^{MEM}\right| \tag{2}$$

Where $U_{no_i}^{CPU}$, $U_{no_i}^{GPU}$ and $U_{no_i}^{MEM}$ stand for the usage of CPU, GPU and memory for edge node P_M ($i = 1, \ldots, n$). $U_{avge_i}^{CPU}$, $U_{avge_i}^{GPU}$, $U_{avge_i}^{MEM}$ denote the average usage of CPU, GPU and memory of all the edge nodes.

Setting of Heuristic Factors
η_{ij} represents the heuristic factor, which mainly represents the expected strength of task i arranged at edge node j. The greater the value of η_{ij}, the greater the possibility that tasks are arranged at this node:

$$\eta_{ij} = Q/M_{D_{ij(t)}} \tag{3}$$

Where, Q is any constant (it is recommended to select the value near 1), $M_{D_{ij(t)}}$ can be defined as the cosine similarity between the required resources of the task waiting to be allocated and the free resources of the node, so the similarity between task i and node j is expressed by the included angle between them. The smaller the included angle, the higher the similarity between the two, and the higher the possibility of task allocation at this node:

$$M_{D_{ij}} = \frac{\sum_{a=1}^{A}\left(S_i^a * Q_j^a\right)}{\sqrt{\sum_{a=1}^{A}\left(S_i^a\right)^2} + \sqrt{\sum_{a=1}^{A}\left(Q_j^a\right)^2}} \tag{4}$$

Where A represents the number of resource types that the edge node can provide for the task (CPU, GPU and memory are taken as the required resources in this paper). S_i^a is the edge node P_{M_i} the idle amount of the a-th resource. Q_j^a is resources requirement of task T_{N_j} for type a.

The allocation between tasks and nodes is a many to one mapping relationship. In task allocation, it is necessary to ensure that the demand of tasks for each resource should be less than the idle resources of nodes. By comparing the demand of tasks for CPU, GPU and memory with the available resources of nodes, it is necessary to prevent tasks from being allocated to nodes with insufficient resources, that is:

$$\sum_i v_{cpu_{ij}} < r_{cpu_i} \tag{5}$$

$$\sum_i v_{gpu_{ij}} < r_{gpu_i} \tag{6}$$

$$\sum_i v_{mem_{ij}} < r_{mem_i} \tag{7}$$

Where $v_{cpu_{ij}}$, $v_{gpu_{ij}}$ and $v_{mem_{ij}}$ are the usage of CPU, GPU and memory for task T_{N_j} on the edge node P_{M_i}.

Update the Pheromone
The pheromone update of the initial ant colony algorithm volatilizes for all paths, which will lead to the pheromone of nodes that are often not passed will be lower and lower or even close to zero. Therefore, the path that has not been traveled is not volatilized, and the specific changes are as follows:

$$\tau_{ij}(new) = \begin{cases} (1 - \rho)\tau_j^i(t) + \rho\Delta\tau(t), & if \ \Delta\tau_{ij} \neq 0 \\ \tau_j^i(t), & otherwise \end{cases} \tag{8}$$

Where ρ represents the volatilization factor of pheromone, $1 - \rho$ denotes the residual factor of pheromone and $\Delta\tau_{ij} = \sum_{k=1}^m \tau_{ij}^k$.

The Framework of the Algorithm

Input: The edge nodes set $P_M = \{p_{m_1}, p_{m_2}, \dots, p_{m_n}\}$, tasks set $T_N = \{t_{n_1}, t_{n_2}, \dots, t_{n_n}\}$, pheromone heuristic factor α, expected heuristic factor β, pheromone volatilization rate ρ.

Output: Optimal task allocation scheme and load imbalance.

Step1: The number of ants AntNum, heuristic factor α and β are initialized, and the required resources of the task are attached to each task according to the order of task submission.

Step2: randomly assign n ants carrying task requirements to random nodes (because different tasks can be placed on the same node, the $Tabu_k$ is only the node that does not meet formula (5) to formula (7)), and calculate the probability that the kth ant assigns task i to node j. Then, a node is randomly selected from the qualified nodes by roulette, and the task is deployed on the node. The probability selection formula is:

$$p_{ij}^k(t) = \begin{cases} \dfrac{[\tau_{ij}(t)]^\alpha [\eta_{ij}(t)]^\beta}{\sum_{k \in allowed_k} [\tau_{ij}(t)]^\alpha [\eta_{ij}(t)]}, & if \ i \in allowed_k \\ 0, & otherwise \end{cases} \tag{9}$$

Step 3: After the kth ant completes all task assignments, it locally updates the assigned nodes according to formula (6).

Step 4: After the deployment of the ant, calculate the load imbalance of the distribution scheme according to formula (2), compare it with the historical records, and record the optimal distribution scheme and the minimum load imbalance.

Step 5: Judge whether all ants are finished. If any ants are not finished, skip to step 2; If all ants have completed this iteration, the global optimal solution is calculated and saved. Finally, the pheromone is globally updated according to formula (8) according to the optimal placement scheme.

Step 6: Judge whether the number of iterations or the preset load balancing degree is met, and the algorithm returns to the optimal path solution at the end of the iteration. Otherwise, return to step 2.

2.2 Computational Resource Scheduling Algorithm

System Description
This paper abstracts the system as a model as shown in Fig. 2. The system contains several computing nodes, the number is M, and the set is $D = \{d_1, d_2, \ldots, d_M\}$. These computing nodes include 1 data center and $M - 1$ edge computing devices, so that the computing device d_1 indicates the data center. Where, node d_i is calculated for any edge. It directly covers several terminal intelligent devices. Each device, as a data producer, will generate a data stream. The data stream will be processed at the edge computing node or forwarded to other computing devices for processing through the edge computing node, that is, the set of data streams generated by the terminal intelligent device covered by edge computing node d_i is Q_{d_i} (Fig. 3).

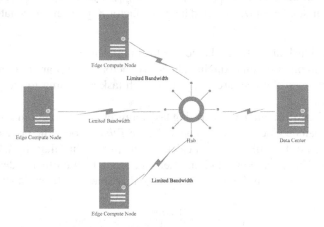

Fig. 2. The abstract model of the system

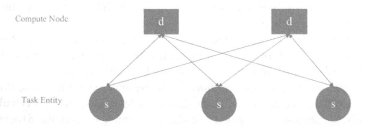

Fig. 3. Bipartite graph composed of task entity and computing node

In the system, the number of stream data processing applications to be deployed is N, that is, the set is $S = \{s_1, s_2, \ldots, s_N\}$. For any stream data processing application s_i, there may be more than one data producer. Each data producer generates a data stream and records its set as Q_{s_i}. There is only one data consumer. This paper uses variable x_{ij} to represent the data consumer of stream data processing application s_i is $d_j \in D$ or not, if yes, then $x_{ij} = 1$, otherwise $x_{ij} = 0$, and each task can only be deployed on a single node. Obviously, there are the following constraints:

$$x_{ij} \in \{0, 1\}; \forall i \in \{1, 2, \dots, N\}, j \in \{1, 2, \dots, M\} \tag{10}$$

$$\sum_{j=1}^{M} x_{ij} = 1; \forall i \in \{1, 2, \dots, N\} \tag{11}$$

Bandwidth Limitation

Since different tasks will compete for bandwidth resources, it is necessary to consider the bandwidth constraints between nodes during task deployment. Let P_{ij}^k denotes the bandwidth cost of node d_k when the application s_i is deployed on the compute node d_j. Obviously, P_{ij}^k can be expressed as:

$$P_{ij}^k = \sum_{q \in \left\{ Q_{s_i} \cap Q_{d_k} \right\}} r_q; \forall i \in \{1, 2, \dots, N\}. \forall j, k \in \{1, 2, \dots, M\}, j \neq k \tag{12}$$

$$P_{ij}^k = \sum_{q \in \left\{ Q_{s_i} - Q_{s_i} \cap Q_{d_j} \right\}} r_q; \forall i \in \{1, 2, \dots, N\}, \forall j, k \in \{1, 2, \dots, M\}, j = k \tag{13}$$

3 Experiment and Results

3.1 Parameter Configuration of Simulation Experiment

In order to verify the effectiveness of the algorithm, simulation experiments are carried out. The polling algorithm (PA), the maximum memory allocation algorithm (MMA) and the algorithm in this paper (IAC) are compared. The simulation is carried out on a computer (four core, 2.5 GHz CPU frequency, 16 GB memory) with Python language programming to verify the performance of the algorithm. The overall load imbalance of the edge node after task allocation and the maximum number of tasks carried by the edge cloud are used as the basis for judging the algorithm.

Since the parameters of ant colony algorithm have a great impact on the performance of the algorithm, various parameter combinations of the algorithm are tested and compared. Using the control variable method, set the values of α, β, ρ respectively, set the number of tasks to 200 (all large tasks, which can make the comparison change more obvious), the number of edge nodes to 100, the number of iterations to 50, and take the average result of 10 times as the final result.

Keep the values of ρ unchanged, respectively set the values of α and β, the specific impact results are shown in Table 1. The larger the α is, the ant is easy to fall into the local shortest path at a certain point. Although the convergence speed will increase, the randomness in the search process will weaken and it is easy to fall into the local optimum; β The larger the size, the easier it is for the ant to choose the original path, reduce the randomness of the search, and fall into local optimization. As can be seen from Table 1, in ρ Without change, $\alpha = 4$, $\beta = 5$, the performance of the algorithm is the best and the load imbalance is the smallest.

Table 1. Impact of ρ on algorithm performance

ρ	The load imbalance
0.05	0.381
0.1	0.378
0.2	0.355
0.4	0.366
0.5	0.36
0.6	0.353
0.7	0.371
0.8	0.362

3.2 Experiment of Edge Computing Resource Allocation Algorithm

In order to simulate the effect of competing bandwidth resources for various types of stream data processing applications, this paper sets the bandwidth required by the data stream to be uniformly distributed in the range of 1–10 Mb/s. At the same time, on the basis of a certain number of edge nodes, the light and heavy system loads are simulated respectively: when the load is light, 16 data streams are generated on all computing nodes; Under heavy load, all computing nodes generate 20 data streams. For all stream data processing applications, the number of stream data processed follows a uniform distribution, and the stream data is randomly distributed on the computing nodes. According to the above process, under different edge nodes: in the light load mode, the number of applications is set to be 4 times the number of edge nodes; In medium load mode, set the number of applications to 5 times that of edge nodes.

In this paper, FFS + IPFs algorithm is compared with ODS, hash and closest algorithms. The specific implementation process is shown in Table 1. Among them, ODC method does not consider edge nodes, hash method maps to any edge node through hash function, and closest method considers deploying tasks to the edge node with the least delay cost.

Since the target V value is the defined total delay cost of the system, this paper analyzes the V values of different algorithms. Figure 4 shows the change of V value of each algorithm with the number of edge nodes under different loads. It can be seen that the FFS + IPFs algorithm proposed in this paper can achieve better results in most cases. Closest operator.

Method can deploy the task at the node with the nearest delay, so it belongs to a heuristic method and can also achieve certain results. The hash algorithm is closer to a random method, so the effect is poor. In all methods, ODC has the worst effect because it does not consider edge nodes, which also explains the role of edge nodes from the side. In conclusion, under different loads, the FFS + IPFs algorithm proposed in this paper can achieve the best results. The average delay can be reduced by 71% compared with ODC algorithm, 39% compared with hash algorithm and 29% compared with closest algorithm.

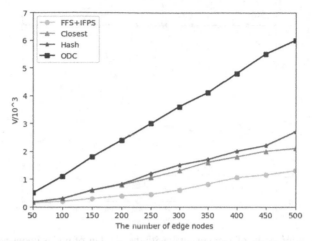

Fig. 4. Variation curve of V value with the number of nodes in light load mode

Figures 5 and 6 show the average transmission delay of the algorithm under different loads and edge nodes. It can be seen that under the light load mode, the average time delay of FFS + IPFs proposed in this paper is 75%, 43% and 34% lower than that of ODC, hash and closest algorithms respectively; In the heavy load mode, the average time delay of FFS + IPFs proposed in this paper is 68%, 34% and 23% less than ODC, hash and closest algorithms respectively, which verifies that this algorithm can achieve good results in different cases.

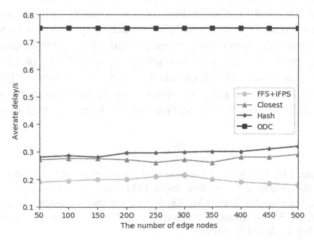

Fig. 5. Variation curve of average delay with the number of nodes under light load

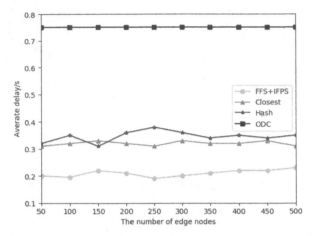

Fig. 6. Variation curve of average delay with the number of nodes under heavy load

4   Conclusion

As the abstraction of physical entity, the accuracy and reliability of mathematical model of chemical process directly affect the design and optimization of chemical process. With the improvement and renewal of chemical process equipment, the increase of complex chemical processes and the increasingly strict requirements of safety and environmental protection, the establishment of mathematical model not only has higher requirements, but also stimulates the development of modeling technology. In order to solve the problems of large amount of data calculation, high requirements for data transmission and difficult to achieve the real-time performance of system modeling in the process of building an efficient chemical dynamic simulation modeling system, this paper proposes a stream data oriented edge computing resource scheduling algorithm and an improved edge computing ant colony algorithm task scheduling model, The problem of efficient data transmission and calculation in chemical dynamic simulation modeling is solved. At the same time, the corresponding comparative experiments of the two algorithms are carried out to verify the effectiveness and robustness of the proposed algorithm.

References

1. Tu, H., Rinard, I.H.: ForeSee—A hierarchical dynamic modeling and simulation system of complex process. Comput. Chem. Eng. **30**(9), 1324–1345 (2006)
2. Marathe, N., Gandhi, A., Shah, J.M.: Docker swarm and kubernetes in cloud computing environment. In: 3rd International Conference on Trends in Electronics and Informatics. Piscataway, NJ, USA, IEEE (2019)
3. Gogouvitis, S.V., Mueller, H., Premnadh, S., Seitz, A., Bruegge, B.: Seamless computing in industrial systems using container orchestration. Futur. Gener. Comput. Syst. **109**, 678–688 (2020)
4. Mandusic, M.: Inference speed and quantization of neural networks with tensor flow lite for microcontroller's framework. In: 5th South-East Europe Design Automation, Computer Engineering, Computer Networks and Social Media Conference (SEEDA-CECNSM). Piscataway, NJ, USA, IEEE (2020)

5. Alexey, S., Semen, Y., et al.: Evaluation of modern tools and techniques for storing time-series data. Procedia Comput. Sci. **156**, 19–28 (2019)
6. Son, J., He, T., Rajkumar, B.: CloudSimSDN-NFV: modeling and simulation of network function virtualization and service function chaining in edge computing environments. Softw. Pract. Exp. **49**(12), 1748–1764 (2019)
7. Yan, Z.H.E.N., Hanyong, L.I.U.: Distributed privacy protection strategy for MEC enhanced wireless body area networks. Digit. Commun. Netw. **6**(2), 229–237 (2020)
8. Yayuan, T.A.N.G., Kehua, G.U.O., Jianhua, M.A., et al.: A smart caching mechanism for mobile multimedia in information centric networking with edge computing. Futur. Gener. Comput. Syst. **91**, 590–600 (2019)
9. Greco, L., Percannella, G., Ritrovato, P., et al.: Trends in IoT based solutions for health care: moving AI to the edge. Pattern Recogn. Lett. **135**, 346–353 (2020)
10. Lorimer, P.A.K., Diec, V.M.F., Kantarci, B.: Covers-up: collaborative verification of smart user profiles for social sustainability of smart cities. Sustain. Cities Soc. **38**, 348–358 (2018)
11. Yang, Y., Lee, J., Kim, N., Kim, K.: Social-viewport adaptive caching scheme with clustering for virtual reality streaming in an edge computing platform. Futur. Gener. Comput. Syst. **108**, 424–431 (2020)
12. Carvalho, A., O'Mahony, N., Krpalkova, L., et al.: Edge computing applied to industrial machines. Proc. Manuf. **38**, 178–185 (2019)
13. Liu, L., Zhaoming, L., Wang, L., Chen, X., Wen, X.: Large-volume data dissemination for cellular-assisted automated driving with edge intelligence. J. Netw. Comput. Appl. **155**, 102535 (2020). https://doi.org/10.1016/j.jnca.2020.102535
14. Cheng, C., et al.: Adoption of image surface parameters under moving edge computing in the construction of mountain fire warning method. PLoS ONE **15**(5), 1–16 (2020)
15. Zahaf, H.E., Benyamina, A.E.H., Olejnik, R., et al.: Energy- efficient scheduling for moldable real - time tasks on heterogeneous computing platforms. J. Syst. Architect. **74**, 46–60 (2017)
16. Verderame, L., Merelli, I., Morganti, L., et al.: A secure cloud-edges computing architecture for metagenomics analysis. Futur. Gener. Comput. Syst. **111**, 919–930 (2020)
17. Kang, Y., et al.: Neurosurgeon: collaborative intelligence between the cloud and mobile edge. ACM SIGPLAN Notices **52**(4), 615–629 (2017)

A Model of Resource Scheduling of Ideological and Political Education in Colleges and Universities Based on Cloud Computing

Ji Rui[✉]

School of Culture and Communication, Shaanxi Radio and Television University,
Xi'an 710119, Shaanxi, China

Abstract. Cloud computing is the allocation and scheduling of Ideological and political education (IPE) resources in CAU(CAU) through certain algorithms in the virtual environment. Firstly, this paper introduces the resource scheduling problem of IPE in CAU, and introduces the research background and significance of the teaching resource scheduling model of Ideological and political theory course in CAU based on cloud computing. Then, the basic theoretical model based on cloud algorithm is proposed. Secondly, it analyzes and summarizes the corresponding countermeasures for the unfair class hour distribution, poor students' autonomy and teachers' one speech hall in the traditional classroom teaching methods. Then the performance of the resource scheduling model is tested. The test results show that the university IPE resource scheduling model based on cloud computing has high practicability and can meet the needs of users.

Keywords: Cloud computing · IPE in colleges and universities · Ideological and political education · Resource scheduling

1 Introduction

With the deepening of the information age, college students are facing more and more challenges in acquiring knowledge and improving their ability. How to improve the efficiency and quality of IPE has become a topic of social concern. In the era of rapid development of information, people acquire knowledge and culture quickly, but the resources mastered by college students are limited. Therefore, how to improve their learning efficiency has become the most concerned and important topic in the IPE in CAU [1, 2]. The traditional teaching mode is that teachers talk about students' listening, teachers and students write notes silently or organize discussion to carry out classroom theoretical narration and exercise training, so as to consolidate the effect of basic knowledge. Cloud computing provides a new technical means to realize networked online learning, and has an impact on College Students' related work by building a virtual service platform on the computer [3, 4].

Many scholars have conducted relevant research on IPE. Some scholars believe that IPE has always been an important part of college education. With the progress and development of society, society has deeper requirements for IPE in CAU, and humanistic care

© Springer Nature Singapore Pte Ltd. 2022
Y. Tian et al. (Eds.): ICBDS 2021, CCIS 1563, pp. 452–460, 2022.
https://doi.org/10.1007/978-981-19-0852-1_35

has become an important content of IPE in CAU. Humanistic care is mainly embodied in people-oriented. The integration of humanistic care in IPE in CAU is not only very helpful to improve teaching quality, but also the reform trend of social development trend. He mainly discusses the lack of humanistic care in CAU, analyzes the importance of integrating humanistic care into IPE in CAU, and puts forward effective measures to integrate humanistic care into IPE [5, 6]. Due to the complexity of the network environment, the current situation of IPE in most CAU in China under the background of network new media is not optimistic. In this regard, some scholars combined with their own teaching practice to make an in-depth discussion on the way of IPE in CAU from the perspective of network new media [7, 8]. Based on the above domestic and foreign literature, we can know that there are still some deficiencies in the research of IPE in CAU in China. First, in theory, China started late in the application field of cloud computing technology. Secondly, there is a lack of in-depth discussion and experience on its development status, prospect analysis and future trend. Then, in terms of relevant foreign research results: they mainly focus on the construction of network resource sharing platform, information security and platform construction in the era of big data, but these results are only in the academic research stage, and there are still deficiencies in the research of IPE in CAU, which need to be further explored and improved.

This paper mainly studies the scheduling of IPE resources in CAU based on cloud computing. In terms of literature retrieval and data collection, after reading and combing the relevant articles at home and abroad, it is found that there are a large number of research results in this field. However, in view of the existing teaching platform, campus network and college students' mobile learning environment, teachers have not formed a unified view on how to organize students to carry out corresponding courses of Ideological and political theory courses. Therefore, it is necessary to establish a resource scheduling model of IPE based on cloud computing technology, which has universal applicability and can meet the conditions of IPE in CAU, and meets the development needs of the current era and the needs of national interests.

2 Discussion on Resource Scheduling Model of IPE in CAU Based on Cloud Computing

2.1 Cloud Computing Resource Scheduling Concept

The resource scheduling of Cloud Computing mainly studies the allocation of resources to different user tasks at a certain time point or time period, which is a decision-making process. Resources are allocated according to single or multiple optimization objectives, including task completion time, cost and resource utilization [9, 10]. Different applications in cloud computing require different resources, and the heterogeneity and dynamics of cloud computing make the resource scheduling problem of cloud computing more complex. As a good scheduling strategy, it should not only improve the utilization of resources, but also minimize the time spent on task completion and improve the overall throughput of the cloud computing system. It can be seen that resource scheduling management should not only meet the service needs of users, but also reduce the operation cost as much as possible and improve the utilization of resources, so as to maximize the interests of cloud computing service providers and users. In addition, cloud computing resource management also needs to use limited physical resources to provide diversified services for more users and meet the requirements of different types of users in terms of real-time, cost and other service quality [11, 12].

2.2 Resource Scheduling Objectives of IPE

In University IPE, teaching resources are an important carrier to carry out ideological and political theory courses. It can also be said to realize classroom knowledge, interactive learning between teachers and students and promote the all-round development of students. However, due to the lack of effective communication mechanism between university teachers and various departments of the University, and the imperfect construction of information sharing platform, many excellent teachers do not have the opportunity to participate in Ideological and political courses, or they can only dispatch IPE resources after completing their teaching tasks part-time. The goal of resource scheduling of IPE in CAU is to connect all stages of various teaching activities with students, teachers and managers, and make them achieve the best through the coordinated management of various teaching activities.

Through the development of cloud computing technology, the resource scheduling objectives of IPE in CAU mainly include the following aspects: (1) realize the integration of teachers' teaching work and students' learning. In the traditional classroom, the interaction between teachers and students is based on the influence of teachers on students. Based on the cloud environment, the platform will change the situation and form a new model -- the mixed teaching mode of "IPE" and "Internet plus classroom". At the same time, it also breaks the previous single and boring teaching form, improves the learning efficiency of Ideological and political teachers and improves the teaching quality. (2) Promote teachers' professional growth and self-improvement ability, improve the management level of IPE, and achieve the goal of Ideological and political course. Therefore, in order to carry out its work better, we must fully mobilize the enthusiasm of all college students. By establishing a good harmonious, democratic and equal development atmosphere, we can stimulate every university teacher and student to participate in teaching, and create a better campus environment and more meaningful and valuable practical activities.

2.3 Characteristics of Resource Scheduling of IPE in CAU

In the traditional scheduling of educational resources, teachers are in the main position and students are passive recipients. Teaching tasks are uniformly arranged and managed by counselors. In this mode, lectures in class have no interaction and discussion function, that is, the lack of communication and communication between teachers and students leads to the problem of low efficiency. At the same time, students' mastery of knowledge is limited and can not meet their personalized needs. The classroom will inevitably be depressed by the teacher's coldness, and even produce resistance, which will eventually affect the learning progress, thus reducing the effect of improving the quality of IPE resources. The resource scheduling model of IPE in CAU is supported by the basic theory and technology of cloud computing, fully considers the factors such as students' living environment and learning style, and takes it as the service object for management optimization. By establishing an efficient and reasonable teaching arrangement system, we can coordinate the relationship and function of various information resources and related personnel in the process of teachers' work.

The characteristics of resource scheduling of IPE in CAU are as follows: (1) pertinence. In the context of the current big data era, information spreads very fast and various information can be transmitted to each other, but there are also problems such as fuzziness and uncertainty, which makes it impossible to process and analyze effectively. Therefore, we must pay full attention to these implied values, so as to make them more practical and accurate, so as to provide basic support for the scheduling of IPE resources in CAU. (2) Principle of scientific effectiveness. In the context of the current big data era, many schools use cloud computing technology to build teaching models. Cloud computing technology can run and manage teaching contents as a virtual server, so as to achieve the purpose of real-time sharing of resources and interactive information. (3) In the current era of big data, information transmission is fast and covers a wide range. Therefore, it is necessary to make full use of various teaching materials and multimedia resources on the network for effective publicity. At the same time, through the students' rationalization of teachers' teaching time, we can achieve efficient management.

2.4 Feasibility of Resource Allocation of IPE in CAU

The scheduling of IPE resources in CAU is a complex and comprehensive system. It needs to consider not only the interior of the school, but also the external environment. Firstly, at present, the teaching content of College Students' Ideological and political theory course in China mainly includes three aspects: first, the national socialist principles and policies. Second, the party's basic line and important spiritual civilization construction. The third is the discussion of social hot topics and current events. These contents are the scheduling of IPE resources in CAU, which involves a large number of practical needs, development needs and future planning needs, so it has strong feasibility.

The feasibility of resource allocation of IPE in CAU mainly includes the following three aspects: (1) under the background of economic and social development, students' Ideological and moral quality, comprehensive ability and practical innovation spirit are indispensable factors in the teaching of Ideological and political courses in CAU. (2) With the continuous improvement of China's market economic system and the acceleration of socialist modernization, the employment situation of college students is becoming more and more serious. (3) Based on cloud computing technology, teaching information sharing can be realized. In the traditional classroom, there is very little communication and interaction between teachers and students. The use of cloud platform for management can effectively solve this problem. It is one of the major advantages of College IPE resource scheduling that teachers release course notices, online and network return visits to collect feedback results for teachers and students to use and complete learning tasks. At the same time, it can also provide more and better services to college students to meet their various needs. Therefore, CAU should make full use of their resource advantages and talent training advantages in IPE and teaching.

2.5 Common Resource Scheduling Algorithms

Traditional scheduling algorithms, including rotation and weighted rotation scheduling algorithms, minimum link and weighted minimum link algorithms, are more traditional scheduling algorithms, but they still have a lot of development space in current products. There are many heuristic scheduling algorithms, such as ant colony algorithm, genetic algorithm, particle swarm optimization algorithm and simulated annealing algorithm. Because of the advantages of constrained optimization, multi-objective optimization, dynamic optimization and multi-solution, heuristic algorithms are applied in many fields. Swarm intelligence algorithms such as ant colony algorithm and particle swarm optimization algorithm have been more and more widely used in the field of computer. The advantages of these swarm intelligence algorithms in solving distributed problems make them continuously applied to the solution of optimization problems. At first, ant colony algorithm was applied to traveling salesman problem and path problem. Later, after continuous research and expansion, ant colony algorithm was also applied to scheduling problem. Compared with the traditional scheduling algorithm, heuristic scheduling algorithm has great advantages, but there are still some limitations. Therefore, people study these limitations, make corresponding improvements to the algorithm itself, or combine two different algorithms, and then apply the improved new algorithm to scheduling.

Here, the classic problem of traveling salesman is used to explain the basic principle of ant colony algorithm. In the TSP problem, n cities are given in advance, requiring travelers to visit from the first city to the last city, and each city must be visited once or only once. Among the feasible paths of these cities, find an optimal path, that is, the shortest path. The specific model is described as follows:

$$
p_{ij}^k(t) = \begin{cases} 0, \text{other} \\ \dfrac{[l(t)][n(t)]}{\sum\limits_{s \in allowed_k} [t_{is}(t)][n(t)]}, if, j \in allowed_k \end{cases} \tag{1}
$$

Where, c is the set of all cities, nij is the heuristic factor, which is the heuristic degree from city i to city j, that is, the attraction of the city to ants, and represents the correlation between the objective function and the selected path. The expression is:

$$
n_{ij}(t) = \frac{1}{d_{ij}} \tag{2}
$$

The heuristic function NIJ (T) represents the expectation of ants to select another city j from one city I, which is inversely proportional to the distance between cities. The smaller the distance, the greater the probability of being selected by ants.

3 Experiment

3.1 Resource Scheduling Model Function

The main function of the resource scheduling model is to analyze the information of IPE in CAU, convert it into a specific and clear data, and realize resource allocation according to cloud computing technology. In this process, various data of different types, different time periods and the same distributed service need to be recorded in detail. First, establish a virtualization system. The platform can provide various forms of literature retrieval and management functions, including user name and use authority; Secondly, the information of IPE in CAU is stored and analyzed. Through the optimal allocation of various teaching tasks in the IPE system in CAU, in order to improve the overall work efficiency of the school, various resources are integrated to form an information base. The resources of IPE in CAU should be distributed orderly, so as to realize sharing among various departments within the school and improve the utilization rate of information. The algorithm can also establish the corresponding hierarchical structure system for different departments, grades and classes. In the system, user types and usage are set according to requirements to divide their management permissions. Then, through data analysis and processing, the goal of each level application object is determined, and the level model file is generated accordingly. Finally, the different attribute distribution functions are transformed into relational resource scheduling mode to realize the function of sharing resources between the IPE information service platform and other departments.

3.2 University IPE Resource Scheduling Platform Based on Cloud Computing

College IPE resource scheduling platform is a public software that provides information services for teachers and students. It can interact with teachers and students in the teaching process, and feed it back to relevant managers. The system can be divided into three parts: the first part mainly includes data acquisition module. The second part mainly includes functional units such as high-capacity server cluster and cloud storage management module in cloud computing environment. The third part completes the resource sharing and allocation through the data collector.

4 Conclusion

4.1 Parameter Setting of Cloud Computing Environment Resource Node

Table 1 is the resource information parameter table.

The resource scheduling model of IPE in CAU based on cloud computing aims at realizing service. On the basis of meeting the needs of users, a dynamic generation algorithm is established to reasonably allocate and optimize various teaching resources. Create a virtual machine and use it as a resource node. The parameter initialization settings of the resource node are randomly selected. Each parameter is shown in Fig. 1. Among them, the resource processing capacity MIPS million instructions per second, the task is in millions of instructions, and the value of resource cost is also random.

Table 1. Resource node parameters

Resource number	MIPS	Number of nodes	Resource price
01	40	3	6
02	30	9	5
03	25	5	3
04	50	5	4
05	102	4	7
06	78	6	5
07	40	3	2
08	40	1	3
09	80	2	14
10	30	4	13

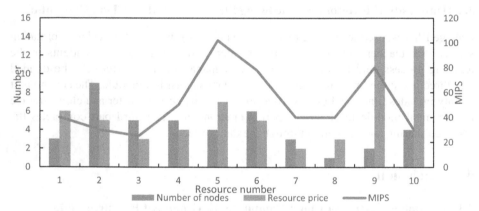

Fig. 1. Parameter settings for the resource information

4.2 System Processing Performance Analysis

As can be seen from Fig. 2, by analyzing the response time comparison diagram, we can conclude that with the increase of the number of services, the response time of both algorithms will increase, but both are within 200 ms. The response time of the two algorithms has no obvious advantages or disadvantages, and general users are not sensitive to the time of milliseconds. Therefore, in terms of response time, the two algorithms perform almost the same.

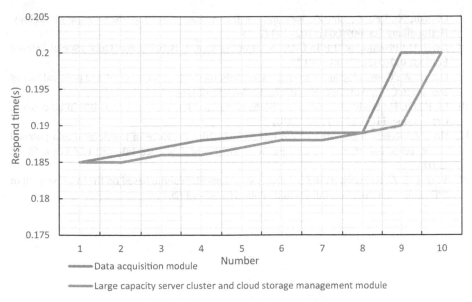

Fig. 2. Response time comparison

5 Conclusion

With the continuous development of education in CAU, CAU put forward higher requirements for talent training mode and teaching resources. According to the learning situation of Ideological and political teachers and students on and off campus under the cloud
computing platform and the feedback information from teachers, this paper establishes
the network model of IPE in CAU, and uses the service virtualization method to build
an efficient, convenient, harmonious and interactive communication environment for
teachers and students based on the desktop (server) or through a third party. It also analyzes and studies the above problems and gives corresponding suggestions to improve
teachers' design and implementation level of teaching resource scheduling scheme.

References

1. Zhi, N.: Recessive IPE in CAU based on the internet. Agro Food Ind. Hi Tech **28**(1), 3233–3236 (2017)
2. Haixia, J.: On the human care of IPE in CAU. Educ. Teach. Forum **000**(042), 30–31 (2017)
3. Yanglin, T.: Research on intellectual and political education in CAU under the view of network new media. J. Jiamusi Instit. Educ. **000**(001), 110–111 (2018)
4. Fei, X.: The influence of the development of new media on the IPE in CAU. Value Eng. **000**(012), 165–167 (2017)
5. Huaping, L.: Research on the application of "four comprehensive" in the IPE in CAU%. J. Xinyang Agricult. Coll. **027**(002), 120–122 (2017)
6. Tang, J.: Research on exploration strategy of IPE resources in CAU. Heilongjiang Higher Educ. Res. **000**(009), 143–145 (2017)

7. Qianyu, X., Lei, Z., Lin, Z.: Research on IPE in CAU from the visual angle of ecology. Heilongjiang Sci. **009**(003), 102–103 (2018)
8. Jiwei, H.: Planning of IPE in CAU in era of big data. J. Hebei Union Univ. (Social Science Edition) **017**(002), 79–81 (2017)
9. Qiong, W.: Combining and thinking on teaching methods of Ideological and political theory courses in CAU. Adv. Soc. Sci. **07**(7), 1048–1053 (2018)
10. Li, F., Fu, H.: Study on college english teaching based on the concept of IPE in all courses. Creat. Educ. **11**(7), 997–1007 (2020)
11. Hou, Z.: Research on value of red resources of Jilin Province in intellectual and political education of universities. J. Changchun Univ. (Natural Science Edition) **028**(006), 58–62 (2018)
12. Yingying, Z.: Research on the construction of domestic culture based on the improvement of IPE quality in CAU. Sci. Educ. Guide **000**(020), 92–93 (2018)

Incomplete Feature Recovery of Cloud Network System Based on Artificial Intelligence

Yuxiang Qiu, Lan Gan, E. Longhui$^{(\boxtimes)}$, Shunwang Xu, Peng Wei, and Yan Cai

Nari Information and Communication Technology Co., Ltd., Nanjing, China
elonghui@sgepri.sgcc.com.cn

Abstract. There are a lot of incomplete multi-modal data in cloud network data, which need to be processed by intelligent analysis method. Recently, there have been a lot of incomplete multi-view studies. Combined with previous studies, most of them are based on multimedia videos, natural images and other aspects to study random missing or view missing. Based on matrix decomposition, non-negative matrix decomposition, Laplacian matrix and other methods, good results have been achieved. Feature extraction can not only rely on general models, but also process data under professional advice. Traditional methods lack pertinence for specific data recovery problems, and are difficult to obtain optimal optimization due to too flexible constraints, so the application effect is not good. By analyzing the data of the complete view of the sample, analyzing the connections within the view and the differences between the views, this paper tries to analyze or learn the structure and probability distribution of the data of multiple views, and then establishes a common subspace or uses GAN to complete the missing values based on the existing data, which proves the effectiveness of the method in the data set. We apply the method to the analysis of cloud network data, and the experiment proves the effectiveness of the method.

Keywords: Artificial intelligence · Data fusion · Feature analysis

1 Introduction

In the context of the era of big data, the forms of data are increasingly rich and the collection methods are increasingly diverse, especially in fields such as computer vision [1, 2], environmental science [3] and imaging [4]. Data often come from different channels or are obtained by different feature extractors and presented in different ways. Similar data with different angles and dimensions are called multi-view data [5]. For example, the same movement of an actor is captured by four cameras at different angles; The same meaning of "you are good" varies from country to country in different languages; A story described in a film consists not only of frame by frame images but also of audio. In multi-view data, the data of different views are descriptions of the same object, and they compose the information of the object in different ways. The information between the multi-view data can overlap and complement each other. The process of using information from multiple views of the same object for learning analysis is called multi-view learning [6–8].

© Springer Nature Singapore Pte Ltd. 2022
Y. Tian et al. (Eds.): ICBDS 2021, CCIS 1563, pp. 461–472, 2022.
https://doi.org/10.1007/978-981-19-0852-1_36

Multi-view classification is one of the most important paradigms in multi-view learning and has great research significance. The goal of multi-view classification is to classify data according to the consistency and complementarity of multi-view data and get better results. Up to now, many multi-view classification methods have been proposed. Among them, most methods are based on the premise of view integrity, assuming that each sample has complete data in all views and a one-to-one correspondence. However, this state of affairs is too ideal for the assumption of a complete view to hold in many cases due to complex realities.

The mutual unification and complementarity of multi-view data can effectively improve the learning performance of the algorithm, and help to improve the analysis accuracy [9]. The loss of multi-view data is an important research branch in multi-view learning, and discarding incomplete data is obviously not the best choice. Therefore, it is an urgent problem to further explore the statistical characteristics and correlation between complete data and missing data. As multiple views are missing to varying degrees in real application, we need to improve their weight in the model according to the characteristics of different views, and design further interpretable algorithms for better intelligent analysis.

In the domain of cloud network, various factors lead to the existence of a large number of incomplete multi-view data [10, 11]. By analyzing the existing cloud network data of patients, the relationship between multi-view data and missing data is explored to reduce the impact of missing multi-view samples to achieve better analysis results, which is the goal of incomplete multi-view classification in cloud network intelligent analysis. This paper uses deep learning method to process multi-view data, recover missing data, and apply it to cloud network system.

2   Related Work

We will introduce some background knowledge related to this paper and some cutting-edge research, including feature extraction, generative adversarial networks and multi-view learning.

Low-rank representation has attracted much attention because of its outstanding feature extraction performance and excellent performance in subspace learning. It combines low-rank constraint with dictionary learning to obtain the solution of the lowest rank of the coefficient matrix rather than the sparse solution. Its self-expression feature can effectively eliminate data redundancy. Low-rank representation can further make full use of the structure information of data on the basis of dictionary learning, which has certain inspiration for us to further learn from multi-modal data to better common representation. We can optimize the coefficient matrix by combining the features, reduce noise, and improve the effectiveness of subspace representation.

A manifold consists of several Euclidean Spaces as local Spaces, which are generally used to describe geometric shapes. High-dimensional data usually contains a large amount of information, but it can also lead to excessive algorithm calculation and even dimension disaster. The data that human can observe is three-dimensional at most.

For the visualization of data, the method of dimension reduction is studied by people. As shown in Fig. 1, this is a higher-dimensional manifold structure. The distance between

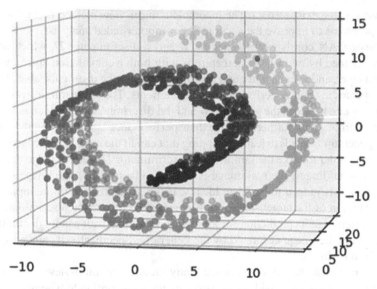

Fig. 1. The manifold structure of the higher-dimensional data

two red points would be very similar if you use the outer Euclidean distance, but if you use the Riemannian distance on a manifold, they are actually far apart. It is assumed that the data are uniformly sampled from a low-dimensional manifold in a high-dimensional Euclidean space, and the purpose of manifold learning is to learn such a low-dimensional manifold. At present, many manifold learning methods have been proposed. It can be divided into nonlinear and linear manifold algorithms. Isomap algorithm uses the curve distance in differential geometry to calculate the distance between high-dimensional manifold data. Only one parameter needs to be determined in the optimization process, which has good stability and global optimality. The Laplacian eigenmaps algorithm uses an undirected graph to represent the structural relations among data, and mines a low-dimensional representation of a manifold by way of graph embedding, trying to preserve the local structural relations in the graph. The LLE algorithm proposed by Roweis et al. believes that all sample points can be obtained according to the linear weighting of k neighboring data, so that the data can still maintain the manifold structure of high-dimensional space after dimensionality reduction.

So far, there have been a lot of incomplete multi-view studies. However, incomplete multi-view learning has not been deeply studied and explored [12]. Due to its professionalism, feature extraction can not only rely on the general model, usually under the professional advice of experts, image segmentation and other processing [13, 14]. Traditional methods lack pertinence for specific problems and images, and due to flexible constraints, it is difficult to obtain the optimal optimization, and the application effect is not good. For different diseases, by analyzing the data of the complete view of the sample, analyzing the connections within the view and the differences between the views, we try to analyze or learn the structure and probability distribution of the data of multiple views, and then establish a common subspace or use GAN [15] to complete the missing values based on the existing data. The incomplete multi-view method is combined with practical problems to improve the accuracy of computer-aided analysis.

The basic GAN consists of a generator G and a discriminator D, which are typically implemented by multi-layer perceptrons with both a convolution layer and a full-connection layer, and the generator and discriminator must be distinguishable. They use alternate updates to achieve performance enhancements. The entire training process can be seen as a game between the generator G and the discriminator D, which is where the name comes from. Both further improve their performance against each other. Among them, the generator G needs to learn a mapping that can fit the input A to the target spatial distribution in order to forge the sample. The discriminator D needs to judge the authenticity of the input image, the real image is judged to be true, and the image generated by the generator is judged to be false. Ideally, if the generator can fit the input exactly to the distribution of the target space, it will be able to confuse the discriminator to the maximum extent that its prediction for all inputs is 0.5, that is, it cannot distinguish the real image from the image generated by the generator. Specifically, it can be expressed as a Max/min problem.

At present, researchers have proposed many incomplete multi-view learning methods, which can be roughly divided into two categories according to whether they complete the missing samples. The first method uses subspace mapping to obtain the common representation of multiple views without processing missing data. Shao et al. [16] calculated the kernel matrix of incomplete view through the kernel matrix of complete view, and then processed the kernel matrix-based clustering algorithm to get the final result. However, this algorithm can only be applied to kernel based multi-view clustering. In order to solve the limitation of this method, some researchers began to pay attention to and study the incomplete multi-view clustering algorithm based on non-negative matrix factorization. Li et al. [17] proposed an incomplete multi-view clustering algorithm (PVC) based on non-negative matrix to learn the common subspace of two views, so as to improve the learning performance of the algorithm. Inspired by this, more incomplete multi-view clustering algorithms based on non-negative matrix factorization are proposed. However, these algorithms still have some limitations in practical application. Firstly, because non-negative matrix factorization (NMF) requires a lot of inverse operations, which are complex and time-consuming, they cannot be used to deal with large-scale incomplete multi-view problems. More importantly, they only consider learning common subspaces, but cannot recover missing data. Therefore, they cannot prove that common subspaces are in every view and have an impact on the ultimate performance of the algorithm. Zhao et al. [18] constructed the relationship between complete samples and missing samples through Laplace matrix, and imposed a global constraint on all samples. Yin et al. [19] optimized the clustering indicator matrix of complete samples by considering the similarity of samples within each view and among different views. Yin et al. [20] added Laplacian graph regularization terms and studied global graph representation and subspace at the same time.

The second method is incomplete multi-view completion, which completes the missing samples to meet the requirements of multi-view learning. Its main idea is to reconstruct the missing data using spatial changes first, and then adopt the complete multi-view learning method. The key point of this method is to predict the missing data. This paper assumes that different views from the same height space, make full use of the observed sample can help restore the missing sample, A matrix decomposition method is proposed to estimate the missing value. Based on weighted non-negative matrix decomposition and L21 regularization term, Shao et al. [21] learned the potential feature matrix of all views and generated consistency matrix, constrained the differences between views and consistency matrix as little as possible, so as to solve the incomplete sample completion problem. Recently, generative adversarial networks (GAN) have attracted much attention due to their excellent performance [22]. GAN can output random noise as a target that needs to be forged. Some recent GAN articles can use mismatched data to learn the relationship between two views. In addition, there are many mature algorithms based on generative adversarial networks for handling different view transformations. Pan et al. used network parameter sharing to ensure that the forged image of the generator was as close as possible to the characteristics of the original image to complete the mutual generation of images [23]. However, all these methods have not been thoroughly studied for all incomplete multiple views in images.

Most of the classification algorithms for multimodal incomplete data rely on image segmentation and labeling, but the segmentation process is costly, and the labeling also needs the intervention of experts. To solve this problem, we propose an incomplete multi-view classification algorithm based on feature completion and classification. GAN is used to generate segmentation manual group features from image features, and existing available manual group features are used as constraints to improve the quality of generated features. Then, we added the category consistency analysis module, which added the label information of samples into the confrontation training process to ensure that the generated features were classifiable. Experiments on data sets show that the proposed method can achieve convincing results.

3   The Complementation and Analysis Method

As an effective means of data analysis, machine learning has been widely used in image analysis, and it has become one of the research hotspots to use machine learning for image analysis. Under normal circumstances, we will collect original data from application scenarios, most of which are images, but also some quantitative indicators. Since images usually have high dimensions and contain some irrelevant or redundant information, they cannot be directly used for classification, clustering and regression task learning. Then the image will be preprocessed manually or using some existing models to get the original features. In this step, multiple groups of original features are extracted for image processing operations such as image correction, image registration and image segmentation. Finally, machine learning algorithm is applied to these original features, feature extraction and other operations, training model, and finally achieve the learning goal. According to the different collection methods and processing methods of original features, multi-view data will be generated. If these data are simply spliced, the problem of "dimension disaster" will be caused due to the excessively large dimension, and the problem of over-fitting will also be easily caused when the sample number is too small.

Incomplete multi-view learning can be applied to datasets with continuous missing or view missing to explore effective information of existing data to the greatest extent, reduce sample discarding, and improve the classification and clustering performance of models. Existing incomplete multi-attempt learning can be divided into two types according to whether the missing view is completed or not. Non-completion algorithms are generally based on matrix decomposition and use the common subspace alignment of multiple views to complete the learning task. The completion algorithm can fill the missing data according to the existing data and use the method of multi-view learning to achieve the final goal. Excellent completion can make data more complete and more separable, so it has become an important direction for researchers to explore. The proposed network is shown in Fig. 2.

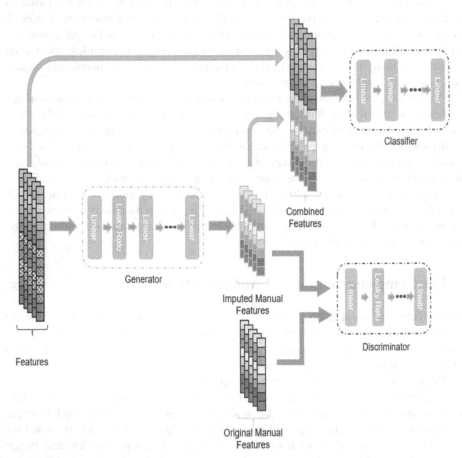

Fig. 2. The complementation fusion network for incomplete multi-modal features

Many incomplete multi-view semi-supervised learning methods and supervised learning methods have been proposed. Aiming at the supervised learning of incomplete multi-view, the method used in this paper makes full use of complementary information between different views, measures the similarity between randomly selected landmark sample set and other samples, and obtains the hidden space of multi-view data through nonlinear projection. Low rank and sparse representation were used to measure the correlation between views. Assuming that there was a linear correlation between the observed complete sample and the observed missing sample, the data of existing views were fully utilized to recover the exact sample according to the learned mapping relationship. However, this method usually uses arbitrary samples and does not consider the features of the completed samples.

In view of incomplete view to analyze problems, this topic first considers the correlation between views. The data can be from various views from their respective mapping in a public space, and each column in the implicit space characteristics of P is for a new sample with the corresponding way. In under the condition of incomplete view, we need to align multi-view data into a discriminant space. At the same time, based on the Laplace matrix, we measure the similarity between samples to obtain the structure between samples in the original sample space, and retain the structural relations of all samples in the hidden space. Finally, considering the linear correlation between samples, based on the assumption the sample can be represented by a key characteristic of public contains, we can use the dictionary matrix D will be a sample expressed as a linear combination of the rest of the sample Z. We put forward under each view, using existing data to fill all the missing data view, at the same time does not change the structural relationship between samples.

The main focus is an in-depth exploration of the interrelationships within views and the structural relationships between views. We will learn by dictionary, so that each sample can be represented linearly by other samples, without introducing new noise. Through the hidden space representation, multi-view data can be aligned, and the overall structure of the sample in the common hidden space can be retained according to its structural relations in their respective views. At the same time, structural constraints can be put on the completion data, and the two can be synergistically optimized to obtain a better solution.

The processing of manual features requires internal algorithms, consuming a lot of time and the support of high-performance computers, which makes this data preprocessing method not widely used. However, the research shows that the multi-view fusion of manual group features and computational group features can effectively improve the analysis accuracy, so we must make the best use of the existing manual group features. Generative adversarial network (GAN) can learn the statistical characteristics and probability distribution of a group of data. Based on this, we preliminarily designed to use GAN to learn the mapping of imaging group features to its corresponding manual group features. The input is a group of imaging features, and the output is its corresponding manual group features. Since the feature dimension of the two groups of features is not very large after pretreatment, the mean square error is used to constrain the real sample and the generated sample to reduce their differences. Considering the classification task, we not only consider the use of discriminators to authenticate the generated data, but also constrain the generated data categories. In order to prevent the occurrence of data drift, labels are added into the training process to ensure that the classification result of the generated manual group features combined with its original features is consistent with the original features.

In this paper, we use the above complementation fusion network for incomplete multi-modal features analysis. We train the network using the antagonistic losses of generators and discriminators. In order to improve the authenticity of the pseudo-samples synthesized by the generator and discriminator, we retain this structure as the base. The antagonistic training between generator and discriminator is realized by binary cross entropy loss (BCEloss). The loss expression is as follows:

$$L = -y\log(D(x)) - (1-y)(\log(1-D(x))) \tag{1}$$

In the discriminator, we require the predicted value of the real sample to be 1, and the predicted value of the generated sample to be 0, so as to maximize the difference between the output results of the real sample and the pseudo-sample. In the generator, we minimize the loss of the manual features generated by the generator via the output of the discriminator and the true values. Thus, the discriminator tries to distinguish between true and false manual group features, and the generator tries to generate manual group features that the discriminator cannot distinguish between true and false. At the same time, the probability distribution of the target space can be understood through the basic generative adversarial network, so that the output manual features conform to the probability distribution of the original space. This is unsupervised adversarial learning. It only ensures that the generated manual features have as much of the same distribution as the existing features. The disadvantage is that the training process is unstable and lacks the principle of one to one correspondence. Just generation of manual features is not enough for our needs. Manual features must correspond to imaging group features. In addition, in this project, all features are low-dimensional data extracted from images, which are not able to see the similarity intuitively like real images. These features are independent of each other in their visual representation, and in fact interrelated. The discreteness of the data obscures the direct relationship between features. The process of generating a generator cannot be well limited only by fighting losses. Therefore, it is not enough to use only against losses. We added the true manual features of the imaging group to the training process. Due to the low dimension of the data, this constraint can reduce the error between the generated data and the actual data and maximize their similarity. The loss function is as follows:

$$loss_G(X_R, X_M, Y; G, D, C) = \log(D(G(X_R))) + \lambda_1 \|X_M - G(X_R)\|_2^2 + \lambda_2 \|Y - C(X_R, G(X_R))\| \tag{2}$$

$$loss_D(X_R, X_M; G, D) = \log(D(X_M)) + \log(1 - D(G(X_R))) \tag{3}$$

This method uses FGAN to align the features extracted from real and fake images to improve the quality of the generated fake images. In our method, the difference is that the input features are already extracted from the CT image, so no additional extraction operations are required. In addition, all training data labels are complete. On this basis, the label is directly introduced into the loss function, which can intuitively ensure that the generated samples also meet the requirements of classification results, and also make up for the over-fitting problems caused by MSEloss. The loss situation is as follows:

$$oss_C(X_R, Y; G, C) = \|Y - C(X_R, G(X_R))\| \tag{4}$$

In GAN, the discriminator tries to distinguish between real and generated manual features, but the generator tries to forge features that the discriminator cannot. The probability distribution of the original space can be learned through generative adversarial network to make the generated manual features conform to the probability distribution of the original space. However, it only goes so far as to ensure that the generated manual features have the same distribution as the existing features. The disadvantage is that the training process lacks stability and the principle of one-to-one correspondence - the generated manual features should correspond to the features of the same sample. These features are interrelated and independent. Due to gradient extinction or gradient explosion, the generator generation process is not well constrained by antagonistic loss. To solve this problem, we added the original manual features corresponding to the input radiology group features as tags to the training process of the generator H and constrained them by mean square error (MSE). Such constraints can greatly reduce the error between the generated data and the real data. Moreover, the similarity between them will be maximized simultaneously at very low cost.

In addition, all training data are labeled. Based on this, we introduced the disease consistency network D for analysis based on categories identified from input data. During training D, the generator is also updated via backpropagation. In this way, the generation of and constraint generators can be further facilitated from the most intuitive point of view, avoiding the occurrence of overfitting. However, distribution drift inevitably occurs between the generated data and the real data. Disease consistency networks trained from real data generally perform poorly in the generated samples due to the occurrence of distribution drift. To solve this problem, we would not simply train D with completely raw or generated features, which would result in poor classification performance on test samples. We train the class-consistent network with real radiomic features and corresponding generated manual features as inputs. In this way, it can effectively avoid distribution drift and improve the accuracy of disease diagnosis. In addition, the trained D can be used directly for the classification of follow-up work.

4   Experiment

To verify the effectiveness of the proposed method, experiments are performed on incomplete multimodal data sets. Experiments include the recognition accuracy of our method and the comparison method under different data missing rates, as well as the recognition accuracy performance of our method under different classifiers. We verify the methods on the benchmark dataset, which contains two different modes of information. Some of the samples are complete in both modes, while the rest only have data in one mode, with some modal data missing. We compared traditional data recovery methods, including low-rank recovery (LRR), sparse representation (SR), principle component analysis (PCA). In addition, the samples with missing data were removed, and only the data with full modal data were used for training and classification. All experiments were cross-validated with 10 folds, of which 1fold was used for test and the rest for training, and the average recognition rate was calculated as the final result. We provide the results in Table 1, and the results show that the identification accuracy of our method exceeds that of all comparison methods. The results show that compared with other data recovery methods, the data we recover may be closer to the real sample data. Compared with the method of directly eliminating incomplete modal data, our method can effectively utilize the correlation between all acquired data to improve the fusion analysis effect.

In addition, we compare the accuracy of different methods in different classifiers. We adopt support vector machine (SVM), decision tree (DT), nearest neighbor classifier (NN), linear discriminant analysis (LDA), kernel based nonlinear discriminant analysis (KDA), etc. Table 2 shows the recognition accuracy of the proposed method on the above different classifiers. The results show that the recognition accuracy of our method on SVM classifier is optimal on this task.

Table 1. The classification accuracies of the methods (%).

Methods	10%	20%	30%
LRR	67.25	65.03	63.83
SR	72.39	70.77	67.58
PCA	47.58	51.29	44.86
Our Method	69.86	73.60	68.27

Table 2. The classification accuracies of the methods under different classifiers (%).

Methods	Accuracy
SVM	69.86
DT	68.24
NN	42.20
LDA	56.74
KDA	65.09

5   Conclusion

There are a lot of valuable data in cloud network. It is very necessary to mine valuable information through intelligent analysis method. In practice, modal data in cloud networks are incomplete, which greatly affects the performance of machine learning analysis methods. This paper adopts a deep neural network data recovery method, which can effectively recover the key data, so as to make full use of the structural information between all samples and improve the performance of fusion analysis. Experiments on benchmark data sets verify the effectiveness of the proposed method, which can obtain high recognition accuracy.

References

1. Hartley, R., Zisserman, A.: Multiple View Geometry in Computer Vision. Cambridge University Press (2003)
2. Kertész, G., Vámossy, Z.: Current challenges in multi-view computer vision. In: Proceedings of Applied Computational Intelligence and Informatics (SACI), 2015 IEEE 10th Jubilee International Symposium on. IEEE, pp. 237–241 (2015)
3. Hofmann, M.: Multi-view 3D human pose estimation in complex environment. Int. J. Comput. Vis. **96**(1), 103–124 (2012)
4. Suk, H.I., Lee, S.W., Shen, D., et al.: Hierarchical feature representation and multimodal fusion with deep learning for AD/MCI diagnosis. Neuroimage **101**, 569–582 (2014)
5. Shiliang, A.: Survey of multi-view machine learning. Neural Comput. Appl. **23**(7–8), 2031–2038 (2013)
6. Sun, S.: A survey of multi-view machine learning. Neural Comput. Appl. **23**(7–8), 2031–2038 (2013)
7. Kan, M., Shan, S., Zhang, H., et al.: Multi-view discriminant analysis. IEEE Trans. Pattern Anal. Mach. Intell. **38**(1), 188–194 (2015)
8. Yang, Y., Wang, H.: Multi-view clustering: a survey. Big Data Mining Anal. **1**(2), 83–107 (2018)
9. Xu, C., Tao, D., Xu, C.: Multi-view learning with incomplete views. IEEE Trans. Image Process. **24**(12), 5812–5825 (2015)
10. Lin, Y., Gou, Y., Liu, Z., et al.: COMPLETER: Incomplete multi-view clustering via contrastive prediction. In: Proceedings of the IEEE/CVF Conference on Computer Vision and Pattern Recognition, pp. 11174–11183 (2021)
11. Jordan, M.I., Mitchell, T.M.: Machine learning: trends, perspectives, and prospects. Science **349**(6245), 255–260 (2015)
12. Xu, M., Li, M., Xu, W., et al.: Interactive mechanism modeling from multi-view images. ACM Trans. Graph. (TOG) **35**(6), 1–13 (2016)
13. Kumar, A., Rai, P., Daume, H.: Co-regularized multi-view spectral clustering. Adv. Neural. Inf. Process. Syst. **24**, 1413–1421 (2011)
14. Li, Y., Wu, F.X., Ngom, A.: A review on machine learning principles for multi-view biological data integration. Brief. Bioinform. **19**(2), 325–340 (2018)
15. Li, C.L., Chang, W.C., Cheng, Y., et al.: Mmd gan: towards deeper understanding of moment matching network. arXiv preprint arXiv:1705.08584 (2017)
16. Shao, W., Shi, X., Yu, P.S.: Clustering on multiple incomplete datasets via collective kernel learning. Int. Conf. Data Min. 1181–1186 (2013)
17. Li, S., Jiang, Y., Zhou, Z.: Partial Multi-view Clustering. In: AAAI, pp. 1968–1974 (2014)
18. Zhao, H., Liu, H., Fu, Y.: Incomplete multi-modal visual data grouping. In: IJCAI, pp. 2392–2398 (2016)
19. Yin, Q., Wu, S., Wang, L.: Unified subspace learning for incomplete and unlabeled multi-view data. Pattern Recogn. **67**, 313–327 (2017)
20. Yin, Q., Wu, S., Wang, L.: Incomplete multi-view clustering via subspace learning. In: Proceedings of the 24th ACM International on Conference on Information and Knowledge Management, pp. 383–392 (2015)
21. Shao, W., He, L., Philip, S.Y.: Multiple incomplete views clustering via weighted nonnegative matrix factorization with local graph regularization. In: Joint European Conference on Machine Learning and Knowledge Discovery in Databases. Springer, Cham, pp. 318–334 (2015). https://doi.org/10.1007/978-3-319-46128-1

22. Zhu, J., Park, T., Isola, P., et al.: Unpaired image-to-image translation using cycle-consistent adversarial networks. In: International Conference on Computer Vision, pp. 2242–2251 (2017)

23. Pan, Y., Liu, M., Lian, C., et al.: Disease-image specific generative adversarial network for brain disease diagnosis with incomplete multi-modal neuroimages. In: International Conference on Medical Image Computing and Computer-Assisted Intervention. Springer, Cham, pp. 137–145 (2019). https://doi.org/10.1007/978-3-030-32248-9_16

A Survey on Service Migration Strategies for Vehicular Edge Computing

Zhiwen Song[(⊠)], Yanfang Fan, and Ying Cai

School of Computer, Beijing Information Science and Technology University, Beijing, China
songzhiwen@bistu.edu.cn

Abstract. Vehicular Edge Computing (VEC) is a promising technology to place services on side of the road to improve the quality of service (QoS) for users. It has advantages over cloud computing in terms of user-perceived latency, security and communication costs. However, due to the mobility of the vehicle and the limited coverage of the edge server, once the vehicle leaves the coverage of the edge server, it will lead to the decrease of the quality of service and the improvement of communication cost. Service migration is expected to solve this problem. The main idea is to continuously move the service to a location close to the vehicle. Due to the dynamically changing network environment, it is a huge challenge to design the optimal migration strategy. To better and quickly know related works, we conduct a survey on service migration strategies for VEC. This paper first introduces the concept of service migration and related technologies. Then the works on migration strategies in recent years are summarized and divided into two categories. One category is based on current location and the other category is based on trajectory information. Finally, some open challenges in service migration strategies are presented.

Keywords: Vehicular Edge Computing · Service migration · Migration strategies

1 Introduction

With the rapid development of Internet of Vehicles (IoV), the demand of vehicle application for quality of service is also increasing [1]. Traditional cloud computing has the problems of high delay, high workload, data insecurity and network bottleneck [2], which cannot satisfy the delay-sensitive [3] and computation-intensive applications in the Internet of Vehicles. VEC based on Multi-Access Edge Computing (MEC) is a promising solution [4] by deploying edge server as close to the user as possible [5], services are migrated from remote clouds to edge servers closer to users, which greatly improves QoS for users and reduce some security risks by reducing data transfer time.

Deploying services in the edge server also faces many new problems. Due to the mobility of vehicles and the limited coverage of the edge server, once vehicles leave the coverage area of the edge server that provides services for them, which will lead to considerable network degradation [6] and further seriously affect the QoS. In order to

© Springer Nature Singapore Pte Ltd. 2022
Y. Tian et al. (Eds.): ICBDS 2021, CCIS 1563, pp. 473–487, 2022.
https://doi.org/10.1007/978-981-19-0852-1_37

reduce the degradation of QoS caused by mobility of vehicles, services must be migrated to a better location [7], namely service migration [8].

Service migration solves the degradation of QoS due to user movement by migrating service entities from one edge server to another. The key question is when and where to migrate. No migration or inappropriate migration strategy may extend the distance between vehicle and service node, which will lead to weak network connection [9] or high migration cost. Therefore, how to design an appropriate migration strategy is an extremely critical issue. Due to the uncertainty of vehicle movement and the difficulty of tradeoff QoS upgrade and migration cost, it is very challenging to make the optimal migration decision. This paper surveys and analyzes the recent literatures on service migration strategies in MEC and relevant computing paradigm scenarios, and classifies and summarizes them.

The structure of this paper is as follows. Section 2 introduces the process of service migration and related concepts. Then Sect. 3 summarizes and classifies the existing work. Sections 4 and 5 present the open challenges and conclusion, respectively.

2   Introduction to Service Migration in VEC

The service migration we explore is caused by the movement of vehicles. Specifically, the works investigated in this paper are the live migration caused by vehicle movement through virtualization technology in VEC.

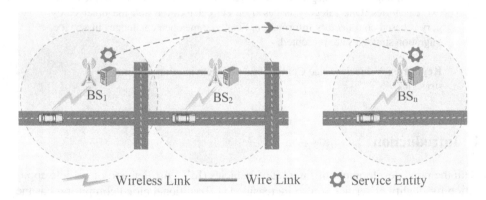

Fig. 1. Service migration example.

Figure 1 shows a simple example of service migration in the VEC. A vehicle is driving on the road, and there is a group of base stations (BS) along the road. Each base station is equipped with one or more edge server on which service entities run to provide services for vehicles. In this scenario, when the vehicle is within the coverage of BS_1, the service entity can communicate directly with the vehicle via a wireless link. There are two ways to continue to get service when the vehicle is out of BS_1's coverage. 1) When the vehicle moves into BS_2's coverage, the vehicle only needs to perform base station handover [10]. Since the edge servers deployed in BS_1 and BS_2 use wire link, BS_1

can provide services for the vehicle indirectly through transmitting data to the vehicle via BS_2. 2) When the vehicle moves into the coverage of BS_n which is assumed to be far enough from BS_1, service migration is necessary because of the intolerable delay caused by the increase in physical distance. The service entity should be migrated from the source edge server to the closer edge server. Once the migration is complete, the vehicle can communicate directly with BS_n to access the service.

The core concept of service migration is to migrate services to a location closer to users as users move. The concept of service migration is akin to handover in cellular networks and live migration in data centers. Compared to handover in cellular networks, service migration requires a larger amount of data to be migrated and does not require migration every time when vehicle moves to a new area, so the considerations are more complex. The biggest difference between live migration in data center and service migration lies in their different concern. The former focuses on downtime, while the latter focuses on the total migration time [11]. Below are some terms and technical descriptions related to service migration.

Service: The element to be migrated in the service migration. It can represent any entity that provides a certain service running on the edge server.

Migration Type: Migrations can be stateful or stateless. Stateful migration means that the running status of the application is also migrated to the target node, whereas stateless migration is not required. Stateful migration is divided into cold migration and live migration. In a cold migration, the service is suspended at the beginning of the migration and resumed when it reaches the target node. And the service remains unavailable throughout the process, known as downtime. Live migration has very little downtime. Because only when the migration is almost done, service will be stopped. It means that in this kind of migration, service can continue to be provided while data is being replicated [8]. If the downtime does not exceed a threshold and the user does not feel the migration directly, it is called a seamless service migration [12]. In VEC, live migration is usually considered.

Virtualization Technology: There are various application component hosting technologies that can provide services for the vehicle in the edge server, including virtual machine technology, container technology and agent technology [11]. Virtual machine technology provides strong isolation because of the migration of the entire operating system. Container technology implements process isolation at the operating system level, which is more portable [13]. The agent [14] has many advantages, such as convenient management, less data transmission and fast start-up. But its application in MEC is still in its primary stage, and there is still a lot of work to be done.

Connection Technology: Communication between vehicles and base stations is using wireless technologies [15], such as cellular, IEEE WAVE, Wi-Fi, 4G/5G [16], etc. Wired link is used among the base stations.

3 Proposed Taxonomy

The migration strategy in the process of service migration is very important and complex. It needs to consider whether to migrate, when and where to migrate. Due to so many influencing factors in the process of migration, it is difficulty to develop a reasonable migration strategy. In general works, the migration problem is firstly modeled as a multi-objective optimization problem, then various algorithms are used to obtain the optimal solution. Finally, the proposed algorithm is evaluated experimentally.

This chapter reviews recent migration papers and divided them into two categories. Category 1 focuses on when to migrate. In this category, researchers aim to design a migration strategy to decide whether to migrate at each time slot. Category 2 focuses on where to migrate. Here researchers aim to maximize the total system utility over the entire trajectory based on the predicted or known trajectory of the vehicle.

3.1 Current-Location Based Service Migration

The works of current-location based service migration make migration decisions based on the current environment conditions. The migration action is to migrate or not to migrate to the edge server that currently covers the vehicle. In other words, these works focus on maximizing long-term system benefits or minimizing system costs by considering the suitability of present environmental conditions for migration. Environmental conditions include channel quality, traffic conditions, vehicle speed, etc. In most schemes, the environmental conditions and optimization objectives are modeled as a mathematical problem, and solved using various algorithms. The algorithms in the migration scheme are the key to the migration strategy. In this section, we distinguish works of using traditional algorithms, reinforcement learning algorithms, and deep reinforcement learning algorithms.

Traditional Algorithm-Based Solutions. Most of current migration papers focus on tradeoffs between QoS and cost. Delay is commonly chosen as the QoS metric in VEC. The delay is usually a combination of the wireless transmission delay between the vehicle and the base station, the computing delay of the edge server, the wired transmission delay between the edge server and the edge server or between the edge server and the cloud server. Cost is usually migration cost and may also include transmission cost and computation cost. In addition to delay and cost, bandwidth [17] and server load [18] are often considered.

In [19], the authors first introduced the Never Migrate Strategy, which has the lowest migration cost, and Always Migration Strategy, which has the lowest end-to-end delay. A threshold-based scheme is proposed that flexibly combines the two baseline schemes mentioned above. The key idea is to keep the end-to-end delay within a threshold, and trigger migration when the delay exceeds the threshold. This scheme minimizes migration overhead while keeping end-to-end delays within acceptable limits.

In addition to delay and cost, the authors in [20] considered more factors and propose a migration strategy for edge computing based on multi-attribute strategy. In the process of migration, if the user goes out of the service range of the server, the migration strategy will be activated. In this strategy, TOPSIS (Technique for Order Preference by Similarity to an Ideal Solution) is used to migrate among multiple servers according to network status, user location, task attributes and server load. The simulation results show that the proposed strategy is superior to the strategy based on non-migration and Markov decision process in terms of time and cost. Furthermore, the authors in [21] considered the problem of increased migration cost caused by I/O interference and multi-user interference, and developed a practical algorithm for designing the optimal JMH (Joint Migration and Handover) policy to solve this problem.

Reinforcement Learning Based Solutions. The traditional solution algorithms have many limitations, including high algorithm complexity and low efficiency. Meanwhile, traditional solution algorithms consume a lot of computing resources and have low fault tolerance, which makes them difficult to be used in large-scale network scenarios. Therefore, in recent years, many studies have used Reinforcement Learning (RL) algorithms to solve the migration decision problem. In RL, agent acquires knowledge of unknown environments through interactions so as to make optimal decisions [22].

The Markov Decision Process (MDP) is used to model the RL problem. The authors in [23] studied service migration in MEC using MDP framework. A new algorithm and numerical technique are proposed to calculate the optimal solution. Experiments using real data sets show that the proposed algorithm is much faster than the traditional method based on standard value and policy iteration, and has better performance in terms of cost.

In [24], the system is also modeled as MDP according to the characteristics of user mobility in MEC network, and a Q-learning method based on RL is used to solve the problem. In the simulation experiment, compared with the genetic algorithm and the other two traditional baseline algorithms, the algorithm based on RL proposed in this paper has better performance. The authors in [25] believe that there is interdependence among services, so service placement schemes need to be reconsidered from different perspectives. In this paper, an active service placement and migration mechanism is proposed, and a model-free RL algorithm is used to make decisions. The effectiveness of the proposed method on the average utilization of server resources is proved by an experiment based on a San Francisco taxi trajectory.

Deep Reinforcement Learning Based Solutions. When the number of servers is large and the state space increases. A huge state space can lead to Curse of Dimensionality, which results in the inability of agent to learn appropriate strategies [26]. Then researchers start to use Deep Reinforcement Learning (DRL) to address this issue. DRL is a combination of deep learning and reinforcement learning that can provide better solutions to decision problems for complex systems.

In [27], the authors designed a service migration model that considers multiple information, which include migration cost, computational cost, QoS, energy consumption of mobile devices and server load information. If a DL-based strategy is used, the algorithm runtime will reach an intolerable level. The authors used a deep Q-learning based algorithm to approximate this complex computing problems. The proposed algorithm is superior to no-migration algorithm, always migration algorithm and Q-learning algorithm in the simulation results. The literature [28] and [29] similarly apply DRL to service migration. In [28], the authors proposed a dynamic service migration scheme considering the impact of speed in a one-dimensional mobile scene, and used a DRL algorithm to maximize the system utility. In the simulation experiment, compared with the migration method without considering the influence of vehicle speed, the proposed algorithm can significantly improve the utilization rate of the system, especially with the increase of vehicle speed, the improvement effect becomes more obvious. The authors in [29] considered the movement support mechanism in fog computing. To support migration tasks for different application requirements, a new container migration algorithm and architecture is proposed. The container migration strategy is modeled as MDP space, and a decision algorithm based on deep Q-learning was designed. Experimental results using real data show that the proposed strategy outperforms the baseline algorithm in terms of delay, power consumption and migration cost.

In distributed mobile edge cloud, the authors, the authors in [30] describe the problem of adaptive service migration as a multi- agent reinforcement learning task, which also uses deep Q learning as the target network. Then proved that a single agent can also learn strategies. Compared with the model-based algorithm, the effectiveness of the proposed algorithm is proved. The authors in [18] believe that in the absence of interaction among multiple agents, it is difficult to evaluate the contribution of a single agent to global reward and learn cooperative strategies. Therefore, the authors introduced a counterfactual multi-agent (COMA) strategy gradient to solve these problems. The so-called counterfactual is to assume existing facts and then evaluate the probability of the occurrence of one of the influencing factors through reverse reasoning. Specifically, the main features of the proposed algorithm can be summarized as the introduction of a centralized evaluator and a counterfactual baseline. The centralized evaluator can calculate each task's contribution to the global goal and then guide each participant's learning. Simulation results show that the average task completion time of the proposed distributed task migration algorithm is reduced by 30–50% compared with the non-migration algorithm and the single-agent actor-critic algorithm (AC) (Table 1).

Table 1. Current-location based service migration.

	Objective	Considered factors	Approach in migration solution	Data sources
[17]	Maximize the average QoS within the constraint of migration time	·Allocated bandwidth ·Memory dirty rate ·Migration time	·Particle swarm optimization ·Genetic algorithm	Synthetic
[19]	Avoid migration at an acceptable and stable latency	·Migration frequency ·End-to-end delay	Threshold-based	Real-World
[20]	Efficiently solve the problem of whether, when and where to migrate	·Bandwidth ·Computing ability ·Latency ·Migration cost ·Energy consumption	TOPSIS	Synthetic

(*continued*)

Table 1. (*continued*)

	Objective	Considered factors	Approach in migration solution	Data sources
[21]	Maximize the sum offloading rate, quantify MEC through-put, and minimize the migration cost	·Communication rate ·Computation rate ·MEC through-put ·Migration cost ·I/O interference	·The sum-of-ratios algorithm ·Hungarian algorithm	Synthetic
[23]	Minimize the long-term expected discounted sum total cost	·Migration cost ·Transmission cost	·MDP ·Modified policy iteration	Real-World
[24]	Reduce the migration probability and maximize the total revenue	·Computation time ·Transmission energy consumption ·Execution resource	·MDP ·Q-learning based	Synthetic
[25]	Improve delay	·Delay ·Server resources	·MDP ·Dyna-Q algorithm	Real-World
[26]	Minimize the end-to-end delay	End-to-end delay	RL-DR method	Synthetic
[27]	Minimize the cost and energy consumption	·Migration cost ·Transaction Cost ·Energy Consumption	·MDP ·Deep Q-network	Synthetic
[28]	Tradeoff the QoS and migration cost	·Migration cost ·Required delay ·Velocity of vehicles ·Memory dirty Rate	Deep Q-learning	Synthetic
[29]	Minimize the total cost	·Delay ·Power consumption ·Migration cost	·MDP ·Deep Q-learning	Real-World
[30]	Learn a cost-minimizing service migration strategy that can adapt to different architectures and cost models	·Latency ·Migration cost	Deep Q-learning	Synthetic
[18]	Minimize the average completion time of tasks under migration energy budget	·Communication times ·Processing time ·Migration time	·Reinforcement Learning ·Counterfactual multi-agent policy gradients Algorithm	Synthetic

3.2   Trajectory Information Based Service Migration

Some works consider migration strategy when the vehicle's trajectory is known or predicted. If the trajectory of the vehicle can be known, unnecessary migration can be avoided, and migration cost and QoS fluctuations can be reduced. The information of trajectory can be obtained by trajectory prediction methods, such as Kalman filtering, which can predict the vehicle movement information in the future period based on the historical movement trajectory [31]. There are also some articles that assume that the trajectory information of the vehicle is known. For example, the trajectory information can be obtained from the navigation software, or it is assumed that the autonomous driving vehicle travels on a fixed trajectory. In Sect. 3.1, the migration action is whether to migrate the service to the server that currently covers the vehicle, while the migration strategies based on trajectory information is to migrate the service to which edge server near the vehicle. That means, it may be the edge server that the vehicle has not reached yet. In this section, we distinguish works based on trajectory prediction and the ones based on known trajectory.

Trajectory Prediction-Based Solutions. Trajectory prediction in VEC is characterized by high speed and regularity [32]. High speed means that the vehicle has a very high moving speed, resulting in a very short stay time in the range of a certain MEC server, which has very strict requirements on migration time and the running time of the strategy algorithm. Regularity means that in the VEC, the road is fixed and the MEC has a fixed coverage area. Then the traffic environment can be further abstracted, and the prediction results obtained after the abstraction will not affect the migration strategy.

In [33], the authors show the value of estimating vehicle mobility when a vehicle moves in a wireless region, meaning the value of trajectory prediction for service pre-migration. The authors proposed a movement prediction algorithm that combines neural networks and Markov chains, and use the output probability vector as the input to the Lyapunov-based online optimizer, which achieves a good balance between the cost of system energy consumption (the number of virtual machines allowed to replicate) and the risk of losing service continuity. Experiments using software to simulate the traffic scene in the city center of Cologne show that the proposed scheme effectively reduces the total energy consumption by more than 50%, compared with the scheme that replicates the virtual machine to all adjacent areas. In [34], the authors predict the user's mobility with Kalman filtering algorithm and then predict the base station load using the historical load information, and select the connected base stations based on the prediction information. And a migration strategy based on DQN is proposed. The experimental results show that the migration cost of the proposed algorithm is better than other related algorithms.

The mobility prediction model relies on the historical data of users' movement between wireless cells, and ignores the changes of users' positions in the service cells. In [35], the authors suggest that the reliability of mobile prediction can be improved by considering the user's movement within the wireless cell in the mobile prediction, and the VM replication strategy can be adjusted dynamically based on the mobile prediction. The authors described the service migration process as a sequential decision problem, and use an angle-of-arrival and learning-based method to predict the movement of vehicles. An online algorithm based on Q-learning is proposed to learn the optimal strategy.

Experiments are carried out on the data sets of telecom base station and taxi trajectory based on Shanghai. The results show that the optimal solution can be found with minimal time delay and migration costs using the offline algorithm based on dynamic programming, while the online algorithm based on reinforcement learning can approach the optimal performance.

In [36], the authors believe that in actual situations, future trajectory could not be accurately predicted, so the prediction accuracy was described in the form of probability. In general, the further away you are from the present, the less accurate your predictions are. In this paper, they first discussed the problem of ignoring the prediction accuracy, meaning all future trajectories and channel capacity information are known, and then propose a solution based on dynamic programming. Then a monotone decreasing exponential function is assumed to describe the prediction accuracy, which decreases with the increase of the prediction time. A partial update migration strategy based on dynamic programming is proposed which combines priority queue and greedy algorithm to solve this problem. In the experiment based on the trajectory of a Roman taxi, the proposed algorithm can approach the optimal solution of the problem.

Known Trajectory-Based Solutions. The authors in [37] made a clever assumption that the destination is already determined when the vehicle is started, and that if the destination is determined, the navigation application will assign a reasonable driving path, i.e., known driving trajectory. And if the vehicle changes its destination or path during the journey, a new route can be planned. In this way, the influence of the uncertainty of vehicle movement trajectory on the service migration decision is controlled to an acceptable range. Specifically, the whole driving trajectory is modeled as MDP, and a service migration decision algorithm based on deep Q-learning that can be dynamically adjusted according to traffic information is proposed. On this basis, a service migration framework composed of neural network is proposed. The training and decision-making parts of the framework are at the cloud server side and the vehicle side respectively. By using the vehicle data of Changsha city, experiments are carried out in the suburban, urban and downtown scenarios, and the effectiveness of the proposed algorithm is verified by comparing with the fixed-hop migration algorithm.

In [38], service migration problem was described as MDP, through the history of the user mobile trajectory to obtain users transition probability matrix. In order to reduce the size of the action set only meet delay condition edge server in this collection. The authors considered the risk of privacy leakage in the process of migration. If an attacker can track the trajectory of service migration in the edge server, then the attacker may track the real moving trajectory of users through the trajectory of service migration, which means user location privacy is at risk of disclosure. The authors define the weighted sum of latency, migration cost, and location privacy risk as the system cost. In this paper, an algorithm based on policy iteration is proposed to find the optimal solution to minimize the long-term total cost. The results show that the proposed algorithm has lower total cost compared with the never migration, always migration and dynamic migration schemes. The service migration problem is translated into defining a sequence of actions over a period of time. Similarly, the authors in [39] believe that avoiding the impact of node or link failures is an important factor in the process of service migration. In this paper, the dynamic changes of the network are innovatively and quantitatively analyzed, and the transfer method based on deep Q learning is used to dynamically perceive the environment and adjust the learning rate adaptively to achieve rapid convergence. The objective of the agent is to maximize the total reward of these time slots by determining the actions from the first time slot to the last time slot, and the policy is defined as the migration action sequence in each state. Simulation results show that this algorithm is superior to the typical solutions in terms of migration success rate.

In [22], the authors innovatively proposed a joint service migration and mobility optimization method, meaning the vehicle will plan its driving path according to the load of the surrounding edge servers, instead of passively migrating the service according to the vehicle's driving path. Therefore, the decision behavior in this paper is which edge server to migrate the service to and the driving direction of the vehicle. A multi-agent DRL algorithm is used to jointly optimize service migration and path planning. In the simulation experiment, compared with the algorithm only carrying out service migration and path planning, the proposed algorithm is effective in reducing system costs and service delays of vehicles (Table 2).

Table 2. Trajectory information based service migration.

	Objective	Considered factors	Approach in mobility solution	Approach in migration solution	Data sources
[31]	Reduce the number of communication handovers and service migrations with guaranteed communication quality and service response time	·Communication delay	Kalman filtering	Q-learning	Synthetic
[33]	Minimize energy consumption at the network level and ensure the continuity of MEC services	·Energy cost ·The risk of losing service continuity	Combines neural networks and Markov chains	Lyapunov drift-plus-penalty framework	Real-World

(continued)

Table 2. (*continued*)

	Objective	Considered factors	Approach in mobility solution	Approach in migration solution	Data sources
[34]	Improve user mobility prediction accuracy and reduce migration costs	·Load balancing ·Migration cost ·Run time ·Number of hops	Kalman filtering	DQN	Synthetic
[35]	Reduce the overall service delay with low costs	·Communication delay ·Migration delay and cost	Angle-of-arrival and learning-based	·MDP ·Dynamic programming-based ·Reinforcement learning-based	Real-World
[36]	Optimize long-term average latency for multiple services with different QoS	·Communication delay ·Migration delay	·A specific look-ahead time-window ·Exponential function of prediction accuracy	·Partial Dynamic Optimization algorithm ·Based on DP merged with the priority queue and greedy algorithm	Real-World
[37]	Reduce latency	·Latency ·The migration frequency	Known trajectory	Deep Q-learning networks	Real-World
[38]	Minimize the total cost	·Migration cost ·User-perceived delay ·The risk of location privacy leakage	Known transition probability	·MDP ·Modified policy iteration	Real-World
[39]	Minimize response latency and migration costs	·Latency ·Link capacity ·Node resource requirements	Planned track	·MDP ·Deep Q-learning	Synthetic
[22]	Meet the service delay requirements with minimum migration cost and travel time	·Wireless transmission delay ·Computing delay ·Total travel time	Route planning	·MDP ·Deep Q-Learning	Synthetic

4 Open Challenges

The previous section summarizes most of the research in recent years. This section lists some of the challenges and research opportunities that exist in VEC.

Service Demand Feature of Vehicle: We observe that almost all studies of service migration treat vehicles as equivalent to other smart devices (e.g., a smartphone carried by a person sitting in a car). And there is no analysis of the difference between the service demands of vehicles and those of other smart devices. However, the different nature of such services may lead to different decision-making behaviors. The service for vehicle requirements continues from the departure of the vehicle to the end of the trip, which means that the service is closely related to the driving or traveling trajectory of the vehicle. However, other smart devices are different. For example, smart phone devices may be active in the same area for a long time, but dormant when moving. In this way, frequent migration services are not needed in the process of moving. Therefore, researchers should design more rational migration strategies to accommodate the specificity of vehicle service requirements.

The Role of Decision Making: Most studies assume that the decision is made by the edge server and a few by the local vehicle, but they do not explain the reason for doing so. And few people pay attention to how to build the service migration management system [40]. The role of decision making is usually the service operator [41], but the interests of the user are not always aligned with the service operator. Service operators are concerned with their own interests or the total interests of all users [42], while individual users make decisions that concern only their own interests. The difference between the two interests will lead to different migration strategies. At present, there are few studies addressing this issue and further research is in great demand.

Priority Among Different Services: In the study of migration strategies, little attention has been paid to the differences between different services, and only a small amount of work [36, 43] has considered priority. However, some safety-critical tasks of vehicles are not allowed to interrupt the service. Therefore, the delay requirements and reliability requirements between safety-critical services and entertainment-related services are very different in the migration process. Also, different applications of the same type are different (e.g., data access frequency) [44], and designing the appropriate application-aware approach is critical for strategy efficiency.

Multiple Service Providers: There may be multiple service providers in an area. The vehicle travels among their respective jurisdictions and the service entity migrates among their servers. The current works consider only one service provider and do not consider the impact of conflicts and cooperation between multiple service providers on migration strategies. The solution to this problem can refer to the roaming service of the telecommunication industry [8].

Security: While VEC brings QoS improvements, it also brings more complex security challenges. It is vulnerability to significant attacks such as DoS (denial of service), false data injection, modification [45]. The strategy of service migration requires the information of the vehicle itself and the surrounding environment, including the status of the nearby edge server and the information of other vehicles. Lack of appropriate protection measures will lead to serious security problems. How to ensure data security while keeping migration decisions fast and efficient is a challenging issue.

5 Conclusion

Service migration can effectively solve the problem of service quality degradation caused by vehicle mobility in VEC. Because of the uncertainty of vehicle moving trajectory and the complexity of surrounding environment, how to make an appropriate migration strategy is a difficult problem. In this article, we first introduce the concept of service migration and related technologies. Then, the works in recent years are analyzed and classified. Finally, we present some open research challenges for service migration in VEC. It is hoped that this review will contribute to the study of service migration in VEC or other similar edge computing scenarios.

Acknowledgement. This work is supported by Qin Xin Talents Cultivation Program, Beijing Information Science & Technology University (No. QXTCP C202111).

References

1. Kaiwartya, O., et al.: Internet of vehicles: motivation, layered architecture, network model, challenges, and future aspects. IEEE Access **4**, 5356–5373 (2016)
2. Xu, J., Ma, X., Zhou, A., Duan, Q., Wang, S.: Path selection for seamless service migration in vehicular edge computing. IEEE Internet Things J. **7**(9), 9040–9049 (2020)
3. Zhang, K., Gui, X., Ren, D., Li, J., Wu, J., Ren, D.: Survey on computation offloading and content caching in mobile edge networks. J. Softw. **30**(8), 2491–2516 (2019)
4. Zhang, K., Mao, Y., Leng, S., He, Y., Zhang, Y.: Mobile-edge computing for vehicular networks: a promising network paradigm with predictive off-loading. IEEE Vehicul. Technol. Magaz. **12**(2), 36–44 (2017)
5. Kekki, S., et al.: MEC in 5G networks. ETSI White Paper **28**, 1–28 (2018)
6. Ha, K., Abe, Y., Chen, Z., Hu, W., Amos, B., Pillai, P., Satyanarayanan, M.: Adaptive VM Handoff Across Cloudlets. Technical Report-CMU-CS-15-113 (June), pp. 1–25 (2015)
7. Refaat, T.K., Kantarci, B., Mouftah, H.T.: Dynamic virtual machine migration in a vehicular cloud. In: 2014 IEEE Symposium on Computers and Communications (ISCC), pp. 1–6 (2014)
8. Rejiba, Z., Masip-Bruin, X., Marín-Tordera, E.: A survey on mobility-induced service migration in the fog, edge, and related computing paradigms. ACM Comput. Surv. **52**(5), 1–33 (2019)
9. Bonomi, F., Milito, R., Zhu, J., Addepalli, S.: Fog computing and its role in the internet of things. In: Proceedings of the First Edition of the MCC Workshop on Mobile Cloud Computing (MCC 2012), p. 13 (2012)
10. Ngo, M.V., Luo, T., Hoang, H.T., Ouek, T.Q.S.: Coordinated container migration and base station handover in mobile edge computing. In: 2020 IEEE Global Communications Conference (GLOBECOM 2020), pp. 1–6 (2020)
11. Wang, S., Xu, J., Zhang, N., Liu, Y.: A survey on service migration in mobile edge computing. IEEE Access **6**, 23511–23528 (2018)

12. Satyanarayanan, M., Bahl, P., Caceres, R., Davies, N.: The case for VM-based cloudlets in mobile computing. IEEE Pervasive Comput. **8**(4), 14–23 (2009)
13. Xu, H.: The Design and Implementation of a Customer-Facing-Service Migration for MEC. Nanjing University of Posts and Telecommunications (2019)
14. Jiang, C.: Research on Mobile Agent-Based Service Migration in Mobile Edge Computing. Nanjing University of Posts and Telecommunications (2020)
15. Aguzzi, C., Gigli, L., Sciullo, I., Trotta, A., Di Felice, M.: From cloud to edge: seamless software migration at the era of the web of things. IEEE Access **8**, 228118–228135 (2020)
16. Sharma, N., Chauhan, N., Chand, N.: Security challenges in Internet of Vehicles (IoV) environment. In: 1st International Conference on Secure Cyber Computing and Communications (ICSCCC 2018), pp. 203–207 (2018)
17. Yang, L., Yang, D., Cao, J., Sahni, Y., Xu, X.: QoS guaranteed resource allocation for live virtual machine migration in edge clouds. IEEE Access **8**, 78441–78451 (2020)
18. Liu, C., Tang, F., Hu, Y., Li, K., Tang, Z., Li, K.: Distributed task migration optimization in MEC by extending multi-agent deep reinforcement learning approach. IEEE Trans. Parallel Distrib. Syst. **32**(7), 1603–1614 (2021)
19. Li, J., et al.: Service migration in fog computing enabled cellular networks to support real-time vehicular communications. IEEE Access **7**, 13704–13714 (2019)
20. Zhao, D., Yang, T., Jin, Y., Xu, Y.: A service migration strategy based on multiple attribute decision in mobile edge computing. In: 2017 IEEE 17th International Conference on Communication Technology (ICCT), pp. 986–990 (2017)
21. Liang, Z., Liu, Y., Lok, T.-M., Huang, K.: Multi-cell mobile edge computing: joint service migration and resource allocation. IEEE Trans. Wirel. Commun. **20**(9), 5898–5912 (2021)
22. Yuan, Q., Li, J., Zhou, H., Lin, T., Luo, G., Shen, X.: A joint service migration and mobility optimization approach for vehicular edge computing. IEEE Trans. Veh. Technol. **69**(8), 9041–9052 (2020)
23. Wang, S., Urgaonkar, R., Zafer, M., He, T., Chan, K., Leung, K.K.: Dynamic service migration in mobile edge computing based on Markov decision process. IEEE/ACM Trans. Netw. **27**(3), 1272–1288 (2019)
24. Wang, D., Tian, X., Cui, H., Liu, Z.: Reinforcement learning-based joint task offloading and migration schemes optimization in mobility-aware MEC network. China Commun. **17**(8), 31–44 (2020)
25. Ray, K., Banerjee, A., Narendra, N.C.: Proactive microservice placement and migration for mobile edge computing. In: 2020 IEEE/ACM Symposium on Edge Computing (SEC), pp. 28–41 (2020)
26. Urimoto, R., Fukushima, Y., Tarutani, Y., Murase, T., Yokohira, T.: A server migration method using Q-learning with dimension reduction in edge computing. In: 2021 International Conference on Information Networking (ICOIN), pp. 301–304 (2021)
27. Park, S.W., Boukerche, A., Guan, S.: A novel deep reinforcement learning based service migration model for Mobile Edge Computing. In: Proceedings of the 2020 IEEE/ACM 24th International Symposium on Distributed Simulation and Real Time Applications (DS-RT 2020) (2020)
28. Peng, Y., Liu, L., Zhou, Y., Shi, J., Li, J.: Deep reinforcement learning-based dynamic service migration in vehicular networks. In: 2019 IEEE Global Communications Conference (GLOBECOM), pp. 1–6 (2019)
29. Tang, Z., Zhou, X., Zhang, F., Jia, W., Zhao, W.: Migration modeling and learning algorithms for containers in fog computing. IEEE Trans. Serv. Comput. **12**(5), 712–725 (2019)
30. Brandherm, F., Wang, L., Mühlhäuser, M.: A learning-based framework for optimizing service migration in mobile edge clouds. In: Proceedings of the 2nd International Workshop on Edge Systems, Analytics and Networking, pp. 12–17 (2019)

31. Tang, D.: The Collaborative Management of Handover and Service Migration in Edge Computing. Beijing University of Posts and Telecommunications (2020)
32. Guan, M.: Research on the Pre-migration Strategy of MEC-Based IoV Applications. Chongqing University of Posts and Telecommunications (2019)
33. Labriji, I., et al.: Mobility aware and dynamic migration of MEC services for the internet of vehicles. IEEE Trans. Netw. Serv. Manage. 18(1), 570–584 (2021)
34. Li, Y.: Design and Implementation of Dynamic Service Placement and Service Migration Path Optimization Algorithm in MEC. Beijing University of Posts and Telecommunications (2020)
35. Wang, S., Guo, Y., Zhang, N., Yang, P., Zhou, A., Shen, X.: Delay-aware microservice coordination in mobile edge computing: a reinforcement learning approach. IEEE Trans. Mob. Comput. 20(3), 939–951 (2021)
36. Yu, X., Guan, M., Liao, M., Fan, X.: Pre-migration of vehicle to network services based on priority in mobile edge computing. IEEE Access 7, 3722–3730 (2019)
37. Wang, C., et al.: An adaptive deep Q-learning service migration decision framework for connected vehicles. In: 2020 IEEE International Conference on Systems, Man, and Cybernetics (SMC), pp. 944–949 (2020)
38. Wang, W., Ge, S., Zhou, X.: Location-privacy-aware service migration in mobile edge computing. In: IEEE Wireless Communications and Networking Conference (WCNC), pp. 1–6 (2020)
39. Zhang, M., Huang, H., Rui, L., Hui, G., Wang, Y., Qiu, X.: A service migration method based on dynamic awareness in mobile edge computing. In: 2020 IEEE/IFIP Network Operations and Management Symposium (NOMS 2020), pp. 1–7 (2020)
40. De Nitto Personè, V., Grassi, V.: Architectural issues for self-adaptive service migration management in mobile edge computing scenarios. In: Proceedings of the IEEE International Conference on Edge Computing (EDGE 2019) - Part of the 2019 IEEE World Congress on Services, pp. 27–29 (2019)
41. Gilly, K., Mishev, A., Filiposka, S., Alcaraz, S.: Offloading edge vehicular services in realistic urban environments. IEEE Access 8, 11491–11502 (2020)
42. Jiao, Q.: Research on Service Migration Algorithm for Edge Computing Based on Reinforcement Learning. Beijing University of Posts and Telecommunications (2020)
43. Lu, Y., et al.: A multi-migration seamless handover scheme for vehicular networks in fog-based 5G optical fronthaul. In: 2019 24th OptoElectronics and Communications Conference (OECC) and 2019 International Conference on Photonics in Switching and Computing (PSC), pp. 1–3 (2019)
44. Bellavista, P., Corradi, A., Foschini, L., Scotece, D.: Differentiated service/data migration for edge services leveraging container characteristics. IEEE Access 7, 139746–139758 (2019)
45. Fraiji, Y., Ben Azzouz, L., Trojet, W., Saidane, L.A.: Cyber security issues of internet of electric vehicles. In: 2018 IEEE Wireless Communications and Networking Conference (WCNC), pp. 1–6 (2018)

Research on the Evaluation Method of Construction Measurement Uncertainty Based on Edge Algorithm

Huali Wang[✉]

Luzhou Vocational and Technical College, Luzhou 646000, Sichuan, China

Abstract. With the rapid development of my country's construction industry, how to control the measurement accuracy of construction engineering has become a research hotspot nowadays. Aiming at the problems of time-consuming, labor-consuming and large error caused by the traditional use of manpower to measure construction projects, this paper proposes a method for evaluating the uncertainty of construction measurement based on edge computing. First, design a construction measurement uncertainty processing and fusion architecture based on edge computing; second, introduce Box-Cox conversion on the basis of the original Zscore data standardization processing, and propose a multi-source data processing method based on generalized power transformation Zscore to achieve various perspectives The unified transformation of measurement; then, the component credibility function is defined to constrain the fusion of uncertain feature attributes in the DS inference process, and a multi-source data fusion model based on conflict-optimized DS inference is constructed to realize the grouping and aggregation of multi-source heterogeneous data; finally, Experimental analysis in a simulation environment verifies the effectiveness of the technology.

Keywords: Construction engineering · Measurement · Precision control · Building quality · Edge computing

1 Introduction

Our country's economy has developed rapidly in recent years. The construction industry also continues to develop and improve. Among them, building survey is an important part of the construction industry. Building survey requirements are very precise and rigorous. Once there is a problem with the construction engineering measurement, the overall quality of all buildings cannot be guaranteed. At the same time, it will also affect the process and speed of later construction. As the so-called "the smallest difference is a thousand miles away", building surveying is a very rigorous work, and there must be no error. The measurement accuracy error may even bring safety hazards to the entire building. Only by ensuring the measurement accuracy of the construction project, can the later design and construction be effectively carried out. Construction engineering survey accuracy control plays a vital role in the construction industry.

© Springer Nature Singapore Pte Ltd. 2022
Y. Tian et al. (Eds.): ICBDS 2021, CCIS 1563, pp. 488–495, 2022.
https://doi.org/10.1007/978-981-19-0852-1_38

Construction engineering survey plays a very important role in construction, and its survey work runs through the entire construction process. Measurement is the foundation of construction engineering, and it also determines the quality of the entire building. Construction engineering surveys have practical applications in the early architectural design, building survey, mid-term construction, and later construction management and supervision. Moreover, these measurement data are the actual basis for the construction of the entire building. Without these actual measurement data, the entire construction project will lose its goal and direction, causing many projects of the construction project to be unable to continue normal operation and construction. In the pre-architectural design stage, it is necessary to measure the topography of the building, the stability of the ground around the building, the starting distance of the building construction equipment, and the ratio of the actual distance between the floors of the building to the daylighting degree. These actual data will affect the entire building design. The actual building measurement can give the most first-line data to the building design, making the design more reasonable and more standardized, and at the same time making the building safer. In the face of force majeure natural disasters, buildings can play their practical role to protect the safety of personnel.

Construction engineering surveying is the most basic step. It not only requires the surveying personnel to have a wealth of professional knowledge, but also requires the construction personnel to be careful and conscientious. However, in recent years, architectural design has focused on architectural appearance design and architectural space collocation, ignoring the most basic construction engineering survey, and construction engineering surveying has not formed a dedicated survey and supervision team. Because building surveying has not received enough attention, there are big problems in measurement accuracy today [7, 8].

Many of the algorithms used in edge detection are based on the principle of differential calculation to extract the required information from the high-frequency part of the image containing noise. However, because traditional edge detection algorithms are more susceptible to noise, the results of edge detection often contain more noise signals, and the required useful information cannot be extracted, resulting in lower detection accuracy [1], for example, Edge detection algorithms such as Laplace, Log, Rewitt, Sobel and Robert [2]. Compared with these several edge detection algorithms, the Canny edge detection algorithm has better detection accuracy, and the detection result has a higher signal-to-noise ratio, so it is widely used in various fields [3].

In summary, the development of intelligent building construction measurement has become an inevitable trend, and edge computing technology provides a feasible solution for this trend. This paper proposes a method for evaluating uncertainty in building construction measurement based on edge computing, and designs a data processing and fusion architecture that fully considers edge computing; proposes various power distribution based on generalized power transformation Zscore (Box-Cox transformation Zscore, BC-Zscore) A unified processing method for the transformation of dimension and order of magnitude of network data sources; through the construction of a multi-source data fusion model based on conflict-optimized DS reasoning (principal components analysis-Dempster Shafer, PCA-DS), the multi-source data fusion model is considered based on multi-dimensional feature factors. The structured data is grouped and aggregated. The evaluation method of construction measurement uncertainty considering edge computing can effectively realize the effective integration of data from multiple measurement angles, and lay a good foundation for improving the measurement and analysis of intelligent building construction. It has important research value and significance.

2 Method

2.1 Traditional Canny Edge Detection Algorithm

The process of the traditional Canny edge detection algorithm is: (1) Use Gaussian filtering to smooth the original image [4]; (2) Calculate the magnitude and direction of the gradient of the image after noise reduction; (3) The magnitude of the gradient Carry out non-maximum suppression; (4) Use the double threshold method to detect and connect the edges to form a complete edge [5].

The Canny edge detection algorithm uses Gaussian filtering to smooth the image, and its principle is the neighborhood average method [6]. The Gaussian function is shown in Eq. (1):

$$G(x, y) = \frac{1}{2\pi\sigma^2} \exp\left(-\frac{x^2 + y^2}{2\sigma^2}\right) \tag{1}$$

Among them, σ is the parameter of Gaussian filtering, and the selection of σ will directly affect the filtering effect. If σ is larger, it will cause serious edge offset and greatly increase the amount of calculation; if it is smaller, although the edge detection accuracy is higher, the smoothing effect of the image is weak, making the noise reduction effect poor. The image smoothing process is as follows: (1) Set a template, in which the weighted average of the gray levels of all pixels is calculated; (2) Assign this value to the gray value of the central pixel of the template; (3)) In the same way, scan each pixel in the image, and then perform the weighted average calculation.

2.2 Optimized Canny Edge Detection Algorithm

Adaptive median filtering is based on traditional median filtering, and adaptively changes the size of the window through the size of the gray value in the window [10]. Set a filter window G_{mid}, which represents the median gray value in the window, and G_{min} and G_{max} represents the maximum and minimum gray values in the window, respectively. If $G_{mid} < G_{max}$ and $G_{mid} > G_{min}$ is satisfied, the size of the window remains unchanged, otherwise the preset window size is increased, and the above process is repeated until a suitable G_{mid} is found, or the window size cannot be increased. Then, verify the gray value G(x, y) of the pixel at the center point, if G(x, y) $< G_{max}$ and G(x, y) $> G_{min}$, then G(x, y) is the gray value of the window, otherwise it is the gray value of the window.

Since the selection of G_{mid} is susceptible to noise, whether it is traditional median filtering or adaptive median filtering, it is impossible to prejudge the noise, resulting in a certain degree of blindness in filtering. Aiming at the above-mentioned shortcomings, this paper proposes an optimized median filtering method, so that the selection of G_{mid} is not affected by noise. The specific steps are as follows.

(1) Find the average of the extreme values in the window $\overline{G}$:

$$\overline{G} = \frac{G_{min} + G_{max}}{2} \tag{2}$$

(2) Compare the gray value of each pixel in the window with. If the gray value of a certain point is $\geq \overline{G}$, it will be regarded as an abnormal point, otherwise it will be regarded as a normal point.

(3) Extract the edge points from the abnormal points. The basis for extracting edge points is the distance between pixel points. Because noise points exist in isolation, while edge points usually exist continuously, the edge points and noise points can be separated according to Eq. (3):

$$\begin{cases} |G(x, y) - G(x + 1, y)| = 1 \ edge \ point \\ |G(x, y) - G(x + 1, y)| > 1 \ noisy \ point \end{cases} \tag{3}$$

(4) Through the above separation method, the noise points can be separated, and the median value of the normal points can be taken as the filtering result.

The traditional Canny edge detection algorithm is sensitive to noise in the calculation of gradient amplitude and direction, which affects the edge detection effect. This paper proposes an optimized calculation method for gradient and amplitude. The specific steps are as follows.

(1) Calculate the partial derivatives in the horizontal and vertical directions, denoted by $P_{0°}$ and $P_{90°}$ respectively:

$$P_{0°}(i, j) = I(i, j + 1) - I(i, j - 1) \tag{4}$$

$$P_{90°}(i, j) = I(i + 1, j) - I(i - 1, j) \tag{5}$$

(2) Calculate the partial derivative in the diagonal (and) direction, denoted by $P_{45°}$ and $P_{135°}$:

$$P_{45°}(i, j) = I(i - 1, j + 1) - I(i + 1, j - 1) \tag{6}$$

$$P_{135°}(i, j) = I(i + 1, j + 1) - I(i - 1, j - 1) \tag{7}$$

(3) Using formula (8) and formula (9) to find the difference $H_{0°}(x, y)$ in the horizontal direction and the difference $H_{90°}(x, y)$ in the vertical direction are:

$$H_{0°}(x, y) = \frac{P_{45°}(i, j) + P_{135°}(i, j)}{2} + P_{0°}(i, j) \tag{8}$$

$$H_{90°}(x, y) = \frac{P_{45°}(i, j) - P_{135°}(i, j)}{2} + P_{90°}(i, j) \tag{9}$$

(4) Obtain the gradient amplitude W(i, j) as

$$W(i,j) = \frac{\sqrt{3}}{2}\sqrt{P_{0°}(i,j)^2 + P_{45°}(i,j)^2 + P_{90°}(i,j)^2 + P_{135°}(i,j)^2 + H_{0°}(i,j)^2 + H_{90°}(i,j)^2}$$

The direction of the gradient $\varphi(i,j)$ is:

$$\varphi(i,j) = \tan^{-1}\frac{H_{90°}(i,j)}{H_{0°}(i,j)} \tag{10}$$

Compared with the traditional Canny edge detection algorithm to calculate the gradient, the above method considers the influence of the partial derivatives in the and two directions, suppresses the noise, and makes the edge location more accurate.

The high and low thresholds of the traditional Canny edge detection algorithm are set based on personal experience. In actual engineering applications, due to various conditions (such as environment, light, etc.), the high and low thresholds set by personal experience will reduce the edge. The accuracy of the test results. Therefore, this paper proposes an improved iterative method to calculate the high and low thresholds. The specific process is as follows:

(1) Use the histogram to get the maximum value of the image gray W_{max} and Minimum W_{min}, and calculate the mean of the two $K = \frac{W_{max}+W_{min}}{2}$.
(2) According to the mean value, the original image is divided into high gray scale area and low gray scale area, the area with gray value > is high gray area, and the area with gray value ≤ is low gray area;
(3) Find the maximum W_1 and minimum W_2 gray levels of the area M, and let $K1 = \frac{W_1+W_2}{2}$.
(4) In the M area, the area with gray value > K1 is a high gray area M1, and the area with gray value ≤ K1 is a low gray area M2;
(5) Find the maximum W_3 and minimum W_4 gray levels in the area M1, and let $K2 = \frac{W_3+W_4}{2}$. According to K2 dividing the area M1 into foreground and background, find the gray mean value G1 and G2 of the two:

$$G1 = \frac{\sum_{E(i,j)\leq K2} E(i,j) \times F(i,j)}{\sum_{E(i,j)\leq K2} F(i,j)} \tag{11}$$

$$G2 = \frac{\sum_{E(i,j)> K2} E(i,j) \times F(i,j)}{\sum_{E(i,j)> K2} F(i,j)} \tag{12}$$

Among them, E(i, j) represents the gray value of the point (i, j) in the image; F(i, j) is the weight coefficient of the point.
(6) According to the method of (5), find the maximum W5 and minimum W6 gray values in the region M2 and the mean K3, according to K3 the gray mean values G3 and G4, which divide the region into foreground and background, respectively:

$$G3 = \frac{\sum_{E(i,j)\leq K3} E(i,j) \times F(i,j)}{\sum_{E(i,j)\leq K3} F(i,j)} \tag{13}$$

$$G4 = \frac{\sum_{E(i,j)> K3} E(i,j) \times F(i,j)}{\sum_{E(i,j)> K3} F(i,j)} \tag{14}$$

(7) Find the new threshold K4, $K4 = \frac{G1+G2+G3+G4}{4}$;
(8) If $\left| K4 - \frac{K2+K3}{2} \right| < T$, T is a preset parameter, then K4 is the high threshold obtained by the iterative method, otherwise K1 = K4, assign the value to, and repeat (4) to (8) until the high threshold is obtained;
(9) In the same way, the low threshold can be found in the N area.

3 Experiment

In order to verify the validity and reliability of the building construction measurement technology based on the edge algorithm, we analyze it through model experiments. In particular, we use GIS to collect the required data. GIS technology is also geographic information system technology. In the process of construction engineering surveying, it is necessary to optimize the design of the survey control network. This is a key step in the construction engineering survey. The use of GIS technology can further ensure the accuracy and reliability of the survey control network and the application of this technology does not need to consume too much cost, and the operation is convenient and the cost is low. In the process of applying GIS technology, input the data information observed by the construction project into the system, and then the system can automatically present the graphic data of a certain area and calculate it. After the calculation is completed, accurate data can be obtained.

In order to avoid the contingency of the processing method, we randomly selected 10 observation numbers to display the results. After the data standardized processing method is processed by the method proposed in this article, the processing result values of the three different formats, dimensions, data types and magnitudes of the data source characteristic attributes are shown in Table 1.

Table 1. Multi-source data processing experiment result values

Number	Source 1	Source 2	Source 3	Source 4	Source 5	Source 6
1	0.33	0.04	−1.00	0.25	0.42	0.84
2	0.52	0.38	0.72	0.49	0.38	0.28
3	0.60	−0.06	0.75	0.37	0.53	0.30
4	−0.81	0.24	0.01	0.22	0.9	0.74
5	0.93	0.17	0.56	0.80	0.78	0.99
6	0.92	0.54	0.32	0.07	0.66	0.58
7	−0.26	0.94	−0.58	0.18	0.63	0.37
8	0.41	0.98	0.16	0.04	0.34	0.28
9	−0.27	−0.43	−0.44	0.72	0.58	0.29
10	0.03	0.65	0.24	0.72	0.65	0.34

Experiments show that by standardizing the continuous raw data within one week of multi-source data, this method effectively realizes the unified transformation processing of the format, dimension, data type, and order of magnitude of the feature attributes of each data source. The experimental results in Table 1 can be it can be seen that the absolute value of each element after the feature attribute transformation of each data source is between 0 and 1, which obviously eliminates the limitation caused by a variety of inconsistent factors, and lays the foundation for subsequent data fusion calculation and information mining.

In addition, we are still using landscape images, ground images and red blood cell images to verify the effectiveness of the algorithms used. The experimental results are shown in Figs. 1, 2, and 3.

Fig. 1. Landscape image effect comparison

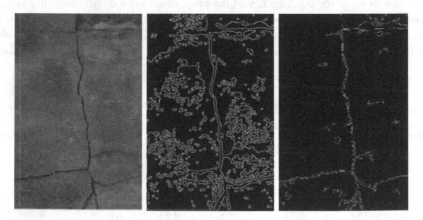

Fig. 2. Ground image effect comparison

Comparing Fig. 1(b) and (c), we can see that the optimized Canny edge detection algorithm can detect more edge detail information, including more wooden bridge details and wooden ship outlines; compare Fig. 2(b) and (c) It can be seen that the optimized Canny edge detection algorithm can better suppress false edge information, so that the edge detection results contain less useless information; comparing Fig. 3(b) and (c), we can see that the optimized Canny The edge detection algorithm can better eliminate the double-edge situation.

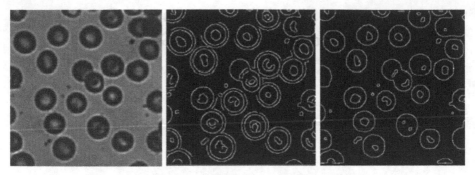

Fig. 3. Red blood cell image effect comparison

4 Conclusion

Aiming at the inaccuracy and time-consuming and labor-consuming problems of traditional building construction measurement, this paper proposes an optimized Canny edge detection algorithm to improve the accuracy of building construction measurement. MATLAB simulation experiment results show that the edge detection algorithm used in this article retains the advantages of the traditional Canny edge detection algorithm, while also significantly suppressing noise, effectively retaining the information of the original image, and eliminating false edges and double edges in the detection results. This makes the test results more continuous and has stronger practicability.

References

1. Sri, R., Retno, D., Hartika, Z.R., Eva, R., Najla, L., Anjar, W.: Prewitt and Canny methods on inversion image edge detection: an evaluation. J. Phys. Conf. Ser. **1933**(1), 012039 (2021)
2. Hernández-Hernández, M., Hernández-Hernández, J.L., Maldonado, E.R., Miranda, I.H.: In: Valencia-García, R., Alcaraz-Mármol, G., Del Cioppo-Morstadt, J., Vera-Lucio, N., Bucaram-Leverone, M. (eds.) CITI 2019. CCIS, vol. 1124, pp. 151–163. Springer, Cham (2019). https://doi.org/10.1007/978-3-030-34989-9_12
3. Xu, Z., Ji, X., Wang, M., Sun, X.: Edge detection algorithm of medical image based on Canny operator. J. Phys. Conf. Ser. **1955**(1), 012080 (2021)
4. Nnolim, U.A.: Automated crack segmentation via saturation channel thresholding, area classification and fusion of modified level set segmentation with Canny edge detection. Heliyon **6**(12), e05748 (2020)
5. Sun, G., Wang, X.: Application of computer virtual reality technology in practical teaching of construction engineering survey. J. Phys. Conf. Ser. **1915**(3), 032072 (2021)
6. Tang, K.: Discussion on the application of modern construction engineering survey technology. Int. J. High. Educ. Teach. Theory **1**(4), 032072 (2020)
7. Cui, M., Li, J., Li, N., Xia, F., Ren, X.: Application of information-based teaching means in the architectural engineering survey training course. In: Proceedings of 2018 International Conference on Education, Psychology, and Management Science (ICEPMS 2018), pp. 1123–1127. Francis Academic Press, London (2018)
8. Shi, C.: Analysis on the manifestation of the green environmental protection concept in architectural engineering survey. In: Proceedings of the International Conference on Future Communication, Information and Computer Science (ICFCICS 2014), pp. 301–303 (2014)

Research on Civil Aviation Economic Pricing Based on Equilibrium Game

Yulin Li[✉]

Dawan Business Aviation Tourism College School, Sichuan Vocational College of Science and Technology University, Guangyuan 620566, Sichuan, China

Abstract. Ticket price is an important factor affecting market demand and passengers' purchase behavior. It is one of the main means for airlines to carry out market competition, and directly affects their profits. However, there has always been the problem of over pricing and single price strategy in the air tickets of civil aviation of China. The essence of civil aviation competition in the transportation market is to maximize benefits. One of the most important aspects of increasing their own benefits is to attract more passenger flow within a reasonable price range. Attracting passenger flow is to change passengers' travel choices through their own marketing strategies, so that passengers are more inclined to their own side when choosing transportation modes. How to attract passengers, we must first determine what factors will affect the choice of passengers, and these factors are directly related to the choice preference of passengers. Therefore, in the process of fare decision-making, we must consider the factors affecting passengers' travel and passengers' choice preferences. This paper selects five influencing factors: rapidity, economy, comfort, convenience and safety, and uses analytic hierarchy process (AHP) to determine the weight coefficient of each index. The gravity model is used to predict the passenger flow between the two places. On this basis, the equilibrium game pricing model of civil aviation is established, and the fare strategy is selected with the goal of maximizing the benefit.

Keywords: Game theory · Analytic hierarchy process · Civil aviation · Nash equilibrium

1 Introduction

Air transportation generally refers to the transportation business of transporting passengers or goods through air routes [1]. The air transport industry involves civil airports, air traffic control departments, airlines and passenger and cargo transport service departments. According to the business attribute, the civil aviation transportation industry can be divided into passenger aviation and cargo aviation. This paper mainly refers to passenger aviation. Civil aviation is not only the tertiary industry, but also the field of infrastructure. It plays a very important role in the development of national economy. Compared with other modes of transportation, the passenger turnover of air transportation is relatively low and its share in the passenger transport market is relatively small,

© Springer Nature Singapore Pte Ltd. 2022
Y. Tian et al. (Eds.): ICBDS 2021, CCIS 1563, pp. 496–506, 2022.
https://doi.org/10.1007/978-981-19-0852-1_39

but civil aviation transportation has always played an irreplaceable role in medium and long-distance transportation. In particular, China has a vast territory, long-distance transportation accounts for a large proportion, and civil aviation plays an increasingly important role [2].

As an advanced mode of transportation, air transportation has attracted more and more attention. After years of development, especially since the reform and opening up, our country has established an increasingly huge aviation network, the transportation capacity of civil aviation has increased significantly, the airport and other infrastructure have been improved, and the air control capacity has been strengthened. China has become a big aviation country. In the process of economic development, civil aviation transportation industry plays a more and more important role.

Air transport plays an important role in China's national economic construction. Excluding the impact of the epidemic in the past two years, the passenger throughput will increase steadily before 2019 [3]. Figure 1 shows the changes of domestic passenger throughput in China from 2012 to 2018.

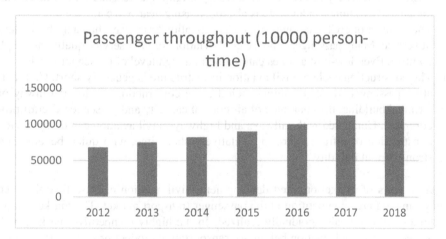

Fig. 1. Passenger throughput in 2012–2018

Figure 1 in terms of passenger throughput and the number of airports from 2012 to 2018, due to the rapid development of civil aviation industry and the continuous growth of the total number of passengers, a certain number of airports will be built every year.

2 Analysis of Influencing Factors

2.1 Characteristics of Civil Aviation Transportation

Air transportation is a transportation mode with the fastest development in recent decades [4]. Compared with other transportation modes, the economic and technological advantages of air transportation are mainly reflected in the following aspects: fast speed, strong mobility, large radiation area, good accessibility, good safety and comfort, short construction cycle, less investment and fast investment recovery [5].

(1) Civil aviation transportation is fast. In all modes of transportation, an important feature of civil aviation is the high cruise speed of passenger aircraft, which generally flies at subsonic speed. This is very important for passengers with high travel time value. These passengers require short travel time on the way and usually choose civil aviation.

(2) The radiation area of civil aviation is large. Due to the influence of topographic conditions, high-speed railway can only run on fixed tracks, which is consistent with the direction and height of tracks. However, civil aviation transportation is relatively flexible. There can be air routes within a certain altitude and safety width. It is very limited by geographical conditions, so the coverage area of civil aviation is very wide.

(3) The safety of civil aviation is good. Nowadays, the aviation technology is more and more advanced, the manufacturing process level is continuously improved, the pilot's driving technical requirements are higher and higher, the aircraft's safe flight guarantee ability is increasing, and various airlines also put safe flight in the primary position. The safety of civil aviation transportation has reached a high level, and the annual aviation accident rate is also decreasing year by year.

(4) The comfort of civil aviation is high. Civil aviation has always had a high standard of service. Many passengers choose civil aviation for their service quality and high comfort. Even low-cost airlines can maintain a high level of passenger service.

(5) The construction cycle of civil aviation infrastructure is generally short. Civil aviation passenger transport mainly includes the construction of airport runway of terminal building, the guarantee of air control capacity and passenger aircraft procurement. Compared with railways and highways, civil aviation can complete the construction of infrastructure in a relatively short time, with quick benefits and strong capital liquidity.

After years of market-oriented development, civil aviation can use flexible price strategy in the fierce competition in the passenger transport market. The marketization of China's railway is also gradually realized. In the highly competitive market, both high-speed railway and aviation belong to transportation product providers. Both sides will provide more competitive transportation products according to passengers' travel preferences and competitors' products [6]. Passengers always want to enjoy the best service with the least money, so they will choose suitable transportation products to maximize their travel utility by integrating factors such as travel cost, total running time, travel comfort, convenience and safety, and in combination with their own travel needs.

In the highly competitive market, price is always in the core position, and price is the most flexible and effective economic lever in the market economy. In the passenger transport market, the price is also at the core. The change of price affects the travel choice of passengers, thus affecting the economic benefits of enterprises and competitors.

The relationship between benefit and ticket price is in line with the trend in Fig. 2. Within a certain range, with the increase of ticket price, the total benefit of the enterprise will also rise. When the ticket price is p*, the enterprise benefit reaches the maximum; When the ticket price exceeds p*, as the price continues to rise, the total passenger flow between the two places will decrease, so the enterprise's own benefits will also decrease.

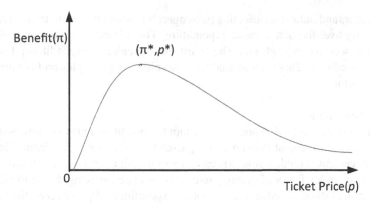

Fig. 2. Relationship between benefits and fares

2.2 Selection of Influencing Factors

When passengers travel between cities, there are usually several modes of transportation to choose. When choosing the mode of transportation, they usually consider their own conditions (such as income level) and the distance of the destination, and combine the differences of various modes of transportation in terms of rapidity, comfort and price, so as to choose the most suitable mode of transportation. Generally speaking, the factors affecting the choice of passenger transportation mode can be divided into the following two categories:

(1) Differences in economic and technical characteristics of various modes of transportation;
(2) Differences in customers' own needs;

As shown in Fig. 3:

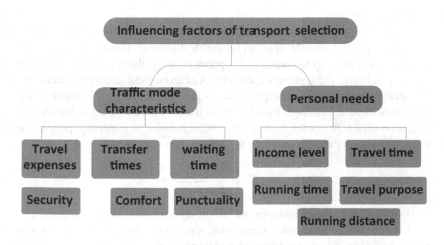

Fig. 3. The influencing factors on passenger transport demand

The factors and indicators affecting passengers' choice of travel mode are divided into the following five: the first is rapid expenditure; The second is economic expenditure; The third is security expenditure; The fourth is convenience expenditure; The fifth is comfort expenditure. This section analyzes the selection principles and connotation of these five factors.

(1) Rapid expenditure

For the convenience of expression, the rapid expenditure index is expressed as X_1. It includes the time cost consumed by passengers in choosing different high-speed passenger travel modes. It is expressed by in transit operation time t. rapidity is an important index factor affecting passengers' decision-making. Since the time variable cannot directly reflect the economic expenditure of passengers, the economic quantitative index of time - economic value w per unit time is introduced, and then the rapidity expenditure is expressed through the calculation of the relationship between them as follows:

$$X1 = w \times t \tag{1}$$

(2) Economic expenditure

The economic expenditure index is expressed as X_2. This expenditure is an important indicator factor affecting passenger decision-making. It includes all the economic costs to be borne by passengers from the starting point to the destination based on the high-speed passenger travel mode they choose. For the sake of simplification, the economic expenditure mainly includes the cost c of arriving at the station from the starting point of travel, the fare p of the selected travel mode, and the cost b of arriving at the destination after leaving the station, excluding other costs. Economic expenditure is expressed as:

$$X2 = b + p + c \tag{2}$$

(3) Comfort expenditure

The comfort expenditure index factor is expressed as X_3. The individual requirements are different, and the demand for comfort is also different. Since the comfort expenditure is not easy to measure, this paper converts the comfort expenditure into time expenditure. The comfort expenditure X_3 can be measured by the recovery time TF spent by passengers on fatigue. The fatigue recovery time T_f required for passengers to choose passenger travel mode is directly proportional to the on-the-way operation time t. According to relevant research findings, generally, people can use the following methods to calculate the fatigue recovery time T_f:

$$T_f = \frac{T_{max}}{1 + me^{-nt}} \tag{3}$$

Where T_{max} is the ultimate fatigue recovery time of passenger travel.

Like the above economic expenditure, since the time variable can not directly reflect the economic expenditure of passengers, the economic quantitative index of time - economic value W per unit time is introduced to represent the comfort expenditure. The expression is as follows:

$$X_3 = w \times T_f = w \times \frac{Tmax}{1 + me^{-nt}} \tag{4}$$

Where: m is a constant and n is the fatigue recovery time coefficient in unit of in transit operation time.

(4) Convenience expenditure

The convenience expenditure index is expressed as X_4, which is measured by the non in transit operation time spent by passengers. The non in transit operation time is represented by T. the non in transit operation time of civil aviation travel mode includes the time when passengers arrive at the airport from the departure place, ticket purchase time, waiting time in the waiting hall, ticket check-in time of ticket clerks, waiting time for boarding, delay time caused by emergencies, and the time when the aircraft arrives at the destination from the airport in the arrival city. Non in transit operation time is a time variable, which can not directly measure the expenditure of passengers. Therefore, the economic quantitative index of time - economic value per unit time w is introduced to represent the convenience expenditure:

$$X_4 = w \times T \tag{5}$$

(5) Security expenditure

The security expenditure index is expressed as X_5. According to Maslow's hierarchy of needs theory, security is the most basic human need. Therefore, whenever and wherever anything happens, the premise is based on personal safety. The safety benefit index X_5 can be expressed by the accident casualty rate index q per 100 million passengers per kilometer of passenger travel mode. According to the experience of current experts and scholars, the relationship between safety expenditure and casualty rate of unit passenger accident can be expressed by the following formula:

$$X_5 = 1 + a \cdot q^b \tag{6}$$

In the formula: a and b are constants respectively.

2.3 Weight Analysis of Influencing Factors

When traveling, passengers will comprehensively analyze the economic and technical characteristics of various transportation modes to choose their own transportation modes. Different passengers have different preferences for various economic and technological characteristics. Therefore, this paper selects analytic hierarchy process to determine the weight of different influencing factors.

Analytic hierarchy process (AHP) is a multi-objective decision-making analysis method combining qualitative and quantitative proposed by American operations research expert Professor T.L. Saaty in the 1970s. People's thoughts and preferences account for a large proportion in the analysis process, so different people will have different conclusions. Through the quantification of qualitative factors, the evaluation tends to be quantitative, so as to compare the data results to draw a conclusion. The whole process can be divided into: decomposition, judgment and synthesis [1]. Analytic hierarchy process quantifies the existing judgment experience to determine the basis of quantitative decision-making. This method plays a role in dealing with some problems that lack necessary conditions and the structure is relatively complex. The basic idea is: the first step is to establish an independent structure describing the characteristics of the system, which has orderly hierarchical levels and the meaning and proportion of corresponding scales; In the second step, the relative importance of each two elements is compared, and the judgment matrix of relative importance is constructed. The judgment matrix is processed accordingly, and the importance sequence of an element to other elements can be obtained; The third step is to test whether the judgment matrix and importance sequence meet the consistency. The use process and steps of analytic hierarchy process are shown in Fig. 4:

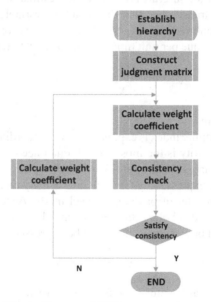

Fig. 4. The use of AHP process and steps

The relative importance of the two elements to the same goal is generally divided into five levels, which are: equally important, slightly important, relatively important, obviously important and absolutely important. In order to facilitate the calculation and comparison results, the five levels of importance are quantified, so that the relative importance of two elements for the same goal can be determined. Use 1–1.5 β Comparison scale. 1–1.5 β The meaning of comparison scale is that the importance of adjacent levels is reflected in the weight of two elements, which is 1.5 times. For example, two elements X_1, X_2; When the importance is the same, the weight ratio $u_2/u_1 = 1.5^0$; X_2 is slightly more important than X_1, and its weight ratio is $u_2/u_1 = 1.5^1$; When it is more important, the weight ratio is $u_2/u_1 = 1.5^2$; The weight ratio is $u_2/u_1 = 1.5^3$; Compared with absolute importance, the weight ratio is $u_2/u_1 = 1.5^4$. In addition, β Taking 0.5, 1.5, 2.5 and 3.5 respectively represents an intermediate state of adjacent relative importance.

According to the above definition, by comparing every two factors, the judgment matrix P can be constructed as follows:

$$p = \begin{bmatrix} a11 & a12 & \cdots & a1j & \cdots & a1n \\ a21 & a22 & \cdots & a2j & \cdots & a2n \\ \vdots & \vdots & & \vdots & & \vdots \\ ai1 & ai2 & \cdots & aij & \cdots & ain \\ \vdots & \vdots & & \vdots & & \vdots \\ an1 & an2 & \cdots & anj & \cdots & ann \end{bmatrix} \tag{7}$$

Where, $a_{ij} = \frac{\mu_i}{\mu_j} = 1.5^\beta$, $a_{ij} > 0$, $a_{ij} = \frac{1}{a_{ij}} i, j = 1, 2, \cdots n$.

(1) Normalize each column of matrix P to obtain:

$$\bar{a}_{ij} = \frac{a_{ij}}{\sum_{k=1}^{n} a_{kj}} \quad i, j = 1, 2, \cdots n \tag{8}$$

(2) Add the normalized matrix by row to obtain:

$$\bar{\delta}_i = \sum_{j=1}^{n} \bar{a}_{ij} \quad i, j = 1, 2, \cdots n \tag{9}$$

(3) Will vector $\bar{\delta}_i = (\bar{\delta}_1, \bar{\delta}_2, \cdots \bar{\delta}_n)^T$. After normalization of ˆt, it is obtained:

$$\delta_i = \frac{\bar{\delta}_i}{\sum_{i=1}^{n} \bar{\delta}_i} \quad i = 1, 2, \cdots n \tag{10}$$

The maximum eigenvalue of matrix P is λ_{max}, introduce the consistency index CI:

$$CI = \frac{\lambda_{max} - n}{n - 1} \tag{11}$$

When CI < 0.1, matrix P is called one-time matrix and eigenvector $\delta = (\delta_1, \delta_2, \ldots \delta_n)$. Is the weight coefficient of each corresponding factor.

3 Equilibrium Game Model

3.1 Concept and Development of Game Theory

Game theory belongs to applied mathematics, sometimes called game theory. It is a basic theory and method to study the phenomenon of social competition. Game theory can also be regarded as an interdependent process of how to make the optimal decision rationally. Rational decision-making means that the subject does not consider moral and emotional factors in the decision-making process, but takes how to obtain the maximum benefit as the standard. The content of game theory itself has strong practicability and practicality in real life. It can play a role in politics, economy, military, transportation, biochemistry, computer science and other fields [2].

In the last century, Zermelo, Borel and von Neumann conducted in-depth research on game theory and gave specific mathematical expressions [3]. In 1938, von Neumann and the economist Oskar Morgenstem jointly published the economic behavior of game theory [4], which began to be applied to the field of economics.

Non cooperative game theory is the basic content of modern game theory [5]. John Nash, an American economist, completed the proof of the general significance and existence theory of Nash equilibrium during his doctoral study at Princeton University, which laid an important foundation for the development of non cooperative game theory, and published two important papers on non cooperative game theory from 1950 to 1951, changing people's traditional understanding of market competition in the past, The concept of Nash equilibrium is defined by using concise words and rigorous mathematical language to prove the existence of non cooperative game solution, that is, Nash equilibrium solution [6].

Nash equilibrium theory is one of the most outstanding products of human wisdom in the 20th century. Its basic ideas and theories have been widely used in politics, economy, management, law, biology, military, computer and other fields. Game theory has developed for decades since it was introduced into China in the 1950s. Chinese scholars have translated some foreign books on game theory and compiled some game theory textbooks. However, as an important branch of operations research [7], the application and research of game theory in China has been relatively backward, and the number of works on game theory is less. After the reform and opening up and the implementation of market economy, people gradually realize the importance of game theory and pay more and more attention to its application in market competition [8]. The development of game theory in China has entered a fast track and gradually become one of the most promising disciplines.

3.2 Establishment of Game Model

Model Assumptions
To establish the competitive game model of civil aviation, we need to make the following assumptions:

(1) It is assumed that only civil aviation transportation mode participates in the game;
(2) Civil aviation can freely price within a reasonable range;
(3) The total passenger volume is affected by the ticket price and is less than the total transportation capacity of civil aviation;
(4) Do not consider the characteristics of passengers, such as gender, age, income, etc.

Nash Equilibrium
Nash equilibrium is a strategic combination of all participants [9–11] and the core theory

of non-cooperative game [12, 13]. When the game reaches Nash equilibrium, for each participant, his strategy is the best strategy when the strategies of other participants are a fixed strategic combination. Nash equilibrium includes pure strategic Nash equilibrium [14] and mixed strategic Nash equilibrium [15]. Due to the problem of civil aviation game pricing, the pricing adopted in each game is a certain value, so this paper adopts pure strategic Nash equilibrium.

The Nash equilibrium is described in mathematical language below. It is assumed that $(S_1^*, S_2^* \ldots \ldots S_n^*)$ is a strategic combination of game $G = \{S_1, S_2 \ldots \ldots S_n; u_1, u_2 \ldots \ldots u_n\}$, where S_i^* is the strategy of the ith participant. If for another n-1 strategy combination, S_i^* is the best strategy, i.e. when the following conditions are met $(S_1^*, S_2^* \ldots \ldots S_n^*)$ is a Nash equilibrium of G.

$$u_i(S_i^*, S_{-i}^*) \geq u_i(S_i, S_{-i}^*), i = 1, 2, \ldots, n \tag{12}$$

Where:S_{-i} represents the strategy combination of other i-1 participants except the i'th participant, i.e. $S_{-i} = (S_1, S_2 \ldots, S_{i-1}, S_{i+1}, \ldots, S_n)$.

When there are only two players in the game, the Nash equilibrium can be simplified to

$$\pi_1(p_1^*, p_2^*) \geq \max_{p_1 \geq c_1} \pi_1(p_1^*, p_2^*) \tag{13}$$

$$\pi_2(p_1^*, p_2^*) \geq \max_{p_2 \geq c_2} \pi_2(p_1^*, p_2^*) \tag{14}$$

Where: π_1 is the income of the first participant; π_2 is the income of the second participant; p_1^*, p_2^* is the optimal strategy price; c_1, c_2 is the operating cost of a single passenger.

According to the definition of Nash equilibrium, we can test whether a strategic portfolio meets the Nash equilibrium conditions. It is very simple to deny whether a strategic combination is a Nash equilibrium. As long as one of the participants has a better strategy, it means that the strategic combination is not a Nash equilibrium.

4 Conclusion

After analyzing the development status of civil aviation in China, this paper analyzes some factors affecting customers' travel from two aspects: the actual situation of customers and the characteristics of modern transportation modes. According to the needs of contemporary people and the current situation of social development, finally, the five factors of rapidity, economy, comfort, convenience and safety are determined as the influencing factors. The weight of these five factor indexes is analyzed by analytic hierarchy process, and then verified by consistency test. Taking gravity model as the starting point, it lays a good foundation for the establishment of game model. This paper uses the related concepts of game theory to simplify the competitive behavior among civil aviation enterprises in reality, and has certain guiding significance for the actual pricing through the equilibrium game model.

References

1. Chen, R.: Application Analysis of Game Theory and Equilibrium Theory in Price Competition. China University of Geosciences, Beijing (2006)
2. Altman, E., Wynter, L.: Special issue on crossovers between transportation and telecommunication modeling - Preface. Biochem. Pharmacol. **24**(1), 963–966 (2004)
3. Jiang H . Network Capacity Management Competition[J], wiadomości lekarskie, 1968
4. Sun, L.J., Gao, Z.Y.: An equilibrium model for urban transit assignment based on game theory. Eur. J. Oper. Res. **181**(1), 305–314 (2007)
5. Neumann, J.V.: Zur Theorie der Gesellschaftsspiele. Math. Ann. **100**(1), 295–320 (1928)
6. Nash, J.: Non-cooperative games. Ann. Math. **54**, 286–295 (1951)
7. Hu, X., Yuan, Y., Zhang, X.: Review and Prospect of the development of operations research. J. Chin. Acad. Sci. **27**(2), 16 (2012)
8. Zong, F.: Research on Evaluation of Traffic Demand Management Strategy Based on Non Aggregate Model. Jilin University (2008)
9. Zhang, R., Luan, W., Zhao, B.: Game Analysis of high-speed railway and air ticket pricing based on the influence of passenger choice. Railway Transportation and Economy (2015)
10. Peng, G., Xiaoqin, Y.: Game theory and Nash equilibrium. J. Nat. Sci. Harbin Norm. Univ. **22**(4), 4 (2006)
11. Guangyong, L., Qiongxiang, C.: Transaction costs, Nash equilibrium and accounting standards. Econ. Sci. **21**(004), 112–116 (1999)
12. Fischer, T., Kamerschen, D.R.: Measuring competition in the U.S. Airline industry using the Rosse-Panzar test and cross-sectional regression analyses. J. Appl. Econ. **6**, 73–93 (2003)
13. Jiang, J.: Research on High Speed Railway Fare Optimization Based on Non Cooperative Game. Beijing Jiaotong University (2012)
14. Chen, X.: Pure strategic Nash equilibrium theory and application. Mall Moderniz. **7**, 2 (2008)
15. Chen, X.: Mixed strategy Nash equilibrium and its application. China Mark. **14**, 2 (2008)

Spinal Posture Recognition Device Using Cloud Storage and BP Neural Network Approach Based on Surface Electromyographic Signal

Yao Wu[1], Yong Lu[1], Chengcheng Ma[1], Xiuyang Zhang[1], Ziyang Pan[1], Xiang Yu[1], and Yameng Zhang[1,2(✉)]

[1] Department of Computer Engineering, Nanjing Institute of Technology, No. 1 Hongjing Avenue, Nanjing 211167, China
yamengzhang@njit.edu.cn

[2] Department of Biomedical Engineering, Nanjing University of Aeronautics and Astronautics, No. 169 Sheng Tai West Road, Nanjing 211106, China

Abstract. The application of medical big data is increasingly popular in healthcare services and clinical research to meet healthcare demands. We designed a spinal posture recognition device with the effective acquisition of surface EMG (sEMG) signal, meanwhile innovatively took cloud storage for visualization and storage, and used BP neural network for classification of different spinal postures. After experiments, the hardware can collect sEMG signals with a signal-to-noise ratio of about 70 dB, and the method can effectively distinguish different spinal postures with a correct rate of greater than 65%. The device is meant for portable big data for scoliosis detection and spinal rehabilitation evaluation.

Keywords: Medical big data · BP neural network · sEMG · Spinal posture recognition

1 Introduction

The paraspinal muscles are one of the important structures to maintain the stability of the lumbar spine. Not only the surface EMG (sEMG) signal of the paraspinal muscles reflects the change of body structure, but also neuromuscular function [1]. In recent years, the sEMG signal of the paraspinal muscles has been widely used in the diagnosis and evaluation of human spine orthopedic diseases. Wang used sEMG technology to compare the muscle function between patients with different subtypes of low back pain and normal subjects [2]. Li employed sEMG signal detection to analyze and summarize the application in the evaluation of low back muscle function [3]. It can be seen that the sEMG signal of the paraspinal muscles is the basis for the assessment of spinal posture.

Y. Tian et al. (Eds.): ICBDS 2021, CCIS 1563, pp. 507–517, 2022.
https://doi.org/10.1007/978-981-19-0852-1_40

Medical big data is a new technology for processing large-scale medical data [4]. Yash Gandhi applied medical big data to personalized medicine to identify accurate diseases or symptoms by studying big data in the health and medical fields [5]. Zhang designed and implemented a secure medical big data eco-system on the Hadoop big data platform, which opened up a new way to improve the intelligence of the medical system [6]. Humans can not only predict the outbreak trend of epidemic diseases, avoid infection, reduce medical costs, *etc.*, but also allow patients to enjoy more convenient services by utilizing the use of big data technology [7, 8].

Therefore, this article aimed at the requirement of medical big data portable diagnostic equipment, and used the sEMG detection technology to develop a set of fast and convenient spinal posture monitoring equipment. The device collected the sEMG signal of the paraspinal muscles on both sides of the human spine in real-time and displayed the original image and the characteristic parameters of the sEMG signal in real-time on the front-end interface. Meanwhile, the device innovatively took Hbase distributed storage and BP neural network to remotely visualize and save the spinal sEMG signal, and effectively distinguish different spinal action postures. The device can provide a new solution for the large-scale detection of scoliosis based on big data technology.

2   Methods and Materials

2.1   Hardware System Design

The whole hardware system design was composed of a preamplifier, filtering circuit and independent power supply, and transmitted the sEMG signal to the computer as seen in Fig. 1.

Power Supply Section
Since the operational amplifier chip of the signal conditioning part required a positive and negative dual power supply, the hardware system used a dual power supplies to meet the power supply of the signal conditioning part. Meanwhile the dual power supplies reduced the noise and improved the stability of signal measurement. Besides, the digital circuit part was powered independently for reducing mutual interference between the digital part and the analog part.

Signal Conditioning Section
Pickup Electrode
The pick-up electrodes are commonly needle electrodes, ball-absorbing electrodes, and surface-mount electrodes. Although the needle electrode can collect more accurate and low-noise deep muscle signals, it is an invasive electrode and cannot collect the overall EMG signal of the entire muscle. The ball-absorbing electrode is convenient and quick, but its bonding effect is not as strong as that of the patch electrode [18]. Above all, in order to ensure the signal quality and reduce interference, the patch electrode was used as the pickup electrode. The patch electrode is firmly fixed and it is difficult to produce moving artifacts. At the same time, due to the conductive gel, the electrode is in good contact with the skin surface, and has the advantages of non-invasive, clean and hygiene.

Pre-amplification
sEMG is a weak signal and requires to amplify the signal for measurement. Moreover, because sEMG is very susceptible to noise interference, the amplifying circuit selected must have the characteristics of high common-mode rejection ratio, low offset voltage, and low noise. The article selected instrumentation of TI amplifier INA828 as the amplifier. The gain calculation formula is: $G = 1 + 50$ kΩ/Rg, and R3 was selected as 1 kΩ, that is, the pre-amplification factor is 51 times. Furthermore, a precision adjustable resistor R8 was added to adapt to different collection requirements.

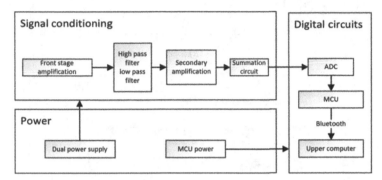

Fig. 1. The block diagram of overall hardware system

2.2 Software Design Based on Big Data Storage

Software Design
The host computer interface was built by wxPython GUI, and the transceiver function of the serial port can receive the collecting sEMG signal and display it in real time. Then the acquisition interface of the system would jumped to the EMG analysis interface by clicking the start analysis button, afterwards the corresponding analysis results graphs (time-frequency graph, spectrum graph, power spectrum graph) was observed visually, the coefficients of time domain eigenvalues (absolute mean value MAV, variance VAR, root mean square value RMS, average power frequency MPF, median frequency MF) were obtained, finally the analysis result of spinal posture recognition would be feed-backed. The serial transmitting port signal and data processing functions are compiled together through GUI, which could easily and intuitively analyze the EMG signal, as shown in Fig. 2.

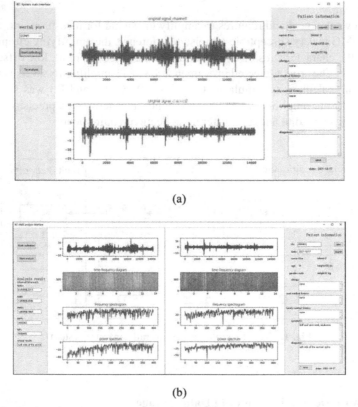

(a)

(b)

Fig. 2. Software interface (a) dual channel of sEMG acquisition interface (b) dual channel of sEMG analysis interface

The control software flow chart of the system is shown in Fig. 3. After the hardware system was powered on, the entire system was initialized first. When the main controller received the begin command, the main controller will perform the A/D collection from the output signal of the signal conditioning circuit. Then the collected data would be processed through format conversion and sent to the PC terminal. Finally, the PC terminal displayed the original signal and the analysis results of sEMG by jumping to sEMG analysis interface.

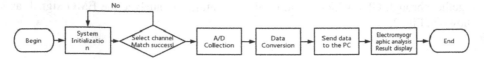

Fig. 3. Flow chart of software control

Data Cloud Storage

In order to meet the demand of big medical and health data, the new technology of distributed cloud storage was adopted to satisfy the real-time analysis and review of spine posture.

This system used the Hbase database, a component of the Hadoop system, which is a real-time distributed database based on "column mode" running on top of HDFS. It is different from the traditional relational database, which uses the big-table data model to store data in the form of a table and divides the table into rows and columns. Row keywords and column keywords together constitute a sparse arrangement mapping table (Key/Value), which can be used for Map/Reduce processing. In the Hbase database, key "doctor" was created to store doctor information, key "patient" was created to store patient information, key "diagnose" was created to the patient's diagnosis results for each time period, key "users" was created to store user names and passwords, and key "statistic" was created to store the original signal, MAV, VAR, RMS, MPF and MF of the patient's sEMG signals. The system is highly fault-tolerant and suitable for deployment on cheap machines. The schematic diagram of the storage design is as seen in Fig. 4.

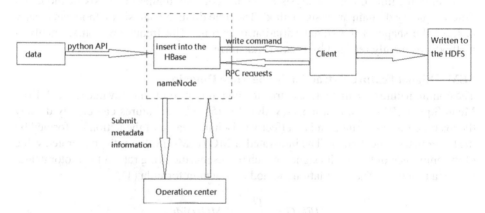

Fig. 4. The schematic diagram of the storage design

Firstly, the HDFS client development library initiated an RPC connection access request to the named node. Then the named node checked whether the file to be created already existed and the creator operation authority, if the check was successful, a record was created for the file, if the check failed, an exception was thrown to the client. When the request wrote by RPC was responded, the client development library cut the file to be written into multiple packets, then applied for new blocks to the named node, and generated a mapping list of local files and HDFS data blocks that were submitted to the named node. Afterwards, the named node returned the configuration information of the managed data node to the client, and the client would write to each data node in sequence in the form of a pipeline according to the IP address of the data node. Finally in the actual operation of data writing, the data in the HBase database can be imported into HDFS through HBase through its own writing tool "hbaseorg.apache.hadoop. hbase.mapreduce.Export".

2.3   SEMG Signal Analysis

SEMG Signal Denoise
sEMG has a narrow amplitude distribution and a wide spectrum distribution, which is easy to be overwhelmed by noise interference. Due to the instability of sEMG, the general traditional analysis method may lose non-stationary parts [12]. Therefore, in order to protect the effective signal as much as possible, the sEMG was processed in the wavelet domain to realize signal denoising. Specifically, this paper selected sys4 as the mother wavelet, decomposed sEMG signal in 5 layers, and deployed the maximum-minimum threshold to perform threshold denoising. According to the sampling theorem, the maximum frequency of the signal obtained by the sampling frequency of 1 kHz is 500 Hz, then the fifth-order approximation frequency band of the signal is less than 15.6 Hz. In this way, low-frequency noise interference can be filtered out by subtracting the reconstructed signal of the fifth-order approximation frequency band from the original signal reconstructed by wavelet.

The commonly used feature extraction methods in the sEMG signal processing mode are mainly the time domain analysis method, frequency domain analysis method, and time-frequency domain analysis method. The time domain analysis method can clearly observe the shape of the signal variation over time. The frequency domain analysis method was mainly realized by Fourier transform.

SEMG Signal Feature Extraction in the Time Domain
The common time domain feature extraction contains absolute mean value (MAV), Root Mean Square (RMS) and Variance (VAR) [13–15]. These features can clearly display the average variation range and an effective discharge value of the action performed by the tester in the time domain. The integrated sEMG (IEMG) value is the integrated value of the amplitude of the sEMG signal, which represents the firing rate of the motor neural unit in a unit time. The calculation method is shown in formula (1).

$$IEMG = \int_{t}^{t+T} |EMG(t)| dt \tag{1}$$

Here, EMG(t) is the sEMG signal, t is the time, and T is the period. In this experiment, we selected the IEMG mean value as the time domain characteristic parameters of the sEMG signal.

SEMG Signal Feature Extraction in the Frequency Domain
Frequency domain signal can show the power of the signal changes with frequency, which is conducive to observing the frequency domain characteristics and avoiding the instability caused by the fluctuation of the signal over time [16, 17]. Common frequency domain feature extraction methods are as follows.

The Mean Power Frequency (MPF) refers to the average power spectrum obtained by the fast Fourier transform of the sEMG signal, which represents the fatigue of the muscle. Its calculation formula is shown in formula (2).

$$MPF = \frac{\int_0^\infty f p(f) df}{\int_0^\infty p(f) df} \tag{2}$$

In the above formula, f is the frequency, and $p(f)$ is the power spectral density of sEMG signal.

The Median Frequency (MF) refers to the half of power spectrum obtained by the fast Fourier transform of the sEMG signal. Its size is related to the fast and slow muscle fibers in the muscle tissue involved in the activity. Its calculation formula is shown in formula (3).

$$MF = \int_0^{MF} p(f)df = \int_{MF}^{+\infty} p(f)df = \frac{1}{2}\int_0^{+\infty} p(f)df \tag{3}$$

Here, f is the frequency, and $p(f)$ is the power spectral density of sEMG signal.

In the experiment, we selected MPF and MF as the characteristic parameters in frequency domain feature to research the spinal posture in different states.

2.4 BP Neural Network

The back propagation (BP) neural network algorithm is a multi-layer feedforward network trained according to the error back propagation algorithm and is one of the most widely applied neural network models [9–11].

A neural network is made up of neurons connected by weights. n stimulus signal, $x_1, x_2, \ldots x_n$ is transmitted to the neuron, which is connected to the neuron through weights w_i. These weights are called the connection weights. After all the signals reach the neuron, the threshold value θ is set and the output of the neuron is obtained through the processing of the activation function, as shown in formula (4).

$$y = f\left(\sum_{i=1}^n w_i x_i - \theta\right) \tag{4}$$

The BP neural network includes an input layer, a hidden layer and an output layer, Where α_h represents the input of the h th neuron in the hidden layer, and the output of the h th neuron in the hidden layer is seen in formula (5).

$$b_h = f(\alpha_h + r) \tag{5}$$

The input of the j th neuron in the output layer is seen in formula (6).

$$\beta_j = \sum_{h-1}^q w_{hj} b_h \tag{6}$$

The output of the j th neuron in the output layer is seen in formula (7).

$$y_j = f(\beta_j + r\Theta) \tag{7}$$

Back propagation is to reverse the residuals layer by layer to the weight parameters between layers. First, the error value of each parameter is solved, and finally the error is corrected in the direction of the gradient of each variable. The magnitude of the correction depends on the learning rate η.

The connection weight of the output layer to the hidden layer is shown in formula (8).

$$\Delta w_{hj} = -\eta \frac{\partial E}{\partial w_{hj}} = -\eta(y_h(t) - y_h)f'(\beta_j + r\Theta)w_j \tag{8}$$

The connection weight of the output layer to the input layer is shown in formula (9).

$$\Delta v_{ih} = -\eta \frac{\partial E}{\partial v_{ih}} = -\eta (y_j(t) - y_h) f'(\beta_j + r\Theta) \sum_{j=1}^{l} f'(\alpha_h + r) x_j \qquad (9.)$$

2.5 Experiments

Before the experiment, the subjects exposed their waists, maintained a standing posture, and wiped the subjects' skin with 75% alcohol. The arms were in a relaxed state. The electrodes 1 and 2 are respectively attached to left and right sides of the midline of the lower spine of the scoliosis arc, 2 cm away from the side. The subject maintained a standing posture for the 20 s, then bent at 45°, and bent every 5 s for 20 s. In order to avoid fatigue induced by a long time of muscle activity to affect the experimental results. After finishing a trial, the subjects rested for 30 s. The experiment was divided into four groups: left bending, right bending, forward bending, and standing upright, which contained 80 trials in each group.

3 Results

The sample result of sEMG signal acquisition and analysis is shown in Fig. 5. Time-frequency and power spectrum of the sEMG signal of the left bend in the right channel were higher than that in the left channel, while time-frequency the spectrum and power

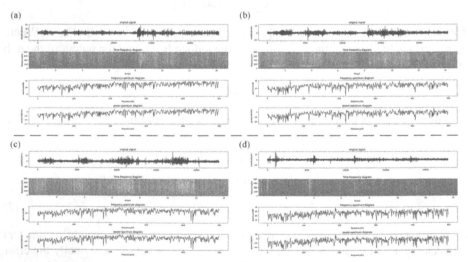

Fig. 5. Comparison of time domain and frequency sEMG signal. Original sEMG signal, time-frequency spectrum, amplitude-frequency spectrum, the power spectrum of left bending in the left channel (a) and right channel (b), Original sEMG signal, time-frequency spectrum, amplitude-frequency spectrum, the power spectrum of right bending in the left channel (c) and right channel (d)

spectrum of the sEMG signal of the right bend in the left channel were higher than that in the right channel, which is associated to the stretching of the muscles on the left and right sides of the spine. The sEMG signal acquisition hardware device designed in this paper indeed collect, store, display, and accurately analyze the corresponding sEMG signal.

In this paper, the software algorithm of the sEMG signal and classification system selected the BP neural network model. A total dataset size was 320, which was divided into four groups including bend left, bend right, bend forward, and upright stand, respectively. Then 75% of the data was the training set, and 25% of the data was the test set. Combined with the signal characteristics of sEMG signal, the characteristic parameters of IEMG, MF, and MPF obtained by dual-channel sEMG signal were selected as the input of BP neural network, then the Softmax transfer function was used as the activation function. When the error is selected as 0.01, the built model has the highest accuracy, and the obtained neural network neural hidden layer node was 9. The final classification result is shown in Fig. 6 and the number of 0, 1, 2, and 3 was the output, which belonged to the 4 categories of the training set.

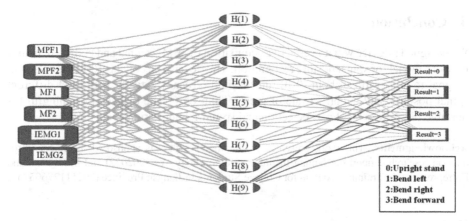

Fig. 6. Structure design of BP neural network

Table 1 showed the accuracy rate of Spinal posture recognition. The results showed that the training model in the upright stand was the best, with a recognition rate as high as 83.3%, and the recognition rate of bend left, bend right, and bend forward were all higher than 70%, which suggested the employ of the sEMG signal for the feasibility of spinal recognition. Afterward, the test set was used to be examined, there was a clear difference between the upright stand and the curvature of the spine, but the recognition rate of bend left and bend right would be significantly reduced to about 60%. It is expected that the one-to-one classification model would be employed in the later stage.

Table 1. Accuracy of spinal posture recognition analyzed by BP neural network with sEMG signal

Classification						
Sample	Measured	Upright stand	Bend left	Bend right	Bend forward	Correct percentage
Train	1	50	3	4	3	83.3%
	3	6	44	3	7	73.3%
	5	5	4	43	8	71.6%
	7	4	4	5	10	78.3%
Examine	1	15	2	1	2	75.0%
	3	3	13	2	2	65.0%
	5	3	2	11	4	55.0%
	7	1	1	2	16	80.0%

4 Conclusion

We designed a device with the effective acquisition of sEMG signal and built a BP neural network model for spinal posture recognition. The device can collect sEMG signals with a signal-to-noise ratio of about 70 dB, and the method can effectively distinguish different spinal postures with a correct rate of greater than 65%. The device is meaningful for portable big data for scoliosis detection and spinal rehabilitation evaluation.

Acknowledgments. This work presented in the manuscript was sponsored by Talent introduction research support of Nanjing Institute of Technology (YKJ202022) and Innovation and Entrepreneurship Training Program for College Students in Jiangsu Province (202111276057Y).

References

1. Wei, T., Cacho-Soblechero, M., Dan, T., et al.: A 4-channel sEMG ASIC with real-time muscle fatigue feature extraction. In: IEEE International Symposium on Circuits and Systems, Daegu, Korea, pp. 1–7. IEEE (2021)
2. Wang, K.: Study on the characteristics of psoas surface electromyography in patients with different types of low back pain. Sun Yat-sen University
3. Li, G., Wang, J., Xu, Z., et al.: Application progress of surface EMG signal detection in the evaluation of low back muscle function. Mod. J. Integr. Tradit. Chin. West. Med. **22**(021), 2382–2383 (2013)
4. Dimitrov, D.V.: Medical Internet of Things and big data in healthcare. Healthc. Inform. Res. **22**(3), 156–164 (2016)
5. Gandhi, Y., Singh, A., Jani, R., et al.: Big data and its application in healthcare and medical field. Data Sci. Intell. Appl. **52**, 161–166 (2021)
6. Zhang, X., Wang, Y.: Research on intelligent medical big data system based on Hadoop and blockchain. EURASIP J. Wirel. Commun. Netw. **2021**(1), 1–21 (2021). https://doi.org/10.1186/s13638-020-01858-3

7. Hamid, H., Rahman, S., Hossain, M.S., et al.: A security model for preserving the privacy of medical big data in a healthcare cloud using a fog computing facility with pairing-based cryptography. IEEE Access **5**, 22313–22328 (2017)
8. Iqbal, U., Hsu, C.-K., et al.: Cancer-disease associations: a visualization and animation through medical big data. Comput. Methods Programs Biomed. **127**, 44–51 (2016)
9. Jin, W., Zhao, J.L., Luo, S.W,, et al.: The improvements of BP neural network learning algorithm. In: International Conference on Signal Processing. IEEE (2002)
10. Ding, S., Jia, W., Su, C., et al.: An improved BP neural network algorithm based on factor analysis. J. Converg. Inf. Technol. **5**(4), 103–108 (2010)
11. Zhu, T., Wei, H., Zhang, K., et al.: Handwritten digit recognition based on AP and BP neural network algorithm. China Science Paper (2014)
12. Roell, J., Sikula, J., Desai, J.: Real-time individual finger movement of a Mecha TE robotic hand using human forearm sEMG signals through hardware-software communication. Sch. J. Eng. Technol. **3**(3A), 252–257 (2015)
13. Bai, D., Liu, T., Han, X., et al.: Multi-channel sEMG signal gesture recognition based on improved CNN-LSTM hybrid models. In: IEEE International Conference on Intelligence and Safety for Robotics (ISR). IEEE (2021)
14. Karnam, N.K., Turlapaty, A.C., Dubey, S.R., et al.: Classification of sEMG signals of hand gestures based on energy features. Biomed. Signal Process. Control **70**(4), 102948 (2021)
15. Xi, X., Jiang, W., Hua, X., et al.: Simultaneous and continuous estimation of joint angles based on surface electromyography state-space model. IEEE Sens. J. **134**(99), 1–7 (2021)
16. Zhang, X., Barkhaus, P.E., Rymer, W.Z., et al.: Machine learning for supporting diagnosis of amyotrophic lateral sclerosis using surface electromyogram. IEEE Trans. Neural Syst. Rehabil. Eng. **22**(1), 96–103 (2014)
17. Deny, J., Raja Sudharsan, R., Muthu Kumaran, E.: An orbicularis oris, buccinator, zygomaticus, and risorius muscle contraction classification for lip-reading during speech using sEMG signals on multi-channels. Int. J. Speech Technol. **24**(3), 593–600 (2021). https://doi.org/10.1007/s10772-021-09816-0
18. Lu, Y., Wang, H., Hu, F., Zhou, B., Xi, H.: Effective recognition of human lower limb jump locomotion phases based on multi-sensor information fusion and machine learning. Med. Biol. Eng. Comput. **59**(4), 883–899 (2021). https://doi.org/10.1007/s11517-021-02335-9

Anomaly Detection of Cloud Network Resource State Based on Deep Learning

Junjie Shi, Fenggang Lai, Weiliang Li, Huaiyu Wang[✉], Xiaoliang Zhang, and Yan Li

State Grid Corporation, State Grid Information and Telecommunication Branch, Beijing, China

Abstract. Nowadays, cloud network resources increasingly exist in different practical systems. Anomaly detection is the important technique in these systems, which is able to monitor the system's status and predict when system maintenance is required. Although many types of data are generated by such systems, time series data is the major type of data which is usually meaningful and worth to analyze. So we mainly consider time series anomaly detection problem in this work. In most cases, the systems are in healthy state, thus the abnormal cases related to cloud network resources are rare, which motivates us to treat this as an unsupervised learning problem. By leveraging the strong learning ability of deep learning, we propose to combine LSTM and autoencoder to detect outliers in cloud network resources. We compare our approach with other basedline models via several benchmark datasets and the effectiveness is verified.

Keywords: Cloud network resources · Anomaly detection · Autoencoder

1 Introduction

Cloud network is better than traditional network in many aspects, thus cloud network resources are increasingly popular in many fields. These possible networks make a lot of data with different types and usages. Among them, time-series data analysis plays an important role. These data are continuously generated, so both its volume and dimension tend to be large. Timely discovery of disordered situation of cloud network resources helps to take quick response to troubleshoot the cause of disorder. Accurately and rapidly detect the abnormal situations are required in cloud network resource management. With this ability, the cost made by anomalies can be reduced.

The research of time series anomaly detection is not new [2,3,5–8]. But this area is active and hot because some challenges like detection accuracy and scalability still exist. The analysis of time series data anomaly detection is more difficult compared to traditional discrete data. The anomaly point in time is

© Springer Nature Singapore Pte Ltd. 2022
Y. Tian et al. (Eds.): ICBDS 2021, CCIS 1563, pp. 518–526, 2022.
https://doi.org/10.1007/978-981-19-0852-1_41

a point whose value deviates with standard, normal, or expected values. The anomaly points are usually generated because of the malfunction of cloud network systems. In general, the amount of measurement data is relatively large. When the data is transmitted, the process is also very susceptible to noise interference, data distortion or loss phenomenon. In addition, there may be complex correlations between different time series data channels. All these factors lead to time series anomaly detection has certain difficulty and complexity. Traditional human discrimination method and the method of delineating the threshold are both unsuitable for our task due to the slow processing speed and lack of flexibility.

With the rapid development of deep learning in recent years, many deep learning models are applied to anomaly detection. Long short-term memory (LSTM) network model is a special model of recursive neural network (RNN). It retains the advantage of standard RNN, so that it can use historical data to infer time series. It has received extensive attention in the field of time series anomaly detection. For example, in aerospace field, NASA combined the powerful nonlinear modeling ability of LSTM and automatic feature extraction capability. The remote control commands and telemetry data are used as input to build the LSTM model, and realize the effective labeling of telemetry data. Time series anomaly detection is a class imbalance problem. Anomalies rarely occur, so the cost of acquiring anomaly labels is high. Therefore, time series anomaly detection methods based on unsupervised learning are more practical.

Autoencoder is a BP neural network. The number of neurons in the input layer and output layer of the model is the same. The middle layer can have multiple layers. Generally, the number of nodes in the middle layer is less than that in the output layer. The middle layer is equivalent to compressing and abstracting data, and to recover and reconstruct the abstract features of the learning data in an unsupervised manner. Only positive sample data is required for training auto-encoder, and no negative sample data are required. In other words, the model only pays attention to the pattern of positive samples. The positive samples are used to train an auto-encoder by means of feature extraction and data recovery data. The encoder is equivalent to a single classification. When predicting a sample, the similarity between the input layer and the output layer can be compared to determine whether it is an abnormal sample, and the similarity threshold is set by itself.

This paper studies a deep unsupervised time-series anomaly detection algorithm. Through integrating LSTM and autoencoder, the abnormal cloud network resources situations can be accurately detected using pure unlabeled data.

2 Related Work

Anomaly detection is worth to study in many fields. An accurate and timely anomaly detection approach is crucial for system security maintenance. Common anomaly detection methods fall into the following categories:

(1) Methods based on statistics. Statistical methods are model-based methods that build a probability distribution model for the data and assume that the normal points basically conform to the distribution model. The probability that an object fits the model will be calculated. Then the objects with low probability are treated as outliers. To use the methods falling into this category, the distribution of the data set must be known in advance. If the initial assumption of the model is wrong, the detection performance will be bad. This is a great limitation.

(2) Proximity-Based Methods. A simple idea for implementing anomaly detection based on proximity is: if an object is anomalous, then it is far from most points. This method is more general than statistical methods, because determining a meaningful proximity measure for a dataset is faster than determining its statistical distribution. An object's outlier score is given by the distance to its k nearest neighbors. The score is highly sensitive to the value of k. If k is too small (such as 1), a small number of nearby outliers may cause a low outlier score; if k is too large, all objects in clusters with fewer than k points may be outliers. To make the scheme more robust to the selection of k, the average distance of the k nearest neighbors can be used. The disadvantages of the proximity detection method are: it takes $O(m^2)$ time and is not suitable for large data sets; the selection of parameters of this method is sensitive.

(3) Density-Based Methods. From a density-based point of view, outliers are objects in regions of low density. An object's outlier score is the inverse of the density around the object. Density-based outlier detection is closely related to proximity-based outlier detection, because density is usually defined in terms of proximity. A common definition of density is to define density as the inverse of the average distance to the k nearest neighbors. If the distance is small, the density is high and vice versa. Another density definition is to use DBSCAN's density definition, where the density around an object is equal to the number of objects within the specified distance d of the object. The choice of d is particularly important at this time. If d is too small, many normal points may have low density and thus get high outliers point score. If d is too large, many outliers may have similar densities (and outlier scores) as normal points. Detecting outliers using any density definition has similar characteristics and limitations as proximity-based outlier schemes. In particular, when the data contains regions of different densities, outliers (anomalies) cannot be correctly detected.

To correctly identify outliers in such datasets, we can use relative density-based outlier detection (LOF technique). First, for a specified number of neighbors (k), the object density (x, k) is calculated, based on which, the object's outlier score is obtained; Then, the point's neighbor average density is calculated, which can be used to calculates the point's average relative density. This quantity indicates whether x is in a denser or sparser neighborhood than its nearest neighbors, and is taken as x's outlier score. For the definition of relative density, there are two common methods: the method used by the SNN density-based clustering algorithm and the relative density method used by the ratio of the density x to the average density of its nearest neighbor y.

Like proximity-based methods, density-based anomaly detection methods necessarily have a time complexity of $O(m^2)$. Using specific data structures for low-dimensional data can achieve $O(mlogm)$. In addition, the parameter selection based on the density method is more difficult. The LOF algorithm avoids the parameter selection problem by observing different k values and taking the maximum outlier score, but it still needs to choose the upper and lower bounds of the k value.

(4) Cluster-Based Methods. The basic idea of cluster-based anomaly detection is to discard small clusters that are far away from other clusters. First, the data is clustered by distribution. After clustering, if it is found that the data sample size of some clusters is much smaller than that of other clusters, and the mean distribution of the data in the cluster is quite different from other clusters, the sample points of this cluster can be considered as abnormal points. For this method, the choice of the number of clusters is highly sensitive. One solution strategy is to find a large number of small clusters. This strategy considers smaller clusters to be more inclined to agglomeration. If an object is an outlier when there are a large number of small clusters, it is probably a true outlier. But this creates the problem that a set of outliers may form small clusters and evade detection. Furthermore, this method requires a minimum cluster size and threshold for distance between small clusters and other clusters.

In the broad field of machine learning, a large number of researches on deep learning have emerged in recent years, and unprecedented results have been achieved in different fields. Deep learning is a subset of machine learning that represents data as a nested conceptual hierarchy for good performance and flexibility. Along with the increase of data scale, the performance of deep learning is better than that of traditional machine learning approaches. In recent years, anomaly detection algorithms based on deep learning are becoming more and more popular and are applied to various tasks. Many research shows that deep learning completely surpasses traditional methods. Anomaly detection methods based on deep learning can also be divided into: (1) supervised methods; (2) semi-supervised methods; (3) unsupervised methods.

Supervised methods based on deep learning. This method uses the labels of normal and abnormal data instances to train deep binary or multi-class classifiers. This anomaly detection method has been used to detect illegal drug names and fraudulent medical transactions. The performance of supervised methods is usually good when sufficient labeled samples exist. However, due to the lack of labeled training samples, such methods are not as good as semi-supervised or unsupervised methods. In addition to this, due to the class imbalance problem, supervised deep learning classifiers are suboptimal (the total number of positive classes is much larger than the total number of negative classes of data).

Semi-supervised methods based on deep learning. In anomaly detection problems, normal data labels are more easier to obtain, so the semi-supervised deep learning technology in the problem of anomaly detection has been widely used. These techniques utilize existing single-class labels (usually positive) to separate outliers. Anomaly detection using deep autoencoders has been used as a common method to perform semi-supervised training on non-anomaly data samples. With enough training samples, for the normal case, the normal class data sample will have a lower autoencoder reconstruction error.

Unsupervised methods based on deep learning. Unsupervised deep anomaly detection techniques rely only on the inherent feature to detect outliers. This method was originally designed to solve the problem that labeled data is difficult to obtain. It is commonly used for automatic labeling of unlabeled data samples. Variety of unsupervised deep anomaly detection models are clearly superior to traditional methods such as principal component analysis (PCA), support vector machine and Isolation Forest. AutoEncoders are at the heart of all unsupervised deep anomaly detection models. These models all assume that the incidence of normal instances is higher than the incidence of abnormal data instances, which will lead to a high false positive rate.

3   The Method Used in This Work

3.1   Problem Statement

Cloud network resource state data is a kind of time-series data $\mathrm{x} = \left(x^1, x^2, \ldots, x^n \right)^T = (x_1, x_2, \ldots, x_t) \epsilon R^{n \times t}$. The value of n represents the $n - th$ feature, and t represents timestamp. Time-series data can be either univariate or multivariate. Univariate case is studied under the unbrella of unsupervised learning in this work. x_u represented unlabeled data. We use autoencoder to reconstruct a new data sequence which is $\tilde{x}_u$. The reconstruction error between x_u and $\tilde{x}_u$ will be calculated and compared with a threshold value. For a sample, if its reconstructed error is greater or equal to the threshold, this sample will be treated as anomaly. Otherwise, this sample will be treated as normal data.

3.2   Our Proposed Model

LSTM autoencoder combines LSTM and autoencoder to inherit their advantages. In addition, the popular attention mechanism is applied on LSTM autoencoder to further improve its performance.

In autoencoder, the input x_t is converted to h_t via encoder. Then h_t will be reconstructed by decoder. For LSTM autoencoder, the time related features will be extracted through the learning ability of LSTM. This is superior to pure autoencoder which is not able to capture time related features. The LSTM autoencoder is shown in Fig. 1.

In LSTM autoencoder, the relationship between hidden state and input time series $\mathrm{x} = (x_1, x_2, \ldots, x_t) \epsilon R^{n \times t}$ is:

$$h_t = f\left(h_{t-1}, x_t \right) \tag{1}$$

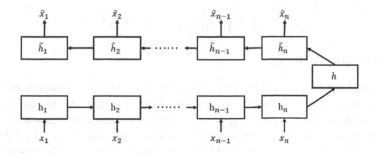

Fig. 1. The LSTM autoencoder.

At time step t, the encoder has the hidden state $h_t \in R^m$. The hidden unit size is m, and the activation function is represented by f. The inputs of LSTM unit include hidden state of previous time stamp, the states of units of previous time stamp, and input of current time stamp. The LSTM unit uses forget gates, input gates and output gates to respectively control the information to be forgotten, the information to be remembered, and the renew. The three gating mechanisms control the output value varies between 0 and 1. When the gated output value is close to 0, the multiplied information cannot be transmitted; and when the gated output is close to 1, the multiplied information can be transmitted almost without loss, so as to realize the control. The process is as follows:

$$
\begin{aligned}
f_t &= \sigma\left(W_f \cdot [h_{t-1}, x_t] + b_f\right) \\
i_t &= \sigma\left(W_i \cdot [h_{t-1}, x_t] + b_i\right) \\
\tilde{c}_t &= \tanh\left(W_C \cdot [h_{t-1}, x_t] + b_C\right) \\
C_t &= f_t * C_{t-1} + i_t * \tilde{C}_t \\
o_t &= \sigma\left(W_o \cdot [h_{t-1}, x_t] + b_o\right) \\
h_t &= o_t \tanh\left(C_t\right)
\end{aligned}
\tag{2}
$$

The loss function below represents the reconstruction error. And LSTM autoencoder can be trained by minimizing this function.

$$
\min \frac{1}{t} \sum_{i=1}^{t} \|x_i - \tilde{x}_i\|_2
\tag{3}
$$

Extracting time related features is crucial for time series data analysis. To this end, we have adopted the sliding window approach to divide a time sequence into multiple data segments. In detail, in our sliding window, the length and step size are both set to one. The original sequential data is $x = (x_1, x_2, \ldots, x_t)$. Through sliding window, multiple data segments $S = \{s_1, s_2, \ldots, s_{t-1+1}\}$ are generated, where $s_i = (x_i, x_{i+1}, \ldots, x_{i+l}), 1 \le i \le t - 1 + 1$. The loss function is updated by the segment and defined as follows:

$$
\min \frac{1}{t-1+1} \sum_{i=1}^{t-1+1} E\left[s_i : \tilde{s}_i\right]
\tag{4}
$$

$$E\left[s_i : \tilde{s}_i\right] = \frac{1}{l} \left\| x_j - \tilde{x}_j \right\|_2 \quad i \leq j \leq i+1 \tag{5}$$

4   Experiments

Public cloud network resource state dataset is not available, instead, we use the hard disk dataset to verify our approach. Hard disk dataset is also a kind of resource state dataset [1,4,9,10]. If our proposed method works on it, we can also implement it on the cloud network resource state dataset in the future.

The public datasets are obtained from Backblaze company. The whole dataset is too big to study, two mamufacturer's hard disk data are selected only. We need to analyze the SMART value of each hard disk to decide this disk is healthy or not. The Data attributes in the experiment are shown in Fig. 2.

Smart ID	SMART Attribute Name	Attribute type
1	Raw Read Error Rate	Normalized
3	Spin-Up Time	Normalized
5	Reallocated Sectors Count	Raw
7	Seek Error Rate	Normalized
9	Power-On Hours	Normalized
187	Reported Uncorrectable Errors	Raw
188	Command Timeout	Raw
190	Airflow Temperature	Raw
193	Load/Unload Cycle Count	Raw
194	Temperature	Normalized
197	Current Pending Sector Count	Raw
198	Offline Uncorrectable Sector Count	Raw
240	Head Flying Hours	Raw
241	Total LBAs Written	Raw
242	Total LBAs Read	Raw

Fig. 2. The SMART data attributes.

The range of above fifteen attributes are different, so all the attributes are normalized to the range $[0,1]$ to reduce the effect of different ranges.

$$x_{norm} = \frac{x_i - x_{\min}}{x_{\max} - x_{\min}} \tag{6}$$

Our proposed method is compared to other two popular unsupervised time series anomaly detection methods: OCSVM and IForest. The F1 measurement is used for evaluating the performance

$$F1 - score = 2 \times \frac{precision \times recall}{precision + recall} \tag{7}$$

The experimental comparison is shown in Fig. 3, which clearly shows the superiority of our proposed approach.

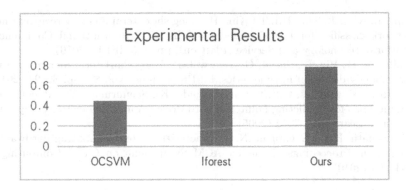

Fig. 3. Experimental results.

5 Conclusions

In this work, we propose a deep learning based method to detect the anomaly states of cloud network resource. Mathematically, we model this as a time-serious detection problem and propose an unsupervised method to solve this problem. Our method is straightforward and easy to deploy. More importantly, it is unsupervised and requires only unlabeled could network resource data. Our method integrates LSTM with autoencoders. LSTM reflects the time dependent of each data. The autoencoder tries to reconstruct each data and compare the difference between original data and the reconstructed data. If the difference is high, we can treat this state data as anomaly data. Finally, the experimental results verify the performance of our approach.

Acknowledgement. This work is supported by Science and Technology Project from State Grid Information and Telecommunication Branch of China: Research on Key Technologies of Operation Oriented Cloud Network Integration Platform (52993920002P).

References

1. Allen, B.: Monitoring hard disks with smart. Linux J. **117**, 74–77 (2004)
2. Chandola, V., Banerjee, A., Kumar, V.: Anomaly detection: a survey. ACM Comput. Surv. (CSUR) **41**(3), 1–58 (2009)
3. Cook, A.A., Mısırlı, G., Fan, Z.: Anomaly detection for IoT time-series data: a survey. IEEE Internet Things J. **7**(7), 6481–6494 (2019)
4. Eckart, B., Chen, X., He, X., Scott, S.L.: Failure prediction models for proactive fault tolerance within storage systems. In: 2008 IEEE International Symposium on Modeling, Analysis and Simulation of Computers and Telecommunication Systems, pp. 1–8. IEEE (2008)
5. Fox, A.J.: Outliers in time series. J. R. Stat. Soc. Ser. B (Methodol.) **34**(3), 350–363 (1972)
6. Goodfellow, I., Bengio, Y., Courville, A.: Deep Learning. MIT Press, Cambridge (2016)

7. Kim, J., Kim, J., Thu, H.L.T., Kim, H.: Long short term memory recurrent neural network classifier for intrusion detection. In: 2016 International Conference on Platform Technology and Service (PlatCon), pp. 1–5. IEEE (2016)
8. Malhotra, P., Vig, L., Shroff, G., Agarwal, P.: Long short term memory networks for anomaly detection in time series. In: Proceedings, vol. 89, pp. 89–94 (2015)
9. Murray, J.F., Hughes, G.F., Kreutz-Delgado, K., Schuurmans, D.: Machine learning methods for predicting failures in hard drives: a multiple-instance application. J. Mach. Learn. Res. 6(5) (2005)
10. Vishwanath, K.V., Nagappan, N.: Characterizing cloud computing hardware reliability. In: Proceedings of the 1st ACM Symposium on Cloud Computing, pp. 193–204 (2010)

Research on Defect Intelligent Identification System Based on Cloud-Fog-Edge Cooperation for UAV Electric Power Inspection

Wenye Liu[1], Haiming Xu[2(✉)], Kegui Guo[1], Nianguo Liu[1], Xuming Tang[1], Jianghui Meng[1], Cifu Zhan[1], Luyao Li[1], and Pin Lu[3]

[1] Huainan Power Supply Company, State Grid Anhui Electric Power Co., Ltd., Huainan 232007, China
[2] Institute of Intelligent Machines, HFIPS, Chinese Academy of Sciences, Hefei 230031, China
hmxu@iim.ac.cn
[3] School of Mechanical Engineering, Hefei University of Technology, Hefei 230009, China

Abstract. UAV patrols have been applied in all walks of life, but at this stage, they mainly depend on manual operation, and the efficiency and intelligence of UAV patrols are not high. Starting from the requirements of power inspection, this paper studies a UAV real-time intelligent inspection system, including an inspection path planning system based on 3D point clouds, a line defect image depth learning and recognition collaborative work algorithm based on UAV onboard computing terminals, vehicle fog computing terminals and cloud high-performance computing platforms, and an intelligent UAV patrol control algorithm driven by target image recognition. The research and development of this system will improve the efficiency of patrol inspection of electric UAVs, improve the degree of intelligence and user experience, and be extended to the fields of transportation, forestry, emergency rescue and so on.

Keywords: UAV · Cloud-fog-edge cooperation · Defect image recognition · Real-time intelligent inspection system

1 Introduction

1.1 Research Background

With the development of the Internet of Things (IOT) and smart hardware terminals, various applications have an increasing demand for high-performance computing. For example, various navigation software needs to load maps of the local region, various virtual reality applications, local face recognition applications, etc., especially various real-time information calculation and real-time control systems, which require higher latency and sensitivity [1, 2].

On November 17, 2005, at the World Summit on the Information Society (WSIS) held in Tunisia, the International Telecommunication Union (ITU) released the "ITU Internet Report 2005: Internet of Things" [3], which officially put forward the concept of the

© Springer Nature Singapore Pte Ltd. 2022
Y. Tian et al. (Eds.): ICBDS 2021, CCIS 1563, pp. 527–544, 2022.
https://doi.org/10.1007/978-981-19-0852-1_42

"Internet of Things". The report pointed out that the ubiquitous "Internet of Things" communication era is coming, and all objects in the world, from tires to toothbrushes, from houses to paper towels, can be actively exchanged through the internet. Radio frequency identification technology (RFID), sensor technology, nanotechnology, and intelligent embedded technology will be more widely used. According to the description of the ITU, in the era of the Internet of Things, by embedding a short-distance mobile transceiver in a variety of daily necessities, humans will obtain a new dimension of communication in the world from any time and any place. The communication connection between people extends to the communication connection between people to things and things to things. From a technical point, the Internet of Things architecture can be divided into a perception layer, transmission layer, and application service layer. The perception layer is the main level of data generation in the Internet of Things. This layer is mainly composed of various sensors and other detection devices, which are responsible for measuring and collecting relevant data information; the transmission layer is responsible for reliable transmission of data and content generated by the perception layer; and the application services layer is responsible for intelligent processing and analysis of the basic information data of the perception layer.

In 2006, Amazon first launched cloud computing services globally, opening a fast path for the development of the Internet. With the improvement and advancement of cloud computing technology, cloud computing has become the infrastructure of the mobile Internet and the Internet of Things, and it is one of the categories of new infrastructure construction. Cloud computing processing services that combine the development of computer technologies such as distributed computing, utility computing, load balancing, parallel computing, network storage, hot backup redundancy, and virtualization [4–6]. In 2011, the National Institute of Standards and Technology [7] clearly defined cloud computing, believing that cloud computing is a business model that charges users according to their actual needs. Too many interactions provide users with convenient and cheap on-demand network access. In the current big data environment, cloud computing is not only a specific calculation but also a new, efficient, and practical data transmission and storage processing mode.

For some special application scenarios, the latency of cloud computing is relatively large. This is mainly due to the influence of network conditions. For example, in some mountainous and remote areas, there is usually no 4G/5G network or stable internet [8]. For some scene image types, the amount of data is large. The calculation resource does not satisfy the need. Therefore, it is urgent to propose a new computing model to solve the deficiencies of the centralized computing model of cloud computing. In 2012, the concept of fog computing was proposed. F. Bonomi defined fog computing [9] in 2014 and proposed the characteristics of fog computing in 2018 [10], mainly referring to the decentralized edge position, supporting mobility, distributed deployment, support for large-scale access of sensor data, real-time interaction, wireless access, and heterogeneous features. In response to the deficiencies of cloud computing, Cisco clearly proposed and defined the network architecture of fog computing in 2015 [11]. Fog computing is an extended concept of cloud computing. The name "fog" comes from the concept of life "fog like cloud but closer to the ground". In this model, data, data processing and applications are concentrated in devices at the edge of the network, rather than almost all stored in the cloud. Fog computing is not composed of powerful servers but is composed of weaker and more powerful servers. It is composed of scattered computers with various functions that infiltrate factories, automobiles, electrical appliances, street lamps, and various supplies in people's lives [12]. Fog computing is a new computing model that extends the traditional cloud computing architecture to the edge of the network. With the assistance of fog computing, delay-sensitive applications can be deployed at the edge of the network, while others (such as high-latency tolerant and computationally intensive applications) can be deployed in cloud computing systems. In addition, fog computing provides many other benefits. For example, for applications with a large amount of data, fog computing can preprocess the data with a filter and denoising algorithm, and then send the result to the cloud server, thereby reducing the burden on the network. Fog computing will bring huge changes to the terminal devices of the Internet of Things, which are mainly reflected in two aspects. First, they are all independently operated terminal devices of the Internet of Things and will almost be connected to the fog node through the network in the future.

The edge computing described in this article mainly includes processing and computing at the front end, such as edge data collection, transmission, and computing. In some documents, edge computing has been included in the category of fog computing. This article specifically refers to computing devices that are bound to edge data collection devices. Edge computing provides terminal computing modes through computing resources deployed at the source of object data. It has the characteristics of high timeliness and responsiveness, but it also has the disadvantages of low computing power and high energy consumption.

Deep learning is a branch of artificial neural networks. Artificial intelligence with a deep network structure is the earliest network model of deep learning. In 2006, Jeffrey Hinton (G. Hinton) proposed the concept of deep learning, and then his team proposed one of the deep learning models in the paper [13], the deep belief network, and gave an efficient semi-supervised algorithm: A layer-by-layer greedy algorithm to train the parameters of deep belief networks, breaking the long-standing deadlock that deep networks are difficult to train. Since its inception in 2006, deep learning has received great attention from scientific research institutions and industry. Initially, the application of deep learning was mainly in the fields of image and speech identification. Beginning in 2011, researchers from Google and Microsoft applied deep learning to speech recognition, reducing the recognition error rate by 20%–30%. In 2012, Jeffrey Hinton's students IIya Sutskever and Alex Krizhevsky used deep learning to defeat the Google team in the image classification competition ImageNet. The application of deep learning reduced the image recognition error rate by 14%. Today, deep learning has been widely used in image, speech, natural language processing, CTR estimation, and big data feature extraction. In March 2016, Google's AlphaGo trained with deep learning artificial intelligence algorithms played a world champion and professional nine-dan player Li Shishi in a man-machine battle, winning a total score of 4–1. On such websites, with the registered account of "Master", it competed with dozens of Chinese, Japanese and Korean Go masters without losing a single game in 60 consecutive rounds. In the world professional Go rankings published on the GoRatings website, its level has exceeded that of the number one player Ke Jie.

1.2   Analysis of Current Situation of UAV Inspection

At present, the inspection of ultrahigh voltage electric transmission lines mainly relies on manual inspection and manual inspection by UAVs as the main mode. This method of manual inspection not only has high work intensity, poor working conditions and low work efficiency but also has personal safety risks. In particular, the inaccurate range measurement of UAVs, complex terrain, and visual fatigue of human eyes increase the difficulty of work. It is impossible to find accidents and abnormalities in time, and it is difficult to meet the inspection cycle specified in the operation regulations.

Multirotor UAVs have the characteristics of flexible maneuverability, good hovering stability and easy control and are currently being popularized and applied in the inspection of power transmission lines. In the actual operation process, the traditional multirotor line patrolling UAV uses high-definition cameras to shoot scenes, which are transmitted to the receiving terminal through the image transmission system and manually checked by the electric staff. This is often time-consuming and laborious and does not completely solve the labor intensity problem. With the development of artificial intelligence technology, deep learning algorithm technology based on image recognition is becoming increasingly mature, which will provide reliable technical support for the autonomous cruise of UAVs and is also the main development direction in the future.

In terms of UAV power inspection, the main method of remote control by the operator is used currently, and the inspector is staring at the returned image to identify the human eye to perform the operation. As shown in Fig. 1, at current stage, three people were basically working together: one aircraft remote control operator, two video inspectors or liaison officers. For large towers or lines, intercoms are needed to direct the UAV operator to perform operations. However, due to the difference in the field of view and coordinate system, communication efficiency is often extremely low. As shown in Fig. 2, because the traditional electric power inspection UAV is greatly affected by wind at high altitudes, the positioning is inaccurate, and the video image is seriously shaken, making human eye detection very difficult.

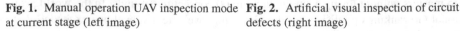

Fig. 1. Manual operation UAV inspection mode at current stage (left image)

Fig. 2. Artificial visual inspection of circuit defects (right image)

1.3 Research and Contribution of This Paper

Limited by the impact of network latency and bandwidth, cloud computing often does not meet the needs of specific application scenarios. Cloud computing, fog computing and edge computing urgently need to work together [14] to meet the characteristics of low latency, high sensitivity, optimal energy consumption [15] and high-performance computing [16]. This article will take the UAV inspection of electric transmission lines as an example to explain the intelligent inspection system by cloud-fog-edge cooperation, providing examples for the practical application of the IOT and artificial intelligence, completely freeing human hands, improving work efficiency, and enhancing intelligence for the electric industry.

2 Principles and Methods

2.1 Intelligent UAV Inspection System Model

The overall structure of intelligent inspections system for the power line includes research on inspection path planning systems based on 3D point clouds, line defects based on UAV onboard edge computing terminals, fog computing terminals, cloud high-performance computing severs, collaborative inspection image recognition algorithm based on deep learning method, intelligent UAV inspection and control algorithm driven by target image recognition, and vehicle-mounted UAV mobile platform (car-based nest, fog computing terminals) system.

The physical components of the UAV intelligent inspection system include the UAV system, the vehicle nest management and control system, and the cloud server system. Among them, UAV systems are divided into two types. One is a system that only includes data collection. It collects information such as latitude, longitude, altitude, flight speed, head orientation, and pictures and then transmits it to the ground control center system, such as DJI P4 RTK. This model can only be interconnected with the mobile phone through remote control. The mobile phone has lower image computing capabilities and can only perform simple data calculations and then interconnect with the car-based nest system and the cloud server system. In addition, one includes an onboard GPU computing system, such as the DJI M300 with a Magic2 GPU. This type can realize real-time front-end recognition, and it can also be directly connected to cloud servers and fog servers through a wireless network (e.g. 4G/5G). The car-based control center system includes the vehicle-mounted machine nest body and control system modules and the vehicle-mounted fog computing system module. The fog computing module is mainly used for the recognition of medium difficulty image deep learning. The cloud server system includes B/S architecture services and databases and high-performance cloud computing modules, which can perform more difficult cloud computing services. These three systems form an overall solution for intelligent system calculations, which can adapt to various working conditions, especially in some mountainous areas or sparsely populated areas (Fig. 3).

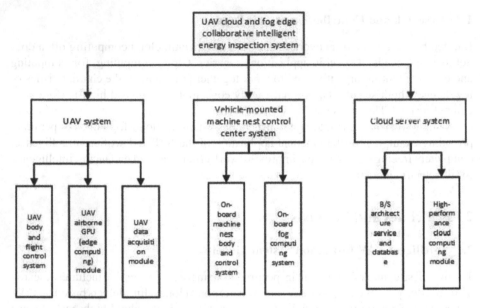

Fig. 3. UAV cloud and fog edge collaborative intelligent inspection system

2.2 Inspection Path Planning System of 3D Point Clouds Based on B/S Architecture

The core of UAV intelligent inspection is the planning of the inspection path. Through laser scanning of the transmission line, a 3D point cloud model is constructed, and the 3D model of the tower and line is accurately recorded. It is carried out through the A* algorithm or artificial potential field algorithm to 3D flight path planning which can not only ensure safety but also realize fully autonomous inspections. Since the 3D point cloud planning system is deployed in the cloud, the generated inspection path file contains the latitude, longitude, altitude, and point action information. This file can be deployed in the fog computing terminal in real time, in order to save uploading and downloading time. The system can formulate a route plan for the detailed inspection of specific poles and towers and modify the flight plan. At the same time, it can also view the route path and simulate flight according to the task plan, assist the ground station (UAV nest, fog computer) in executing the route tasks. The UAV sends the real-time position to the database server, and the web management and control platform can display the aircraft position and inspection trajectory in real time. The three-dimensional display system can simultaneously display the high-definition image transmission pushed by the UAV in real time (Fig. 4).

This paper develops a fine route planning system based on lidar point cloud data, combining two or more UAVs and PZT cameras. According to the requirements of refined UAV inspection, automatic feature point extraction technology is used to output the precise photo point location including the latitude, longitude and shooting angle, and the connection route between each photo point.

Fig. 4. Transmission line 3D point cloud scanned by lidar

2.3 Intelligent UAV Inspection System Based on Cloud and Fog Edge Collaboration

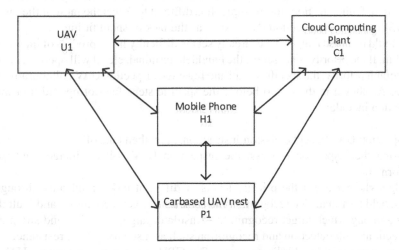

Fig. 5. Cloud-fog-edge collaborative intelligent UAV inspection system architecture diagram

The intelligent UAV inspection system based on cloud-fog-edge collaborative operation is the core scheduling algorithm of this article. It can select computing resources in real time according to working conditions. It mainly includes inspection UAVs, cloud platforms, and fog computing platforms that communicate with each other. The UAV completes inspection tasks according to the control instructions issued by the cloud platform, the UAV nest (fog computing platform), and the handheld terminal. The cloud platform is used to transmit and store the UAV's data, the UAV nest (fog computing platform) is mainly used for the transmission and processing of control instructions and data information with cloud platforms and handheld terminals (Mobile phone); handheld terminals are used for transmission the control commands and information between the UAV nest (P1),Cloud computing plant (C1) and UAV (U1). The control instructions and data information between the fog computing platform (UAV nest) and the cloud platform can remotely control the intelligent inspection UAV system, and supervise the real-time dynamics of the inspection UAV.

Cloud-Fog-Edge Information Collaborative Transmission Algorithm
During the inspection process of high-voltage transmission lines, there are two major categories: target recognition and fault detection. Target recognition mainly refers to the recognition of the target through the image to solve the problem, such as insulator string recognition, hardware recognition, nut recognition, etc. Fault detection is also achieved through images, such as insulator string contamination, missing data, rupture and other issues.

As shown in Fig. 6, Fig. 5, the preset priority levels of different tasks include simple identification tasks (Sm), medium-difficulty identification tasks (Mm), and complex-difficulty identification tasks (Dm). The difficulty is mainly determined by two difficulties. One is the size of the target. The larger the target is, the easier it is to recognize, such as the recognition of insulator strings (Sm); the smaller the target is, the more difficult it is, such as the recognition of tiny hardware (Mm). In addition, target recognition is simpler than fault detection; for example, it is difficult to detect the fault of the insulator string (Mm) and fault detection (Dm), such as the lack of small fittings;

It should be noted that we have already set the difficulty in the process of inputting the algorithm. If the priority is not set for the handheld terminal, etc., it will operate according to the default priority; the specific cloud and fog edge inspection UAV collaborative work method, As shown in the Fig. 6 below, the specific steps for storing and transmitting information include:

1. Inspection UAV accepts mission instructions, and then take off;
2. During the inspection process, the inspection UAV collects images and picture information;
3. Judge whether to set the priority levels of different tasks in advance through the handheld terminal. The recognition tasks include target recognition and fault detection, among which target recognition is insulator target detection and strain clamp detection; fault detection and recognition such as insulator defect, resistance Zhang folder is ectopic, has bird's nest, etc. The GPU (Ug) on the inspection UAV runs simple recognition tasks (Sm); the GPU (Pg) on the vehicle-mounted fog computing platform runs medium-difficult recognition tasks (Mm); the GPU (Cg) on the cloud platform runs complex and difficult recognition tasks (Dm);
4. If the priority level of the preset task is not set in the handheld terminal, the inspection UAV will judge the difficulty of different tasks by itself;
5. Determine whether it is a simple identification task. If it is, the inspection UAV will directly perform the task. After the task is completed, it will return home and transmit the generated data to the airborne fog computing platform and cloud platform for backup;

6. If it is not a simple level recognition task, then judge whether it is a medium level recognition task. If it is a medium-level recognition task, then the inspection task will be transmitted to the aircraft nest fog computing platform through the inspection UAV to run. After completion, the generated data information will be transmitted to the cloud platform and the inspection UAV for backup;

7. If it is not a medium-level identification task, the inspection task will be transmitted to the cloud platform through the inspection UAV for operation. After the task is completed, the generated data information will be stored on the cloud platform and transmitted to the inspection UAV at the same time. Machine and machine nest fog computing platform.

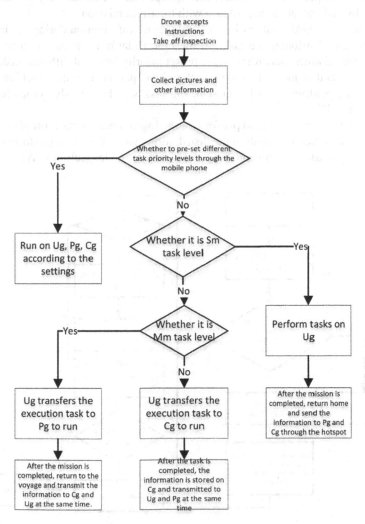

Fig. 6. Cloud-fog-edge information collaborative transmission algorithm

Cloud-Fog-Edge Control Command Collaborative Operation Method

As shown in Fig. 7, the collaborative operation method for cloud-fog-edge control commands has several steps as follows:

1. Set up the UAV inspection flight task on the handheld terminal and send it to the inspection UAV and the fog computing platform of the UAV nest;
2. The UAV and the aircraft nest fog computing platform receive tasks, and the aircraft nest fog computing platform checks whether the patrol UAV meets the normal take-off conditions;
3. If the inspection UAV does not meet the normal take-off conditions, it will not take off; if the inspection UAV meets the normal take-off conditions, it will take off normally and execute in accordance with the flight mission;
4. The inspection UAV collects images and picture information during the inspection process and distributes the tasks to the cloud platform or the machine nest fog computing platform according to the preset priority levels of different tasks;
5. Confirm whether the task is sent to the cloud platform or the machine nest fog computing platform. If it is not sent, the task will be directly completed by the inspection UAV;
6. If it has been sent to the cloud platform or the fog computing platform of the machine nest, the identification result of the distribution task of the cloud platform or the fog computing platform of the machine nest is sent to the inspection UAV;

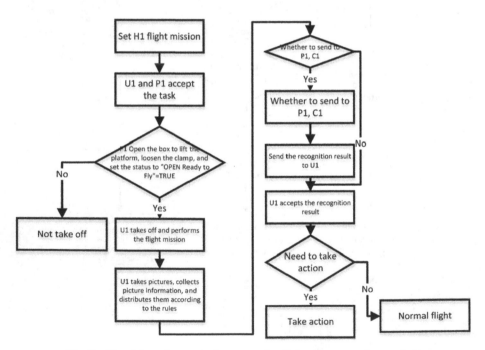

Fig. 7. Cloud-fog-edge control command collaborative operation method

7. The patrol UAV autonomously judges whether the recognition result needs to take action; if necessary, the patrol UAV will take the corresponding action; if not, it will continue the normal flight patrol task.

2.4 Intelligent UAV Inspection Review Algorithm Driven by Target Image Recognition

During the UAV inspection operation, the UAV collects pictures and calls interface of UAV inspection typical target image identification and defect detection system of the transmission line. The algorithm automatically analyzes the pictures, recognizes typical targets and defects, returns the result such as the defect type, location, size, and confidence of the recognition results to the UAV, and sends an alarm if it has defect.

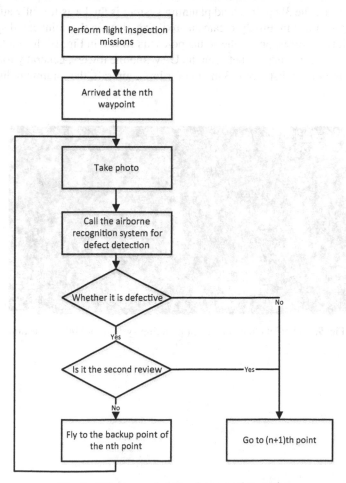

Fig. 8. Trigger mechanism for secondary review

The typical target recognition and defect detection system for UAV inspection of transmission lines will also return flag parameters to the UAV, and the correct flag value is usually 0. When the algorithm finds a suspected defect, but it is difficult to judge, the flag parameter value is 1, indicating that a second review is required.

When the UAV receives the second review flag, it will call the interface of the flight control system to take a second review at a new second backup point, and send a confirm result to the cloud sever (see Fig. 8).

3   Experiment and Analysis

3.1   Inspection 3D Point Cloud Planning

The 3D point cloud planning module is mainly deployed on the cloud service platform. Inspectors can access related modules to plan or edit the inspection paths through the B/S architecture. The 3D point cloud planning system is the basis for fully autonomous inspections, as shown in. Firstly, create an auxiliary plane in the point cloud system and draw the points to correspond to the actual poles, as shown in Fig. 10. It should be noted that to ensure the safe distance between the UAV and the towers, generally for the small aircraft, the minimum distance is 3 m, and for large aircraft, the minimum distance is 5 m (Fig. 9).

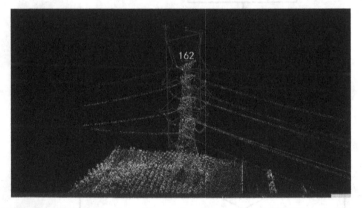

Fig. 9. 3D point cloud intelligent planning system for UAV inspection

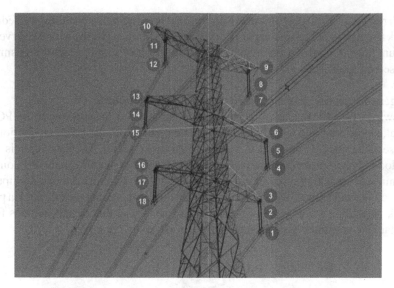

Fig. 10. Actual location for UAV electric power inspection

3.2 Cloud-Fog-Edge Collaborative Work Intelligent Identification System

Intelligent Inspection System Based on Small UAV

As shown in Fig. 11, the server (including database, etc.) interacts with the PC web terminal, car-based UAV nest, and mobile phone app (remote control) in bilateral data interaction. The UAV communicates with the server through the mobile phone app (remote control). Server data are stored in the local database. Among them, the v car-based UAV nest and mobile phone app (remote control) can communicate with the server through the 4G/5G module; the mobile phone app communicates with the UAV

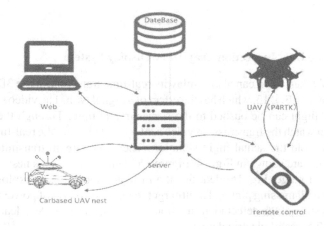

Fig. 11. Interaction model of inspection system based on P4 RTK

through remote control; the computer web terminal is communicated through a dedicated network (including 5G private network or VPN encryption network) with the server; and these functional modules form an intelligent inspection system of electric transmission line based on small UAV.

Intelligent Inspection System Based on Onboard Computer

As shown in Fig. 12, the server (including database, etc.) interacts with the PC web terminal, stable nest, and UAV with onboard computer in bilateral data interaction. The UAV uses the onboard computer to transmit data to the server. The sever data is stored in the local database. Among them, the stable nest and the UAV's onboard computer can communicate with the server through the 4G/5G module; the onboard computer is directly connected to the UAV; the computer web terminal is connected through a private network (including 5G or vpn encryption network). These functional modules form a fixed machine nest intelligent inspection system based on big UAV.

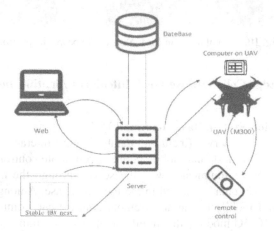

Fig. 12. Intelligent inspection system based on an M300 onboard computer

3.3   Real-Time UAV Inspection Trajectory Display System

After the UAV takes off, it can also display its real-time trajectory in the 3D point cloud system, as shown in Fig. 13, which has the effect of a digital twin. The video stream during the automatic flight can be pushed to the server in real time. Through the monitoring system, we can watch the transmission video sent by the UAV and the real-time trajectory of the UAV to hold the actual flight situation. The video stream transmitted from the UAV in real time are shown in Fig. 14. Figure 15 identifies the bird's nest classed in the abnormal object range, Fig. 16 identifies the insulator spontaneous explosion, Fig. 17 identifies the small missing pins and multitarget recognition effect of power transmission towers. The system of the defect identification algorithm based on deep learning method can identify 17 types of electric defect.

Fig. 13. The real-time trajectory of UAV inspection

Fig. 14. View inspection photo

Fig. 15. Use deep learning to identify abnormal objects in the bird's nest

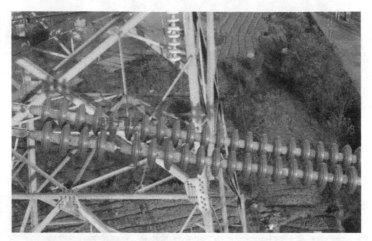

Fig. 16. Identifying the self-explosion of insulators

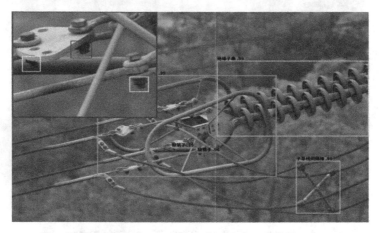

Fig. 17. Multitarget recognition of power transmission towers

3.4 Discussion of Experimental Results

As shown in the following table, we compare the inspection time (taking a 3-level power tower with 26 points as an example), line defect recognition accuracy rate, whether to support secondary reinspection, and inspection methods. As seen from the table below, manual operation method of UAV inspection requires 2 to 3 people to cooperate. The manual inspection time is long, it is difficult to identify small hardware such as pins, and the line defect recognition accuracy rate is 70.27% and cannot be continuous work. Autonomy intelligent inspection based on Phantom 4RTK is fast than the manual method; the spend time is 10 min 14 s because the point information is planned in advance, the inspection speed is faster, and the inspection method is flying first and downloading the pictures after the inspection is completed, and deep learning calculations are performed on the cloud server. The recognition accuracy of this method is more than 95%, but because it cannot be recognized in real time, it does not support automatic second review method. The intelligent inspection based on the M300 with onboard computer, has a lower inspection speed than the Phantom 4RTK solution due to the larger size. The detection accuracy rate is also highest among this 3 method, and since it is real-time identification method, it also supports second review method (Table 1).

Table 1. Comparison of experimental results

Serial number	Test items	Inspection time for a 3-level pole tower (26 point)	Line defect recognition accuracy rate	Whether to support secondary identification check	Inspection method
1	Manually operated UAV inspection (P4)	19 min 23 s	70.27%	Not support	Manual recognition by watching the video, requires 2 or 3 people to collaborate work
2	Phantom 4 RTK Intelligent Inspection	10 min 14 s	95.31%	Not support	Autonomy intelligent inspection method. First fly, download pictures after the inspection, and perform deep learning calculations on the cloud server
3	M300 with local_computer intelligent inspection	12 min and 13 s	97.52%	Support	Use the onboard computer to calculate the picture While flying, support cloud and fog calculation

4 Conclusions

This article aims to solve the problems of inefficiency, inconvenience and inconvenience caused by traditional people operating UAVs in the power line inspection. Facing the important demand for fine automatic inspection of electric transmission lines, we developed the cloud-fog-edge intelligent inspection system based on the Phantom 4 RTK and

M300 platform to realize the 3D point cloud precise planning of the UAV, high-precision navigation and positioning, fully autonomous flight operations, and typical electric line defect identification. Through the integration of the above systems, the entire process of UAV inspection on transmission lines can be automated and intelligent, which will greatly improve inspection efficiency and expand work capabilities.

References

1. Li, L., et al.: Online Workload Allocation via Fog-Fog-Cloud Cooperation to Reduce IoT Task Service Delay. Sensors **19**(18) (2019)
2. Tang, H., et al.: Optimal multilevel media stream caching in cloud-edge environment. J. Supercomput. (10), 1–20 (2021)
3. Heinzelman, W.B., Chandrakasan, A.P., Balakrishnan, H.: An application-specific protocol architecture for wireless microsensor networks. IEEE Trans. Wireless Commun. **1**(4), 660–670 (2002)
4. Armbrust, et al.: Above the clouds: a berkeley view of cloud computing. Science (2009)
5. Foster, I., et al.: Cloud computing and grid computing 360-degree compared. IEEE Computer Society (2009)
6. Subashini, S., Kavitha, V.: A survey on security issues in service delivery models of cloud computing. J. Netw. Comput. Appl. **34**(1), 1–11 (2011)
7. Mell, P., Grance, T.: The NIST Definition of Cloud Computing. Special Publication (NIST SP). National Institute of Standards and Technology, Gaithersburg, MD (2011)
8. Tinini, R.I., et al.: 5GPy: a SimPy-based simulator for performance evaluations in 5G hybrid cloud-fog RAN architectures. Simul. Model. Pract. Theory **101**, 102030 (2020)
9. Bonomi, F., Milito, R., Natarajan, P., Zhu, J.: Fog computing: a platform for internet of things and analytics. In: Bessis, N., Dobre, C. (eds.) Big Data and Internet of Things: A Roadmap for Smart Environments. Studies in Computational Intelligence, vol. 546, pp. 169–186. Springer, Cham (2014). https://doi.org/10.1007/978-3-319-05029-4_7
10. Bonomi, F., Milito, R., Zhu, J., Addepalli, S.: Fog computing and its role in the Internet of Things. ACM (2018)
11. Cisico: Cisco global cloud index: forecast and methodology, 2015–2020 (OL) (2015)
12. Ning, Z., Huang, J., Wang, X.: Vehicular fog computing: enabling real-time traffic management for smart cities. IEEE Wirel. Commun. **26**(1), 87–93 (2019)
13. Hinton, G.E., Osindero, S., Teh, Y.W.: A fast learning algorithm for deep belief nets. Neural Comput. **18**(7), 1527–1554 (2014)
14. Pham, X.Q., Huh, E.N.: Towards task scheduling in a cloud-fog computing system. In: 2016 18TH Asia-Pacific Network Operations and Management Symposium (APNOMS) (2016)
15. Li, G.S., et al.: Energy consumption optimization with delay threshold in cloud-fog cooperation computing. IEEE Access **PP**(99), p. 1 (2019)
16. Du, J., et al.: Computation offloading and resource allocation in mixed fog/cloud computing systems with min-max fairness guarantee. IEEE Trans. Commun. **66**(4), 1594–1608 (2018)

Optimization on Service Function Chain Deployment for Cloud Network Collaborative Operation Platform

Xiaoliang Zhang$^{(\boxtimes)}$, Yan Li, Weiliang Li, Jiaqi Duan, Shunming Lv, and Mei Yan

State Grid Corporation, State Grid Information and Telecommunication Branch, Beijing, China

Abstract. With the involvement of Network Function Visualization (NFV), the operation cost of the cloud network collaborative operation platform can be largely abated. Whereas most service function chain (SFC) orchestration methods cannot simultaneously optimize the resource utilization while minimizing the performance of service delay. In this article, a deep reinforcement learning (DRL) based method of SFC deployment based on a cloud network collaborative operation platform is proposed. By optimizing the SFC sequence and the actual amount of resources being allocated, the proposed framework aims to minimize the resource cost while simultaneously to minimize the end to end delay of the SFC deployment. To solve the multi-objective optimization problem (MOP), a deep reinforcement learning (DRL) based framework is further explored. The MOP SFC orchestration problem is first decomposed into a group of subproblems, and each subproblem is modelled as a neural network, wherein an actor-critic algorithm and a modified pointer network are adopted to solve each subproblem. Pareto front optimal solutions can be acquired directly via the trained models. The experimental results show that the proposed method can efficiently and effectively solve the SFC deployment problem and outperform NSGA-II and MOEA/D in the aspect of solution convergence, solution diversity, and computing time. In addition, the trained model can be applied to newly encountered problems without retraining.

Keywords: Deep reinforcement learning · Multi-objective optimization · Service function chain deployment · Cloud network collaborative operation platform

1 Introduction

National strategies, such as Industry 4.0 and Internet+, drive the upgrading of the whole traditional industry, combine with the Internet, and develop towards the direction of intelligence and scale customization. Such intelligent and large-scale industrial upgrading requires massive data to be concentrated in the cloud, driving the whole society into the cloud era. In the cloud era, flexible and dynamic

© Springer Nature Singapore Pte Ltd. 2022
Y. Tian et al. (Eds.): ICBDS 2021, CCIS 1563, pp. 545–559, 2022.
https://doi.org/10.1007/978-981-19-0852-1_43

network resource allocation and efficient resource utilization are required. Traditional telecom networks need to face more complex and changeable differentiated scenarios and break through the traditional rigid vertical segmentation network system and complex and numerous closed network element architecture. Cloud computing and SDN/NFV technologies are emerging at the right time, providing technological driving force for the transformation of telecom networks. Cloud computing fundamentally changes the service delivery mode. Software Defined Networking (SDN) realizes the separation of control and forwarding and the opening of capabilities on top of the control concentration. SDN technology architecture has the characteristic of the control logic, are used to implement a wide area network (WAN) reconstruction, by focusing on SDN controller, WAN network topological collection, centralized routing calculation, the path of global optimization, global optimization and adjustment, the flow of the concentration of business, issued, can well solve the WAN network not controllable, optimization, efficiency is low, Low resource utilization. Network Function Virtualization (NFV) realizes the decoupling of hardware and software and the virtualization of network functions.

Cloud network collaborative operation platform usually refers to the centralized processing, storage, transmission, exchange and management of information in a physical space. With the application of cloud computing, cloud network collaborative operation platform are comprehensively surpassing and replacing the current data center form. Cloud network collaborative operation platform abstracts and transforms various entity resources in data centers, such as server (CPU, memory), network, storage, etc., to break the uncut barriers between entity structures, so that users can use these resources in a better way than the original configuration. A cloud network collaborative operation platform can also be regarded as a collection of cloud host, network, and storage services provided by cloud computing technology.

The traditional network is integrated by hardware and software, to meet new business requirements, there were growing new closed ceaseless overlay network elements to the already complex and on the basis of the rigid network, produced a large number of independent overlay network and business chimney, vertical segmentation of network cost is high, the resources are not Shared function, coordination and integration. These vertically segmented rigid networks composed of closed hardware network elements eventually lead to high construction and operation costs of network, and it is difficult to provide innovative services to compete with Internet providers, which is the root of the "scissors difference" becoming more and more intense. Although the telecom industry also tries to separate control and forwarding in some professional fields, such as GMPLS of bearer network and IMS of core network, it fails to fundamentally break the vertical segmentation and rigid closed system. In the cloud network collaborative operation platform, the basic network is rebuilt based on the cloud. It is expected that the traditional telecom network can also carry out industrial upgrading and break through the traditional rigid network system of vertical segmentation and complex closed network element architecture. SDN/NFV technology provides the driving force for the industrial upgrading of telecommunication network. It breaks the rigid network system and complex closed network elements from the source, reshapes the flexible and open telecommunication network, builds the next generation of network, and brings huge imagination space to the development of future networks.

Network service chaining, also known as service function chaining (SFC), refers to the capability that utilize SDN and NFV technologies to generate a service chain of network services and connect them in a virtual chaining. Although SFC is more adaptive and flexible in terms of design and deployment in the cloud network collaborative operation platform, currently most SFC orchestration methods cannot simultaneously optimize the resource utilization while minimizing the performance of service delay. SFC orchestration constitutes one of the key problems in cloud network collaborative operation platform, which requires determining the deployment sequence and the amount of resources (computing resource, storage resource, networking resource, etc.) when deploying the SFC. In general, the SFC deployment concerns about two aspects: the amount of resources consumed and the end to end delay of the SFC. The former relates to the network resource utilization (i.e., computation, storage, memory and bandwidth), while the latter refers to the quality of service (QoS, e.g., end-to-end delay). Obviously, these two aspects are conflicting with each other because utilizing more resources can normally reduce the end to end delay, which will in turn increases the QoS for the service. Under such a case, the SFC deployment has to consider the aforementioned factors to ensure the QoS while minimizing the consumptions of various resources in the cloud network collaborative operation platform. Such process can be formulated as an multi-objective optimization problem (MOP). A set of trade-off solutions, denoted as Pareto optimal solutions, are hopefully to be obtained for such multi-objective SFC deployment problem. In addition, to ensure the real-time response of the SFC deployment services, SFC deployment has high requirements for the computation time and generalization ability of the solution. Therefore, multi-objective evolutionary algorithms (MOEAs), which have long been deemed as suitable methodologies to handle MOPs, are not suitable for solving the multi-objective SFC deployment problem.

Facing the challenges mentioned above, the vigorous development of artificial intelligence technology in this round brings new opportunities for Cloud network collaborative operation platform. The ability to control data and information is an important ability for digital transformation of operators. With powerful data analysis and information extraction capabilities, artificial intelligence helps operators transform data bonus into information bonus. The industry hopes that through the introduction of artificial intelligence technology, the internal help to solve the communication network currently encountered various efficiency and capacity problems, external flexible and intelligent to provide integrated digital and information services, so that the communication network has "smart brain", and finally realize the intelligent network. In this article, a deep reinforcement learning (DRL) based method is proposed to efficiently solve the multi-objective

SFC deployment problem. The main contributions of our article are shown as follows:

- To promote the overall quality of the SFC orchestration, the SFC deployment problem is modeled as a multi-objective optimization issue. The focus is on minimizing the total resource consumptions and maximizing the QoS (i.e., minimizing the end to end delay) simultaneously.
- A framework for solving the multi-objective SFC deployment problem by DRL is developed, wherein a neighborhood-based parameter-transfer strategy is utilized to increase the training process. To the best of our knowledge, this is the first time that the DRL-based method is adopted to model and solve the SFC deployment problem.
- Simulations are performed to compare the proposed method with different evolutionary algorithms. The results clearly show that the trained model solves the SFC deployment problem efficiently and effectively, and outperforms other algorithms with respect to solution convergence and solution diversity while consuming less running time.

The rest of this article is organized as follows. Literature review on SFC deployment and MOP problem solving is briefly reviewed in Sect. 2. In Sect. 3, we present the system model of multi-objective SFC deployment and corresponding problem formulation. In Sect. 4, we describe the detailed modeling and training process of solving the problem via DRL-based framework. The validity of the method is presented through experimental evaluations in Sect. 5, and finally we conclude the entire paper in Sect. 6.

2 Related Work

Recently, researchers have witnessed the prosperous of the investigations on the VNF placement or the SFC deployment problem considering the service function chaining restrictions. Normally such problem is considered as a resource allocation problem in SDN/NFV systems, which has been proved to be NP-hard [1]. Also note that for large-scale optimization problems, deriving its solution adopting aforementioned traditional optimization algorithms is cumbersome and even computational intractable, hence heuristic methods are normally adopted as an effective alternative with near optimal solutions but small execution time [2,3]. For instance, in reference [4], a formal model for resource allocation of virtualized network functions within NFV environments is presented and evaluated, a problem they refer to as Virtual Network Function Placement is then formulated. The authors consider a hybrid scenario in which part of the services can be provided by dedicated physical hardware, while part of the services are provided adopting virtualized service instances. Another work can be found in [5], where n NFV network model suitable for ISP operations is provided, and the generic VNF chain routing optimization problem defined and formulated as an MILP.

Recently, a DRL-based method has been proposed to deal with MOPs, which exhibits some encouragingly new characteristics compared to MOEAs (e.g., strong generalization ability, fast solving speed, and promising quality of the solutions) [6]. This paper adopted an end-to-end framework to solve MOPs by using DRL. Yang *et al.* [7] employed an federated multi-agent actor-critic reinforcement learning (ACRL) algorithm to handle the age sensitive mobile edge computing.

3 System Model

In this paper, we consider a cloud network collaborative operation platform aiming to schedule of a number of VNFs, as depicted in Fig. 1. Let $N = \{v_1, v_2, \ldots, v_n\}$ denote the set of VNFs distributed in the cloud network collaborative operation platform. The operator needs to find a sequence of n VNFs and the amount of resources (computation, memory, storage and bandwidth) to each VNF to minimize two cost functions (resource consumption and end to end delay) simultaneously. The SFC sequence vector and the resource consumption vector are expressed as $\rho = [\rho_1, \rho_2, \cdots, \rho_k, \cdots]^T$ and $Q = [q_1^{rec}, q_2^{rec}, \cdots, q_k^{rec}, \cdots]^T$, where ρ_j represents the j_{th} VNF target, and q_k^{rec} means the amount of resources that dispatched to the k-th VNF. We use $k = 0$ to refer to the initial deployment, while $k \in \{1, \ldots, n\}$ refers to each VNF.

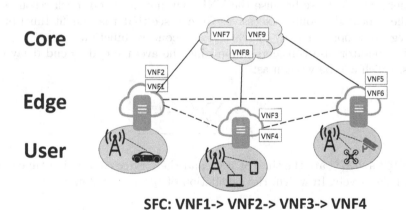

Fig. 1. System descriptions of service function chaining deployment in a cloud network collaborative operation platform.

For each SFC, we have the following constraint:

$$\rho_i \neq \rho_j, \quad \text{if } i \neq j; \ \rho_i \neq 0, \quad \text{and } \rho_i \neq 0, \tag{1}$$

which means that the SFC should not include the same VNF two times. The constraints on minimum and maximum resources allocated are expressed as:

$$0 < q_k^{thre} \leq q_k^{rec} \leq q_k^{ful} - q_k^{ini}. \tag{2}$$

where q_k^{ini} and q_k^{ful} are the resources allocated currently and the maximum amount of resources needed for the k th VNF, respectively. q_k^{thre} represents the minimal amount of resources that k-th VNF demands. In this paper, we assume that each VNF submits a minimal amount of required resources q_k^{thre} rather than the actual amount of required resources. As a result, the actual amount of resources that the k-th VNF will receive is decided by the operator of the cloud network collaborative operation platform, which should be greater than or equal to q_k^{thre} but lower than or equal to $q_k^{ful} - q_k^{ini}$.

The operator first aims at maximizing the average deployment benefits of all VNFs. For the convenience of subsequent presentation, this objective can also be written in the form of cost minimization by expressing as:

$$\min_{Q} f_1 = -\frac{\sum_{k=1}^{N} \log_{q_k^{ful}}\left(\frac{q_k^{ini} + q_k^{rec}}{q_k^{ini}}\right)}{n}, \tag{3}$$

When considering the resource allocation benefit, we introduce the diminishing marginal effect that as the amount of resources increases, the rate of increase in benefit will decrease because the VNF may not need too much resource and find the allocated resource excessive. We can see that the benefit function is a non-negative, monotonically increasing, and concave function.

The operator also considers minimizing the average end to end delay of all VNFs, which can be written as:

$$\min_{\rho,Q} f_2 = \frac{\sum_{k=1}^{N}(t_k^{rec} - t_k^{ini})}{n}, \tag{4}$$

where t_k^{ini} and t_k^{rec} are the time of start and the service completion time of k-th VNF, respectively. In which, the calculation of t_k^{rec} is as follows:

$$t_k^{rec} = t_k^{ini} + \sum_{j=1}^{k} \frac{dist(\rho(j), \rho(j+1))}{v} + \sum_{j=2}^{k} \frac{q_j^{rec}}{\varepsilon}. \tag{5}$$

The end to end delay consists of two parts: the transmission delay and the queuing delay. $dist(\rho(j), \rho(j+1))$ represents the delay between two nodes $\rho(j)$ and $\rho(j+1)$. In this paper, Manhattan distance is utilized to calculate the transmission delay between two nodes. v and ε refer to the transmission bandwidth and the processing rate of the cloud network collaborative operation platform, respectively.

The aim of the multi-objective SFC deployment problem is to determine the VNF sequence and the actual amount of resources allocated to each VNF that maximize the average deployment benefits and minimize the average end to end delay simultaneously subject to the cloud network collaborative operation platform operation constraints, which can be expressed as follows:

$$\min_{\rho,Q} \qquad \mathbf{f} = [f_1, f_2]$$
$$\text{s.t.} \quad (1),(2), \ \rho_1 \in \{0,\cdots,n\}, q_i^{rec} \in \mathbb{R}_0^+. \tag{6}$$

4   The DRL Based Optimization Framework

4.1   The General DRL-Based Framework

Decomposition is a simple but effective way to design the MOP algorithm. Uniformly spread weight vectors $\lambda^1, \cdots, \lambda^M$ is required, where $\lambda^i = (\lambda_1^i, \lambda_2^i)$. Then the original problem is converted into M scalar optimization subproblems, like Eq. (6). After solving each scalar subproblem, the Pareto Front (PF) can be obtained.

The M numbers of optimization subproblems are collaboratively solved via the neighborhood-based parameter transfer scheme, which can increase the training process of neural networks. It is obvious that if the weight vectors of two subproblems are close enough, these two neighboring subproblems will have similar optimal solutions. Thus, the knowledge of one subproblem can help the training process of its neighboring subproblems. Similarly, the network parameters of the i_{th} subproblem can also be utilized for the training of the next subproblem. As a result, the neighborhood-based parameter transfer strategy saves a tremendous amount of time for training the M subproblems. The general framework is presented in Algorithm 1.

4.2   Actor-Critic Based Algorithm

After the SFC orchestration problem is decomposed into a set of subproblems and each subproblem based on the aforementioned framework is solved, each subproblem is solved via the DRL-based framework. In this section, a modified Pointer Network is introduced to model the subproblem, and an Actor-Critic based algorithm is utilized for the training.

First, we introduce the input structure of the neural network. Let the set of input be $X = \{x^1, \cdots, x^N\}$, where N refers to the number of VNFs. Each x^i is represented by a sequence of tuples $\{x_t^i = (s^i, d_t^i)\}$, where s^i and d_t^i are the static and dynamic elements of the input, respectively. It is noteworthy that dynamic elements of each input are allowed to change between the decoding

---

Algorithm 1 The General Framework of DRL-based SFC deployment

---

Initialization: The subproblem model $P = [\omega_{\lambda^i}, b_{\lambda^i}], \forall i = 1, 2, \cdots, M$ weight
    vectors of the problem $\lambda^1, \cdots, \lambda^M$
Output: The optimal model $P = [\omega^*, b^*]$
1: $[\omega_{\lambda^1}, b_{\lambda^1}] \leftarrow Randomly\_Initialized$
2: **for** $i \leftarrow 1 : M$ **do**
3:    **if** $i == 1$ **then**
4:       $[\omega^*_{\lambda^1}, b^*_{\lambda^1}] \leftarrow Actor\_Critic([\omega_{\lambda^1}, b_{\lambda^1}])$
5:    **else**
6:       $[\omega_{\lambda^i}, b_{\lambda^i}] \leftarrow [\omega^*_{\lambda^{i-1}}, b^*_{\lambda^{i-1}}]$
7:       $[\omega^*_{\lambda^i}, b^*_{\lambda^i}] \leftarrow Actor\_Critic([\omega_{\lambda^i}, b_{\lambda^i}])$
8:    **end if**
9: **end for**
10: Return $[\omega^*, b^*]$

---

steps. For example, during the SFC orchestration process, the resource demand
for a VNF becomes 0 after resources allocation, where resources have already
been provided to that VNF. However, the static elements, corresponding to
VNF i's logic location, current resources, and maximum resources needed, do
not change. x_t^i can be viewed as a vector of features that represents the state
of input i at time t. The set of all input states at time t is denoted as X_t. The
output of the model is a permutation of the VNFs $Y = \{\rho_t, t = 0, 1, \cdots, T\}$,
where T refers to the length of decision steps. At every decoding time t, ρ_t
points to one of the VNF, determining the next scheduling target. The process
continues until the termination condition is satisfied when the demand of all
service function chains has been satisfied. This process then generates a variable-
length sequence $Y = \{\rho_t, t = 0, 1, \cdots, T\}$. The reason that the length is variable
is that VNF may further require more resources when necessary. Then decoder
network decodes the code vector to the desired sequence. However, we argue
that the RNN encoder is not necessary because the order of VNF locations
in the input does not affect the outcome. For example, if we swap the order
of two VNFs, the input information should be the same as the original inputs.
Therefore, the embedded layer is utilized to encode the inputs to a vector instead
of an RNN. The method also helps reduce the computational complications
without decreasing the efficiency.

In this paper, the greedy decoder is utilized to select the scheduling target with the largest probability. However, the next visiting target is assigned
according to the sampling from probability distribution during the training process. The proposed model is shown in Fig. 2. In addition to the SFC orchestration
sequence, our model ought to decide the actual amount of resources allocated,
which lies between the minimum amount and maximum amount needed for the
VNF. Assume that the next scheduling target is VNF i. By solving the following optimization problem, the actual amount of resources that VNF i will be
allocated can be determined:

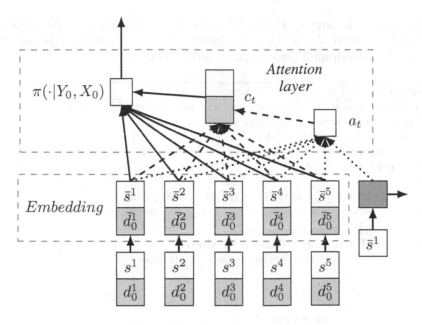

Fig. 2. Neural network model.

$$\max \quad w_1 \cdot \log_{q_i^{ful}}\left(\frac{q_i^{ini}+q_i^{rec}}{q_i^{ini}}\right) - w_2 \cdot \frac{l \cdot q_i^{rec}}{\varepsilon},$$
$$\text{s.t.} \quad q_i^{thre} \le q_i^{rec} \le q_i^{ful} - q_i^{ini}. \tag{7}$$

where w_1 and w_2 refer to the weights of the resources allocation benefit and the end to end delay, respectively. l represents the number of remaining VNFs. $\log_{q_i^{ful}}\left(\frac{q_i^{ini}+q_i^{rec}}{q_i^{ini}}\right)$ denotes the resources allocation benefit of VNF i related to its receiving CPU, memory, and storage resources, and $\frac{l \cdot q_i^{rec}}{\varepsilon}$ represents the overall end to end delay of the remaining VNFs. This is a function that increases first and then decreases. The stagnation point is $s_i = \frac{w_1 \cdot q_i^{ini} \cdot \varepsilon}{w_2 \cdot l \cdot \ln(q_i^{ful})} - q_i^{ini}$. According to s_i, the solution can be obtained as follows:

$$q_i^{rec} = \begin{cases} q_i^{thre}, & \text{if } s_i < q_i^{thre}, \\ s_i, & \text{if } q_i^{ini} \le s_i \le q_i^{ful} - q_i^{ini}, \\ q_i^{ful} - q_i^{ini}, & \text{if } s_i > q_i^{ful}. \end{cases} \tag{8}$$

Encoder encodes the input sequence into a code vector which contains knowledge of the input. Since the attributes of the targets convey no sequential information and the order of targets in the inputs is meaningless, RNN is not necessary to be utilized in the encoder in this work. Therefore, a simple embedding layer is adopted to encode the inputs which decreases the computational compilations without decreasing the efficiency. Different from the encoder, we use RNN to model the decoder network since we need to store the knowledge of previous steps to assist the next VNF. The RNN decoder hidden state can memorize the previously selected VNFs. Then the information combines with the encoding probability. Algorithm 2 presents the training procedure.

Algorithm 2 The Actor-Critic Algorithm
___
Initialization: $\theta, \phi \leftarrow$ initialized parameters given in Algorithm 1
Output: The optimal parameters θ, ϕ
1: **for** $iteration \leftarrow 1, 2, \cdots$ **do**
2:     generate G problem instances from $\{\Phi_{\xi_1}, \cdots, \Phi_{\xi_1}\}$
3:     **for** $k \leftarrow 1, \cdots, T$ **do**
4:         $t \leftarrow 0$
5:         **while** $\phi_{block}^{(\cdot)}$ exists and is not in Γ_i of UE i **do**
6:             select the next VNF ρ_{t+1}^k according to $P(Y|X_0) =$ $\prod_{t=0}^{T} P(\rho_{t+1}|\rho_1, \cdots, \rho_t, X_t)$
7:             **if** next visiting target is EV **then**
8:                 Compute the actual amount of resources q_i^{rec}
9:             **end if**
10:            Update X_t^k to $X_t + 1^k$
11:        **end while**
12:        Compute the reward R^k
13:    **end for**
14:    $d\theta \leftarrow \frac{1}{N}\sum_{k=1}^{N}(R^k - V(X_0^k; \phi))\nabla_\theta \log P(Y^k|X_0^k)$
15:    $d\phi \leftarrow \frac{1}{N}\sum_{k=1}^{N}\nabla_\phi(R^k - V(X_0^k; \phi))^2$
16:    $\theta \leftarrow \theta + \eta d\theta$
17:    $\phi \leftarrow \phi + \eta d\phi$
18: **end for**

The training is conducted in an unsupervised way. The experience instances are generated from distribution $\{\Phi_{\xi_1}, \cdots, \Phi_{\xi_1}\}$. ξ refers to different input features of the VNFs, e.g., the VNFs' locations and its resources demand. G instances are sampled from $\{\Phi_{\xi_1}, \cdots, \Phi_{\xi_1}\}$ for training the actor and critic networks with parameters θ and ϕ, respectively. For each instance, the actor network produces the permutation of VNFs and the reward with the current parameter θ. Then policy gradient approaches use an estimate of the gradient of the expected return to improve the policy in Line 16 iteratively. By reducing the difference between the observed rewards and the approximated rewards, the critic network is updated in line 17 of Algorithm 2.

5   Performance Evaluation and Analysis

In this section, we compare our framework with solutions obtained from classical MOEAs, including NSGA-II and MOEA/D. The effects of different training sizes are also evaluated.

5.1   Parameters and Settings

The evaluation environment is set as a cloud network collaborative operation platform composing of 100 nodes in the evaluation. In each physical node, various kinds of resources for VNFs (such as computation, bandwidth, memory, and storage) are provided. Such resources have various sizes and are utilized to instantiate, transmit and process data. In order to practice the complexity and changeability of a real deployment scenario. Considering the fact that the user's services and the function of VNF instance are variational, each SFC request consists of 3–5 VNFs in series.

5.2   Results and Discussions

We first compare the performance of all the comparison algorithms in terms of end-to-end delay and recourses consumed (i.e., the PFs), as depicted in Fig. 3. All the comparison algorithms show a great ability of convergence. We may easily observe that the solutions created by the proposed method perform much better than those of evolutional algorithms. NSGA-II and MOEA/D show a better ability to obtain a better service function chain, reflected from some subproblems with high weight on end to end delay. However, the large number of iterations cannot lead to a better performance of resources allocation benefits.

As shown in Fig. 3(a) and Fig. 3(b), a hugh number of iterations can lead to less resources allocation benefits in some subproblems. In addition, the large number of iterations will increase the amount of computing time. The computing times of NSGA-II of 500, 1000, 2000, and 4000 iterations are 3.47, 5.98, 11.56, and 23.74 s, and the computing times of MOEA/D of 500, 1000, 2000, and 4000 iterations are 16.87, 30.47, 60.28, and 119.45 s, respectively. In contrast, our method requires only 3.17 s from loading the model to achieve the results.

Overall, the experimental results show that the proposed DRL based method on solving the bi-objective SFC deployment problem is effective. Note that, the obtained model has already studied how to select the next VNF with the given information of VNFs, system status and previous choice. In contrast, NSGA-II and MOEA/D fail to converge by increasing the number of iterations.

We further evaluate the performance of our method on 20-VNF instances. The model is still trained on 10-VNF instances, and it is utilized to approximate the PF of the 20-VNFs instance. The results in Fig. 3(c) and Fig. 3(d) show that DRL significantly outperforms other algorithms. There is an significant gap in performance between DRL and two MOEAs of different iterations.

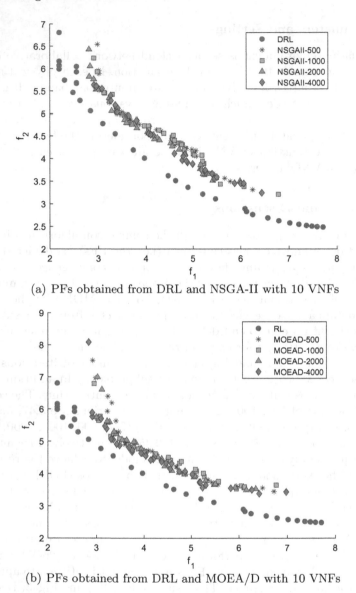

(a) PFs obtained from DRL and NSGA-II with 10 VNFs

(b) PFs obtained from DRL and MOEA/D with 10 VNFs

Fig. 3. A randomly generated 10-VNF bi-objective SFC deployment problem instance: the PF obtained using our method (trained using 10-VNF instances) in comparison with NSGA-II and MOEA/D of 500, 1000, 2000, and 4000 iterations.

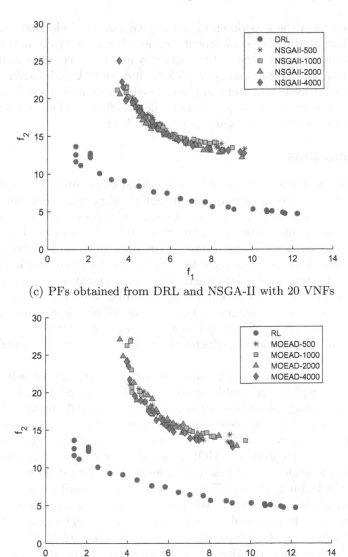

(c) PFs obtained from DRL and NSGA-II with 20 VNFs

(d) PFs obtained from DRL and MOEA/D with 20 VNFs

Fig. 3. (*continued*)

In addition, the running time of DRL is still much lower than those of two MOEAs for 20-VNF instances. It takes 5.88 s for DRL to achieve the PF. However, it requires 3.68, 7.19, 14.25, and 27.90 s for NSGA-II for running 500, 1000, 2000, and 4000 iterations, respectively. The computing time of MOEA/D is even higher, which takes 16.10, 34.11, 68.57, and 137.32 s to reach an acceptable level of convergence.

Observed from the experimental results, we can conclude that our method is able to handle the SFC deployment problem both effectively and efficiently. A better balance between the end to end delay and resources allocation benefits is guaranteed when compared to NSGA-II and MOEAs. Moreover, once the trained model is available, it can apply to newly encountered problems without retraining. In other words, its performance is less affected when confronted with different system circumstances and numbers of VNF's.

6   Conclusions

The Internet of Things, software-defined/virtualization and 5G are important landmarks for the development of the current cloud network collaborative operation platform. The implementation of each technology will bring significant changes to the current network architecture and technology, and at the same time, will bring great challenges to the design, operation and maintenance of the network. Network architecture reconfiguration provides the network with strong flexibility and brings new multi-dimensional management and control complexity. For example, virtual network interact with physical network, manage the life cycle of virtual network, generate a large number of new logical interfaces, and locate faults more easily. This requires a new mode of development, operation, and maintenance coordination, which largely offsets the benefits brought by this mode.

Under such background, this paper provided a new way of solving multi-objective SFC deployment problems adopting the proposed DRL-based framework. By controlling the orchestration sequence and actual amount of resources allocated, the aim of the orchestration scheduling was to minimize the end to end delay of SFC and maximize the resource allocation benefit of VNFs simultaneously. First, we decomposed the MOP into a set of scalar optimization subproblems, wherein a neighborhood-based parameter transfer strategy was adopted to accelerate the training process. Then an actor-critic algorithm and a modified pointer network were adopted to solve each subproblem. Experimental results demonstrate that the proposed method solves the SFC deployment problem efficiently and effectively, as well as outperforms NSGA-II and MOEA/D in terms of solution convergence, solution diversity, and computing time. These results, as we believe, shall provide useful insights helping the deployment of SFCs in the cloud network collaborative operation platform.

Acknowledgement. This work is supported by Science and Technology Project from State Grid Information and Telecommunication Branch of China: Research on Key Technologies of Operation Oriented Cloud Network Integration Platform (52993920002P).

References

1. Mehraghdam, S., Keller, M., Karl, H.: Specifying and placing chains of virtual network functions. In: 2014 IEEE 3rd International Conference on Cloud Networking (CloudNet), pp. 7–13 (2014)

2. Khebbache, S., Hadji, M., Zeghlache, D.: Scalable and cost-efficient algorithms for VNF chaining and placement problem. In: 2017 20th Conference on Innovations in Clouds, Internet and Networks (ICIN), pp. 92–99 (2017)
3. Sang, Y., Ji, B., Gupta, G.R., Du, X., Ye, L.: Provably efficient algorithms for joint placement and allocation of virtual network functions. In: IEEE INFOCOM 2017 - IEEE Conference on Computer Communications, pp. 1–9 (2017)
4. Moens, H., Turck, F.D.: VNF-P: a model for efficient placement of virtualized network functions. In: 10th International Conference on Network and Service Management (CNSM) and Workshop, pp. 418–423 (2014)
5. Addis, B., Belabed, D., Bouet, M., Secci, S.: Virtual network functions placement and routing optimization. In: 2015 IEEE 4th International Conference on Cloud Networking (CloudNet), pp. 171–177 (2015)
6. Li, K., Zhang, T., Wang, R.: Deep reinforcement learning for multiobjective optimization. IEEE Trans. Cybern., 1–12 (2020)
7. Zhu, Z., Wan, S., Fan, P., Letaief, K.B.: Federated multi-agent actor-critic learning for age sensitive mobile edge computing. IEEE Internet Things J., 1 (2021)

Artificial Intelligence/Machine Learning Security

Using Multi-criteria Evaluation of E-learning System: A Methodology Based on Learning Outcomes

Randa Aljably[1]([✉]) and Salah Hammami[2]

[1] Computer Department, College of Science and Human Studies, Shaqra University, Shaqraa, Kingdom of Saudi Arabia
`raljebly@su.edu.sa`
[2] Computer Science Department, King Saud University, Riyadh, Kingdom of Saudi Arabia
`shammami@ksu.edu.sa`

Abstract. Academic research on E-learning system has been widely influenced by COVID-19 pandemic. As evaluating online learning can directly promote the design of more effective learning environments. As evaluating E-learning systems while considering factors such as system content, pedagogical issues, adaptation, learning agents and learning outcomes dimensions can be considered as a complex multi-criteria decision making problem. This paper presents a methodology to support researchers and practitioners in a effectively adopting analytical techniques such as Analytic hierarchy process, Entropy Method, and the Criteria Importance through Inter-criteria Correlation in E-learning evaluation. The paper experiments with multiple learning scenarios and the results provide various alternatives for decision making.

1 Introduction

When the education in the world was affected by the COVID-19 pandemic. The shift to digital environments was the solution to continue the teaching and learning processes. The transition was carried out by complete dependency through the learning management system (LMS), blended E-Learning or Traditional blackboard Teaching-Learning with E-Learning [1].

However, these systems have yet to prove their success in engaging users a quality learning process by providing necessary information in a timely and effective way [2, 3] with respect to pedagogical, learning and adaptation dimensions [4]. To address the evaluation necessity of E-learning systems, this current study attempts to present a systematic and analytical approach to evaluation criteria using analytic hierarchy process (AHP) [5, 6], entropy method (EM) [7], the criteria importance through inter-criteria correlation (CRITIC) [8] and simple derivation weighting (SDW) [9, 10] on the proposed evaluation criteria. The present research is undertaken to accomplish two major objectives, namely:

1. To develop and implement an evaluation model that enables making decisions based on indicators with respect to pedagogical, adaptive, student and course learning outcomes dimensions in a multiple criteria perspective.

© Springer Nature Singapore Pte Ltd. 2022
Y. Tian et al. (Eds.): ICBDS 2021, CCIS 1563, pp. 563–574, 2022.
https://doi.org/10.1007/978-981-19-0852-1_44

2. To generalize the proposed model to be applied under three different scenarios reflecting worse and better conditions of system functionality, student behavior and learning outcomes (LO) to evaluate the impacts of proposed alternatives under different conditions.

This paper is organized as follows. Section 2 presents the previous research in literature on evaluating E-Learning. Section 3 discuss the presented methodology, Next, Sect. 4 experimental setup and results, while a discussion of the findings are presented in Sect. 5. Finally, Sect. 6 concludes the present study.

2 State of the Art of Evaluating E-learning

E-learning systems are multidisciplinary by nature. Many researchers from fields such as computer science, information systems, psychology, education, and educational technology, have been trying to evaluate E-learning systems. There has been a good recognition for the evaluation process even if it's still in its early stages and has dealt only with partial components, each evaluation project or research had its own justification and reasoning. The main categories of the literature are:

Learning during COVID-19 has influence many experts to evaluate the performance of E-learning tools and websites. In [11] the MCDM integration with linguistic hesitant fuzzy sets to evaluate and select the best E-learning website for network teaching. The results indicate that MCDM can be practical and effective when used for website selection under vague and uncertain linguistic environment.

The researchers in [5] employed the analytic hierarchy process (AHP) with group decision-making (GDM) and Fuzzy AHP (FAHP) to study the diversified factors from different dimensions of the web-based E-learning system. The MCDM approach produced realistic results in categorizing each dimension and critical success factors of the E-learning system. This categorization was intended as a decision tool for stakeholders' resources.

On the other hand, when MCDM was used in [12] for problem structuring, it was brought down by weak inter- and strong intra- connection between criteria. And highly affected by criteria definition and the number of criteria in each cluster (cluster size). Another factor that plays a great role in using MCDM is scale selection [13]. In statistical methods and AHP ranking of indicators using a scale of rating [0 to 100], where the higher the rating indicates the higher the performance of the approach under the evaluation criteria.

3 Proposed Methodology

The methodology starts with defining system evaluation criteria and generating alternatives that relate system capabilities to goal. It then follows with evaluating all alternatives in terms of criteria. After applying multi-criteria analysis method. A selection is made on one alternative as optimal. This process iterates until reaching better multi-criteria optimization. So to start with the first step in the research experts and decision makers definition of evaluation criteria we selected the list described in Table 1.

Table 1. The hierarchal structure for evaluation

Dimensions	Level	Criteria
Student Learning Outcomes	Knowledge	C01.Ease of knowledge appliance.
	Thinking skills	C02.Capability of problem definition and analysis.
	Psychomotor	C03.Capability of conducting computer based system design and implementation
		C04.Ease of functioning within teams.
	Community Relationships / Ethics	C05.Perception of ethical and legal responsibilities.
	Generic Learning skills	C06. Ease of communication with teachers.
	Subject content	C07.Undersandment of computing impact.
		C08.Recognition for continuous professional development importance.
		C09. Ability to apply technologies in new context.
Course Learning outcome		C10.Usage of testing strategies.
		C11.Capability of producing soft ware requirements.
System content		C12. Providence of appropriate learning material.
		C13.Suffecient content.
		C14.Latest content.
Pedagogical issues		C15.Fleaxibility of learning.
		C16.Providance of experience to learner.
		C17.Connection between knowledge and realty.
Adaptation	Learning Styles / Motivation	C18.Capability of recording learner's performance.
		C19.Capability of providing gaudiness to learner.
		C20.Capability of controlling learner's progress.
System agents		C21.Privacy of usage and performance.
		C22.Intelctual response to search / Recommending Agents

After defining the criteria, we represent the criteria as scenario indicators which are obtained either from computer simulation models or model results. The model outputs the priority and performance of alternatives under proposed criteria scenario. This study delineates the best alternative on the basis of three different multi-criteria decision making (MCDM) methods, including simple additive weighting (SAW) [9] and compromise programming (CP) [14]. Each method is also applied with a set of criteria weights that represent objective judgments represented by expert's reviews as well as subjective preferences of decision makers.

As for the methodology for calculating criteria values, we suggest that each criterion is specified with a range of values starting from a lower threshold to an upper threshold and measured in a finite amount of time. In this paper the range of the criteria is selected between [0.0–2.0] representing the lower and upper thresholds respectively, in certain conditions these values may be fixed to a specific number to serve better judgment. As for criteria weights, we use AHP [5, 6] as an elicitation technique as one way, the other involves assigning performance scores to each alternative in performance matrix.

In order to derive the preference structure and performance matrix we used analytic hierarchy process (AHP) [5, 6], entropy method (EM) [7], the criteria importance through inter-criteria correlation (CRITIC) [8] and simple additive weighting (SAW)[9]. We choose AHP because of its superiority in performing judgment and scales over others [14]. Using the performance matrix (PM) where the columns correspond to criteria (C1, C2.., Cm) and rows correspond to alternatives (A1, A2, ... An), with the entries (a_{ij}) being the indicators for all alternatives across all criteria. Once the matrix is set up, the next step for the decision process is to define the weights $(w_1, w_2, ...,w_m)$ of the criteria. The value of each alternative or solution will be calculated according to the value n Eq. (1), where A_i represents the suggested alternative or in our case system or solution and where A_{ij}, d_{ik} denotes the performance value of the ith system under criteria j and dimension k respectively.

$$A_i = \sum_{k=1}^{p} d_{ik} = \sum_{j=1}^{n} A_{ij} W_j \qquad (1)$$

When defining weights of Criteria's, these weights in MCDM do not have a clear economic significance, but their use provides the opportunity to model the preference structure. That is why they are assigned by decision makers (DM) using importance weights which represent the relative importance of criteria [15].

In evaluating the current system against the criteria; we will use rating-based and ranking-based methods [16]. Rating-based involves rating an alternative under each dimension then calculating the sum of its weighted performance under each criterion to give it an overall weight with which it will compete with other alternatives [19]. While in ranking-based the alternatives will be pair wise compared with respect to each criterion or dimension to derive normalized relative priorities of each alternative. The overall priority of each alternative and their rankings can then be used as the basis for selection. To apply this on our proposed system, it should be assessed against criteria or dimensions. For each criterion, if its performance value is less than the pre-defined threshold then it indicates that this is an area which needs improvement. However, if there so many areas, then the priority will be given to the area with the greatest weighted distance from perfection, defined by:

$$WDP = CW \, (DW) * (\text{Perfect score} - \text{Performance score}) \tag{2}$$

Where WDP: weighted distance from perfection; CW: criteria weight; DW; Dimension weight.

We depict our implementation for AHP in the following Table 2.

Table 2. Algorithm 1. Procedure of analytic hierarchy process

Algorithm 1. *Procedure of Analytic Hierarchy Process*

This procedure computes the performance evaluation under reference scenario.
 Input:
 C: Criteria Matrix of size n.
 A: Alternative Matrix, of size m.
 Output:
 W: Weights Matrix.
 For each criterion $c \in C$, learn comparison matrix P according to expert reviews or DM.
     -Compute its eigenvector V, repeat steps until difference between successive solutions is less than a predefined threshold.
     -Raise P to powers that are successively square,
     -Obtain N matrix after calculating rows sum of P.
     -Normalize N.
 For on each $c_i \in C$ $(i = 1,2, ... n)$ *learn* $a_j \in A(j1,2, ... m)$, Obtain R_i $(m \times m)$ by calculating pair-wise comparisons of each a_j according to c_i.
 For each R_i compute its eigenvector $E_{j \, ,(j=1,....n)}$.
 Obtain W by Multiplying E $\times$ V.

The next step in the experimental setup is defining the management alternatives as seen in Table 3. The first alternative A01, aims to enhance the educational process and the E-learning performance by adding positive modifications to courses, these modifications are determined after an assessment process for each course to determine its weakness points. Alternative A02 assumes that the deletion of a course is more appropriate as there is no use of modifying it, or that its participation in system performance is significantly poor, this is usually followed by a suggestion for another replacement of the deleted course.

Another alternative similar to A01 is A03, assuming modifications or cancelation A04 are determined and applied to system learning agents to enhance their productivity and there by boost the systems performance, modifications may include change of platform, addition in functionalities, these actions are automated unless necessary.

Alternative A05 is designed and applied to provide an indicator to the decision makers of wither the student or course LO have been written correctly, or need additional revision, sometimes the regression in performance is caused by wrongly written LO which could not by achieved.

If the value for Alternatives A05 or A06 is high, this will be an indicator that improvements are not only necessary for LO but also to course and agents respectively.

Table 3. The alternative matrix

Alternative	Description
A00. Do nothing	No changes are made to the system
A01. Modify Course	Modify course in order to enhance performance
A02. Cancel Course	Replace course with one higher in performance
A03. Modify Agent	Modify Agent in order to enhance performance
A04. Cancel Agent	Replace Agent with one higher in performance
A05. Modify learning outcome (LO)	Enhancing LO in favor of achievement
A06. (A01 + A05)	Improving the course joined by modifying LO
A07. (A03 + A05)	Modify Agent joined by modifying LO

As for the reference scenarios, we based the scenarios on changing factors affecting the E-learning system such as changes in learning outcomes, since it had direct effect on our system and was initially the goal of evaluation. The simulation of evaluation methods is run to identify the impact of changing learning outcomes on our system.

The values that are entered into the performance matrix were obtained by:

A. Pair wise comparison, where it's the responsibility of the decision makers (DM) or experts to make such a comparison between each criterion and the others usually based on their formal or informal judgment.
B. Random distribution of values until a satisfactory state or result is reached.

The first scenario is based on increased demand on the system to fulfill the LOs. The second scenario represents the best conditions containing random values in the range [0.0–2.0] assigned to criteria and alternatives assuming the focus on preserving the current LO achievements with respect to an increase in available agents, content, and courses. Meanwhile the decrease in these mentioned factors were projected in the third scenario represented.

4 Experimenral Results

We start with the performance matrix (PM) for each scenario, containing 6 dimensions versus 8 alternatives, thereby we have 3 matrices shown in Table 4 for the three scenarios.

In scenario (1) the feasible alternatives could by arranged where the top alternatives are A03, A04, A07 these alternatives focus on agents' modification or removal to enhance performance, followed by A01, A05, A06 which focus on modifying course and LO. As for A00 and A02, they were not feasible enough to overcome the domination of other alternatives as their values were slightly less that all others, This indicates that the top alternatives deserve deeper analysis. The same holds for scenarios (2) and (3).

Table 4. Performance matrix for different reference scenarios

Performance matrix for scenario1					
Alternatives	SLO	CLO	Adaptation	Pedagogical issues	System content	System agents
A0	0.56	0.19	0.68	0.19	0.30	0.69
A1	0.68	0.24	0.63	0.25	0.35	0.73
A2	0.55	0.19	0.69	0.16	0.29	0.72
A3	1.88	0.43	0.56	0.17	0.42	0.73
A4	0.80	0.34	0.36	0.15	0.36	0.56
A5	1.72	0.26	0.64	0.12	0.34	0.75
A6	0.89	0.49	0.57	0.18	0.42	0.74
A7	0.81	0.40	0.62	0.19	0.36	0.73
Performance matrix for senario2					
Dimensions	SLO	CLO	Adaptation	Pedagogical issues	System content	System agents
A0	0.66	0.29	0.78	0.29	0.4	0.79
A1	0.78	0.34	0.73	0.35	0.45	0.83
A2	0.65	0.29	0.79	0.26	0.39	0.82
A3	1.98	0.59	0.66	0.27	0.52	0.85
A4	0.9	0.54	0.46	0.25	0.46	0.66
A5	0.82	0.36	0.74	1.22	0.44	0.85
A6	0.99	0.53	0.67	0.28	0.52	0.84

(continued)

Table 4. (*continued*)

Performance matrix for senario2

Dimensions	SLO	CLO	Adaptation	Pedagogical issues	System content	System agents
A7	0.91	0.5	0.72	0.29	0.46	0.83

Performance matrix for senario3

Dimensions	SLO	CLO	Adaptation	Pedagogical issues	System content	System agents
A0	0.46	0.09	0.58	0.09	0.20	0.59
A1	0.72	0.16	0.54	0.02	0.28	0.63
A2	0.45	0.09	0.46	0.06	0.29	0.62
A3	1.78	0.39	0.59	0.07	0.32	0.65
A4	0.58	0.14	0.53	0.15	0.25	0.63
A5	0.70	0.24	0.26	1.05	0.26	0.46
A6	0.79	0.33	0.47	0.08	0.32	0.64
A7	0.71	0.30	0.52	0.09	0.26	0.63

The next step is calculating the criteria weights according to the methods explained before which are: Analytical Hierarchy Process (AHP), Entropy Method (EM), Inter-criteria Correlation (CRITIC) and simple derivation weighting (SDW).These objective weights are displayed in Table 5. The objective weights ranked the most important criteria to assess the alternatives performance as the SLO, Pedagogical issues, CLO in Scenario (1) but this was changed in Scenarios (2) and (3) as the pedagogical issues gained more importance than SLO, followed by CLO, after these come the adaptation criteria in all scenarios.

Table 5. Criteria weights obtained by weighting methods.

Dimensions	Student learning outcomes	Course learning outcome	Adaptation	Pedagogical issues	System content	System agents
Wight matrix for scenario 1						
Entropy method	**0.860**	**0.425**	−0.228	**0.054**	−0.021	−0.091
CIRTIC method	**0.515**	**0.214**	0.085	**0.116**	0.040	0.028
SDW method	**0.350**	**0.240**	0.118	**0.143**	0.089	0.058

(continued)

Table 5. (*continued*)

Dimensions	Student learning outcomes	Course learning outcome	Adaptation	Pedagogical issues	System content	System agents
Wight matrix for scenario 2						
Entropy method	**0.460**	**0.287**	−0.159	**0.485**	−0.013	−0.060
CIRTIC method	**0.170**	**0.083**	0.040	**0.666**	0.022	0.016
SDW method	**0.235**	**0.150**	0.079	**0.437**	0.055	0.041
Wight matrix for scenario 3						
Entropy method	**0.224**	**0.132**	0.030	**0.455**	0.037	0.119
CIRTIC method	**0.082**	**0.073**	0.031	**0.783**	0.016	0.013
SDW method	**0.169**	**0.161**	0.065	**0.527**	0.044	0.031

These criteria were considered important, while the others like system agents or system content were not considered to have a significant role in the decision making process as their scores are less divertive. The sum of these 3 criteria weights derived by the CIRTIC method and SDW ranges from [0.73–0.92] for all scenarios, with one interesting remark was that the pedagogical issues criteria gained importance as the scenarios moves towards better and worst values like in scenario (2) and (3).

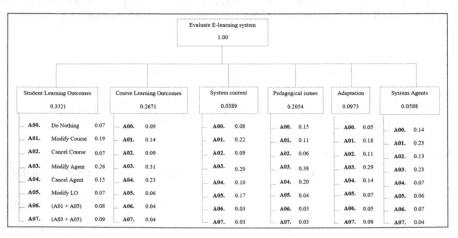

Fig. 1. Results obtained from analytic hierarchy process.

The results collected from the AHP method is illustrated in Fig. 1. The number of performed pair-wise comparisons between the criteria $(6*(6-1)/2 = 15)$ and the alternatives are evaluated against each criterion to determine those who are not considered important in the objective weighting methods. With respect to the preference judgments of DMs who gave priority to environmental effects, SLO were considered to have strong importance over CLO, and demonstrated importance over pedagogical issues.

As for ranking the alternatives according to the distance methods, which calculate the Euclidean distance demonstrated by compromise programming (CP), and simple additive method (SAW). The alternative rankings summarized in Table 6 were as follows:

In Scenario (1), using EM, CIRTIC, SDW; A03, A05 and A06 were given the highest ranking amongst all other alternatives for all methods used. Following are alternatives A07, A04 and A01 while the worst were A00, and A02.

Table 6. Alternatives ranks from different MCDMs.

	SAW-EM	SAW_CRITIC	SAW_SDW	CP_EM	CP_CRITIC	CP_SDW
Ranking for Scenario1						
A00	7	7	7	7	7	7
A01	6	6	6	6	6	6
A02	8	8	8	8	8	8
A03	1	1	1	1	1	1
A04	4	5	5	4	5	5
A05	2	2	2	2	2	2
A06	3	3	3	3	3	3
A07	5	4	4	5	4	4
Ranking for Scenario2						
A00	7	7	7	7	7	7
A01	6	4	5	6	4	5
A02	8	8	8	8	8	8
A03	1	2	2	1	2	2
A04	4	6	6	4	6	6
A05	2	1	1	2	1	1
A06	3	3	3	3	3	3
A07	5	5	4	5	5	4
Ranking for Scenario3						
A00	7	6	6	7	6	6
A01	6	7	7	6	7	7

(continued)

Table 6. (*continued*)

	SAW-EM	SAW_CRITIC	SAW_SDW	CP_EM	CP_CRITIC	CP _SDW
A02	8	8	8	8	8	8
A03	2	2	2	2	2	2
A04	5	3	5	5	3	5
A05	1	1	1	1	1	1
A06	3	4	3	3	4	3
A07	4	5	4	4	5	4

As for AHP the alternatives were arranged according to Table 7 as follow; Alternatives A04, A03 and A01 were giving greater importance according to the DM who were concerned with outcomes criteria in a scenario aimed at enhancing the educational process, the alternatives modifying the agent was most preferable since it will cost less and provide better results than the others. The interesting thing is that when modifying the LO was not preferred by the DM, all alternatives including this choice were given low values and were placed on bottom of the list.

Table 7. Ranking of alternatives using AHP

Alternative	Weight
A00. Do nothing	0.0943
A01. **Modify Course**	**0.1628**
A02. Cancel Course	0.0815
A03. **Modify Agent**	**0.3003**
A04. **Cancel Agent**	**0.1740**
A05. Modify learning outcome (LO)	0.0645
A06. (A01 + A05)	0.0536
A07. (A03 + A05)	0.0581

5   Discussions and Findings

It has become quite important to develop evaluation methods for E-learning systems and be applicable with changing policies and environmental constrains. It is also necessary to focus this evaluation process on systems including their learning agents of all types and layers, in a form of simulator capable of handling all kind of scenarios and producing accurate results to DM, this is an important step in improving such systems.

Considering all presented scenarios, the alternative of modifying system agents was elected as most efficient management alternative followed by combining it with modifications to LOs. By that it would be possible to solve problems vastly if implemented immediately and recover from failure to improve current performance.

Traditional measures such as canceling a course or agents aren't considered efficient for enhancing the learning process and insuring learners' achievement of LOs. All the MCDM methods priorities the alternatives in a similar arrangement, there by the decision that is deduced from any method will be relatively similar to the other. With minor difference based on the method chosen and major difference on the weights assigned to the criteria.

The EM, CIRTIC, AHP, SDW methods can prove reliable in making use of all the information contained in row data, thereby considered reasonable ways in criteria weighting, and guaranteed to produce robust and fair decisions.

6 Conclusion

The success of E-Learning is highly depending upon adaptation and fulfillment of teaching objectives. The factors affecting the E-Learning systems success are many therefore it is essential to evaluate them so that the stakeholders, such as educational authority, students, and instructors, will be able to control the negative effects of each of these E-Learning factors and their dimensions in an effective manner. The Multi criteria decision making (MSDM) approach presented in this paper could prove successful in prioritizing each of the pedagogical, learning and adaptation s dimension according to a presented evaluation criterion. This categorization of factors will help stakeholders in ensuring the continuous improvement in E-learning systems and the design of more effective learning environments.

References

1. Mohammed, H.J., Mat Kasim, M., Mohd Shaharanee, I.N.: Evaluation of e-learning approaches using AHPTOPSIS technique. J. Telecommun. Electron. Comput. Eng. **10**(1–10), 7–10 (2018)
2. Mulla, Z.D., Osland-Paton, V., Rodriguez, M.A., Vazquez, E., Plavsic, S.K.: Novel coronavirus, novel faculty development programs: rapid transition to eLearning during the pandemic. J. Perinat. Med. **48**(5), 446–449 (2020)
3. Barteit, S., Guzek, D., Jahn, A., Bärnighausen, T., Jorge, M.M., Neuhann, F.: Evaluation of e-learning for medical education in low-and middle-income countries: a systematic review. Comput. Educ. **145**, 103726 (2020)
4. Supriyatno, T., Susilawati, S., Ahdi, H.: E-learning development in improving students' critical thinking ability. Cypriot J. Educ. Sci. **15**(5), 1099–1106 (2020)
5. Naveed, Q.N., et al.: Evaluating critical success factors in implementing E-learning system using multi-criteria decision-making. PLoS ONE **15**(5), e0231465 (2020)
6. Taherdoost, H.: Decision making using the analytic hierarchy process (AHP); A step by step approach. Int. J. Econ. Manag. Syst. **2** (2017)
7. Luo, L., et al.: Blended learning with Moodle in medical statistics: an assessment of knowledge, attitudes and practices relating to E-learning. BMC Med. Educ. **17**(1), 1–8 (2017)

8. Abdelkader, E.M.: A hybrid decision support system for holistic evaluation of material alternatives. Int. J. Strateg. Decis. Sci. (IJSDS) **12**(1), 18–36 (2021)
9. Wang, Y.J.: A fuzzy multi-criteria decision-making model based on simple additive weighting method and relative preference relation. Appl. Soft Comput. **30**, 412–420 (2015)
10. Sreelatha, K., Anand Raj, P.: Ranking of CMIP5-based global climate models using standard performance metrics for Telangana region in the southern part of India. ISH J. Hydraul. Eng. **27**, 1–10 (2019)
11. Gong, J.W., Liu, H.C., You, X.Y., Yin, L.: An integrated multi-criteria decision making approach with linguistic hesitant fuzzy sets for E-learning website evaluation and selection. Appl. Soft Comput. **102**, 107118 (2021)
12. Kadin, N., Reɗep, N.B., Divjak, B.: Structuring E-learning multi-criteria decision making problems. In: 2017 40th International Convention on Information and Communication Technology, Electronics and Microelectronics (MIPRO), pp. 705–710. IEEE (2017)
13. Rahmani, F., Ahmadi, H., Ghanbari, E., Khorasani Kiasari, S.M.: Evaluate and ranking the affecting factors in developing E-learning in higher education with fuzzy multi-criteria decision-making approach. Technol. Educ. J. (TEJ) **13**(2), 284–298 (2019)
14. Srinivasa Raju, K., Sonali, P., Nagesh Kumar, D.: Ranking of CMIP5-based global climate models for India using compromise programming. Theoret. Appl. Climatol. **128**(3–4), 563–574 (2016). https://doi.org/10.1007/s00704-015-1721-6
15. Koksalmis, E., Kabak, Ö.: Deriving decision makers' weights in group decision making: an overview of objective methods. Inf. Fusion **49**, 146–160 (2019)
16. Song, Y., Gui, Y., Gehringer, E.F.: An exploratory study of reliability of ranking vs. rating in peer assessment. Int. J. Educ. Pedag. Sci. **11**(10), 2405–240 (2017)

Application of Machine Learning Algorithm in Art Field – Taking Oil Painting as an Example

Kun Huang and Jianlong Jiang(✉)

Anhui Xinhua University, Anhui 230088, China

Abstract. Oil painting production is a very time-consuming task. This article uses the current generation confrontation network popular in machine learning to transfer the style of images, and directly convert real-world images into high-quality oil paintings. In view of the current popular AnimeGAN and CartoonGAN generative confrontation networks, there are problems such as serious loss of details and color distortion in image migration. In this paper, by introducing SE-Residual Block (squeeze excitation residual block), comic face detection mechanism and optimizing the loss function, a new BicycleGAN is proposed to solve the problem of serious loss of details in the AnimeGAN migration image. By adding DSConv (distributed offset convolution), SceneryGAN is proposed to speed up the training speed and eliminate the ambiguous pixel blocks in the CartoonGAN migration image. The experimental results show that compared with AnimeGAN and CartoonGAN, the method in this paper has a significant improvement in training speed, comic image generation quality, and image local realism.

Keywords: Image style transfer · Generative confrontation network · AnimeGAN · CartoonGAN

1 Introduction

With the gradual improvement of people's living standards, there are higher requirements for the living environment. Both residential environment, office environment and public space have the desire of common aesthetic needs. People pay more and more attention to decorating the environment with paintings, especially decorating the home environment with Western world famous paintings. However, it is impossible for world-famous paintings to enter ordinary families. Whether copying or creating an ordinary oil painting, the price is not only high, but also may not make people satisfied and recognized, not to mention low-grade and vulgar paintings. Therefore, simulating world famous paintings is an ideal choice for people.

At present, image wind migration based on deep learning has achieved relatively good results, so deep learning has become a common method of image-to-image conversion [1]. This method is based on the style learning of the Fengli image, and applies the learned style to the input content image to generate a new Fengli image that combines the content of the content image and the Fengli image. These methods mainly use the

Y. Tian et al. (Eds.): ICBDS 2021, CCIS 1563, pp. 575–583, 2022.
https://doi.org/10.1007/978-981-19-0852-1_45

correlation between the depth features and based on the optimization method to encode the visual wind of the image.

In 2016, Gatys et al. took the lead in using deep learning to propose the Neural Style method. The method mainly simulates the processing method of human vision, combined with training multi-layer convolutional neural network (CNN), so that the computer can distinguish and learn the artistic style. So as to use the original image to make the original image full of artistic sense [2]. The method achieves the purpose of wind migration very well, but the migration effect is relatively rigid and content distortion occurs and the generation speed is slow. Therefore, Johnson et al. improved the method proposed by Gatys et al. in 2016. Johnson et al. proposed the Fast Neural Style method, which can generate a transferred art image in a very short time after training a wind model. But this method only improves the speed of generation but still does not significantly improve the quality of image generation [3]. In 2017, Luan et al. strengthened the improvement on the basis of Gatys's work and controlled the details of the wind migration [4]. At the same time, Li. C et al. used the Markov random field model and the trained DCNN network The combined algorithm greatly reduces the inaccurate feature transfer to retain the specific features of the original image [5]. However, no matter how the method is changed, the image generated by the method simply stays in a simple texture transformation and cannot essentially highlight the unique wind and wind characteristics.

Although deep learning is the main method of image wind transfer at this stage, it is similar to the Image Style Transfer Using Convolutional Neural Network (Image Style Transfer Using Convolutional Neural Network) proposed by Gatys et al. in 2016 CVPR. This method is The image texture and image are merged through convolutional neural network to achieve the effect of wind migration, but this is not enough for anime images. The lines of anime characters and the layering of characters and scenes need to be highlighted in anime images. But this method is very difficult to achieve.

GAN (Adversarial Generative Network) is one of the latest methods at this stage [6]. First, the GAN framework is mainly composed of a generator and a discriminator. The generator inputs the generated image into the discriminator to deceive the discriminator, so as to achieve the effect of fitting the real image to the lines and textures of the animation image, so that it will not lose the original image. The content can generate animation images at the same time. Secondly, the parameter update of the GAN generation network comes from the backpropagation of the discriminator rather than the data sample. This can greatly reduce the parameter storage, thereby reducing the memory requirements. In view of the above reasons, this article chooses to use GAN for image wind migration.

In order to solve the shortcomings of existing work. This paper first introduces a Squeeze-Excitation-Residual-Block (squeeze excitation residual-block) and comic face detection mechanism that can realize the channel attention mechanism, and proposes a new ExpressionGAN, and redefines the fusion content loss, counter loss and color The loss function of reconstruction loss and other factors solves the problem of serious loss of face details and color distortion in AnimeGAN. Then, by adding DSConv (distributed offset convolution), a new SceneryGAN is proposed, which speeds up the original training speed and eliminates the ambiguous pixel blocks in the transferred image generated by CartoonGAN.

The convolution method optimizes the problem that the boundary of the Deeplabv3 + generated image is too obvious during fusion. Finally, a new local realism oil painting style migration model that combines ExpressionGAN and optimized Deeplabv3 + is separately processed and fused with the original image characters and environment. The experimental results show that compared with AnimeGAN and CartoonGAN, the method in this paper has a significant improvement in training speed, oil painting image generation quality and image local realism.

2 Method

In this part, we will introduce each part of the proposed method in detail.

2.1 Channel Attention Mechanism

The SE-Residual-Block used in this paper adds SE-Module (squeeze excitation module) to the residual block to realize the channel attention mechanism [7, 8]. Regardless of whether it is a residual block or an inverted residual block, each channel is treated equally, and the importance of each channel is not distinguished. This makes some less useful information affect important feature information, and at the same time there is a phenomenon that important information is lost in violent screening. SE-Module (squeeze excitation module) is equivalent to adding a recalibration mechanism to the network during feature extraction. Through this mechanism, the network can learn and use global information to assign different weights to each channel to achieve selection The effect of sexually emphasizing important feature information and suppressing less useful feature information.

SE-Module specific process introduction:

Input data X through convolution kernel V = {V1, V2, ..., Vc} perform convolution operation Get U = {U1, U2, ..., Uc}. The specific formula of F_{tr} is as Eq. (1);

$$U_c = V_c * X = \sum_{s=1}^{c} V_c^s * X^s \tag{1}$$

Since U_c is obtained by convolution of each V_c, each convolution kernel is equivalent to obtaining information through the local receptive field, so the information obtained by U has limitations. So we hope to compress the global information into a channel descriptor. Therefore, global average pooling in global pooling is used to generate channel statistics. The specific formula for global average pooling is as shown in Eq. (2):

$$z_c = F_{sq}(U_c) = \frac{1}{H * W} \sum_{i=1}^{H} \sum_{j=1}^{W} U_c(i,j) \tag{2}$$

Obtain C z-values through the Squeeze part, and input the C z-values into the Excitation part, which is the $1 \times 1 \times C$ input in the figure. Global average pooling extracts the global channel information, and then enters the information into the excitation section.

2.2 Excitation Section

The excitation part uses the global channel information obtained in the squeeze operation to fully capture the dependencies between channels. It is required that this part can learn the nonlinear interaction between channels in the network, so a simple gating system is adopted. The specific formula is as Eq. (3):

$$s = F_{ex}(z, W) = \sigma(g(z, W)) = \sigma(W_2 \delta(W_1 z)) \tag{3}$$

Where δ is the Relu activation function, σ is the Sigmoid function, and W1 and W2 are the weights used for dimensionality reduction and dimensionality increase of the two fully connected layers respectively. In this paper, W1 = C/16, W2 = C. After the first FC layer is reduced by W1, it is activated by Relu and then restored to the original dimension through W2 of the second FC layer, and then the value learned through the Sigmoid function is normalized and the value is taken from 0 to 1 Between, and finally multiply the normalized value to the original feature U, the formula is as Eq. (4):

$$X_c = F_{scale}(U_c, S_c) = U_c \cdot S_c \tag{4}$$

Among them, X_c is the weighted output of U_c, S_c is the weight on U_c obtained by the incentive part, and V_c is the C-th feature map obtained by convolution.

Pass the channel information into the learning of the Excitation part of the fully connected layer through the Squeeze part, and then recalibrate the original feature map U, thereby increasing the weight of important channel information while reducing the weight of less useful feature channels.

The structure in Fig. 1 is mainly divided into a discriminator and a generator. In the generator and the discriminator, 'k' is the size of the convolution kernel (kernel), 'n' is the number of feature maps, and 's' is Stride. The generator input is a real image, and the discriminator input is a real image. The generator generates an image, an animation image, an animation grayscale image, an animation image that is delineated, and an animation grayscale image is delineated.

The original image input generator first filters the random images in the data set through the face detection mechanism and inputs the detected face images to the generation network. The BicycleGAN generator can be regarded as a codec network, which is mainly composed of standard volumes. Product, depth separable convolution, squeeze excitation residual block (SE-Residual Block), up-sampling and down-sampling modules. The last convolutional layer uses the tanh nonlinear activation function instead of the normalization layer. In the discriminator, the oil painting face detection mechanism proposed in this paper is added. Through this mechanism, the oil painting face is detected on the oil painting image randomly selected from the video, and the picture with the detected oil painting face is selected into the identification network, which is equivalent to the oil painting Image data has been preprocessed, which can further improve the pertinence of network training.

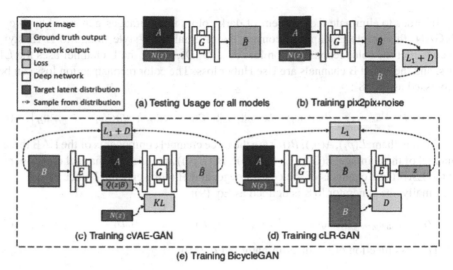

Fig. 1. Bicycle GAN Network structure diagram

2.3 BicycleGAN Loss Function

Bicycle GAN loss function is defined as Eq. (5):

$$L(G, D) = \omega_{adv}L_{adv}(G, D) + \omega_{con}L_{con}(G, D) + \omega_{gra}L_{gra}(G, D) + \omega_{col}L_{col}(G, D) \tag{5}$$

Among them, G stands for generator, D stands for discriminator. $L_{adv}(G, D)$ and $L_{con}(G, D)$ represent adversarial loss and content loss. $L_{gra}(G, D)$ is the gray-scale resistance loss of comic style on the texture and line of the generated image. $L_{col}(G, D)$ is to restore the gray-scale image to construct the color reconstruction loss. w_{adv}, w_{con}, w_{gra}, w_{col} are the weights of each loss function.

The real picture data in this article is defined as $S_{data}(p) = \{p_i | i = 1, 2, ..., N\}$, the oil painting picture data is defined as $S_{data}(a) = \{a_i | i = 1, 2, ..., M\}$, the grayscale image is defined as $S_{data}(x) = \{x_i | i = 1, 2, ..., M\}$, the de-lined oil painting image is $S_{data}(e) = \{e_i | i = 1, 2, ..., M\}$, and the de-lined grayscale image is defined as $S_{data}(y) = \{y_i | i = 1, 2, ..., M\}$.

Among them, the gray-scale anti-loss is specifically as Eq. (6):

$$L_{gra}(G, D) = E_{p_i \sim S_{data(p)}}, E_{x_i \sim S_{data(x)}} \left[||Gram(VGG(p_i)) - Gram(VGG(x_i))||_1 \right] \tag{6}$$

Where Gram represents the Gram matrix of the feature. p_i means the input picture, $G(p_i)$ means the generated picture, $VGG(x_i)$ means the input feature map of the first layer in VGG.

The specific definition of content loss is as Eq. (7):

$$L_{con}(G, D) = E_{p_i \sim S_{data(p)}} \left[||VGG_l(p_i) - VGG_l(G(p_i))||_1 \right] \tag{7}$$

Among them, $VGG_l()$ is the feature map of the first layer of VGG, p_i means the input picture, and $G(p_i)$ means the generated picture is the input data. Both gray-scale confrontation loss and content loss are calculated using L1 sparse regularization.

In order to eliminate the problem of dark colors in the images generated by Bicy-cleGAN, this article attempts to convert the original YUV-style image to LAB-style to construct the color reconstruction loss $L_{con}(G, D)$, where the L channel uses the L1 loss, and the A and B channels are Use Huber loss. The color reconstruction loss can be expressed as Eq. (8):

$$L_{col}(G, D) = E_{p_i \sim S_{data(p)}} \left[|||L(G(p_i)) - L(p_i))||_1 + ||A(G(p_i) \quad c)||_H + ||B(G(p_i) - B(p_i))||_H \right] \quad (8)$$

Among them, $L(p_i), A(p_i), B(p_i)$ are the three channel components of the LAB three-channel of the p_i image, $L(G(p_i)), A(G(p_i)), B(G(p_i))$ are the three channel components of the LAB three channels of the $G(p_i)$ image, and H represents the Huber loss.

Finally, the generator loss is defined as Eq. (9):

$$L(G) = w_{adv} E_{p_i \sim S_{data}} \left[(G(p_i) - 1)^2 \right] + w_{con} L_{con}(G, D) + w_{gra} L_{gra}(G, D) + w_{col} L_{col}(G, D) \quad (9)$$

The loss function of the discriminator is Eq. (10):

$$L(D) = w_{adv} E_{a_i \sim S_{data(a)}} \left[(D(a_i) - 1)^2 \right] + E_{p_i \sim S_{data(p)}} \left[(D(G(p_i)))^2 \right]$$
$$+ E_{x_i \sim S_{data(x)}} \left[(D(G(x_i)))^2 \right] + E_{y_i \sim S_{data(y)}} \left[(D(G(y_i)))^2 \right] \quad (10)$$

SceneryGAN is composed of two convolutional neural networks: one generator G is used to convert real-world pictures into comic pictures; the other is a discriminator, which uses the discriminator used by CartoonGAN. SceneryGAN introduces DSConv (distributed offset convolution) based on the CartoonGAN generator to replace the standard convolution in the original generator. The specific structure of SceneryGAN is shown in Fig. 2.

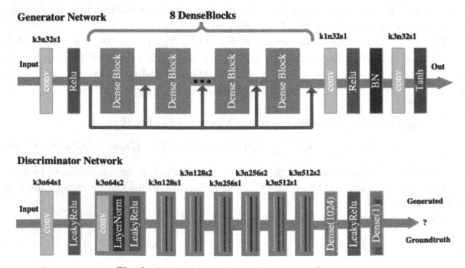

Fig. 2. SceneryGAN Network structure diagram

3 Experiment

In this paper, we uses Pytorch to implement BicycleGAN, SceneryGAN, animation face detection and image edge optimization. The experimental model obtained in the experiment can be provided to other people for subsequent work to make changes. Since the two network models of BicycleGAN and SceneryGAN do not need to match the images in the data set one by one, the data set can be selected by the author according to different comic artists. At the same time, because the animation face detection designed in this paper has high versatility, the requirements for the animation image data set can be further reduced. In order to better compare the images transferred from BicycleGAN, SceneryGAN, and local winds with the latest technology, this article introduces training and test data in Sect. 3.1. In Sect. 3.2, the experimental results after the modification are compared with the previous AnimeGAN and CartoonGAN experimental results. In Sect. 3.3, the optimized local wind migration image is displayed to show the picture effect of the overall model.

3.1 Data Set Introduction

The training data contains real images and cartoon images, and the test images only contain real images. In order to better show the network effect of the changes in this article, the experiment extended the dataset selected by CartoonGAN and AnimeGAN. In BicycleGAN, 6656 256 × 256 real images and 5890 images are used for training and 776 images are used for testing. Among the 6153 real images downloaded from the Flickr website in SceneryGAN, 5402 are used for training and the rest are used for testing. BicycleGAN and SceneryGAN use the same manga image data set. The data set comes from the three animation movies of Hayao Miyazaki and Makoto Shinkai's Spirited Away, Your Name, and The Wind. They are captured by random frame interception. After intercepting, 4,573 and 4,212 animation images of the works of the two artists were obtained.

The photos in Table 1 are 150 real images and 150 real images are generated by BicycleGANand AnimeGAN respectively. Divided into 3 groups with 50 images in each group, the average of 50 similarities in each round was calculated by comparing the transferred image and the real image one by one. From the similarity, it can be seen that due to the restoration of BicycleGAN's facial texture, it has a significant improvement in the characteristics of realistic comics compared to AnimeGAN.

Table 1. BicycleGAN and AnimeGAN Contrast the authenticity of the migration image

Network	Photos	First	Second	Third
AnimeGAN	50	48.13%	46.52%	50.67%
BicycleGAN	50	64.21%	67.17%	58.45%

From the experiment, it is found that CartoonGAN retains the important details of real pictures relatively well during the wind migration, and has a more realistic and good performance in the landscape migration, which meets the current realistic cartoon wind and wind scene needs. However, during the training process, it is found that the effect generated by CartoonGAN will have some unstable pixel blocks, and the training speed is relatively slow, so this article introduces distributed offset convolution (DSConv) in CartoonGAN to obtain SceneryGAN. The original CartoonGAN and SceneryGAN were trained for 200 rounds, and it was found that the speed has been greatly improved and the phenomenon of garbled characters in the generated pictures has been solved. The specific comparison is shown in Table 2 and Fig. 3.

Table 2. Comparison of training times between CartoonGAN and SceneryGAN

Network	Number of epoch	Rounds	Datasets	Single training time	Total training time
CartoonGAN	200	200	Same	0.814 s	22.61 h
SceneryGAN	200	200	Same	0.397 s	12.81 h

Fig.3. SceneryGAN and CartoonGAN Contrast figure

4 Conclusion

This paper is based on BicycleGAN and Scenery GAN, and proposes a new local realism oil painting model, combining BicycleGAN and SceneryGAN to the model to realize local wind migration. Expression GAN's improvements to AnimeGAN are as follows: (1) BicycleGAN. Change the Inverted-Residual-Block in AnimeGAN to Squeeze-and-Excitation-Residual Block. (2). BicycleGAN changes the loss function proposed by AnimeGAN to convert the YUV channel input used in the original text to the LAB channel input. (3). BicycleGAN adds a comic face detection mechanism to the generator and discriminator in the AnimeGAN network. Through the above method, the problem of the loss of facial features of the characters in the pictures generated by AnimeGAN and the problem of dark generated pictures are well improved. The proposed SceneryGAN is modified for CartoonGAN as follows: replace the standard convolution block (Conv) in the original network with a depth separable convolution (DSConv). Through the improvement, the training speed of CartoonGAN is greatly accelerated and the problem of unstable pixel blocks in the generated image during the training process is eliminated.

Acknowledgements. Perspective and Anatomy (Excellent offline course project of Teaching Quality Project of Anhui Education Department, Item number: 2019kfkc160).

References

1. Chen, H., Zhang, G., Chen, G., Zhou, Q.: Research progress of image style transfer based on deep learning. In: Computer Engineering and Applications. Conference 2016. LNCS, vol. 9999, pp. 1–13. Springer, Heidelberg (2016)
2. Gatys, L.A., Ecker, A.S., Bethge, M.: Image style transfer using convolutional neural networks. In: Proceedings of the IEEE Conference on Computer Vision and Pattern Recognition, pp. 2414–2423 (2016)
3. Johnson, J., Alahi, A., Fei-Fei, L.: Perceptual losses for real-time style transfer and super-resolution. In: Leibe, B., Matas, J., Sebe, N., Welling, M. (eds.) ECCV 2016. LNCS, vol. 9906, pp. 694–711. Springer, Cham (2016). https://doi.org/10.1007/978-3-319-46475-6_43
4. Luan, F., Paris, S., Shechtman, E., et al.: Deep photo style transfer. In: Proceedings of the IEEE Conference on Computer Vision and Pattern Recognition, pp. 4990–4998 (2017)
5. Li, C., Wand, M.: Combining Markov random fields and convolutional neural networks for image synthesis. In: Proceedings of the IEEE Conference on Computer Vision and Pattern Recognition, pp. 2479–2486 (2016)
6. Creswell, A., White, T., Dumoulin, V., et al.: Generative adversarial networks: an overview. IEEE Signal Process. Mag. **35**(1), 53–65 (2018)
7. Chen, J., Liu, G., Chen, X.: AnimeGAN: a novel lightweight GAN for photo animation. In: Li, K., Li, W., Wang, H., Liu, Y. (eds.) ISICA 2019. CCIS, vol. 1205, pp. 242–256. Springer, Singapore (2020). https://doi.org/10.1007/978-981-15-5577-0_18
8. Hu, J., Shen, L., Sun, G.: Squeeze-and-excitation networks. In: Proceedings of the IEEE Conference on Computer Vision and Pattern Recognition, pp. 7132–7141 (2018)

Based on Data Mining New Energy Medium - and Long - Term Electricity Market Trading Power Decomposition Strategy

Shuwei Zhang$^{(\boxtimes)}$, Xinghua Yang, Benran Hu, Yongjia Wang, and Huiqi Zhang

State Grid Heilongjiang Electric Power Co., Ltd., Harbin 150090, Heilongjiang Province, China
3474884018@qq.com

Abstract. With the development of China's electricity market reform, electricity transaction is still the main form of mid - and long-term market transaction. Reasonable long-term electricity decomposition strategy can not only guarantee the stable operation of the power system, but also realize the effective connection with the spot market. Aiming at the uncertainty of wind power generation, this paper proposes an optimization decomposition strategy of new energy medium and long term transaction electricity based on wind power fluctuation depth clustering. Firstly, from the perspective of data mining, deep clustering was used to identify wind power fluctuation and construct annual wind power output curve. Secondly, establish the coordination and optimization scheme to meet the medium and long term transaction electricity of new energy; Then, with the principle of preferential consumption of new energy and economic optimization as the goal, the new energy medium and long term transaction electricity optimization decomposition model is established. Finally, an example is given to analyze the power decomposition model proposed in this paper, and the results verify the execution of the decomposition strategy.

Keywords: Medium - and long-term transactions · Deep clustering · New energy consumption · Optimal decomposition

1 Introduction

With the continuous development of economy and industrialization, energy crisis and environmental pollution have become a severe test for China's sustainable development strategy. In the context of China's low-carbon development strategy, in order to effectively solve the problem of further environmental deterioration, a high proportion of renewable new energy represented by wind power has attracted national attention and been rapidly developed, and the proportion of new energy generation will continue to increase in the future. According to the statistics released by GWEC, China's wind power installed capacity accounts for one-third of the world's wind power installed capacity [1]. In 2020, the state formulated relevant policies to further regulate medium and long term market transactions in electricity, and adopted market-oriented transaction measures to

Project Supported by State Grid Heilongjiang Electric Power Co., Ltd.

promote the demand of new energy consumption. At present, the medium and long term electricity market in China's provinces mainly deals with thermal power, supplemented by new energy. The transaction electricity is decomposed gradually to generate planned generation curve on a multi-stage time scale of "year-month-day" [2].

At present, the domestic power grid mainly uses the traditional thermal power unit according to the unit capacity or load proportion distribution to complete the electricity decomposition, but the above decomposition principle is not applicable to wind power. As the uncertainty of wind power has an impact on system operation, when a high proportion of new energy participates in medium and long-term market electricity transaction with a certain scale, the phenomenon of power abandonment will occur in wind power, which leads to the difficulty of connecting decomposition results with daily dispatching and brings losses to the power grid and electricity selling companies. Therefore, in order to ensure the power balance of the power system, it is necessary to improve the accuracy of wind power generation prediction and optimize the decomposition of the generating capacity of new energy and thermal power units in the medium and long term power market transaction has become one of the important problems to be solved in the development of the power market.

Many foreign scholars have a large number of mature studies on promoting wind power consumption and wind power optimal scheduling in the power market. Ref. [3] applies demand side response to the system and establishes a multi-objective optimization model with the lowest cost and minimum air abandonment volume to improve the wind power absorption capacity of the system. Ref. [4] mainly studies the wind power heating system in China, establishes the joint scheduling optimization model of wind-heat system, and improves the utilization rate of wind power. In addition, many scholars have studied the decomposition of medium - and long-term contract electricity. Ref. [5] establishes a multi-objective model according to the priority principle of market transaction, and uses multi-objective programming method to solve it. For hydropower, Ref. [6] proposes a long-term power contract decomposition strategy considering water volume matching constraint to effectively realize the connection with the spot market. Most of the above mentioned units are optimized with economic optimization as the goal, so as to improve the utilization rate of wind power, but the coordination and optimization scheduling problem between wind power and conventional units is not considered.

Therefore, in order to improve the accuracy of wind power prediction, this paper applies the idea of deep clustering to the construction of time series of wind power output, and proposes an optimization decomposition strategy of medium and long-term transaction electricity of new energy based on the deep clustering of wind power fluctuations. Firstly, SOM neural network deep clustering is used to identify wind power fluctuations, build annual wind power output curve, and coordinate and optimize the decomposition of medium and long term transaction electricity of new energy. Secondly, taking the principle of preferential consumption of new energy and economic optimization as the goal, and considering the constraints of unit maintenance, the optimization decomposition model of medium and long term transaction electric quantity of new energy is established to achieve the accurate decomposition of annual transaction electric quantity of new energy. Finally, by using the basic data of IEEE30 node standard test system, the analysis results verify the effectiveness and execution of the decomposition strategy proposed in this paper.

2   Optimization and Decomposition Strategy of Wind Power Transaction Quantity Based on SOM Clustering

2.1   Wind Power Wave Identification Method Based on SOM Clustering

Data clustering is a basic problem in machine learning, pattern recognition, computer vision, data compression and other fields. The purpose of clustering is to divide similar data in the original data into a class cluster based on some similarity measures (such as Euclidean distance). Due to the development of deep learning, deep neural network can transform the original data of wind power fluctuations into a representation more suitable for clustering due to its highly nonlinear characteristics.

Wind power fluctuation process is used to describe the randomness and volatility of wind power, self-organizing Map (SOM) clustering algorithm is used to identify the wind power fluctuation category [7, 8], and the wind power fluctuation is divided into three categories: small fluctuation, medium fluctuation and large fluctuation.

SOM is an unsupervised clustering algorithm based on competitive learning by simulating the signal processing function of human brain. It can map similar sample points in high dimensional space to neighboring neurons in the network output layer and maintain the topology of input samples [9, 10]. The SOM network structure is shown in Fig. 1, consisting of two layers of neurons, input layer and output layer. The number of input layer neurons is determined by the number of features, and each feature has one input layer neuron. The output layer neurons are arranged in matrix or hexagon in two-dimensional space, and the arrangement structure of neurons determines the performance of the whole network. After the network determines the output winning neuron, it determines the position of the input vector in low dimensional space [11, 12].

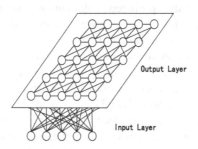

Fig. 1. SOM network structure

The specific learning algorithm process of SOM includes the following steps:

1. Network initialization, normalized input vectors and weights. Samples equal to the number of neurons were randomly selected as the initial weights. The weight vector corresponding to the output neuron is expressed as w_{ij};

2. Iterative training. Let the set of adjacent neurons of j output neurons at time t be $S_j(t)$, and define the maximum training length. In the iterative process, the Euclidean distance of weight vector between input sample and each neuron is calculated;

$$dj(t) = \sqrt{\sum_{i=1}^{n} (xi - wij(t))^2} \tag{1}$$

3. Look for winning neurons. Select the minimum value of all $d_j(t)$, and the output node k with the smallest distance from the sample is taken as the competitive winning neuron, namely, the most matching unit of the input sample. The winning neuron is denoted as N_k^*;

$$\|x - N_k^*\| = \min_i \{\|x - Ni\|\} \tag{2}$$

4. Update the network and re-normalize the processing. Update the neuron set $S_j(t)$ in the topological domain of the most matched node K, and normalize the weight after learning again;

$$w_{ij}(t+1) = w_{ij}(t) + \eta(t)h_{ki}(t)[x_i(t) - w_{ij}(t)] \tag{3}$$

Where, $\eta(t)$ is the learning rate at step t, and $h_{ki}(t)$ is the neighborhood function of k.

5. If the maximum training length is not reached, continue training from step 2.

2.2 Wind Power Output Time Series Modeling

Since wind power output is seasonal, natural months are divided into high, medium and low output months according to the fluctuation characteristics of wind power output obtained in Sect. 2.1. The probability characteristics of all kinds of fluctuations and the transfer probability among all kinds of fluctuations were counted respectively, and the wind power fluctuation categories and statistical parameters were sampled sequentially by month to obtain the simulated time series of wind power output. The specific steps are as follows:

1. The SOM neural network was used to cluster the natural months. According to the duration of large, medium and small fluctuations, a year was divided into three categories: low output months, medium output months and high output months;
2. The transfer probability of wind power fluctuation among three categories in three months was calculated. Markov chain was used to simulate the class conversion in wind power fluctuation process, and the parameters of fitting function of large, medium and small fluctuations were calculated according to month category, and the multi-dimensional distribution of continuous points between wave peaks was established;

3. Sampling is conducted in monthly order, with sequential sampling fluctuation categories. Based on the probability distribution of wind power output trend sequence obtained in Step 2, the sequence of simulated wind power output trend was obtained by sequential random sampling;
4. Connect the simulated wind power output time series of 12 months in sequence, that is, get the output time series of the whole year.

2.3 New Energy Monthly Transaction Preliminary Distribution

According to the transaction situation of theoretical new energy electricity and load electricity consumption in the medium and long term power market, the load electricity proportion and the mean value of theoretical wind power electricity proportion are considered as the proportion of wind power distribution, and the annual transaction electricity of wind power is roughly divided into monthly. According to Sect. 2.2, the theoretical initial value of monthly wind power transaction volume was obtained by accumulating the theoretical power of wind power time by time, and the monthly electricity distribution was updated on a rolling basis. Suppose that the corresponding annual transaction electric quantity from the 1st month to the $(M-1)$st month has been completed, then the algorithm for the initial value of monthly transaction electric quantity of wind power in the M-th month is as follows:

$$\gamma_F(M) = \frac{Q_F^*(M)}{\sum\limits_{m=M}^{12} Q_F^*(m)} \tag{4}$$

$$\gamma_L(M) = \frac{Q_L(M)}{\sum\limits_{m=M}^{12} Q_L(m)} \tag{5}$$

$$Q_c(M) = \min\{\frac{\gamma_F(M) + \gamma_L(M)}{2}(Q_F - \sum\limits_{m=1}^{M-1} Q_R(m)), Q_F^*(M)\} \tag{6}$$

Where: Q_F^* is the theoretical electric quantity of wind power in month M; $\gamma_F(M)$ is the proportion of theoretical wind power quantity in the M month to the sum of wind power quantity from the M month to the end of the year; $Q_L(m)$ is the load electric quantity in the M month; $\gamma_L(M)$ is the proportion of the load electricity of the m month to the sum of the load electricity of the M month to the end of the year; $Q_c(M)$ is the optimized initial value of monthly wind power trading quantity in month M, and its value should not exceed the theoretical wind power quantity in month M, i.e. $Q_F^*(M)$. Q_F represents the annual trading quantity of wind power; $Q_R(m)$ represents the transaction quantity of wind power that has been executed in the m month.

3   New Energy Medium - and Long-Term Trading Power Coordination and Optimization Decomposition Model

3.1   Objective Function

Based on the long-term contract research projects and wind power precision decomposition, consider unit maintenance plan optimization and new energy given priority principle, on the premise of guarantee the unit to complete the contract quantity, reduces the maintenance cost, reasonable arrangement of unit overhaul period of time, and rich in wind resources, reduce the air volume.

The objective function of the decomposition model of electricity quantity coordination optimization in wind power market is composed of two parts. The specific expression of the objective function is Formula (7)–Formula (10). The first part is the unit maintenance cost. This paper comprehensively considers the seasonal distribution characteristics of wind power to make the unit output more stable and efficient while ensuring economic optimization.

$$f_1 = \min \sum_{t=1}^{T} \left[\sum_{i=1}^{N_F} (1 - \mu_F)W_F + \sum_{i=1}^{N_C} (1 - \mu_C)W_C \right] v(i, t) \tag{7}$$

In the above equation, μ_F and μ_C are the maintenance state of wind turbine and thermal power unit respectively; N_F and N_C are the number of stroke power units and thermal power units in the system; $v(i, t)$ is the unit maintenance cost; W_F and W_C are the maximum generating capacity of wind turbine and thermal power unit respectively; T is the planned cycle.

The second part is the minimum deviation of thermal power plant electric quantity completion schedule, which embodies the "three public" scheduling principle.

$$f_2 = \min \sum_{i=1}^{R} (\xi - \xi')^2 \tag{8}$$

$$\xi = \frac{\sum_{t=1}^{j} \mu_C q_C}{\sum_{t=1}^{j} E_i} \frac{\sum_{t=1}^{T} E_i}{W_C} \tag{9}$$

$$\zeta' = \frac{1}{R} \sum_{i=1}^{R} \xi \tag{10}$$

Where, ξ is the progress coefficient of thermal power plant i, namely, the ratio between the utilization rate of the maximum generating capacity of thermal power plant i in the first j time units and the utilization rate of the maximum generating capacity of the power plant in the whole effective period; ξ' is the average progress coefficient of all thermal power plants within time period t; W_C is annual contract electricity of thermal power plant i; R is the number of thermal power plants; E_i is the maximum on-grid electricity of thermal power plant i within time period t.

3.2 Constraint

1. Contract power balance constraints

$$\sum_{t=1}^{T} \mu_n q_n = Q_{ni} \tag{11}$$

Q_{ni} is the annual contract electric quantity of unit I of the power plant.

2. Upper and lower limits of generating set output

$$P_{ni,t}^{\min} \le P_{ni,t} \le P_{ni,t}^{\max} \tag{12}$$

P_{ni} is the power plan of generator set i at t, $P_{ni,t}^{\max}$ and $P_{ni,t}^{\min}$ is the upper limit and lower limit of output of generator set i at t, and is a given constant.

3. Unit maintenance plan constraints

When the unit maintenance time unit is day,

$$d_{i,j} = \begin{cases} 0, j \in [t_s, t_e] \\ 1, j \notin [t_s, t_e] \end{cases} \tag{13}$$

$$d_{i,t} = d_{i,j} \tag{14}$$

$d_{i,j}$ is the operating state of unit i on day j, operation rule $d_{i,j} = 1$ and maintenance rule $d_{i,j} = 0$; t_s and t_e indicate the maintenance start and end days of unit i respectively.

4. Upper and lower limits of line power flow:

$$P_{l\,\min} \le P_l \le P_{l\,\max} \tag{15}$$

$P_{l\,\max}$ and $P_{l\,\min}$ are the maximum and minimum transmission capacity limits of the line l respectively.

3.3 Solve the Problem

The above multi-objective model can be normalized by objective function, as shown in Eq. (16), to eliminate the influence of dimension on the solution of order of magnitude. Then call CPLEX solver to solve, can get the daily trading plan electricity decomposition result.

$$f_i'(x) = \frac{f_i(x) - f_{i,\min}(x')}{f_{i,\max}(x') - f_{i,\min}(x')} \tag{16}$$

4 Methods the Framework

Based on the wind power output curve modeling and long-term transaction electricity quantity decomposition model described in Sect. 1, 2 and 3, the overall process of contract optimization decomposition strategy is shown in Fig. 2, which can be summarized as the following steps:

Step 1: The construction of wind power output curve. SOM neural network clustering is used to identify wind power fluctuations and generate annual output time series. Based on monthly sequential sampling of wind power fluctuation categories, the simulated wind power output curve was constructed.

Step 2: The calculated mean of the proportion of theoretical transaction electricity of wind power and the proportion of load electricity are used as the distribution proportion, and the long-term transaction electricity of wind power is coordinated and optimized as shown in Formula (4)–Formula (6).

Step 3: Solve the result of contract decomposition. In combination with the objective function of Eqs. (7)–(10) and the constraint conditions of Eqs. (11)–(15), the optimization decomposition model of medium and long-term transaction electric quantity of new energy is established considering the constraints of unit maintenance to achieve accurate decomposition of annual transaction electric quantity of new energy.

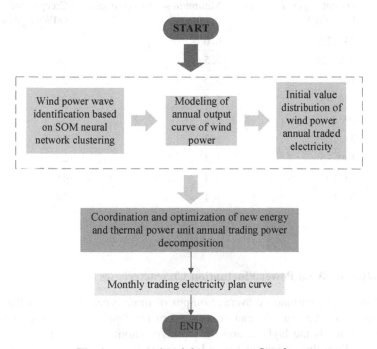

Fig. 2. Contract breakdown strategy flowchart

It is one of the key links to coordinate the connection between annual transaction electric quantity and spot market to decompose the contract electric quantity of new energy to daily. The decomposition algorithm fully considers the optimization of unit maintenance plan and can fairly ensure that the unit can meet the load demand by using its operation characteristics as much as possible. At the same time, the principle of preferential consumption of new energy is considered to reduce the amount of abandoned air, which reflects the rationality of the electricity decomposition strategy in this paper.

5 Example Analysis

5.1 The Boundary Conditions

In this paper, an example analysis is carried out based on the power grid of a city in a province, including 10 thermal power units and 1 typhoon power unit (installed capacity of 500 MW). The thermal power unit data is the data in the IEEE39 node system, as shown in Table 1.

Table 1. Power unit output parameters

Number	Output upper and lower limits/MW	Minimum start-stop time/h	Creep speed $(MW \cdot (15\ min)^{-1})$
1	450, 200	6, 6	50
2	450, 150	5, 5	50
3	165, 50	5, 5	25
4	130, 45	5, 5	20
5	80, 20	3, 3	15
6	55, 10	3, 3	15
7	130, 25	1, 1	20
8	55, 10	1, 1	15
9	55, 10	1, 1	20
10	85, 35	3, 3	15

5.2 Analysis of Wind Power Fluctuation Characteristics

Figure 3 shows the normalized average output of three types of different fluctuations in each month of the year. As can be seen from the figure, the average output with large fluctuations is the highest, and the average output is around 0.5. The average output of medium fluctuation fluctuates between 0.2 and 0.4, and the average output of small fluctuation is the lowest, about 0.1. It can be seen from the figure that wind power fluctuation output is closely related to weather, and different fluctuation categories correspond to different weather, which verifies the rationality of wind power fluctuation category identification.

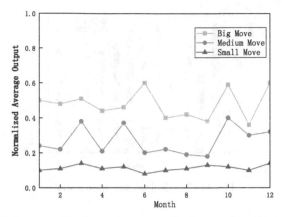

Fig. 3. Various monthly fluctuations normalized average output comparison

SOM deep clustering algorithm was used to classify the natural months, and the persistence ratio of the three types of fluctuations was input in each month. According to the duration of the three types of fluctuations, the annual clustering was divided into low output months, medium output months and high output months, and the clustering results were shown in Table 2.

Table 2. Natural monthly clustering results

Category	Natural month
Big move	February, April,
Medium move	May, October, November, December
Small move	January, March, June, July, August, September,

5.3 Contract Power Breakdown Result

The long-term electricity decomposition model established in this paper is used to optimize the decomposition to obtain the monthly transaction electricity of wind power and conventional units. The decomposition results are shown in Fig. 4. It can be seen from Fig. 4 that in the months with high load ratio, the monthly planned power generation of each unit is high. In high power months, wind power deals are higher. According to the calculation results, the annual cumulative transaction of wind power in this region is 2.23TW·h, and the wind power utilization rate is 91.23%, which verifies the limitation of the model established in this paper.

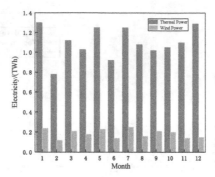

Fig. 4. Electric decomposition result

In order to demonstrate objectively, The decomposing electric quantity results of four units are shown in Fig. 5. It can be seen from the figure that in the month of unit maintenance, the decomposing electric quantity will decrease to a certain extent, and the electric quantity of the unit will be maintained by other units. Therefore, the annual electricity decomposition results obtained by the optimization model proposed in this paper are reasonable and convenient for dispatching departments to arrange power generation plans.

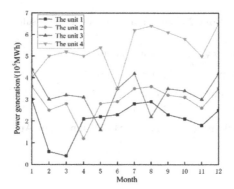

Fig. 5. Unit monthly power decomposition value

6   Conclusion

Considering wind power balance brought by the uncertainty problem, put forward the optimization strategy for medium and long term trading power decomposition, this article from the wind power time, contract electricity output sequence construction coordination optimization decomposition and so on has carried out research and analysis, comprehensive consider the unit performance characteristics and maintenance plan, establish annual trading power coordination optimization decomposition model considering wind power, And the case analysis, the following conclusions are drawn:

1. The proposed method adapts to the optimal decomposition of annual and monthly electric quantity under the principle of preferential absorption of future new energy, and can achieve effective decomposition of medium and long-term transaction electric quantity from annual to monthly while ensuring the maximum absorption of new energy.

2. The proposed method can effectively reduce the execution deviation of monthly electric quantity through rolling coordination and optimization of monthly electric quantity, ensure the effective connection between annual contract transaction electric quantity and scheduling plan, and ensure the execution of daily scheduling level of decomposed electric quantity.

At present, the method proposed in this paper mainly provides a decomposition method for dispatching institutions to execute medium and long term transaction electricity of new energy under the transition period of electricity market. In the future research, market transaction mode should be further optimized according to the actual situation of China's market-oriented construction.

References

1. Chen, X., Yan, R., Liu, Y.: Wind turbine condition monitoring and fault diagnosis in China. IEEE Instrum. Meas. Mag. **19**(2), 22–28 (2016)
2. Yun, J., Yang, M., Shan, Y., et al.: Research on formulation and decomposition of medium and long-term electric power contracts. In: 2020 IEEE 3rd Student Conference on Electrical Machines and Systems, pp. 502–507 (2020)
3. Lu, P., Feng, C., Wu, W., et al.: Optimal modeling of integrated energy system demand response operation considering wind power absorption. In: 2021 6th Asia Conference on Power and Electrical Engineering, pp. 1357–1361 (2021)
4. Zheng, T., Cao, J., Lu, X., Hu, W., et al.: Coordinated control strategy of source-storage-load in wind power heating system considering integrated demand response of power and thermal. In: 2021 IEEE 4th International Electrical and Energy Conference, pp. 1–6 (2021)
5. Wang, Y., Kong, B., Zhou, L., et al.: Multi-objective matching method of bilateral transactions in medium and long-term power markets. In: 2019 IEEE 8th International Conference on Advanced Power System Automation and Protection, pp. 1357–1361 (2019)
6. Xing, Y., Zhang, M., Wang, B., et al.: Midium and long term contract decomposition method considering cascade water quantity matching constraint. In: 2019 IEEE Sustainable Power and Energy Conference, pp. 176–186 (2019)
7. Kim, K.I., Jin, C.H., et al.: Forecasting wind power generation patterns based on SOM clustering. In: 2011 3rd International Conference on Awareness Science and Technology, pp. 508–511 (2011)
8. Wang, L., Liu, J.: Route optimization of wind turbines based on vehicle GPS data. Glob. Reliab. Prognostics Health Manag. **2020**, 1–6 (2020)
9. Wong, M., Abeysinghe, W., Hung, C.: A massive self-organizing map for hyperspectral image classification. In: 2019 10th Workshop on Hyperspectral Imaging and Signal Processing: Evolution in Remote Sensing, pp. 1–5 (2019)
10. Hung, C., Huang, J.: Mining rules from one-dimensional self-organizing maps. In: 2011 International Symposium on Innovations in Intelligent Systems and Applications, pp. 292–295 (2011)

11. Shimomura, R., Kawai, S., Nobuhara, H.: Designing a safe drone with the Coanda effect based on a self-organizing map. In: 2018 IEEE International Conference on Systems, Man, and Cybernetics, pp. 4171–4177 (2018)
12. Tan, K.H., Logenthiran, T., Woo, W.L.: Forecasting of wind energy generation using self-organizing maps and extreme learning machines. In: 2016 IEEE Region 10 Conference, pp. 451–454 (2016ss)

Research and Judgment of Enterprise Energy Consumption Anomaly Based on Massive Data Clustering Algorithm

Zhonglong Wang[✉], Jian Geng, Qing Wang, Han Zhang, Weidong Meng, and Luyan Li

State Grid Shandong Electric Power Company, Tai'an Power Supply Company, Tai'an 271000, China

Abstract. Enterprise energy consumption is not only the main component of national energy consumption, but also an important regulatory object of energy conservation and emission reduction. Aiming at the practical problem of difficult discrimination of enterprise energy consumption anomaly, an enterprise energy consumption anomaly judgment based on clustering algorithm was proposed. Firstly, XGBoost was used for feature selection, and the missing energy consumption data is filled based on the generated countermeasure network; Then, the enterprise energy consumption scenarios are divided by DBSCAN algorithm, and all scenarios are analyzed one by one; Finally, the optimal number of clusters of energy consumption data is determined by SSE-SC index comprehensive decision, and the enterprise energy consumption standard library is divided by K-means++ clustering algorithm; Establish an abnormal energy consumption early warning mechanism to monitor the energy consumption of enterprises in real time.

Keywords: XGBoost · GAN · Enterprise energy consumption standard library · K-means++ · Warning mechanism of abnormal energy consumption

1 Introduction

With the increasing importance of energy to today's social and economic development, the problem of energy shortage has gradually become the focus of national attention. The problem of enterprise energy consumption is the key to affect the comprehensive energy consumption. Therefore, the research on the abnormal energy consumption of enterprises has become the top priority of energy conservation and emission reduction in China.

Literature [1] introduced K-means algorithm and its extension in detail, and proposes an unsupervised K-means algorithm to solve the problems of cluster number and initial cluster center; Literature [2] studies the fault early warning of Gezhouba generator set and establishes the early warning interval; Literature [3] studies the energy consumption of iron and steel enterprises and establishes the corresponding early warning model.

Project Supported by Science and Technology Project of State Grid Shandong Electric Power Company "Research on the key technologies for intelligent research and judgment of energy efficiency anomalies of multi type enterprises based on massive data mining" (5206002000QW).

© Springer Nature Singapore Pte Ltd. 2022
Y. Tian et al. (Eds.): ICBDS 2021, CCIS 1563, pp. 597–606, 2022.
https://doi.org/10.1007/978-981-19-0852-1_47

2 Filling the Missing Value of Enterprise Energy Consumption

The identification and filling of abnormal data and missing data of enterprise energy consumption is of great significance to the establishment of standard database of enterprise energy consumption and the analysis of abnormal data of energy consumption. In order to achieve the accuracy of energy consumption anomaly analysis, this section proposes a data filling method based on generative adjournment network.

2.1 Feature Selection Based on XGBoost

XGBoost [4] is an efficient machine learning function library focusing on gradient lifting, which has fast training speed and good learning effect;

Each iteration of the gradient lifting algorithm will score the importance of each eigenvalue relatively directly. The higher the score, the higher the importance of the eigenvalue; A new tree is established according to the score of the last iteration. [5] Important features can be left through the feature importance score, that is, the purpose of feature selection can be achieved. [6] the specific steps of feature selection based on XGBoost are shown in the following flow chart (Fig. 1):

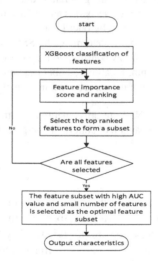

Fig. 1. Feature selection process based on XGBoost

2.2 Filling of Missing Energy Consumption Data

GAN [7] model contains two important components: generator and discriminator, The objective function of GAN is defined as:

$$\min_{G} \max_{D} V(D, G) = E_{x \sim p_{data(x)}}[lbD(x)] + E_{z \sim p_z(x)}[lb(1 - D(G(z)))] \tag{1}$$

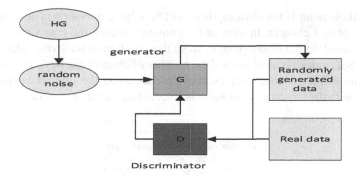

Fig. 2. Actual steps of energy consumption data generation

Fill the missing data based on the generated countermeasure network, as shown in Fig. 2;

step1: Input HG set into GAN;

step2: In GAN, the generator generates data from random noise and sends the real data set of enterprise tons of standard coal into the discriminator for model training;

step3: After the training of the discriminator model, judge the data generated by the generator, and feedback the discrimination results to the generator;

step4: When the data generated by the generator passes the discrimination of the discriminator, the data is verified;

step5: After data verification, fill in the missing data of converted tons of standard coal.

3   Research and Judgment on Abnormal Energy Consumption of Enterprises

3.1   K-means++

K-means [8] algorithm is a typical unsupervised learning algorithm. The similarity of samples is judged by Euclidean distance. The initial value of the centroid of the traditional K-means algorithm is artificially given, and different initial clustering centroids may lead to different clustering results [9]. K-means++ is an optimization algorithm for the above shortcomings. The K-means++ algorithm does not randomly select the initial cluster points, but calculates all the data and selects the centroid points as far as possible [10].

The workflow of K-means++ is as follows:

Firstly, a point is randomly selected from the data as the first centroid point; Then, the distance from the centroid point to each remaining point is calculated, and the remaining centroid points are selected according to the proportional probability of the distance; Finally, the remaining steps are completed according to the k-means algorithm [11].

3.2   Selection of Initial Cluster Number

For traditional clustering algorithms, the number of clusters is given artificially in advance, but it is difficult to give an accurate number of clusters in practical application; The number of disaggregation classes can be calculated by elbow-point, but when the elbow point is not obvious, there will be a large deviation in determining the number of optimal clusters; In view of the above problems, the contour coefficient is introduced based on the elbow-point to solve the problem of unobvious elbow points; Firstly, the SSE index is calculated and the number of clusters can be determined by the elbow-point, then the contour coefficient of the data under the value is calculated, and the k value with the largest contour value is selected as the number of clusters (Fig. 3).

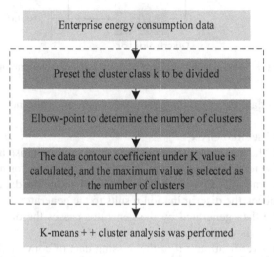

Fig. 3. Judgment strategy of enterprise energy consumption anomaly based on energy consumption standard library

3.3   Generation Strategy of Enterprise Energy Consumption Standard Library

Firstly, the enterprise energy consumption data is divided into scenarios, and each scenario is clustered to obtain the relevant energy consumption standard library;

The generation steps of enterprise energy consumption standard library are as follows:

Step1: scene partition based on DBSCAN clustering;

Step2: Based on the optimal cluster number in Sect. 3.2, K-means++ clustering algorithm is used to cluster the enterprise energy consumption, and three clusters are divided into A, B and C, as shown in Fig. 4.

Step3: Select the cluster with the most data (cluster B in the figure above) as the enterprise energy consumption standard library, and select the average of the centroids of clusters A, B and C as the abnormal boundary value;

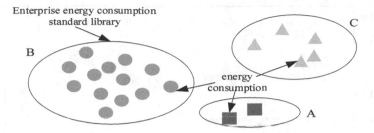

Fig. 4. Schematic diagram of enterprise energy consumption standard library

3.4 Judgment of Abnormal Energy Consumption Based on Standard Library

The previous section analyzes the construction method of enterprise energy consumption standard library. This section will intelligently study and judge the abnormal energy consumption of enterprises in a given time period based on the enterprise energy consumption standard library, as shown in Fig. 5.

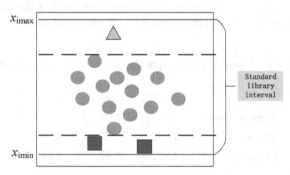

Fig. 5. Schematic diagram of automatic judgment of abnormal energy consumption based on standard library

Take the average of the centroids of cluster classes A, B and C as the abnormal boundary value; The energy consumption of clusters A and C is not in the standard library, but it does not belong to abnormal energy consumption.

4 Example Simulation and Analysis

The real energy consumption data of an enterprise is used as an example. The time span is 7 months (January to July 2021), the sampling frequency is 1 day, and a total of 213 energy consumption data.

4.1 Enterprise Scene Partition Based on DBSCAN Clustering Algorithm

DBSCAN was used to cluster the energy consumption data, and the cluster parameters were Eps = 0.8, MinPts = 7. [12] The clustering results obtained are shown in Fig. 6:

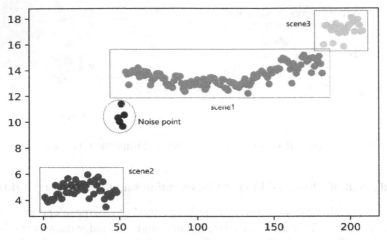

Fig. 6. Result chart of enterprise energy consumption scenario division

Three scenarios can be obtained after the energy consumption data is de-noised, and the corresponding information of the scenarios is shown in Table 1:

Table 1. Distribution of enterprise energy consumption by scene

	Scene1	Scene2	Scene3
Number of point	129	47	27
Max point	15.82	5.98	18.08
Min point	12.22	3.50	16.06

4.2 Automatic Anomaly Identification Analysis Based on Enterprise Energy Consumption Standard Library

The energy consumption standard library of this scenario is obtained by clustering each scenario of the enterprise. Now scenario 1 is selected for correlation analysis, as shown in the figure. If the traditional clustering algorithm is used for analysis, it is difficult to determine the optimal cluster number of samples because the cluster number is a super parameter and needs to be input by human. Therefore, the SSE-SC fusion algorithm is considered to determine the optimal cluster number of enterprise energy consumption (Figs. 7 and 8).

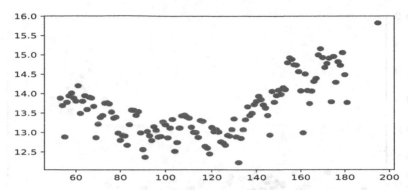

Fig. 7. Schematic diagram of enterprise energy consumption distribution in scene 1

Table 2. Effect comparison of SC algorithm 5

k	2	3	4	5	6	7
SC	0.860	0.811	0.686	0.697	0.702	0.698

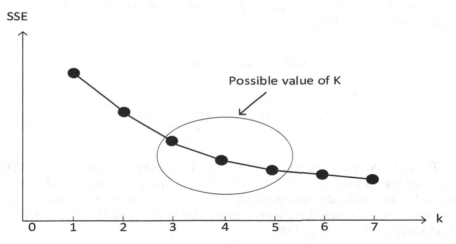

Fig. 8. The SSE values under different cluster numbers

As can be seen from Figs. 8, the SSE values under different cluster numbers are obtained by using the elbow-point alone, but the elbow point is not obvious, and only the possible value bits 3, 4 and 5 of k can be obtained; When the number of clusters is 2 or 3, it is more reasonable, and when k = 2, the contour coefficient is closest to 1; By using SSE-SC fusion algorithm to comprehensively compare the k value under elbow-point and contour coefficient method, it is finally determined that when k = 3, it is the optimal number of clusters (Table 2).

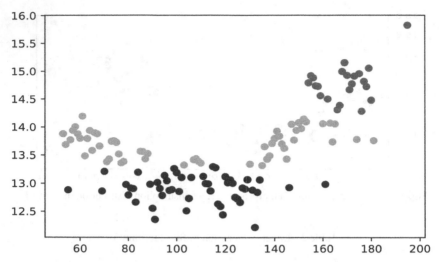

Fig. 9. Clustering results of enterprise energy consumption based on K-means++

The clustering effect is shown in the Fig. 9. The enterprise energy consumption data is divided into three clusters (purple, green and yellow clusters are marked as cluster 1, 2 and 3 respectively) (Table 3);

Table 3. Number of sample data

Cluster	1	2	3
Number	51	22	57

Three clustering centers were determined by K-means++ clustering algorithm. The clustering centers were 12.91, 14.79 and 13.72 respectively; The average value of the centroid is taken as the abnormal boundary value of energy consumption, and combined with the enterprise standard, the early warning line is 13.31, 14.25, 14.41 (enterprise standard) (Fig. 10).

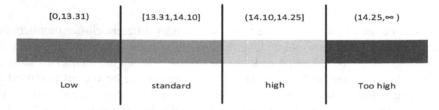

Fig. 10. Enterprise energy consumption warning line

Take [13.31, 14.10] as the energy consumption standard library, judge the real-time enterprise energy consumption according to the early warning line, and take corresponding measures.

5 Conclusion

This paper proposes a clustering algorithm-based method for abnormal energy consumption judgment of enterprises. The main conclusions are as follows:

(1) DBSCAN clustering algorithm is proposed to divide energy consumption scenarios, which can effectively analyze energy consumption in different scenarios.
(2) K-Means++ clustering algorithm based on SSE-SC is proposed to construct the enterprise energy consumption standard library. This algorithm effectively improves the problem that the traditional clustering algorithm is not easy to determine the optimal clustering number, and improves the clustering convergence and efficiency.
(3) Establish a warning mechanism for abnormal energy consumption to monitor the energy consumption of enterprises in real time.

This paper studies the abnormal energy consumption of enterprises. With the increasing energy shortage problem, the energy consumption management of enterprises has become an important direction of energy conservation and emission reduction. Therefore, it is particularly important to study the abnormal energy consumption analysis and early warning. How to put forward corresponding suggestions or strategies for the abnormal energy consumption of enterprises needs further research.

References

1. Sinaga, K.P., Yang, M.: Unsupervised K-means clustering algorithm. IEEE Access **8**, 80716–80727 (2020). https://doi.org/10.1109/ACCESS.2020.2988796
2. Xie, G., Fu, Y., Li, Z.: A real-time fault prewarning approach to generator sets based on dynamic threshold. In: Information Engineering Research Institute, USA. Proceedings of 2013 3rd International Conference on Materials Engineering for Advanced Technologies (ICMEAT2013). Information Engineering Research Institute, USA (2013)
3. Ren, H., Watts, D.: Early warning signals for critical transitions in power systems. Electric Power Syst. Res. **124** (2015)
4. Jiang, Y., Tong, G., Yin, H., et al.: A Pedestrian detection method based on genetic algorithm for optimize XGBoost training parameters. IEEE Access **7**, 118310–118321 (2019). https://doi.org/10.1109/ACCESS.2019.2936454
5. Qu, Y., Lin, Z., Li, H., et al.: Feature recognition of urban road traffic accidents based on GA-XGBoost in the context of big data. IEEE Access **7**, 170106–170115 (2019). https://doi.org/10.1109/ACCESS.2019.2952655
6. Jiang, H., He, Z., Ye, G., et al.: Network intrusion detection based on PSO-Xgboost model. IEEE Access **8**, 58392–58401 (2020). https://doi.org/10.1109/ACCESS.2020.2982418
7. Cho, J., Yoon, K.: Conditional activation GAN: improved auxiliary classifier GAN. IEEE Access **8**, 216729–216740 (2020). https://doi.org/10.1109/ACCESS.2020.3041480

8. Mat Isa, N.A., Salamah, S.A., Ngah, U.K.: Adaptive fuzzy moving K-means clustering algorithm for image segmentation. IEEE Trans. Consum. Electron. **55**(4), 2145–2153 (2009). https://doi.org/10.1109/TCE.2009.5373781

9. Xu, T., Chiang, H., Liu, G., et al.: Hierarchical K-means method for clustering large-scale advanced metering infrastructure data. IEEE Trans. Power Delivery **32**(2), 609–616 (2017). https://doi.org/10.1109/TPWRD.2015.2479941

10. Xu, Y., Qu, W., Li, Z., et al.: Efficient k means++ approximation with MapReduce. IEEE Trans. Parallel Distrib. Sys. **25**(12), 3135–3144 (2014). https://doi.org/10.1109/TPDS.2014.2306193

11. Xiong, H., Wu, J., Chen, J.: "K-means clustering versus validation measures: a data-distribution perspective. IEEE Trans. Syst. Man Cybern. Part B (Cybern.) **39**(2), 318–331 (2009). https://doi.org/10.1109/TSMCB.2008.2004559

12. Shen, J., Hao, X., Liang, Z., et al.: Real-time superpixel segmentation by DBSCAN clustering algorithm. IEEE Trans. Image Process. **25**(12), 5933–5942 (2016). https://doi.org/10.1109/TIP.2016.2616302

State Machine Inference Method of Unknown Binary Protocol Based on Recurrent Neural Network

Yang Chen[1] , Peng Li[1,2](✉) , Yujie Zhang[1] , and Weiqing Fang[1]

[1] School of Computer Science, Nanjing University of Posts and Telecommunications, Nanjing 210023, China
lipeng@njupt.edu.cn
[2] Institute of Network Security and Trusted Computing, Nanjing 210023, China

Abstract. The state machine of binary protocol can effectively reflect the behavior characteristics of the protocol, and its inference results are often not highly influenced by the protocol format information and logical interaction. To solve this problem, a protocol message type recognition and protocol state architecture method based on recurrent neural network is proposed. Based on the previous work of format classification, this paper uses recursive neural network to get the state features of protocol messages, and then uses clustering algorithm to mark protocol message types. Finally, the protocol state machine is constructed and optimized. Experimental results on MQTT and RFID data sets show that the proposed method has high precision of protocol state machine inference.

Keywords: Protocol state machine · LSTM · Clustering · State simplification

1 Introduction

With the rapid development of information technology and increasingly frequent communication, network security threat become more and more serious. According to the data of China National Information Security Vulnerability Sharing Platform [1], the number of network security vulnerabilities recorded in this year increased by 27.9% compared with the previous year, and the number of newly recorded vulnerabilities showed a significant growth trend in the past five years, with an average annual growth rate of 17.6%. As the communication medium of network entity, network protocol plays an important role in network security.

Network protocols are classified into public protocols and private protocols. The protocol specification for disclosure protocols is public. We can use analysis tools such as Wireshark or Fiddler to do things like vulnerability discovering, Fuzz testing [2], and Network Intrusion Detection [3]. In addition, there are also a large number of unknown private protocols in the network. For security, economic interests, privacy and other needs, they do not disclose the details of the protocol, which is easy to produce security loopholes, or used by criminals, threatening network security. Unknown protocols are

© Springer Nature Singapore Pte Ltd. 2022
Y. Tian et al. (Eds.): ICBDS 2021, CCIS 1563, pp. 607–616, 2022.
https://doi.org/10.1007/978-981-19-0852-1_48

mostly private binary protocols, which are difficult to analyze due to their poor readability. This paper mainly analyzes binary protocol state machines [4] from the perspective of protocol interaction.

The state machine inference of binary protocol mainly includes protocol state identification and protocol state machine construction [4], both of which have been studied by many experts and scholars. In PEXT scheme [5], the length of the longest common subsequence is used as a measure for clustering, and the state machine is generated according to the state transition sequence. Finally, the minimum state machine is obtained by merging algorithm. The BFS scheme [6] focuses on the distribution characteristics of each byte, adopts VDV (variance of distribution of variance) to identify the state field, and uses the state separation step to remove the redundant common state when constructing the protocol state machine. Wang Chen et al. [7] depending on the type of protocol message structure is the same message clustering, and then based on the APTA tree building initial state machine, by the state for the same input symbol sequence of state transition and output response to judge the similarity degree, according to the similarity of selecting candidate status and try to merge, and build a test case for validation. Wang Jun [8] proposed a state-related field mining method based on the combination of multi-sequence alignment and value distribution statistics, which used multi-sequence alignment to identify variable length fields and eliminate them, and then used value distribution statistics to mine message type fields. Then, APTA tree [9] is constructed according to the state transition sequence, and the state machine is labeled by heuristic algorithm. Then, the final protocol state machine is obtained by merging similar states. Yan Xiaoyong et al. [10] optimized the way of state field extraction, proposed a recognition algorithm based on the longest common subsequence distance (LCSD), took the behavior logic of the message into consideration in state field extraction, and finally created a protocol state machine through adjacency list and optimized it.

The above research methods are mainly divided into message type annotation from the two perspectives of format similarity and state-related fields. Through analysis, we find that the problems can be divided into the following three aspects:

1) Binary protocol issues. Due to the poor readability of binary protocol and rich distribution of field values, some auxiliary reference information cannot be obtained like text protocol, resulting in low accuracy.
2) Problem of message status identification. In many schemes, message types are marked based on the similarity of protocol packet formats, ignoring the problem that different values of key fields may affect the status of packets when the protocol formats are the same [11].
3) Status field identification problem. State machine fields are generally judged in bytes, but binary protocols are more flexible in design. Different protocols may have different granularity of field segmentation, and not all of them are segmented in bytes [12]. At the same time, many schemes do not consider the protocol interaction logic when selecting the status field, resulting in that the obtained status field cannot completely represent the protocol message type.

At present, recurrent neural network has been widely used in data processing with logical relations, and has made a great breakthrough [13–15]. Therefore, this paper extends it to the field of protocol message. Our article from the perspective of similarity protocol format, taking the binary protocol message sequence as a time series data to analyse, put forward to combining neural networks with k-means the circulation protocol state feature extraction, in order to achieve at the same time consider protocol format and the purpose of the logical sequence of message sequence, Then the protocol state machine is constructed and optimized according to the packets.

2 System Model

2.1 Design Overview

The overall flow of this method is shown in Fig. 1. Considering the interaction logic of protocol packets, this method treats unknown binary packets as time series, extracts state feature vectors through deep learning model LSTM (Long short-term Memory), and obtains message type identifiers through clustering. Finally, protocol state machines are constructed and simplified through packet pairs.

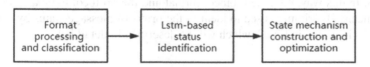

Fig. 1. Overall frame structure

2.2 Format Preprocessing and Classification

General network protocol packets include network layer, link layer, transport layer and other multi-layer network protocols. However, this scheme mainly targets at unknown binary protocols, which are mostly located at the application layer. Therefore, redundant data should be removed first to obtain binary protocol packets to be analyzed. According to literature statistics, the control information of protocol packets is mostly located in the header area of protocol packets. Therefore, for the purpose of extracting state features, this section selects the upper-middle data group of protocol packets as analysis data. The format of protocol data traffic is shown in Fig. 2. Each line corresponds to a packet of the protocol.

```
82 13 00 01 00 0e 73 75 62 6a 65 63 74 5f 63 2b 2b 5f 30 31 00
90 03 00 05 02
10 39 00 04 4d 51 54 54 04 c2 00 3c 00 1e 43 2b 2b 32 63 65 39
61 62 37 36 39 33 38 30 36 35 63 65 39 37 63 61 36 36 61 30 66
37 35 00 08 6d 71 74 74 66 78 30 34 00 03 31 32 33
```

Fig. 2. Binary protocol initial packet

The length of protocol packets is not fixed, which affects the format classification. Therefore, the length of packets needs to be unified. The most common and effective method is to select a fixed length l to delete more than l and add less than l with zero. Set the data set to contain n protocol packets, represented as $(s_1, s_2, \ldots, s_i, \ldots s_n)$. s_i denotes the $i - th$ packet in the data set, and the fixed length L is determined according to Formula (1).

$$l = \max\left(\arg\,\min\left(\sum_i H\left(\frac{\||s_i|-l|}{l}\right)\right), l_{\min}\right) \tag{1}$$

Function H represents the corresponding information entropy and $l_{\min}$ donates the length of the packet with the shortest length in the data set. Then, the format of processed protocol packets is classified based on the similarity of packet formats.

2.3 LSTM-Based Status Identification

In this section, when the protocol format classification has been obtained, the protocol packet sequence is treated as sequence data for processing, and the state feature vector is extracted by the hidden layer state vector in the Long Short-Term Memory (LSTM) algorithm. In this way, both the protocol format and the protocol logic are considered. Then, k-means algorithm is used to identify the protocol message status by clustering. The process is shown in Fig. 3, which will be described in detail below.

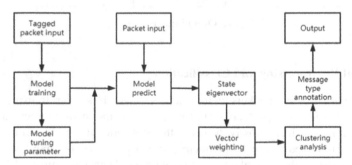

Fig. 3. LSTM - based message status identification process

LSTM is a kind of recurrent neural network (RNN), which is suitable for processing and predicting time series data by adding hidden layer information of the previous moment in the process of hidden layer learning. In this scheme, the protocol message is treated as time series data, and the interaction logic of the protocol message is learned by the transitivity of the hidden layer information, that is, the influence of the pre-message on the protocol state at this time, and the state vector of the message is extracted for analysis.

Since the protocol format classification information has been provided, we can use the format information to label the packets and analyze the packets by considering the format and interaction logic of the protocol through LSTM algorithm. Set training message sample sequence $X = (x_1, x_2, \ldots, x_j, \ldots, x_t)$, x_j represents the message at time j, so the input message sequence of the model is $X[1 : t - 1]$, and the prediction message is $x(t)$. The message data is input into the network in chronological order for learning.

As shown in Fig. 4, in this LSTM network, take the protocol packet $x(3)$ as an example, after the packet enters the LSTM neuron, it will calculate with the state vector $h2$ transmitted by the pre-packet to obtain the state vector $h3$ containing the state information of $x(3)$ and the pre-packet, and $h3$ can be used as the state feature vector at the next moment. And so on, so as to obtain the state vectors of all input messages $(h1, h2, \ldots, ht)$.

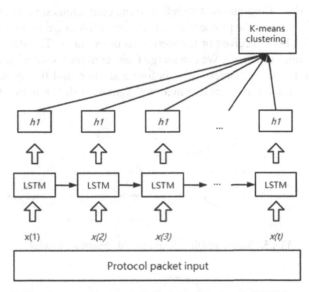

Fig. 4. Feature vector extraction of protocol packets in LSTM network

After the LSTM model training is completed, the protocol message data vector is re-input for analysis to obtain the state vector of each message. At the same time, because the state vector of the same packet is obtained after the second input of the protocol packet, the state vector will appear several times, but its value will be different. We can weight it again to improve the accuracy of the protocol state vector of the packet.

Then, the k-means algorithm [16] is used to cluster the state vector of the message sequence, and the state vector contains both the format features and logical information of the protocol message. For example, if there are two time points p and q, and p Therefore, the clustering result can represent the status type of protocol packets.

2.4 State Mechanism Construction and Optimization

State Mechanism Construction. Protocol message interactions occur between the server and the client in the network, the scheme from the perspective of the server build protocol state machine, because after the server receives the request message and sends a response message for protocol state to complete the process of conversion at a time, so you can use (response message) receives the message, message transformation of identity protocol state machine. As pre-packet has been involved in protocol packet status characteristics, the influence of current received packets on protocol state transformation and the influence of previous key packets are considered in packet pair. We build the protocol initial state machine from the packet pair.

State Machine Simplification. Due to the fine granularity of protocol state identification, the initial state machine constructed in the above way has some redundant states, and these states will be merged and pruned in the following sections.

Continuous Pruning. Continuous state refers to the continuous state in which both the outgo and ingo are one in the protocol state transformation diagram, that is, no transfer of other states has been received or transferred to other states. The state 2–4 in Fig. 5 below is a continuous state path. We can merge these continuous states first. Then prune according to the message characteristics before and after, and finally simplify into a relatively simple protocol state transformation diagram, as shown in Fig. 6.

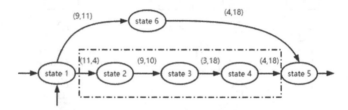

Fig. 5. State transition diagram with continuous states

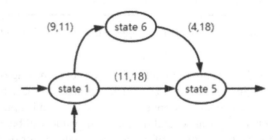

Fig. 6. State transition diagram after merging continuous states

Merger of Similar States. The similar state is a state that is transformed from the same state and turns to the same state through the same input and output. They are in parallel relation and have no connection with other states. In Fig. 7, states 2 and 3 are both converted from State 1 and then transferred to state 4 through the same input and output. In this process, states 2 and 3 play the same role. By combining similar states, we finally obtain a concise protocol state diagram, as shown in Fig. 8.

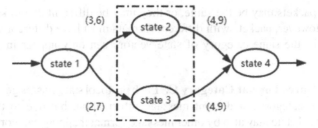

Fig. 7. State transition diagram with similar states

Fig. 8. State transition diagram after continuous state merging

3 Experimental Results

In this section, the proposed model is tested through experiments. The experimental environment and experimental data are first introduced, and then the inference results of the state machine are presented.

3.1 Experimental Environment and Data

The experimental platform uses tensorflow as the back-end keras framework, Python version 3.6, running on Windows 10 operating system. In terms of experimental hardware, the CPU is Inter-core I5 4200 H, the memory is 8 GB, and the GPU is NVIDIA GeForce GTX950.

For the convenience of verification, the data set used in the experiment is known protocol MQTT and RFID protocol data set. The above data sets are collected according to the session under the normal working environment of the protocol platform set up in the laboratory.

3.2 Evaluation Indicators

In the protocol state identification experiment, we input the protocol format characteristic $X = (x_1, x_2, \ldots, x_m)$, m represents the number of protocol format categories, and finally obtains the protocol status feature $Y = (y_1, y_2, \ldots, y_n)$, n indicates the number of protocol status feature categories. Generally, m is less than n. Y contains both format information and pre-packet information of protocol packets. It is difficult to analyze the corresponding real protocol status for a packet set with a large amount of data. So we evaluate it in terms of the relationship between X and Y.

The format category X of the packet is easy to verify in the experiment, and each x corresponds to a format of the packet. Therefore, we divide the packet into two scenarios based on the protocol format. The format of the packets is the same. The status-related vectors of the packets may be the same, or they may be different due to key fields and pre-packets. However, packets with different formats must have different status-related vectors. That is, the same category of state vectors can only appear in one protocol format.

Definition 1. Source Format Category C. Each protocol state classes generated by the protocol format categories and front message information, but due to the abnormal situation, protocol state may also by other message format mapping category. Therefore, for protocol state category y_j, the protocol format category that maps to y_j the most times is called the source format category of y_j.

The following defines accuracy to Preliminary evaluate the generation of protocol state characteristics.

Definition 2. Accuracy Z. The accuracy of calculating the mean probability of a protocol message state vector appearing in its source format class as a protocol state feature. The higher the accuracy is, the more reliable the protocol state feature Y is. Its calculation formula is shown in Eq. (2).

$$Z = \frac{1}{n} \sum_{j \in n} \frac{C_j}{y_j} \tag{2}$$

3.3 Results Analysis

Based on format classification, protocol message state feature extraction results in a series of state vectors, which are the basis of message type annotation. In the experiment, MQTT protocol and RFID protocol are taken as examples, and the accuracy of their state feature vectors relative to format features is shown in Fig. 9.

It can be noticed from Fig. 9 that each message state feature vector has a high similarity with format feature, which is related to the accuracy of protocol format classification, and also indicates the reliability of protocol message state vector.

Taking MQTT protocol as an example, the inference result of its protocol state machine is shown in Fig. 10. It is important to note that due to the potential limitations of the protocol data set, the protocol state machine only contains state transitions when the protocol is working properly. In the inferred result, path 0–1 is the connect process of the protocol, and state 2 is the most frequently used message publishing phase.

In order to verify the validity of the inferred protocol state machine, we test the protocol state machine through MQTT protocol test to calculate the accuracy of the session. In the accuracy test, the adopted test set containing 200 sessions of MQTT journal set and 200 sessions of RFID journal set were mixed and finally all correctly identified.

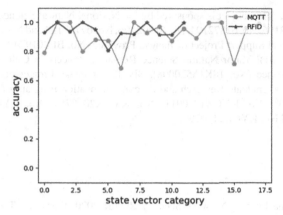

Fig. 9. Accuracy of state feature of MQTT and RFID protocols

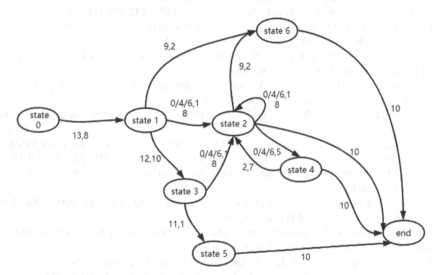

Fig. 10. MQTT protocol state machine inference transfer diagram

4 Conclusion

From the perspective of logical interaction of protocol messages, this paper tries to put forward a protocol message status identification method based on a circular neural network. The protocol messages are regarded as time series data, and the LSTM model is combined with k-means clustering to identify the protocol message status. Finally, the protocol initial state machine is constructed and optimized, and good results are achieved. However, the accuracy of the protocol state vector in this paper is not perfect enough. The next step is to optimize the model to obtain more accurate state characteristics.

Acknowledgement. The subject is sponsored by the National Natural Science Foundation of P. R. China (No. 61872196, No. 61872194, No. 61902196, No. 62102194 and No. 62102196), Scientific and Technological Support Project of Jiangsu Province (No. BE2019740, No. BK20200753 and No. 20KJB520001), Major Natural Science Research Projects in Colleges and Universities of Jiangsu Province (No. 18KJA520008), Six Talent Peaks Project of Jiangsu Province (No. RJFW-111), Postgraduate Research and Practice Innovation Program of Jiangsu Province (No. KYCX19_0909, No. KYCX19_0911, No. KYCX20_0759, No. KYCX21_0787, No. KYCX21_0788 and No. KYCX21_0799).

References

1. CNCERT: China Internet Network Security Report 2020. Posts and Telecommunications Press, Beijing (2021)
2. Weiming, L., Aifang, Z., Jiancai, L., et al.: An automatic network protocol fuzz testing and vulnerability discovering method. Chin. J. Comput. **34**(02), 242–255 (2011)
3. Lingyun, Y., Yi, Y., Dengguo, F., et al.: Syntax and behavior semantics analysis of network protocol of malware. J. Softw. **22**(07), 1676–1689 (2011)
4. Lifa, W., Chen, W., Zheng, H., et al.: Overview on protocol state machine inference: a survey. Appl. Res. Comput. **32**(07), 1931–1936 (2015)
5. Shevertalov, M., Mancoridis, S.: A reverse engineering tool for extracting protocols of networked applications, pp. 229–238. IEEE (2007)
6. Trifilo, A., Burschka, S., Biersack, E.: Traffic to protocol reverse engineering, pp. 1–8. IEEE (2009)
7. Chen, W., Lifa, W., Zheng, H., et al.: Method of protocol state machine inference based on state merging. J. PLA Univ. Sci. Technol. (Nat. Science Edition) **16**(04), 322–329 (2015)
8. Jun, W.: EDSM-based protocol state machine reverse for binary protocol. Harbin Institute of Technology (2016)
9. Comparetti, P.M., et al. Prospex: protocol specification extraction. In: 2009 30th IEEE Symposium on Security and Privacy (2009)
10. Yan, X.: Research and implementation on the key technologies for binary private protocol reverse. Information Engineering University (2018)
11. Wang, Y., Zhang, Z., Yao, D., Qu, B., Guo, L.: Inferring protocol state machine from network traces: a probabilistic approach. In: Lopez, J., Tsudik, G. (eds.) ACNS 2011, pp. 1–18. Springer, Heidelberg (2011). https://doi.org/10.1007/978-3-642-21554-4_1
12. Qin Zhongyuan, L., Kai, Z.Q., et al.: Approach of field format extraction in binary private protocol. J. Chin. Comput. Syst. **40**(11), 2318–2323 (2019)
13. Guorui, W.: Time series data clustering algorithm based on recurrent neural network and its parallelization. Harbin Institute of Technology (2016)
14. Zeng, X.: Traffic anomaly detection method based on improved RNN and density clustering. Beijing University of Posts and Telecommunications (2019)
15. Tian Xianzhong, G., Anna, S.H.: Recurrent neural networks for time series with fuzzy control. J. Chin. Comput. Syst. **42**(02), 241–245 (2021)
16. Gu Chunxiang, W., Weisen, S.Y., et al.: Method of unknown protocol classification based on autoencoder. J. Commun. **41**(06), 88–97 (2020)

Data-Driven Distribution Network Energy-Saving Planning Based on Cluster Division and High-Penetration Renewable Energy Access

Ke Hua[1], Zhichao Wang[1], Baoyin Wu[2(✉)], and Maosheng Fu[2]

[1] State Grid Heilongjiang Electric Power Co., Ltd., Harbin 150090, Heilongjiang, China
[2] School of Electric Power Engineering, Nanjing Institute of Technology, Nanjing 211167, Jiangsu, China

Abstract. In view of the increasing proportion of renewable energy access in the distribution network, traditional distribution network planning methods have been unable to meet the needs of grid development. This paper proposes a data-driven distribution network energy-saving plan based on cluster division with high-penetration renewable energy access. This method firstly optimizes the capacity and layout of high-proportion renewable energy to realize the initial site selection and fixed capacity of renewable energy; secondly, it divides the distribution network based on data-driven clusters to realize the zoning planning of the distribution network, and finally, through a two-level iterative programming model is constructed to realize an optimized decision-making model with cost and energy-saving benefits as the goal. The calculation example uses real power grid data to analyze, and the simulation results show the effectiveness and feasibility of the model and method proposed in this paper.

Keywords: High permeability · Renewable energy · Distribution network · Differentiated energy saving planning · Two-level planning

1 Introduction

In the power system, the loss of distribution network is the most serious, so in the energy saving planning, distribution network has the greatest energy saving potential [1, 2] in the energy saving planning of the power network. At the same time, with the large-scale access of distributed wind energy and photovoltaic, the proportion of renewable energy in the distribution network presents a trend of high penetration [3]. Therefore, it is of practical significance to consider both renewable energy planning and distribution network transformation.

At present, there are many methods for energy-saving transformation of the distribution network. Literature [4] proposed a two-stage stochastic programming model. Literature [5] optimization engine is proposed to minimize the loss of distribution network and improve the voltage distribution of the system. Literature [6] proposes a coordinated

© Springer Nature Singapore Pte Ltd. 2022
Y. Tian et al. (Eds.): ICBDS 2021, CCIS 1563, pp. 617–629, 2022.
https://doi.org/10.1007/978-981-19-0852-1_49

scheme of multiple voltage regulating devices. Literature [7] proposed a random optimal battery storage planning method.

To sum up, the comprehensive transformation of renewable energy and distribution network should be considered in an overall way to achieve the optimal decision.

2   Differential Energy-Saving Planning for Distribution Network

The specific steps of energy saving planning for distribution network are as follows (Fig. 1):

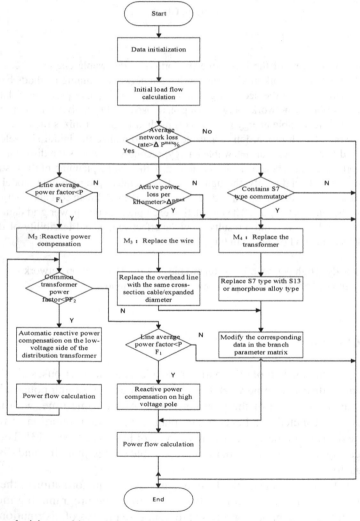

Fig. 1. The decision-making process for the comprehensive renovation of energy-saving and loss-reducing distribution network

Through the energy-saving and loss reduction reconstruction measures shown in the figure above, the loss reduction effect and economy can be taken into account to adapt to complex scenes and achieve the optimal effect.

3   The Impact of High-Permeability Renewable Energy Access on the Distribution Network

Theoretical analysis of network loss changes caused by distributed power supply access [8] (Fig. 3).

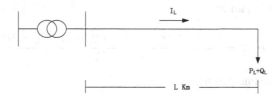

Fig. 2. Ideal distribution network system model

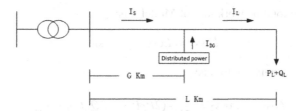

Fig. 3. Distribution network system model with distributed power generation

The system load can be expressed as:

$$S_L = P_L + jQ_L \tag{1}$$

Where: P_L is the active power consumed by the load; Q_L is the reactive power consumed by the load.

The expression of the single-phase current flowing into the load is:

$$\dot{I}_L = \frac{P_L - jQ_L}{3\dot{V}} \tag{2}$$

Where: V is the phase voltage on the line.

The network loss in Model 1 is:

$$Loss_1 = \frac{rL(P_L^2 + Q_L^2)}{3V^2} \tag{3}$$

Where: r is the single-phase resistivity of the system.

The single-phase current in Model 2 is:

$$\dot{I}_G = \frac{P_G - jQ_G}{3\dot{V}} \tag{4}$$

Where: P_C is the active power of the distributed power; Q_C is the reactive power of the distributed power.

It can be concluded from Fig. 2 that the single-phase current flowing into the load is:

$$\dot{I}_L = \dot{I}_S + \dot{I}_G \tag{5}$$

The loss of the first part is:

$$Loss_A = 3rGI_S^2 = \frac{rG(P_L^2 + Q_L^2 + P_G^2 + Q_G^2 - 2P_LQ_L - 2P_GQ_G)}{3V^2} \tag{6}$$

The loss of the second part is:

$$Loss_B = 3r(L - G)I_L^2 = \frac{r(L - G)(P_L^2 + Q_L^2)}{3V^2} \tag{7}$$

Therefore, the total network loss of Model 2 is:

$$Loss_2 = Loss_A + Loss_B \tag{8}$$

The variation of network loss is:

$$\Delta Loss = Loss_1 - Loss_2 = \frac{rL}{3V^2}(2P_LP_G + 2Q_LQ_G - P_G^2 - Q_G^2)(\frac{G}{L}) \tag{9}$$

The rate of change of network loss is:

$$\Delta Lrate = \frac{\Delta Loss}{Loss_1} = \frac{G}{P_L^2 + Q_L^2}(2P_LP_G + 2Q_LQ_G - P_G^2 - Q_G^2) \tag{10}$$

It can be seen from Eq. (10) that the main factors affecting the network loss are the location of the distributed power supply, the size of the capacity and the power factor.

4 Distribution Network Cluster Division Method Based on Data-Driven

The comprehensive indicators of cluster division are defined as follows:

$$\max \rho = \varphi_C + \varphi_P \tag{11}$$

During the trial: φ_C is the cluster modularity index; φ_P is the cluster active power balance index.

(1) Cluster modularity index φ_C:

$$\begin{cases} \varphi_C = \frac{1}{2m} \sum_i \sum_j (A_{ij} - \frac{k_i k_j}{2m})\delta(i,j) \\ A_{ij} = 1 - \frac{e_{ij}}{\max e_{ij}}, k_i = \sum_j A_{ij}, m = \frac{1}{2} \sum_i \sum_j A_{ij} \end{cases} \quad (12)$$

Where, A_{ij} is the electrical distance function of node i and node j, m is the sum of all edge weights; K_i is the sum of weights of lines connected to node i; If node i and node j are in the same cluster, $\delta(i,j)$ is 1; otherwise, it is 0.

For a system with n nodes, the electrical distance based on reactive voltage sensitivity matrix can be expressed as:

$$e_{QV}^{ij} = \sqrt{(S_{QV}^{i1} - S_{QV}^{j1})^2 + (S_{QV}^{i2} - S_{QV}^{j2})^2 + \cdots + (S_{QV}^{in} - S_{QV}^{jn})^2} \quad (13)$$

Where, S_{QV}^{ij} is the element in row i and column j in the reactive voltage sensitivity matrix. The electrical distance based on the sensitivity matrix is defined as:

$$e^{ij} = \frac{(e_{QV}^{ij} + e_{PV}^{ij})}{2} \quad (14)$$

(2) Cluster active power balance index φ_P

$$\begin{cases} \varphi_{clu,i} = 1 - \frac{P_{clu,i}}{\sum\limits_{j \in \Omega_L} S_{L,j}}, \forall i \in H \\ \varphi_P = \frac{1}{H} \sum\limits_{i=1}^{H} \varphi_{clu,i} \end{cases} \quad (15)$$

Where: $\varphi_{clu,i}$ is the active power balance of cluster i; $P_{clu,i}$ is the net power characteristic of cluster i; φ_P is the cluster active balance index of the system.

5 Two-Level Programming Model Based on Cluster Partition

In this section, the planning model is decomposed into two layers for iterative solution. The two-layer optimization architecture is shown in Fig. 4.

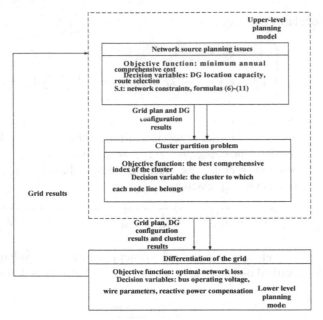

Fig. 4. Two-tier optimization model architecture

5.1 Upper Cost Optimization Model

The upper programming model takes the minimum annual comprehensive cost as the objective and establishes the objective function.

(1) Investment expenses

$$C_I = \frac{r(1+r)^n}{(1+r)^n - 1}(\sum_{i \in NAF} A_L l_i x_{L,i} + \sum_{i \in \Omega_{DG}} C_{I,DG} \overline{S}_{DG,i} x_{DG,i}) \tag{16}$$

In the formula: r is the discount rate, 10% in this article; n is the investment return period; B is the classification set of different lines in the network, B = {EFF, NAF}, and the set represents the existing non-replaceable lines and newly added lines respectively Line; A_L is the investment cost per unit length of the line; l_i is the length of line i; $x_{L,i}, x_{DG,i}$ are 0–1 variables, respectively representing the investment variables of the line and DG, if it is 1, it will be put into construction, otherwise it will not be put into construction; $C_{I,DG}$ is DG The unit capacity investment cost of; $\overline{S}_{DG,i}$ is the planned capacity of DG at node i; Ω_N, Ω_{DG}, and Ω_{DGs} respectively represent the set of network nodes, the set of DG to-be-built nodes, the set of DG-to-be-built and existing nodes.

(2) Operation and maintenance costs

$$C_M = \sum_{i \in B} A_L l_i \gamma_L x_{L,i} + \sum_{i \in \Omega_{DG}} \overline{S}_{DG,i} T_{DG,i} C_{OM} \lambda_{DG,i} x_{DG,i} \tag{17}$$

In the formula: γ_L is the line operation and maintenance cost rate; $T_{DG,i}$ is the annual DG power generation operating hours at node i; C_{OM} is the DG unit capacity operation and maintenance cost rate; $\lambda_{DG,i}$ is the distributed power factor of the i-th node.

(3) Network loss cost

$$C_R = \sum_{clu=1}^{H} \sum_{i=1}^{N_{clu,1}} Z_L l_i I_i C_e T \tag{18}$$

Where: T is the maximum load loss hours per year; H is the number of clusters; $N_{clu,1}$ is the number of lines included in the cluster clu; Z_L is the line impedance amplitude per unit length; I_i and is the current square value of line i, and C_e is the system unit Electricity price.

(4) System purchase cost

$$C_D = \sum_{i \in T} \sum_{clu=1}^{H} P_{clu} C_e \tag{19}$$

In the formula, P_{clu} is the net power flowing into the cluster clu from the network.

(5) Node voltage and line current constraints

$$\begin{cases} U_{i,min} \le U_i \le U_{i,max}, \forall i \in \Omega_N \\ 0 \le I_i \le I_{i,max}, \forall i \in B \end{cases} \tag{20}$$

Where: U_i is the voltage amplitude of node i; $U_{i,min}$ and $U_{i,max}$ are the upper and lower limits of node voltage respectively; I_i is the current amplitude of the line; $I_{i,max}$ is the upper limit of the current allowed to pass through the line.

(6) DG permeability constraint

$$\lambda_{sys} = \frac{\sum_{i \in \Omega_{DGs}} \overline{S}_{DG,i}}{\sum_{i \in \Omega_L} \overline{S}_{L,i}} \tag{21}$$

Where: Ω_L represents the set of load nodes; $\overline{S}_{L,i}$ is the maximum load value at node i.

(7) The DG system permeability constraint is

$$\lambda_{sys} < \overline{\lambda}_{sys} \tag{22}$$

In the formula, $\overline{\lambda}_{sys}$ is the upper limit of penetration rate set by planners.

(8) DG cluster permeability

$$\lambda_{clu} = \frac{\sum_{i \in \Omega_{clu,DG}} \overline{S}_{DG,i}}{\sum_{i \in \Omega_{clu,L}} \overline{S}_{L,i}}, \forall clu \in H \tag{23}$$

In the formula: $\Omega_{clu,DG}$ represents the set of DG installation nodes in the cluster clu, and $\Omega_{clu,L}$ represents the set of load nodes in the cluster clu. This article takes $\lambda_{clu} = 1.0$.

5.2 Differential Transformation Model of Lower Grid

The transformation plan is as follows:

(1) Adjust the bus operating voltage
   The total loss of the distribution network ΔP_Σ is composed of variable loss and fixed loss. The specific formula is:

$$\Delta P_\Sigma = \frac{P^2 + Q^2}{U^2} R_{eqv} + \left(\frac{U}{U_N}\right)^2 \sum_{i=1}^{m} \Delta P_{0i} \qquad (24)$$

   Where: P and Q are load active and reactive power respectively; R_{eqv} is the sum of the equivalent resistance of the distribution line and the distribution transformer load; ΔP_{0i} is the iron loss of the i-th distribution transformer; m is the total distribution transformer in the distribution network Number of units; U_N and U are the rated voltage and operating voltage of the distribution network, respectively.

(2) Change the wire diameter/model
   In the distribution network, the active power loss of the line is:

$$\Delta P_L = 3 \times I_L^2 R_L = 3 \times \left(\frac{P}{\sqrt{3}U \cos \varphi}\right)^2 \times R_L = \frac{P^2 R_L}{U^2 \cos^2 \varphi} \qquad (25)$$

   In the formula: I_L is the current flowing through the component; R_L is the resistance of the single-phase line; U is the line voltage at the same measurement end as P; $\cos \varphi$ is the power factor.

(3) Medium and low voltage reactive power compensation
   Before and after reactive power compensation, the reduction of the active power loss of the distribution network ΔP_φ is:

$$\Delta P_\varphi = P^2 R_L \left(\frac{1}{U_1^2 \cos^2 \varphi_1} - \frac{1}{U_2^2 \cos^2 \varphi_2}\right) \qquad (26)$$

   In the formula, U_1, U_2 and $\cos \varphi_1$, $\cos \varphi_2$ are the operating voltage and power factor before and after reactive power compensation, respectively.

(4) Replacement of high energy consumption distribution transformer
   The active loss ΔP_T of a distribution transformer includes load active loss ΔP_{Cu} and no-load active loss ΔP_{Fe}. The formula is:

$$\Delta P_T = \Delta P_{Cu} + \Delta P_{Fe} \qquad (27)$$

(5) Economics of the transformation plan

The annual network loss fee W_{loss} of the system and the investment payback period Y of the comprehensive transformation plan are as follows:

$$W_{loss} = [(\Delta P_L + \Delta P_{Cu}) \times \tau_{max} + \Delta P_{Fe} \times 8760] \times \beta \qquad (28)$$

In the formula, τ_{max} is the annual maximum load loss hours of 3500h; β is the unit price of 0.6 yuan/kWh.

$$Y = \frac{M_{I,C} + M_{I,L} + M_{I,T}}{W_{loss,1} - W_{loss,2}} \tag{29}$$

$M_{I,C}$, $M_{I,L}$ and $M_{I,T}$ are the cost of newly added reactive power compensation equipment, the cost of transforming the wire and the cost of replacing the transformer.

6 Example Simulation and Analysis

The calculation example uses a real distribution network line for planning, as shown in the figure below. The line contains five loads located on nodes 3, 5, 8, 12 and 14. The actual connection of distributed pv is as follows: Node 6 is connected to a photovoltaic power station of 2000 kW (Fig. 5).

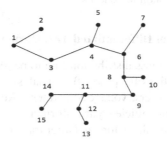

Fig. 5. Actual distribution network diagram

6.1 Analysis of Power Grid Cluster Division

This paper constructs two different planning schemes (Table 1 and Fig. 6).

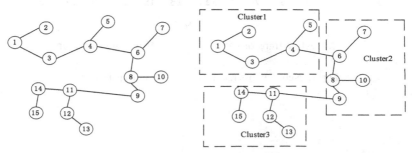

Planning 1 does not consider the network   Planning 2 considers the network planning
planning results of cluster division   results of cluster division

Fig. 6. Network planning results of the two schemes

Table 1. Plan 1 and 2 planning results

Planning	Scheme 1	Scheme 2
Investment cost/10,000 yuan	163.254	158.324
Operation and maintenance cost/10,000 yuan	38.234	33.287
Network loss cost/10,000 yuan	9.854	8.431
Power purchase cost/10,000 yuan	125.384	120.546
Annual comprehensive cost/10,000 yuan	325.584	315.845
DG reduction ratio/%	8.547	2.345
Actual penetration rate/%	82.64	87.57

According to the obvious comparison in the table above, we can see that the costs of plan 2 are significantly reduced, which indicates that cluster division is helpful to reduce network loss and improve economic benefits.

6.2 Analysis of the Effect of Differentiated Transformation

Taking a typical 10 kV heavy loss distribution line to be reconstructed as an example, a day is divided into 24 sections for power flow analysis. The reconstruction scheme includes voltage adjustment (reverse voltage adjustment); Reactive power compensation; Replace wire; Replace the high-efficiency transformer.

Comparative analysis of results before and after transformation (Table 2 and Fig. 7).

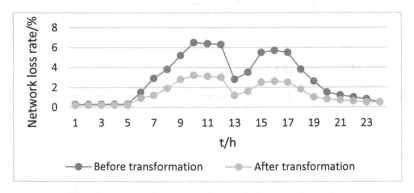

Fig. 7. Network loss rate before and after transformation

Table 2. Comparison of benefits before and after the transformation of distribution lines

Item	Line	
	Before transformation	After transformation
Total active power/MW	4.96	4.34
Total reactive power/Mvar	1.7	1.5
Total active power loss/MW	0.012	0.010
Minimum line voltage/kV	9.49	10.05
Annual network loss/10,000 yuan	1.24	1.11
Payback period/year	6.2	4.66
Average power factor	0.92	0.94
Average network loss rate/%	3.49	2.98

The differential transformation reduces the line loss rate, and it can be seen from the above table that its economic benefits have a significant improvement. Therefore, the line and other conditions are determined through the differential transformation, and the optimal value is selected.

6.3 Influence of High Penetration Distributed Power on Distribution Network Loss

(1) When the penetration rate of distributed power is 10%, the network loss of distributed power connected to nodes 2, 4, 6, 8, 10, 12 is shown in the figure (Fig. 8):

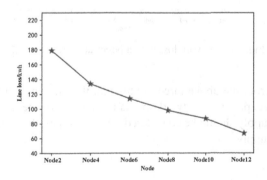

Fig. 8. Network loss with a penetration rate of 10%

(2) When the penetration rate of distributed power is 20%, the network loss of distributed power connected to nodes 2, 4, 6, 8, 10, 12 is shown in the figure (Fig. 9):

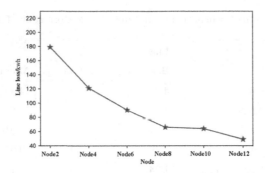

Fig. 9. Network loss with a penetration rate of 20%

(3) When the penetration rate of distributed power is 30%, the network loss of distributed power connected to nodes 2, 4, 6, 8, 10, 12 is shown in the figure (Fig. 10):

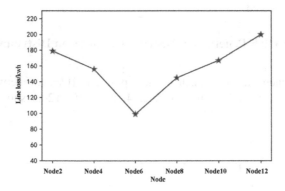

Fig. 10. Network loss with a penetration rate of 30%

It can be seen from the above three figures that the influence of distributed power access location and capacity on network loss is mutually restricted. The capacity of the distributed power supply should be considered when planning the access location of the distributed power supply.

7   Conclusion

The energy-saving planning method of the distribution network, which takes into account the access of high-permeability renewable energy, is proposed in this paper. The established two-layer model realizes the overall optimization of renewable energy planning and energy-saving transformation schemes of the distribution network through mutual feedback and iteration of the upper and lower layers, and achieves the goal of minimizing investment costs and optimal energy-saving benefits. The results of the calculation examples show that the planning method proposed in this paper is beneficial to improve the overall planning and decision-making level of the distribution network, and has certain practical application value.

References

1. Koutsoukis, N.C., Georgilakis, P.S., Hatziargyriou, N.D.: Multistage coordinated planning of active distribution networks. IEEE Trans. Power Syst. **33**(1), 32–44 (2018)
2. Xiang, Y., Liu, J.Y., Li, F.R., et al.: Optimal active distribution network planning: a review. Electr. Power Compon. Syst. **44**(10), 1075–1094 (2016)
3. Dorostkar-Ghamsari, M.R., Fotuhi-Firuzabad, M., Lehtonen, M.: Value of distribution network reconfiguration in presence of renewable energy resources. IEEE Trans. Power Syst. **31**(3), 1879–1888 (2016)
4. Liu, H., Wang, Z.: Research on energy storage and high proportion of renewable energy planning considering demand. IEEE Access **8**, 198591–198599 (2020)
5. Quijano, D.A., Padilha-Feltrin, A.: Optimal integration of distributed generation and conservation voltage reduction in active distribution networks. Int. J. Electr. Power Energy Syst. **113**(1), 197–207 (2019)
6. Manbachi, M., Farhangi, H., Palizban, A., et al.: Smart grid adaptive energy conservation and optimization engine utilizing Particle Swarm Optimization and Fuzzification. Appl. Energy **174**(1), 69–79 (2016)
7. Pamshetti, V.B., Singh, S., Singh, S.P.: Reduction of energy demand via conservation voltage reduction considering network reconfiguration and soft open point. Int. Trans. Electr. Energy Syst. **30**(1), e12147 (2020)
8. Li, Y., Tian, X., et al.: Study on voltage control in distribution network with renewable energy integration. In: 2017 IEEE Conference on Energy Internet and Energy System Integration (EI2). IEEE (2018)

Detecting Hybrid Anomalies Using an Unsupervised Approach in Online Social Networks

Randa Aljably[1][(✉)], Mznah Al-Rodhaan[2], and Yuan Tian[3]

[1] Computer Department, College of Science and Human Studies, Druma, Shaqra University, Shaqraa, Kingdom of Saudi Arabia
raljebly@su.edu.sa
[2] Computer Science Department, King Saud University, Riyadh, Kingdom of Saudi Arabia
rodhaan@ksu.edu.sa
[3] School of Computer Engineering, Nanjing Institute of Technology, Nanjing, China
ytian@njit.edu.cn

Abstract. Over the last decade, there has been significant interest in detecting hybrid anomalies in Online Social Networks (OSN). However, there remain several questions regarding the evaluation of these systems and the nature of anomaly. In order to answer these questions, further research must be conducted on anomaly definitions and development for social networks. This is achieved through datasets that represent a balanced testing environment and contains anomalies with selected characteristics. In this paper, we propose an artificial injection agent as a security solution for evaluating detecting users' abnormal behavior in OSN. The proposed agent creates synthetic anomaly and injects it into the data to utilize the detection accuracy in a Bayesian Network Classifier. We evaluated the effectiveness of the proposed technique concerning the detection of the injected anomalies. Using our approach, we were able to detect the injected anomalies with a success rate of 94% and no false alarm rates.

Keywords: Anomaly detection · Artificial agents · Hybrid anomaly · Injection algorithms · Synthetic anomaly

1 Introduction

Users in Online Social Networks (OSN) generate massive amounts of data. Such data is needed by researchers to conduct experiments on data protection and anomaly detection. A traditional approach is to apply detection systems to publicly available datasets. However, these datasets are usually anonymized and sampled. Unfortunately, this type of dataset preprocessing comes with some shortcomings. First, it changes the data characteristics and consequently the evaluation results. Secondly, the set of normal and abnormal data characteristics that are present in some volumes are limited. Thirdly, if the data was labeled in a supervised manner, it usually introduced bias and errors [1].

© Springer Nature Singapore Pte Ltd. 2022
Y. Tian et al. (Eds.): ICBDS 2021, CCIS 1563, pp. 630–642, 2022.
https://doi.org/10.1007/978-981-19-0852-1_50

With these issues in mind, it becomes essential to understand how to conduct a meaningful evaluation of detection systems; and how do the researchers obtain conclusive information about the origin and nature of anomalies [1].

Furthermore, anomaly meaning is contextual and varies from the application field to another. Thereby converting this definition into parameters and tuning those parameters may be difficult, which triggers the need to specify the appropriate definition of anomalous behavior in online social networks [2].

In an attempt to deal with these challenges, we propose to generate realistic and parameterized anomalous behavior, mimicking that of an adversary, and present it to the detection system. We choose a clean time series of behavioral patterns and system logs and inject varying anomalies to evaluate the detection power of these systems. Our goal is to demonstrate the effectiveness of Bayesian networks (BN) by evaluating it on manually injected anomalies into the dataset. We evaluated the efficiency of the proposed techniques concerning the detection of the injected anomalies.

More importantly, the generation of anomalies will be carried out by an artificial agent. The purpose of choosing this approach is to benefit from agents' heterogenous and autonomous characteristics. Since agents are platform independent and capable of asynchronously monitoring the system entities for target information, this allows our approach to be applied to all detectors relying on behavior data and would not target a specific anomaly detector. However, the problem of detecting the anomalies previously present in the dataset is out of this research's scope. Nonetheless, it still could be used as a tool for conducting a test to answer questions related to anomaly-based detection or classification evaluation.

The contributions of this paper are as follows:

- Our approach proves useful in automatic detection of the hybrid anomaly; the system identified 94% of the injected anomalies with no reported false alarms.
- Second, we show that artificial agents can be used to develop anomalies of social network nature and thus facilitate the detection of anomalous behavior.
- Third, the proposed model is adaptive and flexible so that it can be trained and applied to new datasets and detection systems. Our approach does not target a specific anomaly detector. It is global and applicable to all detectors relying on behavior data. Also, it is well suited for short term modeling.

The rest of the paper is organized as follows: Sect. 2 discusses the primitives needed to understand the construction and implementation of the proposed model and elaborated explanation on artificial agents, anomaly-based detection and Bayesian networks. In Sect. 3, we review the state of the art of security mechanisms for injection algorithms and agent-based applications. Section 4 discusses the proposed injection agent architecture, and Sect. 5 presents the simulation findings. Lastly, Sect. 6 concludes this research and describes avenues of possible extensions to this work.

2 Background

2.1 Anomaly-Based Detection

Anomaly detection has mostly received interest and research for the past decade. The majority of the work focused on robust and complex structures such as networks, graphs, and clouds. According to Hawkins in [2], an anomaly is identified as an event that deviated remarkably from other events and could be inferred that a different mechanism generated it. Following this definition, we can assume that the same anomalous behavior can occur in networks as well as in graphs. Using the notations explained in Table 1, the high-level definition of anomalous vertices and edges:

Table 1. Notation of symbols

Symbol	Description
G	A graph in a fixed time series
V_t	The vertex set in the graph at time point t
v_i	i^{th} Vertex
E_t	Edge set in the graph at time point t
$e_{i,j}$	Edge between v_i and v_j
c_0	A threshold value for normal behavior

Definition 1: (Anomalous vertices). Given G, the total vertex set $V = U_{t=1}^{T} V_t$, and a specified scoring function $f : V \rightarrow \mathbb{R}$, the set of anomalous vertices $\check{V} \subseteq V$ is a vertex set such that $\forall \check{v} \in \check{V}, |f(\check{v}) - \hat{f}| > c_0$, where $\hat{f}$ is a summary statistic of the scores $f(v), \forall v \in V$.

Definition 2: (Anomalous vertices). Given G, the total edge set $E = U_{t=1}^{T} E_t$, and a specified scoring function $f : E \rightarrow \mathbb{R}$, the set of anomalous edges $\check{E} \subseteq E$ is a edge set such that $\forall \check{e} \in \check{E}, |f(\check{e}) - \hat{f}| > c_0$, where $\hat{f}$ is a summary statistic of the scores $f(e), \forall e \in E$ [3].

This approach aims to find a subset of vertices within a set in a graph. Such that, the target vertex in the subset displayed irregular activity compared to the others in the same set. The same definition applies to networks, especially social networks as anomalous users are identified by having an abnormal mode of activity compared to their history. The same applies to the definition of anomalous edges, wherein social networks the difference in an edges weight represents the user's activity toward other users. An anomaly, in this case, can be performing a specific action more/less than usual, such as sending and receiving more/fewer messages than before.

2.2 Bayesian Networks (BN)

Statistical anomaly detection is widely used in many fields, and various methods have been proposed in past years [4]. In this section, we introduce Bayesian networks and provide an overview of the way they function with network structure. Each variable in the dataset is considered a node in the network. A node N has a finite and discrete state space. Its conditional dependence on other nodes is represented as edges. In case the node is a parent, it will be assigned prior probability distribution based on the prior knowledge about this node.

A node N in Bayesian networks, with parents $M_1, M_2, \ldots, M_n$ has a conditional probability distribution

$$P_{cd} = M_1 \times M_2 \times \ldots \times M_n \to N \tag{1}$$

Bayes' Theorem prearranges the distributions:

$$P(n|M) = \frac{P(M|n)P(n)}{P(M)} \tag{2}$$

3 Related Work

The term hybrid anomaly can be interpreted to different meanings in the literature. It is sometimes substituted with the term collective, synthetic or volume anomaly. For example, in [5] hybrid anomaly refers to data that contains different types of attack signatures, such as misdirection or black holes. Another term used for hybrid data is collective anomalies. It considers the occurrence of related data instances together as a collection in a time series to be anomalous concerning the entire data set [6].

The researchers in [5] proposed using K-means clustering algorithm to build patterns of intrusions in an intrusion detection system to tackle hybrid anomalies. Next, the intrusion patterns were matched to the network activities. The injected anomalies in the testing dataset included traffic sent and received and end-to-end delay. The scheme achieved a relatively high detection rate of 98.6% and 1.2% false positive rate.

In more detail, [7] proposed testing the reaction of the evaluation metrics. Whereby the researchers injected two types of anomalies. The first represents a degraded state of a network component to test the network latency or performance. The second anomaly represents a corrupted state of a network service to test network crash. The evaluation was carried out in two phases where the first phase analyses the system operation with regular data, while the second phase analyses the system operation with injected data for the same time interval.

The injection process could be based on a fixed volume of an anomaly. For example, the authors in [8] adopted a traffic generation model that injected synthetic anomalies of fixed size [10, 100, 1000] in each matrix. This is due to the absence of ground truth information about volume anomalies in the Abilene TM dataset. Then they attempted to assess the effectiveness of the network detection systems regarding a total number of detection and false positive rates for the injected traffic. The CUR decomposition detection system achieved better results than PCA-subspace method for volume anomaly detection [8, 9]. Similarly, the study in [10] used injected anomalies to verify that graph-detection systems were able to detect the anomalies with very high detection rates and minimal false positives.

Priebe et al. [11] conducted an experiment based on injecting controlled-anomaly into real graph data and measuring its detectability. The purpose was to study the effect of fusing graph features with statistically inferred and random graph attributes. The results showed that the detectability of some fused data outperformed the situation where separated graph or content features were used. In contrast, other fused data had an adverse effect on signal gain due to additional estimation variance factor. This disproportion indicated the need for expanding the data inference methods beyond graph features and content.

Another anomaly injection approach was presented in [12], in which the authors used correlated and uncorrelated anomalies. The study randomly generated a dataset for one week and injected a different number of correlated and uncorrelated anomaly events into the dataset. To compare the detection accuracy, they injected five correlated anomalies at the same time, then 16 uncorrelated anomalies in random time series. The percentage of anomaly events vary from 0.1%–1% of the total sample population. The result showed a fluctuating performance of the PCA detection system as it distinguished five correlated and two uncorrelated anomalies in a one-week dataset. However, the same seven anomalies were not correctly isolated in two weeks dataset until more correlated anomaly events were injected into the data.

The work in [13] presented a different version of injection scheme, the process randomly selected 5% of the instances in each class, i.e., some files in the dataset, and randomly created anomalous labels for each class. They claimed that experimenting with both raw and injected dataset can be used as a sanity check for detection methods.

Lastly, to evaluate supervised detection in the cloud, the authors in [14] randomly injected anomalies in production data. This approach was deemed necessary to deal with the real-time nature of cloud data. The speed and volume of data made obtaining truly labeled outliers in time series non-practical. Thus, the authors use three factors for anomaly generation: injection time, injection magnitude and anomaly size.

4   Proposed Agent Architecture

In this section, we present our methodology for generating anomalies and injecting them in social network datasets. We define anomaly generation factors that should be considered in the process of creating anomalies. We also outline how anomaly is injected. The first step is to define anomaly in the area of online social networks.

The anomaly can be identified as each unusual event that has a different effect on the social network. Table 2 summarizes five types of anomaly we consider in our system.

Table 2. Types of an anomaly found in communication patterns in social networks

Anomaly class	Description
Additive	A (gradual or sudden) increase in the number of communications between two network users
Subtractive	A (gradual or sudden) decrease in the number of communications between two network users
Interactive	The user is communicating with new users
User-driven	Anomalous behavior is driven outside the user's range of behavior
Platform-driven	Anomalous behavior is driven outside the platform's guidelines and regulations

The first type of anomaly occurs when the user is communicating more in a specific period, while the subtractive anomalous behavior indicates that the user is communicating less in a specific period. This anomaly could be used as an indicator to profile hijacking. The third type is an interactive anomaly where the user expands his network of relationships in an abnormal pattern, which might be an indicator of social engineering. The anomalous value itself may be computed outside the range of actions that are usually performed by a specific user and thereby recognized by the system, regardless of the actions of the social network users. For example, a user may send and receive a range of [365–500] messages over ten days. Any values outside this range may be considered anomalous compared to the user's usual activities. On the other hand, the value may be computed from the platforms specific range of allowed actions—for example, the maximum number of messages sent daily on Facebook.

Regardless of the type of anomaly, some anomaly characteristics must be met. First, the anomaly should be realistic and expresses real-world values. Second, it should be parameterized, in a way that it can be configured to meet the injection objective, such that the parameters that result in the best performance are returned as the output of the anomaly generation agent.

4.1 Injection Operation

To build an anomaly injection agent in social networks, we must attain a deep understanding of anomalous behavior, the network structure, and regular behavior pattern, and data flow within the network. We will define three versions of anomaly generation functions. Then we will present some scenarios for injecting the anomalies on Bayesian detection system and record the results. Table 3 describes the parameters used by the injection agent to create anomalies.

Table 3. Injection parameters

Factor	Values assigned
Anomaly value	[Real-world, user-defined (fixed), randomized]
Window size	[0.1–0.9] of the dataset duration or [5%–10%] of the dataset population [Continuous, independent]
Injection time (Frequency)	[Constant (at the same time), random intervals]
User selection	The selection of particular users to inject their data: Deterministic, probabilistic, or randomized selection
Injection parameter	[Replace original data, incorporate original data in anomalous value]
Value Range	Adapted after determining user or platform driven
Generating function	Correlation () Substitute- value() Gradual-deviation() Additive-Noise ()
Anomaly type	[Correlated, non-correlated]

4.2   Anomaly Generation Functions

Statistical Relation Deduction
In this approach, we generate a statistical relationship between the values in each user's record, then use the relation to deduce outlier values. We first calculate the probability of the first number in the sequence, then the probability of the second number given the first number, and so on.

Additive-Noise
This is appropriate for continuous features, where the injection is performed on parts of the pattern. We Generate a random number in the range [0–2], then multiply the random number with the original value to create noised-value. The noised value is then added to the original value.

Figure 1 illustrate how an injected pattern differs from the original one using additive noise.

Gradual-Deviation
The injection is performed on the entire continuous pattern. An anomalous pattern is generated as a gradual increase or decrease in data. For example, the user's communication pattern will be increased by a factor in the first day, then increased by a multiple of the factor in the second day and so on, and the same for the decrease process. These impressionists a malicious attacker trying to hide his appearance in the social network.

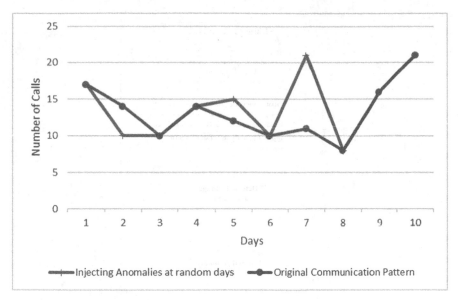

Fig. 1. Injecting anomalies at random intervals

Substitute-Value
Replace a segment of the value (feature/attribute) with a segment from another value (feature/attribute); this could be implied in contextual and categorical data such as users' roles, location, and others.

Inclusion/Exclusion
Add or remove a categorical feature of the dataset.

4.3 Building an Injection Agent

We demonstrate an abstract view of the agent's functionality. As shown in Fig. 2 it starts with initializing the previously mentioned injection factors, then determines the criteria for selecting users, injection functions and other parameters, it generates the synthetic data then injects into the patterns.

After that, the agent tests whether there was any change in the intermediate detection such as the predictive p-values in BN as an indicator to an eruption in the network structure, if not, it will retune the parameters again until the p-values are changed. Lastly, the agent checks if the evaluation metric is achieved and calculates the percentage of a detected injected anomaly compared to the known injected anomaly.

We use a data set adapted from the VAST Challenge 2008 [15]. It represents the unique communication activities of 400 users, throughout ten days. The Bayesian detection model is adapted from [16].

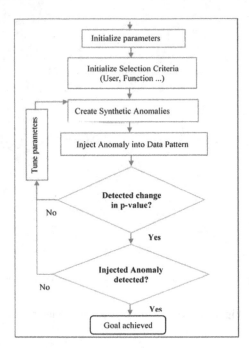

Fig. 2. Injection agent flowchart

4.4 Evaluation Metric

The evaluation of the success of the injection starts with a scenario where at least some of the anomalies are identified. The identification in the Bayesian network could be in many forms: the users with injected data are identified as anomalous, the predictive-p-value for the users has changed, or the projection of the users into the first two eigenvectors of the Laplacian has changed.

Two evaluation metrics are suggested for injection-evaluation. The first metric is the percentage of the detected injected anomalies to the known injected anomalies. The second metric is the percentage of times where at least a portion of the injected anomaly is discovered.

In order to compare the performance of the system between the original dataset and the injected one, we injected the sent and received communication patterns which in turn affect the sending and receiving users. Also, we further replaced the contextual information such as the date of communication and location of users.

5 Simulation Results

In this section, we demonstrate the experiments we conducted on anomaly injection. Each experiment was designed to answer a specific question about the system performance in response to a specific injected anomaly. In the first case, we injected 3% of the communication records with a window size of 2 days randomly distributed. However, none of the anomalies were reported, and the anomalous behavior that was observed on the eighth day as shown in Fig. 3 remained the same. The reason is that the injected volume was not big enough to disturb the social network structure. This means that the dataset with this volume of injection does not contain enough patterns over the ten days to offer a real advantage to the Bayesian network.

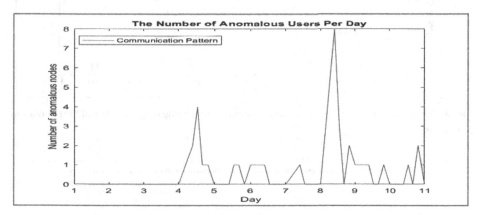

Fig. 3. The number of anomalous users in the VAST dataset without injecting outliers

So, the agent re-tuned the parameters and increased the population of injection to 10% and the duration was two randomly distributed days so that that system could infer more from the statistical pattern. The system detected the injected anomalies, and the number of injected users were added to the anomalous list on the fifth day. The predictive p-value for 934 users out of 1000 users changed, meaning 94% value for the first metric. Another remarkable observation is when the anomaly injection covered users who were classified as anomalous before; the randomized anomaly changed the counting process for the pairs of users' communication model. Since the increments of the counting process are computed according to Bayesian probability. At that point, the injected anomalies resulted in predictive-p values higher than the threshold 0.05. Making the anomalous behavior closer to the previously modeled behavior a thereby undetected. This is seen on the ninth day in Fig. 4.

The agent repeated the same procedure for the receiving users of the communication, again the predictive p-values reflected the changes as well as the set of anomalous users. This could be seen in Fig. 5 and Fig. 6 representing the original p-values for the primary group of anomalous users in Fig. 5 compared to the set after injecting the communication patterns for the same group of users in Fig. 6 In the figures the circular points are the p-values when the number of communication calls is computed randomly, the crosses are the number of communication calls computed from a fixed measure. Both values were affected as seen in the changes that occurred on the (2, 3, 4, 6 and 7)th days.

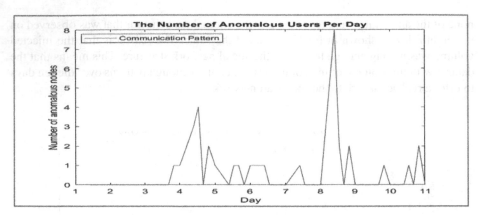

Fig. 4. The number of anomalous users after injecting the sending pattern of 10% of the population of patterns

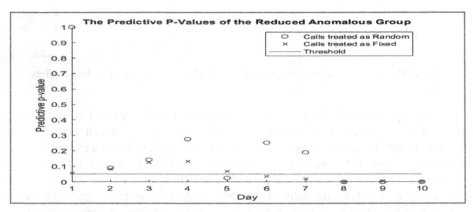

Fig. 5. The predictive p-values of the anomalous set of users under the multinomial model [16] before injecting the set of receiving users

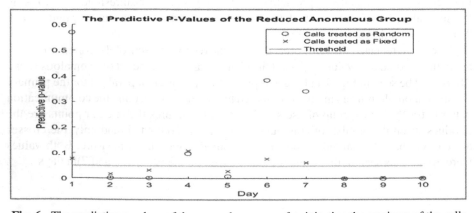

Fig. 6. The predictive p-values of the anomalous users after injecting the receivers of the calls

6 Conclusion and Future Work

In this research, we proposed an artificial agent to create and inject synthetic data into social network datasets. The agent was used as a tool to evaluate the detection performance of Bayesian network classifiers. We conducted a set of experiments, each designed to answer a specific question about the system performance towards a specific injected anomaly. We evaluated the experiments according to the percentage of the detected injected anomalies as compared to the known injected anomalies. We would like to investigate the effect of anonymizing the injected anomalies and the application of the secondly proposed evaluation metric.

Declarations of interest. The authors declare no conflict of interest.

References

1. Brauckhoff, D., Wagner, A., May, M.: FLAME: A Flow-Level Anomaly Modeling Engine. In: CSET (2008)
2. Hawkins, D.M.: Identification of Outliers, vol. 11. Chapman and Hall, London (1980)
3. Ranshous, S., Shen, S., Koutra, D., Harenberg, S., Faloutsos, C., Samatova, N.F.: Anomaly detection in dynamic networks: a survey. Wiley Interdiscip. Rev. Comput. Stat. **7**(3), 223–247 (2015)
4. Zhang, J., Paschalidis, I.C.: Statistical anomaly detection via composite hypothesis testing for Markov models. IEEE Trans. Sig. Process. **66**(3), 589–602 (2018)
5. Wazid, M., Das, A.K.: An efficient hybrid anomaly detection scheme using K-means clustering for wireless sensor networks. Wirel. Pers. Commun. **90**(4), 1971–2000 (2016). https://doi.org/10.1007/s11277-016-3433-3
6. Chandola, V., Banerjee, A., Kumar, V.: Anomaly detection: a survey. ACM Comput. Surv. (CSUR) **41**(3), 15 (2009)
7. Wallschläger, M., Gulenko, A., Schmidt, F., Kao, O., Liu, F.: Automated anomaly detection in virtualized services using deep packet inspection. Procedia Comput. Sci. **110**, 510–515 (2017)
8. Kumar, S.: Classification and detection of computer intrusions. ProQuest Dissertations Publishing (1995)
9. Kumar, A., Saradhi, V.V., Venkatesh, T.: Network-wide volume anomaly detection using alternate matrix decomposition techniques. In: 2017 IEEE International Conference on Advanced Networks and Telecommunications Systems (ANTS). IEEE (2017)
10. Eberle, W., Holder, L.: Anomaly detection in data represented as graphs. Intell. Data Anal. **11**(6), 663–689 (2007)
11. Priebe, C.E., et al.: Statistical inference on attributed random graphs: fusion of graph features and content: an experiment on time series of Enron graphs. Comput. Stat. Data Anal. **54**(7), 1766–1776 (2010)
12. Zhang, Y., Debroy, S., Calyam, P.: Network-wide anomaly event detection and diagnosis with perfSONAR. IEEE Trans. Netw. Serv. Manage. **13**(3), 666–680 (2016)
13. Lu, Y., et al.: An unsupervised approach to anomaly detection in music datasets. In: Proceedings of the 39th International ACM SIGIR conference on Research and Development in Information Retrieval. ACM (2016)

14. Hochenbaum, J., Vallis, O.S., Kejariwal, A.: Automatic anomaly detection in the cloud via statistical learning. arXiv preprint arXiv:1704.07706 (2017)
15. Grinstein, G., Plaisant, C., Laskowski, S., O'Connell, T., Scholtz, J., Whiting, M.: VAST 2008 challenge: introducing mini-challenges. In: IEEE Symposium on Visual Analytics Science and Technology, VAST'08, 19 October 2008, pp. 195–196. IEEE (2019)
16. Heard, N.A., Weston, D.J., Platanioti, K., Hand, D.J.: Bayesian anomaly detection methods for social networks. Ann. Appl. Stat. 4(2), 645–662 (2010)

Community Detection Based on Deep Network Embedding with Dual Self-supervised Training

Yunfang Chen[1], Haotian Mao[1], Li Wang[1], and Wei Zhang[1,2(✉)]

[1] School of Computer Science, Nanjing University of Posts
and Telecommunications, Nanjing 210023, Jiangsu, China
zhangw@njupt.edu.cn
[2] Jiangsu Key Laboratory of Big Data Security and Intelligent Processing, Nanjing University
of Posts and Telecommunications, Nanjing 210023, Jiangsu, China

Abstract. We propose a community discovery method based on deep auto-encoding (DGAE_DST). Firstly, we use the pre-trained two-layer neural network and k-means algorithm to initialize the centroid vector, and then use the DNN module and the GCN module to capture the structure features and attributes respectively. The attribute information is fed to the GCN layer to integrate the structure information and attributes. Finally, DNN and GCN respectively output the reconstructed adjacency matrix and feature matrix, and minimize their loss from the original matrix. The experimental results on four datasets show that the DGAE_DST method has higher stability and accuracy.

Keywords: Complex network · Community detection · Network embedding · Deep learning · Auto-encoder

1 Introduction

A complex network is usually an abstraction of a complex system, and it can usually be represented by graph data. Complex networks commonly have unique community structures. From the perspective of the degree of association and density, the community is also called locally densely connected subgraph or node clusters [1].

There have been a large number of algorithms for community discovery of complex networks. Early studies usually only use network topology information. Most traditional community discovery algorithms need to provide the number of communities, and in some cases even the size of clusters as input, and this information is basically unknown.

Today complex data sets and complex scenarios force us to need more powerful models to handle large-scale networks and high-dimensional data. Deep-learning based network embedding method can encode the feature representation of high-dimensional data [2]. Since we know little about the community in the data, deep learning achieve best perform when meeting unsupervised learning [3]. Taking social networks as an example, the community structure exists objectively, but a certain user in a certain community only interacts with those users who are directly connected to it, but in this community, he interacts with those who are not directly connected to it. These users are actually very

Y. Tian et al. (Eds.): ICBDS 2021, CCIS 1563, pp. 643–656, 2022.
https://doi.org/10.1007/978-981-19-0852-1_51

similar. If you want to recommend friends, users who belong to the same community should give priority to recommendations.

The deep learning model can help us extract richer feature information. It has detection capabilities based on network topology and node attributes to achieve a more robust and better performance. Learning more representative attributes and structural characteristics.

The main contributions:

1) We propose a community discovery method that combines DNN and GCN, and design a transfer operator to input the embedded representation learned by the DNN auto-encoder into the corresponding GCN layer.
2) Our proposed dual decoder and dual self-supervised training method can better express the topology representation and network attributes.
3) The experimental results show that the proposed method can alleviate the impact of over-smoothing, and has higher stability and higher accuracy.

2   Related Works

Previous network embedding algorithms mainly focused on matrix factorization methods [4, 5]. Recently, many node embedding methods based on random walk have also achieved success. Their key idea is to optimize the node embedding, so that nodes on the same random path can obtain statistically similar embeddings. [21] proposed a Deep-Walk network embedding method which is inspired by word2vec, combined random walk with skip-gram algorithm. This method combined with clustering algorithm can be directly applied to community discovery tasks. In 2016, the node2vec [22] algorithm based on biased random walk was proposed. The main innovation of node2vec is to regulate the mode of walking on the basis of DeepWalk, combining depth first search and breadth first search. DFS strategy tends to explore the region far away from the node. The sampling node more accurately reflects the macro view of the neighborhood, which is similar to the "homogeneity" characteristics of the community. The search strategy of BFS tends to traverse directly connected nodes, which reflects "isomorphism". It can be understood that the BFS search strategy can capture the similarity of neighbors. In the community discovery task, the connected edges between nodes are very important, but the connected edges that can be observed in the real network are often a small part, and most of the connected edges or potential connected edges do not appear for some reasons. If there are many common neighbors between two nodes in the network, then the relationship between the two nodes should be relatively close, even if there is no directly connected edge between them. Therefore, the integration of BFS and DFS can achieve both directly and indirectly connected nodes, and can better capture the community relationship between nodes.

With the continuous expansion of network scale and data dimensions, more powerful community detection techniques are needed to maintain effective performance and feasible calculation speed [6]. Taking advantage of CNNs, [7] designed a community detection CNN model. [8] introduces a new convolution in the CNN framework. Autoencoder is also a very powerful deep neural network community discovery model

[9]. Through the work of [10], the modularity maximization model and the normalized cutting model are better integrated into the auto-encoder. Based on this, they proposed a stack auto-encoder framework.

Deep network embedding aims to encode complex networks into low-dimensional feature representations and retain topological features [11]. After getting the embedding vector, downstream can use clustering algorithms to complete the community detection task. [12] proposed a kind of non-negative matrix factorization model of deep auto-encoders. [13] combined deep learning and deep embedding.

In part 1, we introduce the community detection and several typical methods. In part 2, we show the related study from traditional methods to deep learning and GNNs methods. In part 3, we introduce the basic knowledge. In part 4, we introduce the framework and training method in detail. In part 5, we introduce four datasets and analyze the experimental results. In part 6, we make a conclusion.

3 Preliminaries

3.1 Deep Neural Network Module

A deep neural network transform the original input into low-dimensional data, and then reconstructs the input data through the decoder to make it as close as possible to the original data. The stacked auto-encoder is a very powerful method. The model is composed of multiple layers of encoders (Fig. 1).

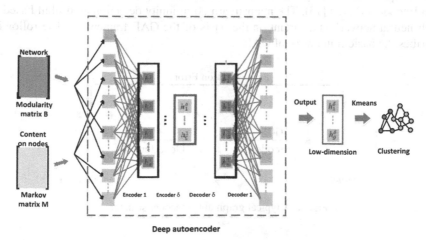

Fig. 1. A typical community detection framework based on deep stack auto-encoder [10], its input matrix $\mathbf{Z}$ is composed of two parts: modularity matrix $\mathbf{B}$ and Markov matrix $\mathbf{M}$.

In the auto-encoding module, joint matrix $\mathbf{Z}$ is input, $\mathbf{z}_i = \left[\mathbf{b}_i^T, \mathbf{m}_i^T\right]^T$. The encoder maps the input data to the low-dimensional hidden layer. $\mathbf{H}^a = \left\{\mathbf{h}_i^a\right\} \in \mathbb{R}^{r \times N}$, where $\mathbf{h}_i^a$ is the embedding of node v_i. The formula is as follows:

$$\mathbf{h}_i^a = \phi(\mathbf{z}_i) = sig(\mathbf{W} \cdot \mathbf{z}_i + \mathbf{d}) \tag{1}$$

Where $\mathbf{W} \in \mathbb{R}^{r \times 2N}$ is weighted matrix, $\mathbf{d} \in \mathbb{R}^{r \times 1}$ is bias vector, $sig(x)$ is sigmoid function $sig(x) = \frac{1}{1+e^{-x}}$. In addition, the decoder utilizes embedding $\mathbf{H}$ to reconstruct input matrix $\mathbf{Z}$. The formula is as follows:

$$z_i^* = \varphi\left(\mathbf{h}_i^a\right) = sig\left(\mathbf{W}^* \cdot \mathbf{z}_i + \mathbf{d}^*\right) \tag{2}$$

Where $\mathbf{W}^* \in \mathbb{R}^{2N \times r}$ and $\mathbf{d}^* \in \mathbb{R}^{2N \times 1}$ are learned parameters upgrated by minimized reconstruction error. The formula is as follows:

$$\delta = \arg\min_{\delta} O\left(\mathbf{z}, \mathbf{z}^*\right) = \arg\min_{\delta} \sum_{i=1}^{N} O(\mathbf{z}_i, \varphi(\phi(\mathbf{z}_i))) \tag{3}$$

$\delta = \{\mathbf{W}, \mathbf{d}, \mathbf{W}^*, \mathbf{d}^*\}$ is the parameter set to be learned.

Finally, k-means algorithm is used to cluster the embedding matrix $\mathbf{H}$ obtained by the deep auto-encoding module for community detection.

3.2 Graph Neural Network Module

The deep neural network embodies the advantages of high accuracy in many fields. In order to apply the deep neural network to the processing tasks of graph data, the method of the graph neural network has been proposed and received wide attention. This type of method can be integrated with clustering algorithms to solve community detection tasks through end-to-end training. Graph Auto Encoder is the most commonly used method based on graph neural network. GAE and VGAE were developed by [14]. It is an unsupervised learning framework based on the graph structure data of Variational Auto Encoders (VAE) [15]. The mainstream community detection algorithm based on graph neural network is a variant on the basis of the GAE framework. The following describes the basic framework of GAE.

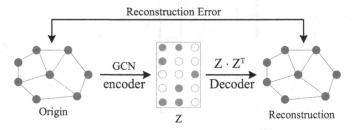

Fig. 2. A typical graph auto-encoder structure

A typical GAE structure [14] (See Fig. 2). Graph Convolutional Neural Network (GCN) is used as the encoder to get the hidden layer representation (or embedding) of the node. This process can be expressed as the following formula:

$$\mathbf{Z} = GCN(\mathbf{X}, \mathbf{A}) \tag{4}$$

Where, $\mathbf{X}$ is attributed matrix, $\mathbf{A}$ is adjacency matrix, output $\mathbf{Z} \in R^{N \times f}$ is hidden layer representation (or embedding). $GCN(\cdot)$ is a function which takes $\mathbf{X}$ and $\mathbf{A}$ as inputs and outputs the embedding.

The decoder in the graph auto-encoder aims to reconstruct the adjacency matrix from the embedding layer, usually using the inner product, which is expressed as follows:

$$\hat{A} = \sigma\left(ZZ^{T}\right) \tag{5}$$

Where $\hat{A}$ is the reconstructed adjacency matrix, $\sigma(\cdot)$ is the sigmoid function. Apply cross-entropy loss function:

$$\mathcal{L} = -\frac{1}{N}\sum ylog\hat{y} + (1-y)log\left(1-\hat{y}\right) \tag{6}$$

Where y is a value of element in adjacency matrix (0 or 1),$\hat{y}$ is a corresponding value of element in reconstructed adjacency matrix ($\hat{y} \in [0,1]$).

Researchers have developed many network clustering algorithms. For example, [16] proposed to integrate the attention mechanism in the graph auto-encoder and combine it with self-supervised training clustering. [17] proposed to use Relaxd k-means to perform clustering supervision on the embedding features of the graph auto-encoder. These clustering algorithms based on graph auto-encoders are also suitable for community detection tasks (Fig. 3).

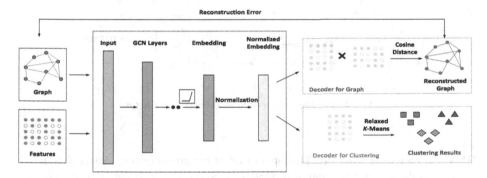

Fig. 3. A typical graph auto-encoder framework [8] based on graph clustering

The graph auto-encoder uses multi-layer GCN layers to encode the adjacency matrix and attributed matrix of the network to obtain the embedding of network. Then the normalized embedding representation matrix is processed in two ways. One is to use the inner product to obtain the reconstructed adjacency matrix and calculate the reconstruction loss. The other is to use Relaxd k-means to enhance the cohesion of the embedding.

4 Model

4.1 DGAE_DST Algorithm

Framework

The paper proposes a community detection model based on Deep Auto-encoder (DAE), Graph Auto-encoder (GAE) and Dual Self-supervised Training (DGAE_DST). The framework is shown in Fig. 4. The input of DAE is the feature matrix. The input of GAE is the adjacency matrix $\mathbf{A} \in \mathbb{R}^{N \times N}$ and the feature matrix $\mathbf{X} \in \mathbb{R}^{N \times d}$. The DNN module encodes the feature matrix through the hidden layer, the output of each hidden layer is used as an input of the GCN encoder.

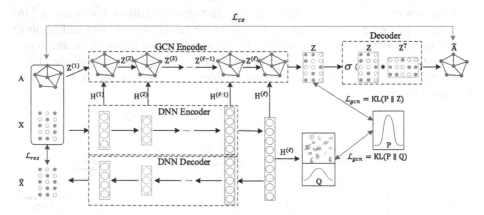

Fig. 4. Dual self-supervised auto-encoding structure

DNN Auto-encoder Module. The input of DNN module is feature matrix $\mathbf{X} \in \mathbb{R}^{N \times d}$, where N is the number of nodes, d is dimension, and vector x_i is the i th node's feature representation.

Assuming that the encoder includes the L layers, the embedding $\mathbf{H}^{\ell}$ can be expressed as:

$$\mathbf{H}^{(\ell)} = \phi\left(\mathbf{W}_e^{(\ell)}\mathbf{H}^{(\ell-1)} + \mathbf{b}_e^{(\ell)}\right) \tag{7}$$

Where ϕ is activation function of full connected layer, $\mathbf{H}^{(\ell-1)}$ is the $(l-1)$ th layer's hidden representation, and $\mathbf{b}_e^{(\ell)}$ and $\mathbf{W}_e^{(\ell)}$ represent the bias and weighted matrix of the l th layer of the encoder respectively. Initialize $\mathbf{H}^{(0)} = \mathbf{X}$.

Decoder reconstructs feature matrix $\mathbf{X}$ by fully connected layer. The formula is as follows:

$$\mathbf{H}^{(\ell)} = \phi\left(\mathbf{W}_d^{(\ell)}\mathbf{H}^{(\ell-1)} + \mathbf{b}_d^{(\ell)}\right) \tag{8}$$

Where $\mathbf{b}_d^{(\ell)}$ and $\mathbf{W}_d^{(\ell)}$ represent bias and weighted matrix of the l th layer of the decoder respectively. $\hat{\mathbf{X}} = \mathbf{H}^{(L)}$ is the reconstruction and it should have the minimum loss with the original data. The object function is as follows:

$$\mathcal{L}_{res} = \frac{1}{2N} \sum_{i=1}^{N} \|\mathbf{x}_i - \hat{\mathbf{x}}_i\|_2^2 = \frac{1}{2N} \|\mathbf{X} - \hat{\mathbf{X}}\|_F^2 \tag{9}$$

Inspired by previous work [18, 19], we set the dimensionality of the hidden layer of the encoder to $[d, 500, 500, 2000, 10]$, and set the dimensionality of the hidden layer of the decoder to $[10, 2000, 500, 500, d]$, where d is the dimension of the feature matrix of the input layer.

GCN Auto-encoder Module. GCN can be used to extract the information in the graph structure, but it is generally used in semi-supervised learning. In order to use it for unsupervised learning, it can be used as a part of the graph auto-encoder and combined with corresponding tasks for training. The encoder is a graph convolutional network. The initial input is the adjacency matrix $\mathbf{A} \in \mathbb{R}^{N \times N}$ and the feature matrix $\mathbf{X} \in \mathbb{R}^{N \times d}$, the representation of the $(l-1)$ th layer is the weighted summation of the feature representation of the $(l-1)$ th layer of the DNN encoder and the structural representation of the $(l-1)$ th layer of the GCN encoder, expressed as follows:

$$\tilde{\mathbf{Z}}^{(\ell-1)} = \lambda \mathbf{Z}^{(\ell-1)} + (1 - \lambda)\mathbf{H}^{(\ell-1)} \tag{10}$$

Then we enter the above results into the GCN layer to learn structural information, and we can get the embedding:

$$\mathbf{Z}^{(\ell)} = \sigma\left(\tilde{\mathbf{D}}^{-\frac{1}{2}}\tilde{\mathbf{A}}\tilde{\mathbf{D}}^{-\frac{1}{2}}\tilde{\mathbf{Z}}^{(\ell-1)}\mathbf{W}^{(\ell)}\right) \tag{11}$$

Where σ is a nonlinear activation function. $\tilde{\mathbf{A}} = \mathbf{A} + \mathbf{I}$, where $\mathbf{I}$ is an identity matrix. $\tilde{\mathbf{D}}$ is the degree matrix of $\tilde{\mathbf{A}}$, where $\tilde{\mathbf{D}}_{ii} = \sum_j \tilde{\mathbf{A}}_{ii}$. GCN takes the adjacency matrix as input, and the encoder finally outputs the embedding $\mathbf{Z}$. The initial input of GCN is adjacency matrix $\mathbf{A}$ and feature matrix $\mathbf{X}$, expressed as follows:

$$\mathbf{Z}^{(1)} = \sigma\left(\tilde{\mathbf{D}}^{-\frac{1}{2}}\tilde{\mathbf{A}}\tilde{\mathbf{D}}^{-\frac{1}{2}}\mathbf{X}\mathbf{W}^{(1)}\right) \tag{12}$$

Utilize softmax function to get the final multi-label output:

$$\mathbf{Z} = softmax\left(\tilde{\mathbf{D}}^{-\frac{1}{2}}\tilde{\mathbf{A}}\tilde{\mathbf{D}}^{-\frac{1}{2}}\tilde{\mathbf{Z}}^{(L)}\mathbf{W}^{(L)}\right) \tag{13}$$

Where $\mathbf{z}_{ij} \in \mathbf{Z}$ represents the probability that the i th node belongs to the cluster center j, and $\mathbf{Z}$ can be regarded as the probability distribution of network nodes.

In decoder, we reconstruct $\hat{\mathbf{A}}$ by performing inner product on $\mathbf{Z}$, the formula is as follows:

$$\hat{\mathbf{A}} = \sigma\left(\mathbf{Z}\mathbf{Z}^T\right) \tag{14}$$

Where $\sigma(\cdot)$ is sigmoid function. The loss of graph auto-encoder is defined as the reconstruction loss of $\mathbf{A}$ and $\hat{\mathbf{A}}$, expressed as follows:

$$\mathcal{L}_{ce} = E_{\Phi(\mathbf{Z}|\mathbf{X},\mathbf{A})}\left[\log p\left(\hat{\mathbf{A}}|\mathbf{Z}\right)\right] \tag{15}$$

Specifically, the cross-entropy function is used to measure the loss of the reconstructed adjacency matrix and the original matrix, which is expressed as follows:

$$\mathcal{L}_{ce} = -\sum_i \sum_j \mathbf{A}_{ij}\log\left(\hat{\mathbf{A}}_{ij}\right) \tag{16}$$

4.2 Train

Duel Self-supervised Training. Inspired by previous works [18, 19], we fit the GCN embedding $\mathbf{Z}$ and the student t-distribution $\mathbf{Q}$ represented by the DNN embedding to the auxiliary distribution $\mathbf{P}$ respectively. We call it dual self-supervised training.

We calculate the similarity between the hidden layer feature $\mathbf{h}_i$ and the community centroid μ_j by using student t-distribution, that is, the probability q_{ij} of assigning sample i to community j can be expressed as:

$$q_{ij} = \frac{\left(1 + \|\mathbf{h}_i - \mu_j\|^2/a\right)^{-\frac{a+1}{2}}}{\sum_{j'}\left(1 + \|\mathbf{h}_i - \mu_{j'}\|^2/a\right)^{-\frac{a+1}{2}}} \tag{17}$$

Where $\mathbf{h}_i$ represents the i th sample's embedding, and μ_j is initialized by pre-training. Refer to previous work [18], we set $a = 1$ and determine auxiliary distribution $\mathbf{P}$:

$$p_{ij} = \frac{q_{ij}^2/f_j}{\sum_{j'} q_{ij'}^2/f_{j'}} \tag{18}$$

Where $f_j = \sum_i q_{ij}$ represents the frequency of cluster j.

We train the model by reducing the KL divergence loss between the predicted distribution $\mathbf{Q}$ and the auxiliary distribution $\mathbf{P}$, the formula is as follows:

$$\mathcal{L}_{clu} = KL(\mathbf{P}\|\mathbf{Q}) = \sum_i \sum_j p_{ij}\log\frac{p_{ij}}{q_{ij}} \tag{19}$$

Similarly, we use the auxiliary distribution $\mathbf{P}$ to supervise the training of the $\mathbf{Z}$ distribution, the formula is as follows:

$$\mathcal{L}_{gcn} = KL(\mathbf{P}\|\mathbf{Z}) = \sum_i \sum_j p_{ij}\log\frac{p_{ij}}{z_{ij}} \tag{20}$$

Model Training. In order to make the learned network embedding more in line with community detection tasks, we design a unified objective function to optimize node embedding and node allocation at the same time. The final objective function is expressed as follows:

$$\mathcal{L} = \mathcal{L}_{res} + \gamma\mathcal{L}_{ce} + \alpha\mathcal{L}_{gcn} + \beta\mathcal{L}_{clu} \tag{21}$$

Where $\gamma > 0$, $\alpha > 0$ and $\beta > 0$ are hyperparameters to balance four loss.

Pre-training. Inspired by previous work [18], we pre-train a DNN for cluster centroid μ_j and initialized parameters of DNN auto-encoder module. Take $W_e^{(\ell)}$ and $b_e^{(\ell)}$ as examples, the parameters are upgrated by backpropagation as follows:

$$W_e^{(\ell)} = W_e^{(\ell)} - \frac{1}{N} \sum_{i=1}^{N} \left(\frac{\partial \mathcal{L}_{res}}{\partial W_e^{(\ell)}} \right) \tag{22}$$

$$b_e^{(\ell)} = b_e^{(\ell)} - \frac{1}{N} \sum_{i=1}^{N} \left(\frac{\partial \mathcal{L}_{res}}{\partial b_e^{(\ell)}} \right) \tag{23}$$

Then we perform cluster algorithm on the output of pre-training DNN to obtain k initial cluster centroids μ. We adopt random initialization for the weights of the graph auto-encoders. Due to the good characteristics of the graph auto-encoder, even the weights initialized randomly can still obtain good results.

Cluster. Our model will output two soft clustering assignment matrices Q and Z when the training converges. In order to better integrate the graph structure and node feature, we weighted the sum of the two soft cluster assignment matrices, and then took the cluster corresponding to the result with the largest value in each row vector (the cluster with the highest probability) as the node corresponding community. The specific formula is as follows:

$$r_i = \arg \max_j \Upsilon_{ij} \tag{24}$$

Where $\Upsilon_{ij} = \frac{\alpha}{\alpha+\beta} z_{ij} + \frac{\beta}{\alpha+\beta} q_{ij}$, where α and β are balance parameter of loss function, represent the contribution rate of GCN and DNN clustering loss to the entire loss function.

5   Experiments

5.1   Datasets

We verified the effectiveness of the algorithm on four real datasets. The statistics of four datasets are shown in Table 1.

Table 1. Statistics of four datasets

dataset	node	edge	feature	class
Cora	2708	5278	1433	7
Citeseer	3327	4552	3703	6
ACM	3025	13128	3025	3
DBLP	4057	3528	334	4

Cora: It is a dataset that studies the citation relationship between documents. 2708 documents in the machine learning direction are selected. These papers correspond to 7 categories. Each paper uses a bag-of-words model with a dimension of 1433 to represent features.

Citeseer: It is a paper citation network. It contains 3327 nodes and is divided into 6 categories. After removing stop words and words with a frequency of less than 10 in the document, 3703 unique words are sorted out to form a node feature matrix.

ACM: It is a subset selected from the network of ACM paper collaborators. Contains 3025 papers published on KDD, SIGMOD, SIGCOMM and MobiCOMM. These papers are divided into 3 categories. Use the bag-of-words feature of 1870 key words to represent the article features.

DBLP: It is a selected subset of the DBLP partner network. The authors' research includes four areas. We selected 4057 articles in the DBLP dataset, and divided the papers into 4 categories according to the conference minutes of these papers. Each paper uses a bag-of-words model with a dimension of 334 to represent features.

5.2 Ablation Study

We set $\gamma = 1$ and discuss the influence of the parameters α and β on the experimental results. Set the value of β to the abscissa, and the ordinate to the corresponding NMI. On each dataset, take α as 0.001, 0.01 and 0.1, and calculate the average value of NMI results from 50th to 100th iterations for each case. See Fig. 5.

We found that when $\frac{\beta}{\alpha} = 10$, the results all perform well on the four datasets and when $\alpha = 0.1$, the experiment obtains the best results.

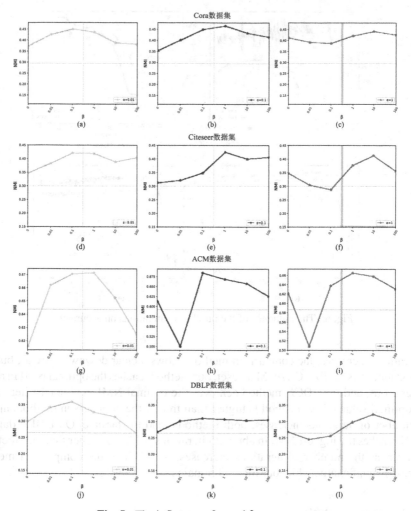

Fig. 5. The influence of α and β on accuracy

5.3 Training Analysis

Over-smoothing is a common phenomenon in GCN, which will cause the clustering accuracy to decrease. In this experiment, all nodes are used for end-to-end unsupervised pre-training of the DNN auto-encoding model, the number of iterations is set to 30, the learning rate is 10^{-3}, and the pre-training results are used to initialize the model parameters. The experiment obtained the following results, where the abscissa represents the number of iterations, and the ordinate represents the NMI value. See Fig. 6.

Experiments prove that the optimal NMI value of the method in this paper is significantly higher than that of the comparison method. Furthermore, the comparison method has a clear downward trend, but our method tends to be stable.

Specifically, on Cora and Citeseer datasets, the optimal NMI of the method in this paper is significantly higher than that of the comparison method, and as the number

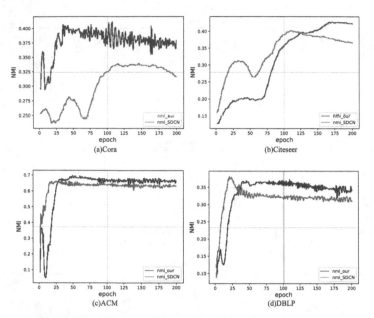

Fig. 6. The influence of the number of iterations on accuracy

of iterations increases, the comparison method shows a clear downward trend, but our method tends to stabilize. On ACM dataset, our method reaches the optimal NMI in about 25 iterations, and the SDCN method achieves the optimal NMI in about 14 iterations. The optimal value of our method is higher than that of the comparison method, and as the number of iterations increases, both methods tend to stabilize. On DBLP dataset, SDCN reaches the highest NMI in about 25 iterations, which is higher than our method. However, as the number of iterations increases, the NMI of the comparison method decreases significantly, while our method remains stable.

5.4 Accuracy Analysis

Table 2 is a comparison between the algorithm in this paper and state-of-the-art methods. For the results on the three datasets of Citeseer, ACM, and DBLP, we refer to the average of results in the paper [20], ignoring the upper and lower floating. The results on the Cora dataset are obtained by performing experiment with the source code and the parameter settings in the original paper. The accuracy of our method ranks among the top two in all datasets (See Table 2).

Table 2. Comparison of NMI results (%)

Algorithm		k-means	GAE	VAGE	SDCN	DGAE_DST
Input		X	A, X	A, X	A, X	A, X
Cora	NMI	23.35	39.70	**40.80**	26.92	40.20
	ARI	16.39	29.30	**34.70**	24.24	**36.98**
	F1	32.91	41.50	**45.60**	33.94	43.23
Citeseer	NMI	16.94	34.63	32.69	**38.71**	40.58
	ARI	13.43	33.55	33.13	40.17	42.87
	F1	36.08	57.36	57.70	63.62	62.40
ACM	NMI	32.44	55.38	53.20	**68.31**	67.59
	ARI	30.60	59.46	57.72	**73.91**	73.56
	F1	67.57	84.65	84.17	90.42	91.01
DBLP	NMI	11.45	30.80	26.92	**39.50**	35.93
	ARI	6.97	22.02	17.92	39.15	33.05
	F1	31.92	61.41	58.69	67.71	68.44

6 Conclusion

In this paper, we design a dual self-supervised model. This algorithm combines a deep neural network (DNN) auto-encoder with a graph convolutional network (GCN) auto-encoder, extracts network features from both the network topology and node feature information, and then utilizes auxiliary distribution to perform clustering. The experiment results on the Cora, ACM, DBLP and Citeseer datasets show that the accuracy of this algorithm is better than state-of-the-art algorithms, moreover, the stability of our method is higher. In addition, it alleviates the over-smoothing phenomenon of the GCN because of the integration of DNN encoding and GCN encoding.

Acknowledgement. This work is supported by National Key RD Program of China (No. 2019YFB2101700).

References

1. Fortunato, S., Hric, D.: Community detection in networks: a user guide. Phys. Rep. **659**, 1–44 (2016)
2. Zhang, Y., Lyu, T., Zhang, Y.: COSINE: community-preserving social network embedding from information diffusion cascades. In: AAAI, pp. 2620–2627 (2018)
3. Tian, F., Gao, B., Cui, Q., Chen, E., Liu, T.: Learning deep representations for graph clustering. In: AAAI, pp. 1293–1299 (2014)
4. Belkin, M., Niyogi, P.: Laplacian eigenmaps and spectral techniques for embedding and clustering. In: NIPS (2002)
5. Kruskal, J.B.: Multidimensional scaling by optimizing goodness of fit to a nonmetric hypothesis. Psychometrika **29**(1), 1–27 (1964)

6. Rosvall, M., Bergstrom, C.T.: Maps of random walks on complex networks reveal community structure. Proc. Natl. Acad. Sci. **105**(4), 1118–1123 (2008)
7. Xin, X., Wang, C., Ying, X., Wang, B.: Deep community detection in topologically incomplete networks. Physica A **469**, 342–352 (2017)
8. Sperlí, G.: A deep learning-based community detection approach. In: SAC, pp. 1107–1110 (2019)
9. Yang, L., Cao, X., He, D., Wang, C., Wang, X., Zhang, W.: Modularity based community detection with deep learning. In: IJCAI, pp. 2252–2258 (2016)
10. Cao, J., Jin, D., Yang, L., et al.: Incorporating network structure with node contents for community detection on large networks using deep learning. Neurocomputing **297**, 71–81 (2018)
11. Xue, S., Lu, J., Zhang, G.: Cross-domain network representations. Pattern Recognit. **94**, 135–148 (2019)
12. Ye, F., Chen, C., Zheng, Z.: Deep autoencoder-like nonnegative matrix factorization for community detection. In: Proceedings of the 27th ACM International Conference on Information and Knowledge Management, pp. 1393–1402 (2018)
13. Li, Y., Sha, C., Huang, X., et al.: Community detection in attributed graphs: an embedding approach. In: Proceedings of the AAAI Conference on Artificial Intelligence, vol. 32, no. 1 (2018)
14. Kingma, D.P., Welling, M.: Auto-encoding variational Bayes. arXiv preprint arXiv:1312.6114 (2013)
15. Jin, D., Yu, Z., Jiao, P., et al.: A survey of community detection approaches: from statistical modeling to deep learning. arXiv preprint arXiv:2101.01669 (2021)
16. Wang, C., Pan, S., Hu, R., et al.: Attributed graph clustering: a deep attentional embedding approach. arXiv preprint arXiv:1906.06532 (2019)
17. Zhang, H., Zhang, R., Li, X.: Embedding graph auto-encoder for graph clustering. arXiv e-prints arXiv:2002.08643 (2020)
18. Xie, J., Girshick, R., Farhadi, A.: Unsupervised deep embedding for clustering analysis. In: International Conference on Machine Learning, PMLR, pp. 478–487 (2016)
19. Guo, X., Gao, L., Liu, X., et al.: Improved deep embedded clustering with local structure preservation. In: IJCAI, pp. 1753–1759 (2017)
20. Van Der Maaten, L.: Learning a parametric embedding by preserving local structure. In: Artificial Intelligence and Statistics, PMLR, pp. 384–391 (2009)
21. Perozzi, B., Al-Rfou, R., Skiena, S.: DeepWalk: online learning of social representations. In: Proceedings of the 20th ACM SIGKDD International Conference on Knowledge Discovery and Data Mining, pp. 701–710 (2014)
22. Grover, A., Leskovec, J.: node2vec: scalable feature learning for networks. In: Proceedings of the 22nd ACM SIGKDD International Conference on Knowledge Discovery and Data Mining, pp. 855–864 (2016)

A Supervised Learning Model for Detecting Ponzi Contracts in Ethereum Blockchain

Ali Aljofey[1,2], Qingshan Jiang[1(✉)], and Qiang Qu[1]

[1] Shenzhen Key Laboratory for High Performance Data Mining, Shenzhen Institute of Advanced Technology, Chinese Academy of Sciences, Shenzhen 518055, China
{aljofey,qs.jiang,qiang}@siat.ac.cn
[2] Shenzhen College of Advanced Technology, University of Chinese Academy of Sciences, Beijing 100049, China

Abstract. Blockchain-based currencies, i.e., Ethereum, have increased in popularity among followers since 2009. However, scammers have customized offline frauds to this new ecosystem depending on blockchain's anonymity. As a result, smart Ponzi contracts are circulating on Ethereum, which appear to be secure investment schemes. We employ data mining techniques to present an effective detection model for smart Ponzi contracts over the Ethereum blockchain. First, we extended the dataset of smart Ponzi contracts and eliminated the imbalanced dataset by performing adaptive synthetic sampling. Next, we defined four kinds of feature sets based on the operation codes (opcodes) of smart contracts such as opcode frequency, count vector, n-gram Term Frequency-Inverse Document Frequency (TF-IDF), and opcode sequence features. It is noteworthy that the feature sets are based on the opcodes of smart contracts, which makes our model more reliable once the smart contract is uploaded to the Ethereum Blockchain. Finally, we designed an ensemble classification model combining Bagging-Tree and XGBoost classifiers, compared to other methods, to increase the detection accuracy of smart Ponzi contracts. The empirical and comparative results show that the ensemble model with only n-gram based features presents the best performance and achieves high precision and recall.

Keyword: Ethereum blockchain · Ponzi contracts · Opcode features · Machine learning

1 Introduction

Blockchain is an open and dispensed ledger that can register transactions between two parties efficiently, demonstrably, and constantly, making it common among investors [1]. Ethereum [2], as an analog work in the second phase of the blockchain [3], allowed the logic and rules of the business to be defined in the Turing Complete programming language, named smart account contracts. When a smart contract is written in high-level languages like Solidity, it must be assembled into bytecode, and then uploaded to

Supported by The Key-Area Research and Development Program of Guangdong Grant No. 2019B010137002.

Ethereum blockchain to be proceed and validated by each Ethereum node. As an open-source, popular blockchain system, Ethereum establishes many smart contracts to carry out a diversity of works. Simultaneously, the technical characteristics come from the incorporation of many sophisticated technologies, which raise the complication of the Ethereum blockchain system and lead to elevated technical impediments among smart contracts and investors. High technical constraints restrain investors from recognition the particular business reasoning of smart contracts running on the Ethereum blockchain. These impediments permit hackers to present a Ponzi scheme in the environment of blockchain investment. The Ponzi schemes potential in smart contracts is more elusive, as they cause more than $7 million in losses to investors [4]. With the growth of online finance, Ponzi schemes have also expanded many new forms in new areas, such as Peer to peer network (P2P), crowdfunding, etc. [5]. Scholars have indicated that Ponzi contracts embedded in the Ethereum blockchain are widespread. However, there are not much researches on detecting Ponzi contracts on the Ethereum blockchain.

Existing Ponzi contracts identification approaches on Ethereum blockchain mostly involve manual analysis or machine learning [6, 7]. The manual analysis methods use etherscan.io, the leading blockchain explorer, search, application programming interface (API), and analytics platform for Ethereum, to restore verified contracts with source code and manually analyze the code to assert the type of contract. However, such identification methods present the defiance of analyzing billions of non-open source smart contracts on the Ethereum blockchain. According to [8], 77.3% of smart contracts on Ethereum blockchain are not open source, so it is impracticable to classify smart contracts only through manual analysis. Recent approaches [9–11] rely on bytecode, opcodes, or trans-action history data of smart contracts using machine learning algorithms to detect Ponzi contracts automatically. However, their approach is based in part on transaction history which is not available in the early days of Ponzi contract deployment. This means that detection based on transaction history data occurs only after the attack has been car-ried out. On the other hand, machine learning techniques for detecting Ponzi contracts face the following challenges: First, it is hard to extract features that can effectively classify them, and statistical work around the features is also unhandy. Second, though some works have been done using machine learning to identify Ponzi schemes in smart contracts, the accuracy is insufficient.

To construct an efficient model for identifying Ponzi contracts without obtaining the source code or transactions data of smart contracts, we first crawled the bytecodes of 4424 verified smart contracts. Then the bytecodes were decomposed into opcodes. Next, four types of feature sets, namely opcode frequency, count vector, n-gram TF-IDF, and opcode sequence features, of these contracts are extracted from opcodes. Finally, an ensemble classification model is proposed based on Bagging-Tree and XGBoost algorithms, compared with many other algorithms (eight of them implemented and compared in the paper).

2 Related Work

With the growth of Internet finance, the Ponzi schemes have also produced many new ways. Recently, online financing models such as crowdfunding and P2P have become very common. Simultaneously, Ponzi contracts such as high-yield investment programs (HYIP) appeared among them, causing a very egregious social impact [5].

Vasek and Moore analyzed 1,780 bitcoin-based Ponzi contracts from http://bitcointa lks.org and indicated that the social interactivity between fraudsters and victims influences the lifespan of scams [8]. Bartoletti et al. [6] analyzed the behavior of a Ponzi contract on Ethereum blockchain, using similarities between contract bytecodes to identify 184 of them. In total, the contracts have raised nearly half a million US dollars from more than 2,000 premium users.

The method of [11] applied data mining algorithms to detect Ponzi contracts implemented on bitcoin. Their best classification model was able to identify 31 out of 32 Ponzi contracts with a 1% false positive. Moreover, it identifies Ponzi contracts using features calculated over the contract's life, narrowing the domain of countermeasures that can be applied versus such Ponzi contracts because the tokens cannot be recovered or marked as stolen. On the other hand, Rahouti et al. [12] reviewed machine learning and data mining-based techniques in abnormality identification in bitcoin, including [11]. Notwithstanding, it inspired [10], which depicts a comparable method using behavior features but also appended opcode frequencies features based on the bytecodes of smart contracts stored on the Ethereum blockchain. They constructed three classifiers, behavior, opcode, and behavior + opcode, using random forest, and the best results come from the opcode classifier, precision at 94% and sensitivity at 73%. While Chen et al. [10] method is the most comparable to ours, we have taken three different stages in building our classification model. First, we expanded the dataset of smart Ponzi contracts verified by etherescan.io. Second, we added more opcode features and compared them. Third, we employed various classification algorithms and attained better performance. Specifics of these features and classification algorithms are in Sect. 3.

3   Methodology

This section presents the methodology used in this study, including the framework workflow, the data acquisition and pre-processing, how to extract features from smart contracts, how to rebalance the data, and the proposed classification model.

3.1   The Framework Workflow

Figure 1 shows the general workflow for this work. To construct an efficient model for identifying smart Ponzi contracts on the Ethereum blockchain, we first get the bytecodes of all the smart contracts in the dataset from etherescan.io. After the duplicate bytecodes are removed, the data is preprocessed by decoding the smart contract bytecodes to the opcodes. The major intention of this work is to fast identify smart Ponzi contracts using accurate features. This is attained by extracting only features from the opcode such as n-gram, count vectors, and frequency of opcodes (i.e., instruction mnemonics) without obtaining the transactions data of smart contracts. Moreover, to balance our dataset, we use Adaptive Synthetic Sampling (ADASYN) technique to the density of the examples in the smart Ponzi contracts class to fit the number of non-Ponzi contracts. In the end, a classification model based on the ensemble method is proposed by combining Bagging-Tree and XGBoost classifiers compared to other methods.

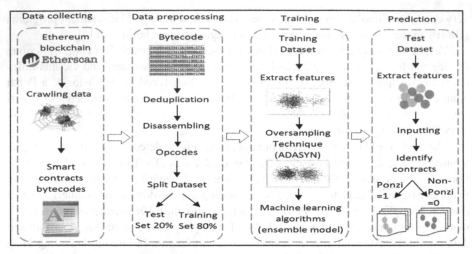

Fig. 1. The workflow of proposed framework for Ethereum security (Ponzi Contracts Detection).

3.2 Data Collection and Preprocessing

At First, A training dataset is needed for both Ponzi and non-Ponzi smart contracts. Data acquisition is often the most arduous for scam identification projects, requiring manual analysis and meticulous research to classify Ponzi from non-Ponzi contracts. Thanks to [6, 10], who provided open-source data including 200 Ponzi contracts and 3580 non-Ponzi contracts provided by W. Chen et al. [10] and 184 verified Ponzi contracts provided by M. Bartoletti et al. [6]. However, part of the collected contracts does not contain bytecode, so we retrieved their bytecodes verified by etherscan.io. We also expanded this data and added 426 Ponzi contracts and 524 non-Ponzi contracts. The Ponzi contracts are collected from [13], whereas the non-Ponzi ones are collected from [14]. After cleaning the data and removing the duplicate bytecodes, we found 4424 unique contracts that were marked as Ponzi contracts (810) and non-Ponzi contracts (3614). Finally, we convert these bytecodes into opcodes using a disassembler named the pyevmasm library,[1] and eliminate the operands after some opcodes, for example, PUSH1 and its operands (such as 0xa0). Table 1 presents the distribution of the Ponzi and non-Ponzi contracts. We divided the data into two sets, where D1 is the expanded dataset, and D2 is the dataset used in existing literature [10]. The database management system (i.e. pgAdmin) was employed with Python to import and prepare the data. The datasets are randomly split into 80:20 ratios for training and testing, respectively.

---

[1] https://github.com/crytic/pyevmasm.

Table 1. Datasets distribution

Datasets	Non-Ponzi contracts (0)	Ponzi-contracts (1)	Total
D1	3614	810	4424
D2	3580	200	3780

The distributions of bytecode length in our data for both Ponzi and non-Ponzi contracts are shown in Fig. 2. As can be seen from the figure, the length of bytecodes ranges from 5000 to 8000 for most non-Ponzi contracts, whereas most of the Ponzi contracts contain less than 5000 bytecodes. The maximum length for non-Ponzi contracts is 45000, and the maximum length for Ponzi contracts is 35000.

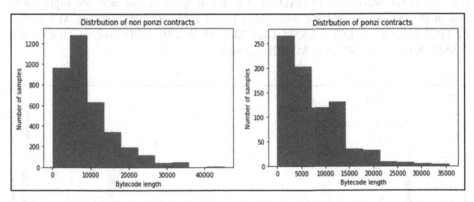

Fig. 2. Distribution of contracts' bytecodes size in D1.

3.3 Training and Feature Extraction

A Python program has been applied, taking smart contract as input and obtaining features from smart contract opcode. These obtained features are fed to the model trained using machine learning algorithms to identify the smart contract either as a Ponzi contract or a non-Ponzi contract. Opcodes have been successfully used in previous studies to analyze different fundamental issues of smart contracts [15, 16]. Thus, we extracted various types of opcode features to evaluate the performance of the proposed method. The opcode-based extracted features are grouped into four sets:

- Opcode frequency features.
- Count vector features.
- N-gram TF-IDF features.
- Opcode sequence features.

Opcode Frequency Features

The occurrence of each opcode in the smart contract is calculated and stored in the database. Each opcode with its own frequency is considered as a feature. We filtered the frequently recurring opcodes such as PUSH, DUP, and SWAP. In general, these stop words do not affect the understanding of the smart contract's logical semantics. Opcodes with frequency less than zero have been removed. Fifty-nine various opcodes are observed in the 4424 contracts' operation codes. Therefore, the component of the opcode features vector is 59 dimensions. The appendix of the Ethereum yellow paper [17] involves a whole list of the EVM opcodes. Figures 3 and 4 show a comparison between Ponzi contracts and non-Ponzi contracts based on the average frequency rate per opcode within each contract in our data. From the two figures, we observed that the ratios of the stop and arithmetic operations (i.e., STOP, ADD, SUB, DIV, etc.), comparison and bitwise logic operations (i.e., GT, EQ, ISZERO, etc.), block information (i.e., TIMESTAMP, NUMBER, COINBASE, etc.), storage and flow operations (i.e., MLOAD, MSTORE, SLOAD, etc.) in the non-Ponzi contracts are higher than that in Ponzi contracts. At the same time, Ponzi contracts contain more ADDRESS, EXITCODECOPY, BLOCKHASH, LT, CALLDATASIZE, CODESIZE, CODECOPY, GASPRICE, GASLIMIT, and MSIZE opcodes.

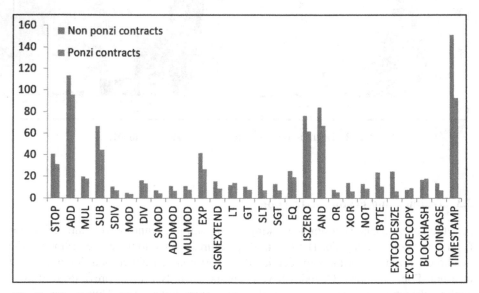

Fig. 3. Distribution of opcode features for both Ponzi and the non-Ponzi contracts in our data.

Count Vector Features

The count vector method is a simplifying impersonation used in natural language processing and information retrieval [18]. The count vector method is usually used in methods of document classification, where the occurrence of each word is used as a feature for training a classifier. It includes two things: A dictionary of known words. A measure of the occurrence of known words. If the new sentences contain new words, then the dictionary size would increase, and thereby, the length of the vectors would increase too. From the empirical analysis, we noticed that the vocabulary size is 76. Here, we implemented this method at the word level on the opcodes corpus.

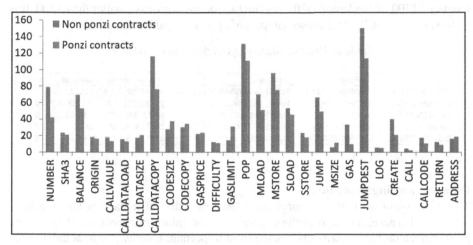

Fig. 4. Distribution of opcode features for both Ponzi and the non-Ponzi contracts in our data.

N-Gram TF-IDF Features

TF-IDF stands for Term Frequency-Inverse Document Frequency. TF-IDF weight is a statistical measure that represents the importance of a term in a corpus of documents. The importance of a term is directly proportionate to the number of times a term appears in a document set. TF-IDF score is calculated by multiplying two terms: the first calculates the normalized Term Frequency (TF), the second term is the Inverse Document Frequency (IDF), calculated as the logarithm of the number of the documents in the corpus divided by the number of documents where the particular term appears [19]. N-grams are the incorporation of N terms together. This matrix demonstrates TF-IDF scores of n-grams. In this section, we analyze the opcode of the smart contracts by splitting the opcodes of smart contract using n-gram without relying on any other expert knowledge to specify its characteristics. We set the length of n-gram between 2 and 3. The primary advantage of n-grams is language independence, as they can be implemented to a new language with no additional effort. However, the vector size can be long for a huge document, leading to enormous computational time. Our empirical analysis noticed that the size of the dictionary is 25256.

Opcode Sequence Features

This section introduces the opcode sequence features extracted from smart contract bytecodes to detect Ponzi schemes. An Ethereum smart contract is a sequence of low-level bytecode, is a hexadecimal representation of a contract that resides in the Ethereum blockchain. First, we transform the bytecode into an opcode, a human-legible layout that is comparable to any natural language. The opcodes consist of instruction mnemonics (i.e., PUSH1, ADD, GT, SHA3, CODECOPY, etc.) and their operands. We then remove the PUSH operations and their operands such as PUSH1, PUSH2, PUSH3, etc. Next, we assembled the opcodes of smart contracts back to their original bytecodes and then converted the bytecodes from hexadecimal format to decimal numbers with a maximum length of 1500. If the length of the contract sequence vector is smaller than 1500, it is padded with zeros. Table 2 shows samples of opcode sequence features.

Table 2. Contract address, bytecode, opcode, and label.

Address	Bytecode	Opcode	Opcode sequence features	Label
0x8d790f3989b...	0x60606040523...	PUSH1 0x60 JUMPI MSTORE...	87, 82, 52, 21, 87, 128, 25...	0
0xeca8d4cb072...	0x60606040526...	PUSH1 0x2 EXP SUB NOT...	87, 82, 128, 57,84, 10, 25...	1
0xc6b13d4186...	0x60606040501...	PUSH1 0x2 100 EXP DUP...	87,82, 243, 57,243, 82, 82...	0
0xf66ca56fc0cf...	0x6000805e64ec...	PUSH1 0X0 CALLDATALOAD...	87, 128, 84, 10, 3, 25, 22...	0
0x1c68f4f35ac5...	0x60606066872f...	PUSH1 0X60 JUMPI PUSH1...	84, 128, 81, 1, 2, 129, 144...	1

Data Resampling Procedure

The challenge of working with unbalanced data sets is that most machine learning algorithms will ignore, and thus perform poorly on the minority class even though their performance on the minority class is the most important. One way to treat unbalanced data sets is to oversample the minority class. The simplest approach includes repeating examples in the minority class, even though these examples do not add any new information to the model. Alternatively, new examples can be synthesized from existing examples. In our training set, the proportion of Ponzi contracts to non-Ponzi contracts is 1:5.27. We use the Adaptive Synthetic Sampling (ADASYN) method oversampling procedure to create more Ponzi contracts to fit the number of non-Ponzi contracts to attain better performance. The main idea of the ADASYN algorithm is to use the density distribution as a criterion to determine how many synthetic samples should be generated automatically for each example of minority data [20]. Figure 5 illustrates the distribution of the non-Ponzi and Ponzi contracts before and after oversampling our dataset.

Classification Model

In this paper, we applied eight classification models (random forest, extra trees, Bagging-Tree, k neighbors, decision tree, AdaBoost, gradient boosting, and XGBoost) as proposed machine learning techniques and then compared their performances. The major aim of comparing various algorithms is to determine the best algorithm appropriate for our feature sets. To apply different machine learning algorithms, the Scikit-learn package[2] is employed, and Python is used to extract features. The empirical results show that bagging tree and XGBoost algorithms perform better than others with significant accuracy and sensitivity. Thus, we chose these two algorithms to create the ensemble model with a soft voting strategy for further experiments.

XGBoost (extreme gradient boosting) is a scalable machine learning algorithm for tree boosting proposed by Chen and Guestrin [21]. Suppose there are N smart contracts in the dataset $\{(x_i, y_i)|i = 1, 2, ..., N\}$, where $x_i \in R^d$ as the extracted features associated

---

[2] http://scikit-learn.org.

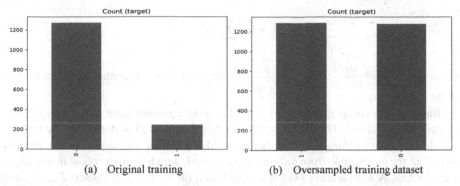

(a) Original training   (b) Oversampled training dataset

Fig. 5. Distribution of non-Ponzi and Ponzi contracts before and after balancing our data.

with the $i - th$ smart contract $y_i \in \{0, 1\}$ is the class label, such that $y_i = 1$ if and only if the smart contract is a labeled Ponzi contract. The final output $f_K(x)$ of the model is as:

$$f_K(x) = \sum_{k=1}^{K} f_k(x) \tag{1}$$

Suppose now we are in Step k, and we use $G_k(x)$ to simplify,

$$f_k(x) = f_{k-1}(x) + \beta_k \omega_k(x) = f_{k-1}(x) + G_k(x) \tag{2}$$

Since all previous $k - 1$ base learners are fixed, so our training Loss function l is as follows:

$$l(y_i, f_k(x)) = \sum_{i=1}^{N} l(y_i, f_{k-1}(x) + G_k(x) + \Omega(G_k(x))) \tag{3}$$

where $\Omega(G_k(x))$ is defined as below. It's a regularization term, T is the number of leaves nodes in the base learner $G_k(x)$, γ is the complexity of each leaf, λ is a parameter to scale the penalty, and ω_t is the output value at each final leaf node:

$$\Omega(G_k(x)) = \gamma T + \frac{1}{2}\lambda \sum_{t=1}^{T} \omega_t^2 \tag{4}$$

Using Taylor expansion to expand the Loss function at $f_{k-1}(x)$, we will have:

$$l(y, f_{k-1}(x) + G_k(x)) \approx \sum_{i=1}^{N} l(y_i, f_{k-1}(x_i) + G_k(x_i))$$

$$= \sum_{i=1}^{N} \left(l(y_i, f_{k-1}(x_i)) + g_i G_k(x_i) + \frac{1}{2} h_i G_k^2(x_i) \right)$$

$$+ \gamma T + \frac{1}{2} \lambda \sum_{t=1}^{T} \omega_t^2 \tag{5}$$

where $g_i = \frac{\partial l(y_i, f_{k-1}(x_i))}{\partial f_{k-1}(x)}$, $h_i = \frac{\partial l(y_i, f_{k-1}(x_i))}{\partial f_{k-1}^2(x)}$ are respectively first and second derivative of the Loss function.

Bagging (bootstrap aggregation) is used to reduce the variance of the decision tree within a noisy dataset. The idea is to create several subsets D of data from the training sample N chosen randomly with replacement. Meaning that the average or the majority vote of all the predictions from different trees is used, which is more robust than a single decision tree. A base learner $b(x)$ is trained based on the random subsets D_{subset_t}, and the output of the final classifier $B(x)$ is voted as [22]

$$B(x) = \arg\min_{y \in \{0,1\}} \sum_{t=1}^{T} XA(b_t(x) = y) \tag{6}$$

where XA is the characteristic function $[b_t(x) = y \in A]$, A is the set of unique class labels, and T is the number of the base learner.

The ensemble voting classifier integrates similar or conceptually different machine learning classifiers for classification by majority or soft voting. In hard voting, we would expect the final class to be named as the class designation most frequently predicted by classification models. The class labels are predicted by averaging the class probabilities in soft voting. We employ bagging tree and XGBoost algorithms to create the ensemble model with a soft voting approach [23].

$$\hat{y} = \arg\max_{i \in \{0,1\}} \sum_{j=1}^{m} w_j p_{ij} \tag{7}$$

where w_j is the weight can be assigned to the $j - th$ classifier and p is the predicted probability for the classifier.

Predication Phase

The predication phase involves building a strong classifier using the ensemble method, bagging, and XGBoost classifiers. The smart contracts are classified into two possible categories: Ponzi and non-Ponzi contracts using a binary classifier. In the training stage, the ensemble model is trained using the feature vector gathered from each instance in the training set. At the testing stage, the model identifies whether a particular contract is a Ponzi contract or not.

4   Experiment and Result Analysis

The proposed model takes suspected smart contract as input and produces the state of the contract as Ponzi or non-Ponzi. A Python custom code has been implemented to obtain the features from the input smart contract. The extracted features are classified into four various feature sets as follows.

- FS1: Opcode frequency features.
- FS2: Count Vector features.
- FS3: N-gram TF-IDF features.
- FS4: Opcode sequence features.

We have evaluated the four features sets mentioned above using different classifiers. To measure the effectiveness of our method, we have used performance metrics such as true-positive rate (TPR) or sensitivity, true-negative rate (TNR), false-positive rate (FPR), false-negative rate (FNR), accuracy, precision, F-measure, and they are defined as below:

$$TPR = \frac{\#of\ Ponzi\ contracts\ classified\ as\ Ponzi}{Total\ \#of\ Ponzi\ contracts} \tag{8}$$

$$TNR = \frac{\#of\ non - Ponzi\ contracts\ classified\ as\ non - Ponzi}{Total\ \#of\ non - Ponzi\ contracts} \tag{9}$$

$$FPR = \frac{\#of\ non - Ponzi\ contracts\ classified\ as\ Ponzi}{Total\ \#of\ non - Ponzi\ contracts} \tag{10}$$

$$FNR = \frac{\#of\ Ponzi\ contracst\ classified\ as\ non - Ponzi}{Total\ \#of\ Ponzi\ contracts} \tag{11}$$

$$Accuracy = \frac{\#of\ correctly\ classified\ Ponzi, non - Ponzi\ contracts}{Total\ \#of\ smart\ contracts} * 100 \tag{12}$$

$$Precision = \frac{\#of\ Ponzi\ contracts\ classified\ as\ Ponzi}{Total\ \#of\ smart\ contracts\ classified\ as\ Ponzi} * 100 \tag{13}$$

$$F\_Measure = 2 * \frac{Precision * TPR}{Precision + TPR} \tag{14}$$

4.1 Evaluation of FS1, FS2, FS3, and FS4 on D1 with Various Classifiers

In this experiment, we extracted opcode frequency, count vector, n-gram TF-IDF, and opcode sequence features from dataset D1 and implemented different algorithms such as k neighbors, decision tree, bagging models (i.e., random forest, extra trees, bagging tree, etc.), boosting tree models (i.e., AdaBoost, gradient boosting, XGBoost, etc.), and the ensemble of XGBoost and bagging tree models to train our proposed method. The major aim of this experiment is to select the best classifier appropriate for our dataset.

The empirical results are shown in Table 3. It is observed that the random forest classifier outperformed the others with adequate accuracy, precision, F_Measure, AUC, and sensitivity in terms of the count vector features (FS2). In contrast, the ensemble classifier was superior to the other classifiers and attained high accuracy, precision, F_Measure, AUC, and sensitivity with respect to opcode frequency features (FS1), n-gram TF-IDF features (FS3), and opcode sequence features (FS4). In Fig. 6, we compare the four feature sets (FS1, FS2, FS3, and FS4) in terms of accuracy, TNR, FPR, FNR, and TPR. Using the ensemble model to predict 362 contracts in our test set, FS3 correctly identifies 195 non-Ponzi contracts and 151 Ponzi contracts and contains 11 FNs and 5 FPs, which is much higher than other features. FS2 and FS4 have 2 and 3 FPs, but 29 and 32 respectively for FNs. However, for FS1, the FNs and FPs are 22 and 6, respectively, which is more impressive than FS2 and FS4. The confusion matrix for the proposed feature sets is constructed as represented in Fig. 7. The receiver operating characteristic (ROC) curve, Fig. 8, shows the true positive rate on the Y-axis and the false positive rate on the X-axis. ROC curves are generally used to observe the behavior of binary classifiers. A large area under the curve (AUC) indicates good classification behavior.

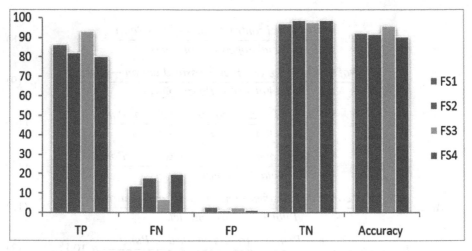

Fig. 6. Performance of the proposed feature sets.

4.2 Comparison with Existing Works

In this experiment, we compare our method (n-gram TF-IDF features using ensemble classifier) with other competing methods in order to evaluate the performance of the proposed method. Note that we have implemented Chen et al. [9] and Chen et al. [10] methods on our dataset D1. Furthermore, we evaluated our method based on the data of Chen et al. [10] based on the three performance measures used in the paper. The comparison results are presented in Table 4. From the results, it is noticed that our model performs better than other models, which indicates the efficiency of detecting Ponzi contracts over the existing models.

Table 3. Performance of the proposed feature sets with various classifiers.

Algorithm	Features	Precision	Sensitivity	F-measure	AUC	Accuracy
K neighbors	FS1	69.18	79.01	73.77	75.25	74.86
	FS2	72.94	76.54	74.69	76.77	76.79
	FS3	71.73	81.48	76.30	77.74	77.34
	FS4	50.47	99.38	66.94	60.19	56.07
Decision tree	FS1	98.17	86.41	87.77	86.41	89.22
	FS2	91.66	81.48	86.27	87.74	88.39
	FS3	92.90	88.88	90.85	91.69	91.98
	FS4	88.23	83.33	85.71	87.16	87.56
AdaBoost	FS1	85.41	75.92	89.39	82.71	83.14
	FS2	84.02	74.69	79.08	81.59	82.32
	FS3	90.97	80.86	85.62	87.18	87.84
	FS4	85.60	66.04	82.14	74.56	79.83
Random forest	FS1	97.82	83.33	90.00	90.61	91.71
	FS2	98.51	82.09	89.56	90.54	**91.43**
	FS3	96.26	79.62	87.16	88.56	89.50
	FS4	95.78	56.17	70.81	77.08	79.28
Extra trees	FS1	98.26	69.75	81.58	84.37	85.91
	FS2	98.11	64.19	77.61	81.59	83.42
	FS3	96.46	67.28	79.27	82.64	84.25
	FS4	96.38	49.38	65.30	73.49	76.51
Gradient boosting	FS1	90.44	75.92	82.55	84.71	85.63
	FS2	93.65	72.83	81.94	84.41	85.64
	FS3	95.45	90.74	93.03	93.62	93.92
	FS4	95.31	75.30	84.13	86.15	87.29
Bagging-Tree	FS1	93.87	85.18	84.17	89.32	90.88
	FS2	93.47	79.62	85.99	87.56	88.39
	FS3	96.71	90.74	93.63	94.12	94.47
	FS4	95.48	78.39	86.10	87.69	88.67
XGBoost	FS1	94.55	85.80	89.96	90.91	91.43
	FS2	95.74	83.33	89.11	90.16	90.88
	FS3	98.01	91.35	94.56	94.92	95.30
	FS4	97.65	77.16	86.20	87.83	88.95

(*continued*)

Table 3. (*continued*)

Algorithm	Features	Precision	Sensitivity	F-measure	AUC	Accuracy
Ensemble	FS1	95.89	86.41	90.91	91.70	**92.26**
	FS2	95.07	83.33	88.81	89.91	90.60
	FS3	96.79	93.20	94.96	95.35	**95.58**
	FS4	97.74	80.24	88.13	89.37	**90.33**

Table 4. Comparison of our method with existing methods

Metrics (%)	Chen et al. [10] (D2)	Our method (D2)	Chen et al. [9] (D1)	Chen et al. [10] (D1)	Our method (D1)
Precision	0.94	0.98	0.94	0.97	0.97
Sensitivity	0.73	0.82	0.85	0.83	0.93
F-measure	0.82	0.89	0.89	0.90	0.95

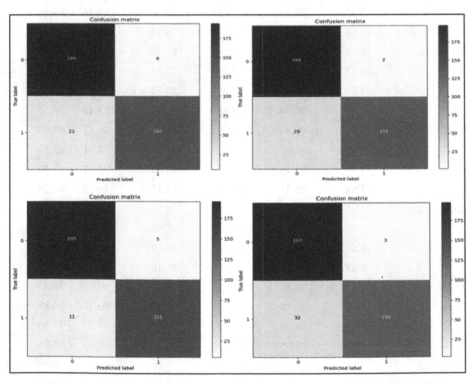

Fig. 7. Confusion matrixes of the proposed feature sets (FS1, FS2, FS3, and FS4).

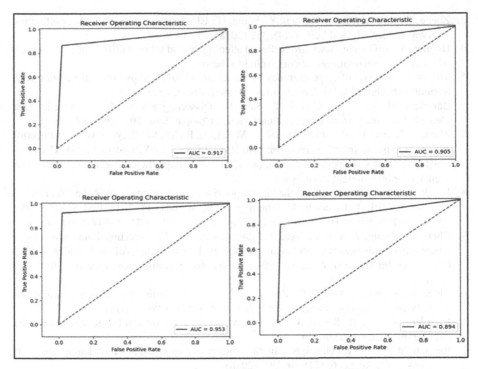

Fig. 8. Receiver operating characteristic of the proposed feature sets (FS1, FS2, FS3, and FS4).

5 Conclusion

Blockchain and cryptocurrency-based financial scams have become serious research issues. With the growth of Ethereum blockchain, Ponzi schemes are now under the guise of smart contracts. In this paper, we propose a machine learning-based method for detecting Ponzi contracts. Firstly, the bytecodes of 4424 verified smart contracts are obtained. Then, four types of feature sets are extracted and compared, i.e., opcode frequency, count vector, n-gram TF-IDF, and opcode sequence features. Finally, based on the superior feature sets and baseline truth data, an ensemble model based on XGBoost and Bagging-Tree algorithms are generated and applied to determine hidden Ponzi schemes in smart contracts. Notably, the feature sets are extracted from smart contract opcodes, which makes the proposed method capable of early detection of Ponzi contracts. In the future, we plan to add more features based on smart contract transaction data in order to improve the classification model against the latest smart Ponzi contracts.

References

1. Iansiti, M., Lakhani, K.R.: The truth about blockchain. Harvard Bus. Rev. **95**(1), 118–127 (2017)
2. Nakamoto, S.: Bitcoin: a peer-to-peer electronic cash system (2008). https://bitcoin.org/bit coin.pdf

3. Zheng, Z., Xie, S., Dai, H.N., Chen, X., Wang, H.: Blockchain challenges and opportunities: a survey. Int. J. Web Grid Serv. **14**(4), 352 (2018)
4. Higgins, S.: SEC seizes assets from alleged altcoin pyramid scheme (2015). https://www.coindesk.com/sec-seizesalleged-altcoinpyramid-scheme
5. Morris, D.: The rise of cryptocurrency Ponzi schemes (2017). https://www.theatlantic.com/technology/archive/2017/05/cryptocurrency-ponzi-schemes/5286
6. Bartoletti, M., Carta, S., Cimoli, T., Saia, R.: Dissecting Ponzi schemes on ethereum: identification, analysis, and impact. Futur. Gener. Comput. Syst. **102**, 259–277 (2020)
7. Zhou, Y., Kumar, D., Bakshi S., Mason, J., Miller, A., Bailey, M.: Erays: reverse engineering ethereum's opaque smart contracts. In: 27th USENIX Security Symposium (USENIX Security'18). USENIX Association (2018), pp. 1371–1385. https://www.usenix.org/conference/usenixsecurity18/presentation/zhou
8. Vasek, M., Moore, T.: Analyzing the bitcoin ponzi scheme ecosystem. In: Zohar, A., Eyal, I., Teague, V., Clark, J., Bracciali, A., Pintore, F., Sala, M. (eds.) FC 2018. LNCS, vol. 10958, pp. 101–112. Springer, Heidelberg (2019). https://doi.org/10.1007/978-3-662-58820-8_8
9. Chen, W., Zheng, Z., Cui, J., Ngai, E., Zheng, P., Zhou, Y.: Detecting Ponzi schemes on ethereum: towards healthier blockchain technology. In: Proceedings of the World Wide Web Conference. International World Wide Web Conferences Steering Committee, pp. 1409–1418 (2018)
10. Chen, W., Zheng, Z., Ngai, E.C., Zheng, P., Zhou, Y.: Exploiting blockchain data to detect smart Ponzi schemes on ethereum. IEEE Access **7**, 37575–37586 (2019)
11. Bartoletti, M., Pes, B., Serusi, S.: Data mining for detecting bitcoin Ponzi schemes (2018). http://arxiv.org/abs/1803.00646
12. Rahouti, M., Xiong, K., Ghani, N.: Bitcoin concepts, threats, and machine-learning security solutions. IEEE Access **6**, 67189–67205 (2018)
13. https://etherscan.io/accounts/label/phish-hack. Accessed 4 Sept 2021
14. https://etherscan.io/accounts. Accessed 4 Sept 2021
15. He, N., Wu, L., Wang, H., Guo, Y., Jiang, X.: Characterizing code clones in the ethereum smart contract ecosystem. arXiv preprint arXiv:1905.00272 (2019)
16. Bistarelli, S., Mazzante, G., Micheletti, M., Mostarda, L., Tiezzi, F.: Analysis of ethereum smart contracts and opcodes. In: Barolli, L., Takizawa, M., Xhafa, F., Enokido, T. (eds.) Advanced Information Networking and Applications. AINA 2019. Advances in Intelligent Systems and Computing, vol. 926. Springer, Cham (2020). https://doi.org/10.1007/978-3-030-15032-7_46
17. Wood, G.: Ethereum: a secure decentralised generalised transaction ledger. http://gavwood.com/paper.pdf
18. Zhang, Y., Jin, R., Zhou, Z.H.: Understanding bag-of-words model: a statistical framework. Int. J. Mach. Learn. Cybern. **1**(1–4), 43–52 (2010). https://doi.org/10.1007/s13042-010-0001-0
19. Bansal, S.: A comprehensive guide to understand and implement text classification in Python. https://www.analyticsvidhya.com/blog/2018/04/a-comprehensive-guide-to-understand-andimplement-textclassification-in-python. Accessed 1 July 2021
20. He, H., Bai, Y, Garcia, E.A., Li, S.: ADASYN: adaptive synthetic sampling approach for imbalanced learning. In: IEEE International Joint Conference on Neural Networks (IEEE World Congress on Computational Intelligence), pp. 1322–1328 (2008). https://doi.org/10.1109/IJCNN.2008.4633969
21. Chen, T., Guestrin, C.: XGBoost: a scalable tree boosting system. In: Proceedings of the 22nd ACM SIGKDD International Conference on Knowledge Discovery and Data Mining, pp. 785–794. ACM (2016)
22. Breiman, L.: Bagging predictors. Mach. Learn. **24**(2), 123–140 (1996)
23. Raschka, S.: Python Machine Learning. Packt Publishing Ltd., Birmingham (2015)

Research on Civil Aviation Economic Security Situation Assessment Model Based on Ant Colony Algorithm

Yulin Li[✉]

Dawan Business Aviation Tourism College School, Sichuan Vocational College of Science and Technology University, Guangyuan 620566, Sichuan, China

Abstract. With the increasing importance of air transportation, more attention is focused on the interactive relationship between air transportation and regional economy. This paper constructs the civil aviation economic security situation assessment and prediction model based on ant colony algorithm, and analyzes the relationship between air transportation and regional economic growth through impulse response and variance decomposition. In order to achieve this goal, this paper uses rough set theory to reduce the conditional attributes of credit card applicants, and discretizes the continuous attribute values combined with the continuous attribute discretization algorithm. Finally, the ant colony algorithm in intelligent algorithm is used to experiment the final data. The experiment shows that the contribution of air transportation to regional economic growth shows a downward trend in the short term; however, in the long run, there is a good interactive relationship between air transportation and regional economy, and the relationship between air transportation and regional economy has entered a new stage.

Keywords: Civil aviation · Economic security · Ant colony algorithm

1 Introduction

When people choose to invest in securities or other risky assets, they are most concerned about two issues: the expected return of assets and risk. In the early stage of the development of financial theory, how to measure the risk and return of investment is an urgent problem for investors. The portfolio theory put forward by Markowitz in 1952 solved this problem well [1], and brought the research of financial theory into the stage of quantitative analysis. Portfolio theory is to study how to effectively allocate assets in a complex and uncertain environment [2–4], maximize returns at a certain risk level or minimize risks at a certain income level, so as to achieve the balance between income and risk. The uncertainty and complexity of the actual environment of financial market determine that the research of portfolio optimization theory needs to involve many disciplines, including economics, operations research and cybernetics. With the development of modern computer technology, the research of finance has entered a new stage. The application of computer technology to the field of portfolio optimization has greatly promoted the development of modern asset selection theory.

© Springer Nature Singapore Pte Ltd. 2022
Y. Tian et al. (Eds.): ICBDS 2021, CCIS 1563, pp. 673–682, 2022.
https://doi.org/10.1007/978-981-19-0852-1_53

1.1 Basic Principle of Ant Colony Algorithm

In recent years, many bionic algorithms have emerged [5], such as ant colony algorithm, immune algorithm, genetic algorithm and so on. These calculations methods solve various complex optimization problems in real life by simulating various natural ecosystems in nature, and the current research results have achieved good results [6]. This paper selects the ant colony algorithm to solve the portfolio optimization problem, in order to get a better method to solve the portfolio optimization problem.

Ant colony algorithm was originally a search algorithm for finding optimal path, which was first developed by Marco, an Italian scholar Dorigo proposed in 1991 that its basic idea comes from simulating the collective foraging process of ant colonies. As we all know, the behavior and ability of a single ant are very simple, but the ant colony composed of these simple individuals can often perform many extremely complex tasks excellently.

1.2 Mathematical Model of Ant Colony Algorithm

The following takes the traveling salesman problem as an example to introduce the mathematical model of the basic ant colony algorithm. The traveling salesman problem is also called the freight forwarder problem and the traveling salesman problem are called TSP problem for short [7]. It is a basic route optimization problem. The problem is to find the shortest path for travelers to start from a starting point, pass through all given points, and then return to the origin.

Notations
Suppose that the ant colony has m ants, and its set is recorded as $X = \{x_1, x_2, \ldots, x_m\}$; N cities, denoted as $C = \{c_1, c_2, \ldots, c_n\}$; the distance between N cities is denoted as $D = \{D_{ij} | c_i, c_j \in C\}$, where D_{ij} is the distance between city c_i and city c_j. The amount of pheromone on the path from city c_i to city c_j is recorded as π_{ij}. At the initial time, the pheromone on all routes is the initial value 1, that is, the initial time of pheromone on all routes is the same.

Movement Rules
To simplify the analysis, it is assumed that each ant moves from one city to the next in each cycle, that is, move only one step [8]. If the ant x_k is currently located in the city c_i, the ant will start from the current city c_i determine the moving direction according to the pheromone distribution on each selectable route. $P_{ij}(k)$ represents the probability that ant x_k moves from city c_i to city c_j. $P_{ij}(k)$ is determined by the following formula:

$$p_{ij}(k) = \begin{cases} \dfrac{\pi_{ij}^{\alpha} \eta_{ij}^{\beta}}{\sum_{k \subset CK} \pi_{ik}^{\alpha} \eta_{ik}^{\beta}}, & if \, j \in CK \\ 0, & if \, j \notin CK \end{cases} \tag{1}$$

Where α and β are constants, the set CK is defined as $CK = \{C_i | the \, ant \, k \, not \, passed \, city \, C_i\}$, η is a heuristic function, which is the reciprocal of the distance between c_i and c_j.

The larger the transition probability of a path, it indicates how many times the ant moves in this direction to get the optimal solution the higher the rate, but the ants do not move directly to the city with the greatest transfer probability. Such a setting will make the ant colony optimization inefficient when the pheromone distribution on each path is more average in the early stage, but it is very necessary. Because this setting can expand the search range of the early ant colony and avoid the ant colony falling into the local optimal solution and ignoring the global optimal solution optimal solution. At the same time, in the later stage of the algorithm, when the distribution of pheromones on each path is quite different, it is different the polarization of the transition probability of the path is obvious, and the transition probability of the effective path is compared with that of other paths big. At this time, this setting has little impact on the search efficiency, and can ensure the diversity of solutions.

Pheromone Update Rule
After each cycle or each ant takes a step forward, the pheromone on the corresponding line needs to be updated. In reality, the pheromone left by the ant colony after passing through a path will volatilize over time [9]. With the passage of time, the pheromone left at the previous moment will have less and less impact on the current ant optimization process. Pheromone update rules are as follows:

$$\pi_{ij}(new) = (1 - \rho)\pi_{ij}(old) + \Delta\pi_{ij} \tag{2}$$

$$\Delta\pi_{ij} = \sum_{k=1}^{m} \Delta\pi_{ij}(k) \tag{3}$$

Where $\pi_{ij}(new)$ is the value of pheromone of the path from c_i to c_j, $\Delta\pi_{ij}(k)$ stands for the number of pheromones left by ant k after passing route ij in this cycle, $\Delta\pi_{ij}$ represents the total amount of pheromones left by all ants passing through path ij in this cycle, that is, the total increment of pheromones on path ij in this cycle, ρ is the Volatilization factor, which represents the reduction rate of existing pheromones, is a constant value in the basic ant colony algorithm. The value of volatilization factor can be adjusted according to different models, and its size is directly related to the volatilization rate of pheromone. If the value is too large, the pheromone left by all ants in the early stage will volatilize too fast, shorten the guiding time of pheromone to ant colony, and reduce the convergence speed and effect; If the value is too small, the pheromone values on all paths will tend to average, making the pheromone lose guiding significance. This situation will also reduce the convergence speed and effect.

1.3 Civil Aviation Economy

As the fifth mode of transportation, the rapid and efficient air transportation has gradually promoted it to become another engine driving economic development [10–13]. With the proposal of the civil aviation power strategy and the strategic concept of coordinated development of Beijing, Tianjin and Hebei, more attention is focused on whether the development of air transportation can adapt to economic development and regional economic development [14]. The novel coronavirus pneumonia outbreak in 2019 also raised a higher-level requirement for the air transport industry. Air transport as an important part of the industrial chain and supply chain shoulders the arduous task of maintaining the stability of the industrial chain and supply chain. Beijing has Beijing Capital International Airport, one of China's three gateway complex hubs, as the most complex airport in China busy route is the endpoint of Beijing Shanghai. Studying the relationship between Beijing air transportation industry and regional economic growth can provide first mover experience and development reference for other regions.

2   Security Situation Assessment Model Based on Ant Colony Algorithm

The basic ant colony algorithm is suitable for solving discrete space optimization problems [15]. In order to model the civil aviation economic security situation, the improved ant colony algorithm must be used [16, 17]. According to the characteristics of civil aviation economic security situation modeling, a multi-objective continuous domain optimization problem with constraints, an improved continuous domain ant colony algorithm is used to solve it.

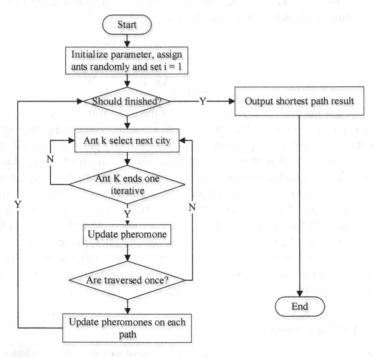

Fig. 1. Flow chart of ant colony algorithm

2.1 Model Establishment and Principle

In order to simplify the analysis, some simplified settings are adopted at the initial stage of modeling, and realistic factors such as transaction cost and minimum transaction unit are not considered temporarily. These assumptions will not affect the correctness of the model. In the subsequent model expansion, these factors can be gradually considered to enrich the model.

2.2 Combination of Objective Function and Pheromone Distribution

Investors pursue the maximization of return when the risk is certain, or the minimization of risk when the return is certain. The model takes this goal as the starting point, combined with the characteristics of ant colony algorithm, sets pheromone change rules, and gradually guides ant colony to find the optimal portfolio.

Assuming that the ant moves in the $\gamma - \delta$ coordinate system, each point in this coordinate system represents the return and variance combination of a security or a combination. The ant colony releases unequal amounts of pheromone at all passing positions, and all ants choose the next moving direction according to the amount of pheromone at each position. Since there is no absolute optimal solution to the portfolio optimization problem, we judge the pros and cons of the solutions by comparing the Pareto relationship between the solutions. After the ant colony finds a new investment portfolio, it first needs to judge whether it is an effective investment portfolio. Comparing the return and variance of the new portfolio with the existing portfolio, there will be three situations: First, in comparison, the return of the new portfolio is higher and the variance is smaller. At this time, it indicates that the new combination is an effective combination, which means that the ant colony has a higher chance of finding an effective combination in this direction. Therefore, it is necessary to assign a higher pheromone value δ_1 at this point to attract other ants to explore in this direction and speed up the convergence speed of the algorithm optimization. The second situation is that compared with the existing portfolio, the new portfolio either has higher risk returns or lower risk returns. According to the shape of the effective front, the probability that the ant colony can find an effective combination in this direction is not as high as the previous case, so in this case, the corresponding point in the coordinate system of the combination is given a slightly lower pheromone value δ_2. The third is that compared with the existing combination, the new combination has higher risks and lower returns. At this time, the ant colony has the lowest probability of finding an effective combination in the direction represented by this point, so it is assigned the lowest pheromone value δ_3. By assigning higher pheromone to the target combination, we can guide the ant colony to move to the target combination, and finally search for an effective investment portfolio. Through the setting of this objective function, we initially combined the portfolio optimization problem with the ant colony algorithm.

2.3   An Improved Continuous Domain Optimization Method is Adopted

In order to prevent the ants from losing the effective combination that has been found during the movement, and to ensure the diversity of the solution, this paper adopts an optimization method based on the guidance of the best experience. The so-called optimal experience guidance is to save all the effective investment portfolios currently discovered by the entire ant colony in a set. All ants can learn the current effective solution distribution from this set, and use this additional information to guide the ants Find the best. In this optimization method, in addition to the guidance of pheromone, ants are also affected by the optimal experience of the entire ant colony. These two methods jointly guide the ant colony to find the optimal solution. Using this method can not only ensure the diversity of the solution, use it together with the pheromone optimization method in the basic ant colony algorithm, but also improve the convergence speed of the algorithm, which is a more effective method.

In the pheromone optimization method, set the transition probability of the ant colony as follows:

$$P_{ij} = \frac{\theta_j \delta_{ij}}{\sum_{j=1}^{m} \theta_j \delta_{ij}}, j \neq i, j = 1, \ldots, N \tag{4}$$

In Eq. (4), P_{ij} stands for the probability of ant moving from combination i to combination j. δ_{ij} is a heuristic factor and can be defined as $\delta_{ij} = 1/d_{ij}$, d_{ij} is the distance between combination i and combination j, the calculate method is as follows:

$$d_{ij} = \sqrt{\sum (X_i - X_j)^2} \tag{5}$$

Where X_i Represents portfolio i, which records the weights of all securities in the portfolio, $X_i = \{x_1, x_2, \ldots, x_m\}$.

In the optimization of the global best experience guidance. It is necessary to establish an effective portfolio collection, and save all the discovered effective portfolios in this collection. When the optimal experience is used to guide the optimization, the ant colony selects a relatively sparse direction in the effective set to move. Because the place with less effective investment portfolio is the less explored part of the ant colony, the probability of continuing to find other effective portfolios in this direction is relatively large.

To this end, first calculate the distance between each effective combination in the set, the calculation method is as formula (5). Assuming that there are P valid combinations in the current set, calculate the distance from each combination to other combinations, and then calculate the sparse function according to the following formula:

$$SS(d_{ij}) = \begin{cases} 1 - \frac{d_{ij}}{\sigma_{share}}, d_{ij} < \sigma_{share} \\ 0, d_{ij} \geq \sigma_{share} \end{cases} \tag{6}$$

In the formula, σ_{share} is the "niche radius", which specifies a range. When calculating the sparse function, only other portfolios within the specified range of this parameter are considered, and combinations outside the range are not considered. After obtaining this parameter, calculate the "niche number" $niche(i)$ according to the following formula:

$$niche(i) = \sum_{j=1}^{p} S(d_{ij}), i = 1, 2, \ldots, p, j \neq i \tag{7}$$

niche(*i*) measures the degree of differentiation between portfolio i and other portfolios. When the difference between the investment portfolio and other portfolios is greater, the number of other investment portfolios within the radius of the niche is smaller, and the number of niches is smaller, and vice versa. The effective portfolio with the smallest number of niches is the direction of movement of the ant colony.

According to the previous movement rules, when the ant finds the direction of the moving target, it does not directly move to the target point, but moves a certain distance in that direction. The improved continuous domain ant colony algorithm stipulates that ants can only move within the radius r. If the distance between the ant and the target point is greater than its range of activity r, the ant can only move a distance of length r toward the direction of the target point. At the same time, a disturbance factor is set to make the movement of ants have a certain random disturbance. The purpose of this setting is to ensure the diversity of solutions. The greater the interference, the smaller the influence of the movement direction found by the model in the last cycle on the subsequent guidance of the ant colony, and the larger the range of the ant colony search. In the early stage of the optimization process, it is necessary to appropriately set a larger interference value, which will help increase the search range and speed up the global optimization. In the later stage, it is suitable for a smaller interference value, which is beneficial to improve the search quality, find the optimal solution in each local range, and accelerate the algorithm convergence.

Suppose we have N securities, an investment portfolio can be expressed as $[x_1, x_2, \ldots, x_m]$, where x_i is the proportion of each security, and the sum of the proportions is 1. If the position of an ant is the combination $[x_1, x_2, \ldots, x_m]^{old}$. Its moving target is ant j, and the combination of the position of ant j is $[x_1, x_2, \ldots, x_m]^{new}$. Then the disturbance coefficient is α, then ant j moves to the position of the following combination:

$$NEW = (1 - \alpha) \cdot \left[k \cdot x(i, :)^{old} + (1 - k) \cdot x(j, :)^{new} \right] + \alpha \qquad (8)$$

According to the above formula, the sum of the proportion of all securities in the new portfolio is still 1.

2.4 Valid Set and Pheromone Update Rules

After the ant finds a new combination, it first needs to judge whether it is an effective solution according to the method mentioned above, and then give the combination in the corresponding position in the coordinate system $\gamma - \delta$ is given the corresponding pheromone value. If the new combination is a valid solution, you need to add it to the valid set. At the same time, it is also necessary to delete all portfolios in which the return is lower than the new portfolio and the risk is higher than the new portfolio. Ensure the correctness and effectiveness of the effective set for ant colony guidance.

3 Experiment and Result

3.1 Evaluation Method

Stationary Test
The series passing the stationarity test can avoid false regression, so the stationarity test must be carried out on the variables before constructing the VAR model. The stability test generally adopts ADF test, also known as unit root test, to judge whether the variable is stable by checking whether there is a unit root.

The inspection results are shown in Table 1. It can be seen from the table that the ADF test values of the two variables are less than the critical value of 5% significance level, and the P values are less than 0.05, indicating that the variables are stable, and the VAR model can be established on this basis.

Table 1. Unit root test

Variable	ADF	critical value (significant level)			P value	results
		1%	5%	10%		
LATS	−3.722091	−3.679322	−2.967767	−2.622989	0.0090	Stable
LGDP	−4.167848	−4.394309	−3.612199	−3.243079	0.0162	Stable

Johansen Cointegration Test
Before establishing VAR model, the most important problem is to determine the optimal lag order of the model. Selecting the optimal lag order can make the best use of the variable information of the model without losing too many degrees of freedom. Determine the lag order, give priority to AIC criterion, and select according to SC criterion if the results are the same. The results are shown in Table 2.

From the results of the evaluation criteria of each order in Table 2, when the lag order is 2, the number of significant variables is the largest, so order 2 is selected as the optimal lag order. The cointegration test results are shown in Table 3. The original hypothesis is rejected at the 5% significant level, and there is at least one cointegration relationship between lats and LGDP, indicating that there is at least one cointegration relationship between air transport scale and regional economic growth at the 5% significant level. For lats and LGDP through one-step estimation, the standardized cointegration equation is obtained as follows:

$$LATS_t = -1.6426 * LGDP_t + 0.0996 \tag{9}$$

The likelihood ratio is 99.7084, and the values in brackets are t statistics. It can be seen from the cointegration equation that there is a long-term stable equilibrium relationship between the scale of air transportation and regional economy. Due to the logarithmic processing of the data, the coefficients before the variables are their respective output elasticity.

Table 2. Model lag order analysis results

Lag	LogL	LR	FPE	AIC	SC	HQ
0	−12.59994	NA	0.009727	1.042853	1.138010	1.071944
1	90.04092	183.2872	8.49e-06	−6.002923	−5.717450	−5.915651
2	98.01073	13.09327	6.43e-06	−6.286481	−5.810694	−6.141028

Table 3. Cointegration test of lats and LGDP

Cointegration rank H_0	Eivenvalue	Likelihood ratio	5% critical value	P value
$r = 0^*$	0.5801	24.2956	19.3870	0.0089
$r \leq 1$	0.1170	3.4844	12.5180	0.8147

4 Conclusion

From the quantitative research, it can be seen that a good interaction mechanism has been formed between Beijing regional economy and air transportation for a long time, and the dynamic relationship between them is long-term and sustainable. Whether short-term or long-term, air transportation can promote regional economic growth. Compared with the one-way interactive relationship obtained by previous scholars studying the dynamic relationship between the two, this is a new discovery. The relationship between air transportation and regional economy has developed into a new stage, but from the variance decomposition diagram of regional economy, it can be seen that the contribution of air transportation to economy is decreasing in the short term and increasing significantly in the long term. It shows that the interaction between air transportation and regional economy has entered such a stage: the role of regional economy in promoting air transportation is a significant normal; Although air transport plays a role in promoting regional economy, it has not been brought into full play. In this paper, we uses rough set theory to reduce the conditional attributes of credit card applicants, and discretizes the continuous attribute values combined with the continuous attribute discretization algorithm. Finally, the ant colony algorithm in intelligent algorithm is used to experiment the final data.

References

1. Hirsch, J.A., Stratton-Rayner, J., et al.: Roadmap for free-floating bikeshare research and practice in North America. Transp. Rev. (2019)
2. Kate, H., Meghan, W.: Who Are public bicycle share programs serving? An evaluation of the equity of spatial access to bicycle share service areas in Canadian cities. Transp. Res. Rec. **2672**(36), 42–50 (2018)
3. Ursaki, J., Aultman-Hall, L., et al.: Quantifying the equity of bikeshare access in U.S. cities. In: Transportation Research Board 95th Annual Meeting, Washington, DC (2016)

4. Goodman, A., Cheshire, J.: Inequalities in the London bicycle sharing system revisited: impacts of extending the, scheme to poorer areas but then doubling prices. J. Transp. Geogr. **41**(1), 272–279 (2014)
5. Shoup, D.: The High Cost of Free Parking: Updated edition. Routledge, New York (2017)
6. Docherty, I., Marsden, G., Anable, J.: The governance of smart mobility. Transp. Res. Part A (2018)
7. Mace, J., Bodik, P., Musuvathi, M., et al.: 2DFQ: two-dimensional fair queuing for multi-tenant cloud services. In: The ACM Special Interest Group on Data Communication. ACM, pp. 144–159 (2016)
8. Wang, Z., Hayat, M.M., Ghani, N., et al.: Optimizing cloud-service performance: efficient resource provisioning via optimal workload allocation. IEEE Trans. Parallel Distrib. Syst. **28**(6), 1689–1702 (2017)
9. Khomh, F., Abtahizadeh, S.A.: Understanding the impact of cloud patterns on performance and energy consumption. J. Syst. Softw. **141**, 151–170 (2018)
10. Ragmani, A., Elomri, A., Abghour, N., et al.: An improved hybrid fuzzy-ant colony algorithm applied to load balancing in cloud computing environment. Proc. Comput. Sci. **151**, 519–526 (2019)
11. Boveiri, H.R., Khayami, R., Elhoseny, M., et al.: An efficient Swarm-Intelligence approach for task scheduling in cloud- based internet of things applications. J. Ambient. Intell. Humaniz. Comput. **10**(9), 3469–3479 (2019)
12. Dupont, L., Dhaenens-Flipo, C.: Minimizing the makespan on a batch machine with non-identical job sizes: an exact procedure. Comput. Oper. Res. **29**(7), 807–819 (2002)
13. Jun, P., Xinbao, L., Baoyu, L., et al.: Single-machine scheduling with learning effect and resource-dependent processing times in the serial-batching production. Appl. Math. Model. **58**, 245–253 (2018)
14. Damodaran, P., Manjeshwar, P.K., Srihari, K.: Minimizing makespan on a batch-processing machine with non-identical job sizes using genetic algorithms. Int. J. Prod. Econ. **103**(2), 882–891 (2006)
15. Gill, S.S., Buyya, R., Chana, I., et al.: BULLET: particle swarm optimization based scheduling technique for provisioned cloud resources. J. Netw. Syst. Manage. **26**(2), 361–400 (2018)
16. Mishra, A., Deb, S.: A GA based parameter meta-optimization of ACO algorithm for solving assembly sequence optimization. In: International Conference on Computers & Industrial Engineering (2016)
17. Mondal, S., Paul, C.P., Kukreja, L.M.: Application of Taguchi-based gray relational analysis for evaluating the optimal laser cladding parameters for AISI1040 steel plane surface. Int. J. Adv. Manuf. Technol. **66**(1–4), 91–96 (2013)

Research on Active Sampling
with Self-supervised Model

Shi-Fa Luo[✉]

College of Computer Science and Technology, Nanjing University of Aeronautics and
Astronautics, Nanjing, China
luosf@nuaa.edu.com

Abstract. In the case of insufficient labeled data, active learning performs very
well by actively querying more valuable samples. Traditional active learning models usually use the target model to select samples in the image classification tasks.
The target model is not only used to find out the crucial unlabeled samples with
massive information but also used to perform prediction. This method does not
use the information of the remaining unlabeled samples, and the efficiency will
also be restricted when using a single model to solve these two tasks simultaneously. We put forward a self-supervised active learning framework to help query
samples in this paper. First, we introduce contrastive learning to construct a new
feature space. Second, a special active sampling strategy is proposed based on the
distance between unlabeled samples and the center of the category clusters. We
update the clusters at each iteration to ensure that the examples most needed can
be selected for labeling. Experiments show the success of our method.

Keywords: Active learning · Contrastive learning

1 Introduction

It is evident that the large size of training data always brings better effects when we
perform a classification task with supervised learning methods. However, it is challenging
to obtain labeled samples in many real-world issues, which requires experts to perform
manual labeling. The time and economic costs are considerable. Moreover, the training
time will be longer when the size of the training sample gets large. Active learning
provides us with the possibility to get a better model with fewer training samples. Active
learning utilizes a certain algorithm to select the most valuable unlabeled samples and
asks the oracle for the true label information. Then it adds their labels into the labeled
set for training and improving the model [1].

In the human learning process, they usually use the anterior experience to acquire new
abilities. Meanwhile, people summarize experience based on the acquired skills, which
accelerates this process in turn. Similarly, machine learning simulates the development
of many industries, using existing knowledge to train models to acquire new knowledge.
Then it modifies the model to become more accurate and useful. Different from passive

© Springer Nature Singapore Pte Ltd. 2022
Y. Tian et al. (Eds.): ICBDS 2021, CCIS 1563, pp. 683–695, 2022.
https://doi.org/10.1007/978-981-19-0852-1_54

learning, which passively accepts knowledge, active learning can selectively acquire knowledge.

The query function is utilized to query one or a batch of the valuable samples. Among various active learning algorithms, the most commonly applied tactics for the design of query functions are uncertainty [2] and diversity [3]. Information entropy is a concept that measures the amount of information, as well as a concept that measures uncertainty. The information entropy increases with the growth of uncertainty, as well as the information inside the sample. In fact, some active learning query functions based on uncertainty are designed using information entropy, such as Entropy query-by-bagging [4]. Therefore, the uncertainty strategy is to find ways to figure out data with maximum uncertainty, since the uncertain samples will help the model converge more effectively. Meanwhile, The selected samples should be dissimilar, which ensures that these samples fully cover the information included in the original data. Each time a sample is picked to be appended to the training pool, the model needs to be retrained to take advantage of the newly acquired information and continue to evaluate the uncertainty of the remaining samples. However, if a batch of samples is selected each time, the diversity of samples should be considered to avoid redundant information.

In the past few decades, plenty of active learning sample selection strategies have been propounded, and most of the related research has concentrated on the amount of information and representativeness of the samples.

Self-supervised learning has become popular since it does not require the label information of the sample and reduces the label cost simultaneously [5]. It can replace real labels with pseudo-labels for experiments, and the converged model can be applied to many other tasks after fine-tune.

Contrastive learning is a significant subfield of self-supervised learning, which has recently achieved fruitful results in image and language processing. It strives for making the positive samples closer in the representation space while trying to augment the distance between embeddings from different samples [5].

In this work, we input all samples into the contrastive learning model to learn a feature representation and design the following query strategy. We estimate the embedding center with labeled data and calculate the distance from the unlabeled embedding to the center of each category. The closer to a certain center, the greater the probability of being classified into a certain category, which means not to be labeled. In this way, suitable samples are actively selected from those unlabeled datasets to be annotated by oracles, and the expanded labeled set is handed over to the original model for classification tasks. Eventually, we obtain excellent experimental effects with a few labeled samples.

The rest arrangement of this paper contains related work, details of the methods and the experiments in Sect. 2 to Sect. 5.

2 Related Work

2.1 Active Learning (AL)

Since actively selected data is more helpful for model training, active learning can learn a model that also has a strong generalization ability with less labeled data, thereby reducing the labeling cost. Active learning research has made significant progress in theory [6], algorithm [7–9], and application [10–12] which has achieved significant results in many practical tasks. For example, in the task of detecting the growth environment of yeast, King et al. used an active learning algorithm to select chemical solutions for labeling, reducing the experimental cost to 1% of the original. This work was published in Nature [13]. In another lung cancer diagnosis task, Liu et al. used active learning strategies to select gene expression files for lung cancer labeling. After obtaining 31 labeled files, the recall rate of the model reached 96%, which saves 82% of resources [14]. In the video classification task, the active learning method proposed by Yan et al. can reduce the error rate to half of the original with the same number of labeled samples [15].

In the past few decades, numerous active learning sample selection strategies have been propounded, and most of the work has been estimating the amount of information and representativeness of the samples. The representative methods of the former consist of selection strategies based on uncertainty, committee query strategies [16, 17], query strategies based on expected model change [18], and expected error reduction [19]. The latter representative method contains clustering or density estimation.

There are already many active learning works that perform well by learning new feature representations. Ran et al. [20] overcome the annotation problem effectively in the well-known Query-By-Committee (QBC) algorithm by mapping the sample to a low-dimensional space, which improves the query speed. Toan Tran uses Bayesian active learning by disagreement (BALD) to sample from unlabeled data sets [21]. After the samples are labeled by oracles, they are processed by the adversarial model VAE-ACGAN to generate new artificial samples with similar information to the input samples. Then the new samples are included in the labeled data set for iterative training of the model. Saito uses generative adversarial auxiliary models in unsupervised domain adaptation to learn new feature representations of samples [22].

2.2 Contrastive Learning (CL)

Self-supervised algorithms include contrastive learning, which means contrastive learning does not need supervision information. On the contrary, it learns knowledge from unlabeled data. Self-supervision in the image field can be separated into two types: generative self-supervised algorithm and discriminative self-supervised algorithm. VAE [23] and GAN [24] are two typical methods of generative self-supervised learning, which requires the model to reconstruct the image or part of the image. This type of task is relatively difficult and requires pixel-level reconstruction. Meanwhile, the image encoding must contain a lot of detailed information. Contrastive learning is a standard discriminative self-supervised method. Compared with generative self-supervised learning, the assignment of contrastive learning is relatively simple. The guiding principle of contrastive learning is: automatic construction of similar and dissimilar examples requires the acquisition of a representation learning Model. It can make the feature representation distance of similar samples smaller, while the distance of negative samples with large differences is larger.

There are many contrastive learning algorithms that have emerged at present. From the perspective of different methods to prevent model collapse, existing methods can be separated into three categories according to the different methods of constructing negative samples: contrast clustering, asymmetric network structure, and the redundancy elimination loss function.

Research shows that the model can be used to distinguish objects using only rough information because of the valid representation space learned from plenty of unlabeled data, which can be utilized in other tasks after fine-tuning. The majority of the previous research in this field employed several classification methods on the instance scope [25–27] with contrastive learning and performs well. On the other hand, recent algorithms such as SwAV [28], MoCo [29], and SimCLR [30] have performed well on ImageNet [31] dataset and attained the same good results as current supervised learning.

3 Problem Setting

3.1 Active Learning (AL)

We assume D^{tr} as the training data set, where $D^{tr} = \{(x_i, y_i)\}_{i=1}^{I}$, such that x_i is the i-th sample and y_i is its label (i.e., class). We search a mapping function $F_\theta : x \to y$ in supervised learning, where x is the input data, y is the output information, and θ is the parameters of the model. The function F_θ is a possible solution of the hypothesis space. We define S as selector, which is the strategy or model to choose samples from candidate data set D^{cdd}. As in Fig. 1, AL uses its selector S to select some unlabeled samples as set B_n from D^{cdd}, gets their labels, and then re-trains the predictor $F_\theta (\cdot)$ by the new D_n^{tr}, where $D_n^{tr} = D_{n-1}^{tr} \cup B_n$.

When selecting only one sample from D^{cdd} to label in each iteration of AL, the selector can be defined as

$$\widehat{X} = arg\max S\left(x_k, D^{cdd}, D^{tr}, \theta\right) \tag{1}$$

where selector $S\left(x_k, D^{cdd}, D^{tr}, \theta\right)$ can be related to D^{cdd}, D^{tr}, θ and even other variations or datasets. Obviously, we can also select some samples $\{\hat{x}_n\}_{n=1}^{M}$ to form the set B_n in each iteration by computing S for D^{cdd} and ranking them [32]. Figure 1 demonstrates the structure of active learning algorithm.

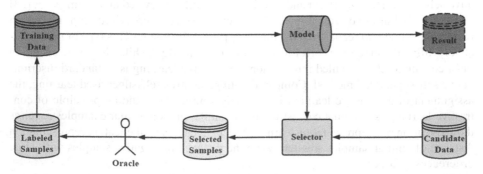

Fig. 1. Active learning.

3.2 Contrastive Learning

We utilize contrastive loss for backpropagation to train an encoder. One method to achieve contrastive learning is to design a metric capable of evaluating the similarity of two samples in the feature space. Cosine similarity is used as the most common similarity metric, which performs as a foundation in many loss functions of contrastive learning methods [5]. The cosine similarity is defined as follows:

$$cos\_sim(A, B) = \frac{A \cdot B}{\|A\| \|B\|} \tag{2}$$

A Noise Contrastive Estimation (NCE) [33] function is a common metric to estimate the different embedding. The definition is written as:

$$L_{NCE} = -\log \frac{\exp(sim(q, k_+)/\tau)}{\exp(sim(q, k_+)/\tau) + \exp(sim(q, k_-)/\tau)} \tag{3}$$

where q is the initial data. k_+ and k_- are positive and negative samples respectively. τ is a hyperparameter used as temperature coefficient in many methods. The sim() function is not restricted to a particular form, however, a cosine similarity is utilized in many cases [5].

InfoNCE is proposed to deal with the diploma when negative samples increase. The Eq. 4 can effectively evaluate the similarity between different samples and assist the neural network to converge when we select an appropriate sim() function and adjust the temperature coefficient.

$$L_{infoNCE} = -\log \frac{\exp(sim(q, k_+)/\tau)}{\exp(sim(q, k_+)/\tau) + \sum_{i=0}^{K} \exp(sim(q, k_i)/\tau)} \tag{4}$$

where k_i is a negative sample.

4   Method

The specific method will be presented in this section. In the traditional active model, the selection is to train a model with labeled data first, then select some samples to be annotated by oracle, and then include the samples to the training pool for followed retraining until the model converges. Obviously, the model we used to select samples is generally the same as the model used for downstream tasks such as classification. We propose a new structure that uses a contrastive learning model to learn the representation space. Then the selected samples are labeled and used in another classification model. We design a corresponding query method to achieve a better sample selection. Figure 2 presents the framework of our model.

First, we use the SimCLR [30] method to input all samples as unlabeled samples into the model to obtain a better representation. Then, the cluster centers of the labeled samples and the embedding positions of the unlabeled samples are calculated on the trained embedding. For each unlabeled sample, the shortest Euclidean distance from each known category cluster is used as the distance to the category. Using these shortest distances, we sort each unlabeled sample category from largest to smallest. The samples with larger distances need to be labeled most. We take the top k samples as a batch and ask the oracle for their labels. The labeled samples are taken from the unlabeled pool and added to the labeled pool. Meanwhile, the class cluster center is updated and iteratively repeated until enough samples are selected to make the classification model converge.

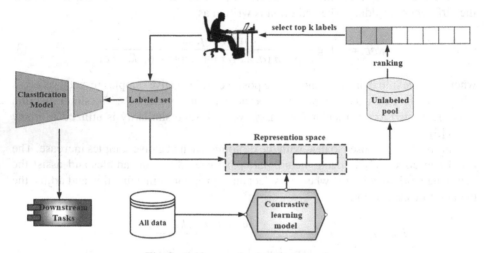

Fig. 2. Self-supervised Active Learning.

4.1 Self-supervised Training

SimCLR is a commonly applied self-supervised training method, which does not require supervised information. Appropriate data augmentation methods are crucial for the model training. Different samples augmented from one sample are regarded as positive samples, while other samples are regarded as negative samples. The specific introduction is as follows.

Assuming that there is a picture x, called Original Image. Data enhancement is performed on it first, and two enhanced pictures X_i, X_j are obtained. There are three ways for data augmentation:

- Cropping the image randomly and resizing the size back;
- Distorting the color randomly;
- Adding random Gaussian noise.

Next, input the enhanced picture X_i, X_j into the Encoder. The two Encoders share parameters to get the representation h_i, h_j, and then we continue to pass h_i, h_j to the projection head to get the representation. The two projection heads here are still shared parameters.

The next goal is to maximize the Z_i, Z_j obtained from the same picture. Figure 3 shows the framework.

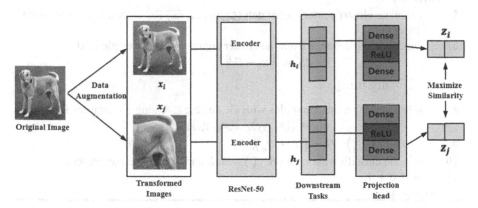

Fig. 3. A simple framework of SimCLR

4.2 Query Strategy

After the contrastive learning model is trained, under the current feature representation, we set up a special query strategy for downstream tasks. Given samples $X_i = (x_{i1}; x_{i2}; \ldots; x_{in})$ and $X_j = (x_{j1}; x_{j2}; \ldots; x_{jn})$, we usually use Minkowski distance as the distance measure.

$$\text{dist}_{mk}(\mathbf{x}_i, \mathbf{x}_j) = \left(\sum_{u=1}^{n} |x_{iu} - x_{ju}|^p\right)^{\frac{1}{p}} \tag{5}$$

When $p = 2$, it turns to be Euclidean distance.

$$\text{dist}_{ed}(\mathbf{x}_i, \mathbf{x}_j) = \|\mathbf{x}_i - \mathbf{x}_j\|_2 = \sqrt{\sum_{u=1}^{n} |x_{iu} - x_{ju}|^2} \tag{6}$$

Algorithm 1 summarizes the steps of querying from a given dataset D and a given contrastive learning model.

Algorithm 1

Input: labeled data set L, unlabeled data set U, candidate sample set n,
              sample category k, query numbers Q

1 **Initialize:** $q = 1$
2   train self-supervised model $f(\cdot)$ with $D = L \cup U$
3   calculate the embedding of labels
4 **while** $q \le Q$:
5   calculate cluster centers separately$(C_1, C_2, ..., C_k)$ for each sample with same
       label in L
6   calculate the distance from the cluster center for each sample in U
$$d_{ji} = \left\| x_j - C_i \right\|_2$$
7      $\lambda_j = \arg\min_{i \in \{1,2,...,k\}} d_{ji}$
8   select and label the n samples with the largest λ_j among all samples in U
$$U_q = \{(x_1, y_1), ... (x_n, y_n)\};$$
9      $L = \left(L \cup U_q\right);\ U = \left(U - U_q\right);$
10   train the classification network g$(\cdot)$ with L and update the parameters
11     $q = q + 1$
12 **return** g$(\cdot)$

---

5 Experiments

5.1 Experimental Setup

Datasets. To estimate the suggested self-supervised active sampling algorithm, We experiment with CIFAR10 and CIFAR100 [34] datasets and we use 50K images for training and 10K for testing. CIFAR10 has 10 object categories, while CIFAR 100 contains 100 categories. Both image size is 32×32. We explore the accuracy and the corresponding label cost.

Baseline. – **Random** selects data from the unlabeled data sets randomly.
– **Entropy** [35] selects the samples with high entropy.
– **All-labeled** uses 100% labeled data.

Data Augmentation. Several data augmentation methods are applied for self-supervised algorithm pre-training. First, Geometric augmentations [36] is utilized: an image is cropped randomly and resized back to the previous size. Then we distorting the color randomly with the change of contrast, saturation, hue and brightness. Random Gaussian noise is appended with a certain probability.

Implementation Details. We implemented this experiment in Pytorch deep framework. We train Resnet18 with the Adam optimizer. We adjust the learning rate to 0.001, and set the training batch size to 128. In the initial self-supervised model training, a total of 200 epochs were trained with all the data. In the subsequent training of the classification model, there are 1% of the labeled samples at the beginning, that is, 500 samples. Each time 500 unlabeled samples are actively selected to be labeled, and the accuracy of the model is recorded after each 5% sample label is added. All used labeled samples are trained for 10 epochs.

5.2 Results

Comparison of Sampling Methods. Figure 4 and Fig. 5 show active learning results on CIFAR datasets. The final results indicate that the proposed method accomplishes the same effect with a lower cost than traditional active learning methods, and can select effective samples faster.

It can be analyzed from the experimental results that our method always surpasses the other two types of sampling methods. In the case of the same amount of annotation, the sampling method we proposed is more accurate. As the number of annotations increases and the model learns enough knowledge, the advantages of our method and the method based on entropy uncertainty gradually shrink. However, it can be seen that only 50% of the original sample size is needed, and our active learning achieves the effect of using a 100% labeling supervision method, which reduces the labeling amount by 50%.

In addition, with the increase of labeled samples, the effect gap between random sampling and ours has become more and more obvious. An explanation is that the redundancy of randomly selected samples is difficult to avoid, resulting in invalid annotations or negative effects on the model. Our method comprehensively examines the uncertainty and representativeness of the sample, and successfully reduces the label cost.

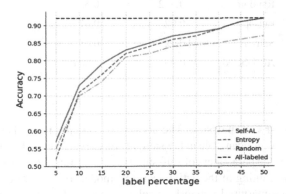

Fig. 4. The performance on cifar10

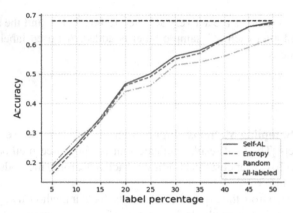

Fig. 5. The performance on cifar100

Table 1 summarizes the comparison of the effects of various methods in the case of 50% labeled data. The method we propose performs well on the two data sets simultaneously, and it is very close to the model performance learned by the supervised learning method.

Table 1. The performance with 50% labeled data

Methods	CIFAR10	CIFAR100
Random	0.852	0.623
Entropy	0.924	0.675
Self-AL	0.927	0.681
All-labeled	0.931	0.684

Network Parameter Comparison. The above experiment proves that self-supervised learning can play a significant role in the sample selection of active learning. In this part, we discuss whether the parameters of self-supervised learning after the model converges are helpful for the training of the active learning model. In the former experiment, we only used the self-supervised network to select the model, and the parameters of the classification network were retrained. Now we compare and retain the weight of the self-supervised network, and continue to use our method to select samples to fine-tune the classification neural network. Table 2 presents the effect of these methods.

Table 2. Performance using self-supervised network parameters or not

Methods	Data	CIFAR10	CIFAR100
All-labeled	100%	0.931	0.684
AL w/o fine-tuning	1%	0.385	0.056
AL + fine-tuning	1%	0.846	0.462
AL w/o fine-tuning	10%	0.732	0.263
AL + fine-tuning	10%	0.893	0.596
AL w/o fine-tuning	30%	0.872	0.567
AL + fine-tuning	30%	0.918	0.635

The results show that the self-supervised network can fine-tune the model parameters with active learning, which can achieve excellent results. It greatly reduces the need for labels and accomplish the effect of supervised training with just 30% supervised information. However, it is worth nothing that fine-tuning the original self-supervised network when the labeled samples increase to a certain scale since our active sampling method can still achieve the final performance individually.

The feature representation trained by the self-supervised network can help the active sampling method. The use of contrastive learning methods can obtain knowledge of unlabeled samples, which provides inspiration for the design of active sampling indicators.

6 Conclusion

In this chapter, we suggest an active learning algorithm combined with a contrastive learning model. We find that the traditional active learning method uses the same model for sample selection and classification. In order to select more valuable samples, we introduce a contrastive learning model to map the samples, which no longer relies on the original model. We also set an indicator to judge whether the sample is valid in this framework. The final results demonstrate that it is quite quick and effective to select samples in the feature representation learned by contrastive learning. Experiments on the CIFAR datasets show the success of the our method. We will extend this active learning framework to other broader tasks to further examine its capabilities in the future.

References

1. Settles, B.: Active learning literature survey (2009)
2. Kapoor, A., Grauman, K., Urtasun, R., Darrell, T.: Active learning with Gaussian processes for object categorization. In: 2007 IEEE 11th International Conference on Computer Vision, pp. 1–8 (2007)

3. Chattopadhyay, R., Wang, Z., Fan, W., Davidson, I., Panchanathan, S., Ye, J.: Batch mode active sampling based on marginal probability distribution matching. In: KDD Proceedings of International Conference on Knowledge Discovery and Data Mining 2012, pp. 741–749 (2013)

4. Copa, L., Tuia, D., Volpi, M., et al.: Unbiased query-by-bagging active learning for VHR image classification. In: Image and Signal Processing for Remote Sensing XVI. International Society for Optics and Photonics, vol. 7830, p. 78300K (2010)

5. Jaiswal, A., Babu, A.R., Zadeh, M.Z., et al.: A survey on contrastive self-supervised learning. Technologies (2021)

6. Wang, L.: Smoothness, disagreement coefficient, and the label complexity of agnostic active learning. J. Mach. Learn. Res. **12**, 2269–2292 (2011)

7. Zhang, L., Chen, C., Bu, J.: Active learning based on locally linear reconstruction. IEEE Trans. Pattern Anal. Mach. Intell. **33**(10), 2026–2038 (2011)

8. Cai, W., Zhang, Y., Zhou, S.: Active learning for support vector machines with maximum model change. In: Joint European Conference on Machine Learning and Knowledge Discovery in Databases, pp. 211–226. Springer, Heidelberg (2014). https://doi.org/10.1007/978-3-662-44848-9_14

9. Yang, Z., Tang, J., Zhang, Y.: Active learning for streaming networked data. In: Proceedings of the 23rd ACM International Conference on Conference on Information and Knowledge Management, pp. 1129–1138. ACM (2014)

10. Li, S., Xue, Y., Wang, Z.: Active learning for cross-domain sentiment classification. In: Proceeding of the 23rd International Joint Conference on Artificial Intelligence, pp. 2127–2133 (2013)

11. Zhang, H.T., Huang, M.L., Zhu, X.Y.: A unified active learning framework for biomedical relation extraction. J. Comput. Sci. Technol. **27**(6), 1302–1313 (2014)

12. Wang, D., Yan, C., Shan, S., et al.: Active learning for interactive segmentation with expected confidence change. In: Proceedings of the 11th Asian Conference on Computer Vision, pp.790–802. Springer, Heidelberg (2012). https://doi.org/10.1007/978-3-642-37331-2_59

13. King, R.D., Whelan, K.E., Jones, F.M.: Functional genomic hypothesis generation and experimentation by a robot scientist. Nature **427**(6971), 247 (2004)

14. Liu, Y.: Active learning with support vector machine applied to gene expression data for cancer classification. J. Chem. Inf. Comput. Sci. **44**(6), 1936–1941 (2004)

15. Lewis, D., Gale, W.: A sequential algorithm for training text classifiers. In: Proceedings of the ACM SIGIR Conference on Research and Development in Information Retrieval, pp. 3–12. ACM/Springer (1994)

16. Beluch, W.H., Genewein, T., Nurnberger, A., Kohler, J.: The power of ensembles for active learning in image classification. In: 2018 IEEE/CVF Conference on Computer Vision and Pattern Recognition, pp. 9368–9377 (2018)

17. Gilad-Bachrach, R., Navot, A., Tishby, N.: Query by committee made real. In: NIPS (2005)

18. Settles, B., Craven, M., Ray, S.: Multiple-instance active learning. In: Advances in Neural Information Processing Systems (NIPS), vol. 20, pp. 1289–1296. MIT Press (2008)

19. Roy, N., McCallum, A.: Toward optimal active learning through sampling estimation of error reduction. In: Proceedings of the International Conference on Machine Learning (ICML), pp. 441–448. Morgan Kaufmann (2001)

20. Gilad-Bachrach, R., Navot, A., Tishby, N.: Query by committee made real. In: Advances in Neural Information Processing Systems, pp. 443–450 (2006)

21. Tran, T., Do, T.T., Reid, I.: Bayesian generative active deep learning. In: International Conference on Machine Learning. PMLR, pp. 6295–6304 (2019)

22. Saito, K., Watanabe, K., Ushiku, Y.: Maximum classifier discrepancy for unsupervised domain adaptation. In: Proceedings of the IEEE Conference on Computer Vision and Pattern Recognition, pp. 3723–3732 (2018)

23. Higgins, I., Matthey, L., Pal, A.: beta-vae: learning basic visual concepts with a constrained variational framework (2016)
24. Goodfellow, I., Pouget-Abadie, J., Mirza, M.: Generative adversarial networks. Commun. ACM **63**(11), 139–144 (2020)
25. Bojanowski, P., Joulin, A.: Unsupervised learning by predicting noise (2017)
26. Alexey, D., Fischer, P., Tobias, J., Springenberg, M.R., Brox, T.: Discriminative unsupervised feature learning with exemplar convolutional neural networks (2014)
27. Wu, Z., Xiong, Y., Yu, S., Lin, D.: Unsupervised feature learning via non-parametric instance-level discrimination (2018)
28. Caron, M., Misra, I., Mairal, J., Goyal, P., Bojanowski, P., Joulin, A.: Unsupervised learning of visual features by contrasting cluster assignments (2020)
29. He, K., Fan, H., Wu, Y., Xie, S., Girshick, R.: Momentum contrast for unsupervised visual representation learning (2019)
30. Chen, T., Kornblith, S., Norouzi, M., Hinton, G.: A simple framework for contrastive learning of visual representations (2020)
31. Deng, J., Dong, W., Socher, R., Li, L.J., Li, K., Fei-Fei, L.: Imagenet: a large-scale hierarchical image database. In: 2009 IEEE Conference on Computer Vision and Pattern Recognition, pp. 248–255. IEEE (2009)
32. Liu, P., Wang, L., He, G.: A survey on active deep learning: from model-driven to data-driven. arXiv preprint arXiv:2101.09933 (2021)
33. Gutmann, M., Hyvärinen, A.: Noise-contrastive estimation: a new estimation principle for unnormalized statistical models. In: AISTATS (2010)
34. Krizhevsky, A., Hinton, G.: Learning multiple layers of features from tiny images (2009)
35. Dagan, I., Engelson, S.P.: Committee-based sampling for training probabilistic classifiers. In: Machine Learning Proceedings 1995, pp. 150–157. Elsevier(1995)
36. Wu, Z., Xiong, Y., Yu, S.X., Lin, D.: Unsupervised feature learning via non-parametric instance discrimination. In: Proceedings of the IEEE Conference on Computer Vision and Pattern Recognition, pp. 3733–3742 (2018)

Research on Intelligent Identification Method of Power Grid Missing Data Based on Improved Generation Countermeasure Network with Multi-dimensional Feature Analysis

Yang Lv[✉], Shiming Sun, Qi Zhao, Jiang Tian, and Chun Li

State Grid Suzhou Power Supply Company, Suzhou 215004, Jiangsu, China

Abstract. With the rapid development of data acquisition system in power grid, the data fusion of power grid has become more and more mature. Aiming at the problem of data missing in power grid, this paper proposes an intelligent identification method of power grid missing data based on generation countermeasure network with multi-dimensional feature fitting. Firstly, based on the fluctuation cross-correlation analysis (FCCA), the correlation between missing data and multidimensional features is analyzed, and the feature data set with strong correlation is selected; Secondly, the kernel principal component analysis (KPCA) algorithm is used to map the feature data set into a low-dimensional vector. Finally, the improved generation countermeasure network (WGAN) is used to reconstruct and distinguish the low-dimensional vector, fill in the missing data of power grid and enhance the identification ability of missing data. The simulation results show that the proposed method has higher data filling accuracy than the traditional data filling method.

Keywords: Fluctuation cross-correlation analysis · Multidimensional features · Generate countermeasure network · Missing data · Nuclear principal component analysis · Intelligent identification

1 The Introduction

With the development of data mining technology, power grid massive data fusion has become the basis of system situation awareness, operation optimization and state evaluation, and the detection of voltage, harmonic and reactive power is beneficial to improve power quality. When the data is missing and the redundancy is insufficient, the analysis of power grid data has a great deviation from the actual situation. Therefore, how to accurately fill and reconstruct power grid data with different missing rates and restore the integrity of power grid data is of great significance [1, 2].

There are two main methods to deal with missing data: deletion method and filling method. In reference [3], proposed an improved random forest filling algorithm, which

Project Supported by the science and technology project of Jiangsu Electric Power Co., Ltd. (J2021046).

is suitable for filling various missing forms of power data. Besides, the filling results have high precision and the model has strong stability, which is conducive to improving the quality of power data. In reference [4], proposed a data filling method combining linear interpolation with LightGBM (Optical Gradient elevator), which can use linear interpolation to deal with short-term missing data and LightGBM to deal with long-term missing data. In reference [5], proposed a data filling method based on incomplete soft set probability analysis, which can avoid the influence of threshold on subjective factors and reduce the further error rate of prediction results to a minimum.

In this paper, an intelligent identification method of power grid missing data based on generative adversarial network considering multidimensional feature selection is proposed. First, based on the wave cross-correlation analysis algorithm, the correlation between missing data and multidimensional features is analyzed, and feature data sets with strong correlation are selected; Secondly, the kernel principal component analysis (KPCA) [6] algorithm is used to map feature data set to a low-dimensional vector. Finally, Wasserstein Generative Adversarial Network (WGAN) [7] was used to reconstruct the low-dimensional vector to fill in the grid missing data and enhance the identification ability of missing data. The simulation results show that the proposed method has higher data filling accuracy than the traditional data filling method. Wave correlation analysis algorithm.

2 Wave Correlation Analysis Algorithm

In order to extend the fluctuation analysis algorithm to two time series, relevant scholars put forward the fluctuation cross-correlation analysis (FCCA) [8] algorithm, FCCA overcomes the defect of DCCA algorithm to determine the fitting between regions. The principle of the algorithm is as follows:

Step 1: Let the two time series be x_i, y_i, where $i = 1, 2, ..., n$, calculate the deviation of the sequence and sum it, namely:

$$\Delta x(l) = \sum_{i=1}^{l} (xi - \overline{x}), \ l = 1, 2, \cdots, N$$
$$\Delta y(l) = \sum_{i=1}^{l} (yi - \overline{y}), \ l = 1, 2, \cdots, N$$

(1)

Step 2: Calculate the forward difference representing the autocorrelation of time series:

$$\Delta x(l, l_0) = x(l_0 + l) - x(l_0), \ l_0 = 1, 2, \cdots, N - l$$
$$\Delta y(l, l_0) = y(l_0 + l) - y(l_0), \ l_0 = 1, 2, \cdots, N - l$$

(2)

Step 3: Calculate the covariance of the sequence:

$$Covxy(l) = \sqrt{\left[\Delta x(l, l_0) - \overline{\Delta x(l, l_0)}\right] \times \left[\Delta y(l, l_0) - \overline{\Delta y(l, l_0)}\right]}$$

(3)

It can be seen from Eq. (3) that when the two sequences are completely identical, FCCA is the same as FA. If there is a correlation between the two sequences, $Covxy(l)$ follows a power distribution $Cov(l) \sim m^{h_{xy}}$; h_{xy} represents the correlation coefficient of sequence x and y, when $h_{xy} = 0$, it means that the sequence x is independent of y; when $h_{xy} > 0$, it indicates that sequence x is positively correlated with y; When $h_{xy} < 0$, it indicates that sequence x is negatively correlated with y.

3   Nuclear Principal Component Analysis

Kernel principal component analysis (KPCA), is the PCA algorithm of nonlinear extension, KPCA can not only reduce the dimension of a data set that can dig out the nonlinear characteristic of the data set contains, so KPCA is often used in nonlinear dimension reduction of data sets. Assuming $x_1, x_2, \ldots, x_M$ is the data sample and the input space is represented by $\{x_i\}$.

Set mapping to $\Phi : R^d \rightarrow F$, the kernel goes through the mapping Φ to realize the mapping of $x \rightarrow F$, therefore, it can be known that the feature space data obtained by mapping meets the conditions of centralization, namely

$$\sum_{\mu=1}^{M} \Phi(x_\mu) = 0 \tag{4}$$

The covariance matrix of the feature space is:

$$C = \frac{1}{M} \sum_{\mu=1}^{M} \Phi(x_\mu)\Phi(x_\mu)^T \tag{5}$$

Assume that the eigenvalue of C is λ, and the eigenvector is v, the following equation can be obtained:

$$Cv = \lambda v \tag{6}$$

That is:

$$(\Phi(x_v) \cdot Cv) = \lambda(\Phi(x_v) \cdot v) \tag{7}$$

Since all eigenvectors can be expressed as the linear span of $\Phi(x_1), \Phi(x_2), \ldots, \Phi(x_M)$, namely

$$v = \sum_{i=1}^{M} \alpha_i \Phi(x_i) \tag{8}$$

In combination with the above equation

$$\frac{1}{M} \sum_{\mu=1}^{M} \alpha_\mu (\sum_{w=1}^{M} (\Phi(x_v) \cdot \Phi(x_w)\Phi(x_w)\Phi(x_\mu))) = \lambda \sum_{\mu=1}^{M} (\Phi(x_v) \cdot \Phi(x_\mu)) \tag{9}$$

Where $v = 1, 2, \ldots, M$. The $M \times M$ dimensional matrix K is defined as:

$$K_{\mu v} = (\Phi(x_\mu) \cdot \Phi(x_v)) \tag{10}$$

Then the above equation can be simplified as:

$$M \lambda Ka = K^2 a \tag{11}$$

the eigenvalues and eigenvectors can be obtained by solving the above formula. therefore, the projection of test samples in the eigenspace is:

$$(v^k \cdot \Phi(x)) = \sum_{i=1}^{M} (a_i)^k (\Phi(x_i), \Phi(x)) \tag{12}$$

4   WGAN

GAN since put forward, in the aspect of data generation advantage is great, GAN has been widely used in image generation, text is generated, and many other areas, and the missing data and image generation is consistent, the network structure as shown in Fig. 1.

In the initial GAN paper, the loss function is defined as follows:

$$\min_G \max_D V(D, G)$$
$$= E_{x \sim p_{data}(x)}[\log D(x)] + E_{z \sim p_z(z)}[\log(1 - D(G(z)))] \tag{13}$$

When the generator weight matrix is fixed and the calculation is reversible, then:

$$E_{z \sim p_z(z)}[\log(1 - D(G(z)))] = E_{x \sim p_G(x)}[\log(1 - D(x))] \tag{14}$$

The loss function becomes:

$$\max_D V(D, G) = \max_D \int_x p_{data}(x) \log D(x) + p_g(x) \log(1 - D(x)) dx \tag{15}$$

Due to the $D = \frac{p_{data}}{p_{data} + p_G}$, V(D,G) is the maximum value, and the loss function is further simplified as:

$$\min_G \max_D V(D, G) = -2 \log 2 + \min_G [2 JSD(P_{data} \| P_G)] \tag{16}$$

As can be seen from the above equation, when the generator effect is too excellent, the loss function is equivalent to JS divergence, and there is an important problem with JS divergence, when the real data distribution does not overlap with the generated data distribution, JS divergence is zero. In order to improve the training effect of GAN, Wasserstein distance was introduced into the loss function.

$$W(p_r, p_g) = \inf_{\gamma \sim \Pi(p_r, p_g)} E_{(x,y) \sim \gamma}[\|x - y\|] \tag{17}$$

Since it is difficult to directly calculate Wasserstein distance between arbitrary distributions, it can be transformed into the following equation:

$$W(p_r, p_g) = \frac{1}{K} \sup_{\|f\|_L \leq K} E_{x \sim p_r}[f(x)] - E_{x \sim p_g}[f(x)] \tag{18}$$

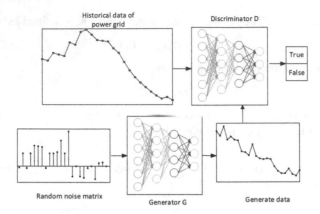

Fig. 1. WGAN network structure diagram

5 Missing Data Filling Based on WGAN

5.1 Data Pretreatment at the Data Location

In order to eliminate the influence of different dimensions between data on model training efficiency, data are often normalized or z-score standardized, its formula is shown in Eq. (19).

$$x^\wedge = \frac{x - a(x)}{s_{td}} \tag{19}$$

Where, x is the original value, $x^\wedge$ is the standardized value, and a(x) is the average value of the corresponding features of x; Std is the standard deviation of all the numbers that correspond to x.

5.2 Data Filling Strategy Based on WGAN Data Filling Strategy

For the problem of missing data in power grid, the overall framework of WGAN-based filling strategy is shown in Fig. 2. The network structure and super parameters are modified according to the test results, the generator of the network structure as shown in Table 1. The network structure of discriminators is shown in Table 2, the network parameters and structure of the discriminator and generator are basically the same, but the only difference is that the activation function of the last full-connection layer is Sigmoid.

First generate a conforms to the gaussian random noise vector to fill the missing data, and constitute the training data and real data sets, in order to improve the training efficiency of network, the dimension of the training set by KPCA algorithm, and the dimension reduction after the generator and generate the training set of input data, and according to the target data loss of discriminant value, Finally, the RMSProp optimizer is used to reduce the loss value and update the network weight iteratively.

Table 1. Generator network structure

The layer number	Network name	Number of neurons	The activation function
1	Full connection layer	32	Relu
2	Full connection layer	64	Relu
3	Full connection layer	64	Relu
4	Full connection layer	32	Relu

Table 2. Discriminator network structure

The layer number	Network name	Number of neurons	The activation function
1	Full connection layer	32	Relu
2	Full connection layer	64	Relu
3	Full connection layer	16	Relu
4	Full connection layer	1	Sigmoid

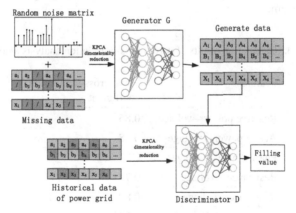

Fig. 2. Data filling flow chart

6 Example Analysis

The example data is selected from a city power grid in east China in one quarter, and the sampling frequency is 10 min, with a total of 12,960 data samples, WGAN adopts Pytorch deep learning framework and constructs the network according to Tables 2 and 3. Due to space constraints, it takes grid voltage data filling as an example. KNN, random forest algorithm and spline interpolation are selected to compare with the proposed method.

6.1 Error Analysis Standard

This paper uses the root mean square error and mean absolute error as the data fill the model of evaluation index, the formula is as follows:

$$E_{rmse} = \sqrt{\frac{1}{n} \sum_{i=1}^{n} (x_i - x_i^*)^2} \tag{20}$$

$$E_{mae} = \frac{1}{n} \sum_{i=1}^{n} |x_i - x_i^*| \tag{21}$$

Where x_i, x_i^* are the true value and the filled value respectively.

6.2 Data Preprocessing Parameter Selection

It can be seen from Table 3 that the characteristics with high correlation with voltage are: reactive power, reactance, phase Angle and resistance; Wave cross-correlation analysis algorithm fully mines the hidden nonlinear relationship between voltage and feature, The correlation between each characteristic factor and voltage is similar to that of the actual power system.

Table 3. Calculation results of wave cross-correlation analysis algorithm

Features	Wave cross-correlation coefficient
Reactive power – voltage	0.85
Active power – voltage	0.68
Phase Angle – voltage	0.79
Resistance – voltage	0.78
Reactance – voltage	0.80
Current – voltage	0.72
Power factor – voltage	0.78

Characteristic variables of different dimensions are selected to study the influence of input variable dimensions on WGAN filling effect. The table below shows the comparison results of voltage loss data filling errors under different WGAN input dimensions.

Table 4. Comparison of WGAN filling errors under different input dimensions

Network input dimension	RMSE	MAE
3	1.95	1.10
4	1.89	1.12
5	1.78	0.93
6	1.85	1.05

As can be seen from Table 4, when the input dimension is 5, WGAN has the smallest filling error and the best filling effect. When the input increases from dimension 3 to dimension 4, the effective information amount of input network increases, and the filling precision increases slightly. When the input increases from 5 dimension to 6 dimension, the redundant information of input network increases and the filling error increases.

6.3 Analysis of Filling Results

The complete sub-sequence is screened from the power grid data, and the missing data with proportions of 10%, 20%, 30%, 40% and 50% are respectively constructed by the method of random deletion. The error variation process of generator and discriminator when the miss rate is 20% is shown in Fig. 3.

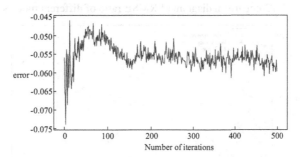

(a)Generator differential error variation diagram

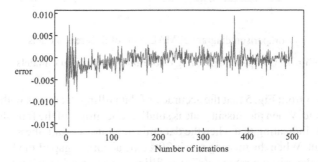

(b)Differential error variation diagram of discriminator

Fig. 3. Variation diagram of WGAN difference error

As can be seen from Fig. 3, with the increase of iterations, the generator error briefly rises and then declines. The discriminator error will eventually stabilize near 0, while the generator error fluctuates up and down within a certain range, indicating that the generated sample data is close to the real data and the weight of the generator tends to be stable.

As can be seen from Fig. 4, MAE and RMSE of data filled by different algorithms have basically the same variation trend. The WGAN filling method proposed in this paper has the smallest RMSE and MAE of data in all miss ratios and the highest filling accuracy. However, with the increase of miss rate, data filling accuracy gradually decreases.

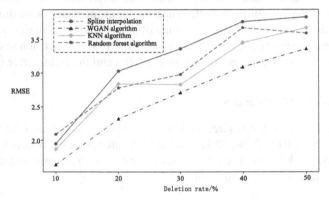

(a)Comparison diagram of RMSE ratio of different models

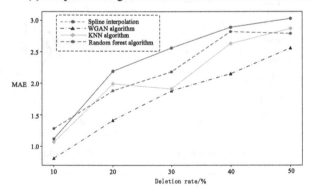

(b) Comparison diagram of MAE ratio of different models

Fig. 4. Comparison of filling error ratio with different models

It can be seen from Fig. 5 that the accuracy of data filling decreases with the increase of the missing rate. When the missing rate is small, the accuracy of the four algorithms can reach over 65%, indicating that when the data missing rate is small, the accuracy of each algorithm is high. When the missing rate is 20%, the accuracy gap of the four algorithms is small. When the missing rate is 40%, the filling accuracy of spline interpolation and WGAN have little difference. When the missing rate is greater than 50%, the filling accuracy of WGAN is obviously higher than that of the other three algorithms.

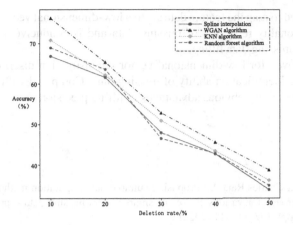

Fig. 5. Comparison of filling accuracy of different models with the same compensation ratio

The data set with a miss rate of 30% was selected and WGAN was used to fill in the data. The filling result and the real value are shown in Fig. 6. As can be seen from Fig. 6, the difference between the filling value and the real value is small, which can restore the missing data well and meet the data filling requirements.

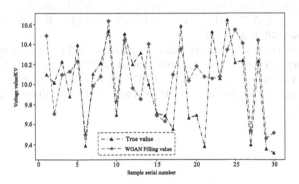

Fig. 6. Comparative analysis of WGAN filling value and real value

7 Conclusion

This paper proposes an intelligent identification method of power grid missing data based on improved generative adversance network with multi-dimensional feature fitting. The main conclusions are as follows:

1) The wave cross-correlation analysis method is used to preprocess the missing data, to obtain the correlation between the missing data and multidimensional features, and to obtain feature data sets with strong correlation with the missing data.

2) KPCA is used to map the feature data set to a low-dimensional vector, which realizes the dimensionality reduction of missing data and is conducive to improving the accuracy of missing data filling.
3) WGAN is given for low-dimensional vector reconstruction discrimination, which improves the identification ability of missing data. Compared with traditional data filling method, it has obvious advantages in filling precision.

References

1. Hemanth, G.R., Charles Raja, S.: Proposing suitable data imputation methods by adopting a stage wise approach for various classes of smart meters missing data – practical approach. Expert Syst. Appl. **187**, 115911 (2022)
2. Zhu, J., Xu, W.: Real-time data filling and automatic retrieval algorithm of road traffic based on deep-learning method. Symmetry **13**(1), 1 (2020)
3. Deng, W., Guo, Y., Liu, J., Li, Y., Liu, D., Zhu, L.: A missing power data filling method based on improved random forest algorithm. Chin. J. Electr. Eng. **5**(4), 33–39 (2019)
4. Huang, G.: Missing data filling method based on linear interpolation and lightgbm. J. Phys. Conf. Ser. **1754**(1), 012187 (2021)
5. Kong, Z., Zhao, J., Wang, L., Zhang, J.: A new data filling approach based on probability analysis in incomplete soft sets. Expert Syst. Appl. **184**, 115358 (2021)
6. Farzana, A., Samira, S., Bassant, S.: Conceptual and empirical comparison of dimensionality reduction algorithms (PCA, KPCA, LDA, MDS, SVD, LLE, ISOMAP, LE, ICA, t-SNE). Comput. Sci. Rev. **40**, 100378 (2021)
7. Zhang, C., Chen, H., He, J., Yang, H.: Reconstruction method for missing measurement data based on Wasserstein generative adversarial network. JACIII **25**(2), 195–203 (2021)
8. Hua, W., Sui, Y., Wan, Y., Liu, G., Xu, G.: FCCA: hybrid code representation for functional clone detection using attention networks. IEEE Trans. Reliab. **70**, 304–318 (2021)

Civil Aviation Etiquette Robot System Based on Decision Tree Model

JinRui He[✉]

University for Science and Technology Sichuan, Chengdu 620500, Sichuan, China

Abstract. With the improvement of people's living standards, the requirements for intelligent services are getting higher and higher. As a kind of service robot, the ceremonial robot is often used in various occasions to receive customers' greeters. It not only reduces the workload of employees, but also provides a good customer service experience. This paper studies the etiquette robots in the civil aviation field, develops a etiquette robot system based on the decision number model, and evaluates the service quality of the etiquette robots. The evaluation results show that the robot's various service indicators are recognized by passengers. The civil aviation robot system can Invest in the civil aviation industry to better serve flight passengers.

Keywords: Decision tree model · Civil aviation etiquette · Etiquette robot · System development

1 Introduction

With the advancement of technology, economic growth and the continuous improvement of people's quality of life, robots will gradually affect various living conditions of human beings. At the same time, robots can also provide people with convenient services. In civil aviation etiquette services, the use of robots is to allow people to experience high-quality services that meet the needs of passengers.

Many scholars at home and abroad have conducted research on the development of civil aviation etiquette robot system based on decision tree model, and have achieved good research results. For example, a scholar has developed a ceremonial robot. The biggest feature of the robot is that it has an advanced navigation system that can help its GPS to indicate the route for users. In addition, infrared detectors and ultrasonic sensors are installed to detect obstacles. Accurate measurement and positioning can be used in airports to guide passengers to take flight routes, and it can also assist cleaning workers in cleaning airport hygiene [1]. A scientific research team used data algorithms to design a robot suitable for reception at the door, and placed the robot at the door of a clothing store. Whether the customer enters the store or leaves, the robot will bow and show good. Through the control of the instruction program, the robot can also let the robot interact with the customer simple dialogue [2]. Although the research results of the development

© Springer Nature Singapore Pte Ltd. 2022
Y. Tian et al. (Eds.): ICBDS 2021, CCIS 1563, pp. 707–715, 2022.
https://doi.org/10.1007/978-981-19-0852-1_56

of the civil aviation etiquette robot system based on the decision tree model are good, there are few practical applications in the civil aviation field. The application of this system should be vigorously promoted to improve the quality of civil aviation services.

This article introduces the functions of civil aviation etiquette robots and the hardware requirements of the robot system design. According to the decision tree model, the structure of the civil aviation etiquette robot control system is designed. An appropriate power supply is placed in the robot body to realize the normal operation of the etiquette robot. Afterwards, evaluate the service quality during the application of the etiquette robot to understand the passenger's satisfaction with the robot service.

2   Civil Aviation Etiquette Robot Functions and System Design Requirements

2.1   Civil Aviation Etiquette Services

Civil aviation etiquette service is the process of providing passenger services to meet the needs of passengers in accordance with relevant matters and regulatory requirements in the airport or cabin as the service place. From a broad perspective, it is further understood that civil aviation etiquette services are the integration of systematic activities, and the perfect combination of technical and normative processes and the service objectives of civil aviation enterprises. The key components of civil aviation services are safety and service. The two factors support and promote each other, improve service quality, create a favorable environment for safety, build development on the basis of quality assurance, and avoid blind pursuit of speed and scale.

2.2   Introduction to the Functions of Civil Aviation Etiquette Robots

(1) Basic functions

The civil aviation etiquette robot is a kind of acousto-optic, electromechanical, and it looks like a human. It has certain visual, tactile and voice functions. It can walk and beckon to hug. It is suitable for greeters who treat passengers at the airport. Combining popular science and increasing entertainment, large robotic animals that simulate human or animal actions are designed to enrich passengers' waiting time. The functions that the civil aviation etiquette robot studied in this article should have are: it can automatically distinguish the arrival or departure of guests, give welcome or farewell speeches, and make corresponding welcome or farewell actions; it can have simple conversations with passengers; it has a distance measurement function, no It can collide with obstacles; it can store the program list, and can sing and dance; through the touch screen on the robot's chest, you can learn about the relevant information of the corresponding unit [3, 4].

(2) Function of multi-sensor system

Before determining the functional requirements of the ceremonial robot multi-sensor system, it is necessary to clarify the various functions of the ceremonial robot. Ceremonial robots can be used in many occasions to serve people. For example, when the flight crew enters the airport, the ceremonial robot can be placed at the door to greet the passenger. When the passenger arrives, it greets the passenger and makes a handshake welcoming gesture. When the passenger leaves, it bids farewell to the passenger and wave goodbye action; In addition, the ceremonial robot can also be moved freely in a certain field, and can actively avoid obstacles during the free movement process, and at the same time can express information with voice. When the robot is moving, it is necessary to avoid collisions with surrounding objects, and emergency stop measures should be taken when necessary. In addition, the ceremonial robot can also guide passengers to the waiting room. During this process, the ceremonial robot can walk along the wall and always keep a certain distance from the wall. In addition, the ceremonial robot can also perform programs for passengers while they are waiting for the flight. Such as singing and dancing. Of course, when to enable the above functions, people need to issue control commands to choose, which requires the human-computer interaction function of the ceremonial robot [5, 6].

2.3 The Hardware Design of the Etiquette Robot System

(1) The design of the host computer

Welcome and free movement are two different states. The robot needs to accept commands and choose to run in an adaptive state according to different occasions, so as to achieve the purpose of real-time control. The host computer should be installed in the body of the robot and move with the robot. Due to the limited space in the robot body, the size requirements need to be met, except for the display and the rest of the touch screen, the size should be as small as possible to save internal space [7].

(2) The design of the main controller module

The main controller is the core of the lower computer, which is mainly responsible for real-time acquisition, processing, and output control signals of multi-sensor information, and communicates with the upper computer and accepts commands from the upper computer. Since the controller is used in the mobile robot, the mobile robot uses an internal power source, and it is necessary to reduce the power consumption of the system under the condition of a certain endurance. In addition, the stability of the system must be guaranteed. System stability is the prerequisite for the normal operation of the system. The more complex the system, the more difficult it is to control it stably. On the premise of ensuring the normal operation of the system, a cost-effective controller should be used as much as possible [8].

(3) Design of sensor module

During the welcoming process, the sensor robot used to detect the entrance and exit of guests is usually placed at the entrance of the hall in the welcoming state, and defaults to a static standing posture. At this time, the robot is required to be able to perceive human movement within at least 3m in front of itself, and determine whether the guest is coming or going out. The infrared pyroelectric sensor can perceive the moving life body in the surrounding environment, which is very suitable for detecting human movement. If there is infrared radiation in the surrounding environment, the surface temperature of the pyroelectric material will change, and the temperature change will cause the surface electric dipole moment to change, thereby generating electric charges. The charge released by pyroelectric materials changes with the change of infrared radiation [9, 10].

(4) Sensors used to detect obstacles in free movement

In the process of free movement, the ceremonial robot should effectively avoid the surrounding obstacles. Since the ceremonial robot can be used for entertainment performances and services, there are usually crowds of onlookers, and the space of the venue will be very limited. In order to save space, the robot should be moved in the process as close to obstacles as possible, it is necessary to select a sensor that can detect obstacles within a short distance. Secondly, because it is mainly used for short-distance detection, the accuracy of the sensor is required to be high. Furthermore, for the obstacle distance within the detection range, an accurate distance value must be obtained so as to adopt different avoidance strategies for obstacles at different distances [11].

2.4 ID3 of Decision Tree Algorithm

The ID3 algorithm uses information entropy as a template to measure the balance of the number of samples in each category in the sample set, and then uses information gain (the reduction of information entropy) as the template selection feature to segment it, so as to achieve tree building and classification [12].

The information entropy calculation formula is as follows:

$$I(X) = -p \log_2^p - (1-p) \log_2^{1-p} \tag{1}$$

Among them, X is the set of examples, and p is the proportion of the number of positive examples in the total number of examples.

The calculation formula of subtree information entropy is:

$$New\_I(X, G_i) = \sum_{j \in V(G_i)} \frac{|X_j|}{|X|} I(X_j) \tag{2}$$

Among them, G_i is the discrete attribute, and X_j is the sample set with $G_i = j$ in the sample set X.

3 Civil Aviation Etiquette Robot System Design

3.1 The Structure Design of the Civil Aviation Etiquette Robot Control System

Figure 1 shows the structure of the control system of the civil aviation etiquette robot. The civil aviation etiquette robot control system is operated by the upper and lower computers together to control the behavior mode of the robot. Since the ceremonial robot must have robust performance to the environment and the ability to transmit information smoothly, it can not only collect environmental information steadily and quickly, but also transmit the external environmental information to the robot control system in a timely and accurate manner. Therefore, a sensor unit is needed. Check environmental conditions. At the same time, the ceremonial robot has a fixed gait mechanism, which can perform multiple sets of different welcoming actions according to different situations, reflecting that the control system needs a fixed drive unit to control the robot's movement. The ceremonial robot has a remote control function, and the user can give instructions to the robot through the remote control, so the control system needs a fixed remote control unit.

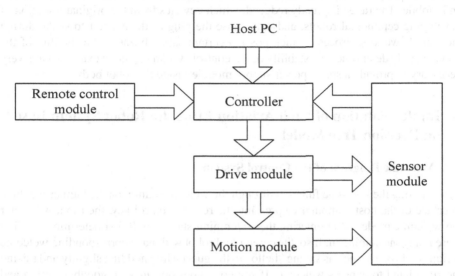

Fig. 1. Architecture block diagram of civil aviation etiquette robot

3.2 Robot Power Supply Selection

Table 1. Battery characteristics

	Nickel-cadmium batteries	NiMH batteries	Lithium ion battery	Lithium polymer battery	Lead-acid batteries
Energy density (wh/kg)	35–40	60–75	85–110	125–135	30–50
Cycle life (times)	350–500	800–1000	500–650	500–600	400–550

Table 1 shows the basic characteristics of different types of batteries. For example, the energy density of nickel-cadmium batteries is 35–40 wh/kg, and the cycle life can reach 350–500 times. The energy density of nickel-hydrogen batteries is 60–75 wh/kg, cycle. The life span can reach 800–1000 times. The civil aviation etiquette robot needs to realize movement, handshake and other actions, energy is the foundation, and the power module is the power source of the robot. The power supply module can be divided into external power supply and internal power supply. The external power supply is the power adapter. The external power supply powered by the cable can provide the necessary energy for the robot and the power needed for PC debugging. However, the length of the power adapter cable is limited, which makes the ceremonial robot flexible and mobile. The range is greatly reduced, which deviates from the original intention of developing ceremonial robots, and may cause the plug of the adapter to shake during the robot's working process, which poses a certain safety hazard. The stability of the power supply determines the stability of the control system to a large extent, so it is very necessary to provide a stable power supply module inside the robot body.

4 Implementation of Civil Aviation Etiquette Robot System Based on Decision Tree Model

4.1 Welcome Program of the Control System

After starting the welcome function through the welcome button on the human-machine interface of the host computer or pressing the remote control key, the robot will enter the welcome mode. After entering the welcoming state, it will first determine whether there is anyone coming in. If so, the ceremonial robot will make corresponding welcome actions and voices, such as saying "hello" to the guest while nodding slightly and raising the right hand to express welcome. If someone goes out, make a goodbye action and voice, such as saying "goodbye, welcome to come again next time" to the guest and beckoning goodbye. If the guest sends an information query instruction through the welcome interface of the host computer, the guest will find the information that he is interested in. If the guest uses the remote control to send instructions to the robot, the robot will complete the corresponding actions in accordance with the received instructions. If the guest issued an instruction for the operation interface, the display screen will show the operation interface. If there is no command signal, it will return to the main program. The flow chart of the welcoming module is shown in Fig. 2.

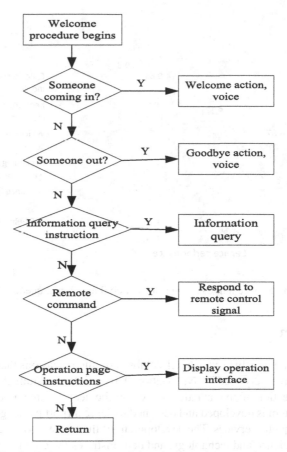

Fig. 2. Welcome process of the etiquette robot control system

4.2 Service Quality Analysis of Civil Aviation Etiquette Robots

The service indicators of civil aviation etiquette robots are scored, and the full score for each indicator is 10 points. The results are shown in Fig. 3. For the robot to quickly respond to customer inquiries, the score is 8.87 points, the service index for keeping the cabin environment clean and tidy is 8.64 points, and the service index for robots welcoming people through infrared heat sensing is 9.17 points, waving and shaking hands with customers to show okay, the service index score for waving goodbye was 9.93 points, the performance score for guiding customers was 9.65 points, and the performance score for customers' checked baggage was 9.8 points. It can be seen that people are more satisfied with the service quality of the civil aviation etiquette robot. The use of the robot can not only reduce the workload of flight attendants, but also meet people's riding needs.

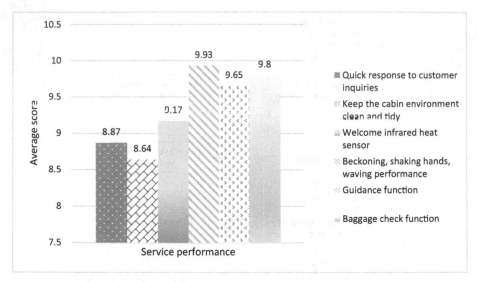

Fig. 3. Service index scoring results of civil aviation etiquette robots

5 Conclusion

Etiquette robots are mostly used in hotels, clubs and other occasions that need to receive guests, but they are rarely used in civil aviation. This article is to study the etiquette robot system in the direction of civil aviation. Based on the decision tree model, the etiquette robot control system is developed and designed to serve airport passengers and improve the quality of etiquette services. The development of this robot also reflects the intersection of modern science and technology, and demonstrates the country's comprehensive scientific and technological strength and level.

References

1. Fazlollahtabar, H., Niaki, S.: Integration of fault tree analysis, reliability block diagram and hazard decision tree for industrial robot reliability evaluation. Ind. Robot. **44**(6), 754–764 (2017)
2. Zhao, Y.: Research on personal credit evaluation of internet finance based on blockchain and decision tree algorithm. EURASIP J. Wirel. Commun. Netw. **2020**(1), 1–12 (2020)
3. Han, Q., Zhang, X., Shen, W.: Application of support vector machine based on decision tree feature extraction in lithology classification. Jilin Daxue Xuebao (Diqiu Kexue Ban)/J. Jilin Univ. (Earth Sci. Ed.) **49**(2), 611–620 (2019)
4. Zinchenko, O., Ogrenich, M., Shepel, M., et al.: Future economists' cultural competence and business English speech etiquette formation. Revista Romaneasca pentru Educatie Multidimensionala **12**(2), 290–310 (2020)
5. Li, H., Strauss, J., Lu, L.: The impact of high-speed rail on civil aviation in China. Transp. Policy **74**(FEB.), 187–200 (2019)
6. Gore, J.: Representing expertise in civil aviation. Comptes Rendus Des Séances De La Société De Biologie Et De Ses Filiales **174**(6), 948–956 (2017)

7. Korber, G.V.: Climate change and international civil aviation negotiations. Contexto Int. **39**(2), 443–458 (2017)
8. Charlotte, A.: The evolution of civil aviation displays. Avionics Mag. **40**(6), 23–27 (2017)
9. Lin, W.: Sky watching: vertical surveillance in civil aviation. Environ. Plan. **35**(3), 399–417 (2017)
10. Zio, E., Fan, M., Zeng, Z., Kang, R.: Application of reliability technologies in civil aviation: lessons learnt and perspectives. Chin. J. Aeronaut. **32**(1), 143–158 (2019)
11. Doisy, G., Meyer, J., Edan, Y.: The impact of human-robot interface design on the use of a learning robot system. IEEE Trans. Hum. Mach. Syst. **44**(6), 788–795 (2017)
12. Feng, H.M., Wong, C.C., Xiao, S.R., et al.: Humanoid robot field-programmable gate array hardware and robot-operating-system-based software machine co-design. Sens. Mater. **31**(6(1)), 1893–1904 (2019)

Chemical Fault Diagnosis Modeling Optimization Based on Machine Learning

Han Zong[✉]

Dongying Vocational Institute, Dongying 257091, Shandong, China

Abstract. With the increasing complexity of modern chemical production processes, chemical operating conditions have become more and more diversified, which has improved the production efficiency of chemical companies and increased the probability of chemical production failures. With the expansion of the chemical industry's scale of development, traditional manual diagnosis methods have been difficult to detect complex fault information. Therefore, the introduction of modern technology has become the key to chemical fault diagnosis. This paper studies chemical fault diagnosis based on machine learning, uses SVM classifier to perform chemical fault diagnosis, and then optimizes the parameters of SVM classifier through three methods of GS, GA and PSO machine learning algorithms. It is found that the diagnosis accuracy rate after GS algorithm optimization is 99.1273%, GA algorithm optimized diagnosis accuracy rate was 99.3548%, PSO algorithm optimized diagnosis accuracy rate was 99.0626%, but from the perspective of fault diagnosis running time, GS algorithm optimization running time is shorter, so GS algorithm is used to optimize SVM classification the parameters of the device more effectively improve the efficiency of diagnosis.

Keywords: Machine learning · Chemical fault diagnosis · SVM classifier · Diagnosis accuracy rate

1 Introduction

Fault diagnosis is the diagnosis of existing faults in the functional components of the industrial process that will cause undesirable or unbearable consequences in the entire system. In order to avoid adverse consequences, more and more intelligent equipment is applied to the faults of the chemical production process. Diagnosis to improve production safety and ensure that chemical equipment is adapted to long-term high-intensity production processes.

Many scholars at home and abroad have conducted research on the optimization of chemical fault diagnosis modeling based on machine learning, and have obtained good research results. For example, the dynamic mapping fault detection method proposed by a scholar is suitable for fault diagnosis in the chemical process. The feature extraction performance of machine learning algorithms can effectively detect the type of chemical production faults, and then optimize the fault diagnosis technology based on neural networks to effectively improve the chemical industry. Failure detection rate [1]. A

© Springer Nature Singapore Pte Ltd. 2022
Y. Tian et al. (Eds.): ICBDS 2021, CCIS 1563, pp. 716–725, 2022.
https://doi.org/10.1007/978-981-19-0852-1_57

researcher established a diagnostic model based on traditional chemical fault diagnosis technology and found that traditional diagnostic technology could not detect the internal faults of chemical equipment. He decided to add a deep network model of nonlinear functions to build a deep fault monitor, and then put the monitor into an industrial process. In, to achieve high-efficiency fault identification [2]. Although the research on chemical fault diagnosis modeling optimization based on machine learning is progressing well, in the face of difficult chemical production and difficult-to-find equipment faults, it is more difficult to find fault information with traditional diagnostic techniques, so machine learning algorithms must be introduced to efficiently detect chemical faults.

This article first introduces several chemical fault diagnosis methods based on machine learning algorithms. Aiming at the chemical fault diagnosis in this article, the SVM classifier is used for fault diagnosis, and then three optimization algorithms are compared to optimize the fault diagnosis accuracy and diagnosis after the SVM classifier parameters are optimized. Run time to find the best optimization algorithm to improve diagnostic performance.

2 Common Chemical Fault Diagnosis Methods

2.1 Chemical Fault Diagnosis Method Based on Machine Learning

(1) Chemical fault detection based on SVM

The SVM-based fault diagnosis method is a data-based fault diagnosis method. Therefore, there is no need to establish an accurate and complex mathematical model in this method, nor does it need to have a thorough understanding of the in-depth physical or mathematical mechanism knowledge of the system process, only through the data information of the system can monitor complex industrial processes. In addition, due to its excellent learning ability, strong promotion ability, nonlinear mapping, strong robustness, avoiding local optima, limiting over-learning, easy operation and other unique advantages, it can meet the requirements of industrial process fault diagnosis, which has received increasing attention and has gradually become a research hotspot [3].

Parameter estimation methods often need to establish accurate process parameter models, and compare the changes between model parameters and corresponding physical parameters to achieve fault detection and separation. Different parameter estimation methods, such as least square method, auxiliary variable method, discrete-time modeling estimation method, etc. These methods all require accurate process dynamic models and have high computational overhead for large-scale processes. At present, in actual research applications, parameter estimation methods are usually combined with other analytical model methods for application, which can effectively improve its performance in fault detection and fault separation.

The basic idea of the equivalent space method is to check the equivalence (ie consistency) of the mathematical relationship of the diagnosed object through the actual value of the input and output (or part of the output) of the system, so as to achieve the purpose of detecting and separating faults. Under ideal stable production conditions, the value of the residual or equivalent equation will be zero. The equivalent space method is to reconstruct the model to achieve the best effect of fault separation. Constantly improve and apply the equivalent space method. The equivalent space method has a better fault diagnosis effect for linear systems.

When the precise mathematical model of the system can be obtained, the state estimation method is the most effective and direct. Its basic idea is to design a detection filter (observer) based on the analytical model of the system and measurable information, reconstruct a certain measurable variable of the system, and then determine the difference between the output of the filter (observer) and the output of the real system Construct the residual, and then analyze and process the residual to realize the fault diagnosis of the system. Among the many analytical methods, the method based on state estimation has the advantages of flexible design, relatively strong robustness, fast response speed, and relatively simple algorithm. Therefore, there are many researches on this method.

(2) Knowledge-based fault diagnosis method
Different from the model-based method that uses mathematical functions to describe the input-output relationship of the process, the knowledge-based method does not require an accurate mathematical model of the process to be diagnosed. Such a fault diagnosis method requires a knowledge base that contains a large number of empirical knowledge rules that simulate human experts, and then uses a computer to perform inference analysis, so it is also called an intelligent diagnosis method. In addition, it also includes some effective search methods to make decisions based on known facts and information. The knowledge-based fault diagnosis method is simply knowledge processing technology, which is the process of fault diagnosis by introducing process-related expert experience knowledge, and then through dialectical reasoning, numerical processing, and algorithm fusion [4].

Expert system is to use the rich experience accumulated by experts for a long time to establish a fault diagnosis knowledge base, inference engine and rule base according to the expert's idea of problem analysis and solution. Through the design of a series of computer intelligent programs, faults can be performed based on the existing knowledge diagnosis. Expert system methods are used in many fault diagnosis. However, the biggest weakness of expert systems is that they cannot obtain all knowledge. The reserve of expert knowledge is not comprehensive enough, and it is difficult to truly express knowledge, which causes the current knowledge base platform to be insufficiently complete. In addition, the expert system still lacks good self-learning ability and cannot automatically improve itself, resulting in the inability to solve new faults and systems, so there are certain limitations.

The biggest feature of neural network is that it has the ability of self-learning, self-organization, associative memory, parallel processing, and distributed storage. Therefore, in nonlinear systems, neural network has obvious advantages and is an ideal fault diagnosis method. Neural networks can overcome the deficiencies of expert systems through self-learning and self-organizing capabilities. The fault diagnosis based on the neural network method is to learn the pattern samples of the fault through the self-learning ability of the neural network, and then reflect the learned knowledge to the weight of the network, thereby establishing a fault diagnosis model. When new test data is input, the corresponding fault diagnosis result can be obtained through network learning.

The biggest characteristic of fuzzy reasoning is to use fuzzy logic concept mechanism to deal with uncertain information and incomplete information in the system. Fuzzy reasoning is more in line with human thinking mode, and the concept of membership degree and fuzzy relationship matrix in set theory is used to solve the uncertain relationship between faults and symptoms, so as to realize detection and fault diagnosis. Fuzzy logic helps the system overcome its own uncertainty and imprecision, so it has obvious advantages in some complex processes. However, the determination of fuzzy relations is often difficult. The conversion of fuzzy membership is artificially established and has a certain degree of subjectivity. If the structure is unreasonable, the correct rate of diagnosis will decrease or even cause failure.

The fault tree method needs to analyze the faults to construct a fault tree. It takes the faults that the system most needs to avoid as the item event, and the cause of the accident as the bottom event, and connects the top event and the bottom event with logical symbols to form A tree structure. Through analysis and comprehensive processing of the fault tree, the set of causes, the probability of occurrence of the event, and the importance evaluation can be obtained, and corrective measures can be proposed. The biggest feature of the fault tree method is its intuitiveness. It is easy to understand the source of the fault. However, once the fault tree is not comprehensive enough or an error occurs, this method loses its meaning.

(3) Fault diagnosis method based on data-driven

Knowledge-based methods need to know some process-related physical and mathematical knowledge or expert experience knowledge in advance, while data-based methods use a large amount of information in process history data, so they are more usable and have a wider range of applications. Data-driven methods are also called statistical process detection methods. Univariate control chart may be the earliest statistical method based on process measurement, and it is widely used in the quality control of early industrial processes. In modern large-scale industrial practice, with the popularity of computers, sensors and other equipment and the improvement of the level of use, many variable data values in the production process will be measured offline and stored, so the data in the process is available. These large number of process measurement values contain a lot of information, especially useful system information will help to effectively monitor the operating status of the process [5]. Due to the large-scale and complex industrial processes, accurate mathematical and physical models are difficult to obtain, or when the specific mechanism knowledge in the process is difficult to obtain, statistical analysis based on system variable data to complete fault diagnosis is an important way. Based on this, many multivariate-based process detection methods have been proposed and have been rapidly developed, such as principal component analysis and partial least squares, which can perform data feature extraction and data compression, and can be used for real-time monitoring and fault diagnosis of industrial processes. In addition, there are rough set theory, cluster analysis and so on. The main advantage of multivariate statistical methods is their better processing ability for a large number of highly correlated variables [6, 7].

(4) Chemical equipment fault diagnosis method based on fuzzy dynamic fault tree

The quantitative analysis of the fuzzy dynamic fault tree of chemical equipment is to determine the occurrence probability of top events and the importance of each bottom event, so as to find out the weak links and key parts of the equipment, and determine the fault diagnosis process. Due to the different mathematical foundations of static gate and dynamic gate in fuzzy dynamic fault tree, it is usually decomposed into independent fuzzy static subtree and fuzzy dynamic subtree, and a model is built for it. Although there are many quantitative models currently used for the two types of fuzzy subtrees, these models have poor versatility and severe constraints, and the accuracy and efficiency of quantitative calculations need to be improved. In view of the shortcomings of the current fuzzy dynamic fault tree qualitative and quantitative analysis methods, combined with the high requirements of chemical companies for the accuracy and efficiency of equipment fault diagnosis, the follow-up work of this article will mainly focus on how to establish a set of high accuracy, good efficiency and general purpose It is highly flexible and suitable for qualitative and quantitative analysis methods of fuzzy dynamic fault tree of chemical equipment.

When the analytical model of the system is difficult to establish, but some of the input and output signals of the controlled system can be measured, the method based on signal processing shows greater advantages, so it is also a fault diagnosis method with a wide range of applications. The methods based on signal processing mainly include: methods based on multivariate statistics, methods based on wavelet transform, and methods based on information fusion.

Method based on multivariate statistics: Considering the scale and complexity of modern production processes, precise mathematical models cannot be established accurately, and each component.

There is a strong non-linearity between the points. In addition, due to the use of a large number of sensors and the upgrading of computers, people can collect a huge amount of data from the control system. The method based on multivariate statistics can effectively extract the useful components in massive data, so it is applied to fault diagnosis in the chemical process.

Method based on wavelet transform: By implementing wavelet transform on the input and output signals of the system to be diagnosed, the singularity can be solved, and the extreme points caused by the sudden change of the input can be eliminated. Then the remaining extreme points reflect a kind of fault state. The wavelet analysis method has the characteristics of frequency domain and time domain at the same time, so it is very beneficial to the fault diagnosis of sensors31. Wavelet transform does not require precise mathematical models, and does not require a large amount of calculations, does not require high input data, has high sensitivity and anti-interference ability, so it is a potential fault diagnosis method.

The method based on information fusion: is to integrate various types of useful information, extract more valuable features from it, and produce judgments and decisions far better than single information. In the diagnosis process, the fault diagnosis of each variable can be realized in a variety of ways, making full use of each information, and comprehensively processing each result, so as to obtain an overall fault assessment.

2.2 Chemical Fault Diagnosis Based on Improved and Optimized SVM

(1) Grid optimization method

The grid search method (GS) is a simple and direct optimization method. Because the penalty coefficient C and the Lagrangian multiplier γ are two independent and unrelated parameters, they can be optimized in the vertical coordinate system. First, select a certain range of values for C and γ respectively, and then perform cross-validation for each point in the selected range, that is, for each pair of C and γ, to get the training under this pair of C and γ parameter values Set verification accuracy rate. Finally, the C and γ values with the highest training set verification accuracy rate are considered to be the best values [8].

(2) Genetic algorithm

Genetic algorithm (GA) is a kind of optimization method that simulates biological evolution phenomenon. It has now been applied in many fields, such as neural network, optimization design and expert system. When dealing with a specific problem, the GA method first compiles possible solutions into individual chromosomes, and then these chromosomes constitute a search space. Randomly select some chromosomal individuals from the chromosome space as the first generation. The fitness of each chromosome structure is calculated by the objective function. The higher the fitness of the chromosome, the better we think this chromosome is, the more likely it is to be selected in the next generation, and crossover and mutation are based on a certain probability. Perform gene exchange or gene mutation operations on chromosomes [9]. In the GA method, selection, crossover, and mutation are continuously performed to generate a new generation to update the population. This evolutionary process will stop only when the termination conditions are met, and the chromosome structure with the greatest fitness in the last generation is considered the optimal solution [10].

(3) Particle swarm algorithm

Particle Swarm Optimization (PSO) is inspired by the common group behavior of birds looking for food. It is an intelligent optimization algorithm. The search for the optimal solution of the problem to be solved is realized by the way that the particle continuously updates its position and velocity [11].

2.3 Support Vector Machine Recursive Feature Elimination

Support vector machine (SVM) maps the vector to the high-dimensional space through the kernel function, and determines the size of the longest space in the space to separate the two types of data to achieve the purpose of optimal classification. SVM is suitable for small sample, high-dimensional and non-linear data problems. It has excellent performance in classification, regression and anomaly detection. Two types of classification problems are known [12].

Suppose there are n pairs of training samples $\{(x_i, y_i)\}_{i=1}^n$, where $x_i \in R^M$ represents the feature vector of the i-th sample, and $y_i \in \{-1, 1\}$ is the category label of x_i. The classification decision function of SVM is:

$$f(x) = \text{sgn}(w^T x + v) \tag{1}$$

Among them, sgn is the symbolic function, the weight vector $w = [w_1, w_2, \ldots, w_m]^T$, and v is the bias. After introducing the kernel function, the dual optimization problem of SVM is described as:

$$\min \sum_{i=1}^{n} \sum_{j=1}^{n} \alpha_i \alpha_j y_i y_j g(x_i, x_j) - \sum_{i=1}^{n} \alpha_i$$

$$s.t. \sum_{i=1}^{n} \alpha_i y_i = 0$$

(2)

Among them is the Lagrangian multiplier and $0 \leq \ \leq C$, i = 1,2,…,n, $g(x_i, x_j)$ is the kernel function, and the penalty parameter C is the trade-off between training accuracy and model complexity, usually derived from experience.

3 Research on Optimization of Chemical Fault Diagnosis Modeling Based on Machine Learning

3.1 Research Purpose

The current chemical production process is gradually moving towards intelligent production, but during the long-term operation of chemical production equipment, various failures occur from time to time. Failure to detect and eliminate chemical process errors in time will block the production process and even cause fires, resulting in property losses and casualties. Therefore, chemical fault diagnosis technology is a technology that needs to be developed urgently. At the same time, the diagnostic efficiency and accuracy of fault diagnosis technology directly affect chemical safety.

3.2 Research Methods

(1) Principal Component Analysis (PCA): It is the dimensionality reduction method to be used in this article. It can get some irrelevant variables based on the original data set and store them in a smaller dimensional space while retaining the original data Most of the information in the set. Because of its simplicity and effectiveness in processing high-dimensional data sets, it has been widely used in many fields, especially data compression.

(2) Comparison method: This article divides several common chemical fault types, namely valve fault, feed fault, reactor fault, classifier fault and stripper fault, and they are numbered as A, B, C, D, E, perform chemical fault detection based on SVM classifier. Then use three optimization algorithms to optimize the parameter values of the SVM classifier, compare the average chemical fault diagnosis accuracy and average running time under different optimization algorithms, select the best chemical fault diagnosis optimization method, and finally introduce the determined optimization method into the SVM classifier Establish a chemical fault diagnosis model.

4   Optimization Analysis of Chemical Fault Diagnosis Modeling Based on Machine Learning

4.1   Chemical Fault Detection Based on SVM Classifier

The Fault Diagnosis Accuracy Rate (FDAR) is the ratio of the number of correctly diagnosed fault samples to the number of all fault samples in the process of chemical fault diagnosis, while the fault detection rate (FDR) refers to the number of fault samples that are correctly diagnosed and the number of fault samples ratio.

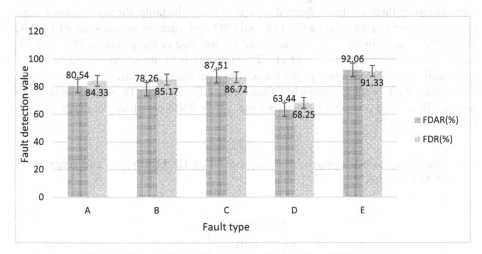

Fig. 1. Chemical fault diagnosis results based on SVM classifier

Figure 1 shows the diagnosis results of five common chemical fault types. It can be seen from the figure that the use of SVM classifier to detect chemical faults has a diagnostic accuracy of 80.54% for valve faults and a fault detection rate of 84.33%; The FDAR for feed failure is 78.26%, and the FDR is 85.17%; the FDAR for reactor failure is 87.51%, and the FDR is 86.72%; the FDAR for classifier failure is 63.44%, and the FDR is 68.25%; for the stripper failure FDAR is 92.06% and FDR is 91.33%. Therefore, the diagnostic accuracy of the SVM classifier for each chemical fault type is low. It is necessary to optimize the parameter values of the SVM classifier to improve the accuracy of the fault diagnosis.

4.2   Comparison of the Effects of Several Optimization Algorithms in Identifying Faults

For the above three commonly used optimization methods, we apply them to the SVM classifier for chemical fault detection, and then select the best method for later use. In this paper, there are 500 samples for fault diagnosis in the experiment. Before putting into the SVM classifier, all the data have been normalized and the PCA method is used for data dimensionality reduction.

Table 1. The fault recognition results of the SVM classifier with 3 methods for parameter optimization

Optimization method used	Mean fault diagnosis accuracy (%)	Average running time (s)
GS	99.1273	264
GA	99.3548	857
PSO	99.0626	745

Table 1 shows the fault recognition results of the SVM classifier with parameter optimization using three methods. According to the data in the table, the average fault diagnosis accuracy rates when using GS, GA, and PSO optimization methods are 99.1273%, 99.3548%, and 99.0626%, respectively, and the average running time is 264 s, 857 s, and 745 s, respectively. The SVM classifier optimized by these three methods has a high fault recognition accuracy, and the accuracy is not much different. However, the SVM using the GS method takes less time to identify the fault. Therefore, choosing to use the GS method to optimize the parameters of the SVM classifier can make the fault diagnosis more efficient.

4.3   Chemical Fault Diagnosis Modeling Based on GS Optimized and Improved SVM Classifier

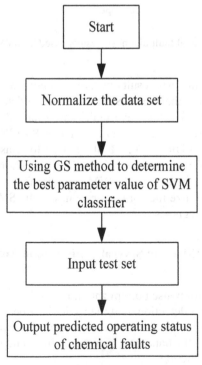

Fig. 2. Chemical fault diagnosis model of SVM classifier based on GS optimization

As shown in Fig. 2 is the chemical fault diagnosis model of the SVM classifier optimized by the GS algorithm. The first step is to process the fault data set. After the principal component analysis method is used to reduce the dimension, the GS algorithm is used to determine the best parameter value of the SVM classifier. After entering the test set of failure information to be predicted, the operational failure status of the chemical process can be obtained.

5 Conclusion

This paper studies chemical fault diagnosis modeling based on machine learning, and applies three commonly used optimization algorithms, GS, GA, and PSO, to optimize SVM classifier parameters. Analyzing the changes in the diagnostic performance of the SVM classifier can be obtained: the SVM classifier with optimized parameters has a higher prediction accuracy. Moreover, when the GS algorithm is applied, the classification diagnosis rate comparable to the other two algorithms can be obtained but the shortest running time is used, so the GS algorithm is more effective.

References

1. Liang, X., He, H., Zhang, Y.: Optimization design of micro-piles in landslide safety protection based on machine learning. Saf. Sci. **118**(1), 861–867 (2019)
2. Han, Y., Zeng, Q., Geng, Z., et al.: Energy management and optimization modeling based on a novel fuzzy extreme learning machine: case study of complex petrochemical industries. Energy Convers. Manage. **165**, 163–171 (2018)
3. Anna, H.R.S., Tavares, F.W., et al.: Machine learning model and optimization of a PSA unit for methane-nitrogen separation. Comput. Chem. Eng. **104**, 377–391 (2017)
4. Zheng, L., Xiang, Y., Sheng, C.: Optimization-based improved kernel extreme learning machine for rolling bearing fault diagnosis. J. Braz. Soc. Mech. Sci. Eng. **41**(11), 1–14 (2019)
5. Ku, J., Kamath, A., Carrington, T., Manzhos, S.: Machine learning optimization of the collocation point set for solving the Kohn-Sham equation. J. Phys. Chem. A **123**(49), 10631–10642 (2019)
6. Wang, N., Li, H., Wu, F., et al.: Fault diagnosis of complex chemical processes using feature fusion of a convolutional network. Ind. Eng. Chem. Res. **60**(5), 2232–2248 (2021)
7. Jiang, X., Zhao, H., Leung, H.: Fault detection and diagnosis in chemical processes using sparse principal component selection. J. Chem. Eng. Jpn. **50**(1), 31–44 (2017)
8. Wu, H., Zhao, J.: Deep convolutional neural network model based chemical process fault diagnosis. Comput. Chem. Eng. **115**, 185–197 (2018)
9. Yang, G., Gu, X.: Fault diagnosis of complex chemical processes based on enhanced Naive Bayesian method. IEEE Trans. Instrum. Meas. **69**(7), 4649–4658 (2020)
10. Liang, M., Zhao, J.: Feature selection for chemical process fault diagnosis by artificial immune systems. Chin. J. Chem. Eng. **26**(08), 7–12 (2018)
11. Wu, H., Zhao, J.: Fault detection and diagnosis based on transfer learning for multimode chemical processes. Comput. Chem. Eng. **135**, 106731.1–106731.13 (2020)
12. Kim, C., Lee, H., Lee, W.B.: Process fault diagnosis via the integrated use of graphical lasso and Markov random fields learning & inference. Comput. Chem. Eng. **125**, 460–475 (2019)

Research and Design of Agrometeorological Disaster Monitoring and Early Warning and Intelligent Service System Based on Data Mining

Wenbo Yang[✉] and Quan Xia

Lanzhou Resources and Environment, VOC-TECH College, College of Meteorology, Lanzhou 730020, Gansu, China

Abstract. At present, insufficient research on the mechanism of agricultural disasters, poor understanding of agricultural disaster processes and key factors, imperfect agricultural disaster monitoring theory and methods, has become the establishment of an effective agricultural disaster monitoring early warning system, the development of disaster space-time dynamic monitoring, as well as the country to make major disaster prevention and mitigation decision-making bottlenecks and obstacles. Among them, agricultural meteorological disaster warning is the most important and challenging problem in the modern world, accurate meteorological prediction often requires the use of more advanced methods and computer models. This paper studies the application of data mining methods in agricultural meteorological disaster warning, and designs an early warning and intelligent service system for monitoring agricultural meteorological disasters based on data mining. The main functions of the system are early warning of agricultural meteorological disaster monitoring and live monitoring of agricultural meteorology. The experimental results also show that the system has good function of meteorological disaster monitoring and early warning and intelligent service.

Keywords: Establishment of an effective agricultural disaster monitoring early warning system · Meteorological prediction · Data mining

1 Introduction

Crop yields are reduced due to extreme meteorological factors. At the same time, disasters have the characteristics of widespread and persistent, often bring certain economic losses and casualties. Therefore, agricultural disaster monitoring is very important to China. With the great planning and support of the national information construction, great progress has been made in the development of sensors, the research of control strategies and the analysis of related data, and the development of agricultural meteorological detection system is becoming more and more mature.

© Springer Nature Singapore Pte Ltd. 2022
Y. Tian et al. (Eds.): ICBDS 2021, CCIS 1563, pp. 726–737, 2022.
https://doi.org/10.1007/978-981-19-0852-1_58

Agricultural meteorological monitoring system is an unattended intelligent agricultural solution that collects agricultural meteorological data collection, transmission and cloud management, and can collect agricultural climate (atmospheric temperature, atmospheric humidity, atmospheric pressure, light intensity, precipitation, wind speed, wind direction, etc.) data in real time during the whole day, and transmit it to the cloud platform in time to form data reports, comprehensively and intuitively present the agricultural climate status and changes of each monitoring site, and achieve real-time online monitoring of regional agricultural climate.

At present, agricultural meteorological disaster prediction technology is divided into the following three aspects:

1) Geographic Information Systems (GIS) forecasting technology that produces only the lowest temperature forecasts for a given period of time and within the region. The principle is to apply geo-information technology and certain indicators, and to modify the forecast values by means of geo-information technology, such as latitude and longitude, altitude, etc., so as to make it easy to draw the temperature forecast values. GIS prediction technology results are very objective, and can provide reasonable guidance for agricultural meteorological disaster prediction. Relevant departments can use the network to publish the forecast results, so that people can do a good job of protection, so as to effectively reduce the actual economic losses. The form of publication is to use the comprehensive nature of agricultural meteorological disaster prediction and release system, so that users in a short period of time to obtain the corresponding information, and geographical situation combined, effectively take preventive and control measures to reduce the actual economic losses. Therefore, the relevant departments need to establish an integrated service system during the meteorological disaster prediction period. In particular, different types of forecasting models should be created in the light of different forecasting conditions, so as to make it easier to actively predict agrometeorological disasters during the determination of agrometeorological disasters and help users offset the risk of agricultural meteorological disasters, thereby reducing the actual economic losses in an all-round way [1]. The University of Florida has established the Agricultural Environmental Geographic Information System, which combines technology and models to enable model simulations to be applied to different climatic conditions [2]. Bilaletdin et al. use a combination of GIS technology and SMART models to monitor and assess the effects of atmospheric subsidence on soil and soil moisture [3].

2) At present, mathematical statistical forecasting has a wide range of applications, mainly using disaster indicators as the main credentials, and using time series and multiple regression methods to reasonably predict meteorological disasters. Time series analysis method, based on the cycle and law of meteorological disasters, can reasonably predict the occurrence of meteorological disasters. During the specific operation, a prediction model of periodic arguments should be created in conjunction with the meteorological disaster homogeneity function. For example, some studies use the area of meteorological disasters as a sample and create model groups [4] to facilitate the rational prediction of disaster forms. Multiple regression analysis can analyze the factors closely related to the occurrence of disasters, and then take the elements as the main basis for rational prediction of disaster situations. The common features of multiple regression analysis include the atmospheric circulation characteristic quantity and

meteorological elements, and the prediction model can be effectively created by the application of discrimination and correlation method. As the main content of research by scholars at home and abroad in recent years, dynamic monitoring of agricultural meteorological disasters can effectively improve the accuracy of monitoring. Zhou et al. according to the time series of agricultural meteorological disasters and the generation of homogeneity function, according to EOF, REOF expansion and other methods to screen the main homogenous function, according to which the regression prediction model with the period as the argument is established [5, 6]. In addition to empirical statistical forecasting models, there are also research methods using physical statistics, taking into account the atmospheric circulation background, weather system and evolving weather climatology characteristics, revealing the precursor signals of disasters, and establishing predictive models [7].

However, in the practical application of contemporary agricultural disaster monitoring technology, there are still many gaps between China's technology and foreign countries, and there are still many areas for improvement. Domestic technology is only in the monitoring and control level of individual environmental factors, but in fact, various environmental factors are interrelated, the changes of various factors are quite complex, therefore, single factor regulation is not enough, so in this case, China still needs to strengthen.

Based on this, this paper studies the application of data mining method in agricultural meteorological disaster early warning, and designs an early warning and intelligent service system based on data mining. The main functions of the system are early warning of agricultural meteorological disaster monitoring and live monitoring of agricultural meteorology.

2 Design of Early Warning Technology for Agricultural Meteorological Disaster Monitoring

2.1 Overall System Architecture and Functional Design

According to the system objectives, according to the idea of combining object-oriented and structured analysis with design method, GIS-based agricultural meteorological disaster monitoring early warning and intelligent service system can be divided into two modules with the support of GIS software and database software: operational monitoring of business systems and meteorological emergency management and early warning signals. The overall architecture and functional design of the system is shown in Fig. 1.

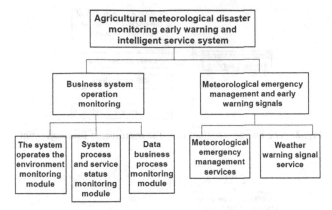

Fig. 1. The overall architecture diagram of the system

2.2   System Architecture Design

The system adopts the mixed architecture of C/S and B/S, the B/S way is the direction and mainstream of network development, it concentrates all the data processing on the server side, has nothing to do with the client, the client is independent, the client uses the browser to make requests to the server side, the server side completes all processing, the results are shown to the user. The main advantages of this approach are in the thousand: (1) the client interface is unified and concise. It does not want to install different customer applications on different clients, as in C/S mode, but simply installs universal browser software, which is simple to maintain; (2) Simplify the development and maintenance of the system. System development does not need to design and develop different customer applications for different levels of users, just implement all the functions on the Web, and set permissions for each group of users on different functions; (3) The system structure is quite flexible. When the system needs to be extended, simply add the corresponding Web hardware and software in the background to meet the requirements of use; (4) Especially suitable for online information publishing and information query functions.

The data acquisition module is designed as a C/S mode, i.e., a customer/server structure. The data exchange between provincial and municipal levels relies on the provincial communication network, using TCP/IP communication protocol, data transmission programming, cross-platform network interconnection, and rapid data transmission and data exchange. Make full use of server resources, put a large amount of data and computing programs on the server, so that the system processing speed significantly improved.

2.3   Business System Operation Monitoring

The distribution of function points for business system operation monitoring is shown in Fig. 2 and is divided into the following three sub-modules, as shown in Fig. 3.

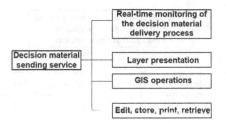

Fig. 2. The business system runs the monitoring function point

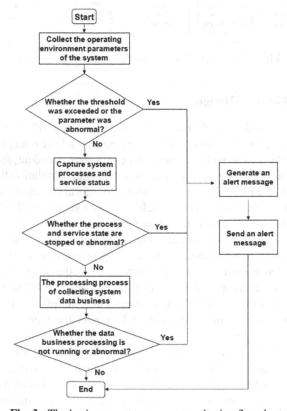

Fig. 3. The business system runs a monitoring flowchart

The System Operates the Environment Monitoring Module. This module captures the system operating environment of the current server, including CPU usage, physical memory usage, disk usage, database size, and network status.

System Process and Service Status Monitoring Module. System process and service status monitoring is a logical processing of system processes or services, when each system process is started directly or indirectly, and at the end of the day, this logical processing is called to record the running status and running results of the system process, and write the log to the job status information table, and for the faulty process, it is necessary to record the cause of the failure.

Data Business Process Monitoring Module. Data business process monitoring is a logical processing of data business processing, when a suspended job file to do business processing, this monitoring will record the process of each process, and the process as a log written to the job file schedule, at the same time, for faulty business processing, need to record the cause of the failure.

2.4 Meteorological Emergency Management and Early Warning Signals

The distribution of meteorological emergency management and early warning signal functional points is shown in Fig. 4.

Meteorological Emergency Management Services. Emergency incident management mainly includes emergency incident start-up, corresponding emergency plan start-up (plan generation), emergency incident tracking, emergency assessment, emergency incident closure, and additions to the handling of emergency events.

Weather Warning Signal Service. Disaster weather includes: such as hail, heavy precipitation, fog, high winds, tropical cyclones, cold and other meteorological important weather, and to achieve a certain intensity of strong weather, the system uses a variety of means such as graphic, literary, sound and multimedia form of alarm prompts, to the early warning command personnel to visually display the latest early warning information; See Fig. 5 for a specific flowchart.

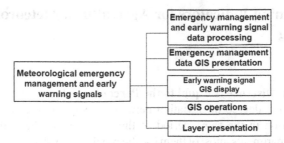

Fig. 4. Meteorological emergency management and early warning signal function points

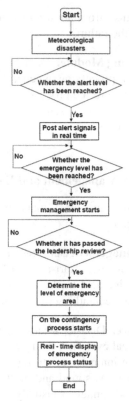

Fig. 5. The flow chart of the main controller controlling the doorbell control module

3 Early Warning Indicators for Agricultural Meteorological Monitoring

3.1 Drought

The Precipitation Distance is Equal to the Percentage. Precipitation distance parity rate [8] refers to the degree of deviation between precipitation in a certain area and average precipitation in the same period of the year, and in the daily operations of meteorological departments, most of them use the precipitation distance equal percentage as an indicator to divide the drought.

$$M_i = \frac{R_i - \overline{R}}{\overline{R}} \times 100\% \tag{1}$$

Here, i represents a time period, M_i is the equal percentage of precipitation distance in the i-period, R_i indicates precipitation during this period, $\overline{R}$ is the average precipitation for many years during the same period。

Precipitation Z Index. The Z-index [9] refers to a period of local precipitation that does not obey the normal distribution, and it is assumed that the monthly precipitation and seasonal precipitation are subject to the Pearson-III distribution, with a probability density of:

$$P(X) = [\beta\Gamma(\gamma)]^{-1}\left[\frac{(X-a)}{\beta}\right]^{\gamma-1} e^{-\frac{X-a}{\beta}} \tag{2}$$

The precipitation X is normally treated, and the probability density function Pearson-ill distribution is changed to the standard normal distribution with Z as the variable, and the conversion formula is:

$$Z_i = \frac{6}{C_s}\left[\frac{C_s}{2}\Phi_i + 1\right]^{\frac{1}{3}} - \frac{6}{C_s} + \frac{C_s}{6} \tag{3}$$

Here, C_s is a bias factor, Φ_i is standardized variables for precipitation. It can be calculated by precipitation data series, and the formula is:

$$C_s = \frac{\sum_{i=1}^{n}(X_i-\overline{X})^2}{n\sigma^3} \tag{4}$$

$$\Phi_i = \frac{X_i-\overline{X}}{\sigma} \tag{5}$$

Here,

$$\sigma = \sqrt{\frac{1}{n}\sum_{i=1}^{n}(X_i-\overline{X})^2} \tag{6}$$

$$\overline{X} = \frac{1}{n}\sum_{i=1}^{n}X_i \tag{7}$$

Here, σ is Average variance, X_i is precipitation in a given year, $\overline{X}$ is average precipitation in n years, n is the number of samples.

3.2 Frost

For frost research abroad, most of them choose the ground temperature less than or equal to $0 \setminus,°C$ as the disaster indicator, and accordingly carry out the study of frost change law. Domestic scholars to the ground minimum temperature to less than $0\setminus,°C$ (including $0 \setminus,°C$) or the minimum temperature to $2 \setminus,°C$ (including $2 \setminus,°C$) as an indicator to study the first frost day, the end frost day and frost-free period of the change characteristics.

3.3 Hail

In view of some forecast indicators of hail, combined with the actual situation in the hail area, there are great advantages in forecasting according to the month, so the vertical accumulation of liquid water content (VIL) is used as an early warning indicator of hail. i.e. (1) May, VIL ≥ 25 kg $\cdot$ m^{-2}, VILD ≥ 3.5 g $\cdot$ m^{-3}, VILH ≥ 15 kg $\cdot$ m^{-2}; (2) June, VIL ≥ 35 kg $\cdot$ m^{-2}, VILD ≥ 3.5 g $\cdot$ m^{-3}, VILH ≥ 20 kg $\cdot$ m^{-2}; (3) July, VIL ≥ 40 kg $\cdot$ m^{-2}, VILD ≥ 3.8 g $\cdot$ m^{-3}, VILH ≥ 20 kg $\cdot$ m^{-2} as forecast indicators for hail.

3.4 Heat Damage

We analyzed the relationship between the occurrence of heat damage, cumulative days and range of occurrence and rice yield under the meteorological and biological indicators, and found that the influence of meteorological indicators on yield changes was more obvious. Thus, in terms of frequency, number of days and range of occurrence, although meteorological indicators reflect a more serious degree of thermal damage than biological indicators, but more practical. This also shows that the biological indicators in determining the degree of thermal damage on rice yield is light and has obvious defects, with meteorological indicators to monitor and warn of rice high temperature heat damage will be more accurate, in the actual production will play a more guiding role. Therefore, meteorological indicators are used as the high temperature thermal hazard indicators of the system. That is, the average daily temperature $\geq 30\ ^{\circ}C$ and the daily maximum temperature $\geq 35\ ^{\circ}C$ continuously appear 3d and above. Depending on the duration, it can be divided into different heat hazard levels: $3 \sim 4d$ for mild duration, $5 \sim 8d$ for moderate, and more than 8d for severe.

4 Experimental Design and Result Analysis

4.1 The Source of the Data

Climate data are data on day-to-day temperatures (including daily maximum and average daily temperature) at 12 conventional weather stations in Area A for 2010–2020, which are divided into three regions: Area B, Area C and Area D in the analysis of spatial characteristics. The rice observation data are the first-quarter rice fertility period and yield data of the three agricultural meteorological observatories in Area A from 2010 to 2020, and when studying the characteristics of rice heat damage and yield loss in the region, the two stations B and D, which have more complete rice observation data and longer data age, were selected from the three stations to analyze as the typical stations in the corresponding region.

4.2 Method

Statistical analysis of rice fertility data from 2 agricultural meteorological observatories shows that the key period of rice extraction - pregnancy spike - and the key period of rice spike-milking from late August to late September was determined. The characteristics of climate warming in different regions of A region are studied by using the determined single-season rice heat hazard index in A region, the spatial and spatial distribution law of rice heat damage in area A is analyzed and its effect on yield, and the effect of climate change on rice heat damage in area A is discussed (Fig. 6) and (Fig. 7).

4.3   Results

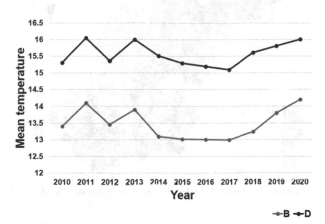

Fig. 6. Average annual temperatures for typical stations B and D in different regions

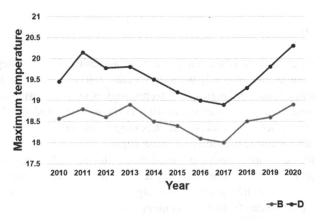

Fig. 7. Typical stations B and D in different regions have the highest temperatures per year

As can be seen from Fig. 1, the average annual temperature and the average annual maximum temperature vary greatly between the two regions for the typical stations in 2 different regions, with the average temperatures of 14.82 °C and 17.12 °C, respectively. The maximum temperatures are 20.39 °C and 21.52 °C respectively. From the graph, it can be seen that the average temperature fluctuated significantly in 2010–2013; Average temperatures stabilized in 2013–2017, showing a downward trend, and after 2018, temperatures gradually increased and fluctuated significantly.

Based on the changes in rice yield in 2 agricultural meteorological observatories, a typical analysis was carried out for the years with significant differences. Select 2019 as the typical year of thermal damage, query the maximum temperature in July 2019, get the following figure.

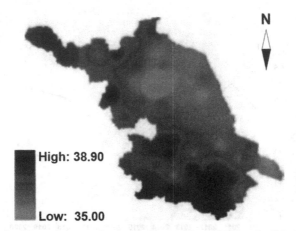

Fig. 8. Chart of the maximum temperature interpolation for July 2019

As can be seen from Fig. 8, for a typical year, the degree of heat damage is found to decrease from southwest to northeast.

5   Conclusion

According to the actual needs of the management of agricultural meteorological disaster meteorological monitoring and early warning service, referring to the mature monitoring service system of other industries, GIS technology is used to design the GIS-based agricultural meteorological disaster monitoring early warning and intelligent service system, which strengthens the analysis and tracking of meteorological service data to provide a rapid and accurate location of meteorological service failures and other functions, and provides a comprehensive and unified monitoring and management platform for meteorological services. There are many local defects in the system, in the future we will refer to other real-time monitoring using some mature technology, put forward further ideas, so that we can further supplement and improve.

References

1. Lan, R., Li, S., Liu, Y., et al.: The status and trends of GIS development. Geospatial Inf. **2**(1), 8–11 (2004)
2. Luyten, J., Jones, J.: AEGIS+: AGIS-based graphical user-interface for defining spatial crop management strategies and visualization of crop simulation results. In: 89th ASA/CSSA/SSSA Annual Meetings, pp. 26–31 (1997)
3. Bilaletdin, A., Lepisto, A., Finer, L., et al.: A regional GIS-based model to prediction-term responses of soil and soil water chemistry to atmospheric deposition: initial results. Water Air Soil Pollution, **131**, 275–303 (2001)
4. Yang, C., Wang, P.: Advances in the research and prediction technology of agricultural meteorological disaster monitoring. Jilin Agricult. **16**, 98 (2018)
5. Zhou, L., Liu, X., Zhou, Y.: Circulation characteristics and prediction of low temperature cold years in Northeast China. J. Shenyang Agricult. Univ. **32**(1), 22–25 (2001)

6. Guo, J., Tian, Z., Zhang, J.: A study of the predictive model of corn heat index in Northeast China. J. Appl. Meteorol. **14**(5), 626–633 (2003)
7. Bi, B.: The temperature anomalies were predicted by using plant weather data. Meteorology **26**(3), 56–57 (2003)
8. Shi, J., Yan, C., He, W., et al.: Overview of the calculation method of meteorological drought index. Agricult. Meteorol. China **28**, 191–195 (2007)
9. Shao, X., Liu, J., Xue, Y.: The determination of dry fishing index and its spatial and 2000 distribution characteristics were studied. J. Nat. Disasters **10**(4), 133–136 (2001)

A Parameter Identification Method of Wind Turbine System Based on Fuzzy Cuckoo Search Algorithm

Jing He[1(✉)], Songtao Zhang[1], Yangfei Zhang[2], Yong Zheng[2], Yuqin Hong[2], and Changyi Huang[2]

[1] State Key Laboratory of Operation and Control of Renewable Energy & Storage Systems (China Electric Power Research Institute), Beijing, China
[2] School of Electric Power Engineering, Nanjing Institute of Technology, Nanjing 211167, Jiangsu, China

Abstract. Aimed at the difficulty of parameter identification of wind turbine system, a parameter identification method of wind turbine system based on Fuzzy Cuckoo Search Algorithm is proposed in this paper. Firstly, the identifiability of wind turbine system parameters is analyzed by the method. Secondly, a fuzzy control method based on Cuckoo Search Algorithm is proposed and applied to parameter identification of wind turbine system, Finally, the real data are used for simulation analysis. The simulation results show that using the fuzzy controller based on Cuckoo Search Algorithm can greatly improve the speed and accuracy of parameter identification.

Keywords: Parameter identification · Cuckoo Search Algorithm · Wind turbine system · Identifiability analysis · Fuzzy controller

1 Introduction

With the continuous and rapid growth of wind power installation and power generation worldwide, it is particularly important to study the modeling and characteristics of wind turbines for power grid operation. The establishment of system model is of great significance to the dynamic characteristic analysis and control strategy research of wind turbines. Therefore, the research on system parameter identification, as the basis of modeling, has attracted extensive attention of researchers [1–4].

The complexity of the structure of wind turbine regulation system is the mechanism modeling method which is usually used in the modeling work. A wind turbine state parameter anomaly identification model is proposed in reference [5], and the parameters are optimized by the joint model of genetic algorithm and BPNN. The simulation results show that the proposed method is effective in wind turbine anomaly identification; In

Project Supported by the Open Fund of State Key Laboratory of Operation and Control of Renewable Energy & Storage System (NYB51201901176).

© Springer Nature Singapore Pte Ltd. 2022
Y. Tian et al. (Eds.): ICBDS 2021, CCIS 1563, pp. 738–748, 2022.
https://doi.org/10.1007/978-981-19-0852-1_59

reference [6], aiming at the problem that it is difficult to model the dynamic characteristics of wind power plants, a linear dynamic equivalent model of large-scale wind power plants is proposed. The proposed equivalent model is compared with the model of real large-scale wind power plant, and the results verify the effectiveness. Reference [7] proposes a wind farm modeling and parameter identification method based on synchronous phasor measurement. The key parameters are selected by sensitivity method. The simulation results show the effectiveness and reliability of the proposed modeling and identification method. Reference [8] proposed a probabilistic pre evaluation method to evaluate the recognition accuracy of target parameters when non-target parameters are inaccurate. A statistical recognition process is used to eliminate the dependence of traditional parameter recognition methods on nontarget parameters. And great results have also been obtained.

In total, there are still some problems in the existed wind power parameter identification algorithms, such as low identification accuracy and slow identification speed. In relevant studies, the identification methods are mostly optimized by genetic or improved intelligent algorithms, and there are few literatures to improve the identification progress by optimizing the fuzzy controller. The key contribution of this paper is that the Cuckoo Search Algorithm is applied to the fuzzy control of wind turbine, so as to realize the accurate and rapid identification of wind turbine parameters.

2 Modeling and Analysis of Wind Turbine System

2.1 Wind Energy Conversion System Model

This paper presents a nine parameter wind energy conversion model with variable pitch, and gives a set of parameters: $c_1 = 0.24$, $c_2 = 116$, $c_3 = 0.4$, $c_4 = 0$, $c_5 = 0$, $c_6 = 5$, $c_7 = 12.5$, $c_8 = 0.08$, $c_9 = 0.035$. Under this parameter setting condition, the variation curve of C_P with λ, as shown in Fig. 1, can be considered as a complex description of the characteristics of variable pitch eight independent parameter wind turbine.

$$P_W = C_P(\lambda, \beta)\rho S v^3 / 2 \tag{1}$$

$$C_P = c_1 (\frac{c_2}{\Lambda} - c_3\beta - c_4\beta^{c_5} - c_6)e^{-c_7/\Lambda} \tag{2}$$

$$\frac{1}{\Lambda} = \frac{1}{\lambda + c_8\beta} - \frac{c_9}{\beta^3 + 1} \tag{3}$$

$$\lambda = \frac{2\pi n R}{v} = \frac{\omega R}{v} \tag{4}$$

Where P_W represents the actual power of the wind turbine; C_P is the wind energy capture coefficient; ρ is the density of air; S represents the area swept by the impeller; R is the radius; v represents wind speed; $c_1 - c_9$ represents wind energy conversion parameters; β is the propeller moment angle; $\frac{1}{\Lambda}$ represents an intermediate variable; λ is the tip speed ratio; ω represents the angular speed of wind turbine rotation; n is the wind turbine speed.

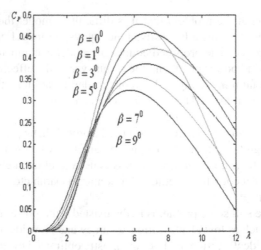

Fig. 1. $C_P - \lambda$ curve of eight parameter model of variable pitch wind turbine

2.2 Transmission System Model

There are many methods to establish the transmission system model of wind turbine, most of which use the equivalent concentrated mass method. This paper adopts the method of equivalent two-mass blocks for doubly-fed wind turbines to model the drive train. The two-mass blocks dynamic model is as follows:

$$
\begin{cases}
H_{\omega t}\dfrac{d\omega_{\omega t}}{dt} = T_{\omega t} - K_{sh}\theta_{sh} - D_{sh}(\omega_{\omega t} - \omega_r), T_{\omega t} = \dfrac{P_W}{\omega_{\omega t}} \\
H_g\dfrac{d\omega_r}{dt} = K_{sh}\theta_{sh} - T_e + D_{sh}(\omega_{\omega t} - \omega_r), T_e = \dfrac{P_t}{\omega_{\omega t}} \\
\dfrac{d\theta_{sh}}{dt} = \omega_s(\omega_{\omega t} - \omega_r)
\end{cases}
\tag{5}
$$

In the above formula: $H_{\omega t}$ represents the equivalent moment of inertia of the wind turbine; H_g represents the equivalent moment of inertia of the generator; $\omega_{\omega t}$ represents the wind turbine speed on the high-speed side of the gearbox; ω_r represents the rotor speed of the generator; ω_s represents synchronous speed of generator; $T_{\omega t}$ represents the mechanical torque of the wind turbine; T_e represents the electromagnetic torque of the generator; K_{sh} represents the stiffness coefficient between the wind turbine and the generator; D_{sh} represents the damping coefficient between the wind turbine and the generator; θ_{sh} represents the twist angle of the transmission shaft; P_t represents electromagnetic power.

Here $H_{\omega t}, K_{sh}, D_{sh}$ are the parameters to be identified in this paper.

3   Parameter Identifiability Analysis of Wind Turbine System

3.1   Wind Energy Conversion System Model

In order to facilitate analysis and reference, the variable pitch nine parameter wind energy conversion model is rewritten into eight independent parameter model. The common expression is:

$$C_P = (\frac{c_1}{\Lambda} - c_2\beta - c_3\beta^{c_4} - c_5)e^{-c_6/\Lambda} \tag{6}$$

$$\frac{1}{\Lambda} = \frac{1}{\lambda + c_7\beta} - \frac{c_8}{\beta^3 + 1} \tag{7}$$

Order:

$$a(\beta) = c_1 e^{c_6 c_8/(\beta^3+1)} \tag{8}$$

$$b(\beta) = -[c_1 c_8/(\beta^3 + 1) + c_2\beta + c_3\beta^{c_4} + c_5]e^{c_6 c_8/(\beta^3+1)} \tag{9}$$

Then there are:

$$C_P = [\frac{a(\beta)}{\lambda + c_7\beta} + b(\beta)]e^{-\frac{c_6}{\lambda + c_7\beta}} \tag{10}$$

Equation 10 is another expression of the eight independent parameter wind energy conversion model.

The parameter of wind energy conversion model in wind turbine, C_P, is related to λ and β. Adjust these two parameters during operation to maximize C_P and ensure maximum wind energy utilization. C_P is a function of λ and β, n, R, v and β can be measured, and λ and P_W can be calculated. Under the same input conditions, the output results of wind turbines with different characteristic parameters are often different. Therefore, the parameter to be identified is $c_1 - c_8$.

(1) Identifiability of c_6

When $\beta = 0°$, there are:

$$C_P = [\frac{a(0)}{\lambda} + b(0)]e^{-\frac{c_6}{\lambda}} \tag{11}$$

Among them, $b(0) = -[c_1 c_8 + c_5]e^{c_6 c_8}$ are constants.

Take three groups of measured quantities v_1, v_2, v_3, n_1, n_2, n_3 and the corresponding calculated C_{P1}, C_{P2}, C_{P3}. The corresponding λ_1, λ_2, λ_3 can be obtained according to Eq. 4:

$$C_{P1}e^{c_6/\lambda_1} = a(0)/\lambda_1 + b(0) \tag{12}$$

$$C_{P2}e^{c_6/\lambda_2} = a(0)/\lambda_2 + b(0) \tag{13}$$

$$C_{P3}e^{c_6/\lambda_3} = a(0)/\lambda_3 + b(0) \tag{14}$$

According to Eq. 12 -14, $a(0)$ and $b(0)$ are deleted:

$$\frac{C_{P1}e^{C_6/\lambda_1} - C_{P2}e^{C_6/\lambda_2}}{C_{P2}e^{C_6/\lambda_2} - C_{P3}e^{C_6/\lambda_3}} = \frac{1/\lambda_1 - 1/\lambda_2}{1/\lambda_2 - 1/\lambda_3} \tag{15}$$

In the above equation, c_6 is unknown and mathematically solvable, then c_6 can be identified and $a(0)$, $b(0)$ can be solved at the same time. If different C_P and λ are selected, c_6 will have different values, but the number of true values must be the highest, so as to determine the unique solution of c_6 and its corresponding $a(0)$, $b(0)$ values.

(2) Recognizability of c_7

Take β as any one measured value γ, we get:

$$C_P = [\frac{a(\gamma)}{\lambda + \gamma c_7} + b(\gamma)]e^{-\frac{c_6}{\lambda + \gamma c_7}} \tag{16}$$

In the equations: $a(\gamma) = c_1 e^{c_6 c_8/(\gamma^3+1)}$, $b(\gamma) = -[c_1 c_8/(\gamma^3+1) + c_2\gamma + c_3\gamma^{c_4} + c_5]e^{c_6 c_8/(\gamma^3+1)}$ are constants. Then take three groups of known conditions, use the same marks, and sort them out according to Eq. 16:

$$C_P(\lambda_1 + \gamma c_7)e^{\frac{c_6}{\lambda_1 + \gamma c_7}} = a(\gamma) + b(\gamma)(\lambda_1 + \gamma c_7) \tag{17}$$

$$C_P(\lambda_2 + \gamma c_7)e^{\frac{c_6}{\lambda_2 + \gamma c_7}} = a(\gamma) + b(\gamma)(\lambda_2 + \gamma c_7) \tag{18}$$

$$C_P(\lambda_3 + \gamma c_7)e^{\frac{c_6}{\lambda_3 + \gamma c_7}} = a(\gamma) + b(\gamma)(\lambda_3 + \gamma c_7) \tag{19}$$

Eliminate with Eq. 17 and Eq. 19, we get:

$$\frac{C_{P1}(\lambda_1 + \gamma c_7)e^{\frac{c_6}{\lambda_1 + \gamma c_7}} - C_{P2}(\lambda_2 + \gamma c_7)e^{\frac{c_6}{\lambda_2 + \gamma c_7}}}{C_{P2}(\lambda_2 + \gamma c_7)e^{\frac{c_6}{\lambda_2 + \gamma c_7}} - C_{P3}(\lambda_3 + \gamma c_7)e^{\frac{c_6}{\lambda_3 + \gamma c_7}}} = \frac{\lambda_1 - \lambda_2}{\lambda_2 - \lambda_3} \tag{20}$$

c_6 can be identified. c_7 in Eq. 20 is unknown. c_7 can be identified according to the same principle as c_6. Similarly, a and B can be obtained.

(3) Identifiability of c_1, c_5 and c_8

From $a(0) = c_1 e^{c_6 c_8}$ and $a(\gamma) = c_1 e^{c_6 c_8/(\gamma^3+1)}$, $c_8 = (1 + 1/\gamma^3)\ln[a(0)/a(\gamma)]/c_6$ can be obtained, then: $c_1 = a(0)/e^{c_6 c_8}$. From $b(0) = -[c_1 c_8 + c_5]e^{c_6 c_8}$, we get: $c_5 = -b(0)e^{-c_6 c_8} - c_1 c_8$. Then: c_1, c_5, c_8 can be identified.

(4) Identifiability of c_2, c_3 and c_4

Identified by, c_6, c_7, c_8, c_1, c_5, let $X = c_2\gamma + c_3\gamma^{c_4}$, by:

$$X = -b(\gamma)e^{-c_6 c_8/(\gamma^3+1)} - c_1 c_8/(\gamma^3+1) - c_5 \tag{21}$$

Then X can be calculated, according to several known β and γ_1, γ_2, γ_3:

$$c_2\gamma_1 + c_3\gamma_1^{c_4} = X_1 \tag{22}$$

$$c_2\gamma_2 + c_3\gamma_2^{c4} = X_2 \tag{23}$$

$$c_2\gamma_3 + c_3\gamma_3^{c4} = X_3 \tag{24}$$

Delete c_2, c_3 from Eq. 22 to Eq. 24, we get:

$$\frac{\gamma_1^{c4-1} - \gamma_2^{c4-1}}{\gamma_2^{c4-1} - \gamma_3^{c4-1}} = \frac{X_1/\gamma_1 - X_2/\gamma_2}{X_2/\gamma_2 - X_3/\gamma_3} \tag{25}$$

Let the right of the equal sign of the above formula be Y, then Y can be calculated, and there are:

$$Y(\gamma_3/\gamma_2)^{C4-1} + (\gamma_1/\gamma_2)^{C4-1} - Y - 1 = 0 \tag{26}$$

In the above formula, c_4 is an unknown number. According to the same principle as c_6, c_7, c_4 can also be identified. From Eqs. 22 and 23, c_2, c_3 can be identified.

To sum up, $c_1 - c_8$ are uniquely identifiable.

3.2 ·Identifiability Analysis of Transmission System Parameters

According to Eq. 5 transmission system model, write the state equation of transmission system in matrix form as matrix 27:

$$
\begin{bmatrix} \frac{d\omega_{\omega t}}{dt} \\ \frac{d\omega_r}{dt} \\ \frac{d\theta_{sh}}{dt} \end{bmatrix} = \begin{bmatrix} \frac{D_{sh}}{H_{\omega t}} & -\frac{D_{sh}}{H_{\omega t}} & -\frac{K_{sh}}{H_{\omega t}} \\ \frac{D_{sh}}{H_g} & -\frac{D_{sh}}{H_g} & \frac{K_{sh}}{H_g} \\ \omega_s & -\omega_s & 0 \end{bmatrix} \begin{bmatrix} \omega_{\omega t} \\ \omega_r \\ \theta_{sh} \end{bmatrix} + \begin{bmatrix} \frac{1}{H_{\omega t}} \\ -\frac{1}{H_g} \\ 0 \end{bmatrix} \begin{bmatrix} T_{\omega t} & T_e & 0 \end{bmatrix} \tag{27}
$$

$$\text{Order}: \quad \begin{cases} X = AX + BU \\ Y = CX + DU \end{cases} \tag{28}$$

Among them,

$$X = \begin{bmatrix} \omega_{\omega t} & \omega_r & \theta_{sh} \end{bmatrix}^T, Y = \begin{bmatrix} \omega_{\omega t} & \omega_r & 0 \end{bmatrix}^T, U = \begin{bmatrix} T_{\omega t} & T_e & 0 \end{bmatrix},$$

$$A = \begin{bmatrix} \frac{D_{sh}}{H_{\omega t}} & -\frac{D_{sh}}{H_{\omega t}} & -\frac{K_{sh}}{H_{\omega t}} \\ \frac{D_{sh}}{H_g} & -\frac{D_{sh}}{H_g} & \frac{K_{sh}}{H_g} \\ \omega_s & -\omega_s & 0 \end{bmatrix}, B = \begin{bmatrix} \frac{1}{H_{\omega t}} \\ -\frac{1}{H_g} \\ 0 \end{bmatrix}, C = \begin{bmatrix} 1 & 1 & 0 \end{bmatrix}, D = [0]$$

Laplace transform Eq. 28 to obtain:

$$G(S) = C(SI - A)^{-1}B + D \tag{29}$$

Among them,

$$(SI-A)^{-1} = \begin{bmatrix} s(s+\frac{D_{sh}}{H_{\omega t}})+\omega_s\frac{K_{sh}}{H_g} & s\frac{D_{sh}}{H_{\omega t}}+\omega_s\frac{D_{sh}}{H_{\omega t}} & -\frac{K_{sh}D_{sh}}{H_{\omega t}H_g}-\frac{D_{sh}}{H_{\omega t}}(s+\frac{D_{sh}}{H_{\omega t}}) \\ s\frac{D_{sh}}{H_g}+\omega_s\frac{K_{sh}}{H_g} & s(s-\frac{D_{sh}}{H_{\omega t}})+\omega_s\frac{K_{sh}}{H_{\omega t}} & \frac{K_{sh}}{H_g}(s-\frac{D_{sh}}{H_{\omega t}})-\frac{K_{sh}D_{sh}}{H_{\omega t}H_g} \\ -\omega_s\frac{D_{sh}}{H_g}+\omega_s(s+\frac{D_{sh}}{H_{\omega t}}) & \omega_s(\frac{D_{sh}}{H_{\omega t}}-s)-\omega_s\frac{D_{sh}}{H_{\omega t}} & (s-\frac{D_{sh}}{H_{\omega t}})(s+\frac{D_{sh}}{H_{\omega t}})+\frac{D_{sh}D_{sh}}{H_{\omega t}H_g} \end{bmatrix} /|sI-A| \tag{30}$$

According to the calculation, Eq. 29 can be written as follows:

$$G(S) = \frac{d(s^2 + es + f)}{s^3 + as^2 + bs + c} \tag{31}$$

Among them, a, b, c, d, e, f are the undetermined coefficient and can be identified in the linear system. And because $H_{\omega t}, K_{sh}, D_{sh}$ can always be represented by a, b, c, d, e, f, $H_{\omega t}, K_{sh}, D_{sh}$ are uniquely identifiable.

4   Parameter Identification Method based on Fuzzy Cuckoo Search Algorithm

4.1   Parameter Identification of Wind Turbine System Steps

Cuckoo Search Algorithm is a new heuristic algorithm [8], which has the characteristics of fast convergence and high precision.

In the optimization algorithm of objective function, each set of solutions is 11 parameters to be identified. Each time the objective function is calculated, run the model with these solutions as parameters once, subtract the operation results from the output results of the actual system one by one, and take the absolute value to obtain the identification error, that is, the objective function of parameter identification of wind turbine system. The parameter identification steps of wind turbine system are shown in Fig. 2.

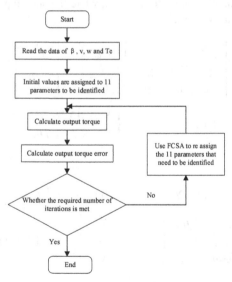

Fig. 2. Flow chart of parameter identification of wind turbine system

In traditional CSA, the discovery probability P_a is usually used with a fixed value, but if the fixed value is large, the convergence of the search may be weakened. On the contrary, the diversity of the global search may be weakened. Therefore, the optimization of P_a value is particularly critical to the convergence speed and calculation accuracy of the algorithm.

4.2 Fuzzy Cuckoo Search Algorithm Flow

The specific steps of cuckoo fuzzy control are as follows: CSA module provides parameters to Dx and Df fuzzy interfaces respectively, and the parameters are passed to the inference system after fuzzification. The corresponding fuzzy parameters can be obtained according to the knowledge base and rule base, and then defuzzified through P_α anti fuzzy interface to obtain the control parameters, which are passed to CSA module for reciprocating cycle. The specific framework is shown in Fig. 3:

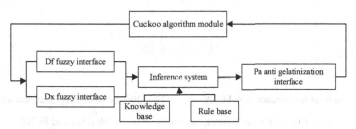

Fig. 3. FCSA fuzzy control framework

5 Example Simulation and Analysis

We will search and optimize 11 parameters which are to be identified in the wind turbine system based on CSA. We set the number of bird's nests to 30, the probability of being found 0.25, and the dimension of the space to 15. Then we get the parameter values of the four types of identification which are shown in Table 1 and the optimization of output torque error which is shown in Fig. 4 by compared CSA and FCSA.

Table 1. Four kinds of identification parameter value statistics table

parameters	CSA (100 generations)	CSA (200 generations)	FCSA (100 generations)	FCSA (200 generations)
c_1	0.8784	0.7020	0.9938	0.503
c_2	187.4688	117.205	172.5911	189.7399
c_3	0.7139	0.2719	0.6829	0.9452
c_4	7.8236	7.0454	2.5415	7.1413
c_5	39.7616	28.4324	43.3309	48.1814
c_6	0.0045	0. 0032	0.01	0.0092
c_7	0.0654	0.0143	0.0844	0.1
c_8	0.0255	0.0327	0.025	0.0919
$H_{\omega t}$	7.302	9.5883	4.6422	7.2856
K_{sh}	1.1273	1.2709	1.1145	1.1261
D_{sh}	2.0924	1.58	1.4963	1.6232

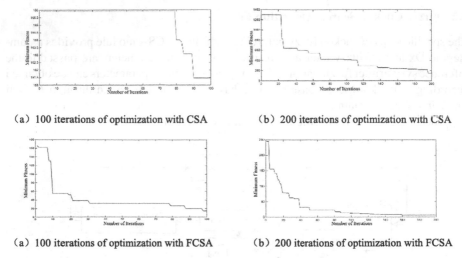

（a）100 iterations of optimization with CSA   （b）200 iterations of optimization with CSA

（a）100 iterations of optimization with FCSA   （b）200 iterations of optimization with FCSA

Fig. 4. Output torque error optimization curve with CSA and FCSA

The comparison of 100 and 200 iterations of CSA and FCSA experiments shows that, the minimum fitness of 100 iterations of optimization of CSA is 161.4625, and the minimum fitness of 200 iterations of optimization of FCSA is 151.2311, The more iterations we do under the same experimental conditions, the closer the experimental value is to the actual value, and the higher the identification accuracy. The same as the result in FCSA. The minimum fitness of 100 iterations of CSA and FCSA are 161.4645 and 14.62 respectively. Under the same number of iterations, the introduction of a fuzzy controller dynamically updates the probability of being discovered, which greatly improves the speed and accuracy of parameter identification.

In summary, the minimum fitness values of the four types of identification are shown in Table 2. The minimum fitness value of 200 iterations of optimization of FCSA is the smallest, and the parameter identification effect is the best.

Table 2. Minimum fitness value of the four types of identification

	CSA (100 generations)	CSA (200 generations)	FCSA (100 generations)	FCSA (200 generations)
Minimum fitness value	161.4645	151.2311	14.62	6.1687

From the analysis of the above results, it can be obtained that the FCSA can not only solve the problem of easily falling into the local optimum with CSA, but also effectively prevent it from falling into the local optimum. If the parameters of FCSA are set reasonable, the algorithm will be able to quickly converge to the global optimal value. If it is ensured that the number of CSA operations is sufficient, it can get the global optimal value out. Among them, the identification process of each parameter in FCSA200 iteration optimization with the best identification effect is shown in Fig. 5.

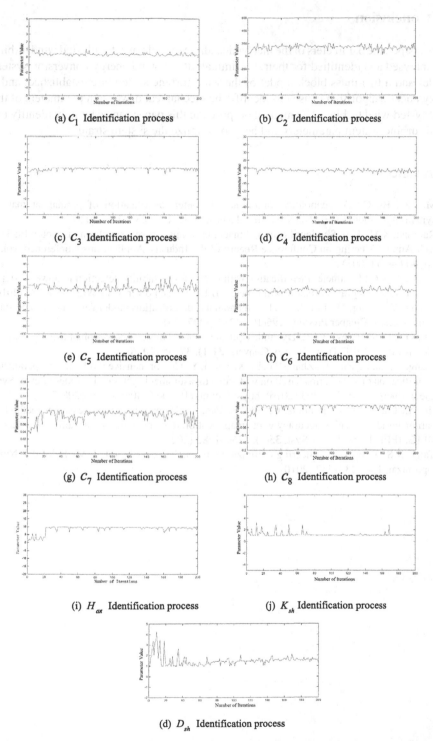

(a) C_1 Identification process

(b) C_2 Identification process

(c) C_3 Identification process

(d) C_4 Identification process

(e) C_5 Identification process

(f) C_6 Identification process

(g) C_7 Identification process

(h) C_8 Identification process

(i) H_{ax} Identification process

(j) K_{sh} Identification process

(d) D_{sh} Identification process

Fig. 5. Identification process of various parameters of wind turbine system based on FCSA

6 Conclusion

In this paper, the parameters of the mechanical drive module of a doubly-fed wind turbine are analysed and identified for their discriminability. A wind energy conversion system model and a two-mass block model of the wind turbine system are established, and a fuzzy cuckoo algorithm is used to identify the mechanical drive train parameters of the doubly-fed wind turbine. The method proposed in this paper can accurately identify the wind turbine system parameters and help to optimize the system strategy.

References

1. Ma, X., Bi, C.: A technology for online parameter identification of permanent magnet synchronous motor. CES Trans. Electrical Mach. Syst. **4**(3), 237–242 (2020)
2. Rahman, K.M., Hiti, S.: Identification of machine parameters of a synchronous motor. In: 38th IAS Annual Meeting on Conference Record of the Industry Applications Conference, vol.1, pp. 409–415 (2003)
3. He, L., Liu, C.: Parameter identification with PMUs for instability detection in power systems With HVDC integrated offshore wind energy. IEEE Trans. Power Syst. **29**(2), 775–784 (2014)
4. Zhang, Y., Zheng, H., Liu, J., et al.: An anomaly identification model for wind turbine state parameters. J. Cleaner Product. **195**(10), 1214–1227 (2018)
5. Kim, D., El-Sharkawi, M.A.: Dynamic equivalent model of wind power plant using parameter identification. IEEE Trans. Energy Convers. **31**(1), 37–45 (2016)
6. Wang, Y., Lu, C., Zhu, L., Zhang, G., Li, X., Chen, Y.: Comprehensive modeling and parameter identification of wind farms based on wide-area measurement systems. J. Modern Power Syst. Clean Energy **4**(3), 383–393 (2016). https://doi.org/10.1007/s40565-016-0208-5
7. Jin, Y., Lu, C., Ju, P., Rehtanz, C., Wu, F., Pan, X.: Probabilistic preassessment method of parameter identification accuracy with an application to identify the drive train parameters of DFIG. IEEE Trans. Power Syst. **35**(3), 1769–1782 (2020)
8. Yang, X.S., Deb, S.: Engineering optimization by cuckoo search. Int. J. Math. Model. Num. Optimizat. **1**(4), 330–343 (2010)

Author Index

Printed in the United States
by Baker & Taylor Publisher Services